Children and Behavior Therapy

Children and Behavior Therapy

ANTHONY M. GRAZIANO

Department of Psychology
State University of New York at Buffalo

KEVIN C. MOONEY

Department of Psychology
Washington State University

ALDINE
Publishing Company
New York

About The Authors

Anthony M. Graziano is Professor of Psychology at the State University of New York, Buffalo. He is the author of *Behavior Therapy with Children, Vols. I and II; Children Without Tomorrow;* and *Handbook of Practical Psychology.*

Kevin C. Mooney is Assistant Professor of Psychology at Washington State University.

Aldine Publishing Company
200 Saw Mill River Road
Hawthorne, New York 10532

Library of Congress Cataloging in Publication Data

Graziano, Anthony M., 1932–
Children and behavior therapy.

Bibliography: p.
Includes index.
1. Behavior therapy. 2. Child psychotherapy.
I. Mooney, Kevin C., 1955– . II. Title. [DNLM:
1. Behavior therapy—In infancy and childhood. WS 350.6
G785c]
RJ505.B4G723 1984 618.92'89142 83-25724
ISBN 0-202-26087-9

Table of Contents

4

CHILDREN'S CONTROL OF FEAR

5

BEHAVIORAL SELF-CONTROL

6

JUVENILE DELINQUENCY

7

FAMILY SYSTEMS

8

BEHAVIORAL INTERVENTIONS IN SCHOOLS

9

SOMATIC SYSTEMS, BEHAVIORAL MEDICINE, BEHAVIORAL PEDIATRICS, AND HEALTH PSYCHOLOGY

10

BEHAVIORAL COMMUNITY PSYCHOLOGY

Preface

This book has been written for students, researchers, and practitioners in education, mental health, medicine, nursing, psychiatry, psychology, and social work. We have reviewed the major developments in child-behavior modification during the period 1975–1981, with some discussions of earlier work where needed. The areas we have reviewed, the studies reported, and their organization in these particular ten chapters reflect our own judgments about the state and direction of the field. Other reviewers would, of course, arrive at other emphases and organization.

Each chapter was written as a review of an area—independently of the other chapters. We have attempted to minimize repetition, although some remains since much of the research is appropriately discussed in several areas. Despite the attempt to develop independent reviews, the chapters maintain several themes, such as our concern for increasing our field's focus on children, concern for other-than-behavioral data and values, and our view of the changing nature of behavior modification with children. This is a vibrant field in transition and in this book we have tried to reflect its changes, directions, and potentials.

Many people have assisted in this work. We wish to thank Susan Alessi, Kathleen Garcia, and Robert Kelly, who contributed to the sections on childhood fears and obesity; Mrs. Erma Rawlings, Mrs. Leann Pawlick, and Gretchen Hill, who did much of the typing; Amy Graziano and Lisa Graziano, who helped in the preparation of the references; and Faith Mooney, for helping in the proofreading tasks. Our acknowledgments are extended also to the library staff of the State University of New York at Buffalo, with particular recognition of the assistance provided by Howard Pikoff, librarian for the Psychology Collection.

Anthony M. Graziano
Kevin C. Mooney

An Introductory Note

Our title reflects this book's starting point in the clinical enterprise of behavior *therapy* with children. With its focus on the amelioration of already existing problems, behavior therapy is but one of several specializations developed within the larger area of behavior modification. One of the major points presented in this book is that by virtue of its major strategies—arranging environmental conditions and predicting human behavior within them—behavior modification is an inherently future-oriented enterprise, and as such is not limited to those past-oriented, pathology-linked, ameliorative therapy endeavors which constitute basic clinical practice. Rather, behavior modification is equally applicable to the enhancement of normal, adaptive, future behavior of individuals and of groups ranging from families to larger social units.

Enhancement and ameliorative goals, of course, are overlapping, and behavior therapy remains an important part of behavior modification. It appears to us that the most promising and exciting developments in this field are those more closely aligned with enhancement, future-oriented, educational goals as distinct from the more traditional clinical treatment or ameliorative focus. Enhancement goals may be seen emerging in the large and still-growing literature on training and educating parents in using behavioral concepts and techniques with their own children; in the growing interest in teaching behavioral skills for achieving, maintaining and enhancing optimum physical health; and in the emergence of a behavioral community psychology with interests in large-scale social interventions. The latter goals are aimed not only toward the prevention of mental and physical health problems but also toward applying behavior modification to concerns such as those for improving environmental quality. We will also assert that, contrary to many critics, behavior modification, perhaps more than our other models of psychological intervention, has an enormous potential for humanizing some of our more insensitive or blatantly coercive treatment and residential settings.

Another point made in this book and reflected in our title is the need for primary emphasis on children. In Chapter 1 we will argue that behavior therapy, like psychodynamic therapy, is essentially an adult-oriented enterprise, having developed from earlier clinical investigations of neurotic adults. The adult-based inferences were later generalized to children. However, adults and children, for all their similarities are functionally and structurally very different. When we begin an entire discipline with a detailed focus on adults then, of course, we are led to adult concerns such as neurotic anxieties over our relationships with other adults. We are not convinced that those issues are at all appropriate in a child-focused discipline. What is needed is an applied field which begins with a focus on children and proceeds to systematic investigations and work with phenomena and applications that are specific to children.

One of the subareas within behavior modification, which emerged in the early 1960s in school settings, began with such a focus on children. Thus, there has been a move away from the more traditional adult-oriented, neuroses-tied behavior therapy, and toward issues that are more appropriately those of growing children, such as acquisition of positive social skills, academic achievement, development of athletic ability and musical and other artistic skills, successfully coping with the common developmental demands of childhood, and so on. In this educationally based subset of behavior modification we find strong emphasis on the development and enhancement of normal, age-appropriate functioning in natural environments. Our point is that the potential for development of a sophisticated and successful *enhancement function* of behavior modification, seems far more appropriate and probable within educational settings than within clinical ones. Consistent with this view, and as developed in Chapter 1, we urge closer alignment of behavior modification with education than has so far been allowed to develop. It appears to us that, in order to increase our child focus, the education and training of child-behavior modifiers should include major emphasis on the psychological discipline of child development which would require supervised practical and internship experience within school settings. These, we believe, are at least as important as our more traditional, clinically based education and experience.

While many behavior modifiers work within school settings, a more formalized conceptual congruence of behavior modification and child development has yet to be constructed. It is, we maintain, a major task for the field over the next several years.

In our judgment, behavior modification is one of the most active and productive fields in education and mental health. It has constructed an impressive empirical data base in the short time of about 20 years—an achievement not matched by any other applied model—giving it a reliable foundation for future development. Much of our potential, we maintain, is in the development of behavioral models and application for the enhancement of normal human functioning. Behavioral enhancement, as distinct from *behavior therapy*, is beginning to emerge as another subset within this field.

1

Children and Behavior Therapy

I. CHILDREN AND RESPONSIBLE PARENTING

Children in the United States appear to occupy a special, even privileged position. Our common knowledge and professed values suggest that childhood is more than a period of physical and psychological growth to maturity; for the child it includes growing, discovering, and learning about oneself and the world, and for the adult it demands selfless responsibility, nurturance, and guidance. The child is commonly viewed as having a special status, enjoying sunny innocence unshadowed by the demands of wordly responsibilities, and having only to flourish under the nurturance of loving parents.

This picture of childhood, of course, may describe only a very small minority, reflecting more eighteenth- and nineteenth-century literary romanticism than modern reality. Many children do not flourish; indeed, many do not even survive. It seems as if children, once conceived, must run a gamut of obstacles—neglect, disease, injury, abuse—as well as coping with the never-ending demands to master all of the normal and greatly varied tasks of growing up. In this process children feel, think, learn, and fail to learn, and out of that long-term mix of people, events, thoughts, and the pains and pleasures of growing, each child becomes immersed in his or her own measure of life quality, very little of which is ever created by the child. And here is an important point that is often overlooked: children live in worlds created and controlled by adults. The child may be well nurtured or neglected, healthy or frail, secure in a loving family, indifferently treated or brutalized, financially comfortable or dulled by poverty, and none is the child's doing. The deciding events are enacted exclusively by the controlling adults or the uncontrolled roll of probabilities, while the child remains unable to create or control the realities of his or her own life conditions. The child's dependency on adults demands adult responsibility and the degree to which adults carry out that responsibility defines virtually all of the child's life quality and even survival. The child's quality of life is in direct proportion to the adult's responsible parenting and, by extension, to the responsible nurturance and guidance of other adults such as teachers and relatives. The overriding reality of life as a child is control by adults.

The child's natural dependence upon adults is as it should be—at least it begins as it should begin. But in our idealizations we do not expect such enthralled dependency to continue. Rather, we anticipate a gradual reciprocal process in which nurturant parental control slowly gives way, step by developmental step, to the child's growing maturity, all toward what is a major idealization expressed by contemporary U.S. democracy: independence and personal self-determination. In other times and other contemporary social and political systems, personal self-determination has not been an idealized goal. But in our society it is, and is loudly professed.

But to be independent one must be skillfully self-directive: capable of emotional control, intellectual discipline, able to reach out and directively construct personal environments of one's own designs, and all in some manner consistent with guiding ethical systems, criteria against which to monitor, judge, and regulate our successes in living harmoniously with other lives, things, and events in our environment. Responsible independence in its idealized form, is a demanding status, indeed.

To achieve that independence is to have completed a transfer of control, a major change in the reality of initial control by adults to greater self-control and independence by the child. One important dimension, then, in adult-child interaction involves parental guidance of the child through acquisition of many skills, with each small acquisitive success presumably bringing with it a small measure more of independence for the child, and correspondingly a small measure less of control by the adult. In essence the parent must actively teach self-control skills toward responsible self-determination by the child, and manage the progressive relinquishing of direct parental control. The process of transferring control or, rather, of teaching directive self-control to children, is a long-term, demanding task for both parent and child, and often requires fine tuning by a perceptive and skillful parent.

The parental responsibility is clear. By virtue of becoming a parent one is subject to a *moral imperative* of assuming full adult responsibility for the child's well-being, and of carrying out that responsibility by nurturing, guiding, and actively teaching the child to achieve independent self-determination. The degree of the child's successful independence is a function of long-term child and adult interaction. Ideally both contribute, both grow and mature, both gain in very personal ways, and one thing is very clear: responsibility resides with the parent, not with the child. The child reciprocates by successfully growing, by actively returning love, and being a continual source of stimulation, joy, and pride for the parents. And when the child is the source of incessant demands and often of concern and sadness, the parents' responsibility remains and their skill and strength are sorely taxed.

II. IN LOCO MAGISTRI

Several points, have been made, all related to the general idea that the child grows in a physical and social natural environment that is, in most respects, not of the child's making. The effective control of that environment lies in the behavior of particular adults. This is a controlling relationship and ideally it changes as the child learns and grows toward greater independence or responsible self-determination. The young child's world of reality is a very small space, indeed, bounded by close confines physically and socially and powerfully controlled by significant adults. The younger the child, the smaller, more confined, and more parentally controlled is the child's real world. As suggested earlier, the overriding reality of life as a child is control by adults.

That reality makes demands on adults, a moral imperative, to engage in responsible parenting. In its most general sense, responsible parenting includes loving nurturance, guidance, and active teaching of the child to develop greater independence and self-control, gradually altering the parental high-control realities. In its specifics responsible parenting includes day-to-day details of decisions and actions, and hard work under demanding conditions. In its idealization this process is carried out lovingly, with care, patience, gentleness, and great enjoyment and reward for parent and child. In its realities it includes also frustration, failures, anger, insensitivity, recalcitrance, disappointment, punishment, meanness, worry, and, too often, sadness.

We have emphasized one dimension of the complex parenting role, that of teaching the child skills toward greater self-control and independence. This function is in addition to all of the other parental functions such as providing love, physical safety, comfort, nutrition, and all of the other basic care responsibilities that we too easily assume are "naturally" carried out by parents. Unfortunately, as every social service department can verify, there are many parents, particularly that growing population of unmarried adolescent mothers, who are barely able to care for themselves, isolated, without a supporting family, and are unable to adequately meet even this very basic level of parenting responsibility. As demanding as those basic responsibilities may be, the parents' function of teaching their children the complexities of successful growth toward responsible independence requires a great deal more sophisticated, future-oriented, and goal-directed interactions between parent and child. Parents teach children through direct demonstrations and the use of contingent rewards and punishments and, in general, through the kinds of direct and indirect learning environments chosen or constructed by the parents or simply allowed to occur by default, such as falling into the pervasive "TV-as-baby-sitter-trap." All are powerful teaching situations.

This dimension of the parenting role, the *parent as a teacher*, is rarely conceptualized or carried out systematically and consistently by parents; the general assumption appears to be that such teaching will occur in the natural course of growing up. But learning responsible self-determination and independence in our contemporary U.S. world of massive external control over individuals exerted by a great variety of social groups such as government agencies, schools, corporations, utility companies, employers, and others, may be too important and complex a task to be left so much to what appears to be social happenstance. Certainly not all of parental teaching can or should be rationally conceptualized, systematic, and consistent but, we argue, it is important that some reasonable portion of the total should be thoughtfully carried out.

Not too long ago we took seriously the notion *in loco parentis*, even at the college level. The concept asserted the importance of parenting to the degree that some parental responsibility and prerogatives could rightfully be assumed by other adults, in the parents' temporary absence. Children in school, even older adolescents and young adults in college, were viewed as incapable of maintaining full responsibility for themselves and thus in need of extended parenting. Teachers and administrators assumed, but did not necessarily demonstrate, that they were more capable and responsible than the students in making decisions affecting even the students' private lives. Thus the notion held that teachers could rightfully operate in place of the parents—*in loco parentis*.

The concept is no longer applicable, perhaps since the 1960s assertiveness of youth. But the parent-teacher affinity remains and we suggest that it needs emphasizing but in the reverse order; that is, not the teacher-as-parent role, but the parent-as-teacher role. We have suggested that among all of the important dimensions of parental responsibility, that of actively teaching the child skills in responsible independence may be among the most important. *In loco parentis* we suggest, has given way to *parens in loco magistri*, the assumption by other adults, here, specifically the parents, of teachers' active roles and prerogatives. *Parens in loco magistri*, parents in place of the teacher, assumes that parents must be as skilled in teaching as they are in providing basic care; it demands that parents recognize and carry out seriously their active teaching responsibility and roles, and suggests that parents be tutored or otherwise trained in effective teaching concepts and methods.

The moral imperative for responsible parenting demands that both parents devote a great deal of time and care to active teaching efforts in addition to all of their other parenting responsibilities, for some sixteen or so years of each child's life. In our contemporary U.S. society there seems little indication that intense, active, and long-term parental involvement in children's learning is on the increase. Indeed it may be decreasing as more children are left for longer periods in day-care centers, as schools seem to be viewed increasingly as the proper places for teaching, and as we experience more one-parent families in which the parenting responsibilities cannot be shared among adults. If there is indeed a real decrease in the social value and practice of responsible parenting then our society may have entered a period of crisis in parenting, with serious implications not only for individuals but for the culture as a whole.

Ideally responsible parenting involves both parents equally in carrying out child care and teaching responsibilities. If this were an important social value we would find living patterns changing, with social supports for a variety of alternate family arrangements in which traditional male/female, homemaker/breadwinner categorizations would give way to more equal sharing of responsibilities, *but with no decline in the quality of parenting*. However, considerations of such "crises" and social changes are beyond the scope of this book; let it be enough here only to have mentioned them.

III. CLINICAL INTERVENTION

The process of development from parental to self-control is here postulated to be one of the important dimensions of childhood, and is assumed to be achieved to different degrees of success by different children and parents, under different conditions. Consistent with its importance in normal child development, control issues are likewise considered to be important—perhaps central—in many of the child-parent problem situations that we address as clinicians. We recognize a disturbed situation when the normal parental or other adult control functions have been disrupted and, therefore, the expected nurturant parenting or other guidance toward the child's responsible self-determination has been prevented. In such instances neither the parent nor the child enjoys the fullest possible rewards of their interactions. Typically children are referred to mental health services when some adult has determined that the child is in some way out-of-control. The hard-to-handle, disruptive, grammar school youngster is referred to the school psychologist; the tantrumous or negativistic, noncompliant child is taken to the clinic by parents who seek help because they no longer know what else to try. The highly phobic or the anxious child is seen as being out-of-control, too often becoming irrational or hysterical. Enuretic or encopretic children, anorexic or highly aggressive children, psychotic children, and delinquents are viewed by adults as operating in some manner outside of normal parental or other social control procedures. The children are referred to the clinics when the responsible adults believe they have reached the limits of their ability to properly control, guide, or teach their child and, in order to carry out their parenting responsibilities, they consult professionals. While normal parenting has been disrupted, these parents nevertheless, by seeking help, are meeting their responsibilities for their children.

Perhaps the most obvious and certainly the most tragic instances of parent-child control disruptions occur in cases of abused children. There the adult exercises overbearing and destructive physical control against which the child is helpless. There is no reciprocation; the child does not gain or grow toward independence and the entire parent-child interaction is viciously perverted. The moral imperative to provide responsible parenting has little value for such adults. If these cases come to professional attention they do so not through the parents' responsible action in seeking help but commonly through the demands of a third party such as a court or social service agency, representing society.

Most of the children who enter the mental health field as potential clients are brought in by their parents who seek help. From the beginning, then, the client may best be conceptualized as a child-parent unit, composed of at least two, but most often more, persons. By their invitation the professional enters a unique and small personal world that is unlike that of any other and which, to a most significant degree, has been created and maintained by the decisions and actions of adults. If it is to be changed, it must be changed by the further action of adults. Whatever the specific problems may be in any individual case two of the important parameters are the adult and the child, and a major dimension of concern is their interaction around the issues of parental control and the child's development of responsible independence. Important here is the suggestion that the client is the parent-child unit.

However, when brought to the clinician, the child usually is the major focus of parental concerns and the problem is most likely defined by parents as residing within the child. By parental definition the child becomes locus, cause, and sustainer of the problems and, it follows reasonably, the target for intervention. The parent seeking professional help does not necessarily blame the child as being *willfully* difficult, although such attributions are often found earlier in the history of the problems as the parents cast about for reasonable explanations. Rather the responsible parent recognizes that the child is in some manner out of their control, perhaps not even under the child's own control. The parents' request for aid, then, is very much a request that the professional help the parents to regain their control over the child by intervening with the child, making the child more amenable to a return to or assumption of parental control.

The parents enter the treatment situation with a mixture of requests, questions, and expectations of frustration or failure, and sometimes the quite perceptive understanding that control issues are involved. But too often the parents enter with a misplaced focus for the expected point of intervention; on the child almost exclusively. Perhaps because they are so closely involved they fail to perceive and to alter their own contributions to the problems. The parents perceive, for example a fearful or aggressive *child*, but only dimly see the adult-controlled fear-sustaining and aggression-sustaining interactions within their child-parent unit.

In many cases the clinician's major task is to educate the parents about their own contributions to the difficulties which they have viewed as the child's problems. The parents' initial expectations that the child is the appropriate point of intervention must in many cases be changed to recognize that the interaction between parent and child is the most important point of intervention. Not only must the child's behavior change but so must that of the parents and often, if it is a school problem, that of the teacher. We cannot now give behavioral prescriptions for how the clinician, in those cases where it is appropriate, swings the parental focus from the child to the child-parent interactions. Certainly it is difficult in many cases and impossible in others, where some parents, persisting in viewing the problems as residing wholly within the child, refuse to make that change.

One point, however, seems clear. When we intervene in this small but complex social system—virtually the entire world of the young child—that child is potentially at risk from some possible abuses and, as with research subjects, steps must be taken to protect the child from those potential risks. Our profession's implicit assumption that the child's welfare is uppermost, is much too general to constitute sufficient protection for the child. To reduce the risks to the child each clinician in each case must, at the very least, carefully consider the potential risks to the child imposed by each particular intervention. As noted by Graziano and Fink (1973) there may be unintended negative effects of psychological treatment, and we must become more sensitive to those possibilities.

The clinician enters a parent-child interaction system in which control functions have been severely disrupted. Parental control in a given case may be over- or underutilized or too rigidly, flexibly, or punitively applied. Whatever the particular direction of the control disruption, the child's development has been interfered with and the parents have sought the clinician, bringing with them some recognition that control issues are involved and often also making the implicit demand that the therapist help them develop more effective parental control. It is here that the potential abuse of therapy and risk to the child may be most severe: that is, when we enter the parent-child system and we construct our interventions, we are imposing upon the system still another controlling adult. The danger lies in the parental invitation to assist in the application of control over the child. That control is applied by mature, trained, and experienced therapists over naive and socially weak children and, as we have argued elsewhere (Graziano, 1975a), control is inherent in every therapy model. Therapists who deny that their particular model imposes control over the clients or who maintain that such control is a danger only in behavior therapy, are insensitive to their own realities. We wonder how perceptive such therapists can be in the rest of their relationship with their clients. The therapist-child social power differences are large, the potential for abuse is great, and the therapist's recognition of that potential is critically important.

While emphasizing that the abuse of control in the name of treatment is a potential problem in all therapy models, it is important to note another point. Since the late 1960s accumulating evidence strongly suggests the power of behavioral approaches to bring about demonstrable changes in children. While direct comparisons with other therapy approaches have seldom been made, this evidence, in conjunction with the general lack of evidence for the effectiveness of other approaches, suggests that behavior therapy is our most powerful treatment, and behavior therapists, as compared with others, have greatest skills in bringing about demonstrable changes in child clients. The potential for abuse may also be greater, and this is the other side of success; the more powerful interventions carry with them the greatest potential for abuse. Therefore behavior therapists, in particular, must be highly sensitive to their own impact upon the child and the parent-child system.

IV. CONTROL ALLIANCES

One of the potential abuses, and perhaps the most common, occurs when the clinician unwittingly enters an alliance with the parent, accepting the parents' implicit goals of increasing their control over the child. Increased parental control is not necessarily harmful for the child but may be if it is the major goal of therapy and has no functional value in enhancing the child's healthy development. Behavioral technology or any other therapy approach is misused when it provides the parent, teacher, group worker, ward aid, cottage parent, or juvenile officer greater skills in controlling children for adults' convenience or for systems' needs, such as for maintaining orderliness without regard for the child's growth. Control alliances between the clinician and the help-seeking adults frequently occur. Many therapists can recall individual cases in which the parents' initial request was to increase their control over the child. Psychologists are often consulted by social agencies such as schools and residential treatment programs and asked to bring high active or disruptive children under better staff control. Too frequently, as discussed by Winett and Winkler (1972), the system benefits more than does the child. As we discuss in Chapter Six, the misapplication of professional control over children and adolescents may be most clearly seen in some treatment settings for delinquent youth, settings which assert powerful control over their residents. In some of those training programs, restrictive control, even including severe physical punishment, has traditionally been considered to be a desirable—even necessary—part of the treatment. The behavior modifier, called into what may be a coercive setting, must guard against introducing sophisticated behavior control technology which might then be used by the traditional staff to deepen their coercive power. However, it should also be pointed out that behavior modification, because of its attention to careful, explicit goal-directed programming and its heavy reliance upon positive contingencies to bring about acquisition of new behavior, is a potentially powerful technology for humanizing residential treatment programs such as those for delinquent youth. This potential humanistic impact of behavior modification compared with other treatment approaches is further discussed in Chapter Six. Thus behavior modifiers must be sensitive not only to potential abuse of control over children, but also aware of their potential for humanizing treatment settings, and must carefully assess the nature of each setting into which we are asked to introduce behavioral sophistication.

V. BEYOND CLINICAL PSYCHOLOGY

To what end, then, do we develop behavior modification with children? Certainly, at least, to help children and their parents or other adults solve difficult, immediately pressing psychological problems, an aim that is in common with that of all therapeutic models. This is part of the traditional definition of psychotherapy as a postdisorder, pathology-focused intervention which attempts to correct existing problems. An immediate and apparent goal of the behavior therapist, then, is to apply professional skills to help ameliorate current problems.

Clinical interventions, however, are applied within the context of a growing, changing child in long-term interaction with a changing adult. Whatever the immediate concerns may be, that context creates an overriding, long-term direction toward optimum development of the child and optimum parent-child interaction. The therapeutic task in every child case is therefore implicitly future-oriented, and herein lies our potential to go far beyond clinical psychology. The clinician's most general task becomes one of interacting with the ongoing parent-child system, entering into that dynamic behavioral flow and carefully synchronizing therapeutic interventions with events in the child's natural environment to bring about not only immediate improvement but to also realign the disrupted interactions, and move them toward future optimum development.

Behavior modification with children, then, is neither implicitly tied to concepts of pathology nor limited to ameliorative after-the-fact therapy applications. In its larger sense this technology is applicable to the enhancement of normal, healthy, optimum development of children individually, and in larger community groups. We can conceptualize behavioral programming to augment children's development in areas such as creativity, self-management, and health-sustaining goals, as readily as we can think of behavioral programs to reduce current pathology. Indeed, the former may be more readily developed than the latter if we would turn our attention to it. An early example of this positive, augmenting function of behavioral intervention is Aylon and Roberts' (1974) procedure to reduce the severe disruptiveness of a fifth grade class. Rather than developing a decremental intervention to reduce disruptive behavior, Aylon and Roberts used an incremental procedure to systematically increase the students' academic skills and to observe the possible salutary effects on disruption. Their attempts were successful. By carefully reinforcing improved academic functioning, they also significantly reduced the severe disruptive behavior. The authors concluded that "a reciprocal relationship may exist between academic performance and disruptive behavior: not the traditionally held 'make them sit still so they will learn,' but rather a 'teach them better and they may sit still' relationship" (p. 76). They had used behavior modification technology to augment positive development of skills rather than enter a decremental child-control alliance with the school. The Ayllon and Roberts methodology begins to use future-oriented, developmental values to guide behavior modification technology. As we discuss in several chapters in this book (schools, behavior medicine, behavior-community psychology), similar concepts are beginning to guide behavioral technology toward focus on large-scale issues such as prevention, physical health enhancement and maintenance, and environmental quality concerns. As we pointed out earlier, behavior modification technology is no longer tied to concepts of pathology nor limited to ameliorative, after-the-fact therapy applications. It has been greatly expanded from its early 1960s identification as a clinical technology tied to the medical model, and is now moving rapidly toward new applications in behavioral pediatrics and behavioral community psychology, going far beyond the limits of clinical psychology. These new areas of behavior modification, discussed in Chapters Six, Eight, Nine, and Ten constitute some of psychology's most important cutting edges in our attempts to contribute to human betterment.

VI. BEHAVIORAL TECHNOLOGY AND THE CONTEXTS OF APPLICATION

We have suggested, in attempting to answer the question "To what ends do we develop behavior modification"?, that these applications potentially go far beyond pathology-linked, therapeutic ameliorative goals and they include potentials for humanizing social settings (see Chapter Six), and enhancing normal, healthy, human functioning. These applications, as ill-defined as they may now be, implicitly demand that many value judgments be made. The behavior therapist who determines that a child will benefit by gaining self-control over fears rather than continuing to demand parental protection, is making value judgments about what is good for the child and the family. The behavior modifier who knows that contingent electric shock is effective in reducing self-injurious behavior in autistic children but decides not to employ it because of moral concerns, has made a value judgment. The behavioral-community psychologist who determines to help counteract large-scale cigarette advertising has weighed health and economic factors, and made a value judgment about what is desirable for the community. The psychologist who initiates a program to increase creative behavior in grammar school children has made value judgments about the desirability of such skills for those children.

But on what bases do behavior modifiers make these and many other necessary judgments? How are we to define, for example, "optimum child development"? Behavioral technology guides us in functionally analyzing and altering behavior, but does that technology provide guiding clarifications of values or definitions of goals such as optimum development?

One of the important ideas basic to this discussion is the view that behavior modification has developed primarily as a technology, although several important personality theories based on behavioral observations and concepts have been developed. These include the early work of Dollard and Miller (1950), Mowrer (1950, 1953), and Sears, (1944, 1951); the behavioral theories of neuroses presented by Eysenck (1947), Eysenck and Rachman (1965), and Wolpe (1958); and the social learning formulations by Bandura and Walters (1963). These and other formulations provide organizations for behavioral observations and empirical constructs to help maintain and predict behavioral events. But these behavioral theories have not yet achieved the level of general acceptance and use as have psychodynamic theories, and the application of behavior modification to human problems remains primarily an empirical undertaking not constrained or guided by personality theories. Indeed this strong empiricism is an important basis for the power of these methods.

At this point in its development, then, behavior modification is primarily a technology. Its major focus is on a large class of events human behavior; its major activity is the development and application of effective and efficient techniques to systematically improve human behavior. Note that we have specified *improvement* rather than *modification* of human behavior. This focus on improvement as a goal immediately introduces value judgments, taking us beyond the more neutral level of "modification." What is important here is to recognize that while the modification of human behavior can be defined by the technology—for example, we can systematically change behavior to increase or decrease its frequency, duration, or resistance to extinction—the improvement of behavior demands value decisions and definitions of the directions of change. Behavior modification, as it now exists, is not a philosophy of life, a theory of personality development, or an ethical or moral system. It is not an attempt to explain all things human. Like applied psychoanalysis it is a technology, albeit hopefully a superior one.

By its nature any functioning technology improves upon its own efficiency and power in its continual pursuit of systematic applications to practical problems. Behavior modification, like any other technology, will also improve its own efficiency. But technology does not justify itself. We can improve the speed and efficiency of mechanical and electronic machines, increase our power to massively reconstruct the earth's surface and change its weather, or sharpen our effectiveness in bringing about systematic behavior change. But throughout all technological progress the Promethean metaphor continues to force the questions, "To what ends do we develop our growing power over nature and what potentials for disaster do we thereby court"? Satisfactory answers have not been found within the details of technological progress because technology guides itself primarily to more technology. We therefore must depend upon values other than those of technology to help define our goals. Behavior modification, like any technology, must derive most of its human values and its direction through association with guiding systems of philosophy, ethics, and other models of human functioning. What is needed is a contextual surrounding for the empirical technology that includes not only moral values, but also information about human functioning and development that is not contained within behavioral technology. Thus far we have only the beginnings of this philosophical-informational surrounding and, we maintain, its development is a major task for this field.

In this regard consider the child psychiatrist or the child-clinical psychologist. It seems reasonable to expect these clinicians to possess modern, empirically derived knowledge about child development as a necessary informational base in order to define criteria of optimum, healthy functioning and to make the many clinical judgments of what may be best for the child. These include judgments of what constitutes pathological, normal, or age-appropriate functioning, and what abilities and skills, understandings and misunderstandings, confusions, fears, and problems are to be expected at various developmental levels and under various other conditions. But one of the unfortunate realities of our modern mental health field is that few child clinicians have mastered or even studied child development, our major contemporary discipline of systematic, empirical study of child growth and psychological functioning. If this is our most complete body of psychological knowledge about children, then the suspicion must be raised that child psychiatrists and child-clinical psychologists—who offer their professional services to the public with the approval of their colleagues and their various state and professional certification boards—may in fact know little of real value about modern children. Although they have not studied child development, these clinicians do, of course, ascribe to theoretical orientations and informational bases. Most commonly these are variants of psychoanalytic theory which evolved by the 1940s primarily from uncontrolled case studies of neurotic, affluent adults. Explanatory concepts, treatment methods, and even whole personality theories were developed from individual case studies of neurotic adults who reminisced about their childhoods and those methods and concepts were then generalized to children. The weaknesses inherent in trying to identify causal factors from uncontrolled case studies, in generalizing from nonrepresentative samples of adults to the whole population of children, and in narrowing the focus almost completely on pathological conditions and then defining health as the absence of pathology all make the entire enterprise very questionable indeed.

The problem is greatest for psychodynamically oriented clinicians who maintain strong adherence to their theories even when supporting evidence is lacking. Perhaps what has become a classic example of believing that something must exist because the theory says it must, despite the lack of evidence, is Anna Freud's reference in *The Ego and the Mechanisms of Defense* (1948) to the latency-period girl whose supposed envy of her little brother's penis entirely dominated her life. However, because the problem was so completely repressed, there was hardly a sign of it and "even in analysis it was exceptionally difficult to detect any traces of it." "Now *that*" comments Arthur Bachrach (1981) "is an interesting observation!," a phenomenon which *must* be there because theory says it must, which completely dominates the child's life but gives virtually no sign of it, and for which the near-total lack of evidence is taken as verification that the phenomenon exists!

Behavior modifiers do not have this particular problem of being blinded by prescientific personality theory. Rather, we can be just as seriously blinded by successful behavioral technology, resulting in our failure to sufficiently question whether some particular behaviors *should* be changed or whether some particular method *should* be used. As different as they may be the two professional models share the same serious limitations of not having empirical, normative information about children to help guide their professional judgments.

When we educate and train our mental health professionals to work with children one of the most important and basic areas of study, child development, is ignored. Few graduate programs in clinical psychology or social work, few psychiatric residencies, clinical psychology internships, externships, or pre- or postdoctoral fellowships pay much attention to this area of study either as active training components of their programs or as requirements for admission. In our view this may be the single most serious failing in the education and training of child mental health professionals.

We have presented the idea that all models of psychological therapy approaches to children are severely limited enterprises whose practicing clinicians have insufficient empirical information about children. To return to the main point of this section, behavior modification is an increasingly powerful empirical technology and requires a contextual surrounding of information and values to help guide its application. The field of child development is our major contemporary area of empirical study of child growth and functioning and, we suggest, can provide much of that needed context. We are not suggesting that an integration of behavior modification and child development is now readily possible, so much as suggesting their interaction. It is hoped that a more formalized statement of the possible interactions of humanitarian philosophy, professional ethics, and child development concepts and data with empirical behavior modification will eventually be developed. A recent paper by Harris and Ferrari (1983) is a beginning attempt to bring together behavior modification and child development.

VII. HISTORICAL DEVELOPMENT

[A more detailed account of the following history is given in an earlier volume (Graziano, 1975a). In this present section we will repeat a few major points, and add some ideas relevant to our discussion of children and behavior modification.]

The modern application of behavior modification to children is not new, having emerged around 1920, but its major development and widespread adoption is less than two decades old, making it at least an apparently recent development. Behavior modification of the 1920s stemmed from earlier investigations by Thorndike, Pavlov, and Watson, and bore resemblance to Witmer's extraordinary—and seldom acknowledged—turn-of-the-century psychoeducational approaches to children. Behavioral concepts and approaches to human functioning were discussed by Haberman (1917), Watson and Rayner (1920), Burnham (1924), Jones (1924a, 1924b), Jacobsen (1929), Gray (1932), Holmes (1936), and Mowrer and Mowrer (1938). The term "behavior modification" seems to have been coined by J. Stanley Gray (1932) in an article entitled "A Biological View of Behavior Modification." As discussed in an earlier paper by Graziano (1970b), Gray urged educators to discontinue their focus on subjective, internal, teleological explanations and, instead, to become more aware of behavior itself. In the early 1920s Sidney L. Pressey developed an automated testing device for college students which he soon realized had considerable value as an automated *teaching* machine. Throughout the 1920s he proposed that further development could lead to a true technology of education. However, despite the now-obvious promise of his prophetic teaching machine Pressey was ignored and in 1932, abandoned his project. During the 1930s some investigators continued to apply behavioral concepts, including Mowrer and Mowrer's (1938) development of the bell-and-pad alarm for training urinary control to enuretic children.

By the beginning of the 1930s, however, the early promise of behavioral approaches to adult neuroses, childhood problems, and education had been overshadowed by the impact of Freud's revival and popularization of the Romantic Psychiatry which had developed more than 100 years earlier (Graziano, 1975a). Psychoanalysis became the major psychological model in the mental health field, reaching its peak of influence in the 1940s, and continuing to dominate the field well into the 1970s.

During the 1930s and 1940s, experimental investigations of behavioral phenomena continued in university psychological laboratories and produced a wealth of data on complex issues of learning. Elaborate learning theories were proposed and many concepts of operant and respondent conditioning seemed applicable to human behavior. Little of this, however, influenced the applied mental health field; psychodynamic psychiatry in mental health, and learning-based psychology in laboratories proceeded contemporaneously but with little interaction.

Not until the personnel demands of World War II brought psychologists into military psychiatry did academic psychology have the opportunity to begin influencing the applied field, and to eventually propose behavioral alternatives to the psychodynamic models. In the 1940s clinical psychologists, at first used to supplement military psychiatry staffs, accepted psychiatry's dominance, trained for and worked within psychiatry's periphery, and adopted the psychodynamic model. By the 1950s, clinical psychology had become established within mental health as a peripheral, ancillary, somewhat lesser-trained psychiatry. In time clinical psychology developed a greater degree of professional independence, but that early adoption of psychiatry's major psychological model continues to characterize clinical psychology. It remains today heavily invested in psychotherapy, using psychodynamic concepts and methods aimed at reversing individual psychopathology.

But however much clinical psychology adopted psychiatry's stance in the 1940s and 1950s, psychologists, unlike social workers and psychiatrists, had a background in learning theory and research, and a strong empirical commitment. This background was brought into the mental health field by the demands of the war and, as more psychologists turned to the issues of human psychopathology, it was increasingly applied. Ullmann and Krasner (1965) commented: "Psychologists who were identified as research workers such as Azrin, Bachrach, Bijou, Ferster, Goldiamond, King, Lindsley, Patterson, and Staats, turned their attention to clinical populations and problems so that the distinction between experimentalist and clinician became blurred" (1965, p. 58). Earlier work by French (1933) and Sears (1936) had already begun to bring together Freudian and Pavlovian concepts, perhaps helping to stimulate Dollard and Miller's classic work, *Personality and Psychotherapy,* which translated psychodynamic theory into Hullian terms. Their work influenced many psychology students and stimulated development toward learning theory and perhaps ironically, away from the psychodynamic theories which they had apparently intended to support.

Another group of theorists (Salter, 1949; Eysenck, 1952, 1960; Wolpe, 1954, 1958) proposed behavioral theories of neurosis as maladaptive habit patterns formed through conditioning and which could be permanently and significantly modified through the systematic application of learning-based technology. Like Dollard and Miller these writers adopted a reinforcement, drive-reduction theory, but they differed in the importance they placed on overt behavior. For Dollard and Miller neurotic behavior is symptomatic of the internal neurotic condition; for Eysenck, Wolpe, and Salter, neurotic behavior is itself the neurotic condition.

Skinner (1953, 1956) regards the label, "neurosis" as an explanatory fiction. Skinner went further than the other writers in rejecting the existence of central conditions, making none of the assumptions about drive, motivation, anxiety, and inhibition which, consistent with Hullian and Pavlovian formulations, were utilized by Eysenck, Wolpe, and Salter.

By the late 1950s several learning-theory based models of adult neuroses and their treatment had been developed, and constituted a small but significant area within the mental health field. All were primarily concerned with adults, with little interest in children, and all, like clinical psychology in general, had adopted the basic psychiatric stance of emphasizing pathology and ameliorative, after-the-fact therapy.

As we noted in an earlier volume (Graziano, 1975a):

> By the late 1950s, then, most of the elements had been gathered for the remarkable surge of behavior modification activity that seemed to appear so suddenly in the early 1960s. One more element must be described—a "spark," perhaps, that seemed to have set off what some consider to have been an "explosion" of activity. In the late 1950s a most dramatic event occurred, the launching of Russia's first sputnik, the first man-made earth satellite (1975a, p. 24).

That first artifical satellite orbiting the earth was a magnificent and thunderously impressive triumph of science and technology—and it was achieved by Russia and not by the United States. This country reeled in paroxysms of self-reproach. Foltz (1961) commented that Russia's success had caused this country to "search for an explanation of how the Soviet peasant under the Bolsheviks had stolen the march on the free American in a democracy . . . many were ready to assume that Soviet education had done the trick, that the solution for the United States lay in a 'crash' program for education . . . (Foltz, 1961, p. 4).

Just as he had been in the center of so many other issues, B. F. Skinner was right in the middle of this one, too. In 1954, more than 30 years after Pressey had announced his teaching machine, Skinner published his important paper, "The Science of Learning and the Art of Teaching." Reminiscent of Gray's 1932 article, Skinner's paper described the direct application of laboratory-based behavior modification techniques to classroom teaching. Teaching machines, similar to Pressey's, had been reinvented. A major difference, however, between Pressey's earlier devices and Skinner's later ones, was Skinner's addition of successive approximations which enabled systematic, step-by-step programming of materials to be taught.

Skinner's proposals (in 1954, 1958, 1968) were made to a vastly different world than were Pressey's in 1924. Americans were on an economic upswing and in an "expansionist" mood after the shortages of World War II. More enamoured of technology than ever before, we were willing to spend our money on it. This generally expansive socioeconomic situation and mood was quite different from that faced by Pressey as America neared the depression years of the late 1920s and early 1930s.

Skinner's programmed learning and teaching machines were caught up as the technology, hardware, and programs for automated instruction, and Americans seized them gladly, hoping for some easy, technical solutions to the educational problems which had caused so much loss of honor. By the 1960s behavior modification—in the form of programmed learning—had become part of the curriculum in many schools. Research and publishing activity in the field grew rapidly and, in 1962 *The Journal of Programmed Instruction* appeared; its purpose was to "advance the techniques, applications, theories, and methods of programmed instruction as a means for furthering scientific knowledge of the learning process and improving the rational basis of instruction" (1962, p. 2). Publishers produced more than 350 new programs in 1963 alone, and variations in teaching machine hardware seemed to abound. Work continued amid a good deal of controversy that seemed much like that which would involve behavior therapy just a short time later. Controversy notwithstanding, programmed instruction became a regular part of many school systems across the country.

Those early teaching machines and programs of the 1960s have been long gathering dust in many school storerooms. Their modern counterparts are sophisticated, interactive, electronic minicomputers with their array of complex programs contained in tiny chips—many long steps from Pressey's 1920s mechanical devices. Other modern descendants are the systematic learning programs developed by Fred Keller and his associates, and used in college teaching.

The early 1960s large-scale acceptance of programmed learning was a major precedent serving to introduce behavioral programming into one of our most important social agencies, the schools, and helping to develop acceptance of behavioral concepts and procedures applied to children. The basic elements of Skinner's learning programs are the same as those involved in current functional analyses of behavior, applied to children or adults:

—Identify the targeted behavioral goal, such as acquisition of a set of facts, concepts, or overt behavior.
—Break down the goal into its constituent parts.
—Arrange them sequentially, in successive approximations toward the goal.
—Identify which is the most appropriate first approximation step for the individual.
—Allow the child to work through the program, systematically progressing along the successive approximation sequence.
—Provide contingent feedback at each step.

The functional analyses, systematic procedures, and contingent reinforcement aimed at the acquisition of new behavior defined programmed learning. Introduced in the schools, it has provided the basic paradigms which have been the foundation for virtually all subsequent behavior modification in the schools. The issues to which these paradigms have been applied have ranged from teaching academic material, through acquisition of social behavior, self-control, and the reduction of negative or disruptive behavior. The main point here is that the development of Pressey's teaching machines in the 1920s and Skinner's programs of the late 1950s turned behavioral laboratory research and concepts into clear behavioral technologies which were introduced into the schools in the early 1960s and became part of educational technology.

Here it is important to compare some aspects of behavior modification developed around issues of adults, and behavior modification which developed from a focus on children. These two lines of development share a strong commitment to empiricism and to behavioral concepts and techniques, and they constitute true alternatives to psychodynamic models of functioning.

However, the two developments also present some sharp differences which make them quite separate subareas. They differ markedly in their clientele, their assumptions about their clientele, the classes of behavior on which they focus, and, therefore, the goals to which the technologies and concepts are applied.

The earlier behavioral theories of personality were adult-oriented, focused upon explanations of psychopathology, and geared to the development of after-the-fact, ameliorative or restorative psychotherapy. This seems particularly true of Dollard and Miller, Salter, Eysenck, and Wolpe. It is clear that in spite of sharp differences between these theorists and the mental health field's prevalent psychodynamic models, they all share the psychiatric stance composed of adult-oriented, pathology-tied, restorative therapy goals. In all of these approaches the presumed pathology is central and the professional aims primarily, but not exclusively, at ameliorating the pathology, thereby restoring the person to a state of health, that is, to an absence of pathology. It is the psychiatric model, albeit with alternative theories and technologies, and they all fit well into the traditional mental health field.

Now consider behavior modification as it developed around children's functioning. The earlier work such as that of Jones (1924a, 1924b) was a restorative-therapy model, focused specifically on fear reduction. In the late 1930s Mowrer and Mowrer (1938) added to that literature their therapy technology for enuretic children. Thus some of the early work with children fits well into the more traditional mental health field along with adult behavior therapy. This line of development—clinical, restorative-oriented child behavior therapy—continues today as an important part of the field.

However, earlier work by Witmer, the urgings of J. Stanley Gray, and Pressey's designs for a new educational technology all pointed to a very different direction of application; and it was this latter tradition that was revived in the late 1950s and ushered into the schools. In this alternative development of behavior modification, investigators focused upon a good deal of behavior other than pathology. Their behavioral goals were those more appropriate for children—academic achievement, acquisition of positive social skills in classrooms, and so on. In Witmer, Pressey, Gray, and Skinner, we do not see an emphasis upon pathology, amelioration, and restoration, but on the *enhancement of normal, age-appropriate positive behaviors*. In this development, pathology is not the central notion. Rather, the child's normal, positive functioning is the central notion.

This discussion returns us to our earlier question, "To what ends do we develop behavior modification with children?" We concluded earlier that the application of behavior modification need not be tied to concepts of pathology nor limited to ameliorative, after-the-fact psychotheraphy; they now include potentials for humanizing social settings and for enhancing normal, healthy human functioning. That brief statement describes two traditions within behavior modification which we will label (A) the psychiatric, pathology-linked, ameliorative tradition in which behavior modifiers have become aligned with the traditional medical profession; and (B) a psychological, normal-functioning, enhancement tradition in which behavior modifiers are more closely aligned with the education profession.

VIII. CHILDREN AND BEHAVIOR MODIFICATION

We now wish to add an additional idea. These two traditions are most clearly represented and distinguished by the behavior modification developed and applied to adults, and that applied to children. In our view it is the child behavior modification development with its psychological enhancement and educational tradition that is the most radical departure from traditional psychiatry and offers the most fertile areas to explore. With its normal-enhancement goals, behavior modification with children leads us quite directly away from after-the-fact restoration, to future-oriented issues and procedures. It leads us to new areas and questions regarding behavioral technology application to enhancement of large-scale behaviors, such as society's collective health-acquisition and maintenance behavior. The tradition of child behavior modification which began with teaching machines in schools is, in our judgment, not only the most radical behavioral alternative to traditional mental health approaches but also our most exciting and promising direction of development. We are not arguing that we ought to limit our behavioral focus to children but are pointing out that by focusing on children this line of behavior modification development has escaped the limits of pathology, and has of necessity had to consider issues closely tied to growth, development, change, learning, and acquisition of normal skills.

In the mental health field the tradition has been to develop intensive clinical studies of individual, pathological adults, and to then generalize the inferences to children. This procedure underlies the entire field of psychodynamic therapy, and is now seen also in some behavior therapy developments. However, that leaves us limited to considerations of self-bounded individuals who are fixed in time. If there is to be any error in generalization from one population to another, we argue that much more will be conceptualized and accomplished by studying children primarily and then proceeding to adults. By doing so we must, because of the nature of the content—children—focus our attention on issues of growth, development, acquisition of normal functioning, and enhancement of healthy behavior. To apply generalizations based on those to issues of adults appears to us to be a potentially useful direction.

Neither do we intend to suggest that ameliorative behavior *therapy* with adults or children has little value. As long as individuals seek restorative help then behavior therapy will be a needed technology. However, we must recognize that whatever number of individual neurotics, smokers or other drug abusers, phobics, psychotics, and so on, are successfully reversed through behavior therapy, our society quickly fills their vacated spaces with still more. After-the-fact therapy may have great value for many individuals, and these services must be maintained; but it has little long-run value for society in general, and additional approaches are needed, including large-scale, community health-enhancement and maintenance approaches. It is our position that child behavior modification, as developed through the educational, developmentally oriented alternative, constitutes one promising path to those larger goals.

To what ends, then, are we to develop behavior modification with children? We believe that development must include both the ameliorative, therapy goals, and the developmental enhancement goals. The latter, we believe, are the most promising, and should constitute our major efforts. This takes us in the direction of applying our technology to large-scale, future-oriented issues and development of an educational and a behavioral community psychology, behavioral health-enhancement and maintenance, and education and training of parents and other child-responsible adults. To achieve these goals will require a far greater alignment of behavioral psychologists with schools and educational professionals, and a corresponding decrease of our growing identification with the psychiatric or clinical stance. It is our belief that our most productive future lies in the development of closer alignment with education, with emphasis on child development, and movement toward a behavioral psychology of enhancing normal child behavior and development.

In the remainder of this book we have tried to review important areas of child behavior modification. Throughout, even when discussing details of behavioral technology, we have tried to maintain our focus on the child, and to follow our own demands to temper behavioral technology with concerns for other values.

2

Autistic Children

I. INTRODUCTION

Despite Witmer's and Healy's early work, substantial interest in treating children generally and childhood psychoses specifically did not emerge until the mid-1930s (Potter, 1933; Despert, 1938). In 1943 Kanner, studying childhood psychoses, described a small sample of children characterized by "extreme autistic aloneness" and stimulated nearly 40 years of professional effort directed at the subgroup of autistic children. Considering the low frequency of autism (Rimland, 1964), this professional interest seems disproportionately high, but this may be due to the generally held assumption that autism is so basic a pathological condition that understanding its development and achieving therapeutic success will have direct and profound implications for all childhood psychoses. This assumption has not been validated and will, of course, depend upon future empirical study.

By the mid-1950s, however, some investigators had arrived at a pessimistic assessment of their therapeutic efforts. Eisenberg (1956, 1957) reviewed the literature and followed up 63 children diagnosed as autistic. He concluded that there was virtually no evidence for the effectiveness of psychotherapy or electrical or chemical shock therapy. Similar conclusions had been voiced by Kanner and Eisenberg (1955) and would be stated again by Brown (1960), Rimland (1964), Rutter (1966, 1968), Havelkova (1968), Yates (1970), and many others. It was clear that traditional psychodynamic therapy—for that matter, any therapy—had little or no effect on severely psychotic children. Further, in those rare cases where improvement had occurred, it appeared to be unrelated to any treatment attempts (Rimland, 1964).

By 1960 a good deal of professional experience with childhood psychoses had developed and with it an increasing conviction that the known, psychodynamic treatments were of little or no use. Alternatives were needed and behavior modification, reemerging at that time, seemed to promise much. In his summary of the early work Leff (1968) noted, "Traditional psychodynamic methods of therapy, in all their diversity, have failed to demonstrate any reasonable degree of efficacy with psychotic children" (p. 135). It was yet to be seen whether behavior therapy would demonstrate any greater success.

With particular reference to autistic children, the accuracy of diagnosis as well as the value of treatment is in question. Although good reliability can be obtained on gross categories, many investigators doubt the validity of the differential diagnosis of early infantile autism (Masters and Miller, 1970). Theoretical and empirical papers on etiology, clinical characteristics, and definitions of autism, with implications for treatment, have appeared, and a number of reviews are available (Rutter, 1968; Gelfand and Hartman, 1968; Leff, 1968; Wing, 1969; Ward, 1970; Churchill, Alpern, and DeMyer, 1971). Other papers, while not full reviews, also discuss issues of etiology and definition (Douglas and Sanders, 1968; Moore and Sheik, 1970; L'Abate, 1972; Rimland, 1971, 1972; Hingtgen and Bryson, 1972). As observed in Rutter's (1968) review, even among those investigators who agree that a definable condition exists, there are major differences in etiological models and thus in the appropriate treatment suggested by those models.

Attempts have been made to differentiate autism from other childhood psychoses on psychological, etiological, social, or biochemical characteristics (Piggott, 1979; Rimland, 1964). These results, however, have been inconsistent and as yet provide only a modest degree of useful information regarding differential methods for the prevention or treatment of these disorders. Our discussion will focus primarily on the deficits or excesses often present across all childhood psychoses.

II. BEHAVIORAL APPROACHES, 1960–1975

The clear failure of traditional psychodynamic therapy with psychotic children was a large factor in the quickened interest in applying behavioral approaches. One of the earlier attempts (Anthony, 1958) reported that autistic children were difficult to condition. Later, operant principles were applied to autistic children by Ferster (1961), Ferster and DeMyer (1962), and DeMyer and Ferster (1962). They presented a functional analysis of the psychotic child's therapy, utilizing an operant, social-learning framework emphasizing a deficiency of positive reinforcement in the child's learning history. A central notion in Ferster's analysis, still unverified, is that lack of positive reinforcement, particularly parental attention, is a major factor in creating many of the autistic child's deficits.

A number of papers soon followed which described the use of positive reinforcement in treatment strategies with individuals and with small groups of psychotic children (e.g. Hewett, 1964, 1965; Davison, 1964, 1965; Dubnoff, 1965; Hingtgen, Sanders, and DeMyer, 1965; Browning, 1967; Ney, 1967; Graziano, 1963, 1967). Several papers described not only contingent positive reinforcement in varieties of shaping procedures but, in line with Ferster's emphasis, focused on the importance of establishing and increasing the general reinforcing value of significant adults such as parents, teachers, and therapists, and, hence, their stimulus control of the child's behavior (Weiland and Rudnik, 1961; Lovaas, Freitag, Gold, and Kassorla, 1965; Metz, 1965). It is interesting that two of the early case studies employing contingent reinforcement (Weiland and Rudnik, 1961; Dubnoff, 1965) as well as a paper emphasizing the schizophrenic child's needs for social rewards and punishment (Goldfarb, 1965) were formulated by therapists working primarily from a psychodynamic framework to which they had added the reinforcement principles.

Other papers described combinations of positive reinforcement and aversive control. The latter included time-out and contingent electric shock, used to decelerate maladaptive surplus behavior, such as self-injury (Wolf, Risley, and Mees, 1964; Lovaas, Schaeffer, and Simmons, 1965; Tate and Baroff, 1966; Marshall, 1966). Ney (1967) compared operant conditioning and play therapy approaches with schizophrenic children. Most of the papers presented operant approaches and one, Graziano and Kean (1968) described group muscle-relaxation training to reciprocally inhibit high excitement responses in autistic children.

Through the 1960s the reemerging behavior modification technology was applied to problems of psychotic children and a sizable literature developed. The early work was exploratory, the results only tentative and suggestive, and no one claimed to have "cured" psychotic children with behavioral methods. Despite the serious design limitations characteristic of the exploratory phases of a developing approach, these early attempts provided workable alternative treatments for psychotic children. They showed that systematic behavioral approaches could effectively reduce severe psychotic behavior such as self-injury, and could teach some important skills such as speech.

Most behavior therapy with severely psychotic children during the 1960s had been carried out on a one-to-one basis, on the assumption that each child must develop basic prerequisite skills *before* interacting in a group setting. However, Graziano (1970a, 1974) described a program that assumed each child would develop basic and sophisticated skills *while* interacting in a group setting. The basic assumption was that the social group setting would provide greater opportunities than would individual treatment for learning across the wide variety of surplus and deficit functionings that characterize these severely disturbed children. The program utilized versions of naturally occurring social settings such as mealtimes and bedtimes to provide much of the necessary structure, social modeling, and specific and generalized reinforcers. Unlike Lovaas, who assumed that the language deficit was the crucial variable and thus emphasized individual language training more than all other training, Graziano's program focused on multidimensional programming, including language training, within the basic social setting. [See Graziano (1974) for a detailed discussion.]

Clearly, the soundest early work in the behavioral treatment of autistic children was carried out by Lovaas, and summarized by Lovaas, Koegel, Simmons, and Long (1973). Lovaas and his co-workers have provided detailed and reliable data on severely psychotic children followed over a number of years. Using detailed behavioral baselines (e.g., self-stimulatory behavior; echolalia; appropriate verbal behavior; social, nonverbal behavior; appropriate play), they applied consistent behavioral programming. Based on their assumption that language was a major deficit and language development a "pivotal" response, 80 percent of their program was devoted to language training. Children were worked with for periods of approximately twelve to fourteen months, and followed up.

According to their results, all children improved in the measured categories, some children minimally, and one of the twenty became "normal." (To our knowledge this is the only published claim, with some substantiating data, of having successfully moved a child from "autistic" to normal.") From their follow-ups they concluded that posttreatment placement is critical: that is, children discharged to hospitals all regressed, while those discharged to parents trained in contingency management continued or maintained their improvement.

The authors concluded that (1) there is so much diversity among autistic children that the overall diagnostic label, autism, is not useful; (2) there was no "key" or "pivotal" response as they had originally thought which, once developed, would serve as the basis for continued improvement; and (3) therapeutic improvement in autistic children comes about through small, slow steps that require extensive and detailed programming.

The last two points are critical; a popular wisdom exists that there is a "key" that will "unlock" autism, and perhaps childhood psychoses in general. This view is shared not only by laymen, but is an assumption implicitly made by professionals. We see it operating in the searches for biochemical bases, in the repeatedly voiced exasperation of the clinician who cries, "If only I could *get through* this child's defenses!" and the general assumption that perceptive interpretations by the therapist will click into action some natural healing psychomechanisms or will readjust out-of-phase internal conditions. It is truly a romantic philosophical notion, grossly simplistic in its application to human beings but, despite the lack of supporting evidence, it persists.

Other authors have made the same point (Graziano, 1974; Fischer and Glanville, 1970; Webster, McPherson, Sloman, Evan, and Kuchar, 1973; Rutter and Bartak, 1973; Wing, 1969; Browning, 1971; Koegel and Rincover, 1974; Browning and Stover, 1971). There has been enough evidence accumulated now to indicate that psychotic children can be helped through detailed, structured, slow, small-step, intensive work by therapists. This may not be as dramatic and romantic as other, earlier, notions of therapy but is undoubtedly more realistic. It remains to be seen whether the degree of improvement can be increased, and whether the gains justify the expenditure of resources.

The programs by Graziano and Lovaas illustrate two variations of behavior modification. They began independently in the early 1960s and were both heavily operant in concept but, because they made somewhat different assumptions about the "nature" of autism, they developed differently. Graziano assumed the most critical characteristic of autistic children was their generalized deficits that would best be treated in a multidimensional operant program within a complex social group setting. Lovaas assumed that the most critical characteristic of autistic children was their language deficit, a key variable that would best be treated through a highly individualized, primarily language-training program.

The repeated demonstration of the modifiability of children's psychotic behavior was perhaps the most significant achievement of the 1960s regarding psychotic children and was a clear advance over the earlier psychodynamic therapies. Behavior modification provided greater specificity and effectiveness, as well as a parsimony in methods and goals that promised to be easily taught to even nonprofessional therapists. Optimistic expectations emerged that if such apparently good results could be generated in only a few years by relatively primitive behavioral techniques and in uncontrolled research settings, further research would surely lead to greater refinements and successes.

Research continued and by 1975 a sizable literature was available on behavioral approaches to psychotic children. By then a number of important reviews of autism had been published including, in chronological order, those by Eisenberg and Kanner (1956), Rimland (1964),

Ward (1970), Moore and Shiek (1971), Wing, (1972), and DeMyer, Barton, DeMyer, Norton, Allen, and Steele (1973). From 1975 to the present, additional important reviews include Harris (1975) on language training, Lichstein and Schreibman (1976) on the use of electric shock, Margolies (1977) reviewing behavioral treatment approaches, and Piggott (1979) reviewing selected basic research studies in autism.

By the mid-1970s many treatment programs had been developed and applied in clinical, educational, and home settings. By that time nearly all investigators accepted the importance of parent training and posttreatment environments. Few have emphasized the family system as clearly as Clancy and McBride (1969) who wrote, "autism can be understood better as a developmental process operating within a social system, the family . . . (which has) many dimensions and levels of organization all interrelated and controlled by feedback mechanism" (p. 233). Other investigators who have emphasized family systems as major treatment setting include Berkowitz and Graziano (1972); Gardner, Pearson, Berkovici, and Bricker, (1968); Graziano (1970a, 1974, 1977); Pinkston and Herbert (1971); Nordquist and Wahler (1973); and Howlin (1973).

Behavior modification for autistic children in classroom settings had been carried out by a number of investigators including Fischer and Glanville (1970); Rutter and Bartak (1973); Koegel and Rincover (1976); and many others. Fischer and Glanville, using programmed teaching, followed the academic progress of 14 autistic children for one year. They noted that progress varied considerably between children and was achieved at a slow pace so that most autistic children would require "some ten years of teaching before they (would be) ready to commence a normal school curriculum" (p. 94). Such small-step progress has also been noted by Koegel and Rincover (1976) in their classrooms, by Browning (1971), and by Lovaas and his co-workers in their residential settings, and by Graziano (1974) in his day-care program.

Prior to 1975 a variety of methods was used in approaching many different behavioral targets as behavior therapists tried to bring about generalized improvements in overall functioning. Therapy programs tried to create major basic changes in overall adjustment, much as the older, more traditional psychotherapies had tried to do. Programs involving the child's full day in special settings were designed to manipulate "key" variables, such as language, that, once developed, would presumably then allow continued natural changes and improvement (e.g. Lovaas et al., 1973), or to train children in multivariable programs for improvement in many behavioral dimensions (e.g. Browning, 1971; Graziano and Kean, 1968; Graziano, 1974). Some children measurably improved in such programs. For example, gains in language and the reduction of severe tantrum behavior were noted. However, there is still no reliably demonstrated success in systematically bringing about overall improvement or "cure" through those programs.

However, if such "total" personality improvement could not be reliably brought about, the behavioral research did make it clear by the mid-1970s that highly detailed, small-step behavioral programming can result in significant improvement in specific behavioral categories, and in many predictable ways. Behavior therapy with severely psychotic children appeared a good deal more promising than had the pessimistic evaluations of psychodynamic therapy by Eisenberg (1956, 1957) and many others.

But if behavior therapy for psychotic children seemed more successful and promising than psychodynamic treatment, it was still not a promise of high efficiency and there was certainly no suggestion of any complete or overall cure. Behavioral programming was limited in its generalization value and required highly detailed, small-step approaches over long periods, perhaps years. The child's extra- and posttreatment environments had to also be programmed to maintain and augment improvements. Limitations notwithstanding, the concepts about successful therapy with severely psychotic children were being drastically changed through behavioral research. The traditional psychodynamic notion of the perceptive psychotherapist healing the sick child in an hour a week of dramatic, one-to-one engagements, was revealed as too naively simplistic to be of any real value. By the mid-1970s and certainly by now as we have entered the 1980s, the question must be raised as to whether individual psychodynamic therapy for psychotic children, particularly autistic children, is indicated *at all* except in special, rare circumstances as adjunct to basic behavioral programming.

III. BEHAVIORAL APPROACHES, 1975–1981

During the years from 1975 to 1981 publication continued at a reasonably high rate with at least 85 papers on the behavioral treatment of autistic children. A dozen were review or discussion papers and 73 reported empirical data. An additional large number of papers on behavior problems such as toileting and self-injury also included data on autistic and other psychotic children, and those papers are presented in another chapter, *Somatic Systems*. Thus it appears that well over 100 papers from 1975 through mid-1981 have reported empirical data on the behavioral treatment of autistic children.

In the following sections, while we will indicate the number of papers we located, space limitations do not permit our reviewing or even listing all of them.

The literature since 1975, inclusive, has been organized into five sections: *Language-Training*, with more than 40 empirical papers and two reviews; *Stimulus Overselectivity*, with 14 papers; *Specific Behavioral Problems*, with 7 papers; *Academic and Classroom Behavior*, with 13 papers; *Reviews and Discussions*, with 10 papers.

A. *Language Training*

1. Operant Approaches to Language Training

This is by far the most active area of behavioral research with autistic children, with more than 45 papers from 1975 to mid-1981, and seems to have been so since the early language-training reports by Hewett (1965), Lovaas, Berberich, Perloff, and Schaeffer (1966), Salzinger, Feldman, Cowan, and Salzinger (1965), Wetzel, Baker, Roney, and Martin (1966), and Wolf, Risley, and Mees (1964). The clinicians' and researchers' interest in language development may have been stimulated and maintained by the two observations that approximately one-half of all autistic children fail to develop speech (Rimland, 1964; Rutter, 1966), and those who do develop some speech by about age five appear to have a better prognosis for improvement than those without speech (Eisenberg, 1956; Rutter and Lockyer, 1967).

The behavioral language-training research has been reviewed through 1974 by Harris (1975), briefly reviewed through late 1975 by Margolies (1977), into 1978 by Goetz, Schuler, and Sailor (1979) and into 1980 by Howlin (1981). The reviewers arrived at quite positive conclusions that, despite a host of difficulties, the behavioral methods have brought about substantial speech and language improvement in many autistic children and acquisition of speech can be facilitated by teaching operant techniques to parents (Harris, Wolchik and Weitz, 1981).

Although approaches varied, a typical sequence of language training proceeded through four stages (Harris, 1975): (1) establishing control over the child's attending behavior; (2) shaping nonverbal imitation; (3) shaping verbal imitation; (4) shaping appropriate spontaneous or functional language. In the typical first training stage (establishing the child's attending behavior), contingent reinforcement is used to teach the child appropriate responses to commands such as "look at me." In this early part of training the child is often restrained to some degree, with the therapist seated very close, or through training in a special training booth (Hewett, 1965). Nonverbal imitation sequences begin with gross motor imitation such as hand-clapping, which is gradually refined to mouth and lip movements. Imitation training continues, shaping vocal and then verbal sounds, and finally proceeds to shaping increasingly spontaneous or functional language.

Among several important conclusions about the language-training research prior to 1975, Harris asserted that generalized responding by autistic children within a given response class such as motor imitation or a given grammatical construct "was relatively easy to establish." But the major weakness in the research was the same problem found in the early 1960s behavior modification; the limits of generalization beyond each response class and across settings. In language training, problems persisted in the transition of new speech and language behavior acquired in the training sessions to the child's natural environment. In this regard, in particular, Harris suggests that training the parents may be an important development.

By 1975, then, behavioral technology was being applied in a commonly used sequence of speech and language training for autistic children; the procedures were demonstrably effective in bringing about specific speech and language goals; and a major remaining problem was the adequate demonstration of generalization of the new skills from the training sessions to reliable performance under other, "natural" conditions.

Since Harris' review (1975), at least 20 speech and language training papers have been published. Several studies have demonstrated the effectiveness of decreasing undesirable speech, such as perseverations (Reichle, Brubakken, and Tetreault, 1976) and echolalia (Carr, Schreibman, and Lovaas, 1975; Freeman, Ritvo, and Miller, 1975; Schreibman and Carr, 1978). Most of the studies focused upon increasing appropriate speech through direct acquisition strategies (Benaroya, Wesley, Ogilvie, Klein, and Meany, 1977; Bonvillian and Nelson, 1976; Carr, Binkoff, Kologinsky, and Eddy, 1978; Casey, 1978; Fulwiler and Fouts, 1976; Handleman, 1979; Hargrave and Swisher, 1975; Hung, 1977, 1978; Kostantareas, Oxman, and Webster, 1977; Kozlowski and Richman, 1977; Miller and Miller, 1973; Stevens-Long, Schwarz, and Bliss, 1976).

Overall, these studies continue to demonstrate, as have researchers for nearly twenty years, that carefully applied behavioral programming can successfully bring about improvement in speech and language in psychotic children. There are two important new aspects to the recent papers: (1) a concern for issues of generalization, apparently heeding Harris' (1975) criticisms of the earlier work, and (2) the exploration of the use of sign language for communicating with autistic children.

Many of the recent studies, unlike the pre-1975 research, have made some attempt to assess the successful generalization of newly acquired speech and language skills from training to other, presumably more natural, settings in the child's life. The generalized skills include both those brought about by the acquisition of new skills and by the decrement of interfering behavior.

In two single-subject studies, generalization was measured across settings: that is, from ward training to school (Reichle et al., 1976) and across stimuli (Stevens-Long et al., 1976). In the latter study a six-year-old autistic boy was trained, using imitative prompts, differential reinforcement with food and praise, and time-out, to describe a series of pictures in grammatically correct, simple, and compound sentences. Substantial generalization was found for both sentence structures when the child was later tested on a new set of pictures. In addition to the measured generalization, teachers noted that the child began to spontaneously use simple and compound sentences in class.

Reichle et al. (1976) compared positive reinforcement, time-out, and a combination of both, to eliminate perseverative verbalizations in a six-year-old psychotic boy. Time-out and the combination of time-out plus positive reinforcement were more effective than use of positive reinforcement alone. The author suggests that in reducing perseverative behavior it may not be necessary to shape appropriate language but, rather, use of time-out in the natural setting such as school appears sufficient. Generalization from the ward to the school setting was demonstrated.

In another single-subject study Hargrave and Swisher (1975) reported the generalization of spontaneous speech from training to home. The generalization, however, was not measured, but was only incidentally observed.

Three papers reported studies using four subjects each. Carr et al. (1978) reported the generalization across therapists of newly acquired signing behavior by four autistic children. Hung (1977) trained four autistic children to use appropriate question-asking or "curiosity" behavior, using variations of "What is . . . doing?" and 'What is . . . for?" Training involved presentation of pictures of common objects and events and included prompting a correct question, such as "What is the stove for?" Positive reinforcement (praise and tokens) was contingent upon asking an appropriate question correctly. Incorrect verbalizations were corrected by the experimenter. After training, Hung examined generalization across settings, time, and response classes. Unlike the other experimenters, Hung reported that little generalization of spontaneous questions and answers occurred outside the training sessions until token reinforcement and appropriate modeling was provided in those other sessions.

Hung's work underscores the importance of actively planning or programming for generalization of new language skills, by providing both appropriate modeling and positive reinforcement in the "natural" settings. Hung suggests that the lack of generalization may have been partly due to the nature of the task, that is, "curiosity" behavior. For autistic children, he suggests, displaying curiosity is unusual, and thus may require particularly well-planned supports if there is to be any generalization from the training sessions.

In recent studies Handleman (1979) and Handleman and Harris (1980) trained seven autistic or "autistic-type" boys to respond appropriately to common questions. The training was carried out in two types of settings; (1) a "restricted" setting, consisting of a small training cubicle, and (2) several "natural" settings within the school, such as a classroom and a lounge. Generalization of their new behavior to the children's homes was tested by having each child's mother ask the various questions at home. Little generalization was found after training in the "restricted" setting (i.e. the training cubicle), but considerably more followed training in the various "natural" settings in the school. Handleman's work suggests the potential value of training autistic children in "natural" or more homelike settings in order to increase the possibility of generalization.

In that regard Graziano (1974) carried out the behavioral treatment of psychotic children in groups rather than individual sessions, utilizing activities and settings that approximated normal home situations, and stimuli that were true natural environment objects and events such as food, furniture, and people, rather than abstracted and artificial pictorial representations. The assumption was that such settings and activities "would increase imitative learning and vicarious reinforcement and should generally facilitate positive transfer of the learned behavior by more closely approximating the 'normal' world" (1974, p. 26). The point has also been made by Goetz et al. (1979) in their recent review of language training. They recommend the "careful . . . selection of responses that are likely to occur in the child's normal interactions with his environment, and which have intrinsic, potentially reinforcing consequences for the child" (p. 399). Such strategies, according to those authors ". . . are gradually moving language instruction away from the artificial stimuli, environments, and trainers that so often characterized early language intervention efforts with the severely handicapped" (p. 340). Lichstein and Wahler (1976) also emphasize the child's natural environment in their detailed "ecological" assessment of an autistic child.

This recent group of studies clearly indicates that researchers have become concerned with the problems of generalization of new speech and language skills from the training sessions to natural environments. The demonstrations of generalization across settings, and people, however, are not always convincing, and must still be viewed as exploratory and only suggestive.

In addition to research issues that apply generally to the field of behavioral training of psychotic children, several issues are specific to generalization of language skills. Future research on the generalization of language skills should continue to attempt to identify variables that will reliably increase the probability of successful generalization to the child's natural environment. When researchers design language training settings it may be advisable to begin by using natural home settings as models, to create training settings as much like the natural setting as can be efficiently managed. In this regard a potentially important procedure for improving generalization is to include parents in the child's training. By training child and parents together in the training setting, the generalization of learned skills to the home might be significantly facilitated. There is a considerable literature on parent behavioral training (Graziano, 1977) but except for Casey (1978), and Harris Wolchik and Weitz (1981), the recent papers on language training of psychotic children seem to have ignored this.

As Hung (1977) pointed out, there may be important interactions between the success of generalization and the type of task demanded of the autistic child. Some categories of speech and language may be much more readily generalizable than others.

A marked lack of information in the recent studies becomes apparent when we question the *maintenance* of generalized speech and language behavior. That is, research must be addressed not only to whether new language skills generalize to the natural environment but, if so, what is necessary to maintain and enhance the skills over long periods of time. The assumption seems to be that once the skills develop and generalize they will be maintained by the "natural" contingencies of the various natural settings. But few data are available to support that important assumption.

In general the behavioral training of psychotic children in speech and language skills continues to be of interest to psychologists, and is progressing. However, considering that Rimland's classic book is nearly twenty years old, there is a nagging suggestion that the progress could, perhaps, occur at a faster rate.

It appears to have been well demonstrated that many autistic children can be taught improved speech and language skills through carefully programmed behavioral approaches. The training remains much the same as the pre-1975 research discussed by Harris (1975), that is, the use of modeling, prompting, contingent positive reinforcement, and time-out to shape progressively more complex behavior, successively approximating speech and language goals. In the past five years the importance of generalization of newly acquired language skills has been recognized by researchers, and strategies to ensure generalization to the child's "natural" environments, such as home and school, are current areas of active research.

2. Sign-Language Training

However, despite the successes reported with many autistic children through operant-based language and speech training, some limitations of the approach have been noted (e.g. Howlin, 1981), primarily around the observation that these procedures have been less successful with autistic children who were mute than with those who were echolalic at the start of training (Lovaas, 1977). Despite intensive and detailed operant-training efforts, many of the mute autistic children still fail to develop speech or language and, if some do, they too often present a repetitious, essentially enlarged echolalic speech. While progress has been made for many autistic children, there still remains some unknown proportion who do not develop speech. We lack the necessary demographic data, but it may still be that even with advances in speech training, some one-half of all autistic children still do not respond well and do not develop speech. As was indicated much earlier by Rimland (1964) and Rutter (1966); their prognoses for improvement, compared with those who do develop speech, are poor.

The inability of many autistic children to develop language has led some investigators to attempt nonvocal, sign-language training, much as had been demonstrated by Gardner and Gardner (1969) with chimpanzees. As reported by Bonvillian, Nelson, and Rhyme (1981), some two dozen research reports have appeared, involving about a hundred autistic subjects ranging in age from 3½ to 23 years, with a mean age of about eight years. In one-half of these studies the subjects had prior operant speech training and in nine studies these prior attempts had failed. It is clear that the most recent research in language training of autistic children has turned to the exploration of sign-language training.

These still early attempts with sign-language training have generated interesting and promising reports, although most lack sufficient experimental control and a sufficiently large sample. Because they employ complex treatment packages, it is difficult to assess the effectiveness of individual treatment components. This work must therefore be considered potentially important but requires further investigation (e.g. Benaroya, Wesley, Ogilvie, Klein, and Meaney, 1977; Bonvillian and Nelson, 1976; Fulwiler and Fouts, 1976; Kiernan, 1981; Konstantareas, Oxman, and Webster, 1977; Miller and Miller, 1973; Schepis et al., 1982).

Carr, Binkoff, Kologinski and Eddy (1978) successfully trained four nonverbal autistic children to correctly use expressive sign labels based upon American Sign Language for the deaf. The sign labels were for commonly encountered items, specifically food (cookies, milk, apple, banana, candy). The training included prompting, fading, contingent positive reinforcement, and stimulus rotation. Two findings, in addition to the training's reported success, were a clear generalization of signing skills across therapists and a savings or learning set phenomenon: after mastering the first ten signs, three of the four children were able to master the next ten signs in many fewer trials. The second set included signs for clothing, toys, food, and grooming items. This suggests that the children were, among other things, "learning how to learn." Similar savings phenomena have been reported in studies of vocal language acquisition (e.g. Lovaas et al., 1973).

In another signing study Casey (1978) trained the mothers of four seven year old autistic children to use manual signs for communicating with their children. Their goal was to help reduce disruptive and other undesirable behavior and to help develop appropriate communication skills. Twenty mother-child training sessions were carried out for each child over a five-week period, with daily observations and recordings made of each child's communicative and disruptive behavior, both in the preschool classroom and during the training sessions. In both settings the children's communicating behavior increased while disruptive behavior decreased. Casey suggests that generalization of the children's improved communication behavior to home and school was facilitated by the manual sign program. The generalization, although described by teachers and parents, had not been systematically observed or measured. The most interesting aspect of this study was its integration of parent training with the new research interest in use of manual signs to communicate with autistic children.

In a review of the sign-training literature, Carr (1979) investigated three important issues involved in training autistic children in signing skills. One issue concerned whether sign training facilitates the development of speech. Carr concluded, after a review of the literature, that sign training has differential effects depending upon whether the autistic child is truly mute or is echolalic. The latter would, presumably, have fairly well-developed speech imitation skills. (Another review may be found in Bonvillian, Nelson, and Rhyme, 1981.) With mute autistic children sign training does appear to effectively teach signing skills and to therefore improve their communication skills. The *speech* of mute autistic children, however, does not appear to improve with sign training. In contrast, echolalic children not only learn signing skills, but many also improve their speech. Carr suggests that mute autistic children display far greater stimulus overselectivity than echolalic children thus visual as opposed to auditory stimuli are attended to and, as a result, the mute autistic child learns the manual signs but ignores the accompanying auditory stimuli, that is, the words spoken by the trainer

At this point, then, it appears that both mute and echolalic autistic children can gain communication skills through sign-language training, and that echolalic children but not mute children also gain in spoken language.

A second issue reviewed by Carr concerned the limits of what can be learned through sign training. It seems clear from the data that noun usage—naming familiar objects—can be taught and used through signing. However, whether more complex language can be taught is still in doubt. Some researchers (Fulwiler and Fouts, 1976; Konstantareas et al., 1977) found little or no improvement in use of prepositions, pronouns, and other more abstract language functions. One unpublished paper cited by Carr (Creedon, 1973) reports some success in teaching more abstract concepts through sign training. At this time, Carr concludes that teaching abstract concepts through signing is uncertain, but continued research, perhaps through long-term training programs, is clearly merited.

Finally, Carr reviewed research bearing upon whether sign-language training is associated with generalized improvement in autistic children. Here again, the findings are equivocal. A few studies report apparent improvement following sign training, in spontaneous communication, reduction of self-injurious and disruptive behaviors, and in improved social behavior (e.g. Benaroya et al., 1977; Casey, 1978; Konstantareas et al., 1977; Schaeffer et al., 1977). These results must be considered promising but very tentative and only suggestive, because they were obtained through complex treatment packages, and the specific contributions of sign training are difficult to assess.

Bonvillian et al. (1981) suggest that sign-language training has not been commonly adopted in programs for autistic children, perhaps partly because of resistance by parents and staff. Parents are often unwilling to allow sign language rather than speech training for their children, believing that it will hamper eventual speech development. Some staff believe that learning sign language will be too difficult for the children, their parents, and, perhaps the staff itself. In this regard we are reminded of the adamant opposition in the 1820s of the faculty, at Houy's Paris school for the blind, to their students' use of Louis Braille's new manual system for reading. The task, they believed, would be too difficult for the sighted faculty, and they forbade its use by their students—including the student Louis Braille himself—who apparently found the system far superior to the older system in use. Similar concerns in our modern context are not supported by data. Bonvillian et al. (1981) suggest that parents be trained in home programs to teach and support sign language to their children. Because the children can master only a few new signs each week, the parent-training time should be minimal, and limited to perhaps only a few minutes weekly. Home parent-child training of sign language appears to be a potentially important development, and more exploration here is urged.

Teaching the use of signs to autistic children is a newly developed area of inquiry and the few studies published suggest strongly that some skills in signing can be successfully taught to autistic children, and thus might prove to be of considerable potential value for those children who do not acquire speech. Future research is needed to investigate the improvement of training methods both for training effectiveness and for generalization from the training settings to natural environments. On the latter point it may be useful to carry out training in a variety of natural environment settings rather than in limited and highly controlled laboratorylike situations.

Beyond the issues of effectiveness and generalization important research questions concern: (1) whether teaching signing will facilitate speech, or (2) will be associated with generalized improvements. As yet (3) there are no clear criteria for predicting which autistic children will benefit from sign training. Finally, (4) we do not yet know the level of language skills that can be taught through signing.

Taken together the research to date on manual sign-training of autistic children is promising, suggesting that both echolalic and mute autistic children can be taught improved communication skills through signing and that echolalic children, in addition, can learn improved speech. To what levels of abstract language use the successful training can be carried, or the effects of manual sign training on generalized improvement, are complex issues and these questions cannot yet be answered.

For researchers and teachers who may be interested in learning this area, Moores (1981) recommends "the classic description of sign language structure by Stokoe (1958)," and literature reviews by Moores (1974), Wilbur (1976), and Stokoe (1976). "The most comprehensive and up to date treatment now available is *American Sign Language and Sign Systems* by Wilbur (1979)" (Moores, 1981, p. 155).

In summary, language training is the most active area of research in autism. Despite many design weaknesses, the research on behavioral methods in language training appears to have brought about substantial speech and language improvement in many autistic children. A continuing issue now being addressed is the generalization of language gains from training to more natural settings.

Many autistic children do not develop speech, even when training has been attempted. Recently some of these children have been successfully trained to use and respond to manual signs. This recent and promising development is of particular potential value with mute autistic children.

B. *Stimulus Overselectivity*

After language training another large group of studies in autism consists of 12 papers focused on stimulus overselectivity.

1. Use of Extra-Cue Prompting in Educational Procedures

One of the most frequent observations made by persons working with autistic children is the children's apparently characteristic narrow focus of attention. In academic, social, therapy or other settings autistic children seem to respond to only a markedly restricted portion of complex stimulus conditions. Earlier research (Lovaas, Schreibman, Koegel, and Rehm, 1971) compared autistic with normal and retarded children on a discrimination-learning task that involved a complex stimulus consisting of the simultaneous presentation of an auditory, a visual, and a tactile cue. After learning to respond correctly to the complex stimulus by pressing a bar, the children were then tested on how well they responded to each of the three cue components of the complex stimulus. That is, in learning to respond to the complex stimulus, had they learned to respond to one, two, or all three of the cues? While the normal children learned to respond correctly to all three of the cues, and retarded children responded in a variable fashion, the autistic children characteristically responded to only one of the three cues. They had "selected out" a single cue from the stimulus complex, learned to respond to it, and ignored the others. In this important research Lovaas et al. demonstrated "stimulus overselectivity" by autistic children.

A number of studies since then have investigated stimulus overselectivity in autistic children (Lovaas and Schreibman, 1971; Koegel and Wilhelm, 1973; Reynolds, Newsom, and Lovaas, 1974; Schreibman and Lovaas, 1973; Schreibman, 1975; Schreibman, Koegel, and Craig, 1977; Schover and Newsom, 1976; Koegel, Schreibman, Britten, and Laitinen, 1979; Kolko, Anderson and Campbell, 1980). As pointed out by Koegel et al. (1979), other research suggests that autistic children respond overselectively also when the multiple stimuli are presented within the same stimulus modality (e.g. Koegel and Rincover, 1976; Koegel and Wilhelm, 1973; Lovaas and Schreibman, 1971; Reynolds et al., 1974; Rincover and Koegel, 1975; Schreibman and Lovaas, 1973).

As a result of the clinical observations and studies of overselectivity, it became generally accepted that stimulus overselectivity is a characteristic behavior of autistic children, may be of a basic nature, and may have important implications for the children's education and training. The overselective responding, if truly characteristic of autistic children, might prevent them from making clear associations among stimuli presented contiguously—such as the stimulus complexes that face normal children all of the time. Overselectivity might thus be a major factor in the autistic child's difficulties with imitation, language acquisition, attention to appropriate cues, and generalization across settings and among stimuli.

One of the most common training procedures used with autistic children is the use of prompting, of providing extra cues to help the child make correct discriminations and other responses. In most training situations the prompts appear to be in direct proportion to the difficulty of the task—the more difficult the task, the greater number and repetition of the extra cues or prompts. Prompting involves the use of extra cues presented contiguously with the major stimulus (be it object, picture card, or a word) that is being taught. The teacher holds up a picture card (visual cue), points to it (another visual cue), says its name (auditory cue), and may even have the child feel the teacher's lips as the sound is produced (tactile cue). During training the various prompts are faded out, leaving only the original major stimulus, the picture, and questions, such as "what is this"? The rationale for the procedure is that all of the extra prompts early in the procedure help to establish the child's attention and correct approximations of the right answer.

But the work on stimulus overselectivity began to cast doubt on the wisdom of the usual prompting situation. If the autistic child overselects, that is responds to only one of the many cues in that prompting procedure, and if that is one of the cues later faded out, then the child will not learn the correct discrimination and response. Schreibman (1975) reasoned that "autistic children may have an attentional deficit" that makes the use of prompting of limited and questionable value. Schreibman tested six autistic children on two prompting procedures; (1) a typical, extra-stimulus prompting procedure consisting of a picture presented, and a prompt of pointing; (2) a within-stimulus prompting procedure that did not use an extra stimulus but, rather, called attention to some aspect of the central stimulus, the picture itself. Schreibman found that autistic children needed prompts to learn the correct discrimination; that while they consistently failed to learn the correct discrimination when the extra-prompt was used, the children did succeed when the within-stimulus prompt was used.

Schreibman concluded that the commonly employed extra-stimulus prompt procedure with autistic children may actually be of little use and the child might "fail to transfer from the prompts" (p. 111). Schreibman recommends that teachers of autistic children use within-stimulus prompts and a progressive fading procedure rather than the commonly employed extra-stimulus prompts.

Further doubt was cast on the use of prompts by Koegel and Rincover (1976) who compared normal and autistic children on their acquistion of discrimination responses through prompting (use of "extra-guiding-stimuli") approaches. Their results appear surprising and very informative: normal children learned better with a trial-and-error procedure than with the extra-stimuli prompting; both autistic and normal children who failed to learn the correct discrimination when prompting was used succeeded when no prompts were used! The experimenters concluded that the use of extra-stimulus prompting for both normal and autistic children is not only of questionable effectiveness, but may actually be "detrimental to the acquisition of training discriminations for all subjects, and particularly so for autistic children. Therefore, the common practice of providing extra guiding stimuli in proportion to the severity of the learning disorder may actually be harmful to the learning of new skills" (p. 60). They continue, "Further it appears that using prompts seems to be more harmful for the more "difficult" discriminations. . . . This seems particularly noteworthy since it is on difficult tasks where it is most common for teachers to use extra guiding stimuli" (p. 70). The authors concluded, "The fact is, based on the data available, one cannot conclude that prompting per se will facilitate learning. In addition, the current trend toward providing extra guiding stimuli for teaching slow-learning children appears to be unfounded. Further, this use of extra stimuli may actually block the acquisition of skills which the child is otherwise capable of learning" (p. 70). Additional evidence that prompts might interfere with functioning is provided by Nelson, Gergenti, and Hollander (1980). They found that extra prompts interfered with the generalization of learning by autistic children.

This research on overselection has practical implications because probably two of the most ubiquitous components of teaching "hard-to-teach" children are extra-stimuli prompts and stimulus fading. It appears that in light of the research, all practitioners such as therapists and teachers of autistic and other special children should reexamine their procedures and results.

2. Mental Age Levels and Learning

In her 1975 article Schreibman attributes overselectivity to an attentional deficit characteristic of autistic children. In general, workers in the field view overselectivity in this way, i.e., as a specific deficit peculiar to autistic condition. Schover and Newsom (1976), however, in an important but largely overlooked study, present data suggesting that the apparently characteristic overselectivity is not so much a function of the psychotic condition as a function of mental age. When they compared 13 autistic children with 13 normal children, matched for mental age, on performance on a complex visual discrimination task, they found the matched children performed to the same levels of accuracy. The autistic children were chronologically older than the normals but functioned as well as their mental age-matched cohorts. Schover and Newsom suggest that overselective attention in autistic children might be better understood "as part of a general developmental lag in cognition . . . than as a specific deficit underlying psychotic behavior." In light of Schover and Newsom's work, other researchers, both before and since, provide data that appear to support that interpretation. For example, normal children typically respond to complex, simultaneously presented stimuli by selecting out only some of the constituent cues (Eimas, 1969; Hale and Morgan, 1973; Ross, 1976). Further, as Koegel et al. (1979) point out, there are clear developmental factors operating, since the number of simultaneous cues responded to by normal children increases with age.

The implications of Schover and Newsom's findings for the training and education of autistic children are of considerable potential importance. That is, rather than assuming that all autistic children have a characteristic overselectivity and thus proceeding to train them in some standard fashion, Schover and Newsom's work suggests that careful discrimination among autistic children along mental age differences may be a necessary prerequisite for planning appropriate teaching strategies for each individual child. They noted, for example, that their use of the Leiter MA measure was more "important" than the presence or absence of language in predicting some of the children's learning. Other researchers have drawn similar conclusions (e.g. Bartak and Rutter, 1976; Frankel, Freeman, Ritvo and Pardo, 1978; Frith, 1972; Fyffe and Prior, 1978; Hermelin and O'Connor, 1970).

It may be that the tasks we typically demand of autistic children to help them make up their obvious deficits are tasks appropriate to higher MA levels and thus beyond the child's cognitive abilities. For example, showing a picture of a cookie, pointing to it, and repeating the word, "cookie," assumes that the autistic child is well able to manipulate the level of abstraction necessary to equate a two-dimensional picture with a real-world, solid, and edible object, called "cookie." In fact, however, we do not even know if the autistic child's perceptual organization of a picture is the same as other children's. That abstraction might simply be too far beyond many autistic children although, on the face of it, the discriminations required might seem simple to an adult. Using real objects in real settings rather than pictorial abstractions might be a more efficient and better generalizable method (e.g. Graziano, 1974), particularly with autistic children at the lower MA levels.

At this time, however, discriminating among autistic children for MA levels as a prerequisite to planning training programs for individual children does not appear to have been well investigated. In light of Schover and Newsom's findings, the lack may be an important omission.

Researchers have continued to investigate the variables that appear to affect stimulus overselectivity in autistic children. Schover and Newsom (1976) suggested that their variable reinforcement schedule might have contributed to a decrease of stimulus overselectivity. Koegel et al. (1979) compared continuous and variable ratio reinforcement. They reported that a VR-3 schedule, as used by Schover and Newsom, was associated with significantly less overselectivity. Thus, in training and educating autistic children, it might be possible to reduce overselectivity by modifying the reinforcement schedule used.

Another line of research (Lovaas et al., 1974; Lovaas and Schreibman, 1971; Schreibman et al., 1977) suggests that overselection might be reduced by modifying the testing procedures so as to include repeated exposure to the testing.

Rincover (1978) focused on the nature of the stimulus characteristics of the discrimination task. Rincover's results tend to support Schreibman's (1975) earlier findings that within-stimulus prompts and fading appears to be a more effective teaching procedure than extra-stimulus prompts and fading. In Rincover's work a "within-stimulus-distinctive-features" fading procedure was found to be best and, he suggested, "the most efficient and productive fading procedure available for teaching autistic children" (p. 550). However, he adds, the prompting and fading procedure is still of limited value and a good deal of research is yet necessary in order to understand stimulus overselectivity and effectively bring it under control. We will undoubtedly continue to see a good deal of research in this area in the 1980s.

C. *Specific Behavior Problems*

There are seven reports of successful treatment of specific behavior problems of autistic children including single-subject case studies (Ives, Harris, and Wolchik, 1978; Luiselli, 1978). Ives et al. described an "autistic like" five-year-old boy who had always refused to eat solid foods. Using a forced-feeding procedure, negative reinforcement, and positive reinforcement in the form of preferred foods, the child was quickly taught to eat a wide variety of solid foods. Only a few other attempts at teaching food-refusing children to accept a wider array of foods have been reported (e.g. Bernal, 1972; Palmer, Thompson, and Linscheid, 1975).

Luiselli (1978) reported a single-case study in which a seven-year old autistic child's fear of riding the school bus was eliminated. A graduated program of positive reinforcement for spending increasing periods of time on the bus, at first while parked and then in motion, resulted in loss of the fear behavior, and maintenance of appropriate bus-riding one year later.

Wells, Forehand, and Hickey (1977) reported success with two autistic children in reducing their stereotyped behavior. Verbal warnings and overcorrection were employed.

The "compulsivelike behavior" of two children was eliminated in a study by Rincover, Newsom, and Carr (1979). For one child compulsive behavior included light-switching, licking, spitting, self-stimulatory rocking, and masturbation. The second child also displayed a variety of compulsive behavior, including "light-switching." It was the latter behavior that was common to both children and on which this particular study focused. The experimenters utilized a procedure they termed, "sensory extinction:" for one child, when the light switch was disconnected and the lights were no longer turned off, light-switching behavior decreased markedly. For the second child, they found, it was the audible "click" of the switch that apparently maintained the behavior. When the switch was modified to prevent any audible sound, even though it was still functional, the second child's behavior also dropped out. The authors comment on the importance of determining the particular factors for each individual child responsible for maintaining compulsive behavior before attempting to decrease the behavior.

The foregoing papers were important demonstrations of behavior therapy for specific problems behaviors of autistic children. One paper (Luiselli et al., 1977) included follow-up one year later. However, they are essentially unreplicated case studies, useful for demonstration of new techniques and generating new "hunches" and ideas for future more controlled study.

The stereotyped behavior of six autistic children was studied by Frankel et al. (1978), who compared low and high IQ autistic children across conditions of high and low environmental stimulation. They reported that for the low IQ group self-stimulation increased under conditions of high environmental stimulation, while it decreased for the high IQ group. This study and others (e.g. Coleman, Frankel, Ritvo, and Freeman, 1976; Schopler, Brehm, Kinsbourne, and Reichler, 197[illegible]) suggest that stereotyped behavior of autistic children may be significantly influenced by immediate external stimuli. To this, Frankel et al. added their findings that the effects of environmental stimuli may systematically vary with the child's intelligence. Like Schover and Newsom (1976), they point out the potential importance of intelligence as a variable in the treatment of autistic children.

D. *Academics and Classroom Behavior*

1. Mainstreaming Autistic Children

Many of the recent papers are particularly relevant to issues of academics and classroom behavior. Largely because of new laws public schools are now more frequently called upon to provide suitable education for autistic and other difficult-to-teach children. The new laws, increased public concern, and even lawsuits on behalf of autistic children will, it is hoped, solve a frequently noted problem: the nearly automatic and complete exclusion of autistic children from public school classes (Brown, 1963; Lovaas and Koegel, 1973; Lovaas, Schreibman, and Koegel, 1974; Rutter, 1971). All of this new activity promises to put increasing numbers of autistic and other special groups of children into the public school system.

Russo and Koegel (1977) point out that research on placing autistic children into the educational system falls into two major categories; the one-to-one teaching setting, and the special class specifically limited to autistic children. Both groups of studies present evidence for their effectiveness and both thus appear feasible and effective, but both, according to Russo and Koegel, are limited. The one-to-one settings are time consuming and expensive. The special classes may allow more efficient use of teachers' time, because they typically include four or more children per teacher. However Russo and Koegel express concern that such special classes are too limited and "may provide merely another form of exclusion [thus depriving the children] of several possible benefits, including the influence of appropriate role models and the exposure to a nonautistic curriculum taught in regular classrooms" (p. 580).

The authors suggest a third alternative, that of integrating autistic children into regular classrooms. The remainder of their article details a single case of a five-year-old autistic girl successfully placed into a normal public school kindergarten with 20 to 30 normal children, one teacher, and an aide. Their procedure included multiple-baseline measurements of three target behaviors: self-stimulation, social behavior, and verbal response to commands. These target behaviors were modified by a therapist within the classroom using token rewards for positive reinforcement of social and verbal behavior, a loud "no" and removal of tokens as punishment for self-stimulation. Later in the process the teacher was trained to continue the behavioral programs using token and, increasingly, social reinforcement. Tokens were gradually thinned out and the therapist faded.

The child's behavior was observed to measurably improve in all three behavior targets to the level where her behavior "was more than adequate, as judged by school officials, to ensure her continuing in the public school" (p. 558). Indeed, the child was promoted to first grade at the end of the year, continued in school, and had no severe problems through follow-ups at first, second, and third grades, all with different teachers. A brief return to self-stimulatory behavior at the start of first grade was quickly controlled and did not occur again.

The researchers concluded that the child was successfully taught to function well enough to remain in the public school, and that the teacher was readily taught to maintain the child's good functioning.

Although this is a single-subject study, it did include multiple-baseline measurements, was systematically carried out, and follow-ups were included for several years. Any of us who have worked intensively with autistic children will recognize this as an extraordinary demonstration of what can be accomplished with careful, individual programming. It is to be hoped that other clinicians and researchers will carefully review Russo and Koegel's procedures, and carry out more such work.

The authors, of course, made the assumption that autistic children in general and that specific child in particular, would gain more in a normal classroom than in a special classroom, such as one limited to autistic children. That is certainly a reasonable assumption, but it is an assumption. The question is one in need of empirical answer, and a good deal of research is needed to determine whether regular or special classes provide the most effective settings for autistic children.

2. Effects of Normal Peer Models

One of the many questions that must arise when we consider placing autistic children in normal classes is whether the children can profit from normal peer models. Given the autistic child's difficulties with social perceptions, it seems doubtful that much could be taught through modeling by normal peers. However, the possibility of learning through observations of normal models was a major assumption in the very early program (1961–1966) for autistic children reported by Graziano and Kean (1968) and Graziano (1974). That program, however, yielded only descriptive data on the effects of such modeling. More recently Coleman and Stedman (1974) described a single case in which an autistic child appeared to have learned some loud-voice modulation through observing a normal peer. Again, the data were only descriptive.

The only experimental investigation of this issue that we located, was reported by Egel, Richman, and Koegel (1981). Four autistic children from five to seven years old were selected because their teacher indicated they were having particular difficulties with various discrimination tasks. Five discrimination tasks, specific for each child, were selected as target behaviors. Using a multiple-baseline design across subjects (Hersen and Barlow, 1976), the experimenters had each autistic child attempt discrimination tasks (baseline, no-modeling condition) in which a teacher/therapist presented instructions and provided reinforcements. Each child then attempted the tasks in a modeling condition, in which the same procedures as in the baseline were employed but with the addition of a normal peer, who modeled the correct responses. Finally, an additional no-modeling (baseline) condition was carried out.

The researchers report that in the peer-modeling condition the autistic children demonstrated greatly improved functioning on the discrimination tasks and maintained the improvements in the final return-to-baseline condition. Thus, at least for these children and those tasks, normal peer modeling appears to have facilitated learning for autistic children.

The authors speculate that the effects may have been due more to novelty than to modeling effects, or perhaps to the relatively high-level functioning of these autistic children compared with many others reported in the literature. Whatever may have brought about the improvement, the observations imply that "moderately impaired autistic children, who are presently placed in segregated classrooms for the severely handicapped, could benefit from the opportunity to observe normal peers" (p. 10).

The data presented by Egel et al. appear to be important in planning autistic children's education. Their major implication is that integrating autistic with normal children, for at least some controlled portions of time, may have beneficial effects. Their finding warrants further investigation of the effects of normal peer models, with other than simple discrimination tasks. To what levels of social complexity, for example, might modeling be effective for autistic children?

3. Improving Education Technology with Teaching Machines and Programmed Learning

The assessment of teacher training in work with autistic children has been investigated by Koegel, Russo, and Rincover (1977). In a planned series of different teaching situations, the behavior of 12 autistic children and 11 teachers was observed and measured. The investigators reported that all 11 teachers were successfully trained in specific behavior modification techniques, while learning "generalized skills effective with a variety of children and target behaviors" (p. 197). This research will increase in importance, particularly as we become more involved in public school placement of autistic children.

With new interest in teaching autistic children academic material in public school classes, the general question of teachers' efficiency and the use of mechanical aids such as "teaching machines" has to be raised. The teaching machine "revolution" occurred in the early 1960s (Graziano, 1971) and a considerable technology of programmed instruction developed, including not only increasingly sophisticated mechanical and electronic hardware, but also development of various types of programs or "software." One major conclusion of early research was that programmed instruction is particularly applicable to special issues, problems, and children, as an adjunct to more traditional teaching approaches. With the wealth of research on programmed instruction and the agreement on its particular applicability to special issues, it is very surprising to find so little use of programmed instruction with autistic children. Some of the early research included that of Colby (1973), Colby and Smith (1971), and Ferster and DeMyer's (1961) now classic work. However, with the exception of some unsystematic approximations of programming techniques used in classrooms and by some therapists, there has been little investigation into what once promised to be a potentially important and productive line of inquiry. We suggest that those working with autistic children begin to seriously investigate this area.

One paper in the recent literature (Russo, Koegel, and Lovaas, 1978) did study the use of a teaching machine with four autistic children. Using a matching-to-sample task, they compared results of teaching the children in three conditions: by a teacher, alone; a teaching machine, alone; a teacher using the machine with the child. The researchers reported that while the teacher-alone and the teacher-plus-machine conditions were effective, the child's use of the machine alone was not. The automated instruction, they concluded, "may at least serve as a valuable aid to teachers of autistic children," but the use of the machine alone will require a good deal more research.

There is a great deal of variety among automated teaching equipment and while the particular apparatus used in Russo et al. was not effective when used alone, some other automated teaching equipment or programs, or feedback mechanisms or reinforcers might, indeed, be effective. But even more importantly, it should be pointed out that automated instruction (or teaching machines or programmed teaching) is not necessarily intended for use by students alone, without supervision. One of the major cries of "despair" in the late 1950s and early 1960s was the automated-instruction proponents' unendingly repeated response to their critics that teaching machines are not intended to be replacements for the live teachers! The apparatus and the programmed material can assist in pacing the pupil, in presenting material in an organized, readily reinforced form, and so on. Indeed, one of the more potentially important effects of using programmed instruction with students might be that it requires the teacher to carefully program the material and to organize its presentation to the student in great detail. Rarely does any teacher, even with special education children, organize his or her lesson plans or curricula to the degree required for good programmed instruction.

Thus the further investigation of programmed instruction with autistic children should be encouraged as a potentially useful teaching tool. Research on the types of material used, the kind of pacing and presentation mechanisms, the reinforcers used, the types of programming, and so on, are all sources of variation within the apparatus named "teaching machine," and careful study should be carried out with all of them.

4. Peer Trainers

As noted earlier, autistic children have been taught in special classes limited to autistic children. Typically in those settings the teacher provides a great deal of individualized attention and structure (e.g. Graziano, 1974), often moving around the room from one child to another, attending to each in turn, while the others presumably continue their own work alone. Studying this situation Rincover and Koegel (1977) found that when the teacher moved on to the next child, the previous child stopped working and, overall, little academic progress occurred in this typical "rotational" system. The researchers then taught the children to continue working after the teacher had moved on, and their academic progress increased. The major implications of this study touches upon the common assumption that autistic children cannot be taught in groups or integrated into regular classrooms because they require nearly constant, one-to-one attention. These researchers demonstrated that autistic children can be trained to continue academic work without constant, individual, teacher attention.

The two final papers in this group of classroom-oriented research are by Etzel and LeBlanc (1979) and Strain, Kerr, and Ragland (1979). In the first paper the authors propose a method for choosing effective, individually geared teaching procedures for autistic and other "difficult to teach" children.

Strain et al. demonstrated ". . . dramatic . . . increases in positive social behaviors" for four low-functioning autistic children. Most interesting in this study is that the "trainer" for the children was an eleven year old, nonautistic boy who had been placed in the school because of "academic and conduct problems." The peer trainer was readily taught how to initiate play between pairs of autistic children and how to verbally prompt and socially reinforce their play. As had been found in previous studies of adult-mediated interaction among autistic children (e.g. Strain, Shores and Kerr, 1976; Strain and Trimm, 1974) no generalization from the training sessions occurred. However, the apparent success of the peer trainer in the training sessions suggests interesting possibilities for working with autistic children in the classroom.

Related to the use of peer trainers in school is training siblings of autistic children for work at home. Schreibman, O'Neill and Koegel (1983) trained three sibling pairs in behavioral techniques to help the autistic siblings learn some discrimination, labeling and language usage tasks. The authors report that the sibling training procedures were effective not only in improving the autistic children's targeted behaviors, but also improving the normal siblings' positive attitudes toward the autistic siblings.

5. Motivation of Autistic Children by Various Stimuli

The reader has by now noted our frequent references to work by Robert L. Koegel at the University of California at Santa Barbara. Koegel's research in autism has been both prolific and important. Among the many issues he and his associates have pursued is the basic, general issue of how to maximize our effectiveness in teaching autistic children. This basic question seems to run through much of Koegel's work that we have already discussed. Four additional papers will be presented briefly.

One recurrent observation about autistic children is that they appear to be little affected by many of the external incentives that operate for normal children. The inference is often made that they are "unmotivated." Dunlap and Koegel (1980) discussed earlier research indicating that stimulus novelty and variation may increase children's responsiveness to educational instructions. They then studied the effects of stimulus variations on the learning of two autistic children. Using a multiple-baseline design across behaviors, they presented tasks to the children in two conditions: a *constant-task* condition in which a single task was repeatedly presented throughout learning sessions, and a *varied-task* condition in which all instructions and procedures were the same as in the constant tasks, but with a variety of tasks presented rather than a single task, repeatedly.

Dunlap and Koegel found "generally declining trends" in response for both children under the constant task condition and substantial maintained improvements in correct responding during the varied-task condition. The authors speculated that the children's motivation may have been enhanced. They also suggest that the commonly used teaching procedure of having autistic children perform a task repeatedly so as to achieve a long string of correct criterion responses might create "boredom" and reduce motivation. Continued research, seeking ways to provide more stimulus variation and novelty in teaching programs for autistic children, is recommended.

6. Arbitrary versus Natural Reinforcers

Another issue investigated by Koegel and his associates is the functional relationship of reinforcers to responses. In operant-based teaching approaches with autistic children, the reinforcer, whether primary or secondary, is almost always provided by the teacher, so as to assure the contingent presentation of the reward. Although attempts are made to individualize the reinforcers so they are effective with each child, most often the reinforcer seems to bear little relationship to the child's functioning at the time, except for its contingent presentation by a teacher. In large measure the positive reinforcer is arbitrary, a choice made by the teacher. When, for example, a bite of food is made contingent upon a correct choice on a color-discrimination task, this teacher-created situation revolves around the arbitrary, implicit demand, "When you give me the correct answer I will give you a bite of food." There is no prior or "natural" relationship between the reward and the child's response. Might learning be enhanced if the contingent rewards were "natural" or functional consequences of the child's behavior chain, or natural elements of the learning situation?

Ferster (1958, 1967) raised this question and distinguished between natural and arbitrary reinforcers. Skinner (1982) has discussed the same issues. Years earlier Guthrie (1935) had discussed the same point, in a slightly different model. Guthrie's discussion was not focused on reward, since contingent reward was not a necessary part of his learning theory. Rather, he discussed natural consequences of behavior that served to end the behavioral act and, because they were contiguous with the act, therefore constituted a single learning event.

The arbitrary-natural reinforcement distinction is made clear in the following lines from Ferster (1967).

> This distinction between arbitrary and natural positive reinforcement becomes practically important when we consider building behavior in children in the natural environment and particularly therapeutically (Ferster, 1958, 1961, 1966). The following is an example of the arbitrary application reinforcement by a therapist: "If you put on your coat, I'll give you a cookie." Such an episode begins with a child who has no disposition to put on his coat and a disposition to eat cookies. The therapist is reinforced when the child puts on his coat but not necessarily when the child eats the cookies. Such behavior benefits the therapist and will cease as soon as he stops giving the cookies. The child's natural environment has never reinforced putting on a coat with cookies and is not likely to do so in the future. The same performance could be reinforced naturally, however, if the coat served to prevent the child from being cold outside (Ferster, 1967, p. 346).

Ferster notes there are many opportunities for a therapist to utilize naturally occurring outcomes as reinforcers in children's learning settings, and suggests that in building programs for children we focus on such natural reinforcers.

This was attempted in an early operant program for autistic children (1961–1966) reported on by Graziano (1974). In that program the physical and temporal structure of the learning environment (e.g. room arrangements and sequencing of events) was aimed at maximizing the availability of natural reinforcers. Thus snacks and lunchtimes, naps, and trips to stores or rides on buses were arranged so as to include natural-environment elements. Lunch time, for example, was arranged to simulate family mealtimes and a host of behaviors, from sitting quietly, to asking for foods, passing items around the table, opening and pouring from bottles and packages, verbally identifying foods, colors, shapes, smells, and textures, using eating utensils, and so on, were stimulated, practiced, reinforced, and, presumably, learned.

For example, the following exchange occurred at a snack time, with four autistic children and two teachers seated around the table:

Ritchie: "Juice, please."
Teacher: "Which juice do you want?" (There was orange juice and tomato juice.)
Ritchie: (pointing) "Red."
Teacher: "O.K. How do we ask for it?"
Ritchie: "I want red juice, please."
Teacher: (handing the tomato juice) "Very good, Ritchie. Here it is. What color is it?"
Ritchie: "Red. It is red!" (Ritchie pours, drinks, obviously enjoying it.)
Teacher: "Mmm, good," (She prompts.)
Ritchie: "Mmm, good." (He drinks more.)
Teacher: "What tastes good, Ritchie?"
Ritchie: "The juice tastes good."
Teacher: "And what does it taste like?"
Ritchie: "Tomato! Tomato juice," he says, loudly.
Teacher: "Right. Tomato juice. It tastes like tomato juice."

This exchange continued and all four children and both teachers were involved. The children were given trials in identifying red, orange, and white colors, all reinforced by appropriate sips of their choice of tomato or orange juice or milk. The teachers were reinforced by the children's good responding.

When possible, such sequences would include the child asking for a specific drink, being passed the container by another child (prompted by the teacher), carefully opening, pouring, and drinking. Each entire chain, it was assumed, would be reinforced by the thirsty child's eventual drinking of his or her preferred juice.

While this program incorporated the natural/arbitrary reinforcer distinction and planned in its attempts to maximize "natural" or functionally related reinforcers, its data were all descriptive, and without controlled, experimental validation.

Concerned with the same issues raised by Guthrie and Ferster and incorporated by Graziano, Koegel and his associates (Koegel and Williams, 1980; Williams, Koegel, and Egel, 1981) provide experimental data showing improved response acquisition by autistic children through arranging that the reinforcer be part of the behavior sequence involved in the task. "For example," they noted, "locating a reward inside a container might be a more efficient way to teach a child to open a container than by handing the child a reward for opening an empty container" (Williams et al., 1981, p. 53).

The researchers compared learning under conditions of arbitrary reinforcement in which, for example, if the target behavior involved a hand movement, the reinforcer might be placed in the child's mouth, "with a functional reinforcement condition." In the latter the tasks were arranged so the "target behavior became directly functional in procuring the reinforcer." (Williams et al., 1981, p. 55). Specific details of trials and tasks are given in the two articles.

The investigators found that under the functional reinforcement condition there was considerably more rapid response-acquisition and maintenance even under a return to arbitrary reinforcement conditions. Their data, although involving only three children in each study, provide evidence that the arbitrary/natural reinforcer distinction as discussed by Ferster (1967) and the development of naturally occurring or functionally related behavior-reinforcement sequences, such as described and applied by Graziano (1974), are potentially important areas for further controlled research, possibly leading to improved effectiveness in teaching methods.

7. Varying Intertrial Intervals

Improved teaching methods have also been researched in regard to intertrial intervals. Many studies have already been carried out on the effects of systematic manipulation of stimulus and reinforcement variables on learning. In addition some researchers have suggested study of events occurring between the manipulated trials, that is, during the intertrial intervals and, in particular, study of the temporal variables, the duration of the intertrial interval and its effects upon learning. Several studies have been carried out with infants and preschoolers (Watson, 1967; Bogartz and Pederson, 1966; Croll, 1970). Carr, Newsom, and Binkoff (1976) reported improved learning and decreased disruptions when nontask stimuli were presented during the intertrial intervals.

Koegel, Dunlap, and Dyer (1980) briefly discussed the above studies and concluded that the literature was at least suggestive that manipulation of intertrial intervals might improve children's learning. They tested the suggestion with autistic children and found that varying the intertrial duration did, indeed, affect task performance. Overall, shorter intervals (about 1 second between the reinforcement of the preceding trial and the presentation of the discriminative stimulus for the next) compared with long trials (4 seconds or more) produced greater percentages of correct responding. The tasks involved a variety of educational tasks that were part of that particular class's learning program: object, verbal, and number discrimination; verbal imitation; color labeling; use of prepositions; and following instructions in sequence.

The authors interpreted their results as support for the hypothesis that intertrial interval duration affects autistic children's performance. But, they caution, short durations may not be better for all autistic children under all task conditions. Rather, some combination of duration and task for particular children resulted in those findings. Further research on the interaction of intertrial duration with task and subject variables is recommended.

In the past five years researchers have paid increased attention to the details of teaching autistic children in classrooms. Over the next five years, with continued social demands for special education in public schools, we will undoubtedly see more research in the classroom teaching of autistic children. Two particularly promising areas in which there is yet little research appear to be (1) the integration of autistic children into regular classrooms; and (2) the investigation of the use of programmed materials and automated teaching equipment. A number of other areas including sign language training and use of peer trainers also appear promising.

IV. REVIEW AND DISCUSSION PAPERS

Several important review articles published in the last five years provide important information for teachers, clinicians, and researchers in autism, and these papers should form a basic part of their libraries. A variety of subjects have been covered in these papers, including: language training (Harris, 1975; Goetz, Schuler, and Sailor, 1979); comparing psychodynamic and behavioral approaches to autism (Helm, 1976; Lovaas, 1979); cognitive abilities and disabilities of autistic children (Prior, 1979); basic physiological, biochemical, etc., research (Piggott, 1979; Ritvo, 1977); behavioral approaches to treatment (Margolies, 1977);

and employing contingent electric shock (Lichstein and Schreibman, 1976). Some of these reviews were included in the above discussions and the main conclusions of the others will be briefly presented here.

Basic studies of autism have been discussed by Ritvo (1977) and by Piggott (1979). Ritvo briefly annotated a number of biochemical studies involving serotonin, tryptophan metabolism, catecholamines, and enzymes. Overall, the studies appear to be exploratory in nature with important research implications, but as yet with insufficient data to generate reliable conclusions. The studies, according to Ritvo, ". . . have raised more questions than they have answered—a sure sign that our science is young" (p. 378).

Piggott more completely reviews physiological, neurophysiological, and biochemical studies in autism and concludes, "There is accumulating evidence that organic disturbances are related to and may be responsible for many of the symptoms seen in various children called autistic. Which and to what degree these disturbances are unique to autism or are also involved in a variety of other developmental deviations is unclear and in need of continued research" (p. 213).

Prior's (1979) review of cognitive abilities and disabilities of autistic children appears to be particularly important for education and training efforts. The author reviews three issues that she considers to be of "major importance in the future investigation of the nature of childhood autism" (p. 357). They are (1) the importance of making distinctions among autistic children for mental ability or developmental level. Prior suggests that future ". . . insight into the autistic disorder is most likely to come from study of the more intelligent subgroup (of autistic children) whose behavior is less governed by severe developmental delay and intellectual retardation" (p. 358). This reflects Schover and Newsom's conclusions (1976) regarding mental age distinctions among autistic children; (2) the importance of correcting methodological flaws in current research, such as the apparently continuing "failure to control for developmental and/or retardation factors"; (3) the etiological implications of the hypothesis of "dysfunction or lack of development of left or language hemisphere functions in autistic children."

The behavioral treatment literature was selectively reviewed by Margolies (1977) and included brief discussions of diagnoses, etiology, and relationship to schizophrenia as well as effectiveness of behavioral interventions. Margolies' review was organized around target behaviors, for example, self-injury, aggression, tantrums, and so on with brief reviews of the research in each target behavior. Margolies concludes that while the literature is largely "preexperimental," that is, largely lacking in experimental or quasi experimental controls (Campbell and Stanley, 1966), the large body of work "cannot be taken lightly and does appear to provide support to justify continued research." Behavioral approaches are still limited but at least at present, they appear to be the most completely researched and best validated approaches to autistic children that we possess.

In a review of the side effects of using contingent electric shock with autistic children, Lichstein and Schreibman (1976) conclude that most of the unintended side effects reported have been of a positive nature, including improved "mood," social behavior, affection, and calmness. Although evidence for negative side effects, such as increased emotionality and temporary suppression rather than permanent decrease, has been published, the evidence for such negative effects is "minimal" and is not characteristic of treatment by contingent shock. Lichstein and Schreibman conclude that response-contingent shock can be beneficial when used correctly and under carefully controlled conditions such as; (1) *immediate* presentation following the maladaptive response; (2) *consistency* or reliability in application to help ensure the child will discriminate the occasion for punishment; (3) with accompanying teaching of positive alternative behavior; and (4) with the active programming for generalization from the training setting to other parts of the child's environment.

The use of contingent electric shock is an extreme treatment for extreme behavior, such as severe self-injury. As the authors conclude, "Treatment for autistic children, regardless of modality, is usually slow and difficult. We cannot afford to abandon any therapeutic approach with this population without a careful analysis of the costs and benefits" (p. 172).

Helm (1976) briefly reviews examples of both psychodynamic and behavioral approaches to childhood autism and concludes that both theoretical positions are included in virtually all therapeutic efforts. "The similarities in methods of intervention found in the work of investigators of very different theoretical persuasions raise the possibility that most treatment methods owe more to empirical clinical experience than to their presumed derivation from a theoretical model" (p. 27).

It seems clear that empirical factors are of major importance in determining treatment approaches and that the basic tasks involved in the adult endeavors of helping autistic children demand, by their very nature, some commonality across theoretical approaches. The psychoanalyst and the behavior modifier, whatever the nature of their theoretical differences, do begin with some basic, common assumptions that the child is "malfunctioning," that the therapist possesses sufficient knowledge and skills to justify attempts to help the child, that "helping" the child is a desirable general goal, and that it can be achieved through some detailed interaction of the therapist and the child.

However, despite those commonalities we believe it may be a serious error to suggest that the theoretical differences in fact make no practical difference, and that the psychodynamic and behavioral treatments are really "all the same." Whether treatment approaches based upon different theoretical positions are "the same" is, of course, an empirical question itself that has not yet been completely answered, although virtually all opinion and unsystematic observations would argue they are not the same. One of the most important empirical issues in comparing approaches to treatment concerns the effectiveness of the outcome of the interventions, and we have yet to see consistently positive, validated outcomes reported in the psychodynamic literature, as we have seen in the behavioral literature. We would certainly expect psychological therapists, of whatever theoretical persuasion, to share some common values, beliefs, and approaches. But the differences between them, derived from their different theoretical positions, may be the important factors that contribute to treatment success or its lack. Lovaas (1979) in contrasting the behavioral and the "illness" models in the treatment of autistic children, notes that if the psychodynamic (i.e. disease) model ". . . had been a viable and effective model for treatment of autistic children, the behavioral model probably would not have seen the light of day" (p. 316).

The point here is that recent interest (e.g. Helm, 1976; Wachtel, 1977) in integrating psychoanalytic and behavioral approaches might effectively obscure the most important differences between the models, those that may be responsible for the apparent successes of the behavioral model. The sharpening of the theoretical differences, at least for the time being, appears to be potentially more productive than what might be a premature leveling process.

V. CONCLUSIONS

Behavioral approaches to autistic children have been explored at least since the early work by Ferster in the late 1950s and early 1960s. Case studies, controlled research on specific issues, and long-term, complex group programs for education and treatment have been developed and reported in the literature. A good deal has been accomplished in these 20 years, as explorations of the behavioral—almost entirely operant—approaches developed.

It has been repeatedly demonstrated that many autistic children, particularly those who were echolalic before treatment, can be taught in carefully organized, educational programs. Children have learned to communicate and to respond to vocal and written instructions, to cooperate with other children and teachers, and to control and reduce their originally frequent tantrum behavior. Self-abuse has been reduced and in some cases, eliminated. Many children have shown academic progress. There is little doubt that behavioral approaches to the education of autistic children has been successful, with a great deal more data and validation of its success than any other educational or treatment approach.

Our success, of course, has been incomplete. Autistic children vary in intellectual levels, language ability, spatial and physical abilities, and physical characteristics, that is, the variation among autistic children is great, indeed, and the same operant approaches that might prove so successful with one child may be ineffective with another. Research within the behavioral framework is still needed to help determine which approaches are most appropriate for which problems of which children. Even in those cases of successful behavioral treatment the children still retain autistic characteristics, such as peculiar speech, poor sociability, and so on. Despite our best efforts this writer at least, has yet to see a single autistic child who has been so successfully habilitated as to appear completely "normal." Some therapists, researchers, and parents may claim to have observed such changes, but to our knowledge no convincing evidence has yet been put forth.

In spite of the limitations we must conclude that at least at this point, operant behavioral programming for the education of autistic children is the treatment of choice. Given our current knowledge and the near-total lack of validation of any other treatment approaches, somatic or psychological, operant programming must constitute the minimum and basic approach to autistic children. At the very minimum, our current data tell us to provide daily, detailed behavioral programming, preferably in educational settings and including goals of academic as well as social skills. Other approaches need to be explored, perhaps somatic treatment or more traditionally psychotherapeutic treatment. But these, if we are to be prudent, must be considered as ancillary to the behavioral programming, and far more tentative and experimental in nature. Indeed we will go so far as to assert that any professional who treats an autistic child in any way other than with behavioral programming *and thereby precludes the child's obtaining such behavioral programming*, is behaving unethically. It is the ethical responsibility of professionals, of whatever theoretical position, to advise the parents or other caretakers of their autistic child-clients that behavioral programming is the treatment of choice, although other approaches may be taken as ancillary or as experimental.

It is to be hoped that our major concern will be to continue providing the most effective treatments known for autistic children. At the same time our research must continue to seek improvements in current treatment methods, and to explore new models and methods. We do not wish to imply that our emphasis on the ethical demand to provide behavioral programming as the basic treatment is a statement that only behavioral treatments will be effective. In our continuing search for effective treatments, progress at any point in time must be viewed as tentative and we must be prepared to discard our models if alternative concepts and approaches are developed and are shown to be superior.

3

Mentally Retarded Children

I. INTRODUCTION

Mental retardation is not a single disease, syndrome, or symptom and the intellectual, behavioral, and physical signs by which it is recognized vary widely in kind and severity. Many factors have been associated with the etiology of mental retardation, including infection and intoxication, trauma, disorders of metabolism and nutrition, brain disease due to pre- and postnatal influences, chromosomal abnormality, gestational disorders, psychiatric disorders, and environmental deficits (Grossman, 1973). Rarely can exact causes be determined, and the condition is often the result of more than one etiological agent.

The extent, variation, and complexity of the conditions labeled as mental retardation are reflected in the large number of research articles, monographs, and books wirtten by researchers from all areas of the medical and social sciences. This chapter will discuss the major behavioral issues in mental retardation. More inclusive and extensive analyses of research on mental retardation can be found in Mittler (1977a, 1977b, 1977c); Snell (1978); Yule and Carr (1980); and Hogg and Mittler (1980).

The most widely accepted classification of the mentally retarded is the American Association on Mental Deficiency's (AAMD) biomedical and behavioral approach (Grossman, 1973). The biomedical aspect separates the retarded according to etiology; the behavioral approach is of primary concern to the behavior therapists, defining mental retardation relative to the intellectual and behavioral norms of development of an individual's chronological age group. The AAMD suggests four major classifications: mild, moderate, severe, and profound retardation.

The exact number of individuals included in each category has been difficult to specify due to frequent changes in definitions and problems of accurate diagnosis and representative sampling in prevalence studies. However, six to seven million persons in the United States are labeled mentally retarded. Parents, guardians, family, teachers, and researchers, intimately involved in the lives of the mentally retarded may number over 20 million persons (Cleland, 1978). Goldenberg (1977) estimated that of retarded people 85% or about 5,900,000 are mildly retarded; 10%, or about 700,000 fall into the moderate category; 4%, or about 280,000 can be categorized as severe; and less than 1%, or under 70,000 fall into the category of profound retardation.

Deficits in both intellectual and adaptive behavior functions are necessary for the classification of mental retardation. The assessment of intellectual functioning utilizes the standard IQ tests such as the Stanford-Binet or the WISC-R. More difficult to assess quickly and reliably than measures of IQ are measures of adaptive behavior. The Vineland Social Maturity Scale (Doll, 1965) and the Adaptive Behavior Scales (Nihira, Foster, Shellhaas, and Leland; 1969) are the measures most widely in use. These rely on evaluations by individuals who are familiar with or who directly observe the child. They attempt to assess the individual's ability to adapt to environmental demands focusing on functional areas such as walking, feeding, social skills, dressing and grooming, toileting, communication, and stereotyped and self-destructive behaviors.

The empirical validity of this classification system is a matter of continuing debate (e.g. Adams, 1973; Balthazer, 1978; Baumeister and Muna, 1975; Brown and French, 1979; Cleary, Humphreys, Kendrick, and Wesman, 1975; Ellis, 1979; Roos, 1979; Taylor, 1980). As Dubose (1978) notes "If the ultimate goal is to change behavior, the IQ score is probably the most trivial bit of information available about a person. By excluding other theories of human adaptation and learning, cultural, motivational, and physiological factors known to account for variability of performance are ignored" (p. 5). Concerning measures of adaptive behavior, Baumeister and Muna (1975) comment that "Adaptive behavior scales often turn out to be a poor man's intelligence test, and they generally enjoy such high correlations with standardized intelligence tests to suggest that these are functionally equivalent measures" (p. 303). Further, the AAMD dimensions of mental retardation are often difficult to distinguish from behaviors associated with autism, learning disability, emotional disturbance, and other syndromes or manifestations of isolated deviance. Where such distinctions are not easily drawn, the diagnosis of mental retardation is dependent largely on the variable commodity of "clinical judgment," although recent research has attempted to arrive at more empirical methods of evaluation (e.g. Freeman, 1979; Krug, Arick, and Almond, 1980; Petersen and Hart, 1978).

These criticisms emphasize the problems with the label "mental retardation." Adaptation and intelligence are only meaningful in relation to the demands of a particular social system. Grossman (1973) cites the deletion of the borderline category of mental retardation as reflecting changing concepts about the social capabilities of persons with low intelligence. How well a person with a low IQ adapts may vary widely from culture to culture, between communities and among families. Individuals cannot be adequately and meaningfully evaluated on such simple dimensions as general intelligence or adaptation as these variables do not necessarily reflect the personal, social, and environmental elements which provide a useful behavioral profile of the individual. This may be particularly true of mild retardation where changes in provision of services, the efficacy of schooling, the availability of employment, and factors related to the assessment process appear particularly crucial (MacMillan, Meyers, and Morrison, 1980; Horner, 1980; Clark, 1977). Cobb (1972) in a review of cross-sectional prevalence and longitudinal follow-up studies of the mentally retarded noted that as age increases there appears to be a considerable drop in the prevalence of mild retardation. This suggests that many persons classified as mildly retarded, be it due to less academic pressure, delayed maturation, or whatever, apparently achieve satisfactory adjustment.

In summary, from a behavior analyst's point of view, even careful use of the AAMD classification according to intellectual and adaptive functioning is misleading. Individuals with the same AAMD diagnosis may differ widely in ability to learn new behaviors, in physical signs, and in a variety of characteristics not included in the evaluations used to arrive at classification. Stereotyping and attempts to limit what retarded individuals can and cannot do seem implicit in the AAMD diagnosis. Behavior modifiers using carefully individualized functional analyses can continue to apply behavioral principles and research to aid children labeled mentally retarded to overcome or augment many of their current behaviors (Throne and Farb, 1978).

II. BEHAVIORAL INTERVENTIONS

Although recent behavioral research with the retarded has questioned the immutability of a child's subaverage IQ [see Farb, Cottrell, Montague, and Thorne (1977) for a review of recent research], the concept of IQ and the label of mental retardation itself implies that a child's behavior is relatively fixed and enduring. These concepts seem not to recognize or emphasize the powerful influences possible through modification of the environment. Emphasizing the "retardedness" of a child instead of the retarded *behavior* of a child may promote a hopeless view of the education and treatment of the mentally retarded. It is behavior, not test scores, that usually precipitate the labeling of the mentally retarded and it is the modification of everyday behavior, not the modification of test scores, that is most relevant to everyday functioning and amenable to consequential change.

However, as noted in Graziano (1975), the field finally seems to be developing a new clinical sensitivity to the selective power of our social environment. Early examples of this include work by Fuller (1949) and Rice and McDaniel (1966) who attempted conditioning procedures with profoundly retarded, "vegetative patients." Rice and McDaniel pointed out that profoundly retarded children with severe metabolic defects, who "function on a near-zero behavioral level," were found to respond differentially to a limited array of reinforcers. Blackwood (1962) reported several cases in which operant shaping procedures modified grossly bizarre behavior in severely retarded patients. Other early reports of operant conditioning with patients usually thought to be "untestable" and "unteachable" include Ellis, Barrett and Pryer (1960); Orlando and Bijou (1960); Spradlin (1962); Gold (1972); and Bellamy, Peterson, and Close (1975). A problem for the behavior modifier has been and remains, not to standardize the mentally retarded individual, but to continually develop and transmit a technology to researchers, teachers, family, and practitioners so they may effectively teach this population.

A. *Intervention Settings and Personnel*

Until recently the school setting was often the only place for the systematic programming of the mentally retarded, with institutional or home environments serving caretaker functions. It was left to the special education teacher in the classroom to properly sequence and fit the school program into the immediate and long-term goals of the home, school, and institution, with little thought to the generalization of skills learned in the school setting to the child's everyday functioning. However, the utilization of alternate personnel in a variety of settings is changing this situation. In the school various paraprofessionals have been used to augment the teacher's classroom role. Examples include Gladstone and Sherman (1975) who used videotaped modeling, rehearsal, and corrective feedback to successfully train high school students to implement behavior modification principles to teach profoundly retarded children to follow simple instructions. Warner and Jones (1968) found it possible to teach elementary school children to be tutors for the retarded. Retarded adolescents have also been utilized as therapeutic agents for their peers and for younger retarded children (Wiesen and Watson, 1967; Whalen and Henker, 1969).

Programming in the institution, where in spite of deinstitutionalization a large number of the severely retarded will spend a majority of their lives, is one area in need of continued progress. Research with retarded and normal infants has shown that the restricted and unstimulating environment of the institution can impair developmental functioning (Francis, 1971; Skeels and Dye, 1939; Skeels, 1966). However, there is also evidence that when the deficient nature of stimulation in institutions is changed the functioning of the retarded is raised (e.g. Horner, 1980; Lyle, 1959).

Whether for mental patients or retarded residents, the institutional environments surrounding the clients are most directly controlled by the ward or residence staff, with the nursing staff perhaps the most crucial. Unlike the traditionally distant administrators and the higher-status but less powerful doctors, nurses occupy a pivotal position in carrying out and supervising daily, direct-care services for residents and occupying a supervisory and decision-making role that largely determines both policy and procedures in their particular ward.

It is encouraging that detailed training programs for nurses in behavior modification have recently come into existence (Closurdo, 1975; Scott, 1977). And, increasingly, the use of ward staff and other paraprofessionals to implement behavioral programs with the retarded is being explored (Carsrud, Carsrud, and Dodd, 1980; Tucker, Hollis, Sailor, Horner, Kelly, and Guess, 1976; Galloway and Larsen, 1976).

The most significant trend in utilizing personnel in the natural environment of the mentally retarded has been to include parents as treatment providers (see also the chapter on Family Systems, pp 187–230). Recently, early and prolonged intervention in the home, using parents as educators, has been shown to have potentially powerful and significant effects upon the early development of both the moderately and severely retarded child (e.g. Ludlow, 1979; de Coriat, Theslencc, and Waksman, 1968; de Lorenzo, 1977; Garver and Heber, 1977; Karnes and Zehrbach, 1977). Such intervention in the home has the benefits of providing long-term, continuous treatment, economy, and training in the environment for which most adaptive behaviors are taught. Further, if families are thought to contribute to the development of some mild retardation, training of such "high-risk" families would presumably provide the environmental enrichment necessary to limit or eliminate the retardation (Stedman, 1977; Ramey and Campbell, 1977; Parmelee, 1977; Montenegro, Lira, and Rodriquez, 1977). There is a growing literature on the training of parents of the handicapped and retarded (e.g. Revill and Blunden, 1979; Menolascino and Coleman, 1980). Baker, Heifetz, and Murphy (1980) report such training can have long-term (one year) benefits. Cash and Evans (1975) used young children as behavior modifiers for their younger, retarded siblings. This involvement of other family members is another interesting development that might be valuable in future intervention programs.

B. *Teaching Academic Skills*

A major issue in research with the mentally retarded has been whether academic skills were too complex for the severely and profoundly retarded to master. Traditionally only the mildly retarded were considered capable of any complex academic skills such as reading or math. Increasingly, such arbitrary judgments based on a child's IQ or AAMD classification have been questioned. The emphasis of most current research on the development of academic skills in the mentally retarded has been to investigate efficient and effective ways to teach individual retarded children, given their unique skills and deficits. As with normal children, the crucial decisions in teaching the mentally retarded do not center around the limits of what can potentially be learned—although for both normal and retarded children there may be definite limits—but rather on how educational resources and training can best be utilized so that the individual child can lead the least restricted, most productive, independent, useful, and fulfilled life possible. Again, such decisions are dependent not only on the available educational technology, but also on the resources, priorities, and values of society.

C. *Teaching Preacademic Skills*

Preacademic skills are often presumed to be critical components in the successful accomplishment of academic goals. Although the utility of modifying preacademic skills instead of academic skills directly has been questioned (see our Schools chapter), preacademic skills-training in both regular and special classrooms still receives considerable attention in the behavioral literature.

Stoudenmire and Salter (1975) implemented a multiple "baseline instructionless" (nonverbal) operant conditioning program for a retarded, nonverbal, hyperactive 3½-year-old girl. The girl was given a light breakfast and then 3 hours' food deprivation. For 20 minutes she was then reinforced with food for "immobile" behavior lasting 5 seconds or more and for another 20 minutes for "attending" to the toys with which she was playing. Stoudenmire and Salter found that both immobile and attending behavior were sensitive to operant control. Although no data on maintenance or generalization were presented, they did report that when the immobile and attending behaviors were being reinforced, the girl's hyperactive behavior diminished.

Systematic teacher praise has been used effectively to increase the on-task behavior of educably retarded children (see Kazdin, Silverman, and Sittler, 1975). Strain and Pierce (1977) examined the effect of such teacher praise on targeted children and also on nontargeted children working alongside the targeted children. They assigned four educably mentally retarded children to two pairs, each pair working at a table. One of each pair was targeted to receive social praise contingent on attentive behavior. Strain and Pierce found that social praise by student teachers increased the attentive behavior of the two targeted retarded preschool children. Spillover effects were noted for the nontargeted children who also increased their attentive behavior, but the treatments, which lasted 20 days, showed less effectiveness for the nontargeted children as the days progressed, suggesting that spillover effects may initiate better behavior but some direct consequences may be necessary to maintain these changes.

Hill and Strain (1977) examined such spillover effects in a classroom with both retarded and nonretarded children. They trained teachers to deliver social praise and attention, contingent on task persistence, to seven retarded children. They found that the reinforcement the teachers provided was functionally related to task-persistent behavior. No spillover effects to mentally retarded or nonretarded children were observed, unlike other studies done exclusively in special classrooms (e.g. Strain and Pierce, 1977). The authors suggest that this lack of spillover effects in a normal class may be due to the low status of the "models" who were labeled "mentally retarded."

Tokens have long been used in the classroom to change a variety of behaviors, with preacademic skills being no exception. Utilizing a token system to increase attentiveness in two young retarded boys, Kazdin and Geesey (1980) found that allowing the reinforcers that back up a token system to be "preselected" by the boys (i.e. selected before the earning of the tokens) led to higher levels of attentiveness than the more remote option of selecting back-up reinforcers after the token had already been awarded. An implication of this study is that the success of the behavior modification of the retarded boys was augmented by their active participation.

In many areas of behavior modification such active participation has been extended to training in "self-control" or "self-management," where the client becomes active controller of his or her own behavior. It is a hopeful trend, in terms of maintenance, generalization, and basic human dignity, that such procedures are beginning to appear in the mental retardation literature (Shapiro and Klein, 1980; Burgio, Whitman, and Johnson, 1980; Horner and Brigham, 1979; Coleman and Blampied, 1977). Still in an early case study stage, the results can only be suggestive. Shapiro and Klein (1980) used and then faded various prompts to build up self-assessment and self-reinforcement in four mentally retarded/emotionally disturbed children which resulted in an increase in on-task behavior. Burgio et al. (1980), in the context of a game, taught two mentally retarded children to focus attention on tasks, thereby decreasing off-task behavior. Coleman and Blampied (1977) and Horner and Brigham (1979) both found self-monitoring to increase on-task behavior with back-up reinforcement by the retarded children (Horner and Brigham, 1979) or others (Coleman and Blampied, 1977), resulting in further improvement. Although issues of the maintenance and generalization of such gains remain largely unexplored, the demonstration of the feasibility of using such procedures with the mentally retarded should go far in changing many limiting stereotypes in the mental retardation field.

D. *Educational Curricula*

A number of incentives, reinforcements, and techniques have been utilized to increase mentally retarded children's performance in academic skills such as mathematics and reading. In a special-class study with 12 educable, mentally retarded 8- to 12-year-old students, Van Houten and Van Houten (1977) compared public posting of individual performance with public posting of the overall class or "team" performance. Daily reading performance was measurably increased over baseline by public posting of individual performance. The addition of posted "team" performances further increased reading levels. In addition, comments made by peers about classmates' reading also increased with public posting as a differential performance feedback.

In a second experiment the investigators enlisted "confederates" from among the special-class children to increase their encouraging comments about classmates' reading. Van Houten and Van Houten found that both reading-lesson mastery and comments by the target peers increased with the classmates' increased encouraging comments.

The fairly simple and economical use of public posting of individual plus group performance as feedback, plus increased, encouraging peer comments were demonstrably effective in improving reading performance for these special-class, educable mentally retarded children. The researchers suggested that the effectiveness of public posting might be, in part, due to its effects on increasing peer comments which, in turn, may serve to reinforce and maintain improved reading.

Whether the systematic manipulation of temporal limits would enhance the academic performance that educably retarded children had already achieved in a token system was investigated by Ayllon, Garber, and Pisor (1976). Three children had been taught to do arithmetic problems for 20 minutes with correct responses exchangeable for a variety of privileges later in the day. They found that if they abruptly decreased the time allowed to work on the problems from 20 to 5 minutes, the rate of correct performance fell 25 to 80%, in addition to causing often disrupting emotional reactions by the children. When the limits were decreased slowly, however, the rate of correct responding increased 125 to 266%. Thus the gradual restriction of temporal limits seems to be a potentially effective way of increasing the rate of academic performance at least in tasks which are reasonably well learned.

In teaching complex academic skills such as reading and math, the subject matter is usually arranged in order of complexity and broken down into small steps (e.g. Resnick, Wang, and Kaplan, 1973; Williams et al. 1978; Braaten, 1979; Snell, 1978). Many teaching programs are now available for teaching specified skills to the retarded (see Wehman and Bates, 1978 for a review). One development that might prove useful is computer-assisted teaching programs (Lally, 1981).

Brown and York (1974), Williams et al. (1978), and others argue that commercially available programs are often not concrete, precise, or relevant for use with the severely or profoundly handicapped. They particularly note that commercially available programs do not usually apply directly to moderately and severely handicapped students. Most programs provide insufficient opportunities for practice and skills instruction; they often employ large-group and worksheet instructional formats; they use abstract tasks to teach skills instead of concrete functional tasks; and often use complex levels of receptive-expressive language. Although procedures for acquiring specific task skills are available (e.g. Wacker, Carroll, and Moe, 1980), the need remains for commercially available educational programs on academic skills which can be taught to the moderately and severely retarded. These academic skills need to be taught in the context of daily, functional use so as to teach more independence in the activities of daily living, recreation, and vocations [see Revell and Wehman, (1978) for a further discussion of issues relevant to vocational training].

E. *Communication*

As preacademic skills have been considered critical in the acquisition of academic skills, prelanguage skills such as head control, eye contact, and related behavior have been considered critical prerequisites to the acquisition of verbal language (Finnie, 1970; Gunn, Berry, and Andrews, 1979). Richman and Kozlowski (1977) investigated the effectiveness of contingent social reinforcement on behaviors prerequisite and collateral to the motor habilitation and beginning language development of a 9-year-old severely retarded, multiply handicapped girl. Appropriate eye contact, head control movements, and the beginning of an implementation of an imitative vocalization language-training program was brought about one behavior at a time through prompting and social reinforcement. Gains maintained over a 6-month follow-up, with the behavior of drooling, although not directly treated, also showing improvement. While such programs, utilizing sound behavioral methods, may be effective in their short-term goal, their necessity as a precursor for training in the acquisition of language is an empirical question open for research.

Language acquisition itself includes both comprehension, the ability to grasp meaning, and production of a linguistic response under stimulus control (Cuvo and Riva, 1980). With nonretarded individuals, a large body of literature suggests that auditory comprehension facilitates and possibly precedes verbal production. A growing body of behavioral literature appears to question the necessity or usefulness of including comprehension procedures in the training of language acquisition with the mentally retarded (Cuvo and Riva, 1980; Miller, Cuvo, and Borakove, 1977; Smeets and Striefel, 1976). Miller et al. (1977) examined generalization and transfer between comprehension and production in mentally retarded subjects. They found that teaching reception did not affect expression, but teaching expression resulted in almost total generalization to reception. Further, the results indicated that there were no savings in trials to criterion on expression-acquisition after having been trained on reception.

The mentally retarded have been shown to have less skill than normal children in being alert to cues from past experience which may be important in the formation of appropriate discrimination skills necessary for proper language acquisition and generalization (Ross and Ross, 1979;

Robinson and Robinson, 1976; Bray, Justice and Simon, 1978). Thus language production may be easier for the mentally retarded to learn than language reception. It may be that encompassing stimulus situations in which language is produced may be easier for the retarded individual to discriminate than a single linguistic utterance with few other relevant stimuli, and possibly many misleading and irrelevant cues present.

To the severely and profoundly retarded as well as the deaf retarded, various manual communication, sign, and symbolic languages have been taught with considerable success and with many positive behavioral side effects, often where attempts to teach verbal language have failed (Berger, 1972; Cornforth, Johnston, and Walter, 1974; Vanderheiden et al., 1975; Hollis and Carrier, 1975; Poultin and Algozzine, 1980; Denmark, 1978; Hodges and Deich, 1978; Rowe and Rapp, 1980). These studies argue that manual communication, sign, and symbolic languages are often easier for the retarded to learn than verbal language. Murphy, Steele, Gilligan, Yeow, and Spare (1977) note that no single language medium may be most effective for the language acquisition of all children. They present a case which involved a 14-year-old moderately retarded boy with an apparently complete absence of receptive or expressive language and unreliable hearing, persistent tantrums, and stereotyped autistic features. He seemed unable to learn receptive or expressive sign language after extensive operant training. However, with an identical training method that employed symbols as pictorial representations of objects, he rapidly acquired a limited 13-symbol language. Other researchers have found that such nonverbal language acquisition can form the basis for the ability to learn verbal language, with the resulting combination of nonverbal and verbal language providing more effective communication than either alone (Barrera, Labato-Barrera, and Sulzer-Azaroff, 1980; Rondal and Hoffmeister, 1976).

Verbal imitation appears to be a key component in the development and acquisition of language. Hung (1976) used verbal imitation as a key component, along with detailed shaping procedures, to train basic verbal responses in three severely retarded children. Clark and Dameron (1978) argue that the acquisition of general imitation skills may aid in the development of verbal imitation. They developed a simplified training procedure which did not require shaping by ward staff in individual sessions to extend verbal imitation of four severely retarded nonspeaking children who could imitate some motor behavior but few vocal responses. Training consisted of interspersing vocal behaviors that retarded children could *not* imitate with vocal and motor behaviors that they could imitate and reinforcing those imitations. Results successfully extended vocal imitation to new vocal behaviors. Such a procedure, using simple reinforcement of imitated behaviors to extend those behaviors, would appear to be easier to implement than a program which uses shaping, fading, modeling, prompting, and reinforcement.

Biberdorf and Pear (1977) found that a two-to-one student/teacher ratio was more effective than a one-to-one ratio in using a picture-naming procedure, suggesting that imitation of peer models may enhance language acquisition. Kelly et al. (1979), utilizing verbal imitation, successfully trained conversational skills with mentally retarded adolescents.

Often conditions within an institution fail to encourage or to provide for daily opportunities for language acquisition and maintenance. Inexpensive procedures have been developed which do encourage such language use and appear able to be transferred to institutional settings. Because of low staff/resident ratios there are often minimal opportunities for the severely retarded to imitate or use language. A major change appears possible by promoting language use by the children in everyday situations. Hart and Risley (1968; 1974; 1975), with nonretarded but culturally disadvantaged preschoolers, utilized such a method during free time at school. Their results suggested that "incidental teaching," where subtle but natural cues by adults are utilized to stimulate a child's language, can be used to promote language usage. In this procedure, the language skills of labeling and describing are taught in naturally occurring adult/child interactions. Language is stimulated by placing toys and activities out of children's reach. The attending adults would then focus their attention on the child as if in anticipation of the child's making a request to play with the toys and games. If the child did not initiate such a request, the adult provided a verbal cue for the child.

With retarded children, Halle, Marshall, and Spradlin (1979) observed that staff would often meet children's needs without ever waiting for a request. They pointed out that in such settings where rigid routines prevail "the language functions of controlling the environment are useless" (p. 431). Typically the children would, with no verbal interaction have their breakfasts and lunches either delivered to them or they would come for it on request with no verbal response on their part. Halle et al. implemented a program with six 11- to 15-year-old institutionalized children with limited verbal repertoires which required the lunch staff in an institution to not immediately serve the children at lunch time. They were instructed to wait 15 seconds or until the child made a request for the tray. If the verbal request was not made, a treatment was implemented: a 15-second delay followed by the request, "Tray, please," modeled by the staff. If there was no request from the child, this procedure was repeated three more times until after a final 15-second delay the tray was given to the child. This simple procedure carried out by the ward staff required minimal intervention and evoked speech in all six of the retarded children. Further, for three of the children this speech generalized to another meal situation. A similar procedure has been used to teach retarded children to request snacks in a natural setting (Simic and Bucher, 1980). Emphasizing the connection between language and the natural environment has also been shown to enhance the generalization of language skills in the mentally retarded (Welch and Pear, 1980). These studies point out that in order to learn to speak, children must have something to say and someone to talk to. In a similar vein, Price (1978), in a review of language remediation procedures for the retarded, notes that this emphasis on the active participation of the child in learning language is critical for a program's success. In particular it can be speculated that the functional utility, the meaningful use of language rather than the structural use of language, is critical for successful language acquisition, maintenance, and generalization.

F. *Teaching Social and Self-Help Skills*

The suppression of retarded and other children's antisocial, inappropriate, and aggressive behavior remains a major area in the literature. Based on case studies by Repp and Deitz (1974) and Risley (1968), Doleys, Wells, Hobbs, Roberts, and Cartelli (1976) proposed "social punishment," a method whose central component appears to be contingent scolding, as an efficient technique for the suppression of inappropriate behavior. Doleys et al. worked with four severely and moderately retarded children who were described by both teachers and parents as being uncooperative and noncompliant. They utilized a social punishment technique in which upon a child's noncompliance with a request or a demand, the experimenter walked over to the child, held the child firmly by the shoulders and in a loud scolding voice said, "You did not do as I asked right away and I don't like it when you disobey me!" The experimenter then released the child, put his hands on his hips, and "glared" silently at the child for 40 seconds. Compared to a 40-second time-out or 40 seconds of positive practice directed by the experimenter, social punishment was most effective in eliminating noncompliance. As the authors pointed out, their results remain difficult to interpret. The 40-second time-out was used in a context where the children had previously been exposed to time-outs in excess of 5 minutes, and the positive practice condition never explicitly provided the child with clear feedback on the consequences of the child's behavior. Most crucial, however, was the lack of maintenance and generalization data. They pointed out that the social punishment appeared to "startle" the children into submission, suggesting that its effects may wear off over time. Further, neither the long-term consequences nor the effects of the modeling of such scolding behavior on the children's social behavior in other situations was examined.

Time-out alone or in conjunction with positive reinforcement continues to be a widely used and researched area both with nonretarded (see the Schools section, Chapter 8) and retarded children. Time-out involves removing a child from a positively reinforcing environment contingent on the child's inappropriate behavior and has proved to be a potent means of controlling behavior (e.g. Brown and Elliot, 1965; Burchard and Tyler, 1965; Hamilton, Stephens, and Allen, 1967; Wolf, Risley, and Mees, 1964). Attempts at investigating the effects of various schedules of reinforcement on the effectiveness of time-out with the mentally retarded remain uninterpretable due to lack of appropriate controls (Clark, Rowbury, Baer, and Baer, 1973; Calhoun and Matherne, 1975). Drabman and Spitalnik (1973) emphasize that it is the "time-out" from positive reinforcement which technically defines time-out and *not* the aversive qualities of the time-out environment to which children are removed, generally an isolated room. To ensure that a classroom was positively reinforcing to begin with, Spitalnik and Drabman (1976), working with two children using a multiple-baseline design, distributed rewards to the children's classroom on a random-time reinforcement schedule. They found that this procedure of using strictly time-out did work in suppressing inappropriate vocalizations.

The assumption underlying time-out, that a child's socially inappropriate behavior may be in response to the child's receiving positive reinforcement from parents, teachers, or peers, may not always be the case. At times inappropriate or aggressive behavior may function as an escape response to terminate demands or other aversive stimuli (Graziano, 1969; 1974; Carr, Newsom, and Binkoff, 1980; Ludwig, Marx, Hill, and Browning, 1969; Patterson, Littman, and Bricker, 1967). In such cases time-out would act as a reinforcer of inappropriate behavior. Carr et al. noted that two nonverbal severely retarded boys would exhibit frequent aggressive behavior in response to demands from the teacher, but when a safety signal indicating that no more demands would be made was presented, aggression fell to near zero levels. It appeared that to these boys aggressive behavior functioned as an escape-motivated response that served to terminate an aversive demand situation. The experimenters reasoned that if aggressive behavior functions to allow a child to escape from an aversive demand situation, then one treatment intervention could center on reducing the aversiveness of such situations. They introduced to the boys a variety of preferred reinforcers contingent on the child's appropriate responding during the demand situation in order to attenuate the aversiveness of that situation. This reduced one child's aggressiveness to near zero, but the other child showed no interest in any of the reinforcers. As an alternate procedure with this child, negative reinforcement was instituted, where demands were terminated by a non-aggressive response. Aggression during this treatment fell to near zero levels. When this child was again permitted to leave the demand situation, aggression again returned to a high level. At another time an extinction procedure was attempted where the child was prevented from leaving the demand situation for 1 hour in spite of high levels of aggression, and his behavior again returned to a near zero level.

Disruptive behavior has also been modified using other means. Barmann, Croyle-Barmann, and McLain (1980), using a negative punishment framework, interrupted music whenever an eight-year-old retarded girl became disruptive on a bus; Deitz, Repp, and Deitz (1976) have reinforced other than disruptive behaviors; and Small, Giganti, and Steinberg, (1978) and Carter, Laz and Russell (1979), in case studies, have suggested the possibility that relaxation through biofeedback may be feasible to reduce multiple-behavior academic problems.

Studies that have attempted to promote the social behaviors of severely and profoundly retarded children and adolescents in schools and institutions report success in using prompts and teacher praise (Petersen, Austin, and Lang, 1979); rewards of food and praise (Whitman, Mercurio, and Caponigri, 1970); modeling techniques alone (Burney, Russell, and Shores, 1977); modeling in conjunction with prompts and positive reinforcement (Paloutzian, Hasazi, Streifel, and Edgard, 1971). Not unexpectedly, generalization of social skills outside of the initial training sessions, when investigated at all, has been marginal (Burney, Russell, and Shores 1977). Petersen et al. (1979) developed some generalization to the natural classroom by using teachers as trainers, but it was unclear whether this generalization was anything more than a carry-over effect as it was measured immediately after training. Clearly, case studies that do not build into their training programs maintenance and generalization features are of little value at this stage in the behavior modification literature. A study by Marburg, Houston, and Holmes (1976) is an exception to the field's notable lack of emphasis on generalization. Working with 32 severely and moderately retarded children, Marburg et al. randomly assigned half to a single-model condition and half to a multiple-model condition. In the single-model condition, one model over a period of three 30-minute sessions reinforced each child with praise for the imitation of ten assorted simple behaviors (i.e. stamping a foot, hugging a BoBo doll) and gave no reinforcement after modeling four different simple behaviors. The multiple-model condition was similar except that a different model was provided for each child in each of the three sessions. They found that: (1) Children trained to imitate by multiple models showed an eightfold higher level of imitative behavior when exposed to a new model who demonstrated new behaviors than children trained by only a single model. That is, multiple models facilitated stimulus generalization or transfer of training. (2) Children trained by multiple models were more likely to generalize and imitate nonreinforced behaviors than children trained by only one model. That is, multiple models facilitated response generalization. (3) Children learned as well with multiple as with single models.

Behavioral principles have been applied to self-help behaviors. Cass and Zimmer-Hart (1978) used a shaping procedure to teach a 4-year-old retarded boy to stand; Richman, Sonderby, and Kahn (1980) were able to use contingent reinforcement in both simulated and *in vivo* meal situations to teach self-feeding skills; and Bacon-Prue, Blount, Hosey, and Drabman (1980) used posting of a photograph as a reinforcement to increase bed-making in an institution. More complex behaviors have also been addressed. Cuvo, Veitch, Trace, and Konke (1978) used instructions, shaping, and modeling to teach money-changing computation to mentally retarded adolescents; Wacker, Carroll, and Moe (1980) used overt self-verbalizations to teach assembly skills to four trainably mentally retarded children; and Kelly, Wildman, and Berler (1980) taught small groups, using instructions, modeling, and behavioral rehearsal to improve job interview skills of mildly retarded adolescents. Again, it would appear that the range of complex social and self-help skills taught to those labeled mentally retarded is one for which the limits remain to be reached.

G. *Reducing Inappropriate Physical Behaviors*

The moderately, severely, and profoundly retarded child is particularly likely to exhibit a number of physical behaviors either injurious to physical health or disruptive to continued training or social acceptance. Probably the most severe type of such behavior can be categorized as self-injurious and may include head-banging, self-biting, hair-pulling, and other self-destructive behaviors. This behavior category, along with problems in toileting and other related behaviors are included in Chapter nine.

Another severe problem often seen in the mentally retarded is "pica" or the eating of small objects. Bucher, Reykdal, and Albin (1976) reported that a "No" followed by 30 seconds of physical restraint contingent on pica behavior was only partially effective in decreasing the pica behavior of a retarded child. A number of other behavioral case studies of other inappropriate physical behaviors which usually have less severe physical consequences than self-injurious or pica behavior but which can, nevertheless, affect the education and social acceptance of the mentally retarded include problems with a protruding tongue (Thompson, Iwara, and Poynter, 1979; Kauffman, Hallahan, and Ianna, 1977); ruminative vomiting (Mulick, Schroeder, and Rojahn, 1980); chronic drooling (Drabman, Cruz, Ross, and Lynde, 1979); excessive nasal discharge (Smeets, Elson, and Clament, 1975); obesity (Rotatari and Fox, 1980); and public masturbation (Cook, Altman, Shaw, and Blaylock, 1978; Luiselli, Helfen, Pemberton, and Reisman, 1977).

Overcorrection has been the most widely used treatment to control and eliminate self-stimulatory and other inappropriate physical behavior [see Ollendick and Matson (1978) for an overview of the extensive overcorrection literature]. Introduced by Foxx and Azrin (1972), it generally consists of: (a) the immediate interruption of the target behavior; (b) an extended period of physically guiding the child in a corrective behavior; and (c) requiring the child to repeatedly practice correct forms of acceptable behavior. Masturbation (Luiselli et al.), excessive nasal discharge (Smeets et al.), and chronic drooling (Drabman et al.) were treated with variations of overcorrection with the retarded to bring about socially acceptable levels of these behaviors, apparently with enduring effects. The suppressed rates of these behaviors then allowed for the reinforcement of socially acceptable behaviors by parents, teachers, and peers.

Other methods of eliminating various physical behaviors include Cook et al.'s, using teachers at school and parents at home as behavior modifiers, to quickly eliminate masturbation in an 8-year-old severely retarded boy by squirting unsweetened lemon juice into the boy's mouth at the initiation of masturbation. Protruding tongue thrust in a 10-year-old severely retarded boy has been successfully treated by Thompson et al. by (a) food being presented only when the boy's tongue was in his mouth; and (b) gently but firmly pushing the boy's tongue back into his mouth when it protruded. Kauffman et al. also successfully treated a 12-year-old severely retarded boy's tongue thrusts by (a) contingent intermittent praise for keeping his tongue in his mouth; and, paradoxically, by (b) the teacher's grabbing the boy's mouth whenever his tongue protruded and protruding the teacher's tongue right back at the boy.

III. CONCLUSIONS

It seems appropriate to conclude this section with a reference to *Christmas in Purgatory*, the provocative title of a photographic essay by Blatt and Kaplan (1966). There, in somber black-and-white photographs that echo an old and recurrent theme, retarded children and adults live in the shadowed institutional worlds created by their keepers. More than a century and a half ago, referring to the patients at the Bicetre, Pinel asked, "How are we to distinguish between the exasperation caused by the chains, and the symptoms peculiar to the illness?" That question suggested a nascent sensitivity to the effects of the external environment—a sensitivity that, while since sharpened by some, is not yet widespread in our profession.

The chains in modern institutions are not forged steel, but patients are most definitely controlled not only by drugs but, more subtly and most surely, by a complex web of differential reinforcement. That web, woven continuously by the caretakers, maintains the patients' entrapment in withdrawn passivity and socially deficient and bizarre behavior. The very behavior maintained by the institution then serves to justify the existence of the institution and the continued incarceration of its inmates. We persist in denying the power of this web of reinforcement, and we remain aggressively insensitive to the environment's selective effects on behavior, insisting that the grossly deficient functioning of the residents is due to "innate mental limitations" wholly independent of and impervious to external environmental conditions. Fully convinced of the residents' "innate mental limitations," the staffs generally have such low expectations that they too often abandon their charges or will not attempt to teach them even simple personal-care skills. The institutions become harborers of pessimism and, as Patterson suggested (1963), vast "teaching machines" that help to maintain patients as patients.

In recent years, our sensitivity to the realities of this environment has increased. We are now beginning to take seriously the notion that environment does significantly affect human functioning—to accept the very old idea that much of what we have considered to be the patients' internal disturbances or irreversible mental limitations may be produced or at least sustained by the very environment that supposedly exists to help them.

As old as the idea may be, it has particularly revolutionary potential with regard to mental retardation, for in no other human category is the internal causation model so solidly entrenched and of such apparent validity. Here, the negative halo created by a label is especially devastating. Once a person is labeled "retarded," his total functioning is "explained" to everyone's satisfaction—every incidence of naiveté, of raucous laughter, sudden anger, exaggerated tale-telling, and momentary loss of control becomes clear once we learn that a person is "retarded." Many of the common behavioral variations exhibited by "normal" people are attributed to external conditions, such as "a bad day at the office" or being cooped up at home with demanding children. But when exhibited by a person labeled "mentally retarded," similar behavior is automatically attributed to an internal condition. The mental retardation explains all. We know, we understand, we are very tolerant.

The tenacity of this view is being challenged. As Lindsley noted (1964), it is perhaps not the population in our care that is retarded but rather the teaching environments we have created for that population. This idea is central to the behavior modifiers' position, and in recent years there has been increased activity and success in the behavioral training of "retarded" populations. Retarded behavior, both mild and extreme, has repeatedly been significantly changed by properly applying the principles of behavior modification.

The environments in which these tasks are taught and used have recently expanded from residential institutions to a variety of settings, including day-care centers, schools, and sheltered workshops. One of the most important recent developments has been the demonstration of the contribution parents can make to the development of the retarded child in the child's home.

An important factor in the increased interest in applying behavioral approaches to the mentally retarded is the recent legal emphasis on accountability in the treatment of mental retardation (Yates, 1977). "Normalization," which implies restoring or moving the retarded person to an equilibrium characterized as "normal life style" (Cleland, 1978), "habilitation," the main point of which is the use of active programming directed toward developing independence through activities of daily living (Repp and Barton, 1980), and "least restrictive environment" (P. L. 94–142, Education for All Handicapped Children Act, 1975) are the legal and professional catchwords of the day and have greatly accelerated the deinstitutionalization of the mentally retarded.

With such an expansion in settings of behavioral interventions with the mentally retarded, new challenges are being placed on the behavioral researcher. Behavioral training may be necessary for an increased number of kinds of behavioral deficits exhibited in the new natural settings. Also, the many levels and facets of the mentally retarded person's delayed intellectual functioning are not the only difficulties for the retarded. Retarded children are also more likely than normal children to possess multiple and overlapping physical handicaps. Most recent research with retarded children has typically categorized the children according to basic IQ groupings, failing to explicitly detail the other strengths and weaknesses of the retarded children studied. Such a detailed analysis and description would be possible in the almost exclusively case-study method utilized by the researchers.

With few exceptions, while behavioral research has proved successful in modifying particular isolated behaviors in specific situations, it has neglected the issue of maintenance and generalization across tasks and across settings. This is a critical issue as a lack of ability to generalize learned behavior has been a long-observed characteristic of the retarded. The maintenance and long-term effects of the training of behavioral skills on retarded children's progress are also largely missing from the field. As educating the mentally retarded is a life-long process, skills should be considered for training in light of the person's ultimate functioning. Objectives relevant to the daily living of the child should be selected, so that the often lengthy time spent in planning and training the children is not wasted. Also taken into account should be how various behaviors will be reacted to and maintained by others in the retarded child's environment, and in what settings the retarded child will be required to perform. The ultimate goal of behavioral interventions should be for retarded individuals to gain the most independent and fulfilled lifestyles in the least restrictive environment possible.

Finally, it is increasingly clear that all such goals must adjust to the perspective that it is the legal-political decision-making process which controls the financial resources of mental retardation programming and decides ultimately whether the "cost" of research in the implementation of programming for the retarded is "worth it" or not (Gross, 1977; Baumeister, 1981). It may be that recent attempts at cost-benefit analyses which distinguish the presumed benefits of prevention and treatment programs for the individual, the family, and for society will have more impact on the legal-political decision-making process than the criterion of what is "best" for the mentally retarded individual.

4

Children's Control of Fear

I. INTRODUCTION

This chapter is a selective review of behavioral treatment of children's fears, an area relatively neglected by behavior therapists and researchers despite their considerable attention to adult fear reduction (Graziano, 1975a). Adults seem to minimize the importance of children's fears, viewing them as common and transitory and thus not a particularly serious part of normal development. But children's fears may not always be transient, and some, such as specific animal phobias (Jersild, 1968; Jersild and Holmes, 1935a; Marks and Gelder, 1966) and fear of physical injury or psychic stress (L. C. Miller, Barrett, Hampe, and Noble, 1972b) may persist as adult problems. Children do experience fears, often intense and disturbing, and the psychological suffering of a fearful child, even if it remits in a few years, is at least as worthy of professional concern as is the suffering of adults. There seems good reason for urging more study of fear reduction in children.

Because of this review's behavioral focus the large psychoanalytic literature is not included. Likewise, school phobia articles, which outnumber those of any other fears by about 25 to 1 (L. C. Miller, Barrett, and Hampe, 1974), have been well reviewed elsewhere (Gelfand, 1978; Hersen, 1971; Kelly, 1973) and are only briefly discussed.

The modern psychological study of children's fears is nearly 60 years old. The literature consists of psychoanalytic and behavioral case studies, normative fear surveys, controlled fear-reduction experiments that are mainly clinical analogs, and a few theoretical articles and reviews.

This chapter was first published as an article by Anthony M. Graziano, Ina Sue DeGiovanni, and Kathleen A. Garcia, Behavioral treatment of children's fears: A review (*Psychological Bulletin*, 1979, *86*, pp. 809–830) and is updated and reprinted here with permission of the American Psychological Association.

Much of the literature is psychoanalytic, but interestingly, the earlier (e.g. Jones, 1924a, 1924b; Watson and Rayner, 1920) and the most recent articles have been behavioral.

Berecz (1968) concluded that the research has been "disappointing," giving "only hints" of the nature and incidence of childhood fears. A decade later, the situation regarding normative research appears much the same. A recent increase in behavioral studies of child fear reduction includes some well-designed research (e.g. Bandura and Menlove, 1968; Kanfer, Karoly, and Newman, 1975; Kornhaber and Schroeder, 1975; Melamed and Siegel, 1975; Murphy and Bootzin, 1973), and a book reviewing the field (Morris and Kratochwill, 1983). Overall, however, the bulk of research still leaves us with hard-to-interpret data, results that are more suggestive than definitive, and an important area very much in need of more empirical research.

One reason for the persistence of uncertain results may be a generally held assumption that knowledge about adult fears is sufficient for understanding fears of children, an assumption that may have encouraged inappropriate concepts and approaches. Piaget's work (e.g. 1929, 1951) on cognitive development should alert one to the dangers of considering children to be miniature adults. Berecz (1968) suggested other reasons, namely, a too inclusive use of the term *phobia* to describe "such a variety of conditions" as to make the term meaningless and definitions of phobias heavily biased by theoretical conceptions.

Ethical restraints, too, make this a difficult area in which to conduct research. For obvious ethical reasons children cannot be subjected to controlled presentations of fear stimuli in order to measure their reactions. Less intrusive measures, such as self-reports, questionnaires, and observations taken in clinical treatment and research, must be used. To these constraints add the problems of obtaining reliable and valid personal information from children, and some of the difficulties become apparent. Accordingly, researchers have tended to tread lightly, using nonintrusive methods that rely heavily on retrospective, subjective reports based on unsystematic self-observations. Virtually all of the normative data were drawn from one form or another of retrospective, subjective report. Frequently the data were from second-person (parents and teachers) verbal reports or were limited to observations made in clinical case studies. These limitations may largely account for the lack of hard data that still characterizes the field despite more than a half century of psychological study.

II. DEFINITIONS: FEARS, PHOBIAS, AND CLINICAL PROBLEMS

Despite these vagaries, there is fairly good general agreement on definitions of *fear* and *phobia*. Fear is commonly thought of as a normal reaction to genuine threat that involves at least three response systems: (a) overt behavioral expressions, (b) covert, subjective feelings and thoughts, and (c) physiological activity. The term *phobia* is commonly used to denote a specific fear in which at least one of the three elements is excessive, persistent, and unadaptive (Marks, 1969; L. C. Miller et al., 1974). Thus it is generally agreed that fear is a normal response to threatening stimuli, whereas phobia is an unreasonable response, often to usually benign or ill-defined stimuli.

Severity ranges from the mildly fearful responses of many children toward darkness, dogs, and so on to disabling, highly intense levels of fear. It is reasonable to assume that fears presented at clinics for professional intervention are the most severe fears. Two questions are raised immediately when one considers *clinical* fears. First, how are clinical fears to be defined other than by virtue of the fact that clients show up in clinics for treatment? Hampe, Nobel, Miller, and Barrett (1973) found that most children, even those with intense fears, overcome them with or without treatment within two years. But some do not, and they might appropriately be classed as having fears of *clinical* duration. Intensity and duration might be important defining characteristics, and we suggest that clinical fears be defined as those with a duration of over two years or an intensity that is debilitating to the client's routine life-style. The second question is, how prevalent are severe fears and should current research be focused only on severe fears or on both mild and clinical levels of the problem? As is shown in the review of controlled studies, most researchers treat all levels of severity the same, working primarily with mildly fearful children and generalizing to all phobic children. A recent review of behavioral treatment of clinical phobias by Mathews (1978) emphasizes the inappropriateness of generalizing from what are essentially analog studies to treatment of clinical fears. This limitation seems to have occurred because both mild and severe levels of fear are important research areas, and mildly fearful children are considerably easier to recruit as research subjects than severely fearful children. However, it seems important to clearly identify the severity of subjects' fears and the limitations that severity places on generalization of the data, especially since one does not know whether mild and clinical fears operate according to identical principles.

We know surprisingly little about childhood fears of high intensity, long duration, and disturbing content. L. C. Miller et al. (1974) estimated that school phobics make up 1 percent of the school-age population, whereas other child phobics may "run as high as 20 percent" (p. 91). In his review, Marks (1969) found little data on the frequency with which phobic children are referred for psychiatric treatment. Graham (cited in Marks, 1969) reported 5 cases of school refusal out of 162 clinical referrals and only ten specific phobias in 239 cases referred to a children's psychiatric hospital. Rutter, Tizard, and Whitmore (1970) screened all 10-and 11-year-old children (N = 2,199) on the Isle of Wight and found only 16 children to have clinically significant and handicapping phobias. Their screening procedure omitted those with monosymptomatic phobias, and thus 16 is a conservative estimate. In the most recent attempt to assess clinical prevalence, Graziano and DeGiovanni (1979) obtained questionnaire data from 19 behavior therapists. They reported a total of 547 children referred within the previous 6 months, of which 37, or 6.8%, were referred for treatment of clinical level fears, as defined above. At present only guesses can be made about the nature and extent of the clinical problem of children's fears.

III. FEAR PARADIGMS

Although several theoretical models have been advanced, none adequately explains the etiology and maintenance of phobias. The major conceptual models are psychoanalytic and behavioral, with ethological theory and a cognitive—developmental model representing less common but potentially important approaches. The major focus of this article is on the behavioral literature.

Behavioral approaches consist of three paradigms, each of which assumes that fears and phobias are learned: respondent conditioning, operant conditioning, and the two-factor theory of learning. In addition, a three-factor model has begun to emerge. The respondent model postulates that anxiety is the central aspect of phobic behavior and that any neutral stimulus present at the time a fear response occurs may become a conditioned stimulus. In future presentations it will elicit the associated fear response. The conditioning occurs if the original conditioning situation was of high intensity or was repeated a number of times. The conditioned fear is presumably maintained in the absence of reinforcement because the avoidance behavior precludes the requirements for extinction, that is, the repeated confrontation of the actually benign conditioned stimulus without its pairing with the unconditioned stimulus. A decrease in avoidance behavior can be achieved by replacing the conditioned anxiety response with a response antagonistic to anxiety (e.g., relaxation) that inhibits or weakens the anxiety. Wolpe's (1974) systematic desensitization is the best known of the therapy procedures based on this *reciprocal inhibition* paradigm. The major problems with the respondent model are that it does not explain why some neutral stimuli seem more likely than others to become conditioned fear stimuli, and, although it attempts to, it does not adequately explain the maintenance of phobic behavior in the absence of reinforcement.

Operant models hold that reinforcement rather than anxiety, primarily social reinforcement such as parental attention, is the central aspect of phobic behavior. Children are presumably taught to be afraid by parents and other significant persons who selectively, albeit unintentionally, attend to and reward fearful behavior. Therapy procedures based on operant models attempt to reduce children's phobic behavior by changing the reward structure in their immediate environments, that is, by teaching parents to ignore phobic behavior and to differentially reward alternative nonfearful approach behaviors. The major problem with the operant paradigm is its failure to adequately account for and therapeutically treat the subjective feelings of intense fear or anxiety and their accompanying thoughts that are often experienced by phobic children.

Modeling, one of the most frequent and promising therapeutic techniques, is based on social learning theory, which is an extension of operant conditioning. Modeling assumes that behavior can be changed through the vicarious experience of rewards (either tangible or cognitive) for new behavior or of the informational value of the modeled behavior. For example, a child's phobic avoidance of dogs may be decreased by his or her vicarious experience of the rewards given to another child (the model) who approaches a dog. Effective rewards can be either objective, such as verbal praise explicitly given to the model for approach behavior, or subjective and nonobservable, such as internal cognitions of social praise generated within the observing child (e.g., "That child is brave for approaching that dog. I will be brave for approaching that dog.") Although both tangible and cognitive stimuli may be equally effective in generating the initial performance of new approach behaviors, it seems likely that reinforcing cognitive self-statements (either those generated by the child spontaneously or those supplied by the therapist) are crucial in maintaining the new approach behavior. Similarly, the acquisition, as well as the therapeutic extinction, of phobic behavior may involve cognitive self-reinforcers, such as "She or he got knocked down by playing with that dog; I will get hurt if I play with that dog." Although the therapeutic effects of modeling with phobic children have been explored (e.g., Bandura, Grusec, and Menlove, 1967), little attention has been given to examining directly the nature and function of cognitive variables in the acquisition, maintenance, and extinction of children's phobias. In light of the role that such cognitions seem to play in phobic behavior, this is a major lack in the current research.

The two-factor theory incorporates both respondent and operant learning concepts. First proposed by Mowrer (1939), it postulates that phobias originate according to the respondent conditioning paradigm and are maintained according to the operant conditioning model. After initial respondent conditioning of fear or anxiety with the conditioned stimulus, anxiety reduction associated with avoidance of the noxious stimulus becomes a positive reward or reinforcer, since anxiety or fear is unpleasant. Thus, anxiety reduction becomes the reinforcement for avoiding the noxious stimulus created by respondent conditioning. Problems with the two-factor theory have been extensively discussed over the last several years (Bandura, 1969; Herrnstein, 1969; Rachman, 1976, 1977, 1978). In brief, (a) the theory assumes that phobias are mediated through the autonomic nervous system, although studies by Solomon and Turner (1962) and Bandura (1969) suggest that behavior is regulated in large part by the central nervous system; (b) it does not explain why people fail to acquire fears in what are theoretically fear-evoking situations (e.g. air raids); (c) it fails to explain the "choice of symptom" issue of why some stimuli are more likely than others to become fear signals, that is, the distribution of human fears is not consistent with the equipotentiality premise of the theory; (d) it accepts the faulty assumption that all fears are acquired directly through classical conditioning, although it has been shown that operant conditioning and observational learning can also indirectly produce fearful behavior; (e) it fails to explain why active avoidance behavior is so persistent and does not extinguish in the absence of further reconditioning or trauma experiences to maintain the anxiety associated with the conditioned fear stimulus. In response to some of these problems, Herrnstein (1969) has reported recent experiments showing that the conditioned stimulus may function as a *discriminative* stimulus for the avoidance response rather than as a noxious stimulus whose removal is inherently reinforcing, as two-factor theory requires.

Rejection of the two-factor theory has significant implications for both treating and measuring phobias, in that it suggests the three major components of fear (avoidance behavior, subjective experience, and physiological disturbance) can covary, vary inversely, or vary independently (Rachman, 1978; Rachman and Hodgson, 1974). Routine tests of these three components should be carried out as a pretreatment measure to determine the amount of synchrony/desynchrony among the three elements and to determine which element(s) does (and does not) require direct treatment. Studies investigating hypotheses based on the concepts of concordance and synchrony have begun to appear in the literature (e.g., Barlow, Mavissakalian and Schofield, 1980; Grey, Sartory and Rachman, 1979). Hugdahl (1981) and Kozak and Miller (1982) discuss some of the difficulties with this emerging three-systems model. Different treatments may tap different elements of a phobia more or less efficiently. Refutation of the two-factor theory also raises the important question of whether one needs to treat each element directly or whether one can assure patients that if one cures one component (e.g., avoidance behavior), the others will follow automatically (e.g., subjective experience). Thus, although the two-factor theory itself does not yield any new treatment techniques, the theoretical and empirical debates over the theory have caused researchers to question both the necessity for and the sequencing of various therapy components based on respondent and operant paradigms.

The major theoretical models reviewed briefly here are not adequate to explain childhood phobias. Two issues that appear to us to be of major importance are not even addressed by the existing models. These issues are (a) the role of cognitions in the origin, maintenance, and reduction of fears, and (b) the influence of developmental issues in childhood phobias. The idea that cognitions may influence phobic behavior is one that is gaining attention both on a theoretical level (Rachman, 1977) and on a treatment-oriented level aimed at fear reduction (e.g., Kanfer et al., 1975; Kissel, 1972; Meichenbaum and Turk, 1976). Developmental issues have long been ignored in this area, although recently some theorists (e.g., Bowlby, 1973; Kissel, 1972; L. C. Miller et al., 1974) have suggested that these issues may be important. Both cognitive and developmental issues deserve further exploration, which might lead to a more complete theoretical model of childhood fears and phobias.

There are two major categories of research in children's fears: normative fear survey research and fear-reduction studies.

IV. NORMATIVE FEAR SURVEY RESEARCH

It seems reasonable to expect that knowledge about the normal fears of children is important in understanding their pathological fears. At least 22 papers since 1932 have reported normative data, but they reveal little clear information. One point, however, is clear: the normative research has focused almost exclusively on the identification of fear stimuli by asking the question "What do children fear?" and then attempting to relate the number, type (content), or intensity of fear stimuli to demographic parameters such as age, sex, and socioeconomic class and to other, presumably pathological, behavior. Most of the studies have focused on the number of fears, and some have focused on the content or type of fear, but very few have dealt with the intensity of fear. Despite many methodological problems, to be summarized later, some consistencies do emerge.

A. *Sex Differences*

One of the most consistent findings is that however fear is measured, girls obtain higher fear scores than boys (Angelino, Dollins, and Mech, 1956; Bamber, 1974; Croake, 1969; Croake and Knox, 1973; Cummings, 1944; Duff, LaRocca, Lizzet, Martin, Pearce, Williams, and Peck, 1981; Klingman and Weisner, 1982; Lapouse and Monk, 1959; Pratt, 1945; Russell, 1967; Scherer and Nakamura, 1968; Spiegler and Liebert, 1970). Although no study reported generally higher fears for boys, three articles (Maurer, 1965; L. C. Miller et al., 1971; Nalven, 1970) found no sex differences.

Though the number of reported fears in relation to sex has been studied, there are uncertain data on the relationship between sex and either the content or the intensity of fears. Lapouse and Monk (1959) found significant sex differences in fear content, specifically in the percentage of children who feared certain objects. Pratt (1945), however, found no sex differences in fear content. MacFarlane, Allen, and Honzik (1954) collected data on fear intensity, but did not report any analysis. Other studies (Bamber, 1974; Russell, 1967; Scherer and Nakamura, 1968) found that girls report a greater fear intensity than boys. Although sex differences in content and intensity are still uncertain, the finding that girls report a greater number of fears appears frequently enough and with no conflicting evidence of reverse findings to be accepted as a reliable finding. Interpreting the finding, however, is difficult. One cannot tell from these data if the girl's higher scores reflect greater fear reactivity or if other factors, such as sex role expectations, operated. Consistent with a general role model of feminine behavior, girls may be more willing than boys to admit their fears. Similarly, in those studies using parents' reports, the adults may incorrectly, but nevertheless reliably, attribute greater fear to girls than to boys. Grossberg and

Wilson (1965) and Wilson (1967) suggested the operation of sex role factors in adult fear scores, whereas Scherer and Nakamura (1968) and Bamber (1974) suggested that similar sex role factors might account for the data on children and adolescents. One would expect, too, that if sex role stereotypes and behavior are changing, future fear surveys might find smaller and less reliable sex differences. In this regard it is interesting that the studies reporting no differences are fairly recent (from 1965 on), which possibly reflects some contemporary changes in sex stereotyping.

B. *Age*

Overall, there appears to be a general decrease from young childhood to late adolescence in the percentage of children who report one or more specific fears (Cummings, 1944, 1946; MacFarlane et al., 1954) and in the simple number of fears reported (Angelino and Shedd, 1953; MacFarlane et al., 1954; Nalven, 1970; Scherer and Nakamura, 1968). But some researchers have found no significant differences in the number of fears reported over the limited age ranges they studied (Croake, 1969; Croake and Knox, 1973; Lapouse and Monk, 1959; Maurer, 1965; Russell, 1967; Ryall and Dietiker, 1979). However, the decrease may not be in simple linear relationship with age, as several studies have shown a sharp increase in the number of reported fears around ages 9 to 11 (Angelino and Shedd, 1953; MacFarlane et al., 1954; Simon and Ward, 1974) or a peak at age 11 (Chazan, 1962; Morgan, 1959). On the other hand, several studies have reported no significant relationships of fear with age (Croake, 1969; Croake and Knox, 1973; Lapouse and Monk, 1959; Maurer, 1965; Russell, 1967).

Some studies suggest that the *type* of fear reported is related to age (Angelino and Shedd, 1953; Nalven, 1970; Scherer and Nakamura, 1968). Jersild and Holmes (1935a) observed that in infancy children's fears arise in response to occurrences in the immediate environment (e.g. loud noises, loss of support). As a child grows older, his or her range of fears grows wider and he or she acquires the ability to dwell on the past and to anticipate the future. Thus many of his or her fears will change to those of an anticipatory nature. This observation seems generally borne out by the data, as reviewed by Scherer and Nakamura (1968). The most consistent findings are an age-related decline in fear of animals, (Angelino et al. 1956; Bauer, 1976; Lapouse and Monk, 1959; Maurer, 1965; Shepherd, Oppenheim, and Mitchell, 1972) and in fears of the dark or of imaginary creatures (Bauer, 1976; Holmes, 1936; Maurer,

1965; Shepherd et al., 1972) and an age-related increase in school and social fears (Angelino et al., 1956; Lapouse and Monk, 1959).

L. C. Miller et al. (1972b), in contrast with most other studies that showed an age-related decline in animal fears, reported that fear of small animals, along with "moral" fears, "emerges more clearly in adult life" (p. 268). L. C. Miller et al. extracted three factors as the "principle dimensions" of children's fear: (a) fear of physical injury, (b) fear of natural and supernatural dangers, and (c) fear of psychic stress (e.g. social events, examinations, etc.). The second factor was found to diminish with age, whereas the other two factors reportedly "emerge early and continue through much of the life span" (L. C. Miller et al., 1972b, p. 268). Similar factors have been reported by other investigators (Russell, 1967; Scherer and Nakamura, 1968).

An important developmental question concerns the relationship between age and degree or intensity of fear. Do children of different ages react differently to the same type and intensity of fear stimuli? It is commonly believed that young children have more intense or all-encompassing fear reactions than do older children. But to date there has been little investigation of this question.

Eme and Schmidt (1978) studied 27 children and found the number and type of fears expressed remained stable over a one-year period. Although more research with larger groups is needed, their study suggests stable fear patterns within individual children, at least over this relatively short period of one year.

Although detailed information on the relationship of age and the number, kind, intensity, and factor structure of children's fears is not known, there is consensus that age is an important variable in fear reactions.

In summary, as children grow older, their fear patterns change, but not in simple linear relation with age. Some fear stimuli remain operative, others lose their value, and some new ones emerge. These tentative conclusions about fear and age are drawn from a mass of research data. They appear reasonable but hardly surprising, and they seem a rather small output for so much research activity.

C. *Socioeconomic Class*

As with age, socioeconomic class (SEC) appears to be an important variable in children's fears, but the details of the relationships are not clear. Several studies have reported SEC differences in the type (content) or number of reported fears (Angelino et al., 1956; Bamber, 1974;

Jersild and Holmes, 1935a; Nalven, 1970; Newstatter, 1938). The more reliable of the two findings is the variation found in content, with lower SEC children reporting more fears of specific events or others such as violence, whippings, dope peddlers, switchblades, drunks, money, rats, and cockroaches (Angelino et al., 1956; Nalven, 1970). In comparison, higher SEC children feared heights, car accidents, train wrecks, and large categories such as poisonous insects or dangerous animals. The fears of the lower SEC children ("ghetto" children in Nalven's 1970 study) strongly suggest the socially determined nature of fear content and an immediacy and reality basis for the expressed fears of the lower SEC children. The data suggest that these children may perceive their immediate environments as far more hostile than do the higher SEC children. This is a hypothesis well worth testing, but it has not been investigated within the scope of the fear literature.

Although it seems clear that fear content varies with SEC, it is not clear whether the number of reported fears also varies. Some studies (Angelino et al., 1956; Bamber, 1974; Croake, 1969; Croake and Knox, 1973; Jersild, Markey, and Jersild, 1933) have found a greater number of fears for lower than for higher SEC children. However, as Garcia, (1977) pointed out, Angelino et al. (1956), a frequently cited study, seemed to misinterpret their own data. The authors concluded that both content and number of fears varied with SEC, but their own data supported only the difference in content. Further, Nalven (1970) made an observation that may have bearing on this issue, namely, that lower SEC children compared with the others tended to list specific fear items rather than more generic groupings. For example, they listed specific animal fears (rats and cockroaches), whereas higher SEC children noted groupings such as dangerous animals or poisonous insects. If this difference in the level of abstraction of the concepts used by different SEC children was reliable, it may have generated a spurious finding of different numbers of fears between the groups. As Garcia suggested, studies that instruct children to simply list their fears are probably most susceptible to such an artifact. Finally, no studies have reported data on SEC differences in the intensity of fears.

D. *Fears and Pathological Behavior*

It seems a reasonable prediction that children's fears are positively related to other behaviors usually considered to be pathological. However, except for the suggestions of such a relationship found in clinical case studies, there seems to be little data to support this prediction. Some case studies (e.g. Tasto, 1969) have even pointed out that the child's severe fear was a specific, isolated reaction, apparently not related to other behaviors. Some studies, however, have shown a relationship between fear and manifest anxiety (Scherer and Nakamura, 1968) and between fear and neuroticism (Bamber, 1974). MacFarlane et al. (1954) reported that children's fears were related to a variety of problems such as general anxiety, irritability, and timidity, all depending on age and sex. Their correlations, however, were low and were not consistent across ages. Hampe et al. (1973) reported a general response to treatment over a two-year follow-up period. As the primary fear reduced in time, so did "a host of other deviant behavior" (p. 451). These authors suggested that not only are fears related to other pathological behavior, but fears are related to other pathological behavior in some causative or mutually sustaining manner.

On the other hand, L. C. Miller et al. (1971) found no correlation between school phobia and other pathological behaviors, and Lapouse and Monk (1959), using detailed individual interviews with a random sample of the parents of 482 children, found no significant correlations between fears and pathological behaviors such as bed-wetting, nightmares, nail-biting, frequent temper losses, and so on. Lapouse and Monk also interviewed a sizable subsample of children to compare their reports with the parents' reports and, again, found no significant relationships between fear and pathological behavior.

Thus there appears to be weak evidence that children's fears may be related to general conditions such as anxiety, but there is no clear support for the relation of fear with specific pathological behavior such as bed-wetting or tantrums. A reasonable hypothesis, not yet explored, is that the intensity rather than the simple number of fears may be positively related to behavior pathology. At this point, however, there is little evidence that childhood fears are related to other pathological behaviors.

E. *Methodological Problems in the Normative Studies*

For the most part methodologies have been fairly straightforward and simple, involving variations of questionnaire and interview methods that range from the earlier studies in which subjects were asked to list their fears to the more recent use of factor-analyzed rating scales. Only Jersild and Holmes (1935a) attempted to obtain normative data by direct observation methods.

In the earlier studies, children or parents were requested to "write down" or "tell me the things you are afraid of" (Maurer, 1965; Pratt, 1945) or to "list the fears of other children in your own age group" (e.g., Angelino et al., 1956; Nalven, 1970). Many studies using this list or list-and-rank method asked the children directly (Angelino et al., 1956; Croake, 1969; Maurer, 1965; Nalven, 1970; Pratt, 1945). Others, however, who sought greater reliability or perhaps more ease in obtaining data, used mothers as informants (e.g., Hagman, 1932; Lapouse and Monk, 1959). Only Lapouse and Monk reported any measure of concurrent validity. They interviewed an additional sample of 193 children and their mothers separately, using different interviewers. Comparing those independent interviews, they found that the largest discrepancy concerned the mothers' and children's assessment of the number of children's fears and worries, with "the mothers, in comparison with the children, underestimating by 41 percent" (Lapouse and Monk, 1959, p. 812). Their results cast doubt on the validity of mothers' or children's self-reports in this and other studies. Marks and Gelder (1966) asked adults to recall the childhood onset of their fears; Abe (1972), in a study carried out in Japan, compared self-report fears of 242 mothers with their childhood fears as recalled and reported by *their* mothers.

Of all the list-and-rank procedures, those of Lapouse and Monk (1959) appear to have been the most carefully executed. Using the Buffalo city directory, they drew a random urban sample and employed trained interviewers to conduct hour-and-a-half interviews with the mothers of 482 6-to 12-year-old children. The interviewers obtained data on the number and kinds of fears, on sex, age, race, and economic status, and on the occurrence of other behaviors such as bed-wetting, nightmares, and a variety of "tension phenomena" such as nail-biting. An additional sample of children and their mothers were also carefully interviewed to compare the children's and mothers' responses. The list-and-rank approach is characteristic of the studies through 1966. The studies did identify fear stimuli, but they share a number of weaknesses. Two of the shortcomings specific to this approach are that one cannot be certain that the lists of fear stimuli are complete, and although data are generated on the number and kinds of fear stimuli, they tell us nothing about the degree of fear-stimulating power of each item or the intensity of the children's fear reactions.

Since 1967 some of the normative studies have been more sophisticated, but still have focused on the essential question, "*What* do children fear?" These later studies used rating scales that provided data not only on the number and types of fear stimuli but also on the relative degree of fear reactions to the different stimuli. In these studies, too, factor analyses were used to identify the presumed factor structure of children's fears.

The major approach in the rating scale studies is to instruct the child (Bamber, 1974; Russell, 1967; Scherer and Nakamura, 1968) or the parents (L. C. Miller, 1967; L. C. Miller et al., 1971; L. C. Miller et al., 1972b) to rate each of the listed fear stimuli for intensity of reaction. The results are then factor analyzed, usually with added demographic or other behavioral measures.

Although fear-survey rating scales provide more information than the earlier approaches and have an advantage of standardization, their reliability and validity are still equivocal (Geer, 1965; Lang and Lazovik, 1963; Manosevitz and Lanyon, 1965). For example, L. C. Miller et al. (1971, 1972b) reported no validity data and only split-half reliability on the Louisville fear survey, perhaps the most often used fear rating scale for children. Although the spilt-half reliability was acceptable ($r = .80$), no data were reported on test-retest reliability or on any form of validity. Split-half reliability and factor analyses, the most commonly reported measures on fear rating scales, are measures of only the internal consistency of the scales. Additional data need to be collected on stability (test-retest) and validity of fear rating scales before any but tentative conclusions can be drawn.

Taken together, the normative studies involve so many procedural differences and methodological problems that clear comparisons and reliable conclusions are difficult to draw. In addition to the difficulties specific to each method already pointed out, the field as a whole suffers from a number of generally shared problems. One major limitation is that the data are essentially subjective, that is, they are usually second-person reports by parents and sometimes first-person reports by children. Further, the adult second-person reports are usually limited to mothers of the children, with whatever sex role biases and attributions may be operative. We do not know, for example, if fathers' reports would generate different results. Perhaps it might be hypothesized that the sex differences would appear even greater, with fathers attributing even less fear to their sons than to their daughters. Whether made by parents or by children, the reports are based on unsystematic observations that are subject to many biases, and the respondents' recall is subject to many distortions. Neither test-retest reliability nor validity measures are routinely taken.

Although normative studies have been reported since 1932, their results are not generalizable because random sampling from the normal child population is seldom attempted. With very few exceptions (e.g. Lapouse and Monk, 1959; L. C. Miller et al., 1971), these are not properly normative studies. Investigators appear to have been interested in limited segments of the population or were restricted in terms of the availability of subjects. For example, some studies (Marks and Gelder, 1966; Poznanski, 1973) used samples drawn from psychiatric populations, and Maurer (1965) used children referred to school psychologists. Abe (1972) used data from a self-selected group of young mothers who were patients in a free medical clinic in Japan; Bamber (1974) studied children in Ireland; and Pratt (1945) studied only rural children. In summary, the basic subjective-report methods have obvious shortcomings: some studies interviewed children, some parents; some required lists, some ratings; the ages of children are not comparable across studies; random samplings from normal childhood populations were seldom taken; reliability and validity data were not reported.

But the major limitation in all of this research is the nature of the questions that have typically been asked. The studies have been virtually limited to identifying fear stimuli, to asking, essentially, "*What* are the common fears of children?" and "To what demographic factors do they relate?" Most studies seem still to be trying to accomplish Hagman's (1932) first aim, that is, "to enumerate and analyze the objects and situations feared" (p. 110). It seems clear that many factors influence the objects or situations chosen as fear stimuli. Some stimuli, as Maurer (1965) pointed out, seem to be merely the subject of the latest adventure story or movie to which the child was exposed; others seem to be stereotypes or culturally conditioned fears, and still others appear to have some significance for the child's life (e.g. Angelino et al., 1956; Maurer, 1965). The type of identification and tracking of fear stimuli that has been done could probably be continued indefinitely. However, the question must be raised as to the point of such an enterprise. In an area as broad and important as fear in children one must ask oneself what kind of research is worth doing and what kind of knowledge is worth having.

The identification of fear stimuli touches on only a small part of what must be a complex fear process. It seems reasonable to assume that children's fears, like other human reactions, proceed through complex paradigms—from fear stimuli that vary in number, type, and intensity and that may be internal, external, or both; through emotional and cognitive operations within the child; through overt fear responses that may act upon and modify both the social and physical environment and that themselves, by means of feedback loops and chaining, may occasion variations in any part of the process. The processes themselves may further vary with developmental factors. Given this reasonable assumption of human complexity, it is clear that the normative research to date has ignored a great deal of it, limiting its view to only one part of the process, that is, identifying fear stimuli. It is as if early researchers took the first reasonable steps toward learning what it is that children typically fear, but then allowed the field to remain on that level, the researchers generating, sharing, and rearranging virtually the same lists of fear stimuli. The research tells us little about the remainder of the paradigm, the nature of children's fear experiences. Remaining unasked are questions concerning the operation of mediating cognitions in children's fear experiences, the degree to which fears are self-or externally generated and maintained, and the effects of fear behavior on the child's social environment and the effects' feedback influence on the child. One must investigate how children in their natural environments typically deal with fearful events and how their strategies vary with developmental level, sex, and so on. One must study the conditions under which natural coping processes fail and fear processes become debilitating, and one must determine the optimum conditions for fear-reduction intervention.

We suggest, too, that there is a related, potentially important issue that has thus far been ignored in the literature: the recognition of the possible adaptive value of childhood fear. Of course one has no clear indication that fear serves any adaptive function at all. It may be that age-linked, transitory fears have important short-term effects on coping with the social environment, on learning how to appropriately sensitize and desensitize oneself. Fear may constitute an important part of children's experiences in learning to successfully cope with problems. The possible adaptive value of fear experiences in children's development may be an important issue, but has been overlooked, clouded perhaps by an implicit, unquestioned value judgment that fears are only disruptive and hence are of negative value.

A great variety of stimuli have been identified as having fear-stimulus value; they range from specific objects (e.g. bees) to abstract and imaginative stimuli such as communism and ghosts. As pointed out by Berecz (1968) and L. C. Miller et al. (1974), almost any event may be a potential fear stimulus. Thus children have access to an inexhaustible supply of them. The normative research suggests that "normal" fear stimuli for children are socially determined and are appropriate for the individual's personal and social situation; for example, the elderly fear loneliness and physical injury, students fear examinations, lower SEC boys fear switchblades and beatings, and young children, still learning the limits of reality, fear ghosts, witches, and darkness. The fears are appropriate to age, social class and role, culture and even moment in history. Thus the normative data suggest that what is feared by children is largely determined by social and historical fashion as well as by individual experiences. Although some fears may be innately determined, it appears that children fear largely what they are taught to fear. It seems that identification of fear stimuli may be limited in its contribution to understanding the processes of learned fears in children, since so many stimuli may be interchangeable. Further research in this direction is of doubtful value, and attention to other parts of the complex fear paradigm would be more profitable. Overall, the normative research only suggests, and with a good amount of conflicting data, that the type and number of fears vary with age, sex, and SEC. The details of the apparent relationships, however, are not clear. There is conflicting evidence concerning the relationship of fears to pathological behaviors, and there are virtually no data on the intensity of fear reactions. The normative research reveals very little beyond the findings of what appear to be a few key studies (e.g. Jersild and Holmes, 1935a, 1935b; Lapouse and Monk, 1959; L. C. Miller, Barrett, Hampe, and Noble, 1972a; L. C. Miller et al., 1972b). The "disappointing research" (Berecz, 1968) may be at least partly due to the ethical problems of fear research with children as well as to a variety of methodological problems that characterize the research. Because of its apparent fixed focus on identifying fear stimuli, the research tells one little about the complete fear processes. Normative data, as Barrios et al. (1981) point out, can be particularly important, given the apparent developmental nature of fears.

V. CASE STUDIES OF FEAR REDUCTION

Like other aspects of the literature in this area, fear-reduction experimental and case studies have a long history. According to Yates (1970), most of the techniques that are now labeled *behavior therapy* were applied in one form or another some 50 years ago, almost entirely in attempts to treat children's fears. Watson and Rayner (1920) suggested, but did not investigate, four possible methods to remove the fear that they had conditioned in Little Albert. Jones's (1924b) treatment of Peter is an early example of the application of learning principles to the remediation of clinical problems. Jones (1924a) studied 70 children in an attempt to discover ways in which children's fears could be reduced or removed. Holmes (1936), stressing the importance of active participation by the child, attempted to eliminate fears of the dark and of heights, whereas Hagman (1932) and Jersild and Holmes (1935b) reviewed methods that parents actually used to deal with fears and suggested a number of more effective techniques.

Unfortunately, as with the normative studies, the promise of the early work was not fulfilled. The vigorous interest in treatment of children's fears seemed to disappear, and except for a few case studies, there was little further activity until Rachman and Costello's (1961) review of the etiology and treatment of children's phobias. They called for "above all a major project to establish the degree and permanence of improvement which may be obtained by these techniques," (p. 104) that is, those suggested by Jones (1924a, 1924b), and by Jersild and Holmes, (1935b). This call has also gone largely unanswered. The amount of research in the behavioral treatment of children's fears since that time has been surprisingly meager in comparison with the amount of behavioral research on adult fears, an area with well over 100 outcome studies on systematic desensitization alone (Wolpe et al., 1973).

Most of the reports on childhood fears are single-case studies, will all of their attendant limitations. However, case studies may offer something that experimental studies do not, that is, examinations of children's phobias at high levels of severity, and may give hints about the nature of phobias and treatment suggestions.

Prior to 1960 there were only a few behaviorally oriented case studies of child fear reduction (e.g. Jones, 1924b; Rodriguez, Rodriguez, and Eisenberg, 1959; Weber, 1936). Since 1960 at least 46 additional papers have appeared, which report on 125 children referred for clinical treatment. Of these papers, 25 were limited to school phobias and account for 77 of the cases. The remaining 21 case studies, accounting for 48 children, involved school phobias plus a variety of other fears such as dogs, water, and noise. Thus, since 1960, excluding school phobias, all other children's fears averaged two case studies per year, a strikingly low average compared with the rest of the behavior therapy field.

Considering the variety of fears reported in normative studies and included in fear surveys, the range of phobias that are presented for treatment is quite small. The overwhelming majority of reported cases involve school phobia, followed by those involving fears of animals, noise, and bodily injury. Even assuming that most of these clinical cases represent severe levels of fear, we note that both the range and the number of severe fears presented for treatment are relatively small. Thus, the important question remains unanswered: Are severe fears largely undetected, or do they simply not occur at a very high rate?

The school phobia literature has been reviewed (Gelfand, 1978; Hersen, 1971; Kelly, 1973), and this section is presented only as a brief overview. School phobia is more prevalent than other childhood phobias (L. C. Miller et al., 1974), a fact that may be due to the high cultural value and legal requirements placed on school attendance. Because it is socially and legally less acceptable for a child to avoid school than to avoid dark places, small animals, and so on, more school phobia cases are likely to be referred for clinical help, that is, the school-phobic child conflicts with social convention more visibly and inconveniently than other fearful children.

Previous reviews suggest that the prognosis for improvement is good with most types of treatment, provided that school refusal has not yet become a chronic pattern. Behavior therapy procedures for school phobia generally are based on both classical and operant conditioning models. Thus, school phobia is seen as avoidance behavior motivated by high anxiety and maintained by reinforcement for not attending school. Four major respondent-based procedures have been reported: (a) systematic desensitization (Chapel, 1967; Lazarus, 1960; Lazarus and Abramovitz, 1962; P. M. Miller, 1972); (b) *in vivo* desensitization (Garvey and Hegrenes, 1966; P. M. Miller, 1972; Olsen and Coleman, 1967; Tahmisian and McReynolds, 1971); (c) flooding (Kennedy, 1965); and (d) implosion (Smith and Sharpe, 1970). Three major operant conditioning procedures were reported: (a) home-based contingency management (Ayllon, Smith, and Rogers, 1970; Cooper, 1973; Edlund, 1971; Hersen, 1970; Kennedy, 1965; Vaal, 1973); (b) school-based contingency management (Brown, Copeland, and Hall, 1974; Hersen, 1970; Rhines, 1973; Weinberger, Leventhal, and Beckman, 1973); and (c) behavioral shaping in the clinic (Hersen, 1970; Patterson, 1965). Most case studies report procedures based on combinations of the classical and operant models, with emphasis on one. The choice of which theoretical model and therapeutic procedure to use seems determined by whether the most pressing therapeutic need is to reduce the child's anxiety with a desensitizing procedure or to avoid reinforcing his or her escape behavior. Follow-up data (ranging from 4 weeks to 2 years) were reported for the majority of cases, although the data were limited either to assessment of continued school attendance or to attendance data plus a verbal report from parents and teachers on the child's social or emotional functioning. Actual behavioral assessment of improvement after return to school was not reported for any case. Whether such follow-up data should be collected is apparently still debatable. Hersen (1971) has criticized behaviorally oriented therapists for not being more rigorous in obtaining data regarding academic, social, and emotional adjustment. However, Ayllon et al. (1970) stated that "school attendance is a legitimate if not the only relevant treatment objective for school phobia" (p. 135).

Behavior therapy procedures for phobias other than school phobias are generally based on a classical conditioning model, that is, the avoidance is seen to be mediated by high anxiety. Two main approaches are used to reduce the inferred mediating anxiety: (a) counterconditioning procedures that pair the anxiety response with a stronger response that is also antagonistic to anxiety, such as muscular relaxation; and (b) extinction procedures in which the anxiety response is repeatedly elicited, but presumably without reinforcement. Therapy for these phobias usually involves a combination of several procedures. The terminology used for the procedures is confusing and overlapping, but the various authors claim that real differences do exist, as summarized by the following four categories: (a) reciprocal inhibition (Bentler, 1962; Freeman, Roy, and Hemmick, 1976; Jones, 1924a; Katz, 1974; Lazarus and Abramovitz, 1962; MacDonald, 1975; Miklich, 1973; Ney, 1968; Tasto, 1969; Van Hasselt, Hersen, Bellack, Rosenblum, and Lamparski, 1979; Wish, Hasazi, and Jurgela, 1973; Wallick, 1979); (b) contact desensitization (Weber, 1936); (c) implosion/flooding (Ollendick and Gruen, 1972; Smith and Sharpe, 1970; Sreenivasan, Manocha, and Jain, 1979); and (d) *in vivo* desensitization plus guided practice (Croghan and Musante, 1975; Pomerantz, Peterson, Marholin, and Stern, 1977; Stableford, 1979). In cases using reciprocal inhibition, the following responses antagonistic to anxiety were used: feeding (Jones, 1924a), music relaxation (Tasto, 1969), playing (Bentler, 1962; Ney, 1968), and emotive imagery (Lazarus and Abramovitz, 1962). Interestingly, playing was included as an integral part of several treatment procedures (Bentler, 1962; Croghan and Musante, 1975; Ney, 1968; Weber, 1936). However, none of these authors stated explicitly that playing was used to teach the child skills of interaction with the feared stimulus. This lack of emphasis on skills-training in case studies is interesting in light of Rimm and Masters' (1974) suggestion that therapists not place sole reliance on decreasing anxiety through desensitization techniques when working with socially inexperienced young children, who often lack the appropriate behavioral skills required to cope with the feared stimulus. Follow-up data were reported in 16 of the 21 recent papers. However, such data were rarely behavioral, making comparisons among cases regarding long-term effectiveness difficult, if not impossible. Rather, follow-up data were obtained in verbal reports of parents or teachers regarding the child's maintenance of his or her new approach behavior.

In summary, we can draw the following tentative conclusions about the clinical treatment of childhood phobias, as reported in case studies. First, given the strikingly low number and narrow range of reported cases, it seems that childhood phobias may not be a significantly large clinical problem, except for school phobia. Second, excluding school phobia, the most frequently used therapy procedures are modifications of those used with adults, that is, systematic desensitization and implosion/flooding. As has been noted elsewhere (Graziano, 1975a), serious ethical and humanitarian questions are raised in using implosion/flooding techniques on children, because children generally have no choice in whether to enter and remain in therapy. Furthermore, as Ullmann and Krasner (1975) have cautioned, the successful use of implosion techniques requires considerable clinical skill and sensitivity so that the highly aversive treatment experience is associated with the avoided object and not with the therapist. In contrast with other phobias, school phobia is again an exception in that its treatment procedures generally include the use of both classical and operant techniques. Thus, this set of case studies may be taken as a comment on the state of the field: with the exception of school phobia, the clinical importance and prevalence of childhood phobias is questionable, and the procedures used are generally copied from work with adult phobics.

Important therapy and research questions raised by these case studies appear to fall into three main categories. First, what procedures not generally used with adults might be useful with children? As noted by Rimm and Masters (1974), young children often lack the appropriate behavioral skills required to cope with the feared stimulus. Thus, the absence of much if any overt skill training in the case reports seems a glaring omission. Such skill training might take the form of guided participation or modeling. Second, what treatment combinations are most effective and efficient for different kinds of phobic children? As pointed out by both Berecz (1968) and Hersen (1971), more controlled research designs are needed to adequately test both the efficacy of any one procedure and the conditions under which it will be most effective, both alone and in combination with other procedures. Case studies are limited in two senses: (a) one has no way to know whether other attempts to treat a phobic child by these authors or other authors using similar techniques were unsuccessful (i.e., how unique is the success of this procedure?); (b) we cannot compare the effectiveness of two or more different procedures because most reports use language that cannot be interpreted in terms of specific behavioral gains (e.g. "has remained in school and continued to improve"). Thus, despite the difficulties, a clear need still exists for more controlled designs using experimental groups or highly systematic multiple studies. Finally, these case studies raise the question of what criteria for success should be used, both at treatment termination and at follow-up. Should one assess only improvement in approach behavior? Or should one also assess improvement in social and emotional functioning? One rationale for collecting social and emotional adjustment data is that these data might help researchers make comparisons among the various techniques, with the ultimate aim of identifying the most rapid and widely effective combinations. At any rate, termination and follow-up data should be collected and reported in terms of behavioral observations as well as in terms of verbal reports from parents and teachers.

VI. CONTROLLED FEAR-REDUCTION STUDIES

At least 36 controlled fear-reduction studies with children have been published, and there are several additional unpublished papers such as those reported in Gelfand's (1978) review. Although far more rigorous and systematic than the clinical case studies, the controlled studies share several common limitations. First, with few exceptions (e.g. L. C. Miller et al., 1972a; Obler and Terwilliger, 1970; Graziano, Mooney, Huber, and Ignasiak, 1979; Graziano and Mooney, 1980); they study what appear to be mild to moderate levels of fear, and the relevance of their findings for treating children with severe fears or phobias has yet to be demonstrated. Second, as with the case studies, the range of fears included has been limited: 14 studies focused on dental/medical fears (Adelson and Goldfried, 1970; Adelson, Liebert, Poulos, and Herskovitz, 1972; Johnson and Machen, 1973; Klorman, Hilpert, Michael, LaGana, and Sueen, 1980; Machen and Johnson, 1974; Melamed, Hawes, Heiby, and Glick, 1975; Melamed and Siegel, 1975; Melamed, Weinstein, Hawes, and Katin-Borland, 1975; Nocella and Kaplan, 1982; Peterson and Shigetomi, 1981; Roberts et al., 1981; Siegel and Peterson, 1981; Vernon and Bailey, 1974; White and Davis, 1974). Animal fears were discussed in seven studies (Bandura et al., 1967; Bandura and Menlove, 1968; Hill, Liebert, and Mott, 1968; Kornhaber and Schroeder, 1975; Murphy and Bootzin, 1973; Obler and Terwilliger, 1970; Ritter, 1968). Fears of social interaction were discussed in five studies (Evers and Schwarz, 1973; Keller and Carlson, 1974; O'Connor, 1969; O'Connor, 1972; Walker and Hops, 1973). Five studies focused on fears of the dark (Graziano et al., 1979; Graziano and Mooney, 1980; Kanfer et al., 1975; Kelley, 1976; Leitenberg and Callahan, 1973). Two discussed test anxiety (Mann, 1972; Mann and Rosenthal, 1969), and one studied fear of water (Lewis, 1974). L. C. Miller et al.'s (1972a) study included a variety of fears, such as fear of school, the dark, heights, germs, nakedness, and storms. However, if one deletes school phobics, the number of children in L. C. Miller et al. who presented fears other than those typically studied totals only 11.

Another general limitation is that most studies use a number of different techniques in complex treatment packages, and it is usually not possible to determine the most effective components of the packages.

The profusion of concepts and methods makes it difficult to organize these studies for discussion. They present a variety of terms, including desensitization, extinction, modeling, reciprocal inhibition, and so on. It is frequently unclear whether a term, systematic desensitization, for example, is used to denote a treatment procedure and is thus part of the independent variable or whether it refers to implicit processes of fear reduction within the child and is thus part of the dependent variable. Likewise, apparently similar processes or procedures are labeled differently by different authors, such as Ritter's (1968) "contact desensitization" versus Lewis's (1974) "participant modeling."

Most authors make their procedures fairly explicit, but only imply their models of fear-reduction processes. However, it appears that all of these authors assumed a disinhibition model, that is, the operation of some process of gradual weakening of the fear response in the course of graduated exposure to the fear stimuli. The graduated exposure may occur actually, imaginally, or vicariously.

The methods used to operationalize gradual exposure fall into three main groups: (a) modeling, (b) multivariable, systematic desensitization or contingency management treatment packages, and (c) a cognitive approach using verbal-mediation strategies. By far, modeling is the most frequently used procedure, accounting for 21 of the 31 controlled studies. Many of the remaining 10 papers seem to have included some forms of modeling, but did not label them as such. Modeling may be implicit in any of the fear-reduction procedures except, perhaps, for imaginal systematic desensitization.

A. *Modeling*

Modeling is largely a development of the last decade; it was stimulated by Bandura's research (e.g. Bandura et al., 1967; Bandura and Menlove, 1968), although precursors of modeling are clearly seen in Jones (1924a). Thelen, Fry, Fehrenbach, and Frautschi (1979) present a comprehensive review of research in videotape and film modeling. At least 23 modeling studies of fear reduction in children have been published in the past ten years. Although there are clear similarities among them, they fall into two fairly distinct groups with a number of important differences. Of these studies, 13, including Bandura's research, dealt with fairly common fears that occur frequently, even daily, for many children in the course of everyday events (i.e. fear of animals, the dark, water in baths, school examinations, and social interactions). In most instances the fears are clearly unreasonable in that there seems to be nothing objectively harmful in the immediate situation. The other ten studies form a distinct group of recent research published in the 1970s. They focused on the specific problems of reducing children's fears and preparing them for dental and surgical procedures. Unlike those in the former group, these fears are highly situation-specific and include often intense, but transitory, anxiety; they occur only at those few times when children are faced with dental or surgical procedures and thus, unlike many other fears, are not frequent or everyday issues. Also, the fears in this group appear more reasonable or reality-based than, for example, fears of the dark. It does not appear to us to be at all unreasonable for a child to struggle against a dentist or surgeon who is going to do unexplained things that, as far as the child knows, will probably hurt a great deal. In fact, we would argue that such self-defensive assertion on the part of a frightened child who is psychologically unprepared for the coming medical treatment is preferable to quiet, but totally frightened, submission. This group of modeling studies focused on the reduction of such fears in these specific situations. They may thus be of immense potential importance for untold numbers of children.

One of the studies in this group (see the listing above) is Melamed and Siegel's (1975) excellent research using symbolic modeling procedures to prepare children psychologically for surgery. The experimenters used a 16-minute film of an initially fearful child who gradually copes with the situation and overcomes his or her own fears. They reported that the children who viewed the modeling film, compared with control group children, showed significantly less "transitory, situational anxiety" on all measures (sweat gland activity, self-reported medical concerns, and overt, anxiety-related behavior). Their data also suggested that experimental group children had fewer postoperative behavior problems than the control group children.

Three important studies were presented by Klorman et al. (1980) who used symbolic modeling to control children's fear of dental procedures. Their results support the effectiveness of symbolic modeling in the dental treatment situation, thus adding to the other experimental evidence in this area. They also clarified an apparent limitation in the use of symbolic modeling in the dental/medical treatment situation—that is, symbolic modeling appears to be most effective, and perhaps effective only, when applied to children approaching their first experience with restorative dental work. Children with prior dental experience, shown the symbolic modeling film to reduce distress in subsequent treatment, do not do as well. Klorman et al. interpret their results as suggesting that restorative dental work on children who are not psychologically prepared may result in traumatic experiences that make the child afraid in subsequent treatment; and that symbolic modeling may have an important function for new child patients as a preventive measure, "inoculating" the children against the possible severe trauma of the first dental experience.

These ten studies give good evidence that brief symbolic modeling may be an effective aid in preparing children for dental and medical treatment, thus reducing their possibly high situational fears. The studies are limited to some degree in that they studied groups of normal children and did not include dental or medical phobics per se; thus, we cannot generalize these results to such chronically fearful children. Further, there is little evidence of the long-term effects of such modeling and yet no differential study of the effect of variables such as cognitive rehearsal, model and subject similarity, age, and so on. But all of those limitations can be avoided in future research.

In all of these studies the strategy was a preventive one; that is, prior to the occurrence of the stressful situation, children were prepared so they could more effectively cope with the stress when it did occur. There are important implications here for preventive and "stress inoculation" approaches, as is briefly discussed later.

Overall, the quality of these 23 modeling studies is high, but generalizations are limited for a number of reasons. First, none of the studies typically included severely fearful children, although Bandura and Menlove (1968) did describe fairly high levels of dog fear in some children, and many of the subjects in the dental/medical fear-reduction research seemed quite fearful. Overall, the children were not selected for severe or phobic levels of intensity or duration of fears. Although modeling appears to be quite effective with mild to moderate fears, its usefulness in reducing phobias or severe fears has not been shown. In order for modeling to be effective, the child must attend to the model. Highly fearful children may find watching any interaction with the phobic stimulus so aversive that they look away, thus avoiding the fear stimulus. Bandura and Menlove (1968) commented on encountering a similar difficulty. Some evidence suggests that modeling may not be as effective when used with children who have had prior experience in the fear situation (Klorman et al., 1980; Melamed et al., 1978). Thus, successful modeling with severely fearful or phobic children has yet to be demonstrated.

All of the studies used behavioral avoidance tests or behavioral observations in their pretreatment assessments. These procedures separate children by fear levels in comparison with other children in a particular study, but do not assess the clinical significance, per se, of the fears. Further, although the subjects' age range was wide (3 to 13 years), selective factors may have operated, for example, the use of children from special university nursery schools (e.g. the Bandura studies) or from parochial schools (e.g. Kornhaber, and Schroeder, 1975) or the use of only black children (e.g. Lewis, 1974) or only poor center-city children (Melamed, Hawes, Heiby, and Glick, 1975). Thus, the subjects in the experimental studies of modeling are not representative of either a clinical population or the normal population of children.

As noted earlier, the range of fears to which modeling has been applied is limited, with ten studies focusing on fears of impending dental/medical treatment, six on animal fears, four on social isolation, and one on fear of water. Thus one must be cautious about generalizing from these modeling studies either to the general or clinical populations or to different fear stimuli.

The basic modeling approach common to these studies consists of fearful subjects' first observing models who demonstrate behavior approach to the fearful stimuli. The subjects then attempt to perform the approach behavior themselves. This basic method has been varied across several dimensions. The modeling has been symbolic, as on videotapes (e.g. Bandura and Menlove, 1968; O'Connor, 1972), or presented by live models (Bandura et al., 1967; White and Davis, 1974); subjects have observed a single model (Ritter, 1968) or multiple models (Bandura and Menlove, 1968); modeling alone has been compared with modeling plus active, graduated contact with models and the fear stimulus (Lewis, 1974; Murphy and Bootzin, 1973; Ritter, 1968); the models have approached single stimuli (e.g. Kornhaber and Schroeder, 1975) or graduated variations of the fear stimulus, such as Bandura and Menlove's (1968) use of a variety of dogs; and the similarity of models to subjects has been explored (Kornhaber and Schroeder, 1975).

Not all of the meaningful combinations of these and other variables have yet been examined, or have sufficient replications of successful studies been carried out. However, some clear consistencies and at least tentative conclusions have emerged. First, therapeutic modeling procedures are in general significantly more effective than control conditions and can override pretreatment differences in "predisposition to emotionality" (Bandura and Menlove, 1968) and in model's similarity to the subject (Kornhaber and Schroeder, 1975). Further, modeling procedures seem effective over a fairly wide age range.

Second, the research suggests that modeling procedures become more powerful as additional controlled components are added to the basic techniques. Thus it seems likely that a highly effective modeling package would include multiple live models who approach a hierarchical range of varied fear stimuli, followed by trials of active contact with models in graduated sequences of progressively bolder contact with the graduated fear stimuli (Murphy and Bootzin, 1973; Ritter,

1968), that is, a modeling plus contact-desensitization package. There is considerable agreement that live modeling combined with progressive contact with models and fear stimuli is potentially a very powerful technique. To date, however, the complete modeling package outlined here has not been tested either against control or against other modeling procedures.

Third, although live modeling appears to be more effective than symbolic modeling, the latter may be equally effective (Bandura and Menlove, 1968) if it involves many trials and includes multiple models and progressively varied fear stimuli. In other words, a symbolic modeling package similar to that described above for live modeling may also be a powerful fear-reduction technique. The significance of this lies in the potential use of symbolic modeling procedures in large-scale, fear-reduction projects, in which direct contact with large numbers of children is not feasible. Thus, to the degree that children's fears may be a large-scale problem, symbolic modeling may offer potentially useful remediation. As of now, the effectiveness of such a program presented, for example, in educational television broadcasts, has not been tested and remains only a possibility.

Fourth, symbolic modeling has important implications for immunological approaches, e.g. stress inoculation (Meichenbaum and Turk, 1976). Although Bandura and Menlove (1968) pointed out the possibility of such preventive strategies as early as 1968, only recently have such approaches been applied to children's fears. Poser and King (1975) reported on a series of their experiments on the reduction of avoidance. In every case, the avoidance inhibitor was brought to bear before rather than after avoidance responding had occurred. One experiment made use of symbolic modeling to inhibit the acquisition of snake avoidance responses in first graders confronted with a live snake for the first time. These approaches deserve much more attention. For example, as suggested by studies such as O'Connor's (1972), might it not be possible to "immunize" entering kindergarten or nursery school children against early school fears? The symbolic modeling studies on reducing dental/mental fears also have clear implications for fear prevention. Large-scale televised symbolic modeling is a potential preventive strategy that has important community mental health implications. It is an area well worth careful attention.

Fifth, some dimensions of model and subject similarity may be important. Kornhaber and Schroeder (1975) found that age similarity (peer modeling) was associated with greater fear reduction for children than adult modeling, although neither attitudinal nor behavioral similarity was an effective variable. Although researchers have investigated model-subject similarity with regard to other behaviors (e.g. Bandura and Barab, 1973; Bandura, Ross, and Ross, 1973; Baron, 1971; Hicks, 1965; Maccoby and Wilson, 1957; Wheeler and Levine, 1967), only Kornhaber and Schroeder (1975) have manipulated model similarity in child fear reduction. Clearly this issue—the relationship between model and subject similarity and the reduction of children's fears—is an area in which more research is needed.

Sixth, Kornhaber and Schroeder (1975) and Melamed and Siegel (1975) also touched upon a related and possibly important issue, that is the relative effectiveness of models portraying a *mastery* versus a *coping* strategy in fear reduction. Several authors (Blanchard, 1970; Rachman, 1972; Ross, 1970) have suggested that modeling effectiveness might be increased if models demonstrated initially fearful behavior that gradually changed to fearless interaction with the stimulus. Hill et al. (1968), Melamed and Siegel (1975), Meichenbaum (1971), and Spiegler, Liebert, McMains and Fernandez (1969) all had their models exhibit some fear during the initial approach. Using adult subjects, Meichenbaum (1971) directly compared coping (initial display of fear) and mastery (no fear modeled) strategies. Meichenbaum found greater fear-reduction effectiveness with the coping strategy than with the mastery strategy. However, in all three studies there was sufficient confounding on variables to make their results uncertain. In the Meichenbaum study, for example, the coping models—but not the mastery models—also demonstrated a breath-control relaxation technique that may have accounted for many of the differences.

Although Kornhaber, and Schroeder (1975) compared a coping and a mastery modeling procedure, their coping models displayed fear throughout the modeling and did not demonstrate a progressive reduction of fear behavior that matched the demonstration of increased approach. Their coping model was thus incomplete. Finally, the coping model procedure used by Melamed, Hawes, Heiby and Glick (1975) was part of the modeling package applied to all experimental subjects and was not compared with a mastery model condition, thus making it impossible to assess the effects that can be attributed to coping strategies per se. Klorman et al. (1980), in the studies introduced above, compared the coping and mastery symbolic models in dental treatment and found the two, coping and mastery, did not differ in their effects. Their suggestion is that effectiveness of modeling may be due to some factor common to both coping and mastery, for example, the information given the child through both procedures. It seems clear that continued systematic investigation comparing coping and mastery models for children's fear reduction and prevention is an area in need of research.

Seventh, although modeling procedures appear to be of a decidedly social nature, they seem to have rarely been used to reduce basically social fears of children such as shyness, severe isolation, fear of speaking in groups, and so on. An exception is O'Connor's (1969, 1972) work with socially withdrawn nursery school children. Using only a 23 minute peer-modeling film that showed progressively more involved social interactions, O'Connor reported dramatic changes in originally shy nursery school children. The children reportedly became normally assertive in class and "indistinguishable" from their non-shy classmates after only one viewing. Control children did not change. O'Connor's results are extremely impressive, but, as discussed by Gelfand (1978), a number of subsequent attempts have failed to demonstrate positive effects of symbolic modeling on social withdrawal. The experimenters, nearly all in unpublished papers, attempted to explain their lack of success by pointing to their own procedural shortcomings (e.g. too disparate model-subject ages, lack of a sound track to accompany a modeling film, a failure to clearly model coping strategies. These failures suggest that modeling may not be as powerful and reliable a technique as is suggested by the published studies. It is most interesting that the attempts to account for the failures suggest a possibly strong presumption of the effectiveness of modeling strategies, a presumption powerful enough to necessitate explaining away the failures as experimental weaknesses. In other words, there may be a tendency to discount negative evidence on modeling.

One of the successful modeling studies on social withdrawal (Jakibchuk and Smeriglio, 1976) reported that the videotaped model's use of a first-person narrative in which the child described himself or herself as initially shy was essential. Their work suggests the operation of important cognitive factors through first-person self-statements as well as the importance of the model's behavioral similarity to the observing child.

Finally, even when modeling is successful in modifying fear behavior, the effects of modeling may disappear in a few weeks for adults (e.g. Bandura, Jeffery, and Wright, 1974) and for children (Keller and Carlson, 1974) if subsequent reinforced practice is not made available to the observer. Like other behavior modification techniques, particularly those used in the 1960s (Graziano, 1975a), modeling with fearful children has repeatedly demonstrated its success in modifying target behavior, but there are yet few data on either the generalization or the maintenance of the new behavior. Further research on these two issues is necessary.

Overall, despite some negative evidence and many yet unanswered questions, the bulk of the research evidence supports modeling as an effective set of techniques and a rich area for further research. Needed are systematic examinations of the effects of several variables (e.g. model and subject similarity, coping and mastery strategies, single and multiple modeling). Three of the more important questions to be answered concern (a) the intensity of fears for which modeling might be effective, (b) the potential use of large-scale symbolic modeling to reduce and, perhaps of greater importance, to prevent particularly common and disruptive fears, and (c) the generalizability and maintenance of behavior newly achieved through modeling. Conspicuously absent in the modeling research to date is direct investigation of the degree to which cognitive factors such as covert competency self-statements are operative.

B. *Desensitization and Contingency-Management Packages*

Eight studies describing complex treatment packages are included here. Two studies (L. C. Miller et al., 1972a; Obler and Terwilliger, 1970) included children with severe fears. Two other studies (Mann, 1972; Mann and Rosenthal, 1969) studied adolescents referred by school counselors for test anxiety who could also be considered at or near severe levels. Obler and Terwilliger used systematic desensitization to pictures of fear stimuli followed by up to 50 hours of *in vivo* contact desensitization to reduce the severe monophobias (of dogs or buses) of 30 "neurologically impaired" children.

L. C. Miller (1972a) compared reciprocal inhibition, psychotherapy, and a waiting-list control condition as treatments in phobic children. The reciprocal inhibition treatment condition was actually a broad array of behavioral approaches, including meetings with parents, restructuring home contingencies, assertiveness training, relaxation and systematic desensitization, and discussions of problems and progress. Psychotherapy treatments focused on inner experience and encouraged the child to talk about his or her feelings and conflicts. There seems to have been considerable overlap in these two treatment conditions. For example, discussions with parents and altering home conditions are similar strategies, and denying the child in the reciprocal inhibition group free access to television at home ("restructuring contingency schedules") to decrease the reinforcement for fear behaviors is similar to the strategy of "removing gratifications" so as to reduce "secondary gains."

Their results are complex and difficult to summarize. Overall, neither treatment was more effective than the waiting-list control treatment. However, when age is considered, the reciprocal inhibition and psychotherapy treatment conditions were equally more effective than the control conditions for children 10 years of age and younger, whereas those 11 to 15 years old did not seem to respond to either treatment condition. In a two-year follow-up (Hampe et al., 1973) the investigators found major effects of age and elapsed time. The younger children had "changed dramatically" immediately following treatment and maintained their improvement. Older children showed a more gradual improvement over the two-year follow-up, as did control children. The researchers concluded that age and time are critical factors in child fear reduction. Younger children tend to lose their fears much more rapidly than do older children; in time (up to two years), children generally lose their fears with or without treatment; nevertheless, treatment, behavioral or psychodynamic, is justified because it "greatly hastens recovery" (p. 451).

Both studies, particularly Obler and Terwilliger's, employed complex treatment packages. Although both research groups labeled their major procedures *systematic desensitization* (Obler and Terwilliger, 1970) or reciprocal inhibition (L. C. Miller et al., 1972a), that is, some variation of Wolpe's (1974) systematic desensitization, they both also included a variety of contingency management techniques, including shaping and probably some modeling. Neither study clearly specified the roles of the therapists, and it is difficult to know just what occurred in the various treatment groups. Further, both studies used parents' reports as the major dependent variable. In fact, Obler and Terwilliger based their analysis on a single item from a ten-item parents' questionnaire. As critiqued by Begelman and Hersen (1971), Obler and Terwilliger's study has methodological problems that make its positive findings highly questionable. L. C. Miller et al. (1972a) and Hampe et al. (1973) are useful studies, in spite of the difficulties noted above. They present important findings concerning fear reduction as a function of age and time, and they include a long-term (two-year) follow-up, a rare occurrence in behavioral research. In essence these three studies together fail to support the differential effectiveness of complex systematic desensitization treatment packages for either severe or more moderate fears. From L. C. Miller et al. and Hampe et al., the safest conclusion is that either behavioral or psychodynamic treatment is helpful in the short term for younger children, who in any event apparently would overcome their fears without treatment in the long term, roughly two years.

The articles by Leitenberg and Callahan (1973) and Kelley (1976) are clinical analogs focused on nursery school and kindergarten children selected for their fear of the dark. Both studies were well designed and used control groups, duration of dark tolerance as pre- and posttreatment behavioral measures, and visual "fear thermometers" for subjective reports by or feedback to the subjects. Neither study employed a follow-up, and no attempt was made to assess the clinical severity of the fears, leaving the possibility that the subjects were only mildly to moderately fearful.

Leitenberg and Callahan used a "reinforcement practice" method in which children were instructed to remain in a dark room for longer periods of time over five trials per session and two practice sessions per week for a maximum of 4 weeks or until the child reached a criterion of two consecutive 5-minute dark-tolerance trials. For each successful trial the children were reinforced with praise and prizes. The authors reported a significant treatment and control group difference on posttraining dark-tolerance tests. However, there were only seven children in each group, and the mean posttraining dark tolerance for the experimental group was only about 3 minutes. Although statistically significant, does a 3-minute dark tolerance have any personal or clinical significance?

Kelley (1976) assigned 40 children who feared the dark to three desensitization treatment groups, one "play placebo" control, and one no-treatment control group and reported no differences between treatment and controls or among the three treatment conditions. The most important finding of this study is the significant effect of a simple demand manipulation, that is, verbal instructions to remain longer in the dark room dramatically increased dark tolerance and was "a far more powerful influence on both behavioral and self-report change scores than three sessions of therapy" (Kelley, 1976, p. 80). In light of Kelley's findings and their implications, we suggest that Leitenberg and Callahan's "significant" reinforced practice effects may have been due simply to their verbal instructions only to the experimental group to remain in the dark room for a longer time on each subsequent trial. Kelley's finding is particularly important because it seems reasonable to hypothesize that demand characteristics are especially salient to children who, because of their immature status, are often in the position of having to comply with the outright and sometimes subtle demands of adults. Certainly these issues need to be explored. The critical research has not yet been done, but it may be that dark-tolerance performance of dark-fearful children can be significantly improved by instruction alone. But would this manipulation, perhaps over repeated trials, change other aspects of fear such as physiological and cognitive responses, and would those changes hold up over time? A potentially important area in need of research is the effects on children's fear behavior of adults' instructions.

In two studies, Mann and Rosenthal (1969) and Mann (1972) compared direct and vicarious desensitization procedures in the reduction of adolescents' text anxiety. Like subjects in Obler and Terwilliger (1970) and some of those in L. C. Miller et al. (1972a), these adolescents, referred by a school counselor for high test anxiety, appear to have been severely fearful. Their major finding was systematic desensitization, whether applied individually or in groups, whether actually or vicariously experienced, was significantly more effective in reducing test anxiety than the waiting-list control condition. The control subjects, when treated later, also improved.

Most interesting about Mann's studies is that the most effective procedure was a vicarious desensitization condition, which actually sounds very much like a symbolic modeling procedure in which subjects observe a videotaped peer model undergoing systematic desensitization and gaining control over the fear. The subjects in the vicarious condition showed greater improvement than those who actually experienced direct systematic desensitization! In Mann's work, then, although called a *desensitization* procedure, the symbolic modeling approach was the most effective with apparently highly fearful subjects. In effect, these two studies of desensitization support the effectiveness of symbolic modeling.

In three modeling studies of shy or withdrawn children, investigators tested whether the addition of direct shaping procedures added any power to the basic symbolic modeling procedure. Evers and Schwarz (1973) found that it did not. O'Connor (1972) reported that although shaping (with praise and attention) was as effective as symbolic modeling, the new interactive behavior of the shaping group soon decayed, whereas modeling group subjects maintained their gains. Somewhat similar findings were reported by Walker and Hops (1973). In their study, the addition of contingency management (tokens for increased classroom interaction) following the symbolic modeling film reliably increased social behavior beyond that produced by modeling alone. However, as Gelfand (1978) pointed out, when tokens were withdrawn, the new behavior degenerated. Apparently, "natural" reinforcers in the classroom did not maintain it. Perhaps a more gradual thinning of reinforcements or the use of more social reinforcements would have produced a more stable level of interaction. The point here is that the success of contingency-management techniques in reducing withdrawn or shy social behavior is still uncertain.

Graziano et al. (1979) and Graziano and Mooney (1980, 1982) included relaxation training and contingency-management techniques in their cognitive self-control fear-treatment package. Although they reported a high degree of success maintained over a three-year follow-up with 41 families and children, their procedures do not allow conclusions to be drawn concerning the specific contributions of the relaxation and of the contingency-management components.

Children's fear of water in a swimming program was treated by Ultee, et al. (1982) using *in vivo* (real-life) and *in vitro* (relaxation and imaginal desensitization) systematic desensitization. They report the *in vivo* method to have been superior to *in vitro* treatment or a control condition. Although providing some evidence for the effectiveness of *in vivo* systematic desensitization, the results are somewhat equivocal because there may have been some confounding of *in vivo* desensitization treatment with live modeling, which may have occurred in the program.

In summary, eight studies have examined complex desensitization or contingency-management treatment packages in the reduction of children's fears, and several other studies have included contingency-management procedures in addition to basic symbolic modeling approaches. Overall the findings are equivocal. One study (L. C. Miller et al., 1972a) found no overall beneficial effects of systematic desensitization compared with other treatments and with nontreated control conditions. Obler and Terwilliger's (1970) study has a number of methodological problems that cast doubt on their conclusions. Kelley (1976) reported no effects of desensitization treatment compared with two control treatments. Leitenberg and Callahan's (1973) results are based on a very small number of subjects and, as discussed earlier, are open to the interpretation that treatment differences may have been due simply to direct instructions. Mann and Rosenthal (1969) and Mann (1972) reported good results with a variety of systematic desensitization treatments, but, on close inspection, their most successful treatment appears to have been symbolic modeling rather than systematic desensitization. Finally, three of the modeling studies (Evers and Schwarz, 1973; O'Connor, 1972; Walker and Hops, 1973) found that the addition of contingency management did not usually improve performance beyond that achieved by symbolic modeling alone, and if it did, the new performance was not maintained.

Unlike the modeling literature, there exists no convincing experimental evidence that approaches developed on respondent-based systematic desensitization or operant contingency-management paradigms are effective methodologies for reducing children's fears.

C. *Cognitive Approaches*

Until 1979, only one published study (Kanfer et al., 1975) used a cognitive self-control approach in child fear reduction. Since then four more have been published: Graziano et al. (1979), Graziano and Mooney (1980), Peterson and Shigetomi (1981), and Siegel and Peterson (1980). In Kanfer et al., children five and six years old rehearsed one of three verbal-mediation responses: (a) sentences emphasizing the child's control or competence [e.g. "I am a brave girl (boy). I can take care of myself."]; (b) sentences aimed at reducing the fear-stimulus value of the dark (e.g. "The dark is a fun place to be"); or (c) neutral sentences (e.g. "Mary had a little lamb"). In dark-tolerance posttests the "competence" group significantly outperformed the others. These children were not representative of a normal population and appeared to be only mildly or moderately fearful; we thus cannot generalize their results to clinical populations. The laboratory dark-tolerance test may have had no relationship to real fears in the children's natural environments, and no behavioral maintenance data were provided. However, despite some shortcomings it was a well-executed study with strong results. The operation of verbal self-control processes was suggested by the authors, although they noted that their study did not specify the details of verbal control mechanisms.

Other hints of the possible effectiveness of verbal mediation are found in case studies (Ayer, 1973; Lazarus and Abramovitz, 1962), in which children rehearsed highly competent, although very imaginative, strategies for coping with fear stimuli. The modeling research by Jakibchuk and Smeriglio (1976) suggests the necessity of a first-person self-speech narrative as an accompaniment to a symbolic modeling film. One possible interpretation of these various hints is that the children's own verbal self-instructions—whether originally received from a film, from specific sentences given to the subjects to rehearse, or from fanciful verbal and pictorial images—on how to successfully deal with the fear stimulus are a central component of the successful interventions.

Among the more recent series of papers on children's fears are those by Graziano and colleagues (Graziano, DeGiovanni and Garcia, 1979; Graziano and DeGiovanni 1979; Graziano, Mooney, Huber, and Ignasiak 1979; and Graziano and Mooney 1980, 1981). Their first paper was a review of the field's research, the original version of this chapter. The authors drew several conclusions, including the following: children's fear-reduction research (a) had not dealt with the issue of clinically significant fears, that is, of high intensity and long duration, and (b) with the exception of Kanfer et al. (1975), had neglected cognitive self-control procedures in child fear reduction. Graziano, Mooney, Huber, and Ignasiak (1979) and Graziano and Mooney (1982) describe two studies in which they attempted to deal with both of those issues. Forty-one families of dark-fearful children were selected from among volunteers for a cognitive, self-control, home-training fear-reduction approach. Selection criteria were age of child (6 to 12), at least two consecutive years of problem duration, and high intensity of nightly fears to the point of serious disruption of the family and the child's behavior. Pretreatment equivalence of experimental and delayed-treatment groups was established for a number of baseline measures that included parents' retrospective reports and rating scales and 7 to 10 days of recorded nightly observations by the parents. In one group meeting for parents and another for children, the families were instructed in a home-training program that was to be carried out nightly for 3 weeks. The nightly practice was to occur just prior to bedtime and it included (a) brief muscular relaxation, (b) rehearsal of images of a pleasant scene, (c) reciting "special words" taken from Kanfer et al. (1975) as verbal self-instruction (e.g. "I am brave; I am not afraid of the dark"), and (d) "bravery tokens" awarded each morning for progressively better sleeping and fearless nighttime behavior. Forty of the forty-one children lost their fears and their success was maintained over a two-year follow-up. One child needed additional training after the first 3-week intervention and he, too, overcame the severe nighttime fears and maintained the improvement over the two-year follow-up.

Graziano and Mooney (1980, 1981) concluded that their intervention package was effective; the effects were maintained over a long period. Although they could not specify which components were most effective, their results suggest that cognitive procedures for some fears, such as nighttime fears, are promising approaches.

Although there are yet few appropriate data on the success of verbal self-controlling manipulations in child fear reduction, certainly enough data and hints are available to alert one that more research in this direction is indicated.

D. *Summary of Controlled Studies*

In summary, experimental fear-reduction research with children has been meager until the past 10 years, during which at least 36 studies have been published. Because of limited sampling procedures, their results cannot be generalized to either normal or clinical populations of children. As for the latter group, we have virtually no data and know surprisingly little about reducing severe phobic levels of children's fears. It has yet to be demonstrated whether the experimental fear-reduction findings are useful in clinical practice.

Only a limited number of different fears have been studied: fear of animals, fear of bodily injury (e.g. fear of dental treatment), fear of darkness, test anxiety, and social isolation. The levels of fear intensity have also been limited, with only 6 of the 35 studies including children with more than mild-to-moderate fears. Only 4 of the studies considered pretreatment fear duration as a measure of seriousness. With the exception of dental/medical fears and nighttime fears, we have virtually no data on fear reduction outside of the laboratory setting and thus do not know if statistically significant changes brought about in the laboratory are related to fear behavior in the child's natural environment or are of sufficient magnitude to be psychologically or clinically significant. Although the experimental reduction of fear behavior has been repeatedly demonstrated, neither generalization nor long-term maintenance of the new behavior has been demonstrated.

Three major fear-reduction strategies have been employed: (a) Most studies (23 of the 36) have used modeling approaches; (b) 8 have used a variety of systematic desensitization or contingency management treatment packages; and (c) 5 studies used a cognitive verbal-mediation strategy. Of the three strategies, the most reliably successful has been modeling (in terms of replications and fairly well-controlled methodology). A number of important research issues in modeling remain to be investigated, including model-subject similarity, coping versus mastery strategies, modeling effectiveness with severe fears, adequate demonstration of both generalization and long-term maintenance of the new behavior in the child's natural environment, and use of modeling in the prevention of fears.

A particularly important issue, not yet systematically investigated, is the operation of cognitive self-controlling mechanisms in successful modeling. Three studies used a verbal-mediation, self-control strategy. Their success is encouraging and should generate a good deal of research.

Unlike the modeling literature, there is no convincing evidence that systematic desensitization or contingency management strategies are effective in reducing children's fears and in maintaining that reduction. Hatzenbuehler and Schroeder's (1978) recent review came to the same conclusion regarding desensitization procedures.

One of the more interesting, if still remote, practical implications of the recent research is the potential use of symbolic modeling in large-scale community mental health fear-prevention programs. A number of common, vexing childhood fears (e.g. fear of starting school and fear of dental/mental procedures) might be prevented on a large scale.

Overall, fear reduction and prevention in children, particularly using modeling and cognitive strategies, is a rich area for research and development. The need for research in many directions in this field is clearly indicated.

VII. CONCLUSIONS

Reaching back almost 60 years, the study of children's fears is old in the history of modern psychology. However, what is most striking is not the field's age but its apparent lack of progress. To paraphrase Berecz's (1968) conclusion, the literature still gives us only hints about the nature of children's fears. After what appears to have been a good start in the 1920s, the field experienced a long hiatus, which appears to be ending. The research of the past ten years has returned to the behavior modification focus of the 1920s and early 1930s.

This review suggests that children's fears, like other human reactions, proceed through complex processes. The many variables involved and their interactions result in a complexity that provides many points at which to focus research. Briefly, fear stimuli may be internal, external, or both and may vary in content, number, intensity, and duration. The child's responses involve combinations of physiological, cognitive, and overt behavioral events, all of which may vary in latency, intensity, and duration and with changes in stimulus conditions. The child's responses, overt or covert, may act on any of the stimulus and response variables, modify them, and thus occasion change in any parts of the process. All of these processes are immersed in social settings that contribute further sources of variation.

Despite this rich complexity, the research over nearly 60 years has focused almost exclusively on the endpoints of the paradigm; that is, normative research has tried to identify fear stimuli, whereas the more recent fear-reduction research has tried to modify the overt avoidance behavior. Virtually all of the variables between, observable or inferred, have been left unexplored, leaving one with little understanding of fear processes in children.

Future research will do well to follow the literature's hints and look more closely at the unexplored areas identified in this review, such as the possible adaptive value of children's fears, fear-prevention strategies, cognitive self-control variables, and developmental factors. In short, we must recognize and test far more complex paradigms of the fear process. Finally, we clearly must correct our continued lack of information regarding severe levels of children's fear.

5

Behavioral Self-Control

I. INTRODUCTION

Clinical and research interest concerning self-control in behavior therapy has been steadily increasing over the past 15 years. This increase has not been without considerable controversy, reflecting greater sophistication and self-criticism as the field of behavior modification matures. Political pressure, theoretical purity, technical concerns, and personal values have played and continue to play a major, and surprisingly explicit, role in the field's development.

As has been discussed by Graziano (1975a), in the early 1960s behavior modification was characterized by fairly discrete, though repeated, demonstrations that disturbed behavior can be brought under external control and predictably modified. Given these demonstrations wider clinical applications followed, encompassing more complex behavior and focusing both on individuals and on people in groups. However, it soon became clear that improved behavior often reverted to earlier levels after treatment ended and that even the most intensive behavioral programs were often limited to the specific setting in which they were implemented. Treatments were needed that not only changed behavior, but that also fostered the maintenance and generalization of that improved behavior. Self-control programs were developed at least in part in recognition of, and as one potential solution to, these problems.

Self-control research interest also arose out of the initial success of behavior modification. An alarming spectre of a behavioral technology out of control was seen by some critics; technology that could insidiously manipulate through subtle reinforcement clients, school children, prison inmates, and society without their knowledge or consent. Committees were formed and laws were passed that protected various populations from the behavior modifer (see Begelman, 1977; Halleck, 1974; Hersen, 1976; Malmquist, 1970; Martin, 1975; and Szasz, 1968). Although the feared power of the behavior modifier was severely overstated (cf. Kanfer, 1965a; Kanfer and Phillips, 1970; London, 1971; Gaylin, 1974), many of the ethical and value issues underlying the concerns are relevant to the behavior modifier or any other person, group, or agency that attempts to influence people. Questions such as: "Are the therapist's skills used to benefit the client, existing institutions, the social order, the goals of the therapist, or some other third party?" "What kind of therapeutic relationship maximizes the client's freedom?" and "What methods best achieve therapy's goals?" are examples of some of the problems that face the behavior modifier. [For further discussion of ethical issues in therapy, see Carrera and Adams (1970); Davison (1976); Erickson (1977); Kanfer (1965b); Kanfer and Phillips (1970); Karoly (1977); Skinner (1968); Sturgis and Adams (1978); and Szasz (1960).] Self-control procedures were seen as a potential solution to some of these problems.

Bandura (1969, 1978) proposed a model of reciprocal determinism that emphasized the ability of people to modify their environment as well as to be acted upon by their environment. This idea is not new (i.e. Skinner, 1953; Mahoney, 1976) and it does not provide clear and testable answers to questions of free will and determinism. It does, however, conceptualize a person as being under self-regulatory control (Shapiro and Zifferblatt, 1976). From such a self-control framework approaches can be developed that have an inherent political value in that the perceived agent of change is the person whose behavior is being altered (Brownell, Colletti, Ersner-Hershfield, Hershfield, and Wilson, 1977).

Self-control has traditionally been viewed in terms of trait concepts (Thoresen and Mahoney, 1974), as internal reservoirs of strength possessed by a person, an inner strength that allows restraint in the face of powerful external forces. *Will power* is the common term for this trait, and people are thought to have or not to have sufficient amounts of it. Unfortunately, the traditional will power concept has little functional value; it does little good, for example, to exhort someone to "pull yourself together," "snap out of it," or "control yourself." To quote from William Long's (1975) discussion, "We are not denying the effectiveness of will power. On the contrary, we are searching for its ingredients. We suspect that what people often label as will power is simply a set of unspecified, yet workable, self-management procedures" (p. 21).

The emerging behavioral concept views self-control as a person's acquired skills in manipulating variables that affect him or herself. The essential idea in this formulation is, not surprisingly, that a person's behavior—overeating, smoking, fear, underachieving, social failure, and so on—is functionally related to a variety of internal and external stimuli, both discriminant and reinforcing. Behavior therapists assume that they can recognize these functional relationships and manipulate the controlling variables so as to modify client behavior. The self-control concept, in essence, asserts that a person can learn to function as his or her own change agent: to carry out the same functional analysis, manipulate the controlling variables, and modify his or her own behavior. In sum, self-control is self-behavior modification.

Self-control research attempts to develop and improve techniques by which people can observe their own behavior, change it if desired, and then continually modify and monitor it according to their needs (Shapiro and Zifferblatt, 1976). It is assumed that a great deal of behavior is under or could be under self-regulation or control in the sense that people monitor their performance, evaluate their efforts gauged against certain standards, and often provide themselves with differential consequences (Thoresen and Wilbur, 1976). A major issue of controversy about self-control among other behavior modifiers is that they are delving into the "lion's den" (Kanfer and Karoly, 1972) of cognitions. Indeed, self-control researchers and their critics have been very cognizant of the major role of cognitive factors in self-control paradigms. Bandura (1978) writes:

> Cognitive factors partly determine which external events will be observed, how they will be perceived, whether they have any lasting effects, what valence and efficacy they have, and how the information they convey will be organized for future use. The extraordinary capacity of humans to use symbols enables them to engage in reflective thought, to create, and to plan foresightful courses of action in thought rather than having to perform possible options and suffer the consequences of thoughtless action. By altering their immediate environment, by creating cognitive self-inducements, and by arranging conditional incentives for themselves, people can exercise some influence over their own behavior. (p. 345)

This emphasis on cognition does not come easy to many behaviorists (cf. Goldiamond, 1976). Often arguments on both sides of the cognitive issue revert to insoluble metaphysical issues, infinite regressions, and "straw man" conflicts. A main point that can be drawn from this discussion, though, is that the usefulness of a cognitive self-control approach is not as self-evident as it may appear. First, self-control is difficult to operationalize; the relationship of the operational definition to the theoretical construct, "self-control," is ambiguous. Even the most cognitively oriented behaviorists realize that self-control research, with its emphasis on cognition, begins with a limited base of empirical support (Thoresen and Mahoney, 1974). In their defense Mahoney (1970) argues, "There comes a time when in the absence of adequate data, inadequate data must temporarily suffice" (p. 272). The controversy is well summed up by Ledwidge (1978).

> Strictly speaking, cognition, to the methodological behaviorist, is a mediational variable. Cognitions do not qualify as behaviors, since they do not meet the prerequisite of objective identifiability. Such hypothetical constructs, however, do have a place in a behavioristic system if and only if they contribute to the functional analysis of behavior by increasing our prediction and control thereof. The utility of such inferred variables in the evolution of behavior therapy techniques is indisputable (e.g. the critical role of anxiety as an inferred variable in the development of systematic desensitization), but whether or not cognition as a mediational variable will also prove useful in the development of efficient treatment procedures remains to be seen. (p. 362)

Until recently self-control research had been carried out primarily with adults. It may be that our assumptions about children prevent much serious investigation in this area. That is, children, are regarded as "immature," and our assumptions about immaturity make the practice of self-control by children a seemingly far-fetched proposition. Further, the very concept of self-control implies that individuals can be controlling agents in their own environment. Children, however, have a subordinate role in society and are subject to control by virtually all adults. To suggest that children be taught skills to more effectively control their own environments is to suggest decreasing control over children by adults such as parents and teachers, and this tampers with a very basic social arrangement (Graziano and Graziano, 1972). It is a suggestion that should be investigated by a society which holds that all competent individuals have an inherent right, as long as they do not abuse it, to the privileges and responsibilities of freedom and autonomy.

We believe that the development of such control by children is desirable and that training children in self-control skills is of great potential importance. We submit that the greater the degree to which children can learn to manage their own lives the more successful they will become in dealing with the variety of unsettling and even destructive controls that beset adults. The implications for preventive mental health are enormous. The greatest potential value of the technology of self-control, we believe, is that it can teach people early in life to intelligently manage their own existence as much as possible. A recent upsurge of interest in self-control with children would seem to reflect this importance. The literature includes a large number of recent general reviews (Karoly, 1977; Meichenbaum, 1979; O'Leary and Dubey, 1979), reviews of various components of self-control (Kendall, 1977; Pressley, 1979; Urbain and Kendall, 1980), reviews of self-control applications in a school setting (McLaughlin, 1975; Rosenbaum and Drabman, 1979; Workman and Hector, 1978), and reviews of self-control procedures with the mentally retarded (Kurtz and Neisworth, 1976; Mahoney and Mahoney, 1976; Polsgrove, 1979).

Although not often explicitly stated and even less often operationally defined, the self-control models that have been proposed and tested generally involve components that include the self-observation, self-evaluation, and self-reward or punishment of behavior as well as various self-regulatory functions posited to change behavior or its consequences, such as self-instruction, stimulus control, imagery, and relaxation (cf. Bandura, 1978; Karoly, 1977; Meichenbaum, 1979).

II. SELF-MONITORING

Self-monitoring or self-observation is usually considered the initial and necessary step in the self-control process and involves attention to various targeted behaviors emitted by oneself. This may include monitoring external or internal behaviors including covert thoughts, or feelings, verbalizations, physiological reactions, and so on, on any number of descriptive dimensions such as frequency, duration, and intensity.

Self-monitoring with children has been studied in classroom settings and has been shown not only to provide self-information but also to be a reactive technique potentially valuable in and of itself for self-control. Improved preacademic skills such as increased on-task behavior, class attendance, and decreased disruptive behavior have resulted from the implementation of the self-monitoring of those behaviors (Broden, Hall, and Mitts, 1971; Clement, Anderson, Arnold, Butman, Fantuzzo, and Mays, 1978; Lovitt, 1973; McKenzie and Rushall, 1974; McNamara and Heard, 1976; Sagotsky, Patterson, and Lepper, 1978) as well as improved academic skills such as the rate and accuracy of responding on tests (Gottman and McFall, 1972; Lovitt, 1973; Nelson, Lipinski, and Boykin, 1978; Sagotsky, Patterson, and Lepper, 1978). On the other hand, other studies have not found self-monitoring itself to have any noticeable effect on the behaviors monitored (Ballard and Glynn, 1975; Iayne, Rickard, Jones, and Lyman, 1976; Santogrossi, O'Leary, and Ironsmith, 1975).

The mechanisms operating during the self-monitoring procedures that cause changes in the targeted behaviors have yet to be investigated. Most researchers assume that self-monitoring is intimately linked with self-evaluative and self-reward or punishment responses that function to change the target behavior (Cautela, 1971; Kanfer and Karoly, 1972; Kazdin, 1974; O'Leary and Dubey, 1979) or it may simply be that the child is attempting to meet the expectations of the investigator.

O'Leary and Dubey (1979) suggest three factors that may influence the effectiveness of self-monitoring procedures: accuracy, the type of child, and the difficulty of the task. Merely because a child is instructed to self-monitor a behavior does not assure that the child will accurately and diligently carry out the procedure. A number of researchers have rewarded children for matching their records to the records of an external observer, resulting in high reliability and presumably accurate self-monitoring (Bolstad and Johnson, 1972; Drabman, Spitalnik, and O'Leary, 1973; Hundert and Bucher, 1978; Nelson, Lipinski, and Boykin, 1978; Wood and Flynn, 1978). One incentive that may be particularly useful in achieving accurate self-monitoring is peer social surveillance (Thomas, 1976). Interestingly, no studies have found a relationship between accurate self-monitoring and improved behavior or performance. Self-monitoring has been effective in changing behavior in a desirable direction even when the reliability of self-monitoring and external monitoring was quite low, a perplexing result that calls for further investigation.

O'Leary and Dubey (1979) speculate that self-monitoring alone may be an effective procedure in changing behavior only when the child already demonstrates a clear motivation to improve the behavior. Thus studies done with unselected "normal" school children might be successful because many of the children might value the expectations of the investigator (e.g. Sagostky et al., 1978). In any case, studies that have involved children with a history of behavioral difficulties have often found self-monitoring alone to be of no avail (Santogrossi et al., 1973; Turkewitz et al., 1975; Layne, et al., 1976).

In regard to the potential effects of the difficulty of the task that is self-monitored, O'Leary and Dubey discuss the study by Peacock, Lyman, and Rickard (1978). This study involved nine boys, ages 12 to 14, at a camp for disturbed children who were required to monitor their cabin-cleaning behavior. When self-monitoring was required but accuracy was not required, the children presented themselves as having completed a greater number of difficult (e.g. bed made neatly; clothes folded and stacked neatly) and easy (e.g. pillow in place; no objects on bed) cabin-cleaning tasks than they actually had completed. When the accuracy of self-monitoring was required, the completion of easy cabin-cleaning tasks increased to the level of the self-monitored behavior that the children had been reporting, while the self-monitoring reports of completion of the difficult tasks dropped to the level the children had been completing all along.

In this study, self-monitoring altered behavior in a positive direction when it involved tasks easily accomplished by the child but had no effect with more difficult tasks. A review of the problem behaviors that have been desirably altered (there have been no published reports of self-monitoring process itself and any corresponding change in behavior will dissipate over time (i.e. Broden, Hall, and Mitts, 1971). The lack of for altering problems of a more serious or "clinical" nature, self-monitoring alone, not unexpectedly, is insufficient.

Another factor that may influence the effectiveness of self-monitoring is the particular technique used for self-monitoring. Although still lacking in experimental support, it may be that data cards and mechanical devices may, in the short term, be more intrinsically interesting while more subtle or covert self-monitoring may generalize better to other situations and be more likely to be internalized and therefore maintained over time.

Many studies have included self-monitoring as an integral component of an entire self-control package. This is reasonable at a clinical level as it is likely that without the addition of other self-control components such as self-reward or of external incentives, the self-monitoring process itself and any corresponding change in behavior will dissipate over time (i.e. Broden, Hall, and Mitts, 1971). The lack of reports of long-term maintenance in the self-monitoring literature is a major weakness.

A few studies have investigated the incremental or augmental value of self-monitoring in a self-control procedure. The incremental effect of self-monitoring in successful token programs has been minimal (Knapczyk and Livingston, 1973) or nonexistent (Salzberg, 1972). In a less successful token program, however, the power of the self-monitoring procedure was demonstrated (Seymour and Stokes, 1976). Seymour and Stokes used a multiple-baseline design to investigate the effects of self-monitoring on four adolescent girls who were doing poorly in the token program at an institutional maximum security setting. They found that adding a self-monitoring procedure to the token program increased the percentage of the teenagers' work behavior in classroom, kitchen, and workshop settings. They also found that this improved work behavior maintained at a high rate for the few days when tokens were eliminated but self-recording was continued. This supports findings by Bolstad and Johnson (1972), who worked with disruptive first and second graders, and Turkewitz et al. (1975), who worked with 7- to 11-year-old students who were behind in academic and social behaviors, that self-monitoring can act as a powerful agent in maintaining behaviors already changed in a token program.

In summary, self-monitoring may be useful in initiating positive behavioral change and in maintaining already changed behavior. Its effectiveness in changing seriously disordered behavior or in making long-lasting changes in behavior without other augmenting procedures appears doubtful. But the importance of self-control training for teaching children to attend to their behavior—of providing them the opportunity to gain information about themselves—is clear.

III. SELF-EVALUATION AND SELF-REINFORCEMENT

In the behavioral self-control paradigm, self-evaluation follows the self-monitoring stage. Self-evaluation involves the individual evaluating his or her performance in comparison with a personal goal or standard of performance (Kanfer and Karoly, 1972; Kolb and Boyatzis, 1970; Shapiro and Zifferblatt, 1976). The selective presentation to oneself of consequences, be they overt or covert, positive or negative, punishment or reinforcement, contingent on one's performance makes up the self-reinforcement state of self-control (Mahoney and Thoresen, 1974; Thoresen and Mahoney, 1974; Shapiro Zifferblatt, 1976). The process whereby one decides whether reinforcement or punishment is deserved for meeting or not meeting the target behavior is included in either the self-evaluation or self-reinforcement stage, depending on the predilection or emphasis of the investigator.

Current research does not warrant separating our discussion of these theoretically distinct self-control processes, as in most studies they are intertwined. We will continue to emphasize the separateness of the self-evaluation and self-reinforcement components as we discuss the literature, but unlike the self-monitoring area, little research has attempted to examine these two components separately. Instead self-reinforcement has been seen as requiring an observation and evaluation of the response in question (Bandura, 1976; Catania, 1975; O'Leary and Dubey, 1979).

A major goal of self-control training is to develop strategies to transfer evaluative and reinforcing functions from the change agent to the individual seeking to change (Anderson, Fodor, and Alper, 1976). A number of studies have investigated how individuals come to adopt internal criteria to evaluate their behavior and determine whether reinforcement is appropriate. Bandura (1969, 1971, 1976, 1977a, 1977b) and others (Lepper, Sagotsky, and Mailer, 1975; Masters and Mokros, 1974) have shown that exposure to self-evalutive standards and self-reward levels modeled by others influence, at least in the short term, children's setting of their own standards and reinforcement levels. Watching peer models obey rules (Toner, Parke, and Yussen, 1978), as well as serving as a model obeying rules, has also increased children's resistance to deviation (Toner, Moore, and Ashley, 1978). An interesting finding related to the literature that models more similar to the children watching the models tend to be most effective (e.g. Bandura and Barab, 1971; Crane and Ballif, 1976; Kornhaber and Schroeder, 1975) is that children watching themselves act appropriately has improved the hyperactive (Dorrick and Raeburn, 1977) and asthma-related (Creer and Miklich, 1970) behavior in case studies of a 4- and 10-year-old boy, respectively.

Instruction also appears to play a role in the setting of standards. Mischel and Liebert (1966) and McMains and Liebert (1968) found that modeling of conformance to stringent standards increased children's performance. When the model verbalized the stringent rule but rewarded oneself leniently, children's conforming to the stringent standard weakened. While children tend to self-select lenient standards (Bandura and Perloff, 1967; Felixbrod and O'Leary, 1973, 1974), Brownell et al. (1977) found that simple instruction was effective in promoting the selection by children of more stringent standards. Karoly and Dirks (1977) rewarded preschool children for correspondence between what they said and what they did. Relevant to self-control strategies is that children who were given the opportunity to say what they were going to do before actually doing it, that is, the opportunity to make a prior commitment, were more likely to carry out their behavior, for example, playing a game, than children who were given the opportunity to play a game and then say that they had.

Glynn and Thomas (1974) found that a cue written on a chart showing when the teacher expected the attention of a third grade class and when the teacher expected them to be working contributed greatly to a self-control program, with baselines of mean on-task behavior of the children to be about 50%, a self-evaluation and token component to bring mean on-task behavior to about 70%, and the addition of a cue to bring mean on-task behavior to just over 90%.

Several naturalistic studies found that the use of rationale, vocalization, and information by parents as a disciplining technique for their child enhanced the development of self-control (Cheyne, 1972; Lavoie,

1973; Peele and Routh, 1978). The importance of information has been clearly demonstrated experimentally by Siegel and Peterson (1980).

Siegel and Peterson randomly assigned 42 low-income preschool children who had experienced no previous dental treatment into three groups. Each group attended an initial check-up. One-half hour prior to the second visit, the children received either a sensory informational treatment (in which the experiences of a restorative dental session were described) including a brief recording of the noise of a dental drill; a coping skills condition in which children were instructed in general body relaxation, deep and regular breathing, pleasant imagery, and self-talk; or an experimenter contact attention control group condition. At the children's second session the child's physiological and overt distressed behavior were measured while restorative dental work that included the injection of a local anesthetic, was performed. Siegel and Peterson found that information given to young children regarding what a dental treatment was like was as effective in reducing stress as self-control training in relaxation, breathing, pleasant imagery, and self-instruction, both being more effective than an attention control group.

It would appear that information, both instructional and demonstrational, can be conveyed via modeling and direct instruction and successfully utilized by children to increase their self-control skills. Modeling seems to be a particularly powerful method of facilitating the generalization of self-control skills (Burgio, Whitman, and Johnson, 1980). It allows one to acquire information on discriminative and behavioral skills in a wide variety of settings without the time constraints and potential hazards of actually participating without proper skills in problem situations.

As with self-monitoring, training in self-evaluation and self-reward has been included as a component to increase self-control (e.g. Bolstad and Johnson, 1972; Drabman et al., 1973). Various contingency programs clearly demonstrate that accurate self-evaluation and self-reward can be attained by most children (Anderson et al., 1976; Bolstad and Johnson, 1972; Drabman et al., 1973; Kanfer, 1971). Studies that have investigated the effects of self-evaluation alone are mixed. Crahay (1977) found self-evaluation to be more effective in teaching children to correct answers and to decrease mistakes than external or unspecific feedback conditions. Spates and Kanfer (1977) taught addition to first graders who could barely do simple arithmetic problems. They found that criterion setting (evaluation) improved performance over self-monitoring or no treatment and that neither the addition of self-monitoring nor self-reward to criterion setting significantly improved performance. Unfortunately, there was no check to see if the technique taught during training transferred to the performance situation. Further, although couched in behavioral terminology, the criterion setting procedure appeared to provide information on how to actually add numbers (i.e. "First I should add two numbers on the right, the middle, then the left"). The inherent importance of knowing how to add may overwhelm any self-evaluative component. In contrast to these studies, Bandura and Perloff (1967), Sagotsky et al. (1978), Santogrossi et al. (1973), and Turkewitz et al. (1975) found self-evaluative standards alone not to influence self-control. Bandura and Perloff (1967) and Felixbrod and O'Leary (1974) suggest that the addition of a self-reinforcement component to self-evaluation may be helpful. Further research is needed investigating what situations or cues serve to activate or inhibit self-evaluation and self-reward.

A critical issue in the literature is whether the "self" component in self-evaluation and self-reward contributes to self-control. With adults, Kanfer and Grimm (1978) found that subjects who perceived that they had freedom of choice in the speed-reading treatment they were to receive had a greater reading speed increase than those who had no choice. With children, Bandura and Perloff (1967), Liebert, Spiegler, and Hall (1970), and Felixbrod and O'Leary (1973, 1974) found that the self-determination condition, where subjects were allowed to choose their own reward standards, was more effective than a no-treatment control group, but did not differ from groups whose standards were set externally by others. However, Birkimer and Brown (1979) found that the addition of a point system that reinforced accurate self-ratings of behavior was more effective than an externally imposed teacher administered point system. Studies by Lovitt and Curtiss (1969) and Brownell et al. (1977) showed the superiority of self-determined over externally determined standards. Brownell et al.'s study, using time on task and number of correct solutions as dependent variables, found that there was a direct relationship between the stringency of standards set and performance output. As might be predicted, subjects who were not allowed to select their own performance standards and who were given maximum reinforcement for minimum work (very lenient standards) spent the most time on task and had the fewest correct solutions. Other interesting results based on sketchy maintenance data suggested that the groups that had stringent standards had lower maintenance of improved behavior, especially if coupled with external determination of standards.

Research conducted on self-reinforcement strategies has also had equivocal findings. Some studies have determined self-reinforcement strategies to be equal in effectiveness (Bolstad and Johnson, 1972; Glynn, 1970) and in maintenance (Johnson, 1970; Johnson and Martin, 1973) with externally imposed reward strategies.

Other studies have found self-determined strategies to be more effective (Lovitt and Curtiss, 1969) and to have better maintaining capacities (Bolstad and Johnson, 1972; Thoresen and Wilbur, 1976). The variables that might account for this discrepancy among studies merit further research.

The child's orienting and personal attributions may be critical in the success of self-control programs. Switzky and Haywood (1974) found that intrinsically oriented children perform better under conditions of self-reinforcement, while extrinsically oriented children perform better under external reinforcement. Bugental, Whalen, and Henker (1977) found hyperactive children who attributed personal causation to academic success after treatment were most affected by a self-control intervention, while those with low perceived causality and those under medication responded best to an external social reinforcement program. Toner, Moore, and Emmons (1980) found that when children were given the label "patient," their ability to delay gratification was decreased. Bugental, Collins, Collins, and Chaney (1978) found that elementary school students after self-control instruction had long-term benefits (6-month) of increased perception of personal control, while a behavioral intervention without a self-control component produced long-term teacher-rated improvements of the students. Such a finding reminds us once again that behavioral changes do not necessarily follow from cognitive changes.

IV. SELF-REGULATION

The label self-control is often applied to those behavior patterns whose immediate or externally visible influences are inconspicuous (Mahoney, 1976). A number of self-control researchers posit that cognitive activity between an external stimulus and response contributes to adaptive or maladaptive behavior (e.g. Beck, 1976; Luria, 1961; Meichenbaum, 1971). Self-control, from this perspective, primarily involves the self-regulation of cognitive activity, that is training children to develop adaptive cognitive responses that are incompatible with previous maladaptive response chains.

The use of a self-instructional approach to regulate one's behavior evolved from the early work of the Soviet psychologists Luria (1961) and Vygotsky (1962) which suggested that verbal commands become internalized and directive of one's behavior according to a developmental sequence. An early study by Lovaas (1964) provided support for this developmental sequence by finding that 5- to 7-year-old children, but not 4- to 5-year-old children, were affected by the semantic content of self-instructions (i.e. the older children pushed a lever more quickly while overtly verbalizing the word "faster" than while overtly verbalizing the word "slower"). Bem (1967) found that even very young children (age three) could be trained to be under the control of the content of self-verbalizations. Other recent research has continued to call into question the necessary developmental sequence of such internalization (cf. Karoly, 1977).

The importance of internalized self-verbalizations in guiding behavior, on the other hand, has received continued investigation and support, largely due to the work of Meichenbaum and his colleagues (e.g. Meichenbaum and Goodman, 1969, 1971; Meichenbaum, 1975, 1977). Their work involves the use of a basic cognitive behavioral model of self-instruction to teach children self-control skills. This model involves: cognitive modeling where the self-instruction targeted task is modeled for the child; overt external guidance where the child is guided through the task with self-instruction; overt self-guidance where the child performs the task while overtly self-instructing; faded overt self-guidance where the child performs the task while whispering; and covert self-instruction where the child performs the task with guidance from internal silent self-instructions. Such self-instructional procedures have been the keystone of self-control research and are included in most self-control studies, for problems ranging from impulsiveness (e.g. Meichenbaum and Goodman, 1971; Bender, 1976) to handwriting skills (Robin, Armel, and O'Leary, 1975) to children's fears (Graziano and Mooney, 1980) to interpersonal problem-solving skills (Spivack and Shure, 1974), to name just a few of the areas.

Delay of gratification and resistance to temptation paradigms of self-control have been used in the laboratory to investigate the influence of a child's focus of attention on self-control behavior. In such situations the actual presence of contingent rewards tends not to facilitate self-control (Mischel and Moore, 1973; Patterson and Carter, 1979), while the symbolic presence of rewards (i.e. slides) (Mischel and Moore, 1973; Yates and Mischel, 1979), the presence of actual rewards while engaged in a task (Patterson and Carter, 1979), and self-instructions that deal with the potential positive or negative consequences of behavior (Hartig and Kanfer, 1973; Mischel and Patterson, 1976; Patterson and Mischel, 1976) have been shown to facilitate self-control. However, self-instructions urging attention to a task while delaying gratification or during temptation with nursery through first grade children did not enhance self-control (Hartig and Kanfer, 1973; Mischel and Patterson, 1976; Moreland, 1978; Patterson and Mischel, 1976), but did enhance the self-control of second graders (Sawin and Parke, 1979). It would appear that self-control in younger and older children is enhanced by self-instruction referring to the consequences of behavior, while over time children's self-instructions acquire the capability of controlling behavior without the need for immediate referral to the direct consequences of behavior.

A number of clinical studies have suggested that attention-focusing tasks such as imagery (Friedman, 1980; Graziano and Mooney, 1980; Robin, Schneider, and Dolnick, 1976), breathing control (Simpson and Nelson, 1974), progressive relaxation (Braud, 1978; Friedman, 1980; Graziano, and Kean, 1968; Graziano and Mooney, 1980; Robin, Schneider, and Dolnick, 1976), and biofeedback (Anchor and Johnson, 1977; Braud, 1978) tend to enhance self-control. Controlled research has investigated some characteristics of attention-focusing techniques that may make them more effective. Masters and Santrock (1976) found that the ecological setting influenced the maintenance of performance in a motor task. Children in a happy room (happy pictures and faces) persisted at a task longer than children in a sad or neutral room. Other investigators have found that instructing children to think "fun things" increased delay of gratification (Mischel and Ebbesen, 1970; Mischel, Ebbeson, and Zeiss, 1972). Kanfer, Karoly, and Newman (1975) also found that statements read to children which emphasize positive affect are more effective than neutral statements in increasing the dark tolerance of mildly fearful kindergarten children. Another finding of Kanfer, Karoly, and Newman (1975) that deserves further research seems to tie in with the importance of self-attributions in self-evaluation and reward as discussed earlier. They found that the self-competency statement "I am a brave boy (girl). I can take care of myself in the dark" was most effective in increasing tolerance of the dark.

V. CLINICAL STUDIES

Most research in self-control with children has utilized the most available large subject pool of children, children in their school settings. The self-control research typically does not deal with all children in the school, but only a select subset which is, not unexpectedly, the same population that school counselors and psychologists have seen: those children who are disruptive, impulsive, or otherwise unmanageable in the classroom. The behavior therapist is applying a new technique, behavioral self-control strategies, to an old problem. The emphasis in these studies, therefore, has been less one of enhancement, and more one of remediation. The enhancement of normal school behavior, the facilitation of the potential of nondisruptive children, or the preventative possibilities of behavioral self-control remain areas of little investigation.

A large segment of the self-control in school literature utilizes a strategy similar to the classic study of Meichenbaum and Goodman that appeared in 1971. These studies utilize an overt to covert verbal fading of self-instruction that is presumed to lead to an internalization of self-instruction and better task performance in a problem situation. In general these self-instructions, as Camp, Blom, Hebert, and vanDoorninck (1977) point out, teach the children to ask four questions when they encounter a problem. These four questions are: (1) What is my problem?; (2) What is my plan?; (3) Am I using my plan?; and (4) How did I do? The training in self-instruction and its verbal fading usually involves: an experimenter modeling a task while stating out loud the self-instruction; the experimenter talking a child through the task; the child and experimenter both talking out loud as the child performs the task; the subject performing that task while self-instructing out loud and then in a whisper; and finally the subject performing the task with covert self-instruction.

Meichenbaum and Goodman (1971) utilized such a procedure in two experiments. The first experiment involved 15 second grade children (ages 7–9 years) who had been placed in an "opportunity remedial class" for behavioral problems such as "hyperactivity" and "poor self-control." Five of the children were trained using cognitive modeling and self-instruction, five were involved in an attention control group and five served as an assessment control group. Their training sessions were limited to four half-hour sessions over a 2-week period. The tasks that were employed to train the children varied along a dimension from simple sensorimotor abilities such as copying line patterns to more complex tasks such as following sequential instructions and completing pictorial series. Generally their results were positive, in that those children who received self-instruction training showed superior performance than did the attention or assessment control groups on a variety of sensorimotor and cognitive tasks, similar but not identical to those involved in the training. However, direct observation of innappropriate classroom behavior and a questionnaire regarding the child's behavior that was completed by a teacher showed no significant differences among the groups. Meichenbaum and Goodman's second study involved 15 slightly younger children selected on the basis of their performance on various sensorimotor/cognitive tasks, as being approximately in the bottom quarter of their kindergarten or first grade class. These "impulsive" children were divided into groups of five that received either cognitive modeling and self-instruction training similar to that used in the first experiment, cognitive modeling alone with no self-instruction training, or an attention control. Their results generally mirrored the first experiment's with cognitive modeling with self-instruction leading to better performance on various sensorimotor and cognitive tasks than cognitive modeling alone or an attention control. No direct classroom observation or teacher rating was taken in this study.

Meichenbaum and Goodman's (1971) emphasis on using self-instruction to increase performance on simple sensorimotor and cognitive tasks has led to other studies that include self-instruction training in interpersonal problem-solving situations that are associated with off-task, disruptive, or aggressive behavior. Camp, Blom, Hebert, and vanDoorninck (1977) utilized a teacher behavior checklist to identify 22 aggressive children who were assigned to either an aggressive-experimental group or an aggressive control group, as well as 12 "normal" boys assigned to another control group. The aggressive-experimental group received treatment similar to that given in Meichenbaum and Goodman (1971) except that they added sequences of interpersonal problem situations during training similar in kind to those developed by Spivack and Shure (1974). Although the training was more extensive than that used by Meichenbaum and Goodman, involving daily 30-minute sessions extending over 6 weeks, the critical comparison of the aggressive-experimental versus aggressive control group resulted in the aggression experimental group scoring significantly higher in only 3 of 19 sensorimotor and cognitive tasks and in improvement in a "low-need achievement" factor on a behavior checklist, while no differences on a three-point teacher rating or an aggressive factor on the behavior checklist were shown.

Coats (1979) followed a cognitive self-instruction program very similar to Camp et al. (1977). Coats taught self-instruction to third grade boys, ages 7–8 years old, who had been selected from normal classrooms by teacher rating and classroom observation because of their impulsiveness, aggressiveness, and general lack of self-control. Two groups of four children each received eight half-hour cognitive self-instruction treatment sessions over a 2-week period, while two similar groups received training without a self-instruction component. The self-instruction training began with sensorimotor and cognitive tasks and progressed to training to solve problematic social situations specific to the behavior of each child.

Like Camp et al. the results appear disappointing. Direct observation of aggressive and off-task behaviors targeted in the training groups, various nontarget behaviors, and teacher ratings did not differ between the two groups. In a staged problematical situation, the self-instruction group showed significant positive differences in waiting and in being less verbally aggressive but the two groups did not differ in requests, negotiation, physical requests, or physical aggression. The authors note that one reason for these disappointing results was that the attention control group showed marked gains between pre- and posttreatment. This suggests that the attention control group was able to learn through cognitive modeling without self-instruction or merely that their behavior regressed to the mean.

Bornstein and Quevillon (1976) trained three highly disruptive preschoolers in one massed session—50 minutes of instruction, a 20-minute break, and 50 more minutes of instruction—dealing with both self-instructional training in sensorimotor and cognitive tasks and interpersonal problem-solving situations. Their results showed highly significant gains with the children's average on-task behavior increasing from about 10% for all three children before training to about 80% after training with maintenance over 90 days. However, the children's own baseline scores were their only comparison, making the results of this study promising, but by no means definitive.

Self-instructional techniques have also been applied to educable mentally retarded children whom their teachers rated as highly distractable and off-task over 50% of the time (Burgio, Whitman, and Johnson, 1980). Burgio et al. gave two experimental children self-instructional training in math or printing tasks. Included was a "distraction-inoculation" procedure, where visual, auditory, and *in vivo* distractors were introduced and the children urged to implement distraction ignoring self-instructions. The training improved off-task performance in the training and classroom settings. No change was observed in academic behaviors.

McCullough, Huntsinger, and Nay (1977) developed a self-control program for an aggressive 16-year-old male brought into an outpatient clinic for his temper losses in school. McCullough et al. implemented a multifaceted self-control program that is an excellent example of a careful functional analysis and self-control treatment program. They were able to obtain the cooperation of the adolescent in the short time of about 30 minutes by pointing out the consequences of his past temper outbursts, using phrases such as "And what did that get you?" They then inquired about antecedent feelings, thoughts, and bodily sensations (e.g., subvocal cursing, tenseness in right arm) prior to an emotional outburst, a procedure that took about 10 minutes. They then spent another 45 minutes role playing and videotaping the boy in angry situations, playing back and discussing the effects of his aggressive demeanor, and role playing appropriate behaviors. The major treatment consisted of 20 minutes of teaching the boy to use (a) thought stopping, (b) relaxation, and (c) walking away from arguments until calm if his right arm remained tense. The boy signed a written contract agreeing to follow the procedures and the school cooperated by allowing the boy to walk away from authority under stressful conditions. This simple procedure resulted in a dramatic decrease in temper losses that maintained over a 6-month period. Although only a single case study, McCullough et al. showed the possibility that direct instruction in self-control procedures could be immediately effective in significantly reducing the frequencies of severe loss of temper, a common problem with many "problem adolescents."

Self-monitoring and self-evaluation have been key components in many school related self-control programs. Broden, Hall, and Mitts (1971) in two case studies with eighth graders, found that study and talking out behavior, respectively, were only minimally affected by a self-monitoring and evaluation procedure. Santogrossi, O'Leary, Romanczyk, and Kaufman (1973), with nine adolescent boys, ages 12 to 15, who were disruptive in a classroom, found points with backup reinforcers to be much more effective than self-evaluation in decreasing disruptive behavior.

Tokens, as has long been shown in various school related studies, can be very effective in changing behavior (Graziano, 1975). Knapczyk and Livingston (1973) with educlably mentally retarded sixth to ninth grade students who were disruptive in the classroom found that a self-monitoring and token system could be easily and effectively administered even by a student teacher with limited information about the system. In another token system, Bolstad and Johnson (1972) found that when first and second graders were allowed to self-monitor and self-reinforce their own behavior such self-regulation appeared to be more resistant to extinction (i.e. the return of disruptive behavior) once backup reinforcers were removed, than teacher control of monitoring and reinforcement.

Generalization and maintenance of appropriate behavior through self-evaluation and token reinforcement was investigated by Turkewitz, O'Leary, Spitalnik, and O'Leary (1973). Eight children between 7 and 11 years of age were involved in an after school reading program and served as the experimental group. These children were at least a year behind in reading and displayed high rates of disruptive classroom behavior. Eight other children in "transitional adjustment classes" were matched for age and reading scores and served as controls.

The study consisted of 12 different conditions over a 4½-month period. These conditions included a baseline condition; a period where reading goals were established and given to each child; a self-evaluative condition with children rating their progress toward their goals; a token phase at which point teachers rated behavior and gave the children points exchangeable for various backup reinforcers (e.g. candy, snacks, small toys); three "matching" phases where 100, 50, and 30% of the children, respectively, were picked out beforehand to have to match or be within one point of the teacher's rating lest they lose their points for the day; a no-match condition where the children would receive points for whatever rating they gave themselves; three "fading" backup periods where 50, 30, and 12½% of the children, respectively, were chosen after the class to receive whatever points they had rated themselves; and a no-backup condition comparable to the earlier self-evaluative condition where no points were given for the children's self-evaluations.

The results showed that the token program resulted in less disruptive behavior throughout the matching, fading, and backup conditions than in the initial baseline, goals, or self-evaluative conditions. The results showed that during the fading backup conditions, disruptive behavior progressively increased, although still well below the initial disruptive levels. Further, the no-backup condition, rather than returning to the initial high levels of disruptive behavior, as in the comparable self-evaluation condition in the early stages of the study, maintained disruptive behavior at a relatively low level.

Generalization was investigated by not instituting the token, matching, and backup conditions in one announced 15-minute period in every hour. The investigators found disruptive behavior to generally remain low even in such a no-reinforcement condition. However, the experimental treatment had no academic or behavioral effects in comparison with the control group of children.

Kendall and Finch (1976) combined a self-instruction and response cost procedure with a 9-year-old impulsive and overactive boy on an outpatient basis. The targeted responses were inappropriate and untimely changes in behavior when in a conversation, playing a game, or setting rules of play. The verbal self-instructions emphasized "follow through" behavior and were cued with a card that reminded the child to "Stop, listen, look, and think before I answer." After the self-instruction training, the child was given 5 dimes that were his to keep unless he "switched" on the targeted behaviors, at which time he would lose one dime and be told the reason it was taken away. The results were very positive, with inappropriate "switches" being almost completely eliminated. Generalization occurred to another room in the clinic, different games, and a new therapist and his latency time and error rates on a cognitive task improved considerably through a 6-month follow-up. Further, his report cards through the year reflected considerable and major improvement in behavior.

Barkley, Copeland, and Sivage (1980) combined self-instruction, self-monitoring, and token reinforcement working with six boys, ages 7–10, referred because of hyperactive and impulsive behavior. The procedures were instituted in a special experimental classroom for 90 minutes every afternoon over 8 weeks, while the children attended their normal schools in the morning. A self-instructional procedure that emphasized problem solving over a variety of academic and interpersonal topics was presented in large and small group work. During individual work, children were instructed to observe their work habits and record their behavior at signaled 1-, 1½-, or 3-minute variable intervals as to whether they were on-task. Reinforcement was received for on-task behavior and accurate self-monitoring.

Results showed that inappropriate behavior in groups was minimally affected. However, the inappropriate behavior during individual work decreased markedly, particularly under the shorter 1- and 1½-minute variable intervals. Other dependent variables of wrist and ankle activity showed no change as a function of treatment. Concurrent on-task behavior in the children's normal classroom improved at the initiation of the program, but did not change in relation to any of the treatment or nontreatment phases, making the generalization results difficult to interpret.

Anderson, Fodor, and Alpert (1976) directly compared the effectiveness of a token fading program, a behavioral rehearsal self-control procedure, and traditional group therapy on classroom on-task behaviors, children's self-reports, and cognitive tasks. Their study involved three groups of six boys each with the boys having been referred by special schools to a day school in the psychiatric hospital because of their disruptive and unmanageable behavior. All treatments involved 1-hour sessions held twice per week for 7 weeks.

The token fading program was similar to that of Turkewitz et al. (1975) and Drabman et al. (1973) which we already described, and involved increasing skills of self-evaluation, prediction of reward consequences, and self-monitoring to obtain points. The behavior rehearsal self-control training primarily involved operating individual GSR units for token points. The children were taught that the tone of the GSR unit depended on their thoughts and feelings. By using relaxation, self-statements, and pleasant imagery, the children were able to decrease the tone on demand. The next stage of this program involved the children receiving token points if during provoking or stressful scenes of conflict with students or teachers they did not let the tone go up. Traditional group therapy primarily involved the discussion of problems.

The results showed that the token fading program generalized improved on-task behavior to other academic classes, while behavioral rehearsal and traditional group therapy had no effect. However, the behavioral rehearsal group's posttreatment performance on cognitive tasks was greater than that of the other two groups. No prepost differences on children's self-report personality measures were found among the three groups. The notion that self-control is not a unitary phenomena, but one that involves many different behavioral skills and response systems is important for future research.

Outside of a school setting, self-control procedures have been implemented for problems as diverse as obesity (Cohen, Gelfand, Dodd, Jensen, and Turner, 1980); self-abusive hair-pulling (Cordle and Long, 1980; Wulfsohn and Barling, 1978); asthma (Creer, Renne, and Christian, 1976); swearing (Friedman, 1980); disruptive outbursts with psychotic children (Graziano and Kean, 1968); severe fears (Graziano et al., 1979; Graziano and Mooney, 1980); dental stress (Siegel and Peterson, 1980); and avoidance of medically ordered exercises (LaGreca and Ottinger, 1979). Self-control techniques have also been taught to parents to enhance the effectiveness of parent-training programs (Wells, Griest, and Forehand, 1980) diminish child abuse, and promote prosocial parent/child interactions (Denicola and Sandler 1980); and to teachers to enhance their appropriate use of behavioral classroom techniques (Szykula and Hector, 1978).

VI. SUMMARY AND CONCLUSIONS

It seems clear that self-control interventions permit children to change a variety of their behaviors considered disruptive or problematic by adults. Although a relatively young area, self-control has become an established part of behavior modification. However, there remain several problems requiring attention from researchers. First, rarely is the choice of behavior to be changed self-selected by the children. Although questions and criticism of the apparent external control of behavior modification helped to stimulate the development of behavioral self-control, rarely does self-control training with children involve instructions on how to make responsible decisions and control their own lives and contingencies. Instead, self-control research has emphasized changing specific behaviors targeted by parents or teachers of the child. It would be interesting, indeed, to compare the self-control priorities of children with those of their parents or teachers. In any case, little research has exploited the potential of training children in general strategies that can be applied to a wide range of situations, thereby increasing the likelihood of problems being prevented or dealt with early. An important exception to this is the work of Spivack and Shure (1974) which utilizes training in problem solving to increase children's ability to make responsible decisions, to generate creative solutions, and to effectively solve social and other problems.

We agree with Urban and Kendall (1980) who after reviewing social-cognitive problem-solving interventions with children state:

> One important implication of the studies reviewed here is their potential applicability for the purposes of primary prevention as well as remediation of interpersonal disturbances in children. Training has been conducted with both clinical and nonclinical groups, although the evidence of any differential outcomes is inconclusive to date (particularly in view of the difficulty of providing long-term follow-up assessments). Clearly, the effectiveness of these methods in efforts toward primary prevention should receive continued research attention (p. 139).

Future research on self-control with children must, like most of the field of behavior modification, pay more attention to the generalization of results. Although the importance of generalization is given lip-service, most often the direct effects of isolated variables in a specific setting are actually studied. Burgio et al. (1980) provide a good example including generalization in their self-control training program. To facilitate generalization of classroom skills, they utilized a storylike instructional procedure, classroom imagery to assist children in recognizing situations where self-instruction was appropriate, and multiple examples of academic tasks encountered in the classroom. A more difficult issue concerns assessing the generalization of treatment to a nontreatment environment. O'Leary and Dubey (1979) note that when generalization was evaluated, positive results were usually reported (Bornstein and Quevillon, 1976; Douglas et al., 1976; Meichenbaum and

Goodman, 1971; Palkes et al., 1968; 1972; Turkewitz et al., 1975). These studies have the common component of self-instructions that were broad and nonspecific in nature. This alone does not appear to assure generalization. Friedling and O'Leary (1979), using a procedure similar to that of Bornstein and Quevillon (1976), failed to find generalization from a training to a classroom setting. Future research must include generalization training and assessment. Although the time, energy, and financial cost of directly observing a variety of behaviors in a child's natural environment may be high, the lack of such data is a major weakness to the entire field of behavior modification and its inclusion is essential. When impossible to assess in the natural environment, generalization in more than one setting is essential. Kendall and Wilcox (1979), for example, have developed a written measure to assess generalization of self-control when direct observation is impossible.

An equally pertinent issue is the maintenance of gains. With few exceptions, follow-up has been limited to a matter of months. As self-control would seem to have the potential for long-term change, investigation of the effect of self-control training over a number of years would be of great interest. The self-control literature has also neglected how relevant individuals in the child's environment, such as parents and teachers, will react to the change in the child's way of monitoring, evaluating, reinforcing, and regulating his or her own behavior. This may be usurping embedded ways of interacting, and the parents may rebuff the child's self-control attempts. Their inclusion in the self-control training, maintenance, and generalization process would seem to be extremely important.

A final point concerning the maintenance and generalization of behavior concerns the fact that self-control research has relatively ignored developmental and naturalistic investigation of self-control, thereby neglecting potential data on the parameters in the natural environment of self-control behaviors, how self-control behaviors are developed, changed, and activated, and the relationship of these findings to a child's age and situation in life. An example of such research is provided by Spivack and Swift (1977) whose findings suggest that a lack of self-control skills may be a key component in predicting later problems in school, but only after children had been in school for some time.

Current theoretical research needs to more accurately define the construct of self-control. Both theoretical and operational definitions are ambiguous in most studies. When self-control is defined as an independent variable, manipulation checks are rarely done. The relationship among self-control situations such as delay of gratification, resistance to temptation, and clinical self-control studies such as decreasing fear or promoting academic skills also deserves closer examination. Research by Kendall and Wilcox (1979) found that delay of gratification did not relate to cognitive self-control, age, or the behavioral observation of self-control. Results of both Kendall and Wilcox (1979) and Anderson et al. (1976) found a limited relationship between self-control as measured by behavioral observation and self-control as reflected in cognitive tasks. Connecting self-control theory with these findings and with the field's diverse methodologies remains a major task for the future. Methodologically, the field appears very aware of its weaknesses and we would be surprised if over the next few years effort is not concentrated on maintenance and generalization.

6

Juvenile Delinquency

I. INTRODUCTION

Children, like adults, engage in a great variety of self-assertive, oppositional, aggressive, and even antisocial behavior. When young, children's small size and inexperience in "efficient" aggression leave them more vulnerable to each other than disturbing to adults. But as they approach young adulthood in size and strength, they become more skilled at moving through social settings and come increasingly under the control of peer-group values and behavior. At this time the disturbing and outright threatening nature of their aggressive behavior becomes far more of a concern for adults. Youthful offenders against adult laws, mores, and desires are often labeled, legally and/or unofficially, as "juvenile delinquents"—a popularized legal term and not a psychological concept. The term denotes a large behavioral category that includes grossly diverse behavior of both youth and adults. There is great variability in types, severity, and duration of the specific behaviors, and in the range of conditions under which identified behavior will be considered "delinquent" or "youthful exuberance." The extraordinary variability within the category indicates that we should not even fleetingly entertain the generally held notion that juvenile delinquents constitute a single, defined population.

Technically, juvenile delinquency is the violation of criminal law by a minor. The laws, their interpretation, and application vary widely from state to state, city to city and even between neighborhoods (Haskell and Yablonsky, 1978). The most complete and widely used compilations of juvenile delinquency data are the FBI's *Uniform Crime Reports* and the national *Juvenile Court Statistics*, both of which attempt to provide reliable, updated crime data. Both compilations are measures of official activity, that is, actual arrests in the *Uniform Crime Reports*, and juvenile court activity in the other. Annual changes in those data may reflect changes in police or court activity, rather than any real changes in criminal behavior per se. Because many offenses go undetected and many offenders unapprehended, these compilations are probably gross underestimates of the actual amount of criminal activity engaged in by youths.

A major category of offenses reported in the *Uniform Crime Reports* are "index crimes," that is, the seven offenses most likely to be known to police: criminal homicide, forcible rape, robbery, aggravated assault, burglary, larceny, and auto theft. Although many other crimes are committed and arrests compiled, the index crimes receive most public attention, and are often used as a measure of the U.S. crime rate.

Youths can be adjudicated as delinquent when found guilty of these major index crimes and/or other criminal offenses, in addition to offenses that do not apply to adults at all, such as status offenses. These include, for example, running away, truancy from school, "incorrigibility," or, even "leading an idle and dissolute life." Thus there may be *at least* two quite distinct groups of delinquents—those found guilty of serious, "adult" crimes such as those included in the crime index, and those who have committed only status offenses, such as runaways.

Despite definitional and reporting problems (many of which may depend upon regional variations among police departments) the *Uniform Crime Reports*, along with other estimates, provide some bases for assessing criminal activity. There is general agreement that both index crimes and other "adult" crimes as well as status offenses by juveniles have increased markedly over the past generation, so that youths now commit a disproportionately high share of all crimes nationwide. Before World War II some two million youths under 21 years of age "came to the attention of the police annually (Vedder, 1979). By 1985 that total may well be close to six million. According to the 1981 FBI *Uniform Crime Reports* more than 2 million juveniles—that is, persons under 18 years of age—were actually arrested. Of that total, 769,508 were arrested for index crimes, accounting for 33.5% of all index crimes committed in the nation. Another 360,846 juveniles were arrested for other crimes, including arson, "other" assaults, and weapons charges. The remaining approximately 1 million juvenile arrests were for a variety of offenses such as prostitution, narcotics violations, drunkenness, and 235,900 arrests on status offenses, such as running away and curfew violations. Vedder noted that ". . . more crimes are committed by children under fifteen than by adults over twenty-one" (1979, p. 37).

Over the last decade arrests for young people have more than doubled, while older groups show only small increases. A wider demographic base of young people is now becoming delinquent, and we see increases in females, rural adolescents, white middle-class males, and ethnic groups, particularly Asian Americans. As Lundman and Scarpitti conclude, "the contemporary crime problem is largely attributable to the actions of juveniles" (1978, p. 207).

Not only has the amount of juvenile crime increased in this generation, but there appears to have been an accompanying escalation of violence. Most of the index crimes for which youths are arrested are property crimes—with nearly 700,000 arrests in 1981 for burglary, larceny, theft and motor vehicle theft. Although there were many fewer arrests for violent crimes—85,853 in 1981 for murder, forcible rape, robbery, and aggravated assaults—the number is still large. These data reflect *arrests* and not criminal activity per se. There may have been more than one violent act for each arrest, more victims of violent crimes by young offenders than the number arrested.

Youth violence is seen most dramatically and viciously in juvenile gangs or "corners," particularly in urban areas in virtually every industrialized country. Instances of savage torture and murder abound, and the sheer depravity of what gang youths have inflicted on their victims before killing them rivals the German's depraved treatment of World War II concentration camp victims.

Juvenile gangs grew in numbers and activity in the immediate post war years of the late 1940s and 1950s, and then seem to have subsided in the 1960s, perhaps partly because of the growth of more peaceful protest groups and the inwardly directed drug culture of the "narcotics" gangs. But now, writes sociologist Clyde Vedder, "In America's large cities, gangs are back . . . older, better armed, more sophisticated, and they operate in deadly earnest. . . . [these newer] gangs are mostly male, terrorizing junior and senior high schools, and [are] . . . more violent than in the 1950s. No longer satisfied with 'zip guns' or 'Saturday Night Specials,' they want top quality, such as a Smith and Wesson .38 like the police have, and have turned schoolgrounds into battlefields. . . . There has been a new addition to gangs of Asian American youth. Hong Kong Chinese, as well as Japanese and Filipino are now equal to Whites in gang members and there is no solution in sight (Vedder, 1979, pp. 161–162)."

The delinquent gangs seem generally to be composed of young males of blue-collar and poverty-level groups, often school failures, largely illiterate, of lower intelligence, and often clearly ethnically identified. A common characteristic seems to be their great satisfaction in "shocking" the rest of society by their behavior. Girls are subsidiary members of the gangs, clearly subservient to the dominant males. As the gangs' violence has increased, so has that of the girls.

Thus, youth crime, whether individuals, small groups, or organized gangs is a serious and growing problem in the United States and in other nations, as increasing numbers of young criinals display an apparently growing willingness to commit aggressive and vicious crimes. Continued economic stagnation, this age group's faster growth compared to the general population, and the growing number and aggressiveness of young offenders leads us to predict that serious youth crime will continue to grow in amount and aggressiveness throughout the twenteth century. Perhaps in another decade or two the very survival of some large cities will depend heavily upon the successful control over and reduction of youth crime. Contemplating the levels that youth crime, particularly that committed by groups and by semiorganized gangs, might reach during the remainder of this century is, at the very least, a disquieting exercise.

II. TRADITIONAL APPROACHES AND PROBLEMS WITH CORRECTIONAL INSTITUTIONS

Society has attempted to deal with juvenile delinquency in four ways: (1) *Punishment-incarceration*: Legal enforcement includes arrest, indictment, trial, and incarceration, removing delinquents from society for some period of time, thus protecting other people. The emphasis here is on punishing the delinquent and protecting society by isolating him. (2) *Rehabilitation*: While the adjudicated delinquent is incarcerated or under legal control, a variety of rehabilitation efforts may be attempted. These include education, vocational training, psychotherapy, and behavior modification. The emphasis here is on remediation of the adolescents' problems through systematic rehabilitative efforts. (3) *Tertiary and secondary prevention*: Attempts, as with urban "youth gangs," to work directly with high-risk groups in their environments with the intention of helping to direct their behavior away from criminal acts. (4) *Economic and other large-scale social approaches*: Control of social issues such as poverty and joblessness that presumably contribute to the development of delinquent behavior, a primary prevention aimed at reducing the incidence of new cases.

Modern society attempts to maintain an enlightened approach by responding quite differently to the young offender than to the adult criminal. As discussed by Haskell and Yablonsky (1978), we hold adults to more demanding standards of personal responsibility for criminal acts. We tend to emphasize concern for the young offender's motivation rather than the behavior itself and supposedly try harder to rehabilitate rather than punish the youth. The entire social response is different for youths than for adults, from the definition of what constitutes "crime," through the court procedures, to the types of sentencing and to the types and degrees of physical control and punishment allowable while incarcerated. There has evolved, at least since the seventeenth century (Haskell and Yablonsky, 1978), an entire juvenile-control legal system quite separate from that for adults, with far more informal procedures, and with the nature of what is "illegal" more loosely defined, than with adults. Unlike adult courts, juvenile courts have a great deal more judgmental leeway and their proceedings are usually closed to the public. This dependence upon the knowledge, compassion, understanding, and good judgment of the presiding judge, while purportedly ensuring more personal and "fair" proceedings for the youth, also guarantees the virtually uncontested right of juvenile court judges to make unchallenged decisions, without clarifying the legal bases. The accused adolescent is rarely represented by legal counsel of his choice; rarely does anyone challenge procedures or decisions; news reporters are barred; only recently, since the Gault decision in 1967, have transcripts of proceedings been maintained; and the records are not available for public scrutiny. The adolescent's fate rests primarily with the decisions of a single, usually unchallenged individual, the judge. The legal proceedings, in the name of humanitarian and personal concerns, may also operate to restrict and even to deny, particularly to those children and youths accused of only status offenses, the same due process of law guaranteed to even the most habitual, violent, and dangerous adult criminals. At present there is state-by-state controversy over the elimination of status offenses as crimes. At this writing only a few states have done so, and the issue is a very long way from resolution. Arrest for status offenses is particularly intrusive for girls, as 70% of the girls incarcerated are held for status offenses, compared with 34 percent of the boys.

The juvenile court ordinarily has a limited range of options in the disposition of a case: probation, commitment to correctional institutions, or ordering custody over the youth by a relative, child-care agency, or foster home (Fox, 1977). Once the custodial agency, under the jurisdiction of its own corrections or social services department, assumes responsibility, the court often has no further power to direct any details of treatment. The youngster is then fully under the control of the corrections agency, and that agency controls all details of the youngster's life during confinement. The correctional agency and its local staff create and implement everyday rules and regulations, the frequency, severity, and duration of punishments within the institutions for any infractions, the quality of food, clothing, bedding, access to education, and training, the hours of required labor, mail, visiting privileges, and so on. The institution thus possesses overpowering control.

There is little evidence that any of the legal and rehabilitative approaches to juvenile justice—alone or in any combination—have appreciably reduced juvenile delinquency. Difficulties involve not only the serious delinquent behaviors that receive most public attention, but also problems of definition: judgmental bias that may incarcerate one youth for many years while giving another only a mild reprimand for the same behavior; the existence of "crimes" that only children and youth can commit; issues of protection under adult-defined and administered laws; the general lack of due process in court; and finally, the too often inhumane but court supported punitive treatment imposed on incarcerated young people in the name of rehabilitation and adult righteousness.

It is difficult to determine the number of juveniles who experience life in a correctional institution in a given year. The FBI *Uniform Crime Reports* shows more than 2 million juveniles arrested, but not all of them are subsequently indicted or go through the court procedures. Of those who do, not all are found guilty. Many of the guilty are placed on probation, given over to the custody of other persons or agencies, or sentenced to a correctional institution. In 1971 the Law Enforcement Assistance Administration (LEAA) conducted its first national census of incarcerated juveniles and found that on June 30, 1971 there were 722 public institutions for juveniles—detention centers, training schools, ranches, forestry camps, farms, halfway houses, group homes, shelters, reception and diagnostic centers, and so on—and that they were holding 57,329 juveniles *on that day*. The inmate population changes daily, with new juveniles entering and others leaving, and the total number of *different* individuals who spend time in the various correctional institutions each year is a great deal higher.

Poulin, Levitt, Young, and Poppenfort (1980), averaging data collected from the 50 states during the mid-seventies, estimated that in any one year 626,223 children and youths spent time in correctional facilities. Juvenile detention centers held 80% of the youths, while 20% were held in jails, usually in towns too small to afford separate juvenile facilities. It is reasonable to expect a much higher number in the 1980s given the increase in the youth-age population. Thus a daily population of 60,000 and a yearly total of nearly three-quarters of a million children and youths in correctional institutions may be taken as an estimate of the correctional populations in the 1980s.

The 1971 census showed more than four times as many boys as girls incarcerated, and for more serious crimes, with 41% incarcerated for felonies and about 35% for status offenses. In contrast, 70% of the girls were incarcerated for status offences, and only 8% for felonies (Vedder, 1979). Girls, then, are a great deal more vulnerable to status offense sentences than boys. In keeping with the proportions of the general population, more than two-thirds of the children and youths, are from urban areas.

Though the institutions and jails housing these predominantly urban juveniles are often located in urban areas, many are found in relatively isolated rural areas where the youths are to enjoy the rehabilitative properties of sunshine, clean air, good food, and healthful work, much of it in a "back-to-nature" style within a somewhat farmlike context of animal tending and gardening. The relevance or effectiveness of the rural setting for these urban youths is yet to be demonstrated.

The institutions are no longer called "reform schools" but, rather are "farms," "ranches," "youth centers," and the like. Many of the buildings are called "cottages," with countrylike small-paned windows rather than steel bars. There are "cottage parents" instead of guards, "clients" or "residents" instead of prisoners, and the whole institutional enterprise is often set in expansive campuslike grounds without walls or fences.

In keeping with our enlightened view of juvenile justice, such as proclaimed by the physical appearances and various labels of the institutions, we have also made a public commitment to provide rehabilitative programs for those youths under our care. As noted by Trojanowicz (1978, pp. 263–304), for example, the following psychological therapies are applied in juvenile institutions:

Psychotherapy	Crisis intervention	Guided group interaction
Social casework	Individual and group counseling	Milieu therapy
Reality therapy		Social environment therapy
Transactional analysis	Group therapy	Direct home intervention
Vocational counseling	Social group work	Family crisis counseling
Behavioral therapy	Social psychotherapy	
Behavioral contracting	Activity therapy	

Dixon (1974) notes that from 1964 to 1974 some 6500 programs were launched in the United States to prevent or reduce delinquency. The number of rehabilitation programs and the variety of therapeutic approaches indicates a social concern for humanitarian ideals.

Our enlightened view, however, may not necessarily penetrate any deeper than the campuslike appearances and impressive lists of therapies. The countrylike, small-paned windows are, in reality, steel-framed and can be opened only a few inches. The youths who stroll across open campuses do so only with official passes, only with an approved destination and time for arrival and are frequently watched as they go. The mix of inmates may be a major self-defeating factor, and has been described by Vedder as follows:

> Institutions must take first offenders and experienced gangsters, boys going through the emotional upheaval of adolescence, runaways, truants, disobedient children, and confine them with burglars, muggers, arsonists, rapists, and even killers. They must accept youths ranging from the feebleminded to the brilliant. They must take sex deviates, perverts, drug addicts, and alcoholics . . . dangerously abnormal personalities, as well as the essentially normal youths; the innocent and immature along with the degenerate; the bully and the weakling. To complicate this situation, many institutions, though very large, are perenially overcrowded. . . . Unless care is exercised, almost any child can be sent to the reform school whether his offense is serious or not (1979, p. 270).

Many of these youth institutions are staffed with political appointees who have patronage jobs with good salaries; there is little demand for good programs or accountability for bad ones. In many institutions the superintendent is virtually an uncontested overlord whose decisions are never publically scrutinized. The staff, protected from public review by layers of self-protective administrations and traditions, operate freely, without accountability, behind closed doors.

Rehabilitation is liberally laced with severe punishments for minor rule-breaking and even for habit problems such as bedwetting. Shaved heads, starvation diets, solitary confinement, severe whippings, and perversely ingenious forms of inflicting pain and humiliation on the young residents appear to be common occurrences.

Nowhere else in society is such rampantly brutal authoritarianism allowed—only in youth institutions and only against children. No adult maximum security prison in the United States today could for very long treat its prisoners to the same beatings or total denial of rights—only with children do we allow it. The homicides in these correctional institutions are appalling and, considering what must be a hopelessly deplorable and frightening existence for many children, we should not be surprised to note that every year some distraught children and youths in the correctional institutions finally escape by killing themselves.

The sheer brutalization of youngsters by the staff that occurs inside too many of these institutions rivals the viciousness of the street gangs themselves. The difference, of course, is that the staff's vicious behavior is well supported by law, social policy, politics, and a great deal of public money.

At a time in history when we seem to have improved the humanity of treatment for adult mental patients and have at least paid some attention to their civil rights, we still find grossly inhumane treatment of children and youths in many institutions—treatment reminiscent of descriptions of the pre-1850s abuses of mental patients. A recent book by Kenneth Wooden (1976) details the severe abuse—physical, sexual, and mental—of youths in many U.S. correctional institutions. Wooden, who devoted some four years, 1972 to 1976, to investigating youth facilities across the country, maintains that a youth correction "industry" has developed in every state, well-protected by political and "industry" power as is any other economic special interest group. According to Wooden's charges, the major goals of this industry are the economic well-being of the many towns that depend upon the youth correctional centers for their economic existence. Necessary for the continuation of the institution—whatever its quality—is a steady supply of children and youths. Wooden charges that political/economic power and secrecy at federal, state, and local levels protect the institutions from public scrutiny and leave them immune to regulatory demands. He describes brutally severe, bizarre punishment of children and youths for even minor infractions. Severe beatings, according to Wooden, are regularly administered to the children. We should note that such physical punishment of adult prisoners is not allowed under the law, but, as the U.S. Supreme Court determined in *Ingraham* v. *Wright* (1977), adults such as school personnel may legally beat children with wooden paddles for "discipline."

Juvenile delinquency, then, involves not only law-breaking by youths, but clearly involves adults' socially solidified value systems, procedures, views, and biases regarding the subservient status of children and youths, an entire set of adult social values that is in many ways similar to the paternalistic and often brutal views toward blacks during the first half of this century. Solving "the problem" of juvenile delinquency will thus entail a good deal more than increased "rehabilitation" efforts for individual children and youths.

We are faced with the social reality of the scope and severity of juvenile delinquency involving more than 2 million youths annually. Still powerful social values relegate children and youths to lower social status, in effect providing them with less protection under the law than adults. In common practice, we define a youth's behavior as delinquent by vague adult criteria rather than clearly defined legal criteria and precedents. It should be clear that the delinquent individual is but one element in a complex chain of complex events and social systems. We must recognize that attempts to rehabilitate delinquent youths constitute only a very small and narrow portion of that overall reality that we call the "juvenile-justice" system or "the problem" of juvenile delinquency. Further, behavior modification programs make up but an even smaller subset of rehabilitation and therefore constitute only a very minimal social response. Even if behavior modification programs were shown to be highly effective in altering the behavior of delinquent youths, the limitations of after-the-fact rehabilitation, no matter how successful, would have a barely perceptible impact when viewed against the social, economic, historical, and philosophical issues of children and youths.

This is not to suggest that rehabilitation programs are not useful for some individuals, or to suggest that behavioral research should be curtailed. Rather, it is intended as a reminder that as we become involved in the details and complexities of behavioral programming and research for a few youths we must not lose sight of the overall reality of the social problem. We, as behavior modifiers, have a degree of expertise to contribute but, as with any professional group, in a very narrow area only. This point might be illustrated by comparing the highly detailed, goal-oriented, carefully programed nature of many of the behavior modification approaches, (Phillips et al., 1973) with the primitive, sometimes bizarrely inhumane treatment in some of the correctional intitutions described by Wooden. Professional operation in this area, perhaps more so than any other in the field, is characterized by extremes, ranging from the inhumanely primitive in which we continue to brutalize our children, to sophisticated integrations of humaneness and behavioral technology. As behavior modifiers further refine our technology, we must not lose sight of the fact that there exist many settings in which the need is for very basic humanitarian reforms, reforms not requiring behavioral sophistication at all.

Thus, a two-fold, potential danger becomes apparent: (1) in helping to make some settings more behaviorally sophisticated we may ignore other, primitive settings in which the basic humanitarian reforms—much like those of the early 1800s in adult mental health—are needed; (2) if sophisticated behavioral control over the children and youths is introduced in those less humane settings by naive psychologists, we may be further solidifying and escalating the already inhumane treatment of children and youths. This point has been made by others such as Winett and Winkler (1972) regarding schools, and by Emery and Marholin (1977) regarding delinquency. What is most important here is for the psychologist to appreciate the nature of each setting into which we introduce new behavioral sophistication. Sarason (1972) discusses the importance of knowing a setting's history, and we highly recommend his book as required reading for behavior modifiers. Reppucci and Saunders (1974) provide a good discussion of a youth behavioral program in light of many of the social and historical issues raised by Sarason.

The behavior modifier, working in the area of delinquency, has a special responsibility to the clients—much more so than in working with adults. The special, nearly powerless status of the incarcerated youth with little due-process protection and generally poor legal representation in the courtroom proceedings that have placed him or her in the rehabilitation settings, the known brutality in some institutions, and the legally allowable physical punishment and control in all juvenile institutions, all contribute to these clients' existence under very special conditions of ever present and severe risks. The behavior modifier must be particularly cognizant of those issues—the nature of the setting and the powerlessness of the clients—and must carefully assess all of the implications and potential risks in introducing sophisticated behavioral technology.

It is wise to keep these cautions in clear view as we now briefly review attempts since the early 1960s to apply behavior modification approaches to the rehabilitation of juvenile delinquents.

III. BEHAVIOR MODIFICATION APPROACHES, EARLY 1960s TO MID-1970s

The application of behavior modification procedures to juvenile delinquency began in the early 1960s with that decade's behavioral revival. Several relatively uncontrolled single-and multiple-case studies appeared along with only a few controlled studies. Zimberoff (1968) and Stumphauzer (1970) provided two early reviews of the literature. Both reviewers concluded that while these applications were "promising" the field was very new and still faced many methodological problems that would have to be solved to justify greater confidence in the results. A few years later Davidson and Seidman (1974) wrote their major review covering the years 1960 through mid-1973. By 1978 three additional and very provocative reviews appeared, Emery and Marholin (1977), Lundman and Scarpitti (1978), and McCord (1978). The last two, not limited to behavioral approaches to delinquency, deal with such basic issues that they are important in any discussion of behavior modification and juvenile delinquency.

Davidson and Seidman organized the literature of some published studies according to three large categories of behavioral targets: that is, educational behavior, within-setting program behavior, and delinquent behavior per se. Within each of these categories the reviewers further grouped the work according to the research design employed: namely, uncontrolled case studies, single-group outcome studies, experimental-control group comparisons, and A-B-A reversal designs. The reviewers' major comments and conclusions are summarized here and the reader is referred to their review for more details and specific references.

Nine studies focused on educational goals: that is, improving classroom or other school-related performance, through some form of operant, contingency management procedures. Tokens or other types of secondary reinforcers were used to reward improvements in daily school work and quizzes. Longer-term criteria such as improved academic achievement test scores were also used in some studies. Overall these studies reported "positive outcomes in a variety of settings." However, the reviewers concluded there was little information on the generalization of the results or of long-term maintenance of the gains. It was not demonstrated that improved academic performance related to improvement in any other category of functioning or much beyond the end of each intervention. As with most of the 1960s behavioral research with children, those academic performance studies concerned themselves with target behavior change, but virtually ignored either generalization or long-term maintenance. This research, then, does not provide evidence that an academic focus has any effect upon delinquent behavior, but rather as have countless others, that academic performance can be enhanced through application of contingency management in the classroom. For delinquent youths, as for any other group of youths in our society, improved academic performance is a worthy goal to pursue, but there is no evidence it will reduce delinquency. Thus, while pursuing academic goals with delinquents, we must also seek other ways to directly alter the delinquent behavior itself.

The second category reviewed by Davidson and Seidman involved selected behavior targets within specific correctional or rehabilitation programs. As with the first group, researchers assumed, but did not demonstrate, that delinquent behavior might be reduced indirectly by teaching the youths to behave in more desirable ways within the treatment setting. These studies were, again, all variations of contingency management approaches, that is, token rewards, time-out, and response-cost procedures. Decremental behavioral goals included reduction of undesirable behavior such as fighting, swearing, destroying property, disobedience, and house-rule violations. Some of the incremental behavior goals included improving self-care, housekeeping, general social behavior within the rehabilitation group, increase of positive self-comments made in group sessions, and improved school and workshop performance. A series of studies has been carried out in various achievement place settings by Phillips and colleagues (for example, Bailey, Fixsen, Phillips, and Wolf, 1970; Fixsen, Phillips, and Wolf, 1972, 1973; Maloney, Harper, Braukmann, Fixsen, Phillips, and Wolf, 1976; Phillips, Phillips, Fixsen, and Wolf, 1973; Timbers, Phillips, Fixsen, and Wolf, 1971). In the achievement place studies, contingency management of juvenile delinquents in group-living situations has been well explored and developed with excellent results in many well-controlled studies, comprising a large and important literature alone.

As with those in the schools chapter, these studies demonstrate the effectiveness of contingency management in a variety of settings but leave unanswered questions of generalization, maintenance, and ultimate importance in terms of the overall social problem of delinquency.

In a final category of 15 studies reviewed by Davidson and Seidman the success criteria specified by the investigators involved actual changes in delinquent, aggressive, or illegal behavior per se. Added to this focus on delinquent behavior were criterion measurements of changes in other categories such as academic behavior, work attendance, positive self-statements, and so on. What seems most interesting and important about the studies in this category is that not only do they focus directly on modifying delinquent behavior, but many of them have progressed from traditional institutional settings, to interventions in more "natural environments" such as families and naturally occurring youth groups or "streetcorner" settings. These studies integrate behavior modification and community mental health approaches, a development that will probably continue in the future. Again as with the other studies, the interventions were virtually limited to contingency-management procedures, but in more complex systems including specific development of contingency contracting within families and other social groups.

Tharp and Wetzel (1969), for example, described a community consultation program with parent and teacher "mediators" of 89 delinquents. They discussed some failures and difficulties in working within family systems, as well as successes. Their follow-ups over a year and a half showed reduction of delinquent offenses, improved grades, and better behavioral ratings. Other studies that focused their programs on natural-environment intervention with delinquents' families include work by Rose, Sundel, DeLange, Corwin, and Palumbo (1970), Alvord (1971), and Alexander and Parsons (1973). This development of complex contracting within the natural environment of the delinquents' families is an important broadening of the application of behavioral technology.

Another setting in which behavioral intervention with delinquents was attempted was described in a number of studies by Schwitzgebel (1964, 1967, 1969), involving "street corner" projects. In addition to improved attendance at regular meetings and in interview content, the delinquent youth in Schwitzgebel (1964), and Schwitzgebel and Kolb's (1964) studies showed significant reduction in arrests and less time in correctional institutions over one-, two-, and three-year follow-ups. These studies demonstrated relatively long-term successes with delinquent youth in natural environments (i.e., noninstitutional) and clearly apply a community mental health focus to the field.

In this category Davidson and Seidman reviewed investigators working largely in community settings, such as families and "street corner" groups, and with a fairly large number of delinquents and families in many of the studies. Of equal importance is their demonstration of improvements in delinquent behavior per se and the maintenance of the improvements for one to three years.

Overall these reviewers concluded that research from 1960 to mid-1973 reported positive and encouraging results. The behavior of delinquents, both delinquent behavior per se but mostly the presumably related behavior such as academic performance has been changed. The research remained mostly suggestive rather than confirmatory, because of methodological weaknesses which seriously limit our confidence in the results. The methodological issues included lack of no-treatment controls, limited baseline measures, the possible effects of bias or expectations on the part of data collectors, lack of long-term follow-ups, and lack of demonstrated generalization of positive changes across settings and from "institutional" to actual delinquent behavior.

Some of Davidson and Seidman's major points are summarized here. Their concluding comments on the field will be discussed later, along with similar commentary by other reviewers.

1. The behavioral studies from 1960 through mid-1973 were encouraging in positive outcomes brought about in a variety of settings.

2. The many methodological weaknesses demand both caution in interpreting the results and improved research efforts to correct them.

3. The positive findings of behavioral improvement have, for the

most part, involved academic, institutional-living, or perhaps "personal" behaviors, for example, improved academic performance, improved housekeeping and reduced fighting in cottages, more positive self-statements in group meetings, and so on. While presumably of value for many youths, *there is no indication that such improvements have any effects in reducing juvenile delinquency.*

4. Aside from a few studies such as the work of Tharp and Wetzel and Schwitzgebel and colleagues, there has been little convincing demonstration of significant, long-term impact of the programs upon delinquent behavior per se.

5. The behavioral research had been too narrowly focused, omitting ". . . such potentially important variables as the role of the change agent, subject and contextual characteristics. . . There is no real sense of an effort toward discovery, rather only the application of a conceptually closed paradigm to a new content area" (Davidson and Seidman, 1974, p. 1008).

6. Continued behavioral research with attention paid to these deficiencies is needed.

Emery and Marholin's review of behavior modification in delinquency appeared in 1977. They searched behavior modification journals from 1968 to mid-1976 and found 27 papers that met their criteria: (1) all subjects were described as delinquent or predelinquent, that is, studies using descriptors *associated with* delinquency, such as "truant" or "aggressive" were omitted; and (2) studies included appropriate research design, response definition, interobserver reliability, and quantified empirical data.

Like Davidson and Seidman they note the generally promising nature of the reported successes in altering the behavior of delinquents. There are, however, a number of serious problems and some of the reviewers' major findings and conclusions are summarized here.

1. Seventy percent of the studies were carried out in community or total institutional settings and 30 percent (eight studies) in natural environments.

2. The age ranged from 8 years 6 months (this could be a seond- or third-grader!) to 16 years. Older delinquent youths were clearly omitted from these 27 behavioral studies.

3. Of all of the target behaviors studied across all years, only 3.7% were delinquent behaviors per se. As indicated in the following table of target behaviors, the delinquency-behavior category was the second-from-last in frequency as targets for study.

TABLE 6.1

Target behavor	Total behavior targets, 1968–1976 (%)
Social/interpersonal	35.6
Program behaviors	21.4
School	17.2
Compliance with authority	11.2
Behavior	
Ecological	7.4
Delinquent	3.7
Vocational	3.5

4. Follow-up information was notably lacking. Only seven studies reported any follow-up at all, with only two reporting follow-ups one year after termination of the program.

5. Less than one-third of the target behaviors in these studies were clearly related to the referral problems.

6. Despite behavior modification's supposed emphasis on carefully individualized functional analyses of presenting problem behavior, only 9% (two studies) individualized the target behavior. In general, target behaviors for the delinquents were not individually selected for each client but, rather, were predetermined and group applied. This failure appears to be particularly important and we will extensively quote Emery and Marholin's comments on it:

> Clearly, applying the same target behaviors to all subjects in an intervention program is far from meeting the requirement of conducting a thorough, individual, functional analysis. In fact, targeting the same behaviors for any heterogenous group of individuals implies that all the members of the group are identical, that they have the same problems, and that the same treatment techniques will help any individual. However, behavior therapists would argue that without a comprehensive functional analysis of each individual client's behavior and without the application of contingencies designed specifically for that individual . . . an intervention program is simply not an applied behavior analysis.
>
> Recent court decisions directed at defining and elaborating the concept of "right to treatment" are particularly relevant to the observed absence of individualized target behaviors. The courts have suggested that group programs characterized by "milieu therapy" in which individuals are not attended to, do not meet the constitutionally required level of treatment adequacy (Martin, 1975; *Donaldson* v. *O'Connor*, *Morales* v. *Turman*, *Wyatt* v. *Stickney*). Furthermore, the courts have stated that individuals can be treated in a group only so long as each has an individual treatment plan, but not if they are simply left to do whatever the group as a whole seems to

> require. Practices such as establishing a token economy that states the same goals and criteria for each client or systematically structuring the interpersonal environment and labeling it a "therapeutic milieu" do not meet the legal requirements for adequate treatment. Thus, the legal decisions of recent years (particularly *Morales* v. *Turman* and *Wyatt* v. *Stickney*) increasingly require that behavior therapists consistently tailor target behaviors to each client's individual needs . . . (1977, p. 866).

In their conclusions the reviewers noted, ". . . most of the reviewed studies on delinquency and behavior analysis were found to be lacking major elements of a true applied behavioral analysis. The failure to individualize programs and the lack of reported follow-up data are both critical omissions. Moreover, a relationship between selected target behaviors and subsequent reductions in the problem of delinquency was not demonstrated. The importance of demonstrating this relationship cannot be overemphasized . . ." (1977, p. 870).

IV. NONBEHAVIORAL APPROACHES TO MID-1970S

Other assessments of programs to rehabilitate delinquent youths or prevent delinquent behavior have arrived at very similar conclusions, even when focusing on nonbehavioral programs. An indication of the importance of the field is Dixon's estimate (1974) that from 1964 to the early 1970s, more than 6500 delinquency prevention programs and studies had been initiated. We expect that by 1980 the number had grown beyond 7000 programs.

Lundman, McFarlane, and Scarpitti (1976) and Lundman and Scarpitti (1978) identified more than 1000 references to delinquency prevention programs from the early 1950s to the early or mid-1970s. Their reference list suggests that they searched almost exclusively in sociological and correction sources, omitting virtually all the behavior modification attempts published since the early 1960s in the psychological and the specifically behavior modification journals. Their review tells us something about the rest of the field and resembles the assessments of the behavioral field made by Davidson and Seidman and by Emery and Marholin.

Of the 1000 citations, Lundman and Scarpitti selected 127 for review—the basis for this selection was not clear in their report—and found that only 40 of the 127 met their criteria that the reports must include "independently interpretable information on both the nature and results of the project" (p. 208). Their major conclusions are summarized here:

1. The selection of subjects or clients was narrow, involving a nearly exclusive use of inner-city, working or lower-class minority youths.
2. Most of the subjects were not adjudicated delinquents at all, but had been labeled "predelinquent" or "delinquent prone."
3. The programs attempted to "correct the presumed causes of delinquency," while only a small minority of studies considered delinquent behavior per se.
4. Most projects had poor experimental designs and were thus incapable of assessing their results.
5. The few projects that did have experimental designs and objective measurements of delinquent behavior had not successfully prevented delinquency" (p. 210).

Lundman and Scarpitti concluded that "there is little reason to believe that past attempts at delinquency prevention have been successful . . . or that a major breakthrough in delinquency prevention is forthcoming" (1978, p. 210).

V. OVERALL VIEW OF BEHAVIORAL AND NONBEHAVIORAL RESEARCH, TO THE MID-1970s

These three reviews, published at about the same time from 1974 to 1978, covered two large areas of literature in juvenile delinquency: the older, more traditional sociological, corrections, psychotherapeutic, and casework approaches (Lundman and Scarpitti, 1978) and the newer behavioral programs (Davidson and Seidman, 1974; Emery and Marholin, 1977). The behavioral literature expressed a good deal more optimism and "promise" than Lundman and Scarpitti in their review of the more traditional work. The behavioral literature has successfully demonstrated improvement in "a myriad of behaviors of delinquent youth" as noted by Emery and Marholin and, as indicated in the behavioral programs of Tharp and Wetzel (1969) and of Schwitzgebel (e.g. 1964, 1967, 1969) fairly long-term improvement in delinquent behavior per se has been demonstrated. These threads of "promise" are fine threads indeed, and the field is overwhelmingly characterized by design problems and failures to adequately demonstrate long-term, significant improvement in delinquent behavior. It is difficult to directly control the events that affect low-frequency and poorly defined behaviors such as delinquency. The investigators' focus on presumably related behaviors—social, academic, personal, verbal, and so on—is certainly reasonable and justified. These have been demonstrably modified many times over for many youths and there is every reason to expect that the same techniques, applied to "delinquents," will also improve their behavior. There is no "breakthrough" here. It will require clear demonstration that changes in the presumably related behaviors are causal events bringing about demonstrable improvement in delinquent behavior per se.

Whatever our field's optimism and promise, the implacable reality remains—our psychological approaches, whether behavioral, psychodynamic, social, or otherwise have so far only rarely demonstrated improvements in some individuals' delinquent behavior and have made no measurable contribution to reducing the overall social problem of juvenile delinquency. If we are going to maintain behavioral research and programming, the social demand upon behavior modifiers is clear—demonstrate that our technology can, directly or indirectly, significantly reduce delinquent behavior itself.

The reviewers agree that research in the field displays a sameness across time, a repetition of weak designs and failures, a continuing demonstration of either no change, or change in other than delinquent behaviors. Procedures did change when behavioral programming began, but that too quickly developed a similar repetitive character. No "sense of discovery" appears, only the repeated application of favored techniques. There is little new understanding of delinquents, their behavior, thinking, development, or the nature and functioning of the social systems in which delinquency is defined, occurs, and is dealt with. In the behavioral field we seem to have repeated attempts to demonstrate the usefulness of contingency-management programs, but the informational value of the research in explicating delinquency seems meager.

A major concern of these reviewers, repeated in our chapter introduction, is experimenters' apparent willingness to accept, work within, and thereby enhance social systems and procedures of questionable value and, by doing so, possibly subject their own clients to high risks. In effect behavior modifiers may be enhancing the status quo and failing to recognize that existing institutions may be in large part designed to implement means and to attain goals in direct conflict with their own. Winett and Winkler (1972) discuss institutions, whose goals of docile and conforming client behavior—in this case school children—might define group-imposed behavioral targets to be brought about by the behavior modifier that prevent individualized functional analyses.

A less obvious example is the common practice in delinquency research of accepting labels such as "predelinquent" or "delinquency-prone," and accepting institutional demands to modify the behavior of children with these labels. Lundman and Scarpitti (1978) noted that most of the juvenile subjects in the studies they reviewed were not adjudicated delinquents but were labeled predelinquent. Because we know so little about the development of delinquency, they argue, predictive accuracy of such labels is in serious question, and their application to individuals may place those individuals at considerable risk. Many behavioral researchers accept the "predelinquent" label with little question, and assume that these children will become delinquent if no intervention is provided.

Perhaps the most extreme recent example of such potential risk-placing is the program suggested by Cortes (1972), described by Lundman and Scarpitti (1978) as ". . . based upon the early—and largely unsupported—theories about the relationship between body type and delinquency" (p. 213). In his book, *Delinquency and Crime: A Biophysical Approach*, Cortes advocates studying all families in Washington, D.C.'s "wickedest precinct," who had not yet had children or whose oldest child was under eight years of age. Using predictive measures such as the Glueck Scales, all of the *potentially* delinquent families would be identified and, whether they were cooperative or not cooperative, would be given psychological "help." Lundman and Scarpitti comment: "Considering the high prediction error rate in the Glueck delinquency prediction scale . . . it is certain that such a project would be unsuccessful. It might well violate the rights of the subjects involved. Such a program might set in motion delinquency-fulfilling prophecies and focus attention on only disadvantaged juveniles" (p. 214). They conclude, "as new prevention programs are developed and implemented, practitioners and researchers must recognize that their juvenile subjects deserve special protections. Generally these subjects have not been found guilty of anything beyond possession of characteristics or behaviors which someone believes are predictive of delinquency. In our zeal to help, we must not lose sight of the fact that juveniles who have not been adjudicated delinquent have the right to refuse that help" (p. 220). We should note here that the situation may be even more coercive than suggested because under a court order, the juvenile might *not* be allowed the right to refuse help!

Unintended negative effects of psychological treatment (Graziano and Fink, 1973) may be of particular concern in delinquency prevention programs because of the addition of powerful and largely uncontested legal constraints imposed on each youthful client, constraints not ordinarily applied to control such large portions of the lives and free movement of outpatient psychological clients. In our review of behavioral literature we have not seen instances in which subjects' rights have been violated or subjects obviously harmed by treatment. Of course there are enumerable instances of direct and severe harm such as described by Wooden (1976) and Vedder (1979) and, in the adult criminal justice system, by Mitford (1973), but these instances from the general field are not presented as bonafide behavioral research. It is hoped that our professionalism and ethics will prevent potential abuses within the behavioral field.

However, one disquieting article points out unintended negative effects that may have occurred in a large delinquency and crime prevention program operated some 30 years ago. McCord (1978) presents a 30-year follow-up of what she describes as having been ". . . one of the most imaginative and exciting programs ever designed in hopes of preventing delinquency" (p. 284). It was not a behavioral program but seems to have been a careful and complete, natural-environment, family-focused program of active intervention in social, psychological, physical health, educational, vocational, and recreational programs. In 1935 Richard Clark Cabot, a physician and social philosopher ". . . established a program (of 506 boys and their families) that both avoided stigmatizing participants and permitted follow-up evaluations" (McCord, 1978, p. 284).

Boys, recommended by schools, welfare agencies, churches, police, and other social agencies, were paired on "delinquency-prone" scores based on a number of measures. Members of each pair were assigned to a treatment group or to a no-treatment, contact-only, control group. The treatment interventions began in 1939, continued for an average of five years, and included regular visits to families by social workers, and where needed, medical and/or psychiatric services, academic tutoring, summer camps, youth groups such as boy scouts and YMCA, and so on. The control group only provided information about themselves.

In 1976, using subsequent records McCord located 410 of the previous clients and obtained questionnaire responses from 113 treatment and 122 control subjects for follow-up. A large number of comparisons of the two groups were carried out using both objective (e.g. court and agency records) and subjective measures of criminal behavior, mental and physical health, family, work, leisure time activities, and beliefs and attitudes. Three major findings were reported.

1. By subjective measures, that is, asking former clients, "In what ways was (the program) helpful to you?" The former clients had high praise for the program, the counselors, and the outcome effects on their personal lives. Subjective reports indicated the program had been highly successful.

2. Overall, comparisons of the treatment and control groups on objective measures failed to support the hypothesis that the intervention programs had been successful for the clients.

3. Most disturbing, of the 57 treatment-control group comparisons, only 7 revealed significant differences and all 7 favored the control group.

Because of the important implications of these findings, we will present the author's discussion in its entirety.*

> This study of long-term effects of the Cambridge-Somerville Youth Study was based on the tracing of over 500 men, half of whom were randomly assigned to a treatment program. Those receiving treatment had (in varying degrees) been tutored, provided with medical assistance, and given friendly counsel for an extended period of time.
>
> Thirty years after termination of the program, many of the men remembered their counselors—sometimes recalling particular acts of kindness and sometimes noting the general support they felt in having someone available with whom to discuss their problems. There seems to be little doubt that many of the men developed emotional ties to their counselors.
>
> Were the Youth Study program to be assessed by the subjective judgment of its value as perceived by those who received its services, it would rate high marks. To the enormous credit of those who dedicated years of work to the project, it is possible to use objective criteria to evaluate the long-term impact of this program, which seems to have been successful in achieving the short-term goals of establishing rapport between social workers and teenage clients.
>
> Despite the large number of comparisons between treatment and control groups, none of the objective measures confirmed hopes that treatment had improved the lives of those in the treatment group. Fifteen comparisons regarding criminal behavior were made; one was significant with alpha less than .05. Fifteen comparisons for health indicated four—from three different record sources—favoring the control group. Thirteen comparisons of family, work, and leisure time yielded two that favored the control group. Fourteen comparisons of beliefs and attitudes failed to indicate reliable differences between the groups.
>
> The objective evidence presents a disturbing picture. The program seems not only to have failed to prevent its clients from committing crimes—thus corroborating studies of other projects (e.g. Craig and Furst, 1965; Empey and Ericson, 1972; Hackler, 1966; Miller, 1962; Robin, 1969)—but also to have produced negative side effects. As compared with the control group,

*McCord, Joan A. a thirty-year follow-up of treatment effects. *American Psychologist*, 1978, *33*, 284–289.

1. Men who had been in the treatment program were more likely to commit (at least) a second crime.
2. Men who had been in the treatment program were more likely to evidence signs of alcoholism.
3. Men from the treatment group more commonly manifested signs of serious mental illness.
4. Among men who had died, those from the treatment group died younger.
5. Men from the treatment group were more likely to report having had at least one stress-related disease; in particular, they were more likely to have experienced high blood pressure or heart trouble.
6. Men from the treatment group tended to have occupations with lower prestige.
7. Men from the treatment group tended more often to report their work as not satisfying.

It should be noted that the side effects that seem to have resulted from treatment were subtle. There is no reason to believe that treatment increased the probability of committing a first crime, although treatment may have increased the likelihood that those who committed a first crime would commit additional crimes. Although treatment may have increased the likelihood of alcoholism, the treatment group was not more likely to have appeared in clinics or hospitals. There was no difference between the groups in the number of men who had died before the age of 50, although men from the treatment group had been younger at the age of death. Almost equal proportions of the two groups of men had remained at the lowest rungs of the occupational structure, although men from the treatment group were less likely to be satisfied with their jobs and fewer men from the treatment group had become white-collar workers.

The probability of obtaining 7 reliably different comparisons among 57, with an alpha of .05, is less than 2%. The probability that, by chance, 7 of 57 comparisons would favor the control group is less than 1 in 10,000.

At this juncture, it seems appropriate to suggest several possible interpretations of the subtle effects of treatment. Interaction with adults whose values are different from those of the family milieu may produce later internal conflicts that manifest themselves in disease and/or dissatisfaction. Agency intervention may create dependency upon outside assistance. When this assistance is no longer available, the individual may experience symptoms of dependency and resentment. The treatment program may have generated such high expectations that subsequent experiences tended to produce symptoms of deprivation. Or finally, through receiving the services of a "welfare project," those in the treatment progam may have justified the help they received by perceiving themselves as requiring help.

There were many variations to treatment. Some of these may have been beneficial. Overall, however, the message seems clear: Intervention programs risk damaging the individuals they are designed to assist. These findings may be taken by some as grounds for cessation of social-action programs. I believe that would be a mistake. In my opinion, new programs ought to be developed. We should, however, address the problems of

> potential damage, through the use of pilot projects with mandatory evaluations (McCord, 1978, pp. 280–289).

McCord has given us an evaluation of one of the few prebehavioral, natural-environment delinquency prevention programs that allows us not only control-experimental group comparisons, but does so with measures that include delinquency per se, and a very long-term follow-up. The most important point for us is the evidence suggesting the possible negative effects of this apparently carefully and well-done program. As McCord suggests, there may have been subtle interactions of the intervention components with parts of the clients' personal and social systems, that resulted in negative effects for some of the clients.

The cautionary note for behavior modifiers is clear: we continue to focus so specifically on immediate target behavior change as to virtually ignore other aspects of our clients' reality. By allowing into our evaluations only a limited range of variables—that is, predetermined, short-term target behavior, by failing to include criminal behavior as a dependent variable and by generally avoiding long-term follow-up evaluations—behavior modifiers might be largely repeating with a different psychological technology the limitations and errors so well discussed by McCord. We seem to have not yet built in a sufficient respect for the complexity of the interacting systems of human functioning. Unintended negative effects of treatment (Graziano and Fink, 1973) are all too possible and it is a ". . . major responsibility of all of us who presume to intervene in the lives of others to recognize that it is, indeed a presumption and it must be tempered by an abiding respect for human complexity and a concomitant prudence when intervening in the human ecology of even one individual" (Graziano, 1975, p. 34).

VI. BEHAVIORAL RESEARCH, 1975 TO 1981

The remainder of this chapter will review the behavioral research with juvenile delinquents published from 1975 to 1981. To avoid overlapping we will limit the discussion to papers published since the review by Davidson and Seidman (1974). We will use the issues in our preceding discussion to evaluate more recent studies. The papers included are grouped into two large categories defined by the nature of the settings—residential institution or community and family—within which the programs were carried out.

A. *Behavior Change Within Institutions*

Eight studies of behavior change within institutions are summarized: two are from the continuing research carried out within various achievement place settings. Maloney et al. (1976) increased appropriate conversations-related behavior in four 13-to 15-year-old delinquent girls in an achievement place token program. The girls assisted in training each other. Although there was no attempt to measure the long-term maintenance of any change, positive changes were reported at posttraining. Further, community members judged the girls' conversation behavior to be more appropriate at posttraining as compared with baseline.

Eitzen (1975) reports positive shifts in boys' "attitudes" as a result of another achievement place program. Attitudinal changes, according to Eitzen, are rarely studied by behavior modifiers who focus on behavioral changes. Here, Eitzen reported, positive attitudinal changes accompanied positive behavior changes. Both of these studies provide additional evidence for the effectiveness of the achievement place programming in bringing about within-program changes in youth.

Three papers reported positive changes in more personal skills: increased positive comments about others in the program, improved communication skills, and improvement in some social skills. Emshoff, Redd, and Davidson (1976) recruited four subjects from a residential home for delinquent and "disturbed" adolescents. Two of the students were to receive "generalized" and two were to receive "constant" training in seven, 30-minute sessions over a 2-week period. The training consisted of an activity during which the student could receive points redeemable for small amounts of cash, and verbal praise for each positive comment the student made. In the generalized training condition, the activity, trainer, location, and time of day were varied, while in the constant training condition these remained the same across all training sessions. Both groups showed large increases in positive comments during the training sessions, but the generalized training group also showed a small tendency to increase their positive comments in their home environment. The authors note that if one were to consider, as is usually done, the students' performance in the training conditions alone, as the assessment measure, the conclusion would be that the two training groups were equally effective, where only the generalized training group in this study seemed at all effective in other than the training situations.

Sanson-Fisher, Seymour, and Baer (1976) trained the staff of a community correctional institution for 14- to 18-year-old girls to alter the adolescents' prosocial and antisocial conversation. All staff were trained in self-recording their own comments. One group of staff was trained to increase positive attention to prosocial comments and ignore antisocial comments made by the adolescents. A second group of staff, working with a different group of girls, was trained to increase positive attention to prosocial comments and to also increase their negative attention to antisocial comments. "Negative attention" was defined as disapproval, rejection, derogatory comments, and discouraging continuation of the topic. This study included 11 staff and 12 delinquent girls, and no inferential statistics were used. Inspection of the pretraining scores between the separate groups of staff and girls showed marked and unexplained differences between the respective groups which limit the findings. Some potential limits of intervening merely in staff's verbal behavior, however, are pointed out. The authors note an increase in prosocial comments by the girls only during training by the staff and not in other conditions or at posttraining. Further, at posttraining, negative attention showed marked increases for the staff member who received it and also for the one who did not. When staff negative attention increased, the girls made fewer positive responses, apparently withdrawing from them and giving increased attention to peers' antisocial comments.

Spence and Marzillier (1979) used a social-skills training package with ten 15-year-old residents in a detention home. For each resident four of five social skills—eye contact, time spent "fidgeting," appropriate head movements, acknowledgements, "question-type feedback"—were selected as subject target behaviors. In a multiple-baseline design each skill was trained in 30-minute sessions. The training sessions involved a combination of instructions, modeling, videotaped feedback, role-playing, target-setting, and social reinforcement. The results showed that the training program seemed particularly effective in increasing eye contact and in decreasing fidgeting movements. The other skills showed variable improvement; "question-type feedback" skills improved least.

Two projects studied the effects of token economies on within-institutional behaviors. Barkley, Hastings, Tousel, and Tousel (1976) operated a token economy in a residential home for eight older, more difficult, delinquents. Three aspects of the program were selected for evaluation: (a) performance of daily chores, (b) littering in the house, and (c) school performance as reflected in daily teacher evalutions. In a multiple, return-to-baseline design, they found that performance of chores and littering returned to baseline quickly after cessation of token reinforcement. School behavior, however, showed maintained improvement at several weeks follow-up.

In an earlier study, Fixsen, Phillips, and Wolf (1972) concluded that self-evaluation alone did not increase room-cleaning behavior in boys in a residential setting. Wood and Flynn (1978), however, in another achievement place setting, found that training and reinforcing accurate self-evaluation as part of a token system to increase cleanliness in rooms improved the effectiveness of token systems.

Davidson and Wolfred (1977) wrote a particularly important paper specifically investigating critical issues in evaluating all of these studies. The seven studies outlined above were carefully executed, with specified behavioral targets, quantitative multiple measures, and controls in the form of experimental-control group comparisons, multiple-baseline, or reversal designs. As a group they seem better controlled than the pre-1975 research, and add evidence to an important finding: namely, specified behaviors of institutionalized "predelinquent" and delinquent youth can be significantly improved through contingency-management procedures. These studies do not give us new information, but do support the earlier findings. However, they share at least three major weaknesses of the earlier work: (1) they still accept the quasijudicial definitions of "predelinquent" and delinquent, adjudicated or not; (2) although somewhat better in this respect than the earlier work, they still, in the main, fail to demonstrate long-term maintenance of the improvements; and (3) most importantly, even the most recent within-institution change programs fail to demonstrate that these improvements, worthy as they may seem, have any effect at all upon reducing delinquency.

These three continuing failures raise important doubts concerning the value of the contribution of behavior modification to reducing juvenile delinquency. In our final assessment we will argue that while behavior modification has not reduced delinquency, it has brought about other, important changes in the juvenile corrections system. Most interestingly, behavior modification as carried out in programs such as the various achievement place settings has demonstrated the feasibility of humane, positively reinforcing programs that are successful in bringing about improvements in the within-institution behaviors. Severe punitive methods, such as occur in many nonbehavioral correctional programs, are clearly not needed to bring about cooperation in daily living settings.

Thus the major importance of behavior modification in the juvenile correctional area may have been its *humanizing* influence. We argue that if this is "all" it has achieved, then its contribution has been of great importance, even though the eventual reduction of delinquency per se is still open to question.

We noted above the particular importance of the Davidson and Wolfred (1977) paper. Their evaluation of a community-based, behavior modification program for delinquency prevention discusses and helps clarify the field's major research issue: the strengths and major weaknesses of behavior modification endeavors with juvenile delinquents. They focus primarily on the earlier conclusion (see Davidson and Seidman, 1974) that within-program, specific target behaviors can be changed, but they specifically ask if such changes can be maintained and if they have any effects on reducing delinquent behavior per se, as measured by recidivism.

The program they evaluated was a community-based, short-term program for "predelinquent or behavior-problem youth" 7 to 17 years of age. Very much in the emerging community mental health tradition the program operated not only within a residential setting but also within other natural environment social systems "that are already important in the child's life." Within that community-based framework the program operated on social learning principles and behavior modification technology such as that in the achievement place settings. The programming utilized behavioral contracting procedures as described by Schwitzgebel (1964, 1967, 1969) and Stuart (1971) and family interventions such as discussed by Tharp and Wetzel (1969). Davidson and Wolfred examined ". . . the efficacy of the techniques used to shape and maintain desired performances and (they evaluated) the generalization of such changes from the treatment setting to natural settings" (p. 297).

This research, then, is transitional—from the earlier, residential treatment settings to the more natural environment, community orientation. In this respect it represents what appears to be a general shift in the child behavior modification field, toward increasing natural environment intervention. Davidson and Wolfred's paper could have been included in another section—community intervention—but it has been included here because of its importance in evaluating effects of residential programs and within-program behavioral change.

Over an 18-month period 53 students completed the program consisting of an "open system" in which they progressed from level one expectations such as room cleaning, attending school, going to bed on time, and so on, through level three functioning that involved increasingly cooperative and responsible social functioning

> . . . where the expectations and privileges faded toward those likely to occur in their targeted discharge settings . . . (such as) more delayed social and activity reinforcers likely to occur in the natural settings. . . . For example, the behavioral expectations for honor-level youth included 100

> percent performance of all first- and second-level behaviors as well as leading group discussion sessions (Fixsen, Phillips, and Wolf, 1973), participation in staff meetings, preparation of discharge plans, practicing performances likely to be important in the natural setting, and meeting individual target performance criteria during brief and extended home visits. Similarly an honor-level student could contract for privileges such as home visits, independent off-ground activities, and assuming responsibility for lower-level students (pp. 298–299).

Detailed results of the program were presented in an earlier paper (Emshoff, Redd, and Davidson, 1976). In the Davidson and Wolfred paper the authors noted success across a number of carefully measured, within-program targeted behaviors and ". . . effectiveness of the contingency system modifying academic and social performance based on operant principles was demonstrated" (p. 300).

Follow-up comparisons were made at 3 and 9 months between the experimental group of youths who completed the program and a no-treatment control group match for age, sex, grade in school, major presenting problem, and date of initial social agency contact. The authors reported that ". . . exact matches were found for 42 of the 53 experimental subjects." Follow-up measures included school grades and attendance, contact with juvenile authorities, criminal contacts, institutional placement, and family or foster home placement. The follow-up results were disappointing, as the researchers found ". . . no desired differences between experimental and control subjects" (p. 302).

Most disturbing—perhaps most ominous—is that their findings echo McCord's (1978) evaluation of that seemingly excellent program of the late 1930s and early 1940s: not only did the data fail to indicate desired improvement in the experimental compared with control clients, but the experimental clients ". . . tended to have more juvenile justice contacts than controls and were more likely to have been placed in institutions" (p. 302).

The overall results of this carefully conceived and carried out program show that within-program behaviors significantly improved during the program, but on follow-ups the experimental clients appear to have done a little worse than the controls! In the author's words, "Namely, experimental subjects were less likely to be placed in their own home and were more likely to be placed in institutions. In addition they were more likely to have had contacts with the juvenile justice system for illegal behavior" (p. 303).

Because of its importance, we will quote Davidson and Wolfred's discussion in its entirety.

By most criteria proposed for effective usage of behavioral principles in applied settings, the in-program results indicated that the CRISIS program was successful in implementing potent behavior procedures (Michael, 1966; Thomas and Walter, 1973). Further, those procedures were effective in producing important changes in the behaviors of predelinquent youth. Given the in-house results, in combination with the extensive research literature reporting positive alterations in the behavior of delinquents (Davidson and Seidman, 1974), it is somewhat disconcerting that the follow-up study produced essentially negative results. Not only were comparisons between the experimental and matched control group negative, but precomparisons to postcomparisons failed to yield changes in the desired direction. Several rather divergent hypotheses need discussion in relation to these findings.

First, it could be argued that the reported data lacked sufficient methodological rigor to produce either clear-cut support for the effectiveness of the in-house program or the failure of the follow-up results. For example, the specific results reported concerning the operation of the in-house classroom contingency quite obviously confounded the effects of instructions and contingencies. Similarly, the outcome study, although following a relatively careful matching procedure, did not include true randomization leaving interpretation difficult due to multiple potential confoundings (Campbell and Stanley, 1966). Although neither argument can be firmly denied, in the case of the former the classroom study was for the purpose of maximizing classroom performance rather than determining the specific role of single variables in producing the high rates of on-task behavior. In the latter the lack of meaningful positive change in the experimental group from preassessment to postassessment reduces its potency.

Second, it is commonly argued that the issue of transfer of behavior change from treatment to nontreatment situations is a problem of generalization (Wahler, 1969). In fact, the failure of newly acquired behavior to transfer from the situation in which treatment took place to other situations has been recognized as a serious limitation of many behavior modification programs (Ullmann and Krasner, 1965; Bandura, 1969; Kazdin and Bootzin, 1972). Given the lack of direct observation of in-program behaviors in follow-up settings, the current research cannot shed direct light on this hypothesis. A related set of hypotheses would suggest that the use of social criteria (for example, school attendance, recidivism) is irrelevant to examining the effectiveness of the behavior modification component of the program, per se. In other words, it might be expected that such global social indicators would be unaffected by changes in the specific performances dealt with in the CRISIS program. If such were the case, it is appropriate that future research efforts begin exploring the functional relationships affecting other critical events in the lives of youths.

A third set of hypotheses would suggest that a variety of social psychological variables, rather than those directly connected with effective behavioral technology, affect the social outcomes (Reppucci and Saunders, 1974). It can be pointed out anecdotally that the staff of the CRISIS program were on many occasions frustrated by other social agencies who had jurisdictional control over the residential and educational futures of the youths involved in the program. For example, even though the staff consistently strongly advocated for target placement within the natural family of the youths, they were on several occasions overruled by the state agency holding wardship. Similar examples could be cited regarding attempts to convince local classroom teachers and administrators to adopt more effective educational strategies. The important point would seem to be that possibly other institutional or community variables need to be critically examined in future research to determine the role that they play in effective outcomes. Although many authors have acknowledged the importance of such variables in implementing successful behavior modification programs (for example, Tharp and Wetzel, 1969; Reppucci and Saunders, 1974), they have usually indicated that such phenomena can be effectively dealt with in a variety of nonspecific strategies. It seems those suggestions are in the spirit of delineating uncomfortable situations that the loyal behaviorist will have to put up with rather than suggesting that the process of implementing innovative programs calls for an open-systems approach to research. Again, if contextual variables play an important role in determining program outcome, they must become the focus of further investigations.

In conclusion, the research reported in this paper indicated the failure of a highly successful behavior modification program in producing desired social outcomes for the youths involved. These results are presented to add a note of caution to previous research on the use of behavioral approaches with delinquent populations (Davidson and Seidman, 1974). It is suggested that not only are additional outcome studies of the efficacy of behavioral techniques needed, but also that future research needs to address itself to broader issues than only the effect of a technology on the specific behaviors targeted (1977, pp. 296–306).

B. *Behavior Change in Natural Environment Settings*

The papers in this section consist of single-case studies and group comparisons. The single-case studies include fire-setting, stealing, and within-family communication problems. Compulsive fire-setting is a destructive behavior posing severe potential danger to other people as well as the fire-setting child. It is a problem behavior difficult to bring under therapeutic control partly because of low frequency and because it is ordinarily not detected until after it has occurred, making immediate contingencies difficult to apply. Although there is little demographic or incidence data on child fire-setters, its low incidence makes group comparisons virtually impossible, leaving only very small numbers of subjects for study in any one project.

Psychodynamic hypotheses about fire-setters traditionally emphasize intrapsychic causes for the fire-setting "symptom" (e.g. Blanco, 1972; Kaufman, Heins, and Reiser, 1961) and therefore assume the necessity of long-term, psychodynamic treatment. However, the problem is of immediate concern in each case, and the leisurely pace of psychodynamic therapy, even if it were ever to be shown effective for this problem, is a luxury that leaves the imminent threat to the child, the family, and/or others unattended for an intolerably long time. The fire-setting child could be institutionalized while psychotherapy is administered, thus placing him or her under close supervisory control. That personal cost, however, might be far too great in light of the generally meager gains so far demonstrated by child psychotherapy.

In light of the immediate demands inherent in this problem behavior, several researchers have investigated behavior approaches to the direct reduction of the fire-setting behavior itself. In addition, several researchers, apparently concerned with the possible negative effects of institutionalizing young children, have attempted the behavioral interventions in the natural family situation (e.g. Holland, 1969; Welsh, 1971). Holland applied a differential reinforcement technique, Welsh used "stimulus satiation." Other attempts include electrical aversion treatment (Denholtz, 1972; Penney, Marcella, and Charlton, 1974). The two most recent case studies are those by McGrath, Marshall, and Prior (1979) and Stawar (1976). In each case the subject was a young boy, aged 11 and 7, respectively, from a multiproblem family.

McGrath et al. reported success with a treatment package including social-skills training, overcorrection, covert sensitization, and fire-safety instruction. Carried out within an institution, it is included here because of the target behavior. In a two-year follow-up no further fire-settings were reported. The procedure appears to have eliminated fire-setting and to have also improved several collateral behaviors, such as social behavior. Of additional interest in this particular paper is the recognition of extra-behavioral issues: specifically, of potential legal problems involved in behavioral treatment of delinquent or "predelinquent" behaviors (see Martin, 1975). The authors noted that each step of the program was "thoroughly discussed with the child's lawyer and by the court . . . in order to judge whether the rights of the child and safety of the community were adequately protected" (p. 70). These added components of legal and judicial review did not impede the program's effectiveness.

Stawar (1976) reports success with a 7-year-old boy through a 2-week program of contingent reinforcement of incompatible behavior, namely, taking any matches he found to his parent, and a clearly cognitive, instructional component. The reinforcement of incompatible behavior was similar to that employed by Holland (1969). Of particular interest in this study is Stawar's use of direct instruction (perhaps somewhat poorly labeled as "operantly structured fantasies") given through a story about a little boy who found some matches and, being a "very good little boy" immediately took them to his parent. The story was told to the child several times, using dolls and a doll house for the setting, until he could generate the story himself and "knew what to do if he found some matches." The boy's mother became the contingency manager at home, rewarding him for bringing matches to her. A 7-month follow-up indicated no further fire-setting.

Although their results are weakened by the usual limitations of single-subject case studies (poor controls, no indication of how many times the procedure may have failed) and the undesirability of reversal designs for this particular problem, both studies included individual functional analyses, focused directly upon the problem behavior itself rather than upon "related" behaviors, approached the behavioral reduction through a multi-variable package, involved "natural environment" systems, and included follow-ups. Given the limitations imposed by this particular behavior, these researchers seem to have been aware of and corrected many of the shortcomings of the earlier research. It remains to be demonstrated if these methods can be validated with larger groups or otherwise improved controls.

Another difficult problem to treat is stealing which, unlike fire-setting, apparently occurs at a high rate in society. Despite the apparently large number of youths who engage in stealing, there have been few reports of systematic attempts to alter their behavior. To our knowledge there have been no group-comparison controlled behavioral studies of stealing. Only two behavioral case studies have been reported (Wetzel, 1966; Stumphauzer, 1976). Surprisingly, systematic behavioral studies of the controlling conditions for juvenile stealing, including demographic, personal, and environmental conditions, and of methods to alter the behavior, have not been carried out.

Treatment of stealing may be difficult because successful theft is presumably self-reinforcing. Further, as Stumphauzer (1976) noted, "aversive controls are usually ineffective" with delinquents, at least partly because punishment "through legal proceedings is variable, intermittent, and delayed" (p. 265).

Stumphauzer reported the successful treatment of a 12-year-old girl with a 5-year history of stealing. The program included self-reinforcement of alternative behavior using cognitive self-statements based on Meichenbaum and Goodman (1971) and Kanfer and Karoly (1972), for example, "I'm trustworthy. I keep my hands to myself, they are not gummy and my mind is on learning at school" (Stumphauzer, 1976, p. 266). Simple family contracts based on Stuart (1971) focused on shifting the attention of the family and school officials from the girl's stealing to nonstealing. Praise, cash allowance, and favorite meals were some of the positive contingencies for successful nonstealing days. Family sessions were also included, in which other problems, such as the girl's apparent social isolation, were discussed and a gradual program to shape more interactive behavior was developed. The stealing ended within 6 weeks of treatment and the authors also reported that "family functioning improved." There was no return of stealing behavior evidenced at 6-, 12- and 18-month follow up.

As with other single-case studies this one, too, is limited in its generalization by the lack of controls and replication. It is suggestive, however, of approaches that might be tested in better controlled research designs with groups of subjects. Of particular interest is Stumphauzer's use of self-statements to enhance self-control while maintaining the interventions within the youth's family, that is, cognitive self-control within the family system. The suggestion is that this type of individual or "solitary" antisocial behavior, as distinct from that which may be peer-group controlled, may be effectively reduced by these individualized cognitive self-control methods. Certainly research in this direction is clearly indicated.

Stuart's (1971) and Tharp and Wetzel's (1969) family contracting procedures have been influential in this field. Lysaught and Burchard (1975), like Stumphauzer (1976), based their case approach upon family contracting. They noted in their case, as did Stumphauzer, the apparently characteristically negative communication patterns within families of delinquents, that is, with parents and juvenile and school officials seeming to force constantly maintained attention upon the youth's undesirable behavior, with little recognition of positive alternatives that might also be characteristic of the youth. Through contingency contracting Lysaught and Burchard decreased the mother's negative commentary regarding the youth's behavior and increased their positive verbal interactions. Their procedure is suggested by the researchers as an aid in helping to "phase" youths back to their families after having been in a correctional program.

Frederiksen, Jenkins, and Carr (1976) also applied contingency contracting within a delinquent's family. They reported family improvements related to the direct contracting interventions. Of particular interest, they found an apparent indirect effect on the adolescent's multidrug abuse. The decrease in drug usage was measured by chemical analyses of urine samples taken at "unpredictable times." The observed reduction of drug use, accompanying improved family interactions, is an interesting and suggestive finding. Controlled research is clearly indicated based on Lysaught and Burchard's single-case findings.

Several experimental-control group comparisons of within-family interventions for delinquent behavior were reported in the late 1970s, and together these papers present somewhat mixed but also quite encouraging results. We will comment more at the end of this section upon this development of within-family intervention in delinquency.

Stuart, Tripodi, Jayaratne, and Camburn (1976) assigned 102 predelinquents to experimental and no-treatment control groups. In the experimental condition contingency contracting was carried out at home and in school. The period of time of the intervention was not clearly indicated. "Soft" measures of change at home and school included Likert-type scale items answered by teachers and parents. Grades and attendance records provided more specific and quantitative outcome data. Overall, the results were disappointing. The results indicated small but statistically significant improvements of experimental subjects compared with controls on most of the parents' and teachers' ratings. Academic performance, however, as measured by grades and attendance, did not improve.

The authors concluded that their single intervention procedure, contingency contracting, may have been too narrow a base for effective intervention. They suggest the advisability of differentiating among families based on demographic characteristics and then providing appropriately differential treatment.

A public school-based social-learning program with 30 experimental and 30 control group "troublesome adolescents" is described by Wodarski, Filipczak, McCombs, Koustenis, and Rusilko (1979). Focusing on predelinquent youth, the one-year school-based program aimed at both a short- and long-range improvement of academic and social skills. The program's development and the posttreatment evaluation have been treated in detail by Filipczak and Wodarski (1980). Of the nine outcome measures seven were statistically significant for experimental-control group differences. Six favored the experimental group (reading comprehension, language skills, mathematics computation and application, disciplinary referrals, and grades). One difference, vocabulary development, favored controls. A one-year follow-up supported the original findings, showing that the experimental group, compared with controls, had better attendance and grades, fewer suspensions, and fewer disciplinary referrals.

In a four-year follow-up, however, using five self-report inventories, the results were mixed, at best, as *t*-tests indicated statistically significant differences for 10 of the 119 variables on which experimental and control groups were compared. Of the ten, seven favored the experimental group and three favored the controls. As the authors pointed out the 119 comparisons would be expected to yield six significant differences by change alone. Since ten were found, seven favoring the experimental group, they concluded that the evidence favoring the experimental group at the four-year follow-up is very meager.

This fairly large community-based project thus demonstrated favorable postintervention outcomes and measures at one-year follow-up that continued to favor the experimental group. The posttreatment changes in this natural environment, community intervention, coupled with the related favorable data one year later, are quite encouraging. Their four-year follow-up, however, failed to show any clear continuation of positive effects, although there was some evidence for such effects.

A final program has been carried out over an approximately 5-year period, and reported in three papers (Alexander and Parsons, 1973; Parsons and Alexander, 1973; Klein, Alexander, and Parsons, 1977). In their research "eighty-six families of delinquents were randomly assigned to one of four treatment conditions: no-treatment controls, a client-centered family approach, an eclectic-dynamic approach, and a behaviorally oriented, short-term family systems approach" (Klein et al., 1977, p. 469).

In this program the integration of behavior modification technology, social-learning theory, and community mental health is clear. The interventions were carried out within families in their natural-environment settings aorally oriented, short-term family systems approach" (Klein et al., 1977, p. 469).

In this program the integration of behavior modification technology, social-learning theory, and community mental health is clear. The inteeinforcement, and contingency contracting emphasizing equivalence of rights and responsibilities for all family members" (Klein et al., 1977, p. 471).

Further, the goals of the program were conceptualized and evaluated in terms of *prevention* as a major intervention strategy, in which the family has been identified as the major socialization force and the principal target for prevention programs (Caplan and Grunebaum, 1967). The program evaluation, then, was conducted as evaluations of primary, secondary, and tertiary prevention effects, that is, this evaluation provided a "multilevel evaluation model for determining the effectiveness of a family system intervention program" (p. 470).

The first evaluation question was whether the family-systems behavioral intervention was indeed effective in changing family interaction patterns: this constituted tertiary prevention (i.e. treatment). The researchers reported that in comparison with the client-centered and no-treatment controls, the behavioral intervention "significantly modified four interaction measures of family conflict resolution and interaction: (a) equality of speech; (b) silence; (c) frequency of positive interruptions; and (d) duration of positive interruptions" (p. 471).

The next evaluation question (the secondary prevention level) was tested at 6 to 18 months following treatment termination, and it compared recidivism rates of the referred, identified delinquents. These researchers, then, unlike most others in this field, focused specifically on delinquent behavior per se of the referred, targeted delinquent, as a dependent variable. They reported that (1) recidivism was significantly lower for the behavioral-family intervention group than for the client-centered, the eclectic-dynamic, or the no-treatment control groups, and (2) the reduction in recidivism was "demonstrated to be statistically related to changes in family process" (p. 471).

The final evaluation, primary prevention, tested the long-range effects of intervention, evaluating the program intervention ". . . in terms of its reduction of the incidence of new cases . . . in the population. Primary prevention, therefore (focuses) either on modifications of the environment that reduce the overall probability of risk or on strengthening the potential recipients or hosts against harmful consequences" (p. 470). It was assumed that deviant behavior in the children was a function of the maladaptive systems within the family, so the ". . . ultimate goal of the therapy process then becomes one of training the family in effective problem-solving techniques in order for the family unit to more adaptively meet the developmental changes inevitably occurring as children reach adolescence" (p. 471). To evaluate the primary-prevention function the researchers analyzed the court records of *siblings* of the initially referred delinquents. The evaluations showed 2½ to 3½ years after treatment termination that the behavioral-family system intervention resulted in a significantly reduced sibling delinquency rate, compared with that for the siblings in the client-centered, eclectic-dynamic, and no-treatment groups.

Their research demonstrates, (a) posttreatment improvements in family process (tertiary prevention or therapy outcome); (b) longer-range (6- to 18-month) reduction of delinquent behavior per se in the referred, targeted youth (secondary prevention); and (c) long-term 2½ to 3½ years, primary prevention of delinquent behavior in new cases, the siblings in the present context. Most notably the researchers have demonstrated immediate and long-term effects on delinquent behavior per se, at a primary prevention level. Of all studies so far reported, this series, based on one intervention program, appears to be the best demonstration of delinquency reduction through behavioral programming. The results provide evidence for direct natural-environment, family-systems behavioral intervention in reducing delinquency.

The central contribution of this research is the suggestion, with good supportive evidence, that delinquent behavior can be successfully modified by applying within-family, behavioral interventions aimed at improved communications and other social interactions. To our knowledge this is the most encouraging research in the field. Replication, with larger groups and more attention paid to initial differential descriptions of types of delinquent behavior involved, is clearly recommended. It may be that these three papers may provide the major prototypes for future delinquency programs, in cases where the family systems are intact and available for the intervention.

VII. SUMMARY AND CONCLUSIONS

This chapter has considered some of the issues in juvenile delinquency with particular focus on the behavior modification research from the early 1960s to mid-1980. A complete review of all of the work in delinquency is not possible in anything less than a multivolume set, so we have attempted only to identify and discuss the major issues of the field. We will limit this summary to the most important conclusions.

1. Juvenile delinquency is a large, serious, still growing problem with the incidence of delinquent acts and the degree of their aggressiveness continuing to rise. There are clear indications that the escalations will continue throughout this century, at least partly because of the continuing increase in the juvenile population. Within the next two decades we may see some of our larger cities seriously threatened by predations of youth gangs and other forms of juvenile delinquency.

2. In general society's attempts to deal with the problems have been failures. Recently, with the advent of behavior modification in programs for rehabilitating juveniles, the prospects appear more encouraging. However, correctional and rehabilitational programming of any kind has to date made no substantiated contribution to reducing juvenile delinquency.

3. Juvenile delinquents comprise a widely heterogeneous collection of individuals, ordinarily grouped together by virtue of a quasilegal label. Despite the obvious heterogeneity, social scientists and correc-

tional workers continue to treat the labeled youth as a homogeneous group, and fail to differentiate among possibly critical demographic, psychological, social, and behavioral characteristics.

The field's implicit assumptions of the homogeneous nature of youth allow correctional and rehabilitational programs to be carried out with the expectations that individual programming is not necessary, and that the same global procedures apply equally to all delinquents. The correctional and rehabilitative programs, particularly prior to the mid-1970s have been notoriously unsuccessful, perhaps in large part due to the failure to develop predisposition differentiation among critical legal, social, psychological, demographic, and other variables, and to the failure to specifically program our rehabilitation efforts so as to be appropriate for those differentiated issues. The variance due to the preintervention individual and subgroup differences may be too great to overcome with the small number of global programs usually attempted. One of this field's major needs is for the systematic development of criteria, measures, and procedures for predisposition differentiation among the labeled delinquents, followed by specific procedures appropriately and differentially applied.

4. Juvenile delinquency is a social problem of great complexity, and even a tentative and superficial attempt to identify significant components reveals several large areas each of which alone constitutes a major area of study. In each individual case of delinquency as well as in the collective social problem, we see the operation of several complex variables:

> *The characteristics of the individual youth*—physical, psychological, and behavioral, the family characteristics and demographics, the specific behaviors for which legal action was taken.
>
> *Cultural and social standards*—laws, values, and biases that define delinquent behavior, allow exceptions for many, and continue to support the use of severe physical punishment for children and youths, alone of all social groups in the country.
>
> *Police procedures* in apprehending and holding juveniles, and police values and biases regarding the young offender.
>
> *Court procedures* that are applied specifically to youths, including all of the procedural and definitional ambiguities, general lack of legal representation for youths, the uncontested exercise of power by the presiding judge, the issues of due process and other legal rights issues for minors.
>
> *Disposition* of the case—including problems of open-ended sentencing, the unchallenged authority of the social service departments that assume jurisdiction over youths following court proceedings.
>
> *The nature of the institution* to which youths are remanded, including correctional institutions, their alleged high prevalence of brutalization, political patronage and economic considerations that allegedly take pre-

cedence over the care of the youthful prisoners, the double-jeopardy reality of the frequent and severe punishments applied within the institution in addition to the punishment by sentence imposed by the judge, the unchallenged authority of the superintendent to control all details of the youthful prisoners' lives, and to exercise, unchallenged, every whim and bias he or she may have in controlling youths; the lack of legal appeal and representation for incarcerated youths, and the general issues of the lack of due process and humanitarianism.

The nature of the vast array of rehabilitation approaches and programs, their ineffectiveness and the need for continued research.

The need for *social reentry and follow-up programs* to help monitor and assure continuation of rehabilitation gains, where those gains might occur.

Primary prevention attempts, to reduce the incidence in the population, are practically nonexistent.

As we noted, each of these is a complicated area of effort, going far beyond social scientists' values of research and objectivity. Each appears to be in need of major reform. Behavior modification is but one set of models and technologies within only one of the many areas, rehabilitation. In light of the realities of the total set of problems, then, behavior modification has made no practical contribution to reduction of the overall problem. Many of the nonpsychological issues of humanitarianism, legal reform, and ethics appear to be far more acutely in need of immediate attention, and any significant reduction of the overall problem, we submit, will require basic reforms in these areas, before any rehabilitation programs can function effectively for any significant portion of this particular population.

In terms of priorities in this field, the humanitarian, ethical, legal, political, and economic reforms are the areas we should be addressing. Behavior modifiers appear little concerned with these nonscience issues.

5. In the rehabilitation area, while nonbehavioral programming has been virtually without demonstrable success—with even some suggestions of unintended negative effects—the behavioral research since the early sixties is a good deal more promising, but still extremely limited. It is clear now that contingency management procedures in controlled institutional settings can successfully increase important skills and behaviors, such as academic performance, social responsiveness, communication skills, positive self-statements, reduced fighting, cooperation in living settings, and so on. While all of these reach for important goals well worth pursuing, they are (a) achievements of behavioral programming that have been demonstrated many times with many youngsters, and they tell us nothing new about delinquents, (b) the

generalization and long-term maintenance of those gains are yet to be sufficiently demonstrated and replicated and, (c) for the most part none of those within-program improvements have been shown to have any effect upon the reduction of delinquent behavior per se. Only rarely and only very recently has data been presented to show that delinquent behavior was reduced over a relatively long term through behavioral programming. The value of continued behavioral research showing within-institution improvements, without relating such changes to long-term reduction of delinquent behavior, is in great doubt. Journal editors, for example, should begin demanding such evidence as a criterion of acceptance.

Behavioral programming, apparently alone of all the rehabilitation models, has demonstrated its effectiveness in improved within-program behavior—and that achievement is an important contribution. However, the critical and thus far elusive criterion for effectiveness of rehabilitation programs is the demonstration of their long-term influence, specifically on the reduction of delinquent behavior per se. Future behavioral research must focus on this issue.

6. The most promising hints that we can glean from the past 20 years of behavioral research with delinquents suggest the following dimensions for future programming and research; (a) highly structured behavioral programming, (b) based on individualized functional analyses, (c) which is carried out in a natural-environment setting, particularly family, (d) where programming, such as contingency contracts, focuses heavily on the modification of the interactions among family members, particularly parents and youth, with special emphasis on communication patterns and on increasing the proportion of positive as opposed to negative communications, (e) where self-control training, such as use of verbal self-instructions, is employed, (f) where long-term monitoring, programming, or other contact is maintained, and (g) where, over long periods of time delinquent behavior per se as well as other behaviors such as academic and vocational functioning, are measured as long-term criteria.

In sum, of all of the research in this field, behavioral and nonbehavioral, *behavioral programming within the natural-environment family-systems model* appears to be the most promising approach, and we recommend that future research focus heavily upon the variables and procedures briefly outlined above.

The need for individualized functional analyses and pretreatment differentiation cannot be overemphasized in this context of family intervention. Clearly, not all delinquent youths can be successfully treated in this way and alternative approaches, some using institutional programs such as achievement place programming, are also needed. The central idea is to make discriminations that will allow successful application of appropriate programming for specific individuals or subgroups.

7. A long-term goal is the integration of community psychology and behavioral technology toward primary prevention programming, that is, reduction of the incidence of delinquency. Thus far few programs offer any data on the success of prevention attempts. One research paper (Klein, Alexander, and Parsons, 1977) appears most promising in this regard and certainly suggests the value of further research to replicate and generalize those findings.

8. In strongly recommending continued research in behavioral programming as a major approach to rehabilitation of delinquents, both in institutions and in family settings, we also urge experimenters to exercise caution in choosing the settings in which they introduce behavioral technology. Unintended second-order negative effects such as inadvertently strengthening an undesirable correctional setting's behavioral control technology must be guarded against. Sharp concern for the legal rights of children, for ethical issues in research and treatment, and for ensuring humanitarian approaches must be maintained.

9. In this regard a comment, perhaps one of some irony, seems appropriate. The application of behavioral technology in correctional/rehabilitation situations such as achievement place has demonstrated significant behavioral improvements in within-institution conduct of the youth. Social cooperation, improved verbal interaction, reduced fighting, increased responsibility for cooperative daily chores such as housekeeping, improved academic achievement and more cooperative classroom behavior, and so on, has been achieved primarily through systematically planned and arranged positive contingencies. Punishments when used, were comparatively mild, consisting mainly of variations of time-out and response costs. Thus what has been demonstrated in a field where the stock in trade seems to be heavy use of aversive control including physical punishment is that good conduct and cooperation can be brought about through positive rewards. The irony, related to earlier criticisms of behavior modification's objective and supposedly less humane stance, is that careful, systematic, behavior modification programming has introduced a high degree of humanization into these correctional systems. And if this is "all" it does—that is, humanize the within-institutional control procedures—then behavior modification has already made an important contribution to this field.

In closing this chapter we return to an important conclusion made by Davidson and Seidman in 1974 which still applies undiminished to 1980s research. They noted, concerning the research to mid-1974, "There is no real sense of an effort toward discovery, rather only the application of a conceptually closed paradigm to a new content area" (1974, p. 1009). As we continue our attempts to reduce delinquent behavior, we must also attempt to learn more about the nature of delinquency itself. This takes us into all of the other, nonpsychological areas as well as examining personal characteristics of delinquent youths. There seem to have been no true breakthroughs, insights, or significant new understandings, and it is to be hoped that as we continue to test our old behavioral technology in this field that we will also allow ourselves to make observations that will help us learn more about the nature of delinquency.

7

Family Systems

I. INTRODUCTION

A. *Implications of New Parental Roles*

One of the major developments in behavior therapy with children has been its application in the child's home with the active and often directive participation of parents trained in behavior change methods. As we will discuss later, training parents to treat their own children's psychological difficulties did not begin with modern behavior modification. The basic idea, however, was not well explored or developed until the major interest of behavior modifiers about 15 years ago. Accordingly, we consider parent training to be a behavior development that has grown rapidly over the past decade and gives every indication that it will not only continue to develop, but will generalize so as to define a large part—perhaps most—of the behavioral approach to child-behavior problems.

Reviewing this literature, we discern a number of important trends. As parent training matures and its trends converge, a field is emerging that is vastly different from the behavior modification of the late 1960s, and radically different from the more traditional psychodynamic and client-centered approaches of pre-1965 child treatment. What seems most exciting is that these changes have occurred in so short a time compared with the more than half-century of psychodynamic explorations. In this process of change some of the basic, traditional professional-client roles and relationships have been redefined to the extent that we now have not only a changed field, but a new field. What

*This chapter is a revised version of A. M. Graziano, Parents as behavior therapists. In M. Hersen, R. M. Eisler, and P. M. Miller (eds.), *Progress in behavior modification*, Vol. 4. New York: Academic Press, 1977, pp. 251–299. The contents have been updated and adapted with permission of the editors and publishers.

are these changes? Briefly, the professional has become more of a family consultant and teacher; the parents and other significant people in the child's environment have become active change agents rather than passive recipients of professional services; the child has begun to edge closer to active assumption of control over his or her own life; the expectations of each concerning the roles of others are different from those of the traditional models; the child's home has become a major setting for intervention, largely displacing the artificialities of the professional's office; and the whole model is easily congruent with the contemporary community mental health focus on *prevention* in natural settings.

These and other changes and their implications have radically recast the psychological treatment of children from traditional child psychotherapy to that in which parents are trained to function as the change agents. These changes require new psychological technology, new personnel and training, new directions in research, and even some new constructions of ethical and legal issues. And all these changes have occurred within our current professional generation. There appears to be more breaking with the past here than in other areas of behavioral treatment of children and adults. We maintain that an overriding reality in this area is that it constitutes a new endeavor, owing little to earlier concepts and procedures.

Although there have been some recent attempts to integrate behavioral and psychodynamic models (e.g. Wachtel, 1977), it appears that at least in child-family intervention the two models have little useful overlap beyond the most basic issues shared by all rehabilitation models: humanitarian concerns for the well-being of the client; commitment to systematic and objective research; use of the most effective methods available; alertness to possible unintended negative effects of treatment; active concern for generalization and long-term maintenance of therapeutic gains, and so on. Those issues help to define the entire rehabilitative and psychological therapy enterprise; they constitute the field's commonality and do not discriminate between the major contemporary models.

An astonishing amount of research has been carried out in the relatively short period of the past 10 to 15 years. In concluding one of our recent reviews (Graziano, 1977) we noted that parent behavioral training might prove to be one of the most important developments in the entire child mental health field. On evaluation this model has been shown to be feasible, relatively economical in application, and ethically acceptable. Like other therapy models, however, it has thus far met only the minimum criteria for scientific evaluation, placing it at about the same level of validation as other major, and far older, approaches. But we discern a sense of greater optimism with the behavioral parent training than with the other models. What leads us to this judgment is its commitment to empirical research, particularly aimed at outcome evaluation. Systematic demonstrations of behavior improvements in children and families have been repeatedly achieved, often in severely disrupted families. As with much of the research in child treatment of any psychological model, here too there are serious procedural and design problems including incomplete controls, questionable reliability of measures, frequent doubts concerning the target behavior's psychological or personal importance to the clients, lack of demonstrated generalization, the long-term maintenance of improvements, and so on. As one reads the literature over the past 15 years there is a definite sense of progression; researchers have become increasingly aware of these problems and are addressing them. There seems every indication that this model of parent training is well into a process of testing to its limits, and such recognition of the limits of an applied model—knowing the conditions under which it is or is not feasible, effective or ethical—is one of the necessary conditions for its continued success. The limits are not yet known, but the research commitment leads us to be optimistic in our expectations for its continued development.

One major point of this chapter is that behavioral training of parents defines a new field with many implications for the mental health profession—its political and other extra-scientific issues as well as its concepts and applications. One of the major extra-scientific implications concerns the new role of parents in the treatment of children. It has been frequently noted that mental health services for children are still of doubtful effectiveness, limited availability, and exorbitant cost (e.g. Berlin, 1975; Colby, 1964; Graziano, 1969, 1974; Hersch, 1968; Joint Commission, 1969; Levitt, 1957; Silver, 1963; Smith and Hobbs, 1966). It has been maintained that those pronounced failures of service may be due more to the profession's political constraints than to the limitations of our scientific knowledge or technical skills (Graziano, 1969, 1974, 1975a). Thus, called into question is not only the effectiveness of therapeutic techniques, but also the wisdom and direction of professional politics that seem to have relegated children's services to the lowest professional priorities.

Mental health services are determined by service givers and political decision-makers, that is, the clinical-managerial level of professionals and bureaucrats and elected officials. The problem is not that these people make significant policy decisions, but rather that mental health services consumers do not. In decision making the goals of these professionals are not tempered by an equally weighted consideration of clients' goals. Traditionally the only decision allowed to clients has been to accept services or not. If not, they are free to consult another clinic where the services will be much the same. We believe this has been particularly true of children's services—where parents have been passive, even docile consumers.

It is on that point, the parents' quiet buying of services that they do not fully understand, cannot evaluate, and in which they have little directive input, that the current serious exploration of parent training in behavior therapy may have its greatest impact. Such training may help reduce some of the ill-defined but no less real social distance between professionals and consumers (Graziano, 1969). Behavior therapists are beginning to bring parents into the therapeutic situation, not as passive buyers of service but as active participants and, often, as cotherapists.

In numerous cases, as reviewed by Berkowitz and Graziano (1972), Graziano (1975a), Johnson and Katz (1973), O'Dell (1974), and Tavormina (1974), parents are being taught some measure of heretofore professional skills, maintained in more continual contact with their child's treatment than is traditionally the case, taught to monitor and evaluate the professional's effectiveness, and finally, given a position of effective input in the therapy paradigm.

If this development is cultivated, parents may become active paraprofessionals in child clinic settings, collectively as well as in individual cases, making several contributions, such as providing another source of personnel or direct access to the child's natural environment. Whatever their technical potential, an equally important contribution lies on the policy-making level. As we have noted elsewhere:

> Although professionals are concerned with the welfare of the children under their care, an element of impersonality must invariably creep in: simply, the professional's commitment to the child cannot be as strong as that of the parents.
>
> The bureaucratization and politicizing of mental health programs have fostered that impersonality by rewarding the professional's commitment to his agency (and profession) far more than his commitment to his client. . . . We do not argue that the professional must have the same intensity of emotional commitment as the parents, but clearly a realignment of values is badly needed in the field so that we will value the child's welfare above that of the (agency). The parents' emotional commitment to their children, given weight in the development of programs, provides another element in the decision-making mix that might be of sufficient influence to pull the professional system toward that realignment of values (Graziano, 1974, pp. 281–282).

An inherent, major objective of mental health technology is its own escalation to large-scale, powerful, and significantly effective social services. Otherwise, what is its point? Such escalation of technology, to be consistent with democratic ideas, must be carried out in an overt, publicly observable manner subject to open review, and remain consistent with prevailing public value systems and procedures. Social programming for mental health services is properly a public policy concern.

As argued above, however, most of the public—and most importantly, those portions of the public that are mental health consumers—have been barred from mental health policy making. Training parents in therapeutic skills, an area previously limited to closed-rank professionals, is a concrete development, a very real change in professional procedure that may force a realignment of policy makers by bringing the parents into the therapeutic paradigm. The point to be made here is that such parent training is far more than a technological development. It has long-range implications for professional conduct and policy making. It may have a profound effect upon the field; it cannot be denied that the field needs profound change. We suggest that this seemingly small step by parents, from one side of the professional line to the other, may very well be the most important single development that has thus far occurred in mental health treatment of children. The potential for major change is present and we are willing to label this parent-training focus as a major, historically important development.

B. *Basic Dimensions of Parent-Training Models*

The emergence of parent behavioral training involves at least three major dimensions, each of which contrasts sharply with prevailing child therapy practice. The therapist (1) directly and actively trains *parents* (2) in *behavior therapy* (3) which they are to implement in the child's *natural environment*. Although the integrated totality of this shift in practice and all its implications are new and important, none of its individual components is new.

Instructions in "better parenting" or managing children's problems are certainly not novel. Child-rearing manuals and even advice-giving newspaper columns have been published for years, although it cannot be claimed that they have been particularly systematic, well-grounded, or sharply evaluated. By and large, most of the parenting literature, until very recently, has been popularizations of "common sense" and frequently conflicting "certainties."

Lightner Witmer, beginning about 1896, was probably the first clinician to train nonprofessional staff, including adult patients as trainers, teachers, and, as one reviews their actual work, psychotherapists (see Brotemarkle, 1931; Levine and Levine, 1970; Sarason, 1972; Sarason, Levine, Goldenberg, Cherlin, and Bennett, 1966). It is not clear, however, if Witmer trained parents to work with their own children, as he trained so many others.

Freud has been credited with the first use of a parent as a psychoanalytic agent. In the case of "Little Hans," Freud's only child analysand, the child's father was supervised by Freud and served as the analytic agent (Freud, 1909). Kubie (1937) reported treatment of a child's phobia, also using the father as psychoanalytic agent. Other psychoanalysts included mothers as observers in their children's sessions (e.g. B. Bornstein, 1935; S. Bornstein, 1935; Burlingham, 1935; Elkisch, 1935; Kolansky, 1960; Schwarz, 1950) and have also used mothers as active therapeutic agents in the home (e.g. Furman, 1957; Gero-Heymann, 1955; Rangell, 1952; Ruben and Thomas, 1947).

Client-centered counseling approaches have also been used to treat children with their parents as therapeutic agents (e.g. Baruch, 1949; Fuchs, 1957; Guerney, 1969; Moustakas, 1959; Pechey, 1955). Fuchs (1957), for example, was supervised by her father, Carl Rogers, and successfully treated her infant daughter's serious constipation. Many variations of family therapy have also involved parents directly and actively (Jackson, 1968; Levine, 1964; Love, 1966; MacGregor, Ritchie, Serrano, and Shuster, 1964; Minuchin, 1965).

Parent discussion groups dealing with child behavior problems have been reported by Davis (1947), MacNamara (1963), and Munro (1952), but although it was believed that parent discussion groups were helpful for the children, none of these papers reported substantial data.

The articles cited above were case studies in which only descriptive clinical discussions were presented. Nevertheless, it is clear that long before the reemergence of behavior therapy in the 1960s many professionals of different therapeutic models were well aware of the value of parents' direct and active involvement in their children's therapy. Despite these early clinical excursions, most child treatment has continued to routinely exclude parents from direct involvement in anything other than mandatory collateral treatment for themselves and, of course, paying the bills. The newly accelerated movement toward parent behavioral training in active therapeutic responsibility is in very sharp contrast with the norms of current practice.

Likewise, behavior therapy (the second important major dimension of parent training noted above) is only apparently new. Although generally perceived to be a development of the last decade, behavior therapy first clearly emerged in the 1920s. It was soon overshadowed by Freud's successful revival and popularization of the intrapsychic focus of 100 years earlier, a development that has been termed "Romantic Psychiatry" (Graziano, 1975a).

Finally, the current fashion of treating the child in the "natural environment" is often mistakenly perceived as another new development of the 1960s. Aside from some problems of definition (Why is the classroom considered to be any more "natural" than the clinic?), we seem to have ignored Witmer's clinical work with children, in which he trained a variety of nonprofessionals to carry out therapeutic and educational programs with child clients, work that he began more than three-quarters of a century ago. Around 1894 Witmer began to develop a psychoeducational approach to children in complete contrast to the dominant psychiatry which focused on the supposed organic pathology of hospitalized adults. Witmer emphasized the normal, adaptive behavior of the child. He utilized systematic, detailed, and programmatic teaching techniques, and enlisted the aid of significant adults in the child's environment to implement a variety of creative remediation programs. Descriptions of Witmer's work have an up-to-date, 1970s cast, but unfortunately are largely ignored by contemporary clinicians.

Thus, this new clinical strategy is actually the current coalescing of at least three old dimensions. The importance of this clinical development lies not in the "newness" or originality of its major concepts but in the contrast of this parent behavior training approach against the background of clinical practice. The contrast exists not only in one respect but in each of its major underlying conceptual dimensions. It is this contrast, this marked difference from prevailing approaches, that provides its current importance and promise.

C. *Implicit Criticisms of Traditional Child Therapy*

The current explorations in parent behavioral training are attempts to overcome the major limitations of traditional treatment. Traditional therapy occupies only a small portion of the child's life and possibly has only incidental relation to it (Graziano, 1971). The therapist's observations of parent–child interactions or of the problem behavior are grossly limited (Hawkins, Peterson, Schweid, and Bijou, 1966). As summarized by Berkowitz and Graziano (1972):

> The therapist's data, then, are usually limited to his one-hour, weekly cross-sectional slice of the total reality of the young client's life, and to the retrospective and often unreliable reports of parents not trained in (direct) behavioral observation. Further . . . the therapist rarely makes useful, practical suggestions, (believing) this to be of less importance than psychodynamic material and, not knowing relevant environmental details, his suggestions may be so technical or general that parents, teachers, and even other therapists are unable to translate them into specific behavior. Some parents, overwhelmed and unable to cope with the demands of a disturbing child receive little practical guidance from the therapist and find no ebbing of their feelings of helplessness, rage, and literal hate (Holland, 1969; Patterson, McNeal, Hawkins and Phelps, 1967). . . . Such intense parental feelings may occasion significant further disorganization in the family's life. Thus, the direct and practical coping with the everyday realities of the disorganized family situation may be an important therapeutic need currently unmet by psychodynamic therapists who deal with inferences and not behavior (p. 298).

The parent behavior training approaches focus largely on overt problems within the family system and assume that a child's maladaptive behavior has been acquired in his natural (i.e., family) environment and can best be changed and the changes best maintained by modifying that environment.

Direct parent involvement in child treatment is not new or limited to behavioral models. As noted above, psychodynamic and client-centered therapists have explored the area. With the reemergence of behavior modification in the early 1960s and its more pronounced focus on an *action* orientation highly sensitive to environmental as well as personal behavior details, both the behavioral model and more practical strategies became available. As a result, training parents as therapists has become far more feasible than before.

In summary, training parents as active agents in their own children's treatment has been explored for many years by therapists from various theoretical orientations. The reemergence of behavior therapy in the late 1950s and 1960s added considerable impetus; the vast majority of the literature has emerged in the past decade as parent behavioral training. This constitutes a true clinical innovation with important implications not only for the techniques of child therapy, but also for ethical issues, professional political issues, and for public health policy making. Seriously utilizing parents as cooperative change agents and training them in therapeutic skills may be the single most important development in the child therapy field.

II. REVIEW OF THE LITERATURE TO 1981

A. *Overview*

Having introduced the area and discussed nontechnical issues, we will now consider major technical and methodological issues. Earlier reviews may be found in Berkowitz and Graziano (1972), Johnson and Katz (1973); O'Dell (1974); and Tavormina (1974).

Two of the earliest descriptions of parental involvement in a child's behavior therapy were presented by Weber (1936) and Williams (1959). Weber successfully treated a 19-month-old girl with a strong fear of her shadow. In what would now be described as a contact desensitization procedure, Weber (1936) cast shadows with a doll and other familiar objects while the child was gradually moved from the reassurance of her father's lap to the floor. Williams (1959) instructed parents in simple extinction of their 21-month-old son's crying. Crying behavior was successfully eliminated in 19 daily extinction trials and no further problems were reported in a two-year follow-up.

Most of the parent-training literature has been published since 1965, with the field showing a marked increase in both publication volume and methodological sophistication. As reviewed by Berkowitz and Graziano (1972), parent training approaches have been applied in considerable variety to virtually all child behavior problems. Parents have been trained individually and in groups, through lectures, assigned readings, programmed materials, group discussions, modeling, and direct coaching. The children involved have been mostly boys. In most papers (1) mothers and not fathers were the primary objects of training, bearing the major responsibility for implementing the home programs; (2) training consisted primarily of operant approaches to contingency management (except for the direct treatment of enuresis, techniques based on respondent paradigms were reported in but a few papers); (3) home programs have been aimed mostly at reduction of maladaptive surplus such as aggressive and hyperactive behavior.

Respondent-based models are seldom used in parent training, except for the treatment of enuresis, using Mowrer (1938) type conditioning devices. Graziano (1974) used a reciprocal inhibition paradigm based on earlier work (Graziano and Kean, 1968) and described four cases in which mothers were taught to train their psychotic children in muscular relaxation. Clement (1970a,b) discussed two cases in which mothers were instructed in a combination of operant and respondent approaches.

Many behavioral strategies have been developed in clinical settings and, as noted by Brown (1971), have been applied to a wide variety of childhood behavior disorders. The development of parent behavioral training has involved the transfer of many of these clinical strategies from professional to parental control. An abundance of child behavioral treatment strategies for virtually all behavior problems are thus being made available to parents and, as concluded by O'Dell (1974), "There does not appear to be any class of overt child behavior that parents cannot be trained to modify" (p. 421).

In the following pages a number of child problem behavior categories in which parental training has been applied will be summarized. Some of these problems are discussed more completely in other sections of this book, and the reader will be referred to those sections when appropriate.

B. *Problems Involving Somatic Systems*

A chapter (*Somatic Systems*) in this book has been devoted to these issues and for the present section we need only note a few major points.

A traditional and major part of parenting is the responsible care of physically ill children. While a good deal of physical child care knowledge has been disseminated among parents, and many public and private medical care resources exist, little systematic attention has been paid to the psychological and/or behavioral aspects of children's illness causality, treatment, and prevention. In a growing new area reviewed in Chapter 9 we see concerns for the behavioral variables involved in common somatic issues such as stomachaches and nausea, diarrhea, encopresis, enuresis, constipation, anorexia, obesity, nail-biting, thumb-sucking, self-abuse, tics, skin disorders, and many other conditions. Some of the more physically serious, sometimes life-threatening, problems include bronchial asthma, ulcerative colitis, and anorexia nervosa.

It is to be hoped that the growing interest of behavior modifiers in behavioral aspects of children's somatic illnesses will lead to dissemination of knowledge and skills to parents and medical professionals for the more effective prevention and treatment of children's physical illnesses. The reader is referred to Chapter 9, for more complete discussion of these matters.

C. *Problems Grouped in Complex Syndromes*

Many children are referred to clinics because of complex, severely disturbed, or markedly deficient and highly generalized behavior. They are often labeled as retarded, brain-damaged, schizophrenic, or autistic (all labels implying some common behavioral syndrome, characteristics of which are supposedly shared by all members of each category). In these cases, although the clinician's focus may be on discrete behavior, it is seldom limited to a single behavioral category. Unlike, for example, the direct treatment of enuresis in otherwise "normal" children, treatment in the present categories involves multiple and highly generalized surplus and deficit behavior. An underlying physiological base might be assumed by the clinician, but the treatment approaches are, in the main, functional.

In the past 15 years most behavioral treatment of children in these diagnostic categories has been conducted in special settings such as hospitals, homes, day-care facilities, and special schools and clinics. A brief historical review of the development of behavioral training in these diagnostic categories can be found in Graziano (1975a).

Increasingly, parental training for treatment and education of the child at home has been utilized. For many years, predating the advent of behavioral treatment in the early 1960s, workers in mental retardation urged parents to assume active training and educational roles for their children. With the techniques of behavior modification, the implementation of parental responsibility has increased. Denny (1966), for example, suggested 2-week workshops to train parents of retarded children in behavioral approaches. In addition, a number of studies of behavioral training or counseling of parents of retarded children have appeared (e.g. Cone and Sloop, 1971; Galloway and Galloway, 1970; Lasser, 1970; Morrey, 1971; Revill and Blunden, 1979; Seitz and Hoekenga, 1974; Tavormina, 1975; Walder, Cohen, Breiter, Daston, Hirsch, and Liebowitz, 1969).

Tavormina (1975) compared the effectiveness of behavioral and reflective group counseling for parents of retarded children. The multiple-success outcome criteria included parent-attitude scales, behavior problem checklists, direct observation of mother-child interactions in the clinic, target behavior ratings by parents, frequency counts at home, and parents' verbal reports. Tavormina found that behavioral counseling was more effective than reflective counseling, and both treatment groups improved more than nontreatment controls.

A great deal of behavioral programming has been conducted with children labeled psychotic, schizophrenic, or autistic, following the early conditioning attempts by Anthony (1958) and Ferster and DeMyer (1962). Many behavioral programs now exist under a variety of sponsorships such as residential hospital environments (e.g. Lovaas, Koegel, Simmons, and Long, 1973), day-care and school environments (e.g. Graziano, 1974), and classroom settings (e.g. Fischer and Glanville, 1970; Koegel and Rincover, 1974; Rutter and Bartak, 1973).

Throughout this development the importance of home programming has become evident. Numerous investigators included some degree of parent training, particularly in preparation for the child's return home. Virtually all behavioral investigators now accept the importance of parent training and the careful development of posttreatment environments inasmuch as such strategies are routinely applied. Clancy and McBride (1969) clearly emphasize the family system: "Autism can be understood better as a developmental process operating within a social system, the family, (which has) many dimensions and levels of organization, all interrelated and controlled by feedback mechanisms" (p. 233).

Nordquist and Wahler (1973) present a single case study in which the parents of a four-year-old autistic child, whose multiple problem behaviors were of such severity that institutionalization had been repeatedly advised, successfully carried out a home treatment program. Success was reported in developing verbal and nonverbal imitation and in decreasing tantrums, whining, crying, and ritualistic behavior. Although limited because it is a single case study (with no baseline data, no descriptions of parental training or parental changes, and no follow-ups), this paper makes two important points: (1) the treatments for an autistic child were totally carried out by parents at home, and (2) it was noted that "weak reinforcers" at home may have been critical in the child's behavior problems. In our own work with seriously disturbed children over a number of years (Graziano, 1974) we have made the same observation: a major factor in a child's disturbed behavior at home may be the weak reinforcing value of the parents. This observation suggests that possibly a critical variable on which to focus is the systematic development of generalized reinforcing value in the parents. This may be as critical in successful parent-administered programs as the generally emphasized precision of contingency management. Our clinical observation has been that parents' general reinforcing value can be developed relatively quickly through direct assertion of control, such as the confrontations that occur in forcing a time-out contingency on severely disturbed children. These observations are worth empirical testing.

Other investigators who have included family systems as treatment settings for psychotic children include: Wolf, Risley, and Mees (1964); Wetzel, Baker, Roney, and Martin (1966); Wolf, Risley, Johnston, Harris, and Allen (1967); Gardner, Pearson, Bercovici, and Bricker (1968); Risley (1968); Peine (1969); Graziano (1970, 1974); Pinkston and Hebert (1971); Webster, McPherson, Sloman, Evans, and Kuchar (1973); Howlin, Marchant, Rutter, Berger, Hersov, and Yule (1973); Lovaas et al. (1973); and Casey (1978). Two reports (Graziano, 1974; Lovaas et al., 1973) show that, upon leaving their respective structured program, autistic children whose parents had been trained in behavioral management skills maintained their gains while those whose parents had not been trained, or who were discharged to nonbehavioral programs, regressed.

It appears that in severe conditions where the disturbed behavior is powerfully overlearned and thoroughly generalized, a total, 24-hour daily programming may be necessary. Accordingly, training parents for home programming to maintain the gains of special treatment settings is also of critical importance. However, the tentative nature of those conclusions is clearly indicated by the discussions of Browning (1971), Lovaas et al. (1973), and Graziano (1974). Lovaas and Graziano both note the disappointing results with some children despite hundreds of hours of detailed programming. Browning (1971) reported the results of a "total behavior modification program" for five autistic children. A variety of professionals and paraprofessionals carried out intensive individual-child behavioral programming in a residential setting. Family therapy was provided for any parents requesting it, and all parents agreed by contract to be continuously involved in the program to an eventual maximum of 20 hours per week. As the child progressed through the program, parents' home programming responsibility increased to its maximum upon the child's full discharge. Programming was intensive and included hefty parental involvement as therapists. After three years of an intensive behavior modification program that encompassed the entire day of each child, the results were very disappointing. Although improvements were observed, Browning (1971) noted that they were able, "at best . . . to train [the] children to perform as variably tractable, but severely retarded and socially dependent children" (p. 326). Further, the maintenance of gains after discharge would require such intensive, highly structured, individual day-long programming as to make it virtually impossible for parents to implement.

Those three reports discuss complex behavioral programming of several years' duration, and they concur that even with intensive programming the gains are hard-won and often of such small measure as to raise the question of the social worth of such high-cost programs.

The task is no less for trained parents than for trained professionals. Indeed, it is undoubtedly greater. At least at this point it appears that training parents to work with severely behaviorally disturbed children, such as autistic children, promises limited effectiveness for even maximum parental effort. It might be, as suggested by Graziano (1974), that parents' strong emotional commitment to their children can provide a good basis for sustaining great efforts in many cases.

D. *Negativistic, Noncompliant, and Oppositional Behavior*

A large portion of behavioral parent training has focused on the reduction of negativistic, noncompliant, and oppositional behavior. Adults seem more disturbed by children's active oppositional behavior than by more withdrawn or deficit functioning. Children viewed by adults as oppositional are believed to display high rates of extremely disruptive surplus behavior that is aversive and demandingly intrusive in adult lives. Episodes both at home and in school involve repeated, often prolonged direct struggle between child and adult. It is no wonder that so much professional attention has been directed at such behaviors, both by the demands of the parents and by the apparently discrete nature of the behaviors, suggesting, misleadingly, ease in bringing it under control.

Research in this area over the past 20 years has developed to fairly sophisticated levels. Earlier work seems to have been characterized by a focus on managing the noncompliant child, where the child's behavior was clearly the target for change. In the most recent approaches, however, there is understanding of the interactive nature of parent-child conflicts, and the functional analyses and interventions involve changes in the parents' behaviors as well. The interactive family system, including siblings, is considered more in recent interventions.

Most early papers reported single-case studies with a few reporting two or three cases. Beginning in the late 1960s and continuing through the 1970s, researchers have reported more controlled group comparisons. The earlier papers reported on instructing parents, almost exclusively mothers, to implement fairly simple contingencies developed by the therapists. They dealt with issues such as excessive crying (Williams, 1959), hyperactivity and extreme aggressive behavior (Bernal, 1969; Hawkins et al., 1966; Johnson and Brown, 1969; Laviguer,

Peterson, Sheese, and Peterson, 1973; O'Leary, O'Leary, and Becker, 1967; Peine, 1969; Sloan, Johnston, and Bijou, 1967; Russo, 1964), manipulative behavior (Wagner, 1968), and fire-setting (Holland, 1969). A few reports on treatment of fire-setting have continued (e.g. Welsh, 1971; McGrath, Marshall, and Prior, 1979; Stawar, 1976).

A series of programmatic research papers by Hanf (1968, 1969) and Forehand and colleagues (e.g. Forehand, Cheney, and Yoder, 1974; Forehand and King, 1974; Forehand, King, Peed, and Yoder, 1975; Hobbs, Forehand, and Murray, 1978; Humphreys, Forehand, McMahon, and Roberts, 1978; McMahon and Forehand, 1978; Roberts, McMahon, Forehand, and Humphreys, 1978; Flanagan, Adams, and Forehand, 1979; Forehand, Griest, and Wells, 1979) have focused on noncompliant behavior by young children. Noncompliance refers to a child's failure to initiate a response to a parental command or failure to inhibit a number of deviant behaviors such as fighting or screaming. It is a large category of behavior and a fairly common problem. In the more recent research there is more recognition by the experimenters of the parents' active part in having created and maintained the child's noncompliance, although the overall concept still appears to define it in terms of the child's lack or deficit. Forehand is one of the most important researchers in this particular parent-training area.

Roach (1958) points out that aggressive and "out of control" children comprise almost one-third of all referrals by teachers and parents for mental health services. The severely aggressive child is sometimes thought of as experiencing a "passing phase" that he will soon "outgrow." However, follow-up studies (e.g. Morris, 1956; Robins, 1966) indicate that these children do not outgrow aggressive behavior very easily but continue to have adjustment problems including fighting, stealing, and a variety of other aggressive behaviors that often remain severe and deviant into adulthood. Severe aggressive behavior in school-aged children is more than a passing phase or source of irritation for adults. It appears to be indicative of serious adult problems, including criminal behavior.

Attempts to reduce severe aggressive behavior, usually in boys, through parent training have been reported in a number of multiple-case studies (e.g. Patterson, Cobb, and Ray, 1972; Patterson, Ray, and Shaw, 1968; Patterson and Reid, 1973; Wahler, 1969; Wahler, Winkel, Peterson, and Morrison, 1965; Wahler and Fox, 1980). A great deal of important programmatic research has been carried out at the Oregon Social Learning Center by Patterson and colleagues. This group's publications are too numerous to cite here, but some of their most recent work includes a summary of their programs since 1965 (Horne and

Patterson, 1980), evaluations of parent training programs (Patterson, Chamberlain and Reid, 1982), accounts of "coercion processes" in families of aggressive children (Patterson, 1979, 1982), and several individual research papers including a study of the maintenance of family treatment effects (Patterson and Fleischman, 1979).

Wahler and Fox (1980) present a particularly interesting suggestion in their research. They studied four aggressive boys aged five to eight and their families, and successfully applied three interventions aimed at reducing the oppositional, rule-violating, and aggressive behavior observed at baseline evaluation. These interventions involved time-out for undesired behavior and contingent rewards for good solitary play, cooperative social behavior, and television-viewing. The most interesting finding was that rewarded experience in quiet, appropriate, solitary play appeared more effective in reducing undesired behavior than reinforced experience in good social interactions. Although not definitive, this suggests the potential value of training oppositional children in how to maintain quiet playing for short periods.

E. *Delinquent Behaviors*

Behavior modification with juvenile delinquents has been reviewed in Chapter 6; only a brief summary will be presented here.

Juvenile delinquency, the violation of law by minors, involves well over two million yearly arrests in the United States. The number of juvenile violations, as well as the aggressiveness and seriousness of their crimes, continues to grow. Society's responses to the problems of delinquency include legal action, incarceration, physical and psychological punishment, and rehabilitation programs. In all of the years of such programming there is virtually no evidence that any of the methods have reduced the social problem.

Behavior modification approaches to juvenile delinquency have been reported since the early 1960s and there have been some indications of limited success with the new behavioral methods. Several reviews of the work have been published. The earliest were those by Zimberoff (1968) and Stumphauzer (1970), followed by Davidson and Seidman (1974) and by Emery and Marholin (1977). These recent reviews have been brought up to the early 1980s in Chapter 6.

Most of the behavioral research in this area has been carried out in special settings such as schools and correctional institutions, with only a minority of studies centered on community or neighborhood groups (e.g. Fo and O'Donnell, 1974; Schwitzgebel, 1964; 1967, 1969; Schwitzgebel and Kolb, 1964) and families (e.g. Alexander and Parsons, 1973;

Alvord, 1971; Rose, Sundel, DeLange, Corwin, and Palumbo, 1970; Stuart, 1971; Tharp and Wetzel, 1969). According to the reviewers most studies involved strengthening social skills, such as improving educational performance in school and increasing cooperative social behavior in correctional and rehabilitation programs. Although improvements in academic and social behaviors in these special settings are worthwhile goals for delinquent youth, there is little evidence that such improvements have any effect upon reducing delinquent behavior itself. The most important criticism of the research to date is its failure to (1) demonstrate improvements in delinquent behavior per se, and (2) demonstrate long-term effects of its methods. A minority of studies were aimed at the direct modification of illegal or delinquent behaviors, and these included family programs carried out in the homes of the youth.

In Chapter 6 we concluded that behavior modification within family systems appears to be one of the most promising approaches developed with this population. Many of the reports of parent training in this area have been single- or multiple-case studies, many of which involved contracting, a procedure suggested by Sulzer (1962). Considering ways to provide better psychological treatment, Sulzer suggested that a clear, businesslike contract between therapist and client be drawn up in order to explicitly state the "exchange of reciprocal benefits between the two parties" (Ayllon and Skuban, 1973, p. 20). Stuart (1971) used contracting techniques in a case study with a 16-year-old delinquent girl. The contract specified both the responsibilities and privileges of the girl and her parents. Stuart reported compliance by both parties, termination of the court wardship, and ending of the delinquent behaviors. Tharp and Wetzel (1969), in a program involving a larger number of families, provided consultations with the families, helping them to specify contractual agreements among members and to carry out contingency management procedures for specific problem behaviors. The authors found that in some families the relationships had so deteriorated that productive verbal interactions were difficult to bring about. In several cases, in order to initiate treatment plans a formal contract was negotiated, drawn up, and signed by the families and their children. The authors conducted follow-ups and reported maintained reductions of delinquent behavior in several cases. Other successful case studies that utilized family contracting include those by Rose et al. (1970), Alvord (1971), Lysaught and Burchard (1975), Stumphauzer (1976), and Fredericksen, Jenkins, and Carr (1976). While those case studies reported successful results, a larger study involving 102 predelinquents was less encouraging. Stuart, Tripodi, Jayaratne, and Camburn (1976) employed contingency contracting approaches at home and in school as their single approach. Although "soft measures" such as Likert-types scales answered by parents and teachers did yield small but statistically significant differences between experimental and control groups, "harder" criteria including grades and attendance showed no differences. The authors concluded that their single intervention procedure, contingency-contracting, may have been too narrow a base for effective intervention.

One of the most important series of studies in this area has been carried out over a four- to five-year period, and reported in three papers by Alexander and Parsons (1973), Parsons and Alexander (1973), and Klein, Alexander, and Parsons, (1977). Eighty-six families with delinquents were assigned to one of four conditions. Forty-six families were assigned to a "short-term behavioral intervention program," 19 to a client-centered family-group program "representative of treatment in many juvenile centers," 11 to a psychodynamic family-group program that "represented exactly the form of treatment that a significant proportion of teenagers (in the county) receive," and 10 to a no-treatment control condition.

In the behavioral group the investigators applied behavioral tactics within a systems model of family interaction for "systematically extinguishing maladaptive interaction patterns and instituting reciprocity instead" (Alexander and Parsons, 1973, p. 221). They applied contingency contracting, modeling by therapists, social reinforcement, and, in some families, token economies and a training manual (a modification of Patterson and Gullion, 1968). In this behavioral group the integration of behavior modification technology, social learning, theory, and community mental health seems clear.

The behavioral intervention group was the most successful when compared with the discussion groups (verbal interactions in group sessions) on process and outcome measures (recidivism 6 to 18 months later), showing a significantly lower recidivism rate (25%). The client-centered and no-treatment controls were equivalent (47% and 50%) while the psychodynamic group showed a 73% recidivism rate. There were some design limitations such as grossly unequal *N*'s (e.g., 46 families in the behavioral group and 11 in the psychodynamic), the reporting of percentages for such small numbers, and the absence of any attempt to control for the experience and ability of the therapists. Regarding therapists, the critical differences might not have been in the therapy models, but perhaps were accounted for by the experience and skill of the therapists or the amount and quality of supervision.

Overall, despite these limitations, these studies provide evidence that carefully detailed, short-term behavioral intervention with delinquents and their families is more effective than traditional client-centered and psychodynamic treatments. The assignment of subjects to a real therapy program (the psychodynamic treatment already existing in the community rather than a laboratory analog) adds power to the demonstrations.

It is of particular note that in this sequence of studies, the investigators assessed the primary prevention effects of their treatment as measured by effects upon the younger siblings of the "targeted" delinquents—upon primary prevention in terms of reduction of new cases in the population. The siblings of the treated delinquents were followed up and results indicated that intervention for the targeted delinquent youth was associated with significantly less delinquent behavior for the siblings as long as 3½ years later. As concluded by the researchers, the family-systems behavioral interventions appear to have altered family interactions so that other than the targeted delinquent youth benefitted. This research suggests that delinquent behavior per se can be significantly reduced by applying within-family behavioral intervention, that the effects are fairly long-term and seem also to have primary prevention value for younger siblings. As we note in Chapter 6, this appears to us to be among the most encouraging research reported in this area. Replication, with larger groups and with more attention paid to initial differential descriptions of types of delinquent behavior, is recommended. It may be that these three papers provide the major prototypes for future delinquency programs, in those cases where intact family systems are otherwise appropriate for this intervention.

F. *Child Abuse*

In aggressive, illegal parent-child interactions the child is not always the aggressor. Child abuse, as described by Bugelski and Graziano (1980) is a crime of violence against children committed by parents or other adults responsible for the child's welfare. In the United States the problem is severe, reaching extremes in which children are beaten, starved, mutilated, tortured, or murdered by their supposed protectors. Each year about 2000 abused children die, and 60 thousand others are seriously injured (Kempe, 1976). The hapless child, as far as any existing data indicate, is a completely innocent victim of adults who behave in what must be described as an inhumane, debased, and thoroughly vicious manner toward the defenseless child. Although child abuse is a tragic and widespread problem in the United States, psychologists, as

Spinetta and Rigler (1972) pointed out in their review, seem little involved in its solution. Recently some papers have attempted social learning analyses of abusing families (Sandler, VanDercar, and Milhoan, 1978; Crozier and Katz, 1979). Few papers have been published in which legally defined child abusers are the targets for training programs (e.g. Tracy and Clark, 1974; Christopherson, Kuehn, and Grinstead, 1976; Sandler, VanDercar, and Milhoan, 1978; Crozier and Katz, 1979). Sandler et al. (1978) described results of training two unmarried mothers who abused their children. Training was aimed at increasing the parents' rates of approval and of positive physical responses to the children. The training procedures are not clearly described and, because they are uncontrolled pre-post case studies, it is difficult to judge the degree or importance of the reported behavioral changes. The reported improvements did appear to have held up over a five-month follow-up.

Crozier and Katz (1979) applied social learning principles to two child-abusing families, and reported important changes in the parents' behavior. The results of these two case studies are only suggestive, but are important because they investigate a new problem area that is much in need of a great deal of research.

G. *Reducing Children's Fears*

As we have noted in earlier papers (Graziano, 1975c; Graziano, DeGiovanni, and Garcia, 1979) in contrast to the vast amount of professional effort that behavior therapists and researchers have devoted to the fears of adults, children's fears have been largely neglected. Adults seem to minimize the importance of children's fears and to view such fears as a common, expected, transitory, and thus not a particularly serious part of normal development. However, childhood fears may be neither transient nor benign (Graziano, 1975c; Jersild, 1968; Marks and Gelder, 1966; Miller, Barrett, Hampe, and Noble, 1972). In any event ". . . the psychological suffering of a fearful child, even if (the child) spontaneously improves in a few years, is at least as worthy of professional concern as is the suffering of adults . . . and there are good reasons, then, for urging more activity by behavior therapists in the study and alleviation of children's fears" (Graziano, 1975c, p. 248).

In their recent review of research in children's fears (see Chapter 4 of this book), Graziano et al. (1979) concluded that of all the behavioral approaches reported, including variations of modeling, systematic desensitization, contingency management, and cognitive, verbal mediation, (a) variations of modeling have been the most frequently used and reliably effective methods reported in controlled studies of children's fear reduction; (b) the effectiveness of systematic desensitization and contingency management is much in doubt; (c) developmental and cognitive variables seem to have been ignored by most of the research; (d) few studies have been reported in which verbal mediation and self-control strategies have been used; (e) with few exceptions the research included only mildly to moderately fearful children in laboratory settings, offering little information on the reduction of severe and highly disruptive childhood fears occurring in the natural environment. Research to date may thus have little relevance in the clinical treatment of severe childhood fears.

The behavioral problem, like childhood obesity, seems particularly suited for parent-administered treatment at home. Unlike psychotic, retarded, or other seriously disturbed children, those who suffer from a variety of fears may have no other serious problems of communication, affect, or relationships. Thus, the treatment of fearful behavior may be relatively uncomplicated, and well within the possibility of reasonable training and parental supervision. However, as with childhood obesity, there has been little research and clinical investigation into children's fears and, more specifically, into the effectiveness of training parents to treat their own children's fears.

Parents have been involved in treatment of school phobia. In several cases, as reviewed by Hersen (1971), parents were trained to various degrees of responsibility for contingency management (e.g. Ayllon, Smith, and Rogers, 1970; Hersen, 1968, 1970; Kennedy, 1965; Patterson, 1965; Smith and Sharpe, 1970). Kennedy (1965) reports on the rapid treatment of 50 school phobics, in which the parents were given the treatment rationale and were carefully instructed on the necessity for firmness in returning the child to school—by force if necessary—on the first treatment day. Other cases involving the integration of "systems" (i.e. home and parents, school, client) have been discussed by Bolman (1970) and Graziano, Hastrup, and Pearlson (1975). In the latter case study, four major treatment dimensions were integrated: reduction of positive reinforcement for staying at home, graded reintroduction to school, reciprocal inhibition, and cognitive self-control training to maintain the behavioral gains. The parents, particularly the mothers, were involved in the first dimension, carrying out fairly simple contingencies by maintaining scheduling limits at home that had been set up by the therapists.

Parents in these school phobia cases were involved in crucial aspects of the treatments, primarily in carrying out relatively simple management strategies. The greatest common demand on the parents in these cases was to become firm and consistent in maintaining behavioral limits at home. In virtually all cases, this was a change in the parents' behavior, and that change was brought about relatively easily through direct discussions with the therapist. None of these parents were required to master sophisticated knowledge of behavioral treatment. For these reasons, despite the limitations of case reports as evidence, these cases do suggest that this particular childhood fear—school phobia—can be relatively quickly treated by professionally supervised parents applying fairly simple behavioral strategies.

Parents have been peripherally involved in other fear treatment for their children, for example, a bodily-injury phobia (Ollendick and Gruen, 1972) and a young child's fear of her shadow (Weber, 1936). Two cases of greater parental involvement were described by Tasto (1969) in which the parents conducted *in vivo* desensitization trials (following both relaxation training and desensitization hierarchies of the therapist's office) to treat a 4-year-old boy's severe fear of sudden, loud noises. Stableford (1979) reported a case study in which a 3-year-old girl's intense fears of sudden, loud noises were eliminated within 2 months by a deconditioning program carried out at home by her parents. Bentler (1962) described a mother's successful treatment of her child's severe fear of water by exposing the child to increasing amounts of bathwater while the child was held by and comforted the mother and surrounded by highly prized, floating, toys.

As reported in three recent papers (Graziano, Mooney, Huber, and Ignasiak, 1979; Graziano and Mooney, 1980, 1981), a parent-administered home program successfully eliminated children's severe and highly disruptive nighttime fears that had been of long duration (mean duration of 4.9 years). In the two treatment studies a total of 41 families (42 children) were treated. In the second study (Graziano and Mooney, 1980) 33 families were randomly assigned to an immediate- and a delayed-treatment group. The families attended these training meetings. Children practiced and self-monitored nightly self-control exercises at home while parents supervised, monitored, and rewarded their efforts at nightly bravery with praise and bravery tokens. Nightly exercises required about 3 to 5 minutes and consisted of (a) muscle relaxation; (b) imagining pleasant scenes; and (c) reciting "brave" self-statements. After 3 weeks of training the experimental group had significantly less nighttime fear than the control group, as measured by parents' direct nightly observations and recordings of fear behavior and by their retrospective reports at the end of training. The delayed treatment group received the same training and exhibited the same improvement. Follow-up at 2, 16, 12, and 24 months showed maintenance of and steady improvement in nighttime fearless behavior.

These studies demonstrated that parents can eliminate their children's severe fears by using a simple and efficient home-training procedure. They demonstrate also that verbal self-control methods are effective, at least with nighttime fears, and the whole problem can be effectively approached through an intervention that emphasizes direct and specific instructions on a rational level, to children and parents. It appears to the investigators that many—perhaps most—parents of phobic children can be readily instructed to conduct and to monitor such treatment for nighttime fears.

H. *Language and Speech Disorders*

Few papers in the behavioral literature describe parent training to treat children's language disorders. Barron and Graziano (1968) describe training parents in clinical settings to conduct collateral speech training at home for retarded children. An interesting aspect of the paper is the suggestion that parent training (if it accomplished little else) might be valuable in mitigating the negative effects that untutored parents might have had through their embarrassed, concerned, reactions to their children's speech limitations, in addition to their frustrated imposition of highly unrealistic speech demands.

Several single-case studies involving parents in some aspects of speech training have been reported with autistic children (Hewett, 1965; Risley and Wolf, 1966), with a "disturbed" and illiterate child (Mathis, 1971), and with cases of elective mutism (Nolan and Pence, 1970; Wulbert, Nyman, Snow, and Owen, 1973).

Although parents of retarded, autistic, and other speech-impaired children have been urged by clinicians to assist in their children's language development, the skills needed to train language acquisition or even to correct relatively minor speech problems are, at present, both complex and not well-known. Before transferring detailed and complex skills to parents, the effectiveness of behavioral language training for disturbed and retarded children must be established. Beyond training parents in straightforward contingency management to support the increase or improvement of already existing speech in their children, more severe speech disorders such as those found in retarded and autistic children seem beyond the present techniques of parent behavior training. Perhaps at this point the most reasonable use of parents with regard to language and speech development is as ancillary support at home in cases of speech problems where there is no other serious, grossly interfering involvement. These appear to have been the conditions under which Morgan (1976) and Morgan and Lyon (1970) approached a related language problem, markedly poor reading in otherwise normally functioning children. Four cases are described in which the mothers were instructed in structuring, pacing, and contingently reinforcing their children's reading.

Well-designed, controlled, group comparison research is needed to establish the effectiveness of parent training in improving even minor speech problems.

I. *Common Behavior Problems in the Home*

Parent behavior training has thus far been a clinical, therapeutic endeavor, in which the behavior problems have had a clear "pathological" weighting. A few investigators have begun to examine parent training to cope with more common issues at home. Hall et al. (1972) reported four case studies in which mild and commonly occurring behavior problems were treated at home by parents, who recorded baseline observations and applied social and token reinforcement. The target behaviors included wearing an orthodontic device, regularly cleaning up a bedroom, a child's persistent whining and shouting, and a five year old girl's mean time of 3 hours and 10 minutes to dress herself in the morning.

Knight and McKenzie (1974) reported the elimination of bedtime thumb-sucking for three children whose parents made bedtime reading to them contingent on nonthumb-sucking. Daytime thumb-sucking was also eliminated in two of the cases without additional programming. Ross (1975) used time-out from television to reduce thumb-sucking in a nine-year-old boy.

Mother-child conflict, a frequently occurring problem of parent-child interaction, often occurs in public places. Both parent and child seem to be at their worst behavior—the child whining, crying, grabbing, and loudly demanding; the mother exasperated, frustrated, demanding, pleading, bribing, and punishing. In extreme cases both mother and child are evicted from the store by the manager. Barnard, Christophersen, and Wolf (1977) and Clark et al. (1977) discuss contingency management programs for five boys and one girl, aged five to ten years, whose parents had indicated that shopping trips were difficult situations. In both papers parents were trained across multiple baselines in use of token reinforcement and response cost as contingencies for "good shopping" behavior. Distracting and disruptive behavior of the children and positive responses of the parents all improved. One of the interpretations was that the parents had apparently held unstated expectations for their children's behavior, but had never before specified and reinforced them. The programming apparently taught the parents as much as it did the children.

It appears to us that to whatever degree such rational and objective contingent reinforcement techniques can reduce the often sharp conflicts that occur in virtually all homes, they are of social value and are potentially useful, particularly in terms of prevention of more serious problems in otherwise normally functioning homes.

J. *Complexity and Severity of Problems Treated by Parents*

Like the behavior modification literature in general, most of the earlier parental training reports involved mild or highly discrete, single-problem behaviors such as tantrums or enuresis. Beginning in the last half of the 1960s, parent training focused increasingly on more severe and multiple-problem behaviors (e.g. Alexander and Parsons, 1973; Eyeberg and Johnson, 1974; O'Leary, O'Leary, and Becker, 1967; Patterson and Brodsky, 1966; Patterson and Reid, 1973; Peine, 1969; Sloane, Johnston, and Bijou, 1967; Tavormina, 1975; Walder, Cohen, Breiter, Daston, Hirsch, and Leibowitz, 1969; Zeilberger, Sampen, and Sloane, 1968). The research by Tharp and Wetzel and by Alexander and Parsons, for example, included very severe and complex behavior of juvenile delinquents. Hanf (1968, 1969), Bernal (1969), and Tavormina (1975) are among several who have focused on complex mother–child interactions rather than limit their investigations to discrete behavior of children. Tavormina (1975), Forehand and King (1975), and Peed, Roberts, and Forehand (1975) have conducted investigations of attitude and behavior change in *parents* as a result of training. These studies indicate a shift from single-problem, discrete, and relatively simple issues in parent training to more severe and complex behavior problems and more complex social interaction.

III. TRAINING

A. *Selection of Parents for Behavioral Training*

As noted by Berkowitz and Graziano (1972), in virtually all of the parent training reports from 1960 to 1975 the mothers were trained, fathers being involved in only a minority of cases. Holland (1969), for example, instructed both parents with the father being largely responsible for implementing strategies to eliminate his son's fire-setting. In several of the school phobia cases reviewed earlier, fathers were instructed to assume the firm, authority role in returning the child to school. Patterson, Shaw, and Ebner (1969) described a case in which the father was specifically instructed to carry out contingency-management procedures with his son. In an earlier paper, Lindsley (1966) reported training 14 fathers of retarded children in group sessions, and indicated some success with 9. Generally, in the larger and more sophisticated parent-training programs (e.g. Alexander and Parsons, 1973; Patterson, McNeal, Hawkins, and Phelps, 1967; Tharp and Wetzel, 1969), more attention was paid to complex family interactions. Fathers appeared more involved, although only Tharp and Wetzel give much space to discussion of fathers' roles in several cases.

From 1975 to 1980 more papers have reported inclusion of fathers although in some papers the fathers were not active in the programming (e.g. Lavigueur, 1976), their roles were not clearly defined (e.g. Frazier and Schneider, 1975; Karoly and Rosenthal, 1977), or they had no special roles distinctly different from the mothers' (e.g. Johnson, Christensen, and Bellamy, 1976). Many were single-case reports (Bach and Moylan, 1975; Johnson, Whitman, and Barloon-Noble, 1978; Stumphauzer, 1976; Frazier and Schneider, 1975; Bornstein and Hamilton, 1978). Some papers reported on groups of families or on several cases (Phillips, 1975; Johnson et al., 1976; O'Dell, Flynn, and Benlolo, 1977; Martin, 1977; Taplin and Reid, 1977). The latter study, Taplin and Reid (1977), involved 25 families with aggressive boys.

Only one paper, Martin (1977), attempted to compare child-behavior outcomes when the father was included and when only the mother was trained. When compared with the wait-control group, both the father-included and the father-not-included treatment groups showed significantly greater reductions of child-behavior problems at posttreatment. Their brief family intervention was effective in reducing child problem behaviors, and the improvements were maintained over a 6-month follow-up. However, of most interest was Martin's finding of no differences in outcome between the father-included and the father-not-included groups. "It did not seem to matter," Martin summarized, "whether the father was included in the intervention." Thus it seems to be sufficient for one of the parents to assume responsibility for carrying out the programs. Perhaps, as Martin suggests, our selective recall of instances in which untrained fathers may have disrupted the intervention might be responsible for the expectation that including fathers may be important for success in family systems. It would be instructive to compare father-only, father-and-mother, mother-only, and a delayed-treatment control group.

On the whole, however, mothers have received most of the training and have carried out virtually all of the home programming. Our social biases seem reflected in the nearly exclusive focus in each case on the mother as the parent expected to bear most child-rearing responsibility, and now we have added the child-*treatment* responsibility. This may reflect social reality—the father is still the major economic provider, while the mother, whether she remains at home to take care of children or goes out to work, still bears the major child-care responsibilities. This reality, as we are increasingly reminded, is itself partly a product of social biases. Our parent behavioral training may be a new technology, but it is being implemented with full deference to some traditional and increasingly questionable conditions.

Parent behavior-trainers may be omitting crucial factors by not examining father–child interactions, comparing skill levels of fathers with those of mothers, and not routinely utilizing these "other" parents. Further, many studies carry the title, "Parent Training" while, in reality, there is only "mother training" involved.

There is little information on the characteristics of mothers who are trained, and virtually no attempts have been made to relate parent characteristics to outcome. Some investigators have commented upon the differential reponse associated with economic status. For example, Salzinger, Feldman, and Portnoy (1970) and Patterson et al. (1972) have noted difficulty in training low socioeconomic status parents, because of the parents' limited education. Zegiob and Forehand (1978) compared mother-child interaction behavior of lower-and middle-class families. They reported that middle-class mothers were less critical, less directive, and they "played more" with their children than the lower class. On the other hand, Hirsch and Walder (1969) and Mira (1970) found that training success was not related to parents' education or socioeconomic levels. O'Dell (1974) has suggested that in the latter two papers the investigators tended to minimize verbal skills in training and, instead, emphasized more "direct" teaching.

There are few data on the effects of parents' personal adjustment on outcome. Wiltz (1969) and Patterson (1965) excluded from training any parents who appeared psychotic. Bernal (1973) suggested screening out families in which there is sharp marital discord. Tharp and Wetzel (1969) commented on the near impossibility of working with some families where there was extreme conflict or excessive rigidity on one parent's part. In one case, Webster et al. (1973) had to discontinue parent training and family intervention because of the mother's "fragile psychiatric state." It is reasonable to expect that the training task will be more difficult if one or more family members exhibit emotional or behavioral problems.

Wahler (1980a, 1980b) and Wahler, Leske, and Rogers (1979) have developed the concept of the "insular mother" and have suggested its importance in parent training. Studying primarily poverty-level families and mothers without husbands in the home, they described the insular mother as having few satisfying personal contacts with other adults. Wahler suggested that it is not the lack of social contacts per se that appears to have been important in these distressed, one-parent families but, rather, the aversive nature of those contacts that they do have. Briefly, these insular mothers are described as having contacts with other people such as adult relatives and social workers who, they find, are seemingly constant in their criticisms, demands, and advice to the mother to change and to improve whatever she is doing in her life. The insular mother seems to lack a sufficient rate of relaxed, noncritical, positive interactions with friends—experiences that might offset the aversive impact of the other, more demanding experiences. Wahler's research suggests that when such "insular mothers" become part of parent-training programs, the behavior therapist might unwittingly fall into the trap of playing the role of another demanding, criticizing, aversive adult, thus reducing the probability of the parent training's success. Wahler's work suggests the importance of careful pretreatment analysis, not only of the parent-child problem behaviors, but also of parent's characteristics, such as insularity, their pretreatment perceptions of the therapist, and their expectations of what the treatment process will be. In this regard, use of some variation of Day and Reznikoff's (1980) pretreatment instructions about therapy, as will be discussed later in this section, seems an appropriate addition to Wahler's findings.

To date, with the exception of some research as briefly presented above, there has been little systematic study of the relationship between parent characteristics and training success—either training of the parents or the parents's training of the children. The parameters for predicting success in parent training have yet to be identified.

B. *Training Settings and Methods*

As discussed by Walder et al. (1969), the major training settings have been individual consultations, controlled learning environments, and educational groups.

Parent training began as a clinical endeavor as reflected in most papers, particularly the earlier case studies in which training was carried out in individual parent-therapist interactions, much like other therapy settings. The therapist might not see the child at all (e.g. Welsh, 1966) or might visit and observe in the home (e.g. Peed et al., 1975; Zeilberger et al., 1968). In these cases, individual supervision of the parents and a detailed focus on that particular child and family were followed.

More systematic and detailed approaches have developed within laboratorylike controlled learning environments where the parents' behavior is systematically shaped by the therapist, sometimes in predetermined training sequences. Audio communications, one-way vision screens, light and sound signals, and videotaping have all been used (e.g. Bernal, Duryea, Pruett, and Burns, 1968; Johnson and Brown, 1969; Patterson and Brodsky, 1966; Terdal and Buell, 1969; Toepfer, Reuter, and Maurer, 1972; Wahler, 1967). Some investigators have begun by modeling appropriate behaviors for parents and then shaping the parents's imitation of the modeled behavior (Engelm, Knutson, Laughly, and Garlington, 1968; Hewett, 1965; Johnson and Brown, 1969; Wagner and Ora, 1970). A particularly interesting development has been reported by Johnson and Katz (1973). Referring to two unpublished papers (Ora, 1971; Wagner and Ora, 1970), they point out that previously trained parents are obligated, as part of their own training, to serve as trainers for parents newly involved in the program. Parent-to-parent consultation in that controlled learning setting is becoming a major aspect of the program.

Among the early systematic investigations in controlled learning environments were those reported by Hanf (1968, 1969) and Bernal, Delfini, North, and Kreutzer (1974). Hanf (1968, 1969) developed parent-training programs and altered specific interactions between mothers and their noncompliant young children in a controlled learning setting. While each mother interacted with the child, the observing therapist shaped the mother's behavior through a fairly standardized, sequenced, two-stage program. Hanf's research was not limited to single, discrete behaviors but attempted to analyze and modify more generalized mother-child interaction systems. The level of parental involvement was high, and mothers were trained to analyze their own as well as their children's behavior.

Parents have been trained in a variety of other special clinic settings, often equipped with two-way mirrors, electronic audio, and video equipment (e.g. Forehand, King, Peed, and Yoder, 1975; Blechman, Olson, and Hellman, 1976; Gardner, Forehand, and Roberts, 1976; Hobbs, Forehand, and Murray, 1978; Zegiob and Forehand, 1978).

Videotaped presentations have been used successfully in parent training (e.g. Koegel, Glahn, and Nieminen, 1978; O'Dell, Mahoney, Horton, and Turner, 1979; Day and Reznikoff, 1980). The first two studies suggest considerable effectiveness with parents when the tapes showed modeling of the desired behaviors. Koegel reported that use of their modeling tape alone, without the presence of a live teacher, was sufficient to teach four mothers of autistic children how to teach their children to develop new behaviors. Use of videotaped instruction, particularly with the modeling component, thus appears to be a potentially important teaching tool for parent training.

An interesting paper by Day and Reznikoff (1980) described the use of a pretraining videotape designed to prepare parents and children for therapy. Comparing families who had viewed the "preparation" videotape with those who had not, the researchers found that the "prepared" group showed increased "correct expectations" about therapy, and fewer canceled and failed appointments. Clients' pretreatment expectations may be important in therapeutic success, but those expectations are seldom controlled for in either treatment or in research. Day and Reznikoff provide some evidence for the success of their approach that focuses upon and "corrects" those pretreatment expectations.

Day and Reznikoff used their pretreatment videotape in a traditional setting, providing individual and group outpatient psychotherapy. The tapes included scenes of children in expressive play therapy and parents in counseling sessions, expressing their "feelings." Although their intervention was traditional psychodynamic therapy, the concept of pretreatment preparation to control for client expectations applies equally to behavior therapy, including parent-child and family interventions. It is hoped that the procedures developed by Day and Reznikoff will be adapted and studied by behavior therapists.

Little of the earlier training was conducted in the home—it was apparently assumed the proper generalization to the home would occur. There was no reporting of clinical material or specification of training, and no reports of baseline to posttreatment comparisons of child behaviors, reinstatements of pretraining conditions, or follow-ups. Therefore the value of the early training programs such as Hanf's to alter clinical problems outside of the training setting was not demonstrated.

In a prolific series of studies, Forehand and his associates have further investigated Hanf's training program (particularly its generalization value and its effects on the parents) and have begun to meet many of these criticisms (Forehand and King, 1974, 1975; McMahon and

Forehand, 1978; Peed, Roberts, and Forehand, 1975). The latter study (Peed et al., 1975), a controlled group comparison, employed direct behavioral observations in both the clinic and homes, together with parent attitude measures. It was reported that parents' attitudes and mother–child interactions in the clinic improved and that the improved interactions generalized to the homes. These data support the effectiveness of Hanf's programming not only for its immediate effects in the clinic, but also its generalization to the homes and changes in mothers' behaviors and attitudes.

Further studies of the generalization effects of parent training have been carried out. Forehand and his colleagues have studied effects of the assessment procedures used (Forehand and Atkeson, 1977) and effects on untreated siblings (Humphreys, Forehand, McMahon, and Roberts, 1978; Resick, Forehand, and McWhorter, 1976). In Humphreys et al. (1978) eight families (mother and child pairs) participated in a standardized clinic program to modify child noncompliance (e.g. Peed, Roberts, and Forehand, 1977). It was reported that after carrying out the program with regard to the targeted child, each parents' behavior toward an untreated sibling also improved, as did the sibling's noncompliant behavior. Generalization of training, then, was demonstrated by the parent from the targeted child to an untreated sibling. The research did not investigate how long the generalized parent changes were maintained; that is an issue for further research. Another important series of research papers reported generalization of effects to nontreated siblings (Alexander and Parsons, 1973; Parsons and Alexander, 1973; Klein, Alexander, and Parsons, 1977).

Koegel, Glahn, and Nieminen (1978) reported two studies of generalization in training parents to work with their autistic children. Miller and Sloane (1976) studied generalization effects in home settings, on children's verbalizations. Reisinger and Ora (1977) reported two studies of mothers and toddlers in which generalization from clinic training to home behavior was demonstrated. Reisinger, Frangia, and Hoffman (1976) noted less generalization by mothers who reported marital difficulties.

Although generalization of training effects has been found under various training conditions, all researchers agree that predicting and ensuring generalization is a difficult task.

Training parents in groups has ranged from relatively unstructured group discussions to comprehensive and fairly well-structured classes. Effective group training has been reported by Rose (1969), Walder et al. (1969), Peine and Munro (1970), Salzinger et al. (1970), Lindsley (1970),

Mira (1970), Cohen (1970), Hall et al. (1972), and Patterson et al. (1972). More recently, group training has been studied by Dolens, Doster, and Cartelli (1976); Glowgower and Sloop (1976); Karoly and Rosenthal (1977); and O'Dell, Flynn, and Benlolo (1977). The most recent research (Christiansen, Johnson, Phillips, and Glasgow, 1980) reported that group and individual parent training were equally effective, using parent ratings of improved child behavior. The group-training condition, however, was considerably more efficient, requiring less than one-half the professional time the individual-training condition did. More research is needed to assess if group training holds up as reliably more efficient and to identify the critical variables.

Several investigators have combined group and individual training (Engeln et al., 1968; Patterson et al., 1972; Salzinger et al., 1970; Wahler, 1969a). In individual or group settings, a "consultation" or structured learning environment, a variety of training methods are employed. Common to all, of course, is the assumption that parents are able to learn specific behavioral techniques and, when necessary, general behavior therapy concepts. Parents may be observed and coached by the trainer as they work with their children. Radio communication, light and buzzer signals, and videotaping for later review and discussion with parents have been used. Lectures, films, programmed texts, daily and weekly assignments to carry out at home, and detailed discussions of specific cases have provided the content of training sessions. Frequently the trainer has modeled behavior to be taught, such as shaping procedures, so the parents can observe, imitate, and rehearse it under supervision.

Although prescribing systematic operant procedures for application to the children, only a minority of trainers have applied the same procedures to support the parents' behavior. It appears that positive reinforcement is generally assumed to occur during the use of programmed texts, as immediate feedback on each item, and as the child's problem behavior improves. It is also assumed that the trainer will, as a matter of course, provide sufficient verbal reinforcement throughout training. Most parent trainers seem to rely on the assumption that the process of training is inherently reinforcing to the parents.

Some investigators see need for more systematic reinforcement of the parents' behavior, such as reducing clinic fees or returning cash deposits contingent upon parents' attendance or completion of assigned work (e.g. Hirsch and Walder, 1969; Patterson, McNeal, Hawkins, and Phelps, 1967; Peine, 1971; Peine and Munro, 1970; Redd, 1969; Reid and Patterson, 1976; Fleischman, 1979). Walder et al. (1967) and Mira (1970) required completion of assigned work in order to be admitted to the next scheduled meeting with the therapist. Patterson et al. (1969) offered to treat the parents to a steak dinner when the father earned a specified number of points working with his son.

The use of written contracts with parents, specifying the target behaviors and the agreed-upon involvement of parents, has been discussed by Walder et al. (1969), Stuart (1970), and Peine (1971).

Whatever the setting, specific techniques, complexity, or sophistication of the training package, therapists have aimed at teaching parents to specify target behaviors, control conditions, use contingency management and monitor results.

C. *Levels of Parental Involvement*

In each case, a decision must be made concerning the degree of involvement and responsibility that parents will assume. If the parents assumed full responsibility for working with the child, they would not be seeking professional assistance. The parent-therapist relationship involves a shared responsibility, and their respective involvement will depend upon many factors (Graziano, 1971, 1974).

In their review, Berkowitz and Graziano (1972) categorized the literature in terms of increasing task complexity. The studies were arranged along dimensions of (1) the nature and complexity of parental involvement, (2) the level of knowledge and sophistication in learning theory principles required of the parents, and (3) the level of rigor and sophistication of the methodologies employed. They reported a considerable range of parental involvement. At its least complicated level there was minimal and brief technique-oriented involvement, where parents implemented the therapist's instructions in simple contingency management to control discrete and relatively uncomplicated problem behaviors. At the level of greatest parental involvement, parents were taught not only specific strategies but also behavior principles in an attempt to develop greater generalized parenting skills. Parents were instructed to observe and record behavior, to plan, carry out, and monitor sequenced programs, and thus became increasingly independent of the therapists. The programs described by Walder et al. (1969) and Patterson et al. (1969) are examples in which greatest parental involvement was demonstrated. The exploratory parent-to-parent consultation, described by Wagner and Ora (1970) and Ora (1971), seems potentially significant in this regard.

IV. EVALUATION ISSUES

A. *Social Standards*

At minimum, any therapeutic approach must demonstrate that it is feasible, consistent with prevailing moral, ethical, and legal standards, and results in at least some stated client satisfaction. These minimum social standards are necessary but far from sufficient conditions and they have been met by virtually all modern therapy systems. In this regard, parent behavior training fares at least as well as any other approach. Therapists and researchers have amply demonstrated the feasibility of parent behavior training applied to a variety of childhood problems, and many parents report satisfaction with the results. Ethical issues regarding behavior modification in general are currently debated, but these issues do not discriminate among the various therapy systems. Rather, they apply as well to all modern therapy (London, 1964).

Parent behavior training has joined the variety of other face-valid clinical approaches and, at this level of evaluation, parent behavior training appears to be at least equal to any other approach.

B. *Research Standards*

Feasibility, ethical consistency, and apparent client satisfaction are the very least to be expected of any therapy approach. When more demanding criteria of effectiveness are applied, parent behavior training shows mixed results, but considerable promise. The available evidence suggests that continued, expanded research is well justified.

The major methodological issues involved in behavior therapy research (e.g. Baer, Wolf, and Risley, 1968; Paul, 1969) and those specific to parent training (Johnson and Katz, 1973; O'Dell, 1974) have been frequently discussed elsewhere. Basically, the criteria demand clear, replicable demonstration of control over selected variables. Generally, in parent-training research, control has been adequately demonstrated over only a limited portion of the important variables—for example over children's targeted behavior—while other important variables remain unexplored. Thus, there has been reasonably good demonstration that certain problem behaviors have improved after parent training, but much is yet to be done to determine reliability of measurements, replication of results, generalization and maintenance of improved behavior, parent characteristics, changes in parent behavior, and clear specification of the antecedent operations (e.g. parent-training procedures and child-therapy manipulations) in order to determine if they are, indeed, responsible for the observed improvements.

Those issues seem to cluster around several main factors: (1) assessment of change, (2) replicability, and (3) relative effectiveness.

1. Assessment of Change

A modern psychotherapeutic approach must at least demonstrate that (see Paul, 1969, p. 41): (a) The client's distressing problems have changed significantly in the desired direction. (b) New problems have not been created (see Graziano and Fink's (1973) discussion of negative second-order effects of treatment). (c) The improved behaviors have generalized and become stable outside the treatment settings. (d) The improved behaviors have been maintained over a substantial time period.

These are the minimum level criteria for therapy validation. Necessary to these criteria is the clear specification of target behaviors and their reliable measurement at least at pre- and posttreatment and at follow-up.

Overall, parent behavior trainers have done quite well in specifying target child behaviors, thus establishing a good basis for the needed assessment of change. This is particularly true with discrete problems such as enuresis (e.g. DeLeon and Mandell, 1966; Lovibond, 1964), self-injury (Allen and Harris, 1966), and thumb-sucking (Knight and McKenzie, 1974). Their discreteness minimizes problems of definition, quantification, reliability, and assessment of generalization and maintenance.

Thus, with many discrete problems, parent training has met this minimum level of validation fairly well, showing good specificity of problem behaviors, demonstrating change, some generalization and maintenance over quite long periods. In the enuresis literature, for example, follow-ups for as long as three years (Loviband, 1964) and four years (DeLeon and Sacks, 1972) have been reported in fairly large group studies, and six years (Graziano, 1974) in a case study.

Specificity of problem behavior has been generally good and the problems of obtaining reliability may be less in behavior modification than in other approaches because of behavioral specificity. However, no matter how clearly the target behavior might be defined, measurement reliability is also needed and, although often reported, has not been consistently demonstrated (O'Dell, 1974). Johnson and Katz (1973), for example, noted that slightly less than one-third of the parent-training studies they reviewed had reported reliability estimates. When reported, reliability estimates usually entail calculating the percentage of agreement, often exceeding 90% between two or more trained, independent observers. Thus, one continuing problem involves the periodic retraining of observers to prevent reliability from drifting downward. Stability of parent observations over time or agreement between parent and professional observations has not been sufficiently studied. Likewise, there has been little investigation of agreement between parent and child observations. Grace (1975) is an exception and reports high parent-child agreement.

Overall, the parent trainers can be commended for their specificity in defining target behaviors, but can also be rightly criticized for not routinely reporting reliability data on their behavioral observations. It is clear that reliability estimates can be easily obtained and there should be no great difficulties involved in including reliability measures routinely in future studies, even in case studies and single-subject designs.

The specificity of target behaviors and the existence of easily applied reliability measures provide an excellent base for subsequent demonstrations of effectiveness. Pre- and postmeasures of behavior, showing improvements, are common in this literature. What has been demonstrated thus far is that many problem behaviors of children have, indeed, been improved through parent behavior training.

However, the remaining criteria at this minimum level of research validation have been less completely met. Are the observed changes significant in a psychological or personal sense? Have they been achieved without creating new problems? Do they generalize beyond the training setting? Are they durable?

Psychological significance and avoidance of unintended negative effects are difficult to assess and, by and large, have not been adequately dealt with by any current therapeutic model. In psychotherapy research, "significance" has been defined in statistical terms and, when demonstrated, has been equated with clinical effectiveness. Lick (1973) and Lick and Unger (1975) have pointed out that, although an experimental manipulation in a factorial design may be significantly more effective according to statistical criteria, it is not necessarily adequate in accomplishing its clinical goal. Those authors argue that the "discovery" or "exploratory" phase of research (Miller, 1972) has been insufficiently developed and requires greater attention from psychotherapy researchers, while the ". . . literature is filled with studies employing multiple control groups and reporting very weak (but statistically significant) treatment effects" (Lick, 1973, p. 34). Parent behavioral training is still largely in this exploratory or discovery phase; it might be valuable for it to remain there for some time. However, there is need to focus on the development of parent-training "packages" for relatively homogeneous subject populations. More importantly, there is the need to show that behavioral changes are both of large magnitude and of clinical significance before moving on to more sophisticated validation of what might be personally unimportant effects. Parent-training packages dealing with enuresis provide examples of large and clinically important changes. But, as discussed by Berkowitz and Graziano (1972), there are still numerous problems involved in clearly specifying the precise variables involved in the treatments.

Negative, second-order, or unintended effects of psychotherapy must also be guarded against, but therapists and researchers seem not to have paid sufficient attention to this issue (Graziano and Fink, 1973). In behavior therapy, "symptom substitution" as a direct result of behavioral treatment does not routinely occur and, until it is demonstrated, is not a serious issue. However, consistent with the argument by Graziano and Fink, there may be numerous possible negative effects of intervening in the complicated ecology of a family or the relationships between a mother and her child. Papers by Wahler (1969a), Sajwaj, Twardosz, and Burke (1972), and Herbert, Pinkston, Hayden, Sajwaj, Pinkston, Cordua, and Jackson (1973) suggest adverse side effects of behavioral training in several cases. The last-mentioned authors studied six mother-child pairs, training the mothers in contingent use of differential attention to reduce maladaptive behavior in their children. Contrary to previous findings, differential attention did not reduce the maladaptive behavior. In fact, for four of the six children, deviant behavior actually increased in a "substantial and durable manner." More to the point of this present section, the authors reported negative "side effects" for all of the children that included: (1) the emergence of new, deviant behavior that had not been in evidence during the baseline evaluations, and (2) for four children, decreases in the appropriate behavior that had been monitored.

The above study clearly cautions against the possible overgeneralization of even "basic" contingency management in family settings, and the assumption that a therapy enterprise is always benign. Thus, although behavioral change associated with parent training has been demonstrated, we have not yet sufficiently demonstrated that those improvements are either clinically or personally significant, or that they have been brought about without creating new problems. Those issues must be dealt with before we invest more confidence in our parent-training "packages."

This field also lacks consistent data on the generalization of observed improvements and their maintenance over time. On the latter point, as discussed by Johnson and Katz (1973), many studies have no follow-ups, few exceed 8 months, and "most were conducted infrequently, informally, and indirectly" (p. 195). The longest follow-ups, as noted earlier, are reported in studies of enuresis.

Generalization of change can be measured in terms of generalizing new behavior (parent's or child's) from one problem to another or from the training setting to other settings. Research by Bernal et al. (1974), Wahler (1969a), Martin (1974), and Johnson, Bolstad, and Lobitz (1974) strongly cautions against the assumption that disturbed behavior, or improved behavior after behavioral training, necessarily generalizes from one setting to others. Generalization of improved behavior, then, must be empirically demonstrated, and not merely assumed to occur. Patterson et al. (1972) found that neither skills taught to parents nor behavior improvements brought about in children necessarily generalize from one child problem to another. Even the most careful research (e.g. Hanf's parent training in controlled learning environments) does not attempt to evaluate the generalization of either parent or child behavior changes. More recently, however, Forehand and King (1974, 1975) and Peed et al. (1975) reported generalization of improved mother-child interactions from the clinical training setting to the home. Forehand and Atkeson (1977) reviewed the research literature on generalization of treatment effects and they concluded as did Graziano (1977) that few studies had systematically examined procedures to institute treatment generalization. Since 1977 there has been more attention paid to generalization issues but it is still apparent that, overall, generalization of improved parent and child behavior has not yet been consistently established.

A related issue, maintenance of improved behavior, has also not yet been well demonstrated. Some recent studies have included data on maintenance effects. McMahon and Forehand (1978) reported maintenance of family changes over a 6-week follow-up; Patterson and Fleischman (1979) summarized 12-month maintenance findings for 50 of the families with which they worked; Alexander and Parsons (1973), Parsons and Alexander (1973), and Klein, Alexander and Parsons (1977) presented data on 86 families of delinquents, showing maintenance effects as long as 3½ years later. Webster-Stratton (1982) reports maintenance up to a year, while Strain et al. (1982) report maintenance for as long as 3–9 years posttreatment. Maintenance of treatment effects for 1 and 2 years were reported by Graziano and Mooney (1980, 1982), following a 3-week home-training parent-child program to reduce children's nighttime fears. As Patterson and Fleischman (1979) concluded in their review, the data on the persistence of treatment effects are very encouraging, but much more research is needed. We need to investigate the contribution to maintenance of treatment effects of specific parent-training and family treatment techniques and of specific, measured behavior changes in family systems and in individual behavior.

We must conclude that parent behavior training only incompletely meets the criteria at even this minimum level of validation. Desirable and predicted changes in well-specified problem behavior has been repeatedly demonstrated, but reliability of measurement, the personal significance of the changes, their generalization and maintenance, and the lack of negative effects have not yet been well established. At this level the strongest part of the literature is that dealing with highly discrete problems (such as enuresis) where definitional and observational difficulties are minimized. That is no small gain, for ameliorating such problems can be of considerable personal value to the children and their families. It is clear that a great deal of research is still needed at this essentially exploratory, minimum level of validation.

2. Replicability

The minimum criteria proposed above leave many other issues unresolved, issues that cluster mainly around replicability. If uniformly met, those minimum criteria would provide evidence that significant, generalizable, stable behavior changes, without negative side effects, follow various parent-training packages. Those criteria do not help to isolate the variables responsible for the observed changes, do not allow for replicability of the studies, and leave no basis for judging the generalization of the methods to individuals and groups beyond those already studied. Continued research must: (a) specify therapeutic operations both in the professionals' training of the parents and the parents' training of their children, and specify changes in parents' behavior, so as to: (i) demonstrate those operations were responsible for the observed improvements, and (ii) make replications possible. (b) Specify both demographic information and child and parent characteristics, so as to: (i) generalize the approaches to different client groups, and (ii) make predictive statements within client groups, that is, discriminate between and predict successful and unsuccessful clients.

Basic, here, is the clear specifications of training and therapeutic operations of demographic, behavioral, and personal characteristics of parents and children. Without such specificity, the necessary demonstrations of control over dependent variables, replications, and generalizations to other groups cannot be made. Overall, when evaluated in accordance with these criteria, parent behavior training does not fare too well.

Two of the major criticisms by O'Dell (1974) are: (1) the marked lack of specific descriptions of the parent-training procedures used, and (2) the lack of data on parent behavior changes. In addition, there is little information provided on parent characteristics.

Johnson and Katz (1973) noted that about 65 percent of the studies they reviewed presented "clear" descriptions of parent-training operations. Overall, however, despite their clarity, the studies presented global rather than specific and operationalized descriptions. Until parent-training procedures are clearly operationalized, replication of the research will not be possible, leaving a string of only vaguely comparable research.

As we noted earlier, some of the more recent studies have included measures of parent changes. These were relatively minor parts of each study, and some were limited to changes in attitude measures. It is yet to be adequately demonstrated that parents' behavior does change through training, that their new behavior is both generalized and stable over time, and that it is, indeed, responsible for improved child behavior.

In addition to the basic and severe limitation of poor specification of training procedures, design weaknesses further reduce the possibility of replications and demonstrations of control over dependent variables. Each of the three earlier reviews cited throughout this chapter noted that most of the studies have been uncontrolled case reports providing virtually no demonstration of control over dependent variables. Johnson and Katz (1973) concluded that in approximately 64 percent of the studies they reviewed, treatment operations were "hopelessly confounded" with extraneous, uncontrolled variables, precluding the "unambiguous interpretation of results" (p. 195).

Experimental control has been demonstrated in a number of studies (e.g. Hall and Broden, 1967; Hall, Cristler, Cranston, and Tucker, 1970; Wahler, 1969a). These have included single-subject or small-sample, single- or multiple-baseline reversal studies. A general problem in many of these studies is the limitation in generalizing from the experimental to the clinical situation. Further, some studies (e.g. Risley, 1968; Wahler, 1967) have introduced successive, multiple treatments, without return-to-baseline conditions, making it impossible to sort out cumulative from individual treatment effects.

A major problem common to all of the single-subject and small-sample case studies and experiments is their limited sampling, which makes it impossible to draw inferences about populations. As O'Dell (1974) points out, the sampling procedures throughout this literature are weak, often consisting of volunteers or clinic referrals. Systematic, unbiased sampling procedures, adequate sample size, and information concerning demographic characteristics are needed.

3. Relative Effectiveness

If all of these criteria were met, the effectiveness of various specific parent-training procedures with known populations would be well established. However, tests against other criteria would still be necessary to determine the social value of the procedures. If these procedures are effective, what are their costs? Are they any more effective than other currently available therapeutic approaches to children?

Neither of these two issues has been frequently studied but, as reviewed by Johnson and Katz (1973), some estimates are available of the time required to train parents (e.g. Alexander and Parsons, 1973; Herbert and Baer, 1972; Mira, 1970; Patterson et al., 1967; 1969; Tahmisian and McReynolds, 1971; Wahler and Erickson, 1969). Overall, the investment of time in each parent-training case seems surprisingly small, and suggests good efficiency. But as we discussed earlier, with severely disturbed or psychotic children a vast expenditure of professional time is required to bring about even minor gains. The difference suggests that what is required to adequately evaluate efficiency is a careful analysis of the distribution of time over many cases, grouped by problem behavior, and demographic variables. Data are needed for the professional time required to train parents and the parents' time required to train children. Further, the total time must be gauged against the magnitude and personal or clinical significance of the observed behavioral gains, a difficult assessment that requires the comparison of very different classes of events. Finally, an analysis of time required by different therapeutic approaches is needed.

One attempt at economic cost-effective analysis of a parent-implemented mental health program was reported by Hester (1977). The analysis was carried out by a university industrial engineering department, which concluded that the state of Tennessee realized a gain of well over a million dollars over expenditures for the three years of operation that were studied. These gains were largely those brought about by that outpatient's service precluding the necessity of institutionalizing approximately 64 seriously disturbed children, and by the savings from the parents' participation, compared with costs of professional time that would be needed to provide those services. Hester discusses program evaluation in terms of economic costs-benefits, evaluation of specific organizational goals, client objectives, data-based assessment of child progress, and accountability to a consumer-based evaluation committee. Her proposed evaluation system is ambitious and promising, and we would hope to find future discussions of its utility.

Despite such promising beginnings at cost-efficiency evaluation, the data are yet too sparse to permit clear assessment of the efficiency of parent behavior training, and the field is still very far from answering that question. The same holds for its effectiveness relative to other therapeutic approaches, for example, psychodynamic child therapy. Approaches based on different models might be compared directly in factorial designs, or indirectly, against some known standard of "natural" improvement of specific behavior problems. Few investigators have made such comparisons, and when they do, there are often design problems that seriously limit the conclusions.

Walder et al. (1967, 1969) compared behavioral and psychodynamic parent counseling but did not adequately specify training and therapy procedures for behavioral data on children and parents. DeLeon and Mandell (1966) reported that an automated buzzer conditioning device applied by parents with minimal professional supervision or training was superior to professional psychodynamic psychotherapy in treating enuresis. The design problems included grossly unequal group size of the two treatment conditions, uncontrolled parent-child interactions, and failure to specify the psychotherapy procedures, making it difficult to attribute the observed improvements solely to the superiority of the conditioning apparatus.

Papers by Alexander and Parsons (1973), Parsons and Alexander (1973), Tavormina (1975), and Bernal, Klinnert and Schultz (1980) provide more complete, better designed group comparisons but their results, too, are somewhat equivocal. In the latter study, for example, both parent training and the client-centered counseling were specified and controlled by the researchers, and the therapists were specifically trained, a considerable improvement over the earlier research. However, because of problems in obtaining subjects, the no-treatment control group was not randomly assigned, and thus the only reliable comparisons are those between the two treatment conditions. It is not known from this study if either treatment was superior to no treatment. Their major finding was that behaviorally trained parents reported more child improvement and more satisfaction with the outcomes than did the client-centered counseling group. However, behavioral observations made in the home did not support the reported differences, and found no measurable difference in outcome between the two treatment conditions. Further, at two-year follow-up the parental report differences had disappeared. Thus, while parental reports indicated greater effectiveness for behavioral training in comparison with client-centered treatment, the observation data indicated no difference, and the researchers concluded that, when viewed at the two-year follow-up, "behavioral therapy was no more effective than client-centered therapy in reducing child conduct problems" (p. 688, 1980).

Client-centered parent counseling appears to be a fairly common approach in the applied clinical field. It is feasible and appears to be quite effective when evaluated, as reviewed by Tavormina (1974). Data such as presented by Bernal et al. (1980) suggested client-centered parent counseling and parent behavioral training do not differ in outcome effectiveness. Further controlled comparisons of these two approaches appear critical in our continuing efforts to evaluate behavioral parent training.

The data available, with all of their design limitations, tend to support the effectiveness of parent behavioral training over other approaches. However, the differences, as in comparisons with client-centered parent counseling, may be too small to be of practical significance or may be only temporary. As with nearly all other evaluation issues this field is still a long way from clear, unequivocal answers.

V. CONCLUSIONS

Parent-child behavior training as developed over the past two decades may be the single most important development in the child mental health field. Its critical commitment to empirical research has evolved from earlier, uncontrolled case-study demonstrations of behavioral change to more recent, sophisticated and well-controlled investigations. It has done this in an impressively short time, compared with other models. Improvements in child behavior across a wide variety of child problems have been repeatedly demonstrated. The field's continuing commitment to research pushes toward the model's limits and is actively testing beyond demonstrated effectiveness in behavior change. As the research continues, concern is seen with the personal significance of those changes, their maintenance and generalization, comparative effectiveness and cost-efficiency. It may be that no other model of psychological treatment of children's problems has ever been scrutinized so closely or completely as the child-parent behavioral training model is now.

This commitment to research, with its continually growing body of knowledge, tempts us to suggest, albeit with considerable caution, particularly in comparison with client-centered parent counseling, that child-parent behavioral training may become the most appropriate general mode of psychological treatment for children. Of greatest importance are those research attempts to answer the question of specificity: under what conditions (what problem behaviors, family situations, etc.) are which technologies most effective and appropriate? The very prospects for success and continuing research refinements must, however, also carry a strong cautionary admonition: we hope that the field's strong commitment to research will continue to guard against uncritical, overgeneralized, clinical application.

8

Behavioral Interventions in Schools

I. INTRODUCTION

A. *The Child in School*

In Chapter 1, we discussed the reemergence of behavior modification, largely in public schools, during the late 1950s and early 1960s. Its later rapid application outside the schools was to a large degree, triggered by the successful application of operant conditioning principles to the teaching of academic material through programmed learning. Later developments were fed back into the schools and are now applied not only to academic matters, but also to the correction of social and personal "problem" behavior.

Over the past 15 years, it has been demonstrated that contingent reinforcement, such as teacher attention or the use of tokens, is effective in modifying schoolchildren's behavior. The use of rewards in education is a very old idea, but the *systematic*, contingent "awarding of prizes or rewards on a *frequent* basis in the classroom" (O'Leary and Drabman, 1971) is a more recent development.

There is little doubt that systematic application in regular classrooms will bring about significant behavior change. The research, though reasonably good, has probably witnessed a too avid application of behavioral techniques for limited goals without an adequate assessment of the total setting.

Regular classes constitute a special environment, in some ways resembling home, in others a factory or large office. In the child's life school is unique, having its own physical settings, rules, rewards, punishments, and bureaucratic structures, and children are at the very bottom of the decision-making hierarchy. In effect, children are required by law to spend a major portion of their lives within a huge bureaucracy which has, dangling from various points in its structure, innumerable small clusters of children, presided over by adults. Each child's particular teacher and classmates become a mandated social reality—like it or not—for a consecutive 10 months each year.

In each classroom, teachers and children are participant observers of behavior that ranges from the amusing to the bizarre. In their complex daily interactions, teachers and pupils alike function smoothly, often with good humor, enjoyment, and success. They also become bored, upset, lose control, and behave irrationally and disruptively. But only the children are "corrected" for such behavior.

From the early 1960s to the early 1970s behavior modification was largely employed in such "correctional" services, focusing narrowly on interventions to reduce disruptive classroom and to increase on-task behavior. In regard to the latter concept Madsen, Becker, and Thomas (1977) seemed to have spoken for many behavioral researchers by claiming that successful on-task behavior was the functional converse of disruptive behavior. As reviewed by Klein (1979), many researchers used a small variety of on-task measures, such as number of correct answers to some standard academic assignment in a given period of time, as the major and sometimes sole independent measure of intervention success.

Such a limited focus was soon criticized on a number of grounds, including concern for the ethical implications of applying sophisticated behavioral interventions largely to increase the teacher's control in an already rather autocratic setting.

Considering the many criticisms of those goals (e.g. Kanfer, 1973; Silberman, 1970; Winett and Winkler, 1972), behavior modifiers may have in some ways impeded improvements in education. Winett and Winkler found that many recent behavioral studies in schools focused on goals such as reducing disruptive or inappropriate behavior—being out of one's seat, running, talking to peers—and increasing "appropriate behavior"—attending to the teacher, remaining seated, and working quietly.

Behavioral technology appears to have been too frequently used to teach a narrowly defined class of "appropriate" behavior—obedience, docility, and general physical inactivity—none of which appears to be particularly healthy for young children. Ironically, despite their public stance of "innovation" and the continued battles with "traditional" values and approaches, behavior modifiers do not appear to have been significant change agents in the schools. Their use of new technology to support old goals and values is not surprising, since behavior modifiers are in the schools at the invitation of school personnel (principals and teachers) who define, or at least transmit, the goals.

Most critics would argue that the goals must be changed. But to speak of goals in education is to refer to a vast hodgepodge of often conflicting directions, all tied to a variety of special and community interests. Ostensibly, the schools' overriding goal is to teach academic material to children. In fact, society imposes multiple goals on the schools, focusing not only on education (e.g. teaching academic subjects, citizenship, home economics and handyman skills, appropriate sex roles, and other desired social behavior), but on other social functions as well, such as day-care services for the parents and the creating of a vast number of jobs, ranging through administrators, teachers, maintenance crews, architects, building contractors, real estate agents, bus fleet owners, trade union members, security officers, and crossing guards. Schools constitute not only an academic educational system for teaching children, but also have extraordinarily important political, social, and economic functional value—goals and rewards that make competition for control over parts of the vast system a constant and major reality. Though educational goals are paramount, they actually comprise only a small subset of goals within a vast system. Significant changes in educational goals might have little effect on the rest of the system and, indeed, might be nullified by other factors. New technology will be acceptable so long as it does not conflict with the existing goals and values heavily supported by the vast surrounding school system. The essential point made by Winett and Winkler (1972) and by Kanfer (1973) is that the application of behavioral technology has been limited to traditional, too often questionable goals; we have as yet challenged only the teaching methods and not the essential goals.

Behavior modifers are not compelled to maintain a narrow view of behavioral goals for schoolchildren and may be in a particularly good position to help shift the emphasis to other goals. Some questionable educational practices can perhaps be changed through careful functional analyses of *what* is being taught, *how* it is being taught, and *why* it is being taught (Kanfer, 1973).

In addition, the growing behavioral literature on self-control seems to offer particularly promising techniques for training schoolchildren in active self-regulation skills that contrast with their current passive-recipient role. Functional analyses and systematic programming using contingent reinforcement are not limited to teaching factual material or quiet obedience, but can also be used to teach active questioning, creative seeking, and self-regulated learing. We believe that behavior modification can make its most significant contributions to the schools in this direction.

The 1970s saw a growing diversity of research, perhaps partly because of the earlier criticisms. Research has grown beyond the narrow limits of on-task behavior or reduced disruption as major dependent variables (Klein, 1979). Over the last five years, the continued high rate of research output has been concerned with a variety of issues, such as the now almost traditional one of postresponse contingency management, as well as new concerns for the importance of antecedent conditions, peer effects, self-control, and the enhancement of normal child behavior, such as creativity. While a good deal of research is still concerned with reducing classroom disruption, there has been a growing breadth of interest in other issues and procedures.

B. *Reactivity to Classroom Observation*

In many of the studies of classroom behavior researchers have relied on direct observations of children made in the classroom. It is usually assumed that such "natural environment," direct and immediate behavioral observations are valid, reliable, of greater value than more retrospective teachers' ratings or other testing methods, and provide a solid basis for generalization. A central assumption in these in-class observations is that children do not react to the observers or, if they do, soon adapt to the observer's presence and return to preobservation baselines. Considering the many studies using in-class observation, these assumptions have been insufficiently investigated.

Three recent papers have investigated reactivity to in-class observational procedures, two dealing with conduct-problem children (Dubey, Kent, O'Leary, Broderick, and O'Leary, 1977; Weinrott, Garrett, and Todd, 1978), and one focusing on normal children in a regular class (Nelson, Kapust, and Dorsey, 1978). The investigators used similar procedures: in-class observations were made across multiple-baseline conditions and were compared with observations made surreptitiously from behind one-way screens. The three studies report little or no reactivity by students or teachers to the in-class observational procedures. The nonreactivity was found not only in studies limited to observations (Dubey et al., 1977 and Nelson et al., 1978) but also in the behavior-change research where six socially aggressive children were observed and a token reinforcement system implemented to change their classroom behavior (Weinrott et al., 1978). Thus, in-class observation, whether in nonintervention baseline situations or during actual behavior-change interventions, appears to be a nonreactive procedure with these studies supporting in-class observations in both regular and special class settings. Caution, of course, is still needed, as the results of these three studies might not be generalizable to other situations.

Reactivity to in-class observations might be affected by previous social experience (Marsh and Hedley, 1975); by the intrusiveness or status of the observer (e.g. the principal or parent); by knowledge of what behavior is being observed; or by age, with older children perhaps being more sensitive to the observer than younger ones (Nelson et al., 1978). Little data are now available concerning these possibilities. Nonetheless, with caution, in-class observation, taking advantage of the natural setting, appears to be a feasible, nonreactive methodology for generating reliable data on children's behavior.

While some data indicate that children appear little affected by in-class observers, little information exists concerning the effects on teachers. One study by Sattler and Swoope (1976), reported that teachers trained in contingency-management procedures administered significantly more positive reinforcement (tokens) while being observed than when not being observed. It appears that the reactivity of the in-class-observed children may be minimal but the teacher's reactivity might be an important and, as evidenced by the studies to be reported in the remainder of this section, apparently almost always overlooked variable. Clearly, more research is needed.

C. *Manipulating Antecedent Conditions*

A sizable literature now exists on the effective use of contingency-management procedures in classrooms. However, behavior is also controlled by antecedent conditions, and little research has been reported on the systematic manipulation of antecedent conditions to influence academic performance. In the few reported studies, instructions to children have been manipulated as antecedent conditions, while other, potentially effective stimulus conditions seem to have been ignored. Rainwater and Ayllon (1976) point out that research in clinical treatments has employed antecedent stimulus conditions other than instructions—such as the use of a metronome to pace stutterers' speech or to help hyperactive subjects lower blood pressure. They hypothesized that if a timing or pacing device such as a metronome has been effective in decreasing or eliminating behaviors, a similar timing device used as an antecedent stimulus condition might be effectively used to increase schoolchildren's behavior, such as the response rate of academic performance.

Using a timer as the antecedent condition, and math and reading rates as dependent variables, Rainwater and Ayllon found that four low-achieving first graders increased their rates of math and reading performance. No reinforcement contingencies had been used and the increased academic performance appeared to be due to the antecedent timing or pacing device. They concluded, "Perhaps the most valuable conclusion one can draw from this study is that antecedents in the form of a timing device can increase rate of behavior, thus extending the findings of Brady (1971) regarding the behavioral effects of a pacing device. In a classroom this knowledge is extremely valuable. Rather than bringing in costly and difficult-to-implement contingency-management programs, teachers may achieve the same results by introducing a simple antecedent" (p. 677).

As will be seen, virtually all the behavioral interventions in schools utilize postresponse contingency-management procedures. Rainwater and Ayllon's results suggest that researchers would do well to investigate the limits of applicability of preresponse stimulus-control procedures.

The remainder of this chapter will report on major research published from 1975 to mid-1981 in five major sections: increasing academic behavior; decreasing disruptive behavior; special problem behaviors; enhancing normal behavior; self-management.

II. INCREASING ACADEMIC BEHAVIOR

Behavior modification in schools has focused on many target behaviors, primarily in the two large categories of academic achievement and social functioning. The direction of the desired behavioral change has varied with the particular values associated with classes of behavior: interventions are aimed at decreasing disruptive behavior and increasing academic and cooperative social behavior. We will briefly summarize recent interventions that have focused their procedures directly on increasing academic behavior; we will discuss them in three groups according to intervention: performance feedback, vicarious reinforcement, and peer intervention.

A. *Performance Feedback*

Performance feedback to students is a commonly used classroom procedure. Feedback has been provided in various ways including traditional grades and test scores released days, weeks, or even months after the completion of the material; immediate verbal or written feedback by a teacher; tokens; printed comments or instructions in programmed materials; and various right/wrong signals in automated instructional devices. An additional recently investigated method is the public posting of performance feedback. As reviewed briefly by Van Houten and Van Houten (1977) public posting of performance feedback has been systematically used to improve the performance of psychiatric aides, and of swimmers, tutors, and elementary school children (e.g. Van Houten, Hill, and Parsons, 1975; Van Houten, Morrison, Jarvis, and McDonald, 1974).

In a study with a special class of 12 educable, mentally retarded 8- to 12-year-old students, Van Houten and Van Houten (1977) compared public posting of individual performance with public posting of the overall class or "team's" performance. Daily reading performance was measurably increased over baseline by public posting of individual performance. Posted "team" performances further increased reading levels. Peers' comments about classmates' reading also increased with public posting.

In a second experiment the investigators enlisted "confederates" from the special class children to increase their encouraging comments about classmates' reading. Van Houten and Van Houten found that both reading lesson mastery and peer comments increased with increased encouraging comments.

The fairly simple and economical public posting of individual-plus-group-performance feedback plus increased encouraging peer comment were demonstrably effective in improving reading performance for these special-class, educable, mentally retarded children. The researchers suggested that the effectiveness of public posting might be partly due to its effects on increasing peer comments which, in turn, may serve to reinforce and maintain improved reading.

Six children from regular and special education classes displayed a marked tendency to reverse letters and/or numbers, for example, saying "p" for "q"; writing 31 for 13, and so on. Stromer (1975) successfully altered the reversals using specific modeling of correct letter and number usage, with differential experimenter feedback. The feedback included immediate verbal praise for correct usage plus informing the students when reversals occurred. The procedures appeared effective in eliminating reversals for all six children.

In some research, tokens have been used to provide or augment performance feedback. A paper by Rowbury, Baer, and Baer (1976) focused on seven preschool children with marked behavior problems, and variously described as autistic, retarded, emotionally disturbed, or brain-damaged. Because of their severely disruptive behavior some of the children had already been dropped from preschool classes, others threatened with expulsion, and others required to postpone entry to public schools until they were under better control. For the baseline portion of their research, Rowbury et al., designed a token reinforcement system. The children earned tokens by completing specified tasks, such as a puzzle, and the earned tokens could then be used to purchase 5 minutes of free-play time in one of several highly reinforcing play areas. This research utilized what has been termed the "Premack Principle"; behavior of high probability or value—e. g., playing with toys—serves as the effective reinforcer for a lower probability behavior like the completion of some specified preacademic task.

The researchers found that access to play areas, via the earned token, was "an effective reinforcer in establishing and maintaining sustained levels of completion of the preacademic tasks in the work area" (p. 91). The children who had originally displayed seriously disruptive behavior were able to carry out a variety of preacademic tasks. Access to play as a preschool classroom reinforcing system was well demonstrated. The authors concluded that teacher attention, in the form of systematically applied guidance, was an important component of the system. They noted that the combination of teacher guidance and the "token-mediated activity reinforcer" was critical in the children's initial acquisition of the preacademic tasks used in the study.

Rapport and Bostow (1976) also reported success with a similar performance-feedback procedure. With a regular class of third graders access to varied recreational activities was made contingent upon meeting specified academic performance criteria. All 19 of the children improved in the targeted daily tasks, which included writing, copying words, spelling, and dictionary skills.

Tokens can be presented contingently upon occurrence of the specified behavior—immediate positive reinforcement—or as a response-cost procedure in which tokens are subtracted for failure to achieve behavioral criteria. In a study with six elementary school children Hundert (1976) found that token reinforcement, whether as a positive contingency, a response-cost contingency, or as a combination of both, effectively increased attentive behavior and arithmetic performance. The different modes of token systems did not differ from each other in effectiveness. The small number of subjects in Hundert's study leaves the relative effectiveness of the token systems still uncertain but the study suggests, in effect, that tokens are powerful stimuli in each system.

B. *Vicarious Reinforcement*

In any classroom situation the positive reinforcement given by the teacher to one or a few children, whether by verbal praise, public posting, tokens, or other forms of reinforcement, can be readily observed by the other children in the class. What are the effects upon the peer observers of their observations of others being rewarded? Is there, as reported by Bandura (1971) and Kanfer (1965), an effect of vicarious reinforcement? Several researchers have reported that vicarious reinforcement results in the nonreinforced, observing peers' behavior changing in the same direction as that of the directly reinforced child (e.g. Broden, Bruce, Mitchell, Carter, and Hall, 1975; Christy, 1975; Drabman and Lahey, 1974; Kazdin, 1973; Kazdin, Silverman, and Sittler, 1975). In a more recent experiment Kazdin (1977b) again found evidence for the power of vicarious reinforcement in altering the behavior of an observer. However, Kazdin reported that the direction of change in the observer did not necessarily follow that of the reinforced target child. The observing peer's behavior improved when the target child was reinforced for *either* attentive or inattentive behavior.

In an analogous classroom situation, Okovita and Bucher (1976) investigated the effects of the token reinforcement of a preschool child's attending behavior on two nearby peers. From their multiple-baseline design, the results show that (a) the reinforced child's attending is increased during reinforcement conditions but quickly extinguishes during return to baseline observations; (b) initially, the surrounding children's level of attendance increases when the target child is reinforced but after a return to baseline their attending behavior remains at a baseline level. Due to confounds in the design, this latter result lends itself to two explanations. It is possible that the surrounding peers' behavior increased during the initial reinforcement condition because the target child was between them and they had little opportunity to interact with each other, while in the second observation condition, the two surrounding peers were adjacent to each other and better able to interact. However, it is also possible that their initial expectation was that they would be reinforced for attending like the targeted child and when this proved unlikely, their attending behavior dropped out. In any case, it is important to note that in no condition did the reinforcement of the targeted child cause a decrement in surrounding children's attending behavior.

It seems quite clear that children who observe their classmates being rewarded will alter their own behavior, and vicarious reinforcement in the classroom appears to be a real phenomenon. But the details of the functional relationships between the reinforced and the observer child are not clear. The effects of vicarious reinforcement might vary with factors such as the status of the target child, the behavior being reinforced, and the nature of the reinforcement. On the latter point Christy

(1975), for example, reported the effects of vicarious reinforcement to be only transitory, unlike the presumably long-term effects reported by earlier researchers. Christy suggested that the difference in effects might have been due to the different kinds of reinforcement used in her study—tangible rewards—compared with the less specific, less tangible verbal rewards applied in many of the other studies.

Finally, Kazdin (1977b) suggested that what we have termed vicarious reinforcement might not constitute "reinforcement" at all. Rather the effective component might be the operation of stimulus control. The concept here is that the observation by one child of another being rewarded might provide a discriminative stimulus, a cue, to the observing child that his or her own behavior might also be rewarded soon. The observers might then improve or in some way alter their behavior in accordance with the expectation, set by the discriminative stimulus, of possible reinforcement.

As several of the researchers have suggested the systematic use of vicarious reinforcement in the classroom might prove to be an effective set of interventions. The research into possibly important variables such as type of reinforcement, status of the rewarded student, behavior being rewarded, and so on, has yet to be completed.

C. *Peer Tutors*

Having school children tutor their peers is not a new development. For example, it was discussed 50 years ago by Horst (1931) who described a high school peer-tutoring program. More recently a number of papers have reported that children show academic gains from being tutored by other children (e.g. Cloward, 1967; Frager and Stern, 1970; Johnson and Bailey, 1974) or by age-mates (e.g., Harris, Sherman, Henderson, and Harris, 1973; Harris and Sherman, 1973). Gartner, Kohler, and Riessman (1971), as part of their interest in paraprofessional or nontraditional manpower in the human services, reviewed peer-tutoring and maintained that the tutor, as well as those receiving the tutoring, would gain from the experience. Similar suggestions were made concerning this "double effect" of peer-tutoring, by Cloward (1967); Harris et al., (1973); Harris and Sherman (1973); and Stokes and Baer (1976). All suggested that children who tutor will make academic gains, as well as those who receive the tutoring.

Testing that suggestion Dineen, Clark, and Risley (1977) worked with three children, nine to ten years old, in a small class of normal intelligence children, who showed both reading and mathematics deficiencies. The children were put on a rotating schedule in which each child tutored another, was tutored by another, or was not involved in either giving or receiving peer-tutoring. The dependent measure was the acquisition of spelling words. The experimenters found that peer-tutoring was effective in mastering spelling words and, most interestingly, that essentially the same gains occurred when the child functioned as the tutor, as when the child received peer tutoring.

Jason, Ferone, and Soucy (1979) instructed, modeled, and prompted first- to third-grade children in learning "tutoring" skills. The children, grouped into triads, were taught to use prompts, corrective feedback, and other "tutoring" behaviors and to keep score of a fellow group member's responses. Each group would consist of a tutor, a "tutee," and a scorekeeper. These roles would switch every 5 minutes. Sessions were 15 minutes long and centered on curricula of arithmetic and spelling. There were about 25 sessions. Results showed that the children increased their appropriate tutoring behaviors from baseline at the successive introduction of each skill. In general an increase in arithmetic and reading grades and appropriate classroom behavior occurred after treatment. Almost all of the children enjoyed participating in the "tutoring" sessions.

In another special-class application of peer-tutoring, Stokes, Doud, Rowbury, and Baer (1978) demonstrated the effectiveness of having two five-year-old deviant preschoolers teach preacademic skills to each other. In their training sessions the child in the peer tutor role presented stimulus materials and provided consequences for the other child's responses. The children systematically reversed roles and effectively taught each other to correctly identify prepositional relationships in pictures, such as a boy *in* or *out* of a wagon. As with the Strain et al. (1979) paper, discussed earlier in Chapter 2, this study is particularly interesting because of peers' success in teaching disturbed children. It seems clear that even in special-class situations, with children who display serious behavior problems, peer-mediated teaching provides a strategy for potentially successful intervention. In the Stokes et al. paper a further value was demonstrated: the use of peers may have aided in generalization of new skills from the training sessions to other settings where the peer trainer was present. Generalization of new skills is a major concern in behavior modification approaches, and the use of peers as trainers might be of value in many cases. Further research on the limits of peer-mediated training for children with psychological difficulties is clearly indicated.

It is clear that a variety of behavior modification procedures, directly focused upon improved academic functioning, can enhance the educational approaches ordinarily applied in both regular and special classes. These behavioral interventions, primarily incremental in nature, employ various contingent positive reinforcers and are consistent with ordinary class structure, are aimed at standard academic goals, and appear to be fairly easy for teachers to initiate and maintain.

III. DECREASING DISRUPTIVE BEHAVIOR

The decrease of disruptive classroom behavior continues to be a major concern of behavior modifiers. This category includes any school-time behavior noxious to teachers, administrators, or other children. Disruptive behavior creates measurable upset and interference with normal classroom activities, and includes loud voices, "out-of-seat" behavior, interrupting other children or the teacher, failure to follow commands, particularly those pertaining to "comportment," aggressive behavior, talking-out without permission, and so on. In other words, the familiar annoyances that vex the teacher's day.

While it seems obvious that many children exhibit such classroom disruptive behavior, it is interesting to note that the identified disruptor is virtually *always* a child and seldom or *never* a teacher! A major, tacit agreement among school personnel and psychological researchers is that "disruptive behavior" labels the functioning of children only; in the school-researcher's world, only children are disruptive. No studies have investigated the effects upon children of the disruptive teachers, administrators, aides, custodians, and other personnel.

As noted earlier there are serious dangers in focusing our behavioral skills so narrowly upon bringing about "good," decorous or otherwise "nice" behavior as defined by the wishes of any teacher or administrator. At the same time such behavior is what the label denotes: disruptive of classroom functions and children's progress. Decreasing disruptive behavior is therefore a reasonable and potentially helpful goal, whose major dangers appear to lie in the attributions made and the procedures employed by teachers and behavior modifiers, rather than its nature. That is, focusing on children's disruptive behavior invites the attribution of all "cause" for the disruptions to the children or, more likely, to specific individual children. Such attribution might obscure the contributions of the teacher, other personnel, or school conditions, and lead to methods applied only to the children that are so decremental in nature as to be punitive and restrictive, thereby interfering with positive learning. Focusing on reducing children's disruptive behavior may be useful and important, provided that the teachers and behavior modifiers become sensitive to, and take care to avoid, possibly restrictive attributions and procedures that are, in fact, disruptive themselves.

In the past five years researchers appear to have become increasingly aware of these issues and to have attempted more positive approaches to reducing disruptive behavior. We briefly consider recent research on decreasing disruptive behavior through (1) increasing on-task behavior; (2) increasing academic behavior; (3) training or otherwise involving parents; and (4) creating token systems with their heavy reliance on contingent positive reinforcement.

A. *Increasing On-Task Behavior*

In many studies the negative influences of in-class disruptive behavior are assumed to be primarily upon the child's on-task behavior. Measures of on-task or off-task behavior are often taken as indices of effects of disruption or used as a measure of academic behavior (e.g. Aaron and Bostow, 1978; White-Blackburn, Semb, and Semb, 1977). Aaron and Bostow report a strong relationship between on-task behavior and academic productivity. When on-task behavior defined as a percentage of completed academic tasks was contingently rewarded with a free-time condition, the academic performance of three "educably" handicapped children increased markedly. White-Blackburn et al. used a contingency (good behavior) contract that specified good and unacceptable behavior, and associated rewards and penalties. Application of the contingencies increased on-task behavior, improved weekly grades, and decreased disruptive behavior. Similar results of good-behavior contracting were reported by Warner, Miller, and Cohen (1977) and by Marlowe, Madsen, Bowen, Reardon, and Logue (1978). The latter study reports that systematically applied teacher attention, verbal praise of good behavior and of on-task behavior, accompanied by ignoring disruptive behavior—was highly effective. Teacher attention was considered to be more effective than extra-class client-centered or behavioral counseling sessions. Further, the effects of differential teacher attention to desirable behavior were strongly enhanced by the addition of clear token contingencies. The major practical conclusion was that professionals might serve better as consultants concerned with improving the natural classroom environment than as out-of-class counselors or therapists. This notion, central in the Community Mental Health approaches to schools (e.g. Cowan and Zax, 1969; Levine and Graziano, 1981) appears to have been tacitly adopted by many behavior modifiers working in schools.

A paper with similar implications by Switzer, Deal, and Bailey (1977) reports on a second-grade intervention program to reduce stealing by children. The researchers compared two interventions: (1) anti-stealing lectures to the children once weekly with no contingencies or other systematic intervention applied; (2) a daily classroom contingency of free time each morning in which nothing in the class had been stolen and loss of free time if stolen items were not reported or returned. The lecture intervention was noneffective while the classroom contingency management intervention "immediately decreased and eventually eliminated stealing" (p. 271). The immediate effects of the contingencies were striking; there is no doubt that the intervention was very successful. However, as with most behavior modification research, neither long-term maintenance nor generalization were demonstrated.

It should be pointed out, too, that the success of the program depended upon the teacher's daily check on whether items had been stolen, reported, and returned, and on her application of the appropriate contingencies. In other words, the control of stealing was elevated in importance to an issue of daily regular attention and effort by the teachers and all class members.

Stealing, a vexing problem in many schools, was quickly eliminated by a simple intervention that had immediate and significant effects which continued over the approximately 3 months of the study. Long-term effects and generalization to other settings still need to be studied.

The "good behavior game" is a procedure reported by Barrish, Saunders, and Wolf (1969) and subsequently studied by Darch and Thorpe (1977), Medland and Stachnik, (1972), and Fishbein and Wasik (1981). In this procedure a highly disruptive class such as that described by Fishbein and Wasik, is divided into teams and each team awarded points by the teacher for "good behavior." Criteria for good behavior are specified and the children usually have some involvement in helping to define the criteria and to select reinforcers. The winning team is reinforced with some pleasant activity at a designated time during the week, while the losing team must continue usual academic work during that time. In most applications, both teams can earn enough points to reach the criteria of good behavior and, when that occurs, a tie is recorded and both teams are reinforced. The good behavior game seems to be an effective group-oriented contingency-management approach that focuses on the development of positive classroom behavior.

An interesting study with toddlers (18 to 34 months old) in a day-care center was reported by Porterfield, Herbert-Jackson, and Risley (1976). They used what appears to have been a live modeling technique, although they named it "contingent observation," to significantly decrease the disruptive behavior in this group of toddlers. The disruptive behavior appears to have been at about normal levels for children of this age and not at any severe or pathological level. The authors were seeking a "gentle" and humane procedure to teach these very young children how to behave without disruptive and conflicting or aggressive behavior.

Their "contingent observation" procedure was used whenever a child was observed to behave disruptively, such as aggressing against another child or taking a toy from another. The teacher or "caregiver" would verbally correct the child, describe to them the appropriate behavior, move the child to the sidelines of activity, and instruct the child to "sit here and watch how the other children ask for toys they want." After a brief period of usually less than a minute of the child's watching appropriate play, the caregiver would invite the child back, asking, for example, "Do you know how to ask for the toys you want"? When the child indicated he or she did, then they were brought back into the group. If they did not, they were told to "sit here and watch the children until you think you can ask for the toy you want."

Clearly, the procedure includes elements of first interrupting the disruptive behavior, verbal explanations and instructions, a mild time-out, live modeling for observation, and subsequent verbal reinforcement for the appropriate behavior. From the description this sequence was carried out in a "soft" and not a punitive, manner.

Contingent observation was compared with "redirection" in which the disruptive child would be verbally corrected and then redirected to some other activity. For example, the adult might say, "No, don't take toys. Come over here and listen to a story." According to the researchers various forms of redirection are the most commonly used methods in young children's groups, and perhaps in early grade schools, too, to deal with disruptions. Thus their "contingent observation" was being compared to what they believe is the present, typical approach.

The "contingent observation" was far more effective than the redirection procedure in controlling children's disruptive and aggressive behavior. The design of the study does not allow conclusions as to which variables—interruption, observation of live modeling, verbal explanations, time-out, reinforcement for appropriate behavior, or some combination of them—was most responsible for the superiority of the procedure over the commonly used "redirection." The researchers seem to have developed an appropriately gentle, positive way to teach appropriate social behavior to very young children. The patience, support, and careful guidance of the caregiver implicit in this procedure certainly appeal to this writer.

B. *Increasing Academic Behavior*

We begin with a brief consideration of the classroom disruptions attributed to children considered to be "impulsive." In these studies the earlier attribution of some condition of disorder like impulsivity and its concomitant focus on methods to reduce that impulsivity, have at least partly given way to procedures that attempt to focus directly upon improving academic performance while largely ignoring, or not even inferring, the "impulsive" condition.

Impulsivity, a common descriptive label applied to many children with behavioral and learning difficulties in school, suggests that these children's strategies in problem solving are characteristically nonreflective, with careless, rapidly given, frequently incorrect answers. The overall social behavior as well as the academic functioning of many children may also be described as "impulsive." Inferences have been made about "cognitive tempo" and distinctions between children who seem characteristically impulsive and those who appear more reflective. As discussed by Cullinen, Epstein, and Silver (1977), impulsive children seem to perform relatively poorly on cognitive tasks, perceptual skills, discrimination learning, and on academic tasks such as reading and arithmetic. Groups of handicapped children such as those labeled "hyperactive or brain-damaged," are also frequently described as being more impulsive than normal children (Campbell, 1973; Ollendick and Finch, 1973; Hallahan, Kauffman, and Ball, 1973). The academic and behavioral difficulties of such impulsive children have often been studied, and many attempts have been made to modify the children's impulsive behavior. As noted by Cullinen et al., (1977), researchers with impulsive children have focused primarily upon the direct teaching of how to slow down their responding, and taught them careful, slower, responding by punishing errors, modeling careful problem solving, and using self-verbalized problem-solving instructions. In general, these attempts seem to have been somewhat successful in slowing the children's response time and, to some extent, in reducing errors.

In a study of 33 impulsive, learning-disabled boys, 9 to 12 years old, selected from special classes, Cullinen et al. (1977) compared videotaped modeling, with the same modeling plus self-verbalizations of reflective instructions. The modeling tape depicted a boy engaged in careful, reflective problem-solving behavior. Compared with controls, both modeling groups improved their accuracy of response. A 3-week follow-up, however, showed that the improvement had not been maintained. This study adds to the evidence that impulsive problem-solving behavior can be modified, although maintenance of the improved behavior in the child's natural environment, a very common problem in behavior therapy, is still difficult to achieve. What is most interesting about this study is that while the children's accuracy improved, they did not increase response time, suggesting that speed of response may be more resistant to change than accuracy of response. Most importantly the study suggests that programs to modify impulsive functioning might better focus on improving accuracy rather than the more frequent target of slowing down response time.

A reflectivity-impulsivity dimension was proposed by Kagan, Rosman, Day, Albert, and Phillips (1964), who suggested that impulsivity may be a result of the child's high fears of failure on any given task. With later evidence Kagan (1966) revised that position and speculated instead, that the impulsive child may be, through personal experiences, "resigned" to failure. Thus, rather than being overly concerned about making errors, impulsive children might actually be insufficiently concerned about errors. It can be hypothesized, then, that increasing impulsive children's focus on or concern with their errors, might be effective.

That hypothesis was tested by Brent and Routh (1978) with reading-disabled children. The experimenters hypothesized that a response-cost strategy would increase the children's concern about making errors, and thus help improve their reading performance. Response cost has been effectively used in classrooms but Brent and Routh's study appears to be one of the only applications of a response-cost strategy, contingent upon academic accuracy "to improve performance on specific academic tasks such as reading" (p. 213). Studying 30 fourth-grade children severely deficient in reading (1.5 years below grade level) the experimenters compared a no-treatment control condition with a positive reinforcement condition (paying one nickel for each correctly read word) and a response-cost condition (taking away 1 of 40 nickels for each incorrect word). They reported that while positive reinforcement successfully slowed down impulsive reading, it did not help improve accuracy. The response-cost procedure, however, both increased latency and reduced errors. Brent and Routh interpret their findings as providing support for Kagan's (1966) hypothesis that impulsive children are characteristically insufficiently concerned about making errors in academic work.

Although employing different strategies, Cullinen et al. (1977) and Brent and Routh (1978), using a modeling film and response cost, respectively, both focused children's attention on response accuracy rather than attempting to increase response latency, (i.e. "slowing down"). The studies lend support to strategies aimed at directly improving academic performance, rather than attempting to decrease interfering or disruptive behavior.

Additional support for this approach is provided in a paper by

Marholin, Steinman, McInnis, and Heads (1975) in a study of six institutionalized, highly disruptive, conduct-problem children ranging from 11 to 14. This study focused on the effects of the teachers' presence or absence on the children's disruptive and on-task behavior, and on the accuracy of their academic work. The researchers found that the presence of the teacher markedly affected on-task and disruptive behavior but had no effect on academic accuracy. When the teachers were absent, even for short periods of time, class disruption increased markedly. While it is not surprising that school children are more disruptive when their teacher steps out of the room, the most important finding was that during the teacher's absence the level of disruptive behavior varied with the nature of the behavior being reinforced at the time. That is, when reinforcement was contingent upon academic accuracy and rate, rather than being either noncontingent or contingent upon on-task behavior, the disruptions during teacher absence were reduced. The authors suggest that even with children "institutionalized as severe management problems . . . the reinforcement of academic behavior rather than on-task behavior or classroom social behavior" appears to be the most effective approach. The findings lend support to the notion that teachers might find it effective to focus more heavily upon the amount and quality of academic work while paying less attention to various problem behaviors.

Several writers have commented upon the desirability of focusing on improving academic behavior rather than on the reduction of disruptive behavior. Winett and Winkler (1972), as noted earlier, argue that decremental approaches may only serve to underscore the teachers' power to force children to remain quiet, orderly, docile, and obedient, which might not be either appropriate or ultimately beneficial. Ferritor, Buckholdt, Hamblin, and Smith (1972) reported that academic achievement does not necessarily improve when disruptive behavior is successfully reduced. These and other investigators (Marholin et al., 1975) provide a rationale for aiming interventions at increasing academic behavior through positive reinforcement, and then observing if disruptive behavior decreases as a result. At least three studies have supported the suggestion that positive reinforcement of increased academic behavior will result in decreased disruptive behavior (Page and Edwards, 1978; Hundert, Bucher, and Henderson, 1976; and Ayllon and Roberts, 1974).

Ayllon and Roberts (1974), who worked with a highly disruptive fifth-grade class of 38 students provide the most interesting results. Selecting the five most disruptive children as ranked by the teachers, they created a whole-class token economy system designed to increase academic achievement. Tokens were awarded for meeting academic criteria, defined in terms of percentage of correct answers in daily performance sessions. A back-up reinforcement menu was available from which children could select privileges and items for purchase with their earned tokens.

Reinforcement of academic behaviors did significantly improve those behaviors for the five children. Disruptive behavior, not specifically aimed at by the token contingencies, significantly decreased as academic performance was strengthened. Ayllon and Roberts concluded, "A reciprocal relationship may exist between academic performance and disruptive behavior: not the traditionally held 'make them sit still so they will learn,' but, rather, a 'teach them better and they may sit still' relationship" (1974, p. 76).

Over the past five years a number of published studies have focused on the targeted behavior of increased academic performance, in both special and regular class settings. The subjects have ranged from preschoolers through adolescents—retarded, psychotic and normal—and have included those with behavioral problems in addition to academic deficiencies, as well as normal children without behavioral or academic difficulties. In the latter instances behavioral approaches have been used to augment highly desired skills such as improved language and increased creative behavior. Thus, behavioral approaches have not been entirely limited to "problem" behaviors.

In nearly all studies the major intervention approach has been some variation of contingency-management strategies, including public grade posting, frequent progress reports sent home to parents, immediate verbal feedback by teachers, and token reinforcement with response-cost, and various back-up menu items such as free play.

The contingencies have been managed successfully by teachers, aides, parents, and even peers, in mutual tutoring sessions.

Only one study (Rainwater and Ayllon, 1976) explored the systematic use of antecedent stimulus conditions to increase academic performance rather than the more commonly used postresponse contingency management. They found that a timer, used without reinforcing contingencies, was effective. Their paper appears to be among the more interesting and suggests a promising alternative area for researchers.

Another of the more interesting hints provided by recent research is that when there is a choice between reducing interfering behavior or focusing upon increasing desirable behavior, the latter may be the more effective. Thus, with impulsive children we might ignore the rapidity of their response, not attempt to slow it down at all but, rather, concentrate upon improving their response accuracy. With children with behavior problems we might focus on improving the desired academic behavior rather than proceeding along the assumption that we must first bring the disruptive behavior under control. This decision—whether it is desirable to bring disruptive or problematic behavior under control before attempting to increase desired behavior—was seen earlier in Chapter 2.

Overall it appears that a direct focus on improving academic functioning is effective with special as well as normal children, and may have positive covariate effects in reducing undesirable behavior. In effect, the message we begin to hear, not yet listened to by very many is that if we focus on improving positive behaviors, the behavioral system might "automatically" take care of the interfering behaviors. It is a notion well worth exploring.

C. *The Hyperkinetic Syndrome*

Hyperactivity, or the hyperkinetic syndrome, is generally considered to be a behavioral problem with organic bases and is ordinarily included in discussions of neurologically based issues. We depart from that organization for two reasons: first, the diagnosis of hyperactivity and its inferred neurological basis are far from certain; second, the problems of children's overactive behavior are most evident, most troublesome to others, and least tolerated in school. Accordingly most of the behavior modification treatment has been applied in a school setting. Hyperactivity, in large part a school problem, is thus included here as a special case of disruptive behavior. It is not clear to us if what makes these children special cases is some true difference between them and other disruptive children, or only the attributions made by the adults who apply the hyperkinetic label.

Despite difficulties with the diagnostic label there is, at least in the United States, an apparently growing willingness of parents, teachers, pediatricians, and mental health professionals to label children with "hyperkinetic syndrome." The diagnosis is much less frequently used in Europe and England (Shaffer and Greenhill, 1979). The syndrome is thought to include excessive and inappropriate gross motor behavior, short attention span, low frustration tolerance, academic and social difficulties, and aggressive behavior, all of long standing, usually in a child of normal intelligence.

In their excellent review Shaffer and Greenhill (1979) point out four major issues: (1) hyperactivity or the hyperkinetic syndrome has become a commonly diagnosed childhood problem; (2) the major features, as described by Cantwell (1977), are all behavioral, that is, the child is observed to be overactive, inattentive, easily distractible, and shows a marked lability of mood; (3) there is evidence for reasonably good response of hyperactive children to treatment by stimulant medication (Barkley, 1977; Shaffer, 1977; Whalen and Henker, 1976); (4) there is a common belief that the observed hyperactive behavior is caused by organic or neurological problems and, "is associated and indeed synonymous with, so-called minimal brain damage" (Shaffer and Greenhill 1979, p. 61).

To this list we will add a fifth point—one already made—that hyperactivity is almost always diagnosed and treated within the school setting, suggesting that the observed childhood condition may be as much "caused" by school as by organic impairment.

Whalen and Henker (1976) point out that up to 20 percent of the school-aged population are considered hyperactive and, once so labeled are most likely recommended for treatment by "psychostimulant medication, usually methylphenidate (Ritalin) or dextroamphetamine (Dexadrine)" (p. 1113). Despite growing public concern over widespread use of medication to control children's behavior, the research suggests that drug treatment has desirable effects in "slowing down" children in most cases. However, several cautions are in order: first, up to 40% of the children do not improve with treatment; second, many who show behavioral gains do not maintain them after the end of treatment; third, those who improve may suffer negative physiological effects. As reviewed by Barkley (1977) the most frequent temporary negative effects are weight loss, irritability, and abdominal pains. A long-term effect noted on some children is suppressed height and weight. Few clear data have been gathered on negative effects. Fourth, improvements due to drug treatment do not necessarily support the organic or neurological etiology hypothesis, since such improvements are by no means limited to hyperactive children. Fifth, as Whalen and Henker (1976) discuss, there may be serious social and psychological effects upon children who use drugs to control their behavior, effects on their self-concepts and their attributions to personal control over their own functioning. Sprague and Sleator (1977) reported that methylphenidate, while effective in reducing hyperactivity, also interfered with academic performance. These, like the possibility of negative somatic effects of long-term drug use, have not yet been adequately studied.

At first glance hyperactivity appears to be a fairly simple concept: a person behaves in some obviously excessive manner at a much higher rate of gross motor activity than seems appropriate under the circumstances. Hyperactive behavior is not limited to children; adults, from normal through various psychiatric conditions can often be observed to so behave, particularly under stress. Hyperactive adults, however, are not labeled with the "hyperkinetic syndrome." All children, across all psychiatric categories, of all ages and levels of intelligence, display hyperactive behavior.

How much of this represents a normal childhood capacity for thorough involvement in grossly overstated motor activity? Much of the children's normal exuberance is "excessive" in the adult eyes, many of whom find children's boisterousness barely tolerable. Lapouse and Monk (1958), for example, found that more than 50% of the mothers in their survey of the general urban population of Buffalo, New York, thought their sons were "overactive." Similarly Rutter, Tizard, and Whitmore (1970) found a high proportion (one-third) of normal boys in their survey to be described by parents or teachers as "overactive or inattentive." Shaffer and Greenhill (1979) found the base rate of perceived overactive behavior of children in the normal population to be so high as to make "the symptoms of little value for the purposes of diagnoses (or to) discriminate between children with different types of psychiatric disorders" (p. 63).

A good portion of the hyperkinetic syndrome, we submit, is "in the eye of the beholder." We suspect that in adult-supervised or adult-dominated situations such as the schoolroom, dinnertime at home, visits from relatives, and so on, adult tolerance for children's normal activity level is low, indeed. The more the situation is adult constrained, such as with classroom demands to sit still for long periods, then the narrower and more inflexible are those adult limits of tolerance. As adults' tolerance limits shrink, the children's normal activity levels must increasingly conflict with those limits and begin to stand out as clear perceptual figures against the adult-defined ground.

If we assume for the moment that children's motor activity levels are normally distributed within any particular age group, then some children will be located toward the extremes. As the adult's tolerance shrinks toward allowing lower levels of activity then, of course, increasing numbers of children will be identified as "hyperkinetic."

The diagnosis of the hyperkinetic child, then, may be based in the limitations of the particular adult, be it teacher, parent, pediatrician, or psychologist, who defines the proper or normal limits. Accordingly professionals called in to examine, treat, or provide remedial education for a "hyperactive" child should exercise caution before too readily accepting the description and assuming a hyperkinetic disorder. Considering the doubtful validity of the concept and the general unreliability of the diagnosis, each case should be examined to determine the extent to which the label reflects the reality of the child or the intolerance of the adult. This caution is particularly addressed to behavior modifiers who are becoming increasingly involved in the treatment of hyperactivity.

Two other factors seriously compound the problems of improper labeling. First, drug treatment is frequently, perhaps most often, prescribed for a child labeled "hyperkinetic." Public attention has been drawn to cases where, with little diagnostic care, drugs have been prescribed for large proprotions of the children in a school system. In our view such instances of unwarranted general use of behavior-control drugs constitute child abuse, carried out by professionals and commercial interests. Second, the label, hyperkinetic, as uncertain as it is, leads many to make an even more tenuous inference that the child, because of the imposed label, is suffering *minimal brain damage* (MBD). This inference then becomes the probable "cause" of the supposedly hyperactive behavior.

Thus there may be highly doubtful diagnoses based on tentative and unsystematic observations such as are made in school, and causal inferences regarding the presence of an even more nebulous condition, MBD. Once that statement is made, and those initials are indelibly stamped into a child's school records, the nebulous inference takes on the significance of factual reality. The negative impact on the child's school career of being known by teachers as "having" brain damage, "being" hyperactive, and "needing" medication, may be enormous.

Any diagnostic label may obscure individual differences among children so labeled; hyperactivity or hyperkinetic syndrome is no exception. Children so labeled comprise a heterogeneous group, with each child having personal strengths and weaknesses. Although overactivity may be the characteristic most vexing for the teacher, a child may have other problems of much more personal significance: academic deficits, general or specific social-skills deficits, and so on. Rather than viewing hyperactivity as an all encompassing class of behavior diagnostic of MBD and controllable by medication, it is important for the psychologist to conduct a careful functional analysis and to specify skill deficits as well as apparent inappropriate surplus behavior. Such analysis may demonstrate that each child presents a personal combination of skill deficits and, we should add, of strengths. Then, rather than approaching hyperactivity as a generalized surplus to be reduced—as is implicit in the drug-treatment model—we may approach each child positively in terms of developing new or better skills in individually important areas. This ideographic emphasis satisfies a major criterion of work on children's disruptive behavior: a focus on incremental rather than decremental interventions.

Some children's noxiously high rates of motor activity invite a repressive response from adults who attempt to suppress, slowdown or reduce the behavior. These decremental strategies depend upon punishment, extinction, and differential reinforcement of suppressed functioning such as sitting still. Drug treatment, for example, is a powerful decremental procedure for many children.

In 1974 Ayllon and Roberts reported the classic research on the issue of choosing between decremental or incremental strategies with disruptive children (see pages 248–249). Breaking with the standard approach, instead of using strategies to decrease disruptive behavior, they systematically reinforced academic performance. As academic achievement improved, disruptive behavior decreased. Classroom common sense leads most teachers to believe that orderliness and quiet, attentive behavior are prerequisites to academic learning. But Ayllon and Roberts have demonstrated a relationship operating in the other direction. Teaching academics can help the children control motor behavior with improved academic achievement as a bonus.

Ayllon developed these findings further by asking if similar procedures would be effective with children at the disruptive extremes: children regarded as clinically hyperactive who were being controlled by use of drugs. Ayllon, Layman, and Kandel (1975) worked with a girl and two boys, aged eight, nine, and ten. The children, all highly disruptive, were of at least average intelligence, had been diagnosed as chronically hyperactive, and were under drug (Ritalin) treatment.

With the cooperation of the parents, school officials and physicians, the investigators obtained 17 days of baseline measures of hyperactivity and academic performance in arithmetic and reading, all while the children remained on their usual medication.

On the eighteenth day medication was withdrawn and three days (a long weekend) were allowed for the drug's effects to wear off. During the next three schooldays, with the children off medication, measures were again taken of hyperactivity and academic performance.

The reinforcement intervention was carried out while the children remained off drugs. It consisted of six days of systematic reinforcement of arithmetic performance, followed by six days of reinforcement during reading lessons with no attempts made to directly reduce hyperactivity. The measures of academic performance and hyperactive behavior continued during these training phases.

The findings were striking. While on medication, being taught in the usual manner, the children's hyperactivity was high, and their academic achievement was low, nearly to the point of not existing. When Ritalin was withdrawn and the usual teaching methods continued, the children's hyperactivity sharply escalated, doubling or tripling its initial level. Academic performance remained at its previous low level. However, when reinforcement was systematically and contingently applied to arithmetic (six days) and then to reading (six days) not only did academic achievement markedly increase in each academic subject, respectively, but hyperactivity dropped "to a level comparable to the initial period when Ritalin chemically controlled it (Ayllon et al., 1975, p. 142).

These results demonstrate the suppression of hyperactivity by reinforcing academic performance. Further, ". . . the academic gains produced by the behavioral program contrasts dramatically with the lack of academic progress shown by the children under medication" (Ayllon, et al., 1975, p. 143).

Because of its importance Ayllon and his colleagues' work deserves to be quoted at length:

> It usually took only one session for each child to learn that academic performance was associated with reinforcement while hyperactivity was not, suggesting that in the absence of medication these children react to reinforcement as normal children do. The classroom with reinforcement procedures now sets the occasion for academic performance rather than hyperactivity.
>
> The present results suggest that the continued use of Ritalin and possibly other drugs to control hyperactivity may result in compliant but academically incompetent students. Surely the goal of school is not to make children into docile robots either by behavioral techniques or by medication. Rather, the goal should be one of providing children with the social and academic tools required to become successful in their social interactions and competent in their academic performance. Judging from the reactions and comments of both parents and teachers, the goal was achieved during the reinforcement period of the study. The parents were particularly relieved that their children, who had been dependent on Ritalin for years, could now function normally in school without the drug. Similarly, the teacher was excited over the fact that she could now build the social and academic skills of the children because they were more attentive and responsive to her than when they were under medication (Ayllon et al., 1975, pp. 143–144).*

The work of Ayllon and his colleagues is an important and stimulating demonstration. Research on similar methods with larger numbers of children and with measures of generalization and long-term effectiveness (over at least a year) will be of great value.

A number of investigators have continued this focus on incremental strategies with hyperactive or seriously disruptive children. None of these studies made controlled comparisons of their methods with use of medication, as did Ayllon, Layman, and Kandel (1975). Therefore it is not known if these methods are effective alternatives to medication. All were carried out with children free of medication at the time of study.

In 1976, O'Leary, Pelham, Rosenbaum, and Price treated nine children described as hyperactive, while eight others served as controls. The therapist met with parents and teachers to explain and discuss their various roles in the teacher-managed program. Daily goals were specified for each child by the teacher. The teacher rated the child's success in achieving those goals at the day's end. The teacher's daily report was sent home to the parents who rewarded progress toward the goals.

An important point, in keeping with the Ayllon et al. (1975) focus, is that the goals and procedures were all incremental and included academic achievement and positive social behaviors. O'Leary et al. did not focus on the decrement of hyperactive behavior. The treated children improved over the 10-week procedure, as measured by a variety of rating scales. A major problem, however, was that observed improvements were based on the teachers' ratings made before and after they applied the program. A repetition of this study, using independent observers, is in order.

In the studies by O'Leary et al. and Ayllon et al. hyperkinetic behavior was successfully reduced by focusing on two different categories of behavior. O'Leary et al. and several previous investigators assumed that by increasing "attending" behavior and decreasing "nonattending" behavior, hyperactivity would decrease. Ayllon and Roberts (1974) and Ayllon et al. (1975) focused directly on academic skills and observed a decrease in hyperactivity. Both were contingency-management approaches, depending upon continued systematic reinforcement by parents and teachers.

Douglas, Parry, Marton, and Garson (1976) suggest that it may be "unwise to rely solely on operant techniques to train hyperactive children" (p. 390). As we noted above there are no generalization or long-term maintenance data. Douglas et al. (1976) also suggest that a reliance on externally controlled contingency management might create problems for hyperactive children in an argument similar to that presented by Levine and Fasnacht (1979) against the possible problems with token reinforcement procedures. Douglas et al. noted that some of their own observations as well as those of others (Cohen, 1970; Douglas, 1975; Firestone, 1974; Firestone and Douglas, 1975; Friebergs and Douglas, 1969; Parry, 1973) suggest that use of positive reinforcement with hyperactive children "may increase impulsivity and attract their attention away from the task and toward the reinforcement or the reinforcing adult" (Douglas et al., 1976, p. 390). Hyperactive children, they suggest, compared with normal children, appear to respond to external reinforcement in "unique ways," such as showing greater performance disruption than normal children when presented with partial or noncontingent reinforcement. These suggestions of course are open to further testing, which might be valuable for this field.

Given these possible limitations of externally controlled contingency management, Douglas et al. suggest self-control training with focus on "the development of inhibitory control and the teaching of strategies for deploying and sustaining attention" (p. 391).

Douglas et al. trained 18 boys ranging from six to ten years of age who were described as seriously hyperactive. The training program consisted of two sessions weekly for 12 weeks (24 sessions), a total of 12 sessions with parents and 6 with teachers. Children's sessions were focused on cognitive problem-solving skills and verbal self-reinforcement. Specific training, in skills such as careful visual scanning of written material, was included. Experimental-control group comparisons indicated that on several cognitive measures the treated group improved significantly more than controls. On a ten-point hyperactivity rating scale filled out by teachers, the treated children showed a significant pre-post improvement; the controls did not. Direct posttreatment comparison of experimental and control subjects was not carried out.

Cameron and Robinson (1980) and Bornstein and Quevillon (1976), each including only three children, present further evidence for effectiveness of self-control training. Cameron and Robinson found significant improvements in on-task behavior for three children, as well as improved academic performance (math) for two of the three children. There was suggestion that cognitive skills may have generalized to oral reading, an area in which specific training had not been carried out.

Barkley, Copeland, and Sivage (1980) included six hyperactive boys in a self-control training program. "Misbehavior" and "attending to tasks" improved but only during individual seat-work and not during group instruction. Activity level was not improved by the procedure.

While these and other recent studies (e.g. Bugental, Whalen, and Henker, 1977; Camp, Blom, Herbert, and Van Doorninck, 1977; Conners and Wells, 1979) have shown some positive effects of cognitive behavior training for school-age children, only one, Cohen, Sullivan, Minde, Novak, and Helwig (1981), has tested the procedures with pre-school, hyperactive children. The investigators selected 24 children described as hyperactive by parents and teachers and assigned them to three treatment and one no-treatment control groups; Methylphenidate (eight children); cognitive, behavior modification training (six children); combined drug and cognitive training (six children); no-treatment control (four children). The cognitive-training procedure was designed to be "an individualized, total push treatment" program similar to that described by Douglas et al. (1976). It consisted of twice-weekly, 1-hour individual training sessions in which the basic aim was to "teach each child to slow down, to develop a more systematic approach in problem-solving situations, and to evaluate his or her own performance" (p. 46).

Because of the small number of children in each group Cohen et al. presented a descriptive analysis that indicated two interesting findings: (1) there were no treatment-effect differences among medication, cognitive behavior modification, the combined treatments, and no treatment; (2) these preschoolers improved significantly over a year's time, unrelated to any treatment. The researchers concluded that while these treatments appear effective with school-age hyperactive children, they are not effective with preschoolers. Their results add to our need for caution in too readily diagnosing and treating children, particularly preschoolers, as hyperactive. It may be best to leave the supposed hyperactivity alone, and continue to teach the children, undifferentiated from "normals," usual preschool and school-readiness skills, while normal maturational processes occur and help the children over time.

These studies of self-control for hyperactive children are important steps toward further research. However promising they may be, there are still questions to be answered. First, their superiority in improving academic performance over contingency management, as employed by Ayllon, Layman, and Kandel (1975), has not been demonstrated or even tested. Thus there is no evidence that the self-control procedures avoid the problems suggested—but not demonstrated—as possibly occurring with externally controlled contingency management. Further, two of the most important reasons for moving to a self-control training procedure are the expected potential for skills generalization and long-term self-maintenance. However, neither advantage has been well demonstrated in these self-control studies. Only Cameron and Robinson's data suggest some classroom-appropriate generalization, and that was with only three children. While all these studies have shown changes associated with self-control training, none has demonstrated long-term effectiveness.

Thus self-control strategies seem a reasonable development, needing much more research, as do the more direct contingency-management procedures, particularly in generalization and maintenance effects. Because direct comparisons have not been made, no data indicate the superiority of the more complex self-control procedures, over relatively uncomplicated and more direct contingency-management approach used by Ayllon et al. (1975), to strengthen academic skills. What seems clear is that incremental-training approaches do seem effective with "hyperkinetic" children in school. Whether the improvements are of personal significance, whether they generalize in any important manner or are maintained over long periods of time, or whether the addition of self-control and cognitive training are significant additions, are all subjects for further research. We suspect that the next five years will provide some answers.

In summary, there may be too great a physical and psychological cost to children, particularly preschoolers, to warrant our continued use of medication in any but those cases most resistent to alternative treatments. The act of labeling children as "hyperkinetic" and inferring the existence of an undefinable "MBD" causal condition may also generate more negative than positive effects upon the children. Incremental psychological and educational approaches are being developed. Aimed at building up identified skills in specific deficit areas rather than reducing the generalized hyperactivity as decremental approaches have, these methods may prove to be effective alternatives to medication. The specification of deficits, such as in math or reading, may prove to be more useful to the child than the diagnostic label of "hyperkinetic syndrome."

One more point should be made. Incremental approaches depend partly upon increased stimulation, rewarding the child with more, for doing more rather than less. Some researchers and teachers would object because hyperactive children are traditionally thought of as being "overaroused" and are thus thought to be in need of reduced stimulation and reduced activity. Prevailing educational practice still recommends reducing classroom stimulation to decrease hyperactivity and increase attention to tasks, thus allowing academic learning to proceed. Recently, however, some data have suggested that understimulation rather than overstimulation may be a major factor in generating hyperactive behavior (Zentall and Zentall, 1976; Zentall, 1980). These findings support an underarousal rather than overarousal theory of hyperactivity. This conception is consistent with incremental approaches, such as those of Ayllon et al. as well as with making more academic demands.

All these issues surround the hyperkinetic syndrome: underarousal or overarousal models, incremental or decremental strategies, contingency-management and self-control approaches, medication versus psychological training, and the reliability and validity of the hyperkinetic diagnosis itself, particularly for preschoolers. They yield many important directions for research.

D. *Training Parents*

Training parents to carry out behavioral programs for their own children is a large, growing, and important area of inquiry (Graziano, 1977) that is more fully presented in Chapter 7. Three of the papers in this present section report programs that include parents' participation to improve their children's academic and, in some cases, classroom behavior. Kent and O'Leary (1976) report on second, third and fourth graders with both academic deficiencies and conduct problem behaviors. They compared a treatment group of 16 children with an equal number of randomly assigned "no-contact" controls. The treatment package was quite complex, involving a 20-hour program over several months that included structured, successive phases of assessment, school intervention, home intervention, and withdrawal. School and home interventions included instructions to teachers and parents regarding appropriate, systematic positive reinforcement, and reduction of inappropriate attention, threats, and reprisals. The parents were also instructed in tutoring.

Kent and O'Leary found that at the program's end treated children's social behavior improved significantly more than the untreated controls', but not their grades or achievement test scores. The results thus supported use of the total package to improve social behavior. However, at a 9-month follow-up, the control's behavior had improved and the differences had disappeared. At the same 9-month follow-up the treated children showed significantly better academic grades than did the no-contact controls. The results suggest that the treatment package may have speeded up some naturally occurring process of improved social behavior and contributed to a gradual, long-term improvement in academic performance. Because the treatment package was not experimentally "dismantled" it is not known which components contributed most to the changes. The package as a whole, however, appears to have been effective.

A daily home-report card method was used by Schumaker, Howell, and Sherman (1977) with young adolescents with academic and school-conduct problems. They found mailing privileges and other rewards contingent upon improved classroom conduct, classwork, daily grades, and teacher satisfaction considerably improved conduct and academic performance.

The home reports in the above studies were presented on a fixed time schedule, predictable by the students. In a study of third graders Saudargas, Madsen, and Scott (1977) found that students completed more academic work when home reports were sent on a variable time schedule in which the students could not predict on which days their reports would be sent home, than when the reports were on a fixed schedule. There was no parental involvement other than their receiving the reports. These studies suggest that frequent progress reports to the home, particularly on a variable time schedule, may be a relatively simple, effective method for improving children's, academic performance and classroom conduct. It remains to be determined how much further improvement might be brought about by systematically increasing parental involvement in home contingencies based on those reports.

E. *Token Reinforcement Systems*

Varieties of token systems continue to be used in classroom behavior modification. Prior to 1975 a large literature had already reported many demonstrations that the basic token system can be varied in many ways and can be highly effective with a large number of social and academic target behaviors, in regular or special classes, with normal, retarded, psychotic, delinquent, or other groups of children, and across virtually all school ages. The common procedure in all token systems, regardless of the diversity in target behaviors, clients, or settings, includes awarding tokens as valuable exchange media, contingent upon behaving in some specified manner. The tokens earned can then be exchanged or "cashed in" to purchase valued back-up reinforcers that include objects, privileges, play or free time, and so on. Some of the most consistent findings in the use of token systems are summarized here.

Token systems can be powerful behavior change intervention strategies, and they appear to have specific effects upon clearly specified behavior. For example, tokens awarded contingent upon improved specified social behavior will help to strengthen that targeted social behavior but will not necessarily help to increase academic behavior. A complete token system for improving disruptive, low-achieving students would best include contingent token reinforcement for both specified academic and social behaviors.

In many studies peers have served as effective token "managers," presenting cues and contingently awarding or withdrawing tokens for other children (e.g. Surratt, Ulrich, and Hawkins, 1969; Willis, Morris, and Crowder, 1972; Winett, Krasner, and Krasner, 1971).

While individual children seem to have been most frequently studied on the token systems, many researchers have studied group token systems. O'Leary and O'Leary (1976) described a continuum of token systems in which target behaviors and contingent rewards range from individual to group involvement. At one end the behavior of all children in class contributes to total class target behavior and contingent rewards. Each child, for example, contributes to the group's academic "average" in arithmetic, or contributes to the control over classroom noise levels. At the other end specific children may be reinforced for individual target behavior, and the entire class shares in the rewards.

As research has continued we can see the increased use of "natural" rather than "contrived" or "artificial" rewards. That is, the use as back-up reinforcers of valued objects or events that already exist in the school system, is increasingly considered more appropriate and, possibly, more effective as reinforcers. These would include prized activities such as free time, working on particularly interesting projects, and so on. Another development in token systems is the growing interest in integrating school performance and home contingencies through the use of daily progress records sent home and appropriate home reinforcement, controlled by parents.

Since 1975 journal discussions of token systems in schools have appeared quite frequently. Recent work continues to provide evidence for their effectiveness while not seeming to add much new in method, applications to new groups or problem behaviors, or classification of our understanding of the processes involved. Token systems continue to be effective interventions in classrooms, as already demonstrated prior to 1975.

Recent papers have focused on using token systems to decrease disruptive classroom behavior and additionally in some papers, to help improve academic achievement. As did earlier studies, these papers also focus on classroom contingency management of small numbers of elementary school children; few have studied classes of older children. For example, a growing problem is serious misconduct in junior high schools. Many of these older, conduct-problem adolescents are two or more years behind their age-mates academically, largely because so many have been retained in earlier grades. Retention-in-grade is a highly destructive intervention strategy that, despite clear and overwhelming evidence that argues against its use, is still one of the most commonly used interventions by educators (Levine and Graziano, 1981). In many schools this group misconduct becomes seriously disruptive and requires a good deal of teacher and administrator time and attention. Heaton, Safer, Allen, Spinnoto, and Prumo (1976) tested a token system for them, designing a contingency-management program within the normal setting aimed at improving conduct and academic performance. These adolescents were thereby maintained in the system, rather than transferred to special school settings for conduct problems.

Their system included teacher rewards and parent-controlled reinforcements, contingent upon improved academic performance and in-class behavior. At the end of the academic-year's intervention the differences between the 14 treated and 32 control children were striking. Most notably, the untreated controls had continued their serious misconduct and, before the year's end, almost half had been dropped from school. In contrast, only one of the 14 treated children had dropped out.

In another study of token systems in junior high school, Main and Munro (1977) demonstrated improved classroom behavior and academic performance. While thinning out the reinforcements, they demonstrated maintenance of gains over a 4-week follow-up.

Token systems continue to be shown effective in reducing disruptive behavior. Systems awarding tokens contingent upon the desired behavior (positive reinforcement) and removing tokens upon the occurrence of the maladaptive behavior (response cost, e.g. Swanson, 1979), appear to be equally effective (Baer, Ascione, and Casto, 1977). Baer et al. (1977) hypothesized that the two procedures might be equally effective because of the instructions given to children explaining the conditions under which tokens would be earned and/or lost. The demonstrated equivalence of the two methods might thus be due to the common instructions. Baer et al. compared the two procedures for four disruptive elementary school children without instructions and found that awarding tokens for desirable behavior was not effective in decreasing disruptive behavior, but combining token rewards and response cost was effective for three of the four children. Their results not only support the superiority of combined token-reward and response-cost procedures but also suggests the importance of clear instructions.

It appears, too, that token systems are more effective when used in conjunction with other interventions, such as in combinations of token rewards, social reinforcement, and response cost (Walker, Hops, and Feigenbaum, 1976). These authors report a sudden rather than gradual improvement in performance when the combined program was applied. In an interesting variation with 18 disruptive second graders, Robertson, DeReus, and Drabman (1976) awarded tokens for decreased disruptive behavior in the morning school session. The children's "tickets" could then be used to admit them to a daily tutoring period with fifth-grade or college-student tutors (contingent tutoring condition) or served only as "feedback" information. In this condition the students received tutoring, but the tokens were not necessary for admission to the tutoring sessions (noncontingent tutoring condition). Of most interest to our present discussion is that when the "tickets" had redeemable value and were necessary for tutoring, the children's disruptive behavior decreased. Tutoring was thus an effective backup reinforcer. Further, there were no differences in this effect between fifth-grade and college-student tutors.

But there have been critics of the token system research. Levine and Fasnacht (1974) for example, cautioned that token rewards can be seriously misused, with possible negative effects on children. If, they argued, extrinsic rewards such as tokens are applied to activities already of some intrinsic interest to children, the net result might be an undermining of intrinsic value of that activity and a decrease in that behavior. Notz (1975) presented data to support that prediction. Another criticism (Levine and Fasnacht, 1974; Levine, Fasnacht, Funabiki, and Burkart, 1979; O'Leary and Drabman, 1971) points out a lack of evidence for long-term maintenance effects of token systems. To date only a few studies (O'Leary, Becker, Evans, and Saudargas, 1969; Sulzer, Hunt, Ashby, Koniarski, and Krams, 1971; Wasserman and Vogrin, 1979) have provided data showing long-term maintenance effects; this, clearly is a needed area for research.

Overall, despite the criticisms it appears that systematically applied token-reinforcement systems, with clear instructions as generalized antecedent conditions, are effective intervention procedures in schools. It may be that among token systems' most important effects is the continual clarification of what the desired behavior is, and their built-in opportunities for continual student monitoring of personal success. In this interpretation the token economy system may be seen as being at least in part a reactive self-monitoring system, as well as an operant reinforcement system. This interpretation brings the token procedures within a self-control conception that suggests other areas of investigation. For example, it would be instructive to explain the mechanics of a token system to a group of children, set up a program and allow them to experience it, and then allow the children to expand the system by determining the target behaviors and the nature of the back-up reinforcers for themselves. Control of the program, then, would be increasingly in the children's hands.

There seems little doubt that research in classroom token systems will continue to be a common area of inquiry. The previous five years of research have served to replicate earlier findings, giving added support to the already known effectiveness of the procedures. Future research is needed on the long-term maintenance of effects. As suggested above, conceptualizing the token procedure within a self-control paradigm and emphasizing self-monitoring aspects might lead to interesting new data and uses.

IV. SPECIAL PROBLEM BEHAVIORS

In addition to large, varied categories such as academic and disruptive behavior, researchers have also investigated special behaviors in which one behavioral characteristic appears to be the dominant problem. Hyperactivity, impulsivity, elective mutism, and social withdrawal are examples. Hyperactivity and impulsivity have been discussed on pages 250–259. Presently we will briefly consider recent research on elective mutism, socially withdrawn behavior, and mild problem behaviors.

A. *Elective Mutism*

Elective or voluntary mutism refers to an inappropriate, total lack of speech in certain stimulus situations but not others. Typically, it involves children who speak to their mothers and other immediate family members but not in the presence of other relatives, teachers, neighbors, or classmates. Williamson, Sewell, Sanders, Haney, and White (1977) have pointed out that many studies labeling children as "electively mute" have actually described children who exhibit a low frequency of speech rather than no speech in the stimulus situation. They differentiate this problem from elective mutism and have labeled it "reluctant speech." Children described in both elective-mutism and reluctant-speech cases vary widely as to whether and under what conditions they speak to some or all of their family, friends, and teachers. Although we will maintain a distinction between elective mutism and reluctant speech whenever possible, the appropriateness and usefulness of such a dichotomous categorization merits further investigation.

Electively mute and reluctant-speech children are usually in preschool or the early elementary grades when brought to the attention of mental health professionals. Some of the children are described as shy or withdrawn (e.g. Nash, Thorpe, Andrews, and Davis 1979; Scott, 1977; Williamson, Sewell, et al., 1977). With the exception of mild social insults (Nash et al., 1979; Scott, 1977), the studies described a surprising lack of problems connected with this absence of speech. Academic difficulties reflected by the children's written work were rarely reported. Some reports emphasized how well the children, their families, classmates, and teachers adjusted to this problem, making no demands on the children to speak to others (Scott, 1977; Van der Kooy and Webster, 1975), which may partially account for why only three case studies dealing with a total of four electively mute children and three case studies dealing with a total of six reluctant-speech children have been reported in the behavioral literature from 1975 to 1980.

As noted by Reed (1963) and Straughan, Potter, and Hamilton (1965), traditional psychotherapy has proved to be notably ineffective in the treatment of electively mute children. Starting in the mid-1960s successful treatment using a variety of behavior modification techniques were reported in electively mute and reluctant-speech children. These studies comprise the research on these disorders today, with clinicians and researchers still expanding on various behavioral techniques and programs used to treat these multifaceted problems.

Attempts to promote the gradual development of speech through shaping have used prompts, modeling, and rewards and have proved either remarkably difficult or unsuccessful. Williamson, Sanders, Sewell, Haney, and White (1977) used a shaping and modeling procedure with two electively mute children where imitation by the children of progressively more speechlike activities modeled by the experimenter was reinforced with money or toys, and lack of compliance was punished by time-out. These activities ranged from eye contact, to blowing, to prespeech sounds such a "ah" or "mmm." In one case the goal of prespeech sounds was not reached. In the other case prespeech sounds were imitated, but even with the addition of a considerably larger reward, no full-word responses were achieved. Thus for both cases, as shaping/modeling proved largely ineffective, it was necessary for alternate strategies to be employed.

Nash, Thorpe, Andrews, and Davis (1979) used a contingency-management program for three children with reluctant speech. They structured a hierarchy of responses for each child consisting of (a) nonverbal compliance beginning with eye contact and ranging through commands to "stand," "sit," "pick up toys," and so on; (b) sound verbalizations which began with simple sounds and progressed to single and multiword responses; and (c) normal conversations with the experimenter, teachers, and classmates. Within each hierarchy prompting, chaining, and role-playing were used to stimulate the desired response. The requests were made repeatedly and correct responses were followed by verbal praise and tokens. Tokens could be used for various reinforcements distributed by the parents at home, such as snacks before bed. When considered necessary, punishments or negative reinforcements were administered in the classroom. Of particular interest was the apparent difficulty with which correct responses were brought about. For example, one 6-year-old girl required 23 requests to "stand up," followed by being forcibly stood up by the teacher before she complied with the help of a prompt to the request. That same girl also required 1495 prompts over 2 days to stimulate the "h" sound. A two-year follow-up showed that two of the children maintained "normal speech" and one regressed to baseline measures.

Attempts to obtain whole-word responses from children have proved most successful. Straight contingency-management programs have been successful with children described as having "reluctant speech." Williamson, Sewell, et al. (1977) report two cases of reluctant speech using contingency-management techniques. One boy's reluctant speech, particularly to classmates, led these investigators to set up a program at recess where verbalizations to other children immediately received a token toward earning a party for his class. On the first day of treatment the classmate response to the reluctant-speech boy when he spoke was so overwhelming that he withdrew and refused to talk. This problem was countered by forming a small group of friends to respond initially to him, which was then expanded to comprise the entire class. After the class party, tokens could be exchanged for privileges and improvement was maintained.

Williamson, Sewell et al.'s (1977) other reluctant-speech case was implemented in the clinic and at home. For prompt or spontaneous speech, tokens to be exchanged for various toys and privileges at home were given to the experimenter in the clinic and to persons outside the boy's immediate family at home over a 7-week period. A 2-month follow-up showed greatly improved speech in the clinic and at home and a one-year follow-up showed a continued lack of any reluctant-speech problem.

Griffith, Schnelle, McNess, Bissinger, and Huff (1975) trained a teacher and aide to operate a contingency-management program for a boy with reluctant speech in school. Reinforcement contingencies, with tokens earned for speaking to a peer being exchanged for free time, were instituted sequentially in three separate classes. This contingency proved effective in only the first class as the tokens apparently became inflated, that is, came to have less value as more were earned. A response-cost contingency for nonspeaking in the other two classes, which could take away tokens earned in the first class was effective and a 3-month follow-up after cessation showed maintained verbal behavior.

Using rather persuasive contingency-management methods, Van der Kooy and Webster (1975) instituted normal speech in an electively mute child in an intense 1-week program at summer camp. Speech was first initiated in the child as a necessary avoidance response: counselors would dunk or splash him unless he said, "No!" or "Go away!" These responses were gradually expanded by demanding that the child be more specific and by setting out tasks requiring speech for the child.

Speech was also reinforced by obeying his spoken requests and by attending to his verbal behavior. A 6-month follow-up showed the child speaking appropriately and fully in social and academic settings in school.

Other studies have been more gradual, spreading treatment over a longer period of time. Scott (1977) instituted a treatment program with an electively mute girl. The theoretical framework was based loosely on Wolpe's (1958) method of reciprocal inhibition in conjunction with more operant procedures. The girl was observed to be comfortable and relaxed when alone in a room speaking into a tape recorder. The relaxing response in the reciprocal-inhibition paradigm, carried out after each trial, was the child listening to her own voice while sitting on the experimenter's knee. With this base, the experimenter moved into sight and gradually over trials moved closer to the child until the two were face to face as the child spoke into the recorder. The tape recorder was then removed and more complex verbal face-to-face interactions were begun. New adults, including the child's school teacher, were gradually and progressively brought into the room on subsequent trials until the child was able to ask questions of four adults in the clinic room. An initial teacher-run generalization to the classroom, requiring the child to respond in front of the teacher in sight of another student, was not successful. The experimenter then attempted an even more gradual generalization, and within two hours the child was able to answer questions in front of her entire class. Selected classmates were then instructed to encourage her continued speaking through appropriate questioning and the mother was encouraged to ask the child questions at home in front of other adults. A 3-month follow-up showed the child still lacking in spontaneous speech, but previous progress had been maintained and further improvement was continuing.

Williamson, Sanders, Sewell, Haney, and White (1977) after failing at promoting speech through shaping and modeling "preword" responses with two electively mute cases attempted a variety of techniques centered on whole-word responses. A child who would talk and answer questions freely when alone with her mother was encouraged to speak to her mother when the experimenter was partly visible in another room. The experimenter gradually became more visible, and came closer, until with the promised use of a pair of roller skates contingent on responding (called a reinforced sampling procedure), the child was willing to answer the experimenter's direct questioning. Generalization did not extend, however, to a second experimenter. Generalization did occur in the classroom when coupled with the promise of being able to keep the roller skates, contingent on reading a 10-minute passage in front of her class. Gradually faded individual and group reinforcements were then used to maintain such speech in the classroom. A 1-month follow-up showed continued maintenance.

For the other child, an "escape-time-out positive-reinforcement" procedure was used to facilitate the production of a one-word response. Contingent on a one-word response to a prompt, this child was given a positive reward and also was able to "escape" from the 2-hour session in the clinic for 10 minutes to be with his mother. Lack of a verbal response resulted in a contingent 20-minute time-out. This technique was successful with both one and two experimenters present. However, similar contingencies in the classroom in front of teachers and students were not successful in bringing about a verbal response. To promote generalization a gradual shaping procedure was implemented in which the number of persons present was progressively increased and the physical environment shifted from the clinic to the classroom. The child's repertoire of responses was also increased through modeling and reinforcement. Finally, the modeling, prompts, and reinforcements were discontinued and 2-week and one year follow-ups showed continued improvement, including spontaneous speech.

Sanok and Striefel (1979) report their work with an 11-year-old girl of normal intelligence and academic achievement who had been electively mute for some six years. A particularly difficult case, the child spoke freely to family members and at home, but to no one else and not outside the home. Previous attempts, including positive reinforcement in school, had all failed, and she remained mute in school. Using a combination of contingent reinforcement and response cost, the researchers tried to establish verbal responses in five categories: single, "yes" or "no" answers to questions; single-word responses, other than "yes" or "no"; multiword responses; reading sentences aloud; verbally prompted speech. Pennies—identified previously as effective reinforcers for this child—were presented or withdrawn in contingent-reward and response-cost procedures.

The training resulted in fairly rapid acquisition of verbal behavior in the first four of the five categories. Verbally prompted speech, however, was not developed. Stimulus control was transferred from the first trainer to another adult trainer (stranger 1) who then used the same procedure to transfer control to stranger 2. In addition, generalization across settings (school and home) was reported to occur very readily. The use of pennies as reinforcers was faded as verbal reinforcement was emphasized.

A 10-month follow-up showed maintenance of the gains. The child was willing to use multiword responses to people outside the home. Her verbal responses in school increased, as did her level of academic achievement. However, spontaneous speech outside the home did not develop.

The authors point out that the single-subject nature of the study does not permit the assumption of generalization to other children. They do suggest, however, that because their task of having the children read sentences aloud was so readily mastered, that particular procedure may prove useful with other resistant cases.

Behavior therapy has been shown to be effective both in the treatment of elective mutism and reluctant speech. To date, due to the reports consisting exclusively of uncontrolled and unsystematic single-case studies, firm conclusions regarding the superiority of one particular method over another must remain speculative. This is particularly true of the active components of therapy involved in the original initiation of verbal responses to strangers or in public. This component, which differentiated between treatment programs of elective mutism and reluctant speech, seemingly accounts for the time difference in children's programs. Electively mute children's programs normally contained many more sessions than reluctant-speech children's programs. Anxiety-provoking cognitions and personal sense of control might be crucial here (Bandura, 1978), so a self-control treatment paradigm might prove particularly beneficial.

Once speech is initiated in the child in a particular setting, straightforward contingency management seems able to expand the child's repertoire. However, generalization of speaking from one setting or person to another, particularly when the repertoire of speech with strangers or in public is low, is more variable. As with initiation of speech, a cognitive component may be mediating here.

Unlike most behavior therapy literature, natural contingencies seem to quickly replace experimenter-induced reinforcers; maintained and continued improvement with minimal formal planning has been generally reported. The one exception to this was the oldest child reported in these studies, a 9-year-old girl, who regressed to baseline. This suggests that the early treatment of elective mutism may be crucial.

B. *Withdrawn Behavior*

Withdrawn behavior is characterized by inappropriately low rates of social interaction. Researchers have selected subjects primarily by observing children's interaction rates in class (Gottman, Gonso, and Schuler, 1976; Gottman, 1977; Weinrott, Corson, and Wilchesky, 1979) or in free-play situations (Evers-Pasquale and Sherman, 1975; Strain, 1977; Strain, Shores, and Timm, 1977; Kandel, Ayllon, and Rosenbaum, 1977), and have chosen those rated as being least socially interactive. In addition to low rates of interaction, some studies have used other criteria to select subjects, including sociometric analysis (Gottman, 1977; Gottman et al., 1976; Whitehill, Hersen, and Bellack, 1981; Gresham and Nagie, 1980) and teacher's checklists of withdrawn behavior (Weinrott et al., 1979). Subjects included nursery school children (Gottman, 1977; Evers-Pasquale and Sherman, 1975; Kandel et al., 1977; Strain, 1977; Strain et al., 1977) and early elementary school children (Kandel et al., 1977; Weinrott et al., 1979; Gottman et al., 1976).

Researchers and teachers are often concerned about the "low interacting" child in class and assume that for such children intervention is desirable. In a recent review, however, Shenfeld (1980) questions what she views as too easily made assumptions about the nature of the "quieter" children and the desirability of intervention. Shenfeld writes,

> [The fact] that treatment strategies are being devised for these children suggests that professionals are concerned with the current or future adjustment of isolated and withdrawn children. This statement, however self-evident, introduces the crucial question whether treatment is in fact warranted for these different populations. No doubt, there is something intuitively disturbing about the withdrawn child who interacts infrequently with his peers. Similarly, it is tempting to infer that the child who has few friends or is outwardly rejected by his peers must be sad and lonely. Nonetheless, since children do not usually have the freedom to choose whether to accept treatment and typically do not volunteer for such programs, it is incumbent upon the researcher or treatment provider to demonstrate that these children actually could benefit from, or are in need of, treatment (Shenfeld, 1980, pp. 5–6).

Shenfeld discusses the major assumptions made about less interactive children. These include assumptions that the child whose social interaction rate is low necessarily lacks social skills; that the child would "really" prefer to be more interactive and thus would welcome the intervention; that such children are mildly "unhappy" or dissatisfied; that solitary play for preschoolers, the group for whom most of the "social isolation" research has been developed, is less desirable than socially interactive play; that such children will have greater future problems in adjustment. These are all, according to Shenfeld's review, only assumptions, largely untested and, in some cases, challenged by data. Researchers and teachers would be prudent to concern themselves with the issues raised and discussed by Shenfeld.

Between 1975 and 1980, there have been four controlled experimental studies of "withdrawn" children actually treating a total of about 176 children. All of these studies have selected children from regular classrooms (Gottman, 1977; Gottman et al., 1976; Evers-Pasquale and Sherman, 1975; Weinrott et al., 1979). There have been three case studies dealing with 11 children which have selected withdrawn children with additional problems (Strain, 1977; Kandel et al., 1977; Strain et al., 1977).

As a base Gottman (1977) and Evers-Pasquale and Sherman (1975) used a film that O'Connor (1969) had found successful in significantly increasing withdrawn children's social interactions as compared with a control group. The film consisted of 11 scenes showing children interacting with others, first in passive non-threatening situations and progressively in more active and threatening situations; these interactions were followed by reinforcing consequences. O'Connor (1972) later found that the addition of a shaping procedure to the film did not enhance the child's social interaction. Evers and Schwarz (1973) also replicated these results, showing that teacher praise did not enhance the film's usefulness. Gottman (1977), comparing only prefilm intervention scores with a 7-week postintervention follow-up, found no differences on sociometric or observed social interaction scores between an experimental group which saw the film and a control group which saw a travel film.

Before showing the O'Connor film to an experimental group and a neutral film to a control group, Evers-Pasquale and Sherman (1975) divided the groups of children into peer-oriented children (those who chose to play or be with a peer in responding to a series of questions) or non-peer-oriented groups (children who chose to be alone or with adults). They found that at 2-day and 4-week postassessments, both the peer-oriented and non-peer-oriented groups had increased significantly in observed social interaction over the control groups. Further, the peer-oriented experimental group changed more in observed social interaction than the non-peer-oriented experimental group. The peer-oriented and non-peer-oriented control groups did not exhibit changes on these pre-to posttests. Although a formal statistical analysis was not done, a 3-month follow-up showed continued improvement in the peer-oriented and non-peer-oriented experimental groups. Interestingly, the peer-oriented controls at this time had also markedly increased in observed social interaction, suggesting that over time, peer-oriented children are capable of attaining acceptable levels of peer interaction without intervention. The non-peer-oriented control group exhibited no change.

The differences between the Gottman (1977) and Evers-Pasquale and

Sherman (1975) and other film modeling results is striking. There are many possible reasons for these differences, on which future research is needed. One reason might be that Gottman's observations of social interaction were taken in a more structured classroom environment where the effect of structured classroom activities might overshadow meaningful and consistent differences in social interaction, the observations of Evers-Pasquale and Sherman were made in a less structured free-time classroom situation. Evers-Pasquale and Sherman also showed that peer-orientation might prove to be a variable of considerable importance in treating withdrawn children. Gottman's selection process, which used a sociometric analysis, may well have selected out peer-oriented individuals and individuals with whom peers may have responded to their increased social overtures at posttreatment.

Strain (1977) and Strain et al. (1977), in multiple-baseline case studies, attempted to ameliorate withdrawn behavior among behaviorally disordered preschool children. Strain et al. (1977) trained age peers to deliver social initiations to these children which resulted in increased positive social interactions in the 20 tested situations. Strain (1977) replicated this effect (at least with two out of three children) and also assessed target behaviors 1 day later in a free-play situation. They found that the same two children who had increased their social interaction in response to peer initiations appeared to show some generalized improvement. Unfortunately, the most severely withdrawn case at baseline showed no treatment effect or generalization effect, thus calling into question the efficacy of this method with severely withdrawn children.

Taking a different approach, Kandel et al. (1977) viewed isolated or withdrawn behavior as a response associated with extreme anxiety. They hypothesized that withdrawn children consider peers a fearful stimulus. With a 4-year-old boy described as aggressive, hyperactive, and chronically anxious, they instituted a flooding procedure whereby 15 classmates were told to play with the withdrawn child for 2 minutes before they could use a new toy or earn a piece of candy. Seven days of such flooding saw a drastic increase in the boy's social interaction and a drastic decrease in his self-talk in the classroom. These results did not generalize to the playground. A similar flooding technique was then used for 3 days with successful results. Approximately 1-month and five-month follow-ups showed continued maintenance of treatment gains. A similar procedure was instituted with a diagnosed autistic 8-year-old boy who exhibited bizarre and ritualistic mannerisms. The original flooding attempt produced a highly emotional negative reaction from the child. Hence, a systematic exposure technique was instituted in which two socially skilled children would help the child interact and participate with him in activities. Seven days of such systematic exposure on the playground did produce an increase of social interaction on the playground but did not generalize to another situation in the school. Five days of similar systematic exposure in the school along with continued systematic exposure on the playground also produced increased social interaction in the school, while the social interaction on the playground was maintained. A 3-week follow-up showed continued maintenance of high levels of social interaction in both situations and a 9-month follow-up on playground behavior only also showed continued maintenance. Kandel et al. (1977), Strain (1977), and Strain et al. (1977) all illustrate the importance of generalization training in the treatment of withdrawn children. What is less clear is the difference between the Kandel et al. (1977) follow-ups which showed continued maintenance and Strain and his colleagues' (1977, 1977) studies which showed return to baseline after intervention. One possible reason is that Kandel's procedure seemed to build in a modeling social skills component whereas Strain and colleagues stopped primarily at attempting to initiate social interaction.

Gottman, Gonso, and Schuler (1976) and Weinrott, Corson, and Wilchesky (1979) both trained withdrawn children in social skills. Gottman et al.'s (1976) treatment of two children was divided into three stages, supervised by an adult. The first step attempted to teach children how to initiate social interaction. This was accomplished by watching a film of four social interactions, similar to the one used by O'Connor in 1969, with the addition of a cognitive coping self-statement sequence similar to that used by Meichenbaum and Goodman (1971). Next, the children role-played with their adult experimenter various friend-making sequences while receiving training in attentive listening and the reinforcement of others' behavior. The third stage involved giving instructions to a puppet and role-playing as a teacher and was aimed at helping the child take the perspective of the listener. The treatment lasted 30 minutes a day for 5 days and the child chose someone in his or her class on which to practice his or her new skills. A control group of two children merely conversed with an adult experimenter on various topics. A 9-week follow-up showed modest results, with the two experimental-group children showing improvement. There was no overall change in the frequency of social interactions for either the treated or control children. Gottman et al. also discusses possible interactions due to the treatment of frequency of social interaction increasing with some types of peers and decreasing with others, but such conclusions would appear to await further research with a larger experimental group.

Weinrott et al. (1979) trained 20 teachers to implement behavior modification programs for a selected withdrawn child in their classes. Five more teachers did not receive training, and they and their selected withdrawn students were used as matched control groups. The study consisted of six stages and lasted approximately 5 months. The first stage was a 2½-week baseline. The second stage consisted of a 2-week demand condition in which the teachers were asked to make their target child appear as outgoing as possible during the observation period without deviating from the normal classroom routine. The third stage was a 2-week return to baseline. There were then two intervention stages, labeled early and late interventions, which lasted 5 weeks apiece. Treatment procedures in these stages were presented sequentially in terms of complexity and elaborateness and implemented only when target child improvement was deemed unsatisfactory by the teacher. The early intervention program consisted of (a) attending to the withdrawn child contingent on the child's interaction with the teacher or others; (b) developing a reinforcement menu; (c) showing films of a withdrawn child that increasingly coped and was rewarded for increased social interaction in a way similar to O'Connor (1969); and (d) developing a point system which served as a basis for a positive or negative reinforcement. The second, late-intervention stage started out by modifying the children's point programs to permit the addition of group rewards. To increase peer interaction, both the targeted child and the child's peers could receive points for initiating social interactions with each other. This then changed to where the targeted child needed to accept the peer's initiation for the peer to receive points. Finally, teachers were to implement and carry out a fading procedure for contrived reinforcements and contingencies within 3 weeks. At the end of treatment and at 3-, 4-, and 5-week follow-ups, the treated groups' interaction rates were equal to that of peers, while the control group had not changed. The difference between the experimental and control group was also significant. The demand condition also increased scores of appropriate interaction with peers, but not as much as the interventions. Other measures of withdrawn behavior, such as teacher checklist, volunteering, and attention in class, were less striking, but in the predicted directions.

Bornstein, Bellack, and Hersen (1977) recruited subjects who exhibited problems with interpersonal interaction, and whom they labeled "unassertive." Teachers referred four children and described them as excessively cooperative, conforming, shy, passive, and unassertive. The four children, who ranged in age from 8 to 11, were also rated for (a) eye contact during speech, (b) loudness of speech, (c) number of requests to others to change their behavior, and (d) overall assertive behavior during a role-play situation where they were instructed to respond to an experimenter as they would act in certain interpersonal situations. All the children were rated as unassertive and deficient on all three of the specific targeted behavior areas.

Following baseline assessments, the children received 3 weeks of social skills training consisting of three 15- to 30- minute sessions per week. During the first week, the children received training geared toward increasing their loudness of speech. During the third week, they focused on increasing the number of requests. The social skills training consisted of presentation of the same role-play situations used in the original assessment followed by prompts, feedback, modeling, specific instructions, and rehearsal to an acceptable criterion. The results for all three children were similar and consisted of assessments of the targeted behaviors and overall assessment on the training scenes and three generalization scenes (i.e. scenes not used during training). The targeted behaviors showed improvement on both training and generalized scene role-plays. Training in one targeted behavior did not generalize to other targeted behaviors. Overall assertiveness typically increased during training and stayed at a high level after the training was accomplished. A 2- and a 4-week follow-up showed maintained improvement.

In summary, children considered socially withdrawn by their teachers or psychologists have been approached through a variety of techniques including filmed modeling, flooding, direct social skills training of children, and teacher training. The goal has typically been to increase the children's interactive social behavior and is based on a number of assumptions about children observed to be relatively inactive in social situations. The assumptions need verification and researchers are cautioned against too quickly intepreting these children's adjustment as "problematic." In this area the most important future research might not be in attempts to sharpen our ability to modify children's behavior toward increasing rates of social interaction but, rather, in sharpening our ability to differentially select from among the "quieter" children, those whose relative social inactivity is, in fact, problematic *for the child*.

C. *Mild Problem Behaviors in School*

Behavior modification in schools has focused on children who exhibit clearly disturbing behavior ranging from markedly psychotic behavior and the severe limitations of mental retardation through a variety of overt problem behaviors that disrupt classes and interfere with children's academic and social development. These children are typically viewed as involved in problem behaviors that depart radically from normal, enhancing, or age-appropriate functioning and development.

Teachers are also commonly faced with children who appear to function within the generally accepted "normal" limits in most respects, but depart—moderately or only mildly—in others. These would include, for example, the frequently noncompliant child who exhibits mild refusals to act on teachers' requests or instructions; children too often tardy or absent from school; children who might have mild difficulty in relating to their peers, and so on. These children are not easily described as "problems" and yet appear to exhibit mild difficulty in some areas. In several studies researchers have tried to bring such children closer to age-appropriate functioning: a sample is presented here. It should be noted that in all the studies the behavioral difficulty is constituted by some fairly mild behavioral deficit rather than surplus.

Two studies, Barber and Kagey (1977) and Morgan (1975), modified attendance behavior. Barber and Kagey (1977) had teachers reward first, second, and third graders with partial or full admittance to a class party and "fun rooms" for good attendance. Comparing attendance at baseline with previous school years and with other schools in the district, they found that their program, which included daily class attendance, charting, and contingent parties, had a significant positive effect on daily attendance.

Morgan (1975) attempted to increase the attendance of K-5 children with excessive unexcused absence. Morgan compared the effectiveness of three treatment groups and a control group. In one treatment group, two friendly and well-attending peers of each targeted child and the targeted child would receive tokens for the targeted child's attendance. These tokens were given on a generally increasing variable ratio schedule so as to better resist extinction and were exchangeable for various toys and candy. Another treatment group was not matched up with peers and was merely given the opportunity to earn tokens for toys and candy using a similar schedule as described above. The remaining treatment group received no tokens or material reinforcement; instead the teacher kept a daily attendance chart and praised the child's attendance in front of the class using a schedule similar to that in the other treatment groups. Treatment for all groups lasted 40 days; there was an extinction period where the teacher monitored attendance for 20 days. The results show that while their reinforcement schedule was in effect, all three treatment groups increased attendance greater than a control. Their analysis leaves unclear how well such gains were maintained.

Goetz, Holmberg, and LeBlanc (1975) compared the effect of three reinforcement conditions on the compliance to teacher requests of a rather noncompliant, although otherwise normal, preschool girl. In a multiple-baseline design, the teacher would (a) move into close physical proximity (within 3 feet) of the girl and contingent verbal praise for compliance; (b) come into close proximity regardless of the girl's compliance—after compliance verbal praise consisted of general pleasantries not related to the requested behavior; or (c) move into close physical presence with the girl contingent upon noncompliance and then verbally excuse the noncompliance. The contingent or noncontingent presence of the teacher for compliance or noncompliance were the independent variables investigated and analyzed, although the verbal responses in the three conditions also differed. They found that the condition in which the child was reinforced by teacher presence for compliance decreased noncompliance and increased compliance. Both of the other conditions decreased compliance and increased noncompliance. The condition in which the teacher's presence was made dependent on noncompliance increased noncompliance more quickly and to a higher level than the condition in which the teacher's presence or absence did not depend on compliance or noncompliance.

LaGreca and Santogrossi (1980) designed a group-oriented social skills program for elementary school children who evidenced difficulty in relating to peers. This 4-week program included videotaped peer modeling by a variety of peers in many different situations: coaching, behavioral rehearsal, videotaped feedback, and discussion. The children were also given homework assignments to practice their social skills with peers outside group meetings. They trained the children in the eight skill areas of smiling/laughing; greeting others; joining ongoing activities; extending invitations; conversational skills; sharing and cooperation; verbal complimenting; and physical appearance/grooming. The children were chosen for the program by their having received less than peer acceptance ratings on sociometric measures. Both pre- and posttreatment the experimenters conducted social skills measures of verbal problem-solving when faced with a social problem, role-playing, direct behavioral observation in a variety of school-related situations, and sociometric analysis. These results were compared to attention-placebo and waiting-list control groups. At posttreatment, sociometric analysis revealed no differences between the groups and no pre-post differences. The other results were mixed. The children's verbal skills knowledge and the role-playing performance of those who had received treatment was much higher than for those who did not receive treatment. Generalized behavioral change according to direct observation was generally in the predicted direction, but differences tended to be small and often not significant. No follow-up data were gathered. This well-controlled and carefully designed and run study does show the feasibility of a program to effectively teach social skills to elementary school children. However, the study failed to fade out reinforcement or to reinforce the improved behavior in a variety of school settings and situations. This failure is disappointing and further research is needed to investigate the potential for maintenance and generalization of these new skills.

Besalel-Azrin, Azrin, and Armstrong (1977) combined a wide variety of behavioral procedures into what they labeled a "student-oriented classroom" program with a normal fifth-grade class. The number of student- and teacher-defined problems and observations of students' compliance with rules were recorded. Besalel-Azrin et al. then seated one-half of the classroom's students on one side of the room to receive regular instruction from a student teacher and the other half of the students in the other side to participate with their regular teacher in their student-oriented classroom program. After 1 month the same measures assessed initially were again assessed and the side of the class which had received regular instruction was also included in the behavioral program. Five months later the teacher- and student-defined problem assessments were again taken, including a measure of parent, teacher, and student happiness with the program. The results may be suspect due to the inherent weaknesses of this design in not controlling for teacher differences, the lack of a long-term follow-up control group to assess the possible "novelty" effect which might quickly wear off and normal long-term baseline change. However, the study is of interest both for its technical combination of many behavioral procedures into one program, as well as for the issue it raises concerning student self-management.

Initially, both the teacher and the students listed class-wide rules they would like each other to follow. The rules listed by the teacher for the students to follow primarily concerned school problem-conduct areas, such as no hitting in school, finishing work on time, and so on. The rules listed by the students were primarily procedural or structural rules for the teacher to follow in running the program, (such as frequent individual conferences in which the teacher would give them constructive, not critical feedback on their following the program, allowing students to self-correct mistakes without penalty, and so on). Whenever possible the teacher and student were instructed and urged to phrase all statements in a positive framework of what should, as opposed to should not, be done. These rules were modified continuously in individual conferences between the teacher and student and both signed a formal written statement of their agreements.

This program, unlike most contingency programs carried out in schools, relied primarily on positive reinforcement. By following the agreement the students were allowed to choose from a list of previously agreed-upon reinforcements, such as leaving early for recess or lunch, going to the library, and so on. They were allowed to make up or self-correct misbehavior by formal apologies to the injured party, restating the appropriate correct rule of behavior, and verbally committing themselves to future compliance. If an incident occurred repeatedly, in addition to the above make-up procedure, the students practiced correctly following the rules for 5 to 10 minutes as positive practice. Only on refusing to perform the make-up and positive practice was the student then directly punished by being required to remain in his or her seat until compliance. Weekly reports on the students' performance were also sent to the students' parents, who were encouraged to praise their children for their efforts and performance. In addition, the students' records were posted on a class bulletin board.

In addition to the practice of relying primarily on positive reinforcers, this program was also unusual in that a large degree of teacher-student reciprocity was included. To promote this feeling of mutual helpfulness, the teacher and students were required to (a) alternate requests; (b) never directly refuse requests, but offer alternative solutions; (c) emphasize a satisfactory aspect of any situation before requesting improvement in the situation; and (d) when making requests, also offer specific procedures for arriving at a solution. The method of preceding any request for criticism with a statement of something satisfactory or pleasant that the other person is doing was also role-played and students were encouraged to use this approach when requesting a change of behavior of other students or with the teacher.

This reciprocity, though, did have a limit. As with most studies, the teachers were the ones to assess the students' compliance with the procedure and requests in their formal agreement, but neither the students nor anyone else monitored the teacher's compliance. Also only the students received direct positive reinforcements for their efforts. The apparently implicit assumption that the students' behavior was the only behavior to be assessed was also present in the original list of rules where the student was required to actually change problem-conduct behaviors and follow the structural obligations of the program, while the rules for the teacher were centered almost exclusively on his or her behavior in implementing the program.

In any case, the results showed that students who had participated in the program for 1 month had fewer student- and teacher-defined problems and more observed following of the rules than their classmates in the control group. At 6 months, after the control group had participated for 5 months, both the experimental and control groups showed improvement according to the number of student- and teacher-defined problems. According to the satisfaction questionnaire taken at this time, the parents, teacher, and students were, on the average, very happy with the program.

V. ENHANCING NORMAL BEHAVIOR

Although behavior modification in the schools has emphasized children's problematic behavior, it has not been entirely limited to that category with its essentially therapeutic or remedial goals. Several recent studies have been concerned with augmenting and enhancing normal children's already existing skills in attempts to take those children beyond "normal" or average levels of skills. The target behaviors have included creativity, language skills, assertive behavior, cooperative behavior, sharing, and even improving appropriate dinnertime conversation at home.

In the first of seven studies to be briefly outlined here, Parsonon and Baer (1978) investigated the direct teaching of creative behavior. To a number of critics the idea of "behavior-modifying" creativity is virtually a contradiction in terms (e.g. Cole and Parsons, 1974; Crary, 1969) and not only presumably cannot be done, but perhaps *ought not* to be done. Despite skepticism there is now a small but growing literature on behavioral approaches to increasing creative behavior (see the brief review by Parsonon and Baer, 1978).

The latter authors studied the ability of five preschool children to improvise or create novel solutions to problems. Specifically the three experimental tasks involved pounding on a peg-bench, storing marbles in a container, and lacing a shoe. Each task, however, required that the child improvise effective tools—hammers for pounding the pegs, containers for the marbles, and substitutes for shoelaces—from a variety of available nontool items. The major point of this particularly interesting study was to test whether training could improve the children's ability to creatively improvise tools. The children were trained to improvise in one tool class (hammers) and tested for improvisation within the same class and in the other tool classes. The experimenters found that (1) without training the children increased their improvisation; (2) with training all children increased their improvisation of tools; (3) generalization of the new improvisational behavior occurred within the class of tool in which training had occurred but not across different classes of tools; and (4) follow-up "probes" immediately following the study and 3 months later showed that the increased improvisation due to training was durable.

Parsonon and Baer conclude ". . . the results . . . clearly showed that preschool children could be trained, using explicit generalization programming techniques, to display diverse, novel, and generalized improvisation skills . . . behavioral diversity can be trained systematically" (p. 379). They caution, however, that while their procedures appeared effective, they were personnel intensive, with one-to-one interactions, and would have to be made a good deal more efficient before any wider scale applications could be considered.

This study, and those comprising the small literature noted by Parsonon and Baer, provide another important area of inquiry where we hope there will be a growing interest in behavioral approaches to teaching creativity to children.

Hart and Risley (1975) used an "incidental teaching" procedure they had developed earlier (Hart and Risley, 1968, 1974), with 11 preschool children from low-income families. Daily samples of spontaneous speech over an 11-month period had been recorded for each child. The incidental teaching procedure was defined as ". . . the interaction between an adult and a single child, which arises naturally in an unstructured situation such as free play and which is used by the adult to transmit information or give the child practice in developing a skill" (p. 411). There are countless everyday opportunities for incidental teaching of children, such as are provided whenever a child seeks assistance with dressing, eating, manipulating toys and other objects, or solving interactional conflicts with other children or adults. In this study Hart and Risley selected language skills of labeling and describing objects and activities, and their use in compound sentences. Children's requests for assistance in a variety of conditions were used by the teachers as opportunities to model and teach more complete use of compound sentences, while interacting with the children around the specifics of each request. Following the incidental teaching procedures the 11 preschool children measurably increased their "unprompted use of compound sentences," and "spontaneous variety in speech." The latter appears to be a particularly important suggestion of this research because, by utilizing a variety of naturally occurring events for language teaching we might improve generalization of newly learned responding, and avoid producing stereotyped responding in the children. This may prove particularly important in working with autistic and retarded children, as discussed in Chapter Two.

Vogrin and Kassinove (1979) reported a successful assertiveness-training procedure for normal third-grade children. They demonstrated improved assertive skills as measured by two paper-and-pencil tests constructed by researchers. One test, for example, described ten situations requiring assertive responses, such as refusing unreasonable requests. Thus the behavior that improved in the assertiveness training consisted of verbal responses to a test much like a standard academic achievement test following some particular lesson. The research did not demonstrate any functional utility of the improved assertive verbalizations in the children's everyday activities. The authors conclude that implementing such assertiveness training in school mental health programs at this time is premature.

The use of videotaped models to increase cooperative behavior in preschool children was reported by Geller and Scheirer (1978). They found that with disadvantaged children videotaped modeling alone or with the addition of an extensive verbal component generally did not result in greater prosocial behavior in laboratory or natural environments over a control condition. However, a middle-class sample of preschool children did show a gain in prosocial behavior under similar videotaped modeling conditions, with a verbal component again not adding to the prosocial behavior. The variables underlying these differences remain unclear.

Barton and Ascione (1979) attempted to facilitate sharing in preschool children. They instructed the children to (a) ask to play with a toy with another child (the verbal sharing training condition); (b) play with a toy with another child (the physical sharing condition); or (c) ask to play with a toy with another child and to actually play with another child (verbal and physical sharing condition). These specific behaviors were then modeled for their respective conditions. For each group they prompted and praised only those behaviors appropriate to that group, ignoring the others. The children's sharing was then immediately measured in a free-play situation. They found that during training phases all three groups' physical sharing increased from a baseline condition and relative to a no-treatment control group. Only the two groups with a verbal sharing training component showed improvement on return to baseline and in a 4-week follow-up condition. There appeared to be a small amount of generalization during the training conditions to a setting where the children played with art materials which was generally lost on return to baseline or follow-up conditions. Verbal sharing was also increased only in the groups trained with a verbal sharing component but, in contrast, none of the training conditions showed improvement on return to baseline or follow-up conditions. Further, there appeared to be no generalized effect to the setting with art materials. These results are interesting in that instructing, modeling, and reinforcing requests and participation in verbal sharing showed maintained physical sharing effects in preschoolers while such procedures with physical sharing alone showed no maintained effect. Further, no maintenance of verbal sharing was found even in groups which specifically trained verbal sharing. Apparently in specific situations these children's words can be translated into deeds but not the reverse.

Jewett and Clark (1979) trained and reinforced four preschool children to participate in appropriate dinnertime conversation with their parents and older siblings. The training consisted of simulating appropriate dinnertime conversations in school and in reinforcing the child for the use and accurate verbal reporting of appropriate dinnertime conversation by the children at home, particularly in the training sessions and to a lesser extent after the withdrawal of school feedback and reinforcement.

VI. SELF-MANAGEMENT

A study by Switzer et al. (1977) to reduce stealing in a second-grade class was discussed earlier (see page 244). Although the entire successful intervention was teacher-planned and controlled, the most interesting part of it was the brief period of time each day when the children were left alone in the classroom. From the authors' description the children were apparently highly motivated and very active in carefully checking to see if any items were missing and to ensure their return, in order to obtain the token reinforcement. In effect, the children briefly assumed control over the situation: they monitored their own behavior, arranged the classroom conditions, recorded the essential information, and controlled the token reinforcement. This daily behavior constitutes a self-management component of the procedure, and it would not be too difficult to refine the Switzer et al. methods into a more complete self-management approach in which the children themselves define specific target behaviors, carry out their own daily monitoring of collective class behavior, record and evaluate their behavior, and arrange for their own reinforcement. Could a collective, class self-regulation procedure be successful across a variety of behavioral goals? The specific research suggested here, involving a total class self-management package, has not been carried out, but would provide interesting data.

A study such as the one suggested here would fall into a growing area of research interest, children's self-regulation. Over the past two decades we have seen ample demonstration of significant modification of children's classroom behavior through externally imposed, systematically varied, teacher-controlled procedures. In contrast to the teacher-controlled methods most recent studies of self-regulation have explored procedures to teach children to regulate their own behavior.

In the self-management research a commonly assumed model conceptualizes self-management as a sequence of complex processes that include self-monitoring, self-evaluation, and self-reinforcement (none of which have yet been sufficiently studied). Self-monitoring is typically considered to be a critical starting point in the self-regulation process, without which the remainder of the sequences could not effectively occur. Self-monitoring itself is assumed to be a process in which a person keeps track of his or her own behavior through self-observation and recording. Recent research has demonstrated that children can effectively self-monitor (e.g. Broden, Hall, and Mitts, 1971; Bolstad and Johnson, 1972; Glynn and Thomas, 1974; Thomas, 1976), and self-reward by controlling reinforcement contingencies (Ballard and Glynn, 1975; Bolstad and Johnson, 1972; Drabman, Spitalnik, and O'Leary, 1973; Glynn, 1970; Glynn and Thomas, 1974; Glynn, Thomas, and Shee, 1973; Johnson and Martin, 1973; Wall and Bryant, 1979). Other parts of the self-regulation processes have also been demonstrated (e.g. Brownell, Colletti, Ersner-Hershfield, Hershfield, and Wilson, 1977; Drabman, Spitalnik, and O'Leary, 1973; Felixbrod and O'Leary, 1973; Glynn, 1970; Lovitt and Curtiss, 1969; Spates and Kanfer, 1977; Turkewitz, O'Leary, and Ironsmith, 1975).

Nearly all of this research has utilized positive self-reinforcement as the end process in the self-management sequence. One recent study, however, Humphrey, Karoly, and Kirschenbaum (1978), studied the effects of self-regulated punishment on children's classroom behavior. The punishment contingency used in their study was a response-cost procedure within a token-reinforcement system. Previous research in the early 1970s as reviewed by Humphrey et al. (1978) and by Kazdin (1972) had shown that externally imposed response-cost procedures have been successful in increasing positive behaviors and weakening undesirable behaviors without the negative side effects frequently expected with the use of punishment contingencies. Humphrey et al. took baseline measures of classroom disruption and academic behavior, established a classroom token economy, and compared groups that self-managed positive token reinforcement with groups that self-managed token response-cost. The experimenters found that both positive reinforcement and response-cost self-regulation conditions were associated with improved academic and classroom behavior, "although self-reward improved reading rates and workbook performance to a somewhat greater extent" (p. 592). It is clear the response-cost self-regulation procedures, although apparently effective, are not a good substitute for self-regulated positive reinforcement. Yet to be investigated, however, is whether the two self-regulation procedures used together might interact and provide a "package" more powerful than self-regulation or positive reinforcement alone.

Two papers have studied self-management procedures in reducing disruptive classroom behavior. Epstein and Goss (1978) discuss a single case study of a ten-year-old boy with a history of high rates of disruptive behavior. The intervention included earning points by engaging in specified "good" behavior, and receiving social reinforcement. In addition to a fairly standard teacher-controlled reinforcement system, a variety of self-monitoring was included in which the child estimated the number of points he was earning and thus, at least implicitly, assessed his own behavior. The procedures were reportedly eagerly adopted by the child and significant improvements were noted in a variety of disruptive behaviors.

Because of its single-case nature, generalizations from this study are limited. However, an interesting suggestion is provided by the results in that the self-monitoring aspect, as small a part of the procedure as it may have been, appears to have helped the child maintain his improved behavior over a fairly long period of time, after the formal token-reinforcement program ended. The suggestion, of course, is that a self-monitoring component added to a token-reinforcement system might effectively serve as one possible way of building in long-term maintenance of improved behavior.

Another study that included concern for maintenance of improved behavior brought about by a self-management package is reported by Bornstein and Quevillan (1976). The authors reported success in increasing the on-task behavior of three "overactive" preschool boys, and in maintaining the improvement over a fairly long time. Their program involved a 2-hour self-instructional training program that included verbal self-instructions for problem solving. Wall and Bryant (1979) reported maintenance of gains in a self-reinforcement procedure with fourth and fifth graders for a 3-week follow-up. Those authors point out that longer maintenance follow-ups are needed.

Self-management strategies in schools have been applied primarily to alter children's functioning but, in a small number of studies, they have been applied also to teachers (e.g. Hannum, Thoresen, and Hubbard, 1974; Herbert and Baer, 1972; Szykula and Hector, 1978). While success is reported in these studies, it is too early yet to draw any conclusions about the effectiveness of self-control training for teachers or of the impact of such approaches on the classrooms. We hope this area will continue to be investigated.

In another interesting and somewhat more heavily investigated area, self-management concepts have been applied to improving interactions between children and their teachers. Most importantly, in these studies some degree of self-management training or instructions was carried out with the children, and the *teachers'* behavior was targeted for change. Children were taught skills to control some important aspects of adult's behavior (e.g. Cantor and Gelfand, 1977; Graubard, Rosenberg, and Miller, 1971; Polirstok and Greer, 1977; Sherman and Cormier, 1974; Stokes, Fowler and Baer, 1978).

In the latter study the experimenters taught eight 4- to 6-year-old children to judge the quality of their own academic work and to then provide appropriate prompts or cues to their teachers to increase the teachers' comments on and reinforcement for the children's work. The children, according to the experimenters, were taught self-management skills that enabled them to ". . . contact a sometimes dormant but readily available natural community of reinforcement, i.e., to recruit an increase in cued praise and schedules of praise for their good work" (p. 285).

This research seems to carry children's self-management training to a very different level than we usually find, in which at least some of the control traditionally exercised by the teacher is being assumed by the children. Although it is too early to draw many conclusions about this research, it may be of potential significance for the development of children's independence.

These studies and a number of earlier papers (the introductory reviews in Bornstein and Quevillan, 1976; Epstein and Goss, 1978; and Humphrey et al., 1978) provide evidence for both feasibility and effectiveness of several self-management procedures in classrooms. The evidence suggests that both behavioral improvement and improvement maintenance can be brought about through self-regulation training procedures. An additional contribution of this work is the move toward child-controlled procedures which, in contrast to other-controlled procedures, might also be more generalizable to other natural settings for the child. Both issues of maintenance and generalization need to be researched. Finally, these self-management directions might also help overcome concern still voiced by some over the apparent degree of external control imposed upon children in many behavior modification procedures.

VII. CONCLUSIONS

The success of behavior modification within school systems has been a major impetus for the development of the entire behavioral field. Systematic behavioral programs have been applied to the solution of a variety of problems in school, including academic and social behavior as well as more traditionally considered clinical problems such as aggressive and withdrawn behavior and mutism. Programming has also aimed at enhancing normal behavior and teaching self-management skills to children. It seems clear that many children have benefitted from behavioral approaches in schools, and that this area of behavioral application will continue as one of our most important endeavors.

Schools are complex social system that are unique in many ways, and various forms of adult and child behavior that are appropriate within the school environments are demanded nowhere else in society. Thus some of the problems to which behavior modification procedures are applied involve issues that occur only in school settings. Herein lie two problems: (1) the behavior modifier may be pressed to alter children's behavior so as to serve the special needs of the school, needs which may sometimes conflict with what might be to the child's benefit; (2) adaptive behaviors that are of value only within some limited intraschool environment have, by definition, no generalization value for adaptive functioning in other social settings. Thus when powerful behavioral technologies are brought to bear on this essentially captive population, subject to the special needs of the setting, the behavior modifier must be particularly alert to avoid negative impacts of the procedures.

9

Somatic Systems, Behavioral Medicine, Behavioral Pediatrics, and Health Psychology

I. INTRODUCTION

Psychophysiological reactions of children ordinarily involve a single organ system, usually under the control of the autonomic nervous system. This category has traditionally included: accident-proneness, headaches, stomachaches; manipulative motor habits such as nail-biting, thumb-sucking, and tics; skin disorders; and problems of elimination, enuresis, encopresis, and functional constipation. Some of the more serious, life-threatening psychophysiological reactions are thought to include bronchial asthma, ulcerative colitis, and anorexia nervosa. In each condition the somatic disorder is thought to be caused or at least exacerbated by functional variables. The presumed causal relationship is not clear, nor are the mechanisms whereby psychological processes interact with somatic systems.

Traditionally psychophysiological reactions have been treated medically or through a psychodynamic model, the latter assuming that the somatic problems are symptoms, the results of repressed emotionality. Consistent with that model, psychodynamic treatment has aimed at uncovering the repressed material, thus reducing the psychic tension that, in turn, had caused the somatic symptoms.

More recently both respondent and operant conditioning models have been applied to psychophysiological reactions, assuming that conditioning is one major factor in a causal chain leading to actual tissue damage. The classical conditioning model assumes that affective states such as chronic anger serve as unconditional stimuli eliciting physiological responses such as high blood pressure which, in turn, lead to structural change (Zax and Cowan, 1972). Clinical case descriptions (Noyes and Kalb, 1963) and experimental data (Dekker, Pelser, and

Groen, 1957) support a classical conditioning model. Noyes and Kolb, for example, describe a case where asthmatic attacks were precipitated not only by real roses, but also by papier-mâché roses. In other cases asthmatic attacks were precipitated by specific songs or occurred only at specific times of the day. Although not providing hard evidence, those descriptions suggest that those reactions had been respondently conditioned.

Some investigators have demonstrated that autonomic responses can be conditioned instrumentally as well as respondently (Kimmel, 1967; Miller, 1969). Their findings suggest that a large variety of natural reinforcers can potentially shape psychophysiological disorders. Miller (1969), for example, suggested that the secondary gains resulting from a somatic illness might be of such reinforcing power in many cases.

If operant or instrumental conditioning can, in fact, shape autonomic responses, increasing them from a "normal" baseline to a high level of stimulus control by external stimuli, then behavioral treatment utilizing contingency management should be effective with psychophysiological reactions. The growing interest in the psychology of physical illness has led to the recent emergence of behavioral medicine.

A. *Behavioral Medicine*

Behavioral medicine is a field only recently recognized and defined. Its emergent date is usually given as February, 1977 when Yale University hosted the first conference on behavioral medicine. Its goal was to formally establish this new field. Since then we have seen the publication in July, 1977 of *The Journal of Behavioral Medicine*, and the formation in November, 1979 of the Society of Behavioral Medicine. A special training branch of the National Institutes of Health has been established and some professional organizations such as the Association for the Advancement of Behavior Therapy, have established special divisions. Several universities and medical centers, including Harvard, Johns Hopkins, Mississippi, University of Pennsylvania, Stanford, and Yale have established programs in behavioral medicine (Weiss, 1978) and a number of others are planning to.

Of course investigations into psychological factors in physical illness have been conducted for a long time. But the organizers of the Yale conference judged that the amount and type of research had reached critical levels which required the integrative step of being recognized as a new area, that had been formed by the merging of several lines of development. One of those developments was the reemergence of behavior modification in the early 1960s. Behavior modification is very much a central foundation for behavioral medicine. This can be seen in the definition of the new field arrived at by the Yale conference: "Behavioral medicine is the field concerned with the development of behavioral science knowledge and techniques relevant to the understanding of physical health and illness and the application of this knowledge and these techniques to prevention, diagnosis, treatment, and rehabilitation. Psychosis, neurosis, and substance abuse are included only insofar as they contribute to physical disorders as an end point" (Schwartz and Weiss, 1978, p. 7). Clearly the defined focus of efforts is on *behavioral science development,* toward understanding, preventing, and treating physical illness. That emphasis is also suggested by the sponsorship of the conference: the Yale Department of Psychology as well as Psychiatry, the School of Medicine, the Lung and Blood Institute, and the National Institutes of Health.

Another indication of the centrality of behavioral science in this new area has been discussed by Pomerleau (1979). In essence, Pomerleau argues that the Yale conference defined the field too broadly by including earlier work such as that in psychosomatic medicine and psychodynamic personality therapy. Pomerleau and Brady (1979) offer a definition of behavior medicine that strongly emphasizes its "origins in modern behaviorism" (Pomerleau, 1979, p. 655). For those authors, "Behavioral medicine can be defined as (a) the clinical use of techniques derived from the experimental analysis of behavior—behavior therapy and behavior modification—for the evaluation, prevention, management, or treatment of physical disease of physiological dysfunction; and (b) the conduct of research contributing to the functional analysis and understanding of behavior associated with medical disorders and problems in health care" (p. xii).

Despite these definitional differences, there is essential agreement that behavioral medicine is the field concerned with the interplay of human behavior and physical illness, and its major concepts and methods are those of behavioral science. While concepts of psychosomatic medicine and psychophysiological disorder carry some resemblance to behavioral medicine, they are not equivalent concepts. Both apply more narrowly than behavioral medicine, and both assume underlying psychological causality for certain somatic conditions, such as ulcers and bronchial asthma. The field of psychosomatics is heavily infused with psychodynamic concepts of unconscious motivation, while psychophysiological disorders are seen as being related to the operation of uncontrolled anxiety. Behavioral medicine is concerned with the relationships among behavior and illness, and the term "behavior" includes individual micro- as well as macrobehavior, and social as well as individual behavior. Thus large-scale public education programs to urge children to properly clean their teeth, or to convince adults to reduce smoking, are well within the purview of behavioral medicine, but are not problems for psychosomatics or psychophysiology. Recognizing Pomerleau's (1979) admonition that any definition at this early point in the field's history must be taken as a tentative statement, we will try to outline the scope of the field as currently—and tentatively—seen.

1. Behavioral medicine is practiced by a variety of professionals representing different disciplines, including: the medical (e.g. dentists, physicians, nurses, physical therapists); the psychological (e.g. psychologists, various psychotherapists, psychological aides); the sociological (e.g. social workers, medical sociologists, and public health workers); and the educational (e.g. health education teachers and administrators, teachers and supervisors in professional programs, internships).

2. Behavioral medicine research may be carried out by all of the professionals noted above. It is anticipated, however, that Ph.D. psychologists, because of their research training, will be the major researchers in the field.

3. Behavioral medicine's major concepts and interventions are those of behavioral science, with specific emphasis on behavior modification and applied behavioral analysis. These will include operant- and respondent-based approaches as well as more social and cognitive concepts of social learning theory. The major general goal it to modify health- and illness-related behavior.

4. The clients for behavioral medicine practitioners and the subjects for its researchers form a large and heterogeneous group. They include: (a) traditional patients, those with some physical illness to be treated, at least in part, by behavioral methods (e.g., obesity, asthma, hypertension, etc.); (b) special groups such as children and pregnant women, and the public at large, whose behavior can be modified toward better personal health care and primary and secondary prevention; (c) health professionals themselves, who are to be retrained or further trained in behavioral medicine procedures.

5. Its major goals are suggested by the nature of the clients or recipients of service as noted above.

1. Treatment

Treatment interventions are applied to the illness-related behaviors of medical patients so as to help alleviate the medical illness. Training a severely asthmatic child in deep muscle relaxation and in self-control methods to respond appropriately to early signs of asthmatic attacks, or the use of biofeedback with hypertense patients, are examples.

2. Maintenance

This entails modifying patients' behavior so as to increase their skills in maintaining proper treatment behavior. Examples would be maintenance of dieting behaviors after weight loss, of nonsmoking, or of proper exercise and diet for postcoronary patients.

3. Prevention

Secondary and primary prevention is sought by reducing patients' high-risk behaviors so as to reduce probabilities of recurrence of the illness (secondary prevention) and reduce risks to special high-risk groups, such as sedentary, overweight, middle-aged men, so as to reduce the probabilities of a first coronary or similar physical problems.

4. Professional Education

Modifying the behavior of health-care professionals so as to improve their service delivery is an important goal.

Behavioral medicine involves the use of behavioral concepts and methods toward four major change goals: treatment, maintenance, prevention, and education. Its clients include individual patients, special-patient or high-risk groups, the general public, and health-service professionals. Its practitioners and researchers are drawn from several professional disciplines. Its overall focus is the systematic investigation of the relationships between human behavior and physical illness and health.

B. *Behavioral Pediatrics*

Behavioral pediatrics is that subarea of behavioral medicine in which the patients are defined in terms of age, that is, children and adolescents. The other characteristics of behavioral medicine discussed above apply equally to the behavioral pediatric area. The term, "behavioral pediatrics" was used at least as early as 1970 by Friedman, who argued for greater integration of behavioral science and pediatrics, although the behavioral science referred to was traditional psychodynamic psychiatry. Friedman anticipated the importance of behavioral medicine to children, and was among the first to call for this development. There have been many behavioral studies since the early 1960s that can properly be categorized as behavioral pediatrics, none of which were so labeled at the time of their publication.

C. *Behavioral Health and Health Psychology*

Another definitional attempt has been offered by Matarazzo (1980). In his presidential address to the Division of Health Psychology of the American Psychological Association, Matarazzo noted that the emerging area of behavioral medicine has its focus primarily on behavior-related pathological conditions, but does not sufficiently stress illness prevention, positive physical health attainments, and maintenance. Arguing, as did Knowles (1977) that these positive health goals are individual, corporate, and public responsibilities, Matarazzo pointed out the need to define a field of systematic inquiry and practice in behavioral health. Matarazzo proposed, "Behavioral health is an interdisciplinary field dedicated to promoting a philosophy of health that stresses *individual responsibility* in the application of behavioral and biomedical science knowledge and techniques to the *maintenance* of health and the *prevention* of illness and dysfunction by a variety of self-initiated individual or shared activities" (p. 813).

It appears to us that behavior modification may offer much in this enterprise by helping to identify both health- and illness-related behaviors to determine effective procedures to bring about positive behavior changes and health-behavior maintenance. Concepts and procedures in the area of behavioral self-control may be appropriate for developing individual skills in both the prevention of disorders and maintenance of health. As Matarazzo noted the field is not yet well developed and has as yet little progress to offer, but is potentially a significant contributor to the welfare of our society.

It is not our intention to review this entire literature, as that is a task too large for our present purposes but, rather, to at least briefly discuss recent studies in several areas of behavioral pediatrics. We may omit areas that other investigators believe are important, or may include some deemed inappropriate by others. This attempted organization is offered, echoing Pomerleau's 1979 admonition, as a tentative statement, a working paper, very much subject to change.

The areas we have selected are: respiratory problems (asthma); physical injuries (self-inflicted and child abuse); food-related problem behaviors (obesity, anorexia, rumination); bladder and bowel-control problems; sleep disturbances; seizures, tics, hyperactivity. In a concluding section (additional issues), a number of other problems will be briefly discussed (e.g., behavior modification in medical procedures, smoking prevention).

II. RESPIRATORY PROBLEMS—ASTHMA

Recognized since antiquity, and known to occur on a worldwide basis, asthma at present appears to be principally a disorder of urbanized populations. In industrialized cities in the northern United States, asthma is the most important single disease requiring an emergency room visit or hospitalization during certain times of the year. Estimates of the prevalence of the disease vary, depending upon the methodology of the survey and, particularly, the differing criteria used to define asthma by various investigators. However, at some time, approximately 5 to 10% of children have respiratory tract signs and symptoms compatible with the diagnosis of asthma. It is the leading cause of chronic illness in children.

There is general consensus that the incidence and severity of asthma relate to many variables beyond the issues of medical/physiological treatment. For example, the reduction of urban air pollution might be a significant public health measure in general (Foster, 1972) as well as an aid in reducing asthma in particular, but the issues involved in such measures are more political and economic than medical.

The point is this: If one asks the crucial question, "What variables bring about, heighten, and maintain asthmatic responding?" then even a cursory view of the evidence reveals that not only medical but also physiological, psychological, sociological, political, and economic factors are involved.

The most parsimonious view of the literature is that (1) psychophysiological factors are most central in asthma, and medical treatment is thus the most basic treatment; (2) there may be a common disorder in asthma but there are great variations in ". . . clinical patterns, severity, and natural history of asthma . . . in the pathophysiological, immunological, and psychological aspects of the disorder, and in the precipitating causes for the attacks" (Williams and Phelan, 1975, p. 119); (3) psychological factors may be powerfully involved and for some patients the original physiological disorder becomes escalated into a massive physiological-plus-psychological problem.

Many children are "allergic" or otherwise hyperreactive to various stimuli such as household chemicals, dust, pollen, animal fur and dander, particular foods and spices, cold temperatures, and even physical exertion and stress. Physiological responses include skin rashes, stomach upsets, teary eyes, blocked nasal passages, and perhaps hyperactive behavior. Individual children respond characteristically through some particular organ system and for the asthmatic child that response involves the respiratory system. Once triggered, the asthmatic response involves a swelling of airway tissues causing the child increasing difficulty in breathing. Parents whose children are asthmatic recognize the condition by the pronounced wheezing sounds from the chest as the child tries to pull air through restricted passages. Labored breathing, faintness, and pallor are additional signs of a serious asthmatic condition. Some children develop a permanent "pinched" and round-shouldered posture from their repeated breathing difficulties.

Asthma can appear suddenly and at any age. The attacks may be frequent or occasional, and may continue for many hours or only minutes. For children whose asthma began before age 13, some 70% improve in adolescence and young adulthood. Many, however, do not improve and must remain on controlling medication for life. Although not usually fatal, asthma produces some deaths, at a rate of 1.5 per thousand.

In addition to its physical dangers and discomforts, asthma can have highly disruptive psychological effects—both immediate and long term, for the child and the parents. Each attack can be an extremely frightening experience for a child struggling to breathe and who recognizes that the breathing difficulty is rapidly worsening. The anxiety can escalate to extreme levels of panic for a child and parent, both of whom may fear the gasping child will die at any moment. The panic adds its own disruption and the attack's overall severity takes a significant turn for the worse. The repeated midnight rush to find emergency hospital treatment, the family's continual apprehension of new attacks, the child's feelings of helplessness, the frequent interruption of school attendance, the common reduction of physical activity such as school sports or the rough and tumble play of children, and the possible development of self-perceptions of weakness and physical inferiority all contribute to what can be a severely disruptive, chronic condition of physical and psychological illness.

For many children the acute attacks can be quickly reversed by the timely use of medications such as those dispensed through inhalers which dilate the swollen air passages. A continued regime of anti-allergy medications can reduce the frequency and intensity of attacks, as can systematic avoidance of the particular triggering stimuli. As King (1980) observed, pharmacological treatment includes use of aminophylline and theophylline, isoproterenol, epinephrine, cromolyn sodium, and corticosteriods. "The pharmacologic management of childhood asthma is far superior to psychological treatment including behavior therapy" (p. 176). And, we will add, it is clearly the treatment of first choice.

These pharmacological treatments constitute both emergency and long-term self-control over the asthmatic condition and require systematically obtained information about the relevant variables accounting for the condition, and careful training in the various components of self-control methods appropriate to the asthmatic condition.

The behavioral medicine issues, then, involve: (1) identification and amelioration of the psychological variables that accompany asthmatic conditions; (2) teaching new skills in recognizing and avoiding triggering stimuli and appropriately using self-administered pharmacological treatments for the immediate reversal of acute episodes and/or their long-term prevention or lessening; and (3) public health campaigns aimed at the reduction of large-scale contributing factors such as air pollution. Behavior modifiers have done nothing toward that third issue, perhaps not even perceiving such public campaigns as being properly within their professional jurisdiction. The other two areas, however, have been approached with behavioral methods.

Asthma has long been considered a psychosomatic condition in which psychological variables, such as hypothesized infant dependency needs, are thought to be causal agents, as in the classic psychoanalytic model of asthma (French and Alexander, 1941). There is, of course, no evidence to support that explanation or to recommend psychotherapy as the major treatment. More recently we have viewed psychological issues such as anxiety, operant and respondent conditioning processes, and so on, as more the results rather than the causes of the basic pathophysiological condition. Even psychologists are beginning to believe that while psychological treatment of asthma-associated behaviors may be important, the basic condition is a physiological one and the clear treatment of first choice is pharmacological.

In recent years there has been increased interest in the use of behavioral models primarily in the adjunct treatment of asthmatic children, and a corresponding decrease in the use of psychodynamic concepts and approaches. The field is moving toward an increasing emphasis on the use of respondent and operant conditioning models and social learning theory to study the relationships between physical and psychological (primarily behavioral) variables. In general, researchers do not assign primary etiologic value to psychological variables. However, there is increasing recognition that psychological variables are critical in aggravating and escalating the primary physiological condition. Psychological escalation may in some cases be so severe as to result in massive family disturbance. The effects not only of asthma but other chronic illnesses on a child and his or her family can be devastating, and it is likely that much of what has been recognized as behavioral problems in both chronic asthmatics and in other chronically ill children may result from, rather than be the cause of the disease.

As reviewed by Creer (1976), two of the major groupings in the recent literature are those studies of variables that precipitate and/or aggravate asthmatic responding, and studies investigating variables that ameliorate the symptoms.

In the first category Creer notes that a large variety of instigating and aggravating stimuli have been identified. However, the lack of standard criteria for selection of subjects and for assessing severity, and the many procedural and methodological differences among the studies, make their results difficult to compare. What seems clear is that many variables, psychological and physical, can instigate and aggravate asthmatic symptoms and that they are largely idiosyncratic variables.

The second group of studies discussed by Creer includes a wide variety of intervention strategies to ameliorate asthmatic responding. These include temporarily removing the child from the home (Peshkin, 1959; Faillers, 1970; Purcell, Brady, Chai, Muser, Molk, Gordon, and Means, 1969), suggestion and hypnosis (Smith and Burns, 1960; Moorefield, 1971; Maher-Loughan, et al., 1962; Smith, Colebatch, and Clarke, 1970).

Perhaps the most rapidly growing area is the use of behavioral strategies in individual and family approaches to reduce asthmatic responding. Relaxation training has been used alone (Alexander, 1972; Alexander, Miklich, and Hershkoff, 1972; Sirota and Mahoney, 1974; Davis, Saunders, Creer, and Chai, 1973; Philip, Wilde, and Day, 1972) and as part of systematic desensitization strategies (Walton, 1960; Cooper, 1964; Sergeant and Yorkston, 1969; Moore, 1965; Yorkston, McHugh, Brady, Serber, and Sergeant, 1974). In their review of behavior therapy for asthma, Knapp and Wells (1978) concluded that relaxation training, compared with no treatment controls, ". . . has consistently produced statistically significant improvement in subjects' respiratory function measures" (p. 108). When relaxation training is compared with systematic desensitization," the latter procedure has always proved superior" (Moore, 1965; Yorkston et al., 1974, p. 111).

In a carefully designed study with chronic, severely asthmatic children, Alexander, Cropp, and Chai (1979) found that relaxation training did not help to improve the children's pulmonary functioning. Their findings are at odds with the common practice of advising asthmatic children to "relax" and with the earlier suggestions of relaxation's possible effectiveness (e.g. Alexander, 1972; Alexander et al., 1972; Davis et al., 1973; Tal and Miklich, 1976), as reviewed by Knapp and Wells (1978). Alexander, Cropp, and Chai used standard relaxation training methods. Heart rate measurements indicated the children did attain a relaxed state. A number of physiological measures of pulmonary function were taken, in a carefully controlled study that used the subjects as their own controls. They noted, "The effects of relaxation on pulmonary mechanics obtained in these severely asthmatic youngsters were consistently unremarkable" (p. 32). Their conclusion is that relaxation training appears to be of no clinical value for improving pulmonary function of severely asthmatic children. Their results cannot be generalized to either moderately and mildly asthmatic children or to adults although, as the researchers noted, there is little reason to expect good results with these groups, either. Indeed, they suggested that a case can be made to the effect that physiological relaxation may even be counter-indicated for asthma because relaxation may involve a decrease in sympathetic and adrenergic activity, a condition that may be detrimental to asthmatics.

The researchers concluded that relaxation training may be effective in reducing a child's fear of asthmatic attacks, and thus may have some utility in total treatment, but relaxation appears to have no beneficial effects upon pulmonary function in asthma. This point is also made by Alexander (1980) who concluded there are little data to support the direct effectiveness of any psychological variables on the mechanics of pulmonary functioning.

Perloo (1976) noted that a small number of studies have employed biofeedback procedures in asthma research. This small number is surprising compared with the flurry of biofeedback studies in other clinical disorders (Blanchard and Young, 1974; Shapiro and Surwit, 1976). Biofeedback procedures have been used as part of relaxation training (Davis, Saunders, Creer, and Chai, 1973; Greene and Pranke, 1973; Scherr, Crawford, Sergeant, and Scheer, 1975; Khan, Staerk, and Bonk, 1973; Feldman, 1976). Vachon and Rich (1976) found reliable and statistically significant improvement with mildly asthmatic, young adult subjects, when biofeedback was used without relaxation instructions.

The rather consistent success in this small number of studies is certainly encouraging, but caution must still be maintained when interpreting and generalizing to their clinical significance (Creer, 1976; Alexander, 1972; Alexander et al., 1972; Vachon and Rich, 1976). Vachon and Rich, for example, cautioned that their results, although statistically significant, should not be overestimated, since the magnitude of the changes they found "is equivalent to that observed after one inhalation of Isoproterenol . . . [and] . . . few asthmatics would be satisfied with this level of clinical relief" (p. 1976, p. 129). This issue of the clinical versus statistical significance in treatment research has been well discussed by Lick (1973), Lick and Unger (1975), and Alexander et al. (1979) and must be borne in mind when interpreting any treatment research findings. In sum, research data on biofeedback techniques in asthma do indicate both immediate and follow-up improvements; these are encouraging results, and continued research efforts are clealy indicated. However, it is yet to be demonstrated that it is equal to or better than pharmacological treatment.

Psychological intervention in family systems has been reported by a number of investigators from a psychodynamic model (e.g. Liebman, Minuchin, and Baker, 1974) but mostly with the more recently developed social-learning model (e.g. Alexander et al., 1972; Creer and Renne, 1976). Despite theoretical differences, these two groups show considerable agreement in the active goals employed with the families (Creer, 1976). Both focused on (a) alleviating asthma symptoms; (b) identifying critical family interaction patterns; (c) teaching family members to recognize and modify those patterns; and (d) monitoring the family for reasonably long follow-up to prevent symptom recurrence.

The studies of family intervention in asthma have incomplete control procedures, are largely single-case studies, and are still too few to form definitive conclusions. However, as with the relaxation-systematic desensitization and the biofeedback approaches, the available tentative information on family intervention is somewhat encouraging.

Researchers have employed a variety of psychological paradigms to teach improved breathing control. Much of this research has been reviewed by Creer (1976), and the studies include use of positive and negative reinforcement, punishment, extinction, satiation, time-out, and response-cost.

The implications of these studies in the use of specific behavior-change techniques are, again, cautiously promising, and continued research is indicated. Overall, the psychological research literature—only very briefly summarized here—suggests a number of important research avenues:

1. Asthmatic responding appears to be easily conditioned. The importance of that suggestion is that in normal settings, such as in most families, asthmatic responding can easily come under stimulus control of a great variety of commonly occurring stimuli.

2. The stimulus control is highly idiosyncratic, varying greatly be-

tween individuals, between families, and perhaps within individuals and families over time and place.

3. The idiosyncratic stimulus control can function to accelerate or decelerate asthmatic responding, probably depending upon the quality of family interactions.

4. Individualized clinical case studies of families, while posing problems for experimental methodology, are still needed to identify the idiosyncratic *S-R* variables and relationships.

5. Behavior modification paradigms (e.g. systematic desensitization, operant and respondent conditioning) and the use of biofeedback techniques are promising, and must be pursued.

6. The common element in all of these varied psychological studies of asthma is their focus on learning processes at both voluntary and involuntary levels. With regard to the amelioration of psychological escalation of asthma, learning implies the necessity of teaching, and the two together demand the active participation of both teacher (clinician) and learner (patient). One major thrust of this modern, psychological asthma literature is toward teaching the patient to learn improved skills in asthma self-management.

In summary, despite the preliminary work and reviews, such as that of Knapp and Wells (1978), recent reviews of the behavioral treatment of asthma (Alexander et al. 1979; King, 1980) cast doubt on its effectiveness for improving respiratory function. The most important research in this regard is that of Alexander et al., (1979) who concluded that respiratory function improvements due to psychological treatment appears to be so slight as to be of no demonstrated clinical significance. Far more effective (and efficient) treatment is provided through relatively simple use of medication.

Although some future value may be found in behavioral treatment of respiratory function, and some researchers will continue their investigations, at this point there seems little to justify any major expenditure of research effort in this direction. The behavioral model might be better directed at other aspects of the problem of asthma. These could include research in deconditioning asthmatic responses to a variety of *conditioned* stimuli; contingency contracting in families to alter social reinforcement of "sick role" behavior of the asthmatic child; self-control training in the effective use of prescribed medication and the systematic avoidance of triggering stimuli; public health campaigns to educate school personnel and parents about the characteristics and the effective treatment of asthma; and renewed efforts to control contributing large-scale factors such as air pollution. It is a potentially rich field for behavioral research and application.

III. PHYSICAL INJURIES

Each year many children are injured or killed, in a variety of situations from public highways to private homes, involving catastrophic events, accidents, child and adult carelessness and neglect, and even deliberate attacks on children.

It is clear that emergency and long-term treatment of the physically injured child is a medical responsibility. But what profession is most appropriately concerned with the large variety of human factors that constitute the conditions under which those injuries occur? Those factors, of course, are behavioral events. The child-neglecting and/or abusing parent, the manufacturer of dangerous toys, clothing, and processed foods, the school principal who allows a dangerous building condition to remain unrepaired are, among many others, engaged in behaviors that often prove harmful to children. Those human behaviors are proper concerns for behavioral medicine in general, and for the small but growing area of behavioral pediatrics.

We have suggested a wide array of human behavior as proper content in our investigation of physical injuries to children. They include self-injurious behavior of the children themselves, parental neglect and abusive behavior, adults' carelessness, and a wide range of behaviors dangerous to children largely because of adults' ignorance of their effects on children. Thus behavioral medicine should properly be concerned not only with treatment of specific behavior, such as self-injurious behavior, but also with the reduction of current child abuse, prevention of future child abuse, and the education of the public toward awareness of the many forms of adult behavior harmful to children. A too common example is the parent who leaves a young child, unrestrained, sitting or standing on the front seat of a moving automobile, all the while virtually immersed in the parent's cigarette smoke. However, most of what we suggest as our proper concern has not yet been explored by behavior modifiers. In this section we will deal with two areas of behavioral research, children's self-injurious behavior and adults' child-abuse behavior.

A. *Self-Stimulatory and Self-Injurious Behavior*

Self-stimulatory behavior is a large category of excessive and usually bizarre behavior including grimacing, gesturing, arm-flapping, head-waving, rocking, bouncing, jumping, spinning, giggling, and screaming. At its most severe levels, it includes self-injurious behaviors (SIBs) such as hair-pulling, head- and face-banging, skin-digging, arm-, lip-, shoulder-, and knee-biting, eye-gouging and punching, rectal digging, setting oneself on fire, and so on. Such behavior is usually associated with psychotic and retarded children. However, self-stimulatory and injurious behavior is not limited to such populations and otherwise normal children have been treated by behavior therapists for hair-pulling, nocturnal rocking, head-banging, self-biting, self-excoriation (self-caused skin ulcers), and thumb-sucking.

Within the diversity of self-stimulatory behavior, from bizarre grimacing through eye-gouging, there are several common elements: the behavior is repetitive, stereotyped, of obvious intensity, often involving considerable force, high rate, and prolonged duration; it inhibits adaptive behavior; it is often paradoxical, as, for example, when self-inflicted pain appears to have reinforcing value. While exhibiting SIBs the child appears to be in a general state of high excitement and is apparently oblivious to normal social stimuli. SIBs are not only highly resistant to extinction, but often appear to be self-reinforcing, independent of external environmental contingencies, and apparently maintained by the immediate sensory effects of the behavior on the child.

Self-stimulatory behavior is highly aversive to others and can be powerfully disruptive in treatment programs or at home. A screaming child forcefully banging his head against a concrete wall or busily digging out his own self-inflicted wounds will disorganize any parent, clinician, or program, and may also produce permanent, serious physical damage to himself. Even milder self-stimulation, such as loud giggling, interferes with school and treatment programs and with social interactions at home. Lest some readers think we are being overly dramatic, we refer to case descriptions by Watson (1967), Bucher and Lovaas (1968), Tate and Baroff (1966), Hamilton, Stephens, and Allen (1967), Hamilton and Standhal (1967), Gardner (1969), Corte, Wolf, and Locke (1971), Tate (1972), Bachman (1972), and Graziano (1974).

Therapy has generally failed to deal with these problems, commonly leaving that difficult task to institutional caretakers and parents, whose major recourse has been to impose various restraints to protect children from their own behavior. Unfortunately, these caretakers have been observed to unwittingly reinforce and help maintain the very behavior they try to reduce (Bachman, 1972). A therapeutic technology is needed that can rapidly decelerate self-stimulatory behavior, removing it as an interfering, prepotent response and increasing the likelihood of more adaptive behavior.

It is improbable that such technology will be developed within traditional psychoanalytic or psychodynamic models, since such concepts do not easily lead to specific procedures. For example, as noted by Corte, Wolf, and Locke (1971), earlier psychoanalytic explanations suggested that SIBs are a manifestation of a death wish (Ferenczi, 1956), the product of anaclitic depression or severe guilt (Spitz, 1953), a derivation of "the archaic biological reflex of autonomy" (Fenichel, 1945), or a reflex "producing abandonment of an injured organ for a substitute organ to be regenerated" (Corte et al., 1971, p. 201). The therapeutic application of such concepts requires many inferential steps and the communication of abstractions to the client on a level of sophistication far beyond the capacities of the screaming, head-banging child. The concepts have been of no demonstrated effectiveness with severely disturbed self-injurious children. Carr (1977) has examined and evaluated the evidence of the major hypothesis of the etiology and maintenance of SIBs. Carr's emphasis is that SIB is a most complex behavior, most likely multiply determined. For those interested in this area of SIB research his article is highly recommended.

The clinical problem of self-stimulatory activity is seen here as a class of maladaptive surplus behavior, and the essential therapeutic task is to decelerate that behavior. Of the numerous behavioral strategies for decelerating behavior (see Reese, 1966), those most frequently applied to self-stimulatory behavior are response prevention through physical restraint, extinction, punishment (both as response-contingent application of aversive stimulation and as response-contingent withdrawal of reinforcement), and differential reinforcement of alternative behavior.

We will first examine the treatment strategies used with primarily institutionalized children diagnosed as mentally retarded or psychotic, and then examine separately the self-stimulatory and injurious behaviors reported in otherwise normal children.

1. Response Prevention through Physical Restraint

This has been used with self-stimulatory, aggressive, and other classes of severe, "out-of-control" behavior. The degree of restraint usually varies with the severity of the behavior. Given the lack of behavioral technology to reduce self-stimulation activity, institutional caretakers have utilized a variety of protective and restraining strategies, including helmets, mittens, bandages and other protective clothing, or tied children's arms to their sides, or the children themselves to chairs, carts, or beds. In some cases, restraint has immobilized the child for years, risking atrophied muscles and interrupted development. The caretakers are in a sad dilemma; by restraining the child or not, negative results are likely.

Tranquilizers and other medication provide more subtle restraint. Although more acceptable to caretakers because the imposed restraint is less apparent and, viewed superficially, less "inhumane," drugs have been of little success in eliminating SIBs (Berkson, 1965; Rudy, Himwich, and Rinaldi, 1958), though limited success with tranquilizers has been reported with relatively mild self-stimulatory activity (Hollis, 1968; Davis, Sprague, and Werry, 1969).

Although it does not solve the behavioral problem, restraint not entailing harsh or punitive elements might be of some value in producing temporary response prevention. Children whose intense self-stimulation is prevented by restraints are often observed to be relatively calm, at least potentially more responsive to social stimuli, and less disruptive to a given program. When the restraints are removed, however, the children resume their self-stimulation (Bucher and Lovaas, 1968; Lane and Dormath, 1970; Carr, Newsom, and Binkoff, 1976; Favell, McGimsey, and Jones, 1978). In terms of long-term effects, the use of restraints to prevent SIBs might reduce the cumulative physical injury, but there is no evidence that it brings about any lasting decrease in self-stimulatory behavior when the restraints are removed.

While restraint as a temporary response-prevention strategy has been a commonly used ward-management technique, it has not often been systematically studied as a possible therapeutic technique. Some case studies describe the use of restraint as one aspect of more complete treatment programs. Graziano (1974) described cases in which physical restraint, as an aversive stimulus, was manipulated as a negative reinforcer. Physical restraint, such as holding the child's arms, was immediately contingent on "high excitement," "aggressive," or "out-of-control" behavior, and was released immediately contingent upon the child's progressively better approximations of "relaxation" responses. Restraint was gradually faded and eliminated as relaxation came under, first, the therapist's verbal control, then the child's verbal self-control.

Saposnek and Watson (1974) reported the use of mild restraint in blocking a child's arms to prevent head-slapping; Henriksen and Doughty (1967) held a child's arms to interrupt and reduce wild mealtime behavior; Singh (1980) covered a baby's face with a terrycloth bib for 3 seconds contingent on thumb-biting; Hamilton, Stephens, and Allen (1967) combined restraint in a behavioral chain with 30 minutes of time-out to reduce SIBs in one child and other self-stimulatory activity in four other children. Other researchers have used restraint in conjunction with other punishments contingent on the antecedents of the SIB cycle (Griffin, Locke, and Landers, 1975) or contingent on SIB in conjunction with positive reinforcement for alternative behavior (Schroeder, Petersen, Solomon, and Artley, 1977). Interestingly, Favell, McGimsey, and Jones (1978) observed with two profoundly retarded children that restraint appeared to be rewarding (i.e. allowing the children back into their restraints would stop their crying and screaming) and was thus a possible reinforcer. Along with contingent punishment for SIB (a squirt of lemon juice) and distraction, the children were allowed to return to their restrained condition contingent on increasing intervals of more appropriate "other than SIB" behavior. Such an addition was more effective than the use of lemon juice alone as a punishment. Many other writers who describe time-out procedures generally pass over the fact that physical restraint is often necessary to interrupt the undesirable behavior and place the child in the time-out situation. Restraint, then, is probably frequently incorporated in treatment strategies, but seldom discussed or systematically studied as a potentially effective response-prevention strategy. More systematic research might reveal carefully programmed, highly contingent, and brief physical restraint to be an important element in treatment programs aimed at the reduction of self-stimulatory activity.

2. Extinction

This is the progressive weakening of behavior by withholding reinforcement. It has been applied with mixed success in a number of clinical cases: by Williams (1959) to reduce operant crying of an infant; by Wolf, Birnbrauer, Williams, and Lawler (1965) to reduce vomiting and temper tantrums in a retarded child; by Graziano (1974) to reduce "mildly upset" behavior in psychotic children; by Bucher and Lovaas (1968) with SIBs; by Birnbrauer, Bijou, Wolf, and Kidder (1965) in a classroom of retarded boys. Spradlin and Girardeau (1966) suggested that extinction might be the most effective procedure to reduce aggressive behavior, including tantrums and SIBs.

The successful application of extinction procedures requires that the target behavior continue to occur while the effective reinforcers are withheld. Thus, extinction is an appropriate technique only where prolonged trials do not threaten physical injury, and where the discriminative and reinforcing stimuli can be clearly identified and controlled by the therapist. Extinction procedures may therefore be appropriately applied to problem behavior, such as tantrums, screaming, and most of the self-stimulatory activity, such as arm-flapping, and so forth, in which no physical injury is threatened and in which the controlling stimuli can, in fact, be withheld. On the latter point, it should be noted that there are serious difficulties in applying extinction procedures in social settings, such as classrooms and therapy groups. Graziano (1974), for example, noted that social groups provide so many sources of uncontrolled reinforcement for the children's disruptive activity that too often it may be the clinician's behavior, rather than the child's, that weakens through extinction.

Extinction procedures are not appropriate where physical danger threatens or the controlling stimuli cannot be withheld. Most obviously, the clinician cannot allow severe self-injurious behavior to continue, as would be required in extinction trials. Even though SIBs might be maintained by social reinforcement, as has been suggested by Ferster (1961), Spradlin and Girardeau (1966), and Moore and Bailey (1973), an extinction strategy could result in serious injury (Lovaas, Freitag, Gold, and Kassorla, 1965; Bucher and Lovaas, 1968; Gardner, 1969). Bucher and Lovaas (1968, p. 91), for example, were concerned that one child might have "killed herself during an extinction run" had extinction been used. Further, SIBs may be largely and paradoxically maintained by their physical effects on the child and not by any social consequences. If so, withholding social reinforcement will have little useful effect. Corte, Wolf, and Locke (1971) provide some supporting data, although with only four children. They compared three methods of reducing SIBs, including extinction by withholding social reinforcement, and reported no decrement with the extinction procedure.

In summary, extinction procedures appear to be of value, but are often difficult to apply, for relatively mild and noninjurious self-stimulatory activity. They are not appropriate for severe self-stimulation, including SIBs.

3. Punishment

The contingent application of aversive consequences and the contingent withdrawal of positive consequences unfortunately constitute the most common, popular, and socially accepted methods used by adults to control children in natural environments. Our present discussion is specifically limited to the use of punishment to reduce self-stimulatory activity. The reader is referred to Gardner (1969) and to Harris and Ersner-Hershfield (1978) for a more complete discussion of the use of punishment with a wider variety of behavior problems. Ethical issues in the use of punishment have been discussed by many behavior modifiers, including Rachman and Teasdale (1969), and by virtually every writer presenting data on the use of punishment with humans. In addition, the experimental literature has been well summarized by Azrin and Holz (1966).

Contingent aversive stimulation, primarily electric shock, has been successfully used to reduce SIBs (Lovaas, Freitag, Kinder, Rubenstein, Schaeffer, and Simmons, 1964; Lovaas, Schaeffer, and Simmons, 1965; Bucher and Lovaas, 1968; Risley, 1968; Tate and Baroff, 1966; Hamilton and Standhal, 1967). Corte, Wolf, and Locke (1971) compared three methods to reduce SIBs in four institutionalized, profoundly retarded adolescents: extinction by eliminating social consequences, differential reinforcement of non-SIB behavior, and contingent electric shock. Only electric shock eliminated SIBs in all four children. However, its effects did not seem to generalize, but remained specific to the situation in which the shock was used. Corte et al. suggested that to eliminate the SIBs of severely retarded children it may be necessary to apply shock in the variety of settings in which these SIBs occur.

This issue of generalization was approached by Birnbrauer (1968) and by Bucher and King (1971). In the latter study, treatment of a retarded schizophrenic boy was designed to achieve generalized suppression of the child's dangerous and persistent behavior of playing with and destroying electrical equipment, such as the ward television sets. Electric shock was contingent on touching forbidden electrical appliances in a series of 16 experimental situations that represented the range of environmental settings in which the child's time was spent. The response was effectively suppressed, but it quickly reappeared with each new setting, a finding that supported previous work showing the specificity of punishment effects. With continued punishment in the various settings, the behavior was significantly reduced, and some measure of generalization was achieved. The authors point out too, that although the behavior was significantly reduced, it was not eliminated, and their data do not allow conclusions concerning the long-term effects of the treatment. In contrast Griffin, Locke, and Landers (1975) reported the successful suppression of SIB in multiple settings and over a three-year follow-up in a blind, profoundly retarded male using multiple forms of punishment including electric shock, hair tugging, and restraint. However, Favell, McGimsey, and Jones (1978) report a case where treatment with electric shock only temporarily reduced SIB. Carr, Newsom, and Binkoff (1976) report electric shock to have been unsuccessful in reducing various SIBs.

Other aversive stimuli have been used as contingent punishments to suppress a variety of behaviors—cayenne pepper (Blackwood, 1962; Blackwood et al., 1971); lemon juice (Favell et al., 1978; Rapoff et al., 1980); Listerine (Lamal, 1976); physical restraint (Whitney and Barnard, 1966; Hamilton, Stephens, and Allen, 1967; Henriksen and Doughty, 1967; Graziano, 1970, 1974; Griffin et al., 1975; Saposnek and Watson,

1974); aversive tickling (Greene and Hoats, 1971); a squirt of aerosol shaving soap in the mouth (Conway and Bucher, 1974); water from a plant sprayer in the face (Dorsey, Iwata, Ong, and McSween, 1980); smelling ammonia (Rapoff et al., 1980; Singh et al., 1980); a tug at the hair (Banks and Locke, 1966; Griffin et al., 1975); spanking or slapping (Moore and Bailey, 1973; Cavalier and Ferretti, 1980); social isolation (Drabman and Spitalnik, 1973). Conditioned aversive stimuli, such as verbal disapproval and facial expressions, were also included as part of treatment packages by Whitney and Barnard (1966), Henriksen and Doughty (1967), Graziano (1970, 1974), and Moore and Bailey (1973). Romanczyk (1977) also found that, as predicted by learning theory, intermittent punishment produced resistance to extinction superior to punishment contingent on every occurrence of self-stimulatory behavior.

Based on Foxx and Azrin (1973b), Harris and Romanczyk (1976) implemented both in a treatment center and at home an overcorrection procedure for the head-banging of an eight year old trainably retarded boy. It required that the boy's head be forcibly guided in an up-down, left-right pattern contingent on the occurrence of a SIB. Their results show a sudden decline in SIB at the onset of treatment which continued at near zero levels over 9 months of treatment. Azrin, Gottlieb, Hughart, Wesolowski, and Rahn (1975) combined a similar overcorrection procedure with the addition of positive reinforcement contingencies in a multiple case study of ten mentally retarded individuals, ranging in age from 6 to 26, and one 15 year old male, diagnosed as schizophrenic. They used 20 minutes overcorrection contingent on SIB which they gradually decreased until only a warning or reminder was given to the client for any attempt at self-injury. In addition, at first continuously and then intermittently, they used verbal praise, snacks, and stroking, to reinforce the clients' positioning their hands away from their heads and their clients' outward-directed physical and social activities. Overall, after 3 months of treatment, 99% of the original SIBs were eliminated. Similar procedures have proven effective with various self-stimulatory and self-injurious behaviors (Harris and Wolchik, 1979; Wells, Forehand, Hickey and Green, 1977; Coleman, Whitman, and Johnson, 1979; Kelly and Drabman, 1977; Singh, 1980; Conley and Wolery, 1980). However, other studies report little or no success using overcorrection (Rapoff, Altman, and Christophersen, 1980; Measel and Alfieri, 1976; Cavalier and Ferretti, 1980). Coleman et al. (1979) found little situational generalization using overcorrection and Matson, Ollendick, and Martin (1979) call into serious question the long-term maintenance of gains through overcorrection.

Punishment by the contingent withdrawal of positive reinforcers has been somewhat less controversial. Interestingly, it appears as if a schedule of differential reinforcement has been operating on some larger scale, and behavior modifiers, criticized for one mode of punishment, have shifted toward the other. This second mode includes time-out and response-cost. Response-cost, a procedure in which a response is suppressed by the contingent withdrawal of conditioned reinforcers (e.g. tokens, privileges), has been studied by a number of investigators and reviewed by Kazdin (1972). From Kazdin's review, it can be seen that response-cost procedures have been used with a variety of behavioral problems and clinical populations and that they appear to be quite successful in decreasing undesirable behavior. However, the lack of long-term follow-up studies and the need to carefully examine possible negative side effects permit only tentative conclusions about the clinical effectiveness of these procedures.

Both response-cost and time-out depend on the manipulation of external reinforcers, and if self-stimulatory activity is, indeed, self-reinforcing, then neither response-cost nor time-out will be effective. However, self-stimulatory behavior may have multiple reinforcers, and external reinforcement may play some part in supporting it or in serving as a learned discriminative stimulus setting it off. Time-out and response-cost may thus have limited value in reducing self-stimulatory behavior in severely disturbed or retarded children, but may be of greater value in children for whom a variety of conditioned reinforcers have already been developed.

Time-out is conceptually similar to response-cost but differs strategically from it, involving either the suspension of positive reinforcers by the therapist or the removal of the child to a neutral situation. In either case, there is a contingent period of time away from positive reinforcement.

Carr, Newsom, and Binkoff (1976) observed that the rate of SIB of an eight year old mildly retarded and schizophrenic boy, increased during classroom situations. Using a multiple schedule design, they found that during free time and during times of "tacts" (simple verbal statements from an adult which did not require a response from the child) the rate of SIB was relatively low, about one SIB per minute. However, during times of "mands" (a time intended to approximate a structured classroom or therapy session in which the child was presented with simple commands) SIBs increased to a high rate in excess of 50 SIBs per minute. Thus, in this case, it appeared that SIB was greatly increased by the environment. This conclusion received even stronger support in showing that at the end of the "mands" situation, the statement "OK let's go" caused the hitting to drop to near zero while the statement "the sky is blue" caused no such drop.

Another finding of the study was that if the commands in the "mands" situation were interspersed with a positive context such as the animated and cheerful reading of a simple story instead of silence, the SIB decreased to rather low levels of about two to ten SIBs per minute. This study, along with the previously described study of Favell, McGimsey, and Jones (1978) which utilized "distraction" in its treatment program, hint at the potential importance of the general pleasantness of the situation in influencing SIB.

Duker (1975) used a time-out procedure carried out by hospital staff to reduce the head-banging and hitting of a profoundly retarded 15-year-old girl to near zero. The procedure involved confining the girl, contingent on head-banging, into a small bathroom for 10 minutes with the added requirement that confinement would be extended until the last 2 minutes of confinement were free of head-banging. Meanwhile the girl was put on an intermittent schedule of reinforcement where attention and the chance to manipulate plastic and suede items were provided for incompatible alternative noninjurious forms of behavior.

Myers (1975), however, found that a time-out procedure involving removal of attention by the teacher and aide for a 12-year-old trainably retarded boy was ineffective in eliminating self-biting. Also a DRO (differential reinforcement of other behavior) token system in which tokens were earned for common compliance behavior but withheld during SIB had only a minimal effect. The addition of a response-cost procedure, however, in which, in addition to a verbal reprimand, tokens were taken away, caused SIBs to drop drastically and then decrease gradually to a near zero frequency after 20 days of treatment and to remain at near zero over a 12-week follow-up.

It appears that the contingent presentation of aversive stimulation, specifically electric shock, is best supported by data as an effective punishment technique for reducing self-stimulatory behavior (Corbett, 1975). The clinical use of electric shock is still clouded by ethical and empirical issues. Among the latter, three appear to be most important. First, in virtually all the studies using electric shock, an alternative response was possible and a differential reinforcement paradigm was in operation. Thus, the effects of the shock alone are difficult to assess; perhaps the behavior changes were brought about as much by the positive reinforcement of the alternative response as by the punishment of the target behavior (Gardner, 1969). Second, punishment is of limited generalization (Corte, Wolf, and Locke, 1971; Bucher and King, 1971). Third, its long-term effects are still uncertain.

Other punishment and paradigms, such as time-out and response-cost, and more general social disapproval and withdrawal of social approval, appear to have received varying success. More empirical tests are needed to decide if these techniques can generally be of value.

4. Developing Alternative Behaviors

Decreasing self-stimulatory activity by accelerating alternative behavior is a strategy, used implicitly or explicitly, in most approaches. Behavior modifiers generally agree that directly decelerating maladaptive behavior, whether by restraint, extinction, or punishment, is not sufficient and that some form of more adaptive, alternative behavior must also be strengthened.

Much of the self-stimulatory activity of institutionalized children may occur because of a general lack of support for varied alternative behaviors in the insidious and nonrewarding environment found in most children's institutions. Berkson and Davenport (1962), Berkson and Mason (1964), and Guess and Rutherford (1967) observed a marked reduction of institutionalized retarded children's self-stimulatory activity when more toys were made available to them. Thus, such activity should decrease if the caretakers simply enrich the environment by adding manipulable, rewarding objects, such as carefully chosen toys. Watters and Watters (1980) noted that the self-stimulatory behaviors of autistic children decreased after physical exercise.

The role of specific sensory reinforcement in maintaining self-stimulation has been tested by Rincover and his associates (Rincover, 1978; Rincover, Cook, Peoples, and Packard, 1979). Rincover (1978) has extended suggestions by Berkson (1967) and Berkson and Mason (1964) that the tactile and kinesthetic stimulation of SIB and self-stimulatory behavior acts as its own reinforcement. Rincover (1978) tested whether the sensory consequences of self-stimulation maintained the self-stimulatory behavior. If so, the removal or masking of specific consequences of self-stimulatory behavior (e.g. removing the noise of a spinning plate; masking the propioceptive feedback of finger-flapping and object manipulation; making visual feedback impossible), a process they called sensory extinction, should decrease the self-stimulatory behavior associated with that sense. In a multiple-baseline design with three developmentally delayed children, sensory extinction caused a rapid decrement in self-stimulatory behavior. Rincover (1979) extended this study and found that not only did certain children appear to be reinforced by the sensory feedback of their self-stimulatory activity, but that specific toys which provided similar sensory feedback to the child's original self-stimulation were preferred over toys which provided different sensory feedback. These findings agree with a distinction made by Carr (1977) in his review of motivational factors in SIB. Carr suggested that the treatment of SIB could be usefully dichotomized into those in which the source of reinforcement is intrinsic to the child and those in which the source of reinforcement is extrinsic to the child. Extrinsically motivated SIB would be controlled primarily by the social reinforcement of the behavior. Intrinsically motivated SIB would imply that the source of reinforcement for the SIB would be within or a direct consequence of the behavior itself. Rincover's procedure would seem to offer one alternative treatment of such intrinsically motivated SIB that could be used in conjunction with attempts to provide a variety of additional reinforcements to compete with the reinforcement. The effectiveness of tailoring specific sensory reinforcement to children's specific self-stimulatory behavior deserves further attention.

Focused attempts to reduce self-stimulation by shaping alternative behavior have also been reported. In some instances, the alternative behavior was physically incompatible with self-stimulation (Lovaas, Freitag, Gold, and Kassorla, 1965; Allen and Harris, 1966; Graziano and Kean, 1968; Hollis, 1968; Mulhern and Baumeister, 1969; Myers, 1975; Duker, 1975; Graziano, 1974). Moore and Bailey (1973), noted that positive reinforcement of incompatible behavior, while "rarely sufficient" to modify extreme behavior, "is often helpful." Behavior incompatible with self-stimulation includes physical relaxation, as described by Graziano and Kean (1968) and Schroeder et al. (1977) and such responses as keeping the arms down at the sides or the hands engaged in activities like playing with clay, paints, or puzzles. These responses are incompatible with head-banging, arm-flapping, and other self-stimulation involving hands and arms, and their contingent positive reinforcement may succeed in reducing self-stimulation.

Other reports (Azrin et al., 1975; Cavalier and Ferretti, 1980; Rapoff et al., 1980; Guess and Rutherford, 1967; Peterson and Peterson, 1968; Graziano, 1974) suggest that the alternative behavior need not be physically incompatible with self-stimulation, although in some cases the data are confounded. On this point, Bachman (1972) suggested that, rather than incompatibility, a major factor may be the degree to which the alternative behavior successfully produces positive reinforcement. An earlier point needs repeating here: virtually all the studies, using contingent electric shock to suppress SIBs actually included the reinforcement of alternative behavior, and the apparent effect of the contingent shock was confounded with the effects of differential reinforcement.

Dorsey, et al. (1982) reported success in reducing chronic S.I.B. of three mentally retarded persons, using differential reinforcement and contingently used protective clothing.

All this suggests that differential reinforcement of alternative adaptive behavior may be a potentially powerful and largely uninvestigated strategy to reduce self-stimulation, perhaps even including SIBs. Contingent shock is apparently the most successful strategy, but it is confounded. Before allowing its apparent effectiveness to soften our moral concern over inflicting pain on children, we should investigate more completely the strategy of strengthening alternative behavior. A hefty application of positively reinforcing stimulation, without the use of aversive control, contingently applied in programs of successive approximations, may prove to be both effective and efficient.

We suggest that the main elements of a technology to reduce problematic self-stimulation should include a programmed and "rich" differential reinforcement of alternative adaptive behavior and, for SIBs in particular, a combination of protective restraints and clothing to prevent injury and reduce the stimulation value of the behavior, gradually faded as alternative adaptive behavior is progressively strengthened.

5. Self-Injurious Behavior in Nonpsychotic and Nonretarded Children

Many self-stimulatory or self-injurious behaviors of children who are not psychotic or retarded appear similar to the behaviors already discussed, but typically lack the all encompassing prepotency and self-absorption found among retarded and psychotic children. The children remain aware of and generally responsive to the web of social and other reinforcements in their environment.

The most frequently reported SIB of otherwise normal children is trichotillomania (hair-pulling)—a problem largely considered secondary to the many other problems of retarded and psychotic children. The literature on hair-pulling, for both adults and children, consists entirely of case studies and is well reviewed in the introduction by Gray (1979). Treatment of all but one child resulted in total or near total elimination of the problem. The one exception was a 15-year-old girl in which treatment was successful through a 6- but not 9-month follow-up (Mastellone, 1974).

Treatment has varied considerably in complexity and type. Mastellone (1974) utilized the punishment of self-administered wrist-snappings of a rubber band. Shapiro, Barrett, and Ollendick (1980) used an overcorrection procedure. Anthony (1978) found self-monitoring to be a sufficient intervention to eliminate hair-pulling in a 9-year-old boy. Sanchez (1979), with the youngest subjects—including a 27-month-old boy—combined a time-out procedure contingent on hair-pulling with social and food reinforcers for behavior incompatible with hair-pulling. This treatment was only partially successful and the child continued to pull his hair while in time-out. Noticing that in the well-developed chain of responses the boy's hand would go into his mouth after he pulled his hair, they added a simple component of applying tape to the boy's fingers, thereby interrupting this response. This added component eliminated hair-pulling through a 12-month follow-up.

Other research has combined token economies and punishment. Evans (1976) found that tokens for not pulling hair along with time-out for pulling hair was an effective treatment with an 8-year-old girl. Gray (1979) found that tokens and social reinforcement for not pulling hair helped minimally with a 5-year-old girl. The addition of the punishment of four hand-slaps for hair-pulling, however, caused the behavior to drop to near zero.

Another problem which appears of little interest to those who work with retarded and psychotic children is thumb-sucking. Ross (1975) decreased to near zero the thumb-sucking of a 9-year-old which had caused noticeable malocclusion of his front teeth and was delaying dental treatment. The boy sucked his thumb primarily at night and while watching TV. The night thumb-sucking was decreased by the simple application of medication to the thumb. The day thumb-sucking involved the parent turning the TV off for 5 minutes if the child was thumb-sucking while watching. Unintentionally, this treatment also involved heavy reinforcement by siblings for nonthumb-sucking as they did not like the TV turned off. Lassen and Fluet (1978) found in a case involving thumbsucking at night that the application of medication to the thumb had a minimal effect. Success was achieved by the simple procedure of requiring a thin cotton glove be worn on the offending hand. The elimination of thumb-sucking, even after wearing the glove was terminated, was maintained through 6- and 12-month follow-ups.

Cases have also been reported of otherwise normal children exhibiting the kinds of SIBs most commonly associated with psychotic and retarded children. Matson, Ollendick and Martin (1979) developed a treatment package for nine young children, ages 18 months to 3½ years, who exhibited low-frequency self-biting behavior. These children received a spray of Listerine mouthwash from the parents contingent on bites and attempted bites and were reinforced through verbal praise and physical hugs for nonbiting behavior. All of the parents reported maintained success at 6-month follow-up, except for one mother who refused to continue the treatment.

Latimer (1979) eliminated the self-excoriation (self-caused skin ulcers) of a 12-year-old girl. A behavioral analysis of the girl's picking found that: (a) the picking had become the major source of interaction between the girl and parent; (b) the girl was often unaware of her picking; and (c) TV and lying in bed appeared to have become discriminative stimuli for picking. The treatment included reinforcing appropriate behavior, giving noncritical feedback, instructing the girl to engage in the incompatible behavior of pressing her thumb and finger together for 60 seconds whenever she caught herself picking, and the development of a token economy for not picking with the parents refraining from scolding. This treatment caused a gradual decline in picking until the nineteenth week, by which time the behavior had been eliminated. This was maintained through a three-year follow-up.

Martin and Conway (1976) treated a 25 month old girl for a problem they labeled "infant nocturnal rocking." This problem involved head-banging in bed. Martin and Conway hung a 100-watt bulb over the child's crib which was activated by the noise of the head-banging and remained on for 5 seconds. This decreased the head banging to a low rate over 6- and 12-month follow-ups.

Dougherty and Lane (1976) implemented a punishment procedure to eliminate head-banging in bed by a three-year-old girl. They instructed the parents to (a) withdraw the pacifier of the child as soon as the head-banging was heard and say "Bang head, loose pacey," and (b) leave the room and wait for no head-banging for at least 1 minute at which time they would return the pacifier and say "Good! Don't bang head, can have "pacey" back." After two consecutive trials, the interval required to get the pacifier back was increased to 4 minutes. After 19 days of treatment, no more SIBs were noted through a one-year follow-up.

Linscheid et al. (1981) used overcorrection with incompatible behavior to reduce chronic severe SIB in two otherwise normal children. The children were hospitalized during treatment and they and their parents were taught to continue the overcorrection procedure after hospital discharge.

In summary, the treatment procedures applied to the self-stimulatory and self-injurious behaviors of nonpsychotic and nonretarded children are similar to those used for retarded and psychotic children. However, there have been greater applications of the reinforcement of alternative behaviors, the use of social reinforcement, and the use of self-control strategies. Even in cases where punishment was used, these children, unlike the retarded and psychotic children in institutions, appeared to receive increased natural reinforcements from their environment. As mentioned previously, this increased reinforcement may play a critical role in ensuring the generalization of effects to other situations and to increased maintenance.

B. *Child Abuse*

Zigler (1980) and Graziano, Gallipeau, and Graziano (1981) have made a similar observation: although an estimated 2000 children are killed each year through abuse and another 60,000 injured (Kempe, 1976) it is not the numbers involved that make child abuse so serious a social problem. Rather it is the fact that one of our most basic and cherished relationships of trust—the child's trust in its parents—is being seriously violated. A single child's terror and pain when violated by a parent is a serious criticism of the stability of human integrity; the many tens of thousands of such violated children confirm the seriousness of an indictment that could be made on the basis of a single case.

Alvy (1975) began his discussion of child-abuse prevention by defining two alternative general approaches: (1) a comprehensive view that defines the child-abuse problem as one of social and institutional functioning as well as one of individual behavior; (2) a more focused approach that views child abuse as a matter of individual deviant behavior only.

Most social service agencies appear to approach the issues in Alvy's "focused" or "limited" sense, as individual and separate cases, viewing each as the result of a particular parent's psychopathology or weakness under extreme conditions such as severe economic frustrations. Case-by-case approaches, once emergency medical treatment has been provided for the child, typically result in therapy or homemaker services for the abusive parent *but little or no direct help for the probably still abused child.* There is no convincing evidence yet that psychotherapeutic approaches have in any significant way alleviated this social problem.

Increasingly, it seems, professionals are taking a larger view, considering child abuse as not due to a single parent's psychopathology but as a set of behaviors in many ways encouraged and supported by our social values (Gerbner, Ross, and Zigler, 1980). Blatt (1980), Feshback (1980), Graziano et al. (1981), and many others have commented upon the apparent social supports for child abuse and the need for legislation and large-scale social programs to promote concern for and protection of children and their rights. Potentially helpful attempts could include public and legislative activity that will increase children's rights and protect them from various forms of abuse such as corporal punishment in schools. Graziano et al. (1981) have reported that 92% of the 600 college students they surveyed indicated they had been spanked as children. The investigators suggested that our society's acceptance of spanking, even severely painful spanking, for "disciplinary" purposes provides a "high floor" of permissible violence toward children, making additional steps from what many consider "proper discipline" to overt abuse very easy to take and likely to occur.

However necessary legislative action and public campaigns may be to prevent future abuse, we are still faced with the thousands of children who are abused and with the humanitarian demands to intervene in each known case so as to end that child's suffering. Such individual treatment will not prevent new cases from occurring. However many cases we may treat, even if all were successful, new cases will still continue to appear. At this point we have not yet developed successful primary prevention methods, and our typical professional response remains on the individual, family level. As such it remains humanitarian, but also remains a grossly limited, inadequate professional response with no primary prevention value.

The procedures available for individual family intervention are few, perhaps only four: (a) immediate emergency medical treatment of the abused child; (b) separating parents from the child by removal of the child into protective custody and/or sentencing of the parent to prison; (c) keeping the family intact while helping the parent to learn better child-rearing skills; (d) continued protective custody, such as foster care, combined with long-term psychological, social, and educational treatment and training of the child to help overcome the psychological damage due to the earlier abuse.

Most social service agencies seem to combine the first three approaches: immediate medical care, if necessary; temporary protective custody of the child followed by returning the child to the parents; and psychological treatment and economic or other support for the parents. This standard approach has serious limitations: it has no primary prevention value; there is virtually no evidence that the psychodynamic-based therapies or economic supports used are effective in reducing child abuse; these approaches do little or nothing to protect the child who must remain with the often still abusing parents while the social workers support and treat those parents. Finally, in this type of approach virtually no help is given the child either immediately or in the long term, for psychological, social, and educational programming to help the child develop more normally and so overcome or mitigate the effects of the abused early history.

Recently as reviewed by Isaacs (1982) behavior modification has been used in child-abusing family treatment approaches. The criticisms noted above apply to these behavioral programs. These recent behavioral interventions have substituted behavioral-functional analyses and contingency-management programming for the traditional psychodynamic therapies. It remains to be shown whether such behavioral treatment is any more effective than the psychodynamic treatment in reducing child abuse. What is clear, is that the newer behavioral approaches contribute no more than their predecessors to primary prevention, to the direct protection of the child or to long-term service to the child. Thus, however effective behavior therapy may be in the studies published to date it is, like all of the previous social and psychodynamic work, yet of little or no demonstrated value in curbing the social problem. In Alvy's (1975) definition, then, behavior therapists have adopted the "narrow approach" to this problem.

In a recent review of the behavioral treatment of child abuse McKeethen (1981) identified nine papers, most of which were published since 1977. Two papers had appeared in 1973 to 1974. Behavior therapists' interests in these problems are very recent. McKeethen notes similar procedures in the studies: functional analysis of parent-child interactions, complete with baseline recordings, and interviews to determine the parents' child-rearing methods, paying particular attention to the use of punishment. From the functional analyses the major conditions under which punishing and abusive behaviors occur are identified. Treatment then proceeds to not only alter those behaviors under those specific conditions, but also in many of the studies, to improve the parents' general child-rearing skills.

Papers by Sandler, VanDercar, and Milhoan (1978), Denicola and Sandler (1980), and Crozier and Katz (1979) described quite similar treatments for abusive parents in their homes. Each project included only two families. Sandler et al. (1978) and Denicola and Sandler (1980) studied single-parent families (mothers) while Crozier and Katz (1979) worked with both parents in each of their two families. Each intervention attempted to increase the parents' use of positive reinforcement with their children. In addition to the basic program Denicola and Sandler (1980) included parents' coping-skills training to help them recognize and to control their own anger arousal and expression.

In his critical assessment of these three studies McKeethen points out an ethical "trap" into which the researchers were led by their procedures. In each of the six cases the mothers had abused their children, frequently in some cases. The researchers used baseline assessments, some as long as 6 weeks, during which the children were still possibly being abused. McKeethen believes that the lengthy baselines were not necessary to establish reliability. Research values, he argues, were distorted to the degree that they appear to have taken precedence over the children's welfare.

Reavley and Gilbert (1979) reported 27 cases of individual counseling plus home record keeping. Outcome success was measured by therapists' ratings on a nine-point scale ranging from "no change" to "complete success." The mean therapist rating of outcome was 5.8 or "75%

success," and a follow-up showed that 25 of the 27 patients had maintained their treatment gains. It is interesting to note that the rating scale included only positive outcome; that is, there was no recognition that, as Graziano and Fink (1972) argued, some clients become worse in treatment. We do not know if, for example, any of the therapy dropouts of the program had actually increased their child-abuse behavior.

An interesting case study is described by Mastria, Mastria, and Harkins (1979). Three 40-minute mother-child play session baselines were videotaped on three consecutive days. In the clinic-based treatment, portions of the videotapes, showing the creation or sustaining of mother-child conflicts, were played back. Unlike the other studies summarized here, Mastria et al. (1979) did not attempt to develop a general improvement in child-rearing skills but, rather, focused specifically on altering the conflicting aggressive and potentially abusive interactions. In individual sessions the mother and therapist reviewed the videotapes. Verbal feedback and modeling were used to teach the mother to praise her son's cooperative behavior, ignore his aggressive behavior, or to divert the boy's imminent aggressive behavior. The mother was instructed to practice at home and, when she believed she detected her own imminent loss of control, to leave her son with a cooperative neighbor until she had calmed herself.

Posttreatment and follow-up videotapes were made of mother–child interactions and trained observers rated appropriate and inappropriate behaviors of mother and child. Although this is a case study and generalizations cannot be made to other cases, the procedure appears to have been carefully worked out and executed, and may offer some suggestions for researchers and clinicians.

The papers so far outlined reported individual treatment cases, totaling 34 families. Mothers were the sole clients in 32 families, and both parents participated in only two cases. An alternative, behavioral treatment of groups of parents, has been reported in three papers. Use of a group rather than individual settings is potentially more cost efficient and may provide important social cues and reinforcers for improved parenting (Ambrose, Hazzard, and Haworth, 1980). In their hospital-based program Ambrose et al. provided "cognitive behavioral" treatment for child-abusing parents in eight weekly group sessions. The program included teaching basic information in child development, and skills in managing problem behavior and their own anger control. Procedures included group discussions, lectures, videotaped presentations, and some homework assignments. Unfortunately, the only assessment of results included changes in attitudes during group meetings and parental self-reports. No follow-up was reported.

Doctor and Singer (1978) and Wolfe, Aragona, Kaufman, and Sandler (1980) reported more complex treatments that involved group counseling and training sessions, and home monitoring and evaluation visits. Although Doctor and Singer had no objective evaluation and Wolfe et al. used only ratings of "success," their two papers make an interesting but tentative suggestion: parents who were in the program involuntarily—by court order—appeared to have made considerably more progress than those who were voluntary participants. McKeethen (1981) suggests that the apparent differences are striking enough to suggest the value of better designed and controlled studies of the comparative effectiveness of court-ordered and voluntary participation by child-abusing parents.

Overall, behavioral approaches to child abuse do not yet appear to be demonstrably useful in reducing the problem. One major general limitation is a continuing commitment to an after-the-fact, individual-case treatment approach logistically impossible to provide to all child-abusing parents. Thus, even if successful in every therapy case, the treatment would do little to reduce the number of new cases; the approach has no primary prevention value. Current behavioral approaches, like traditional psychodynamic treatments, persist in viewing child abuse as a problem of individual functioning or, in its largest-group sense, a problem of mother-child interaction. Accordingly they have so far provided little to identify and change the social factors that may be involved. Such an issue, widespread throughout all levels of society, cannot reasonably be conceptualized and dealt with as multiple instances of individual psychopathology or behavioral malfunctioning.

Furthermore, in individual cases the behavioral approaches show little convincing evidence of success. The studies are all limited in their assessment of treatment effects and provide little convincing data that much had been accomplished. Controls were weak or lacking, objective data sparse, and follow-ups were rare.

The most severe error is the lack of objective, physical evidence of a reduction in child maltreatment. No one seems to have physically examined the children to determine if old wounds were healing, old bruises fading, or if there were no new injuries. General physical health, body tone, weight, coloring, activity, growth, alertness, and so on, all seem to have been ignored as the clinical researchers presumably accepted the parents' self-reports, or rated improvements in contrived and videotaped parent-child interactions. If the overriding concern is the quick and effective elimination of child abuse and neglect, we must fault behavioral studies for their failure to consider the most basic and important dependent variable—the condition of the children. In general these behavioral studies, like their psychodynamic counterparts, paid little attention to the children themselves, to their physical conditions, to their fears and possible resentments, to their interrupted social, personal, and educational development, and did little to help those children to overcome the negative effects of their abusive treatment.

A paper by Tracy and Clark (1974) appears to be an exception. In a hospital-based, home-intervention program they included continued monitoring of the child for physical injuries and signs of abuse and neglect. The abused children were medically treated for their injuries and, after release, were physically examined on each of their outpatient visits to the hospital's clinic. Records on each child provided continual objective monitoring to assess any further physical abuse so as to provide immediate help if needed. Tracy and Clark's procedures should be examined by workers in this field.

IV. FOOD-RELATED PROBLEM BEHAVIORS

Children are plagued by a number of behavioral problems associated with food and resulting in nutritional deficiencies or other somatic illnesses. Many children overeat and become obese; some refuse to eat adequately and lose so much weight that it becomes life-threatening. Some children persist in ingesting inedible and harmful substances such as hair and soil (pica). Others eat, but then, with little apparent distress, deliberately bring up their food, often reingesting some of the vomitus (rumination). These and other food-related problems have been studied and treated by behavior modifiers; we consider three: obesity, anorexia, and rumination.

These are genuine behavioral medicine issues: problems in which somatic disorders are brought about primarily by human behavior. Further, as successful treatment requires modifying the contributing problem behaviors, the necessity of a behavioral component in treatment seems clear.

These somatic disorders are among the more obvious in this food-related category; others of equal importance have not yet been identified as problems for behavioral medicine or phenomena to be studied by behavior modifiers. The question posed here is, "*What* additional human behaviors relevant to food contribute to *what* kinds of somatic disorders?" Several tentative answers immediately come to mind: chewing heavily sugared foods such as candy and many breakfast cereals contributes to tooth decay and gum-tissue disorders; poor shopping and cooking skills contribute to imbalanced diets and poor nutrition; the use of lead solder by food processors to seal cans accounts for an estimated 50% of the lead in the American diet (Settle and Patterson, 1980) and contributes to increased risks of brain damage; consumer persistence in demanding food additives including colorings, flavors, and sweeteners such as saccharine contributes to increased risks of cancer; industrial pollution of drinking sources and contamination of entire food chains, such as the 1973 Michigan polybrominated biphenyl (a fire-retarding agent) disaster, contributes to increased cancer risks. These and other relationships among behavior, food, and somatic illness involve the public's everyday behavior and touch upon public policy and legislation, public education, and the monitoring of and control over industrial and other business practices. These large-scale issues ordinarily excluded from our professions' legitimate functions, share in the behavior-food-somatic illness relationships: their solutions depend upon appropriate behavior change, though not that of individual clients, but of a large class of consumers, politicians, policy makers, and industrial managers. The client population ranges far beyond our usual clinic clients; the society-wide scope of the needed changes cannot be approached by any of our current clinical systems. But the issues are well within the proper scope of behavioral medicine.

A. *Overeating and Obesity*

Adult obesity has been of professional concern for many years; interest in childhood obesity is quite recent. Behavioral approaches to adult obesity were among the first attempts by psychologists to deal with a traditional medical problem (Wooley, Wooley, and Dyrenforth, 1979); the psychologists "had picked one of the most perplexing and refractory of all disorders" (p. 3). Medical researchers have identified obesity as a major health problem for adults, rejecting "the idea that it was constitutionally determined" (Wooley et al., 1979). As the earlier psychodynamic therapies proved ineffective, obesity seemed a possible "testing ground" (Wooley et al., 1979) for reemerging behavioral approaches. Since the mid-1960s literature on the behavioral treatment of obesity has grown rapidly and now constitutes a major area of interest. Wilson (1978) suggested this remarkable growth may be due partly to the expansion of behavior modification in general during that period, but also because (a) the problem offers a very clear and easily measured dependent variable: weight loss; and (b) there are many potential subjects willing to cooperate in studies and weight-loss programs. Combined with the large-scale apparent seriousness of the problem, it was an attractive problem for behavior modifiers.

The overall success of behavioral approaches to obesity has been disappointing, although somewhat more effective than the older psychodynamic therapies. In general a variety of environmental and self-control strategies have been applied, resulting in small weight losses which, although statistically significant in many studies, appear to have been too minor to be of any personal importance or satisfaction for the dieting subject. Further, the weight reductions were on a decreasing curve and, following treatment, subjects often gained back all or most of the weight, in many cases, surpassing their pretreatment weights.

The common assumption in these studies is that obesity is due to excess calories. Thus some combination of ingesting excess calories and expending insufficient calories (overeating and underexercising) is usually targeted for change. Most behavioral programs focus their attempts directly on modifying eating patterns such as rate of chewing, size of bite, number and place of meals, and availability of high-calorie foods. Self-control attempts included making ultimate aversive consequences (becoming fatter) more immediate by imagining oneself in a grossly unflattering shape whenever the urge to overeat occurs. Attempts were made to increase self- and social reinforcement for successful weight loss, and so on: appropriate—but only modestly effective—behavioral interventions.

In the many recent obesity-control studies the original behavioral assumptions have come to be seen as having been about as naive as the earlier psychodynamic speculations. Although environmental and self-control interventions did result in weight loss, the process was a great deal more complex than first thought. As one loses weight through behavioral programs, the body may physiologically adapt to lessened intake, perhaps by conserving energy expenditure, and might continue to store fat despite the lowered caloric intake. Thus it may be that as one loses weight, a counterreaction begins, causing the person to slow the weight loss and perhaps even to gain weight. One early simple, apparently reasonable assumption was that fat people eat more than normal-weight people. Subsequent research, however, has shown there may be little difference in amounts eaten by obese and normal weight people (Garrow, 1974; Wooley et al., 1979).

The more critical variable may not be caloric intake but energy expenditure, largely a matter of metabolism that may vary with physiology, genetics, eating patterns, and rates of intake. However, eating patterns and rates of intake seem to vary greatly among the obese (Stunkard, 1959); as a group there may be few differences between obese and normal weight subjects in that regard. It may not be total calories ingested but patterns and rates of eating as combined with patterns and rates of exercise that are the major behavioral determinants of obesity.

Obesity is a multidetermined problem in which behavioral, cultural, social, and personal values and physiological and genetic variables all appear to be important. Obesity now appears to be a far more complex issue than thought just ten years ago; these important complicating factors are discussed in the excellent review by Wooley, Wooley, and Dyrenforth (1979).

It may be assumed that obesity in children is no less complicated, with comparable difficulties in successful intervention and factors particularly important for children. For example, because children are largely under parental control, they are far more influenced by family factors than adults: obese children may benefit more from changed family behavior and environmental control procedures.

One difficulty in measuring success with children is their normal growth and weight gain over time. Weight loss may not be a good dependent variable at all (Edwards, 1978). Obese children who successfully slim down over a 6-month period or longer might not lose any weight at all.

A factor not taken into consideration in behavioral weight control with children is children's consistently strong, negative evaluation of their obese peers. Wooley et al. (1979) report that obese children "are judged negatively on nearly every dimension studied" (p. 18); they are seen as ugly, stupid, mean, sloppy, lazy, and dishonest (Lerner, 1973). These often intense, negative evaluations seem to increase in adolescence, particularly with girls, who often try to diet. It is reasonable to assume that such evaluations, held by the obese children and/or by their peers, must affect the weight-related behavior. Behavioral programs to date have not taken this as a potentially important variable.

Behavioral Research in Childhood Obesity*

Between 1971 and 1975 over 45 articles were published on behavioral procedures for adult obesity. A review of research by Jeffery et al. (1978) states that behavioral interventions in adult obesity have produced consistent, but only modest, weight losses. A more disheartening prologue by Gillick (1973) contended that the behavioral work done with obese adults is inappropriate for use in children since these programs tend to rely rather heavily on still developing behavioral repertoires.

Nevertheless, approximately ten years after the inception of behavioral therapy for adult obesity, systematic behavioral treatments for childhood obesity were introduced. Based on the supposition that effective weight control requires major changes in eating behavior, it is examined in relation to its antecedents and consequences. Behavioral treatment aims to modify antecedent stimuli (stimulus control), to

*This section has been written by R. J. Kelly, Department of Psychology, State University of New York at Buffalo.

regulate the act of eating per se, and to reinforce these behavior alterations.

We will consider published reports of behavioral treatments of childhood obesity. Reported data was evaluated in relation to the following important characteristics: the type of study (group versus case), presence or absence of control techniques, the general and specific behavioral treatments employed, subject variables such as sex, age, and number of subjects and drop outs, the criterion for the label obesity, the length of treatment, the degree of obesity among subjects, the effectiveness of the program, and follow-up data. As noted above, a true evaluation of the effectiveness and maintenance of weight programs with children cannot be based solely on pre- and posttreatment weight levels since children's weight increases developmentally. Thus, a successful program might show a child actually gain weight. For this reason the data must be evaluated in terms of the subjects' age, the length of treatment, and the time lapse before follow-up.

In an early behavioral treatment of childhood obesity Dinoff, Rickard, and Colwick (1972) successfully applied behavioral contracts in a weight-reduction program for a bright, emotionally disturbed, 10-year-old obese boy attending a therapeutic summer camp. Their procedure consisted of constructing written agreements between this 194-pound boy and his counselor in terms of food intake. Daily weigh-in sessions served as immediate reinforcing events, while the boy was also granted predetermined major reinforcing events each time he lost 10 pounds. These larger reinforcements involved playing with a one-way mirror, operating a videotape machine, and using the camp dictaphone. After only 7 weeks the boy lost 30 pounds. However, his participation in a total treatment program makes it impossible to assess the direct effect of the contracts; unfortunately, the authors failed to report any follow-up data on this encouraging case study.

Schoenwetter (1978) implemented a behavioral program for weight control with a 12-year-old, 125-pound (eighty-ninth percentile) girl with Downs syndrome. Baseline data on her eating behavior and general daily activity showed chronic overeating and little physical activity. The strategy employed involved goal-setting along with many stimulus cue modifications. A special chair and smaller plates were used for eating, while the child's pace of eating was slowed by suggesting that she put her fork down and count to ten between bites, use chopsticks on some nights and her left hand on other evenings, and take a 2-minute break in the middle of her meals. The girl's adaptive physical education teacher in school involved her in a motor program to increase her physical activity in the classroom and in gym. In addition, the child was taught effective responses to children who called her "fatty" or offered her food. After 7 months, the child's weight was approximately the same as at the program's inception. Perhaps this study's most important contribution was pointing out the special problems of dealing with retarded children via self-control methods. The program consisted of nonnutrient food reinforcers, and also involved both the home and school environments. No follow-up data could be gleaned at the time of the report.

Altman, Bondy, and Hirsch (1978) combined self-monitoring with contingency contracting in their extremely successful work with two obese, mentally retarded adolescent females with Prader-Willi syndrome. Contingency contracting between the children and their parents/caregivers was used to specify consequences for daily self-monitoring, reduced caloric intake, weight loss, and exercise. In addition, punishment was administered for stealing food. A multiple-baseline design across the two subjects showed no significant weight loss (average, 3.5 pounds) during a self-monitoring-only phase. However, the subjects lost an average of 44 pounds during subsequent phases involving reinforcement for decreased caloric consumption and weight loss, reinforcement for weight loss only, and maintenance procedures. Follow-up checks at 3, 6, and 9 months (plus a one-year check on one subject) found almost complete maintenance of this weight reduction. Key elements may have included putting primary responsibility for change with subjects and their caregivers along with emphasizing long-term weight loss.

A 7-month nutritionally based school program for the control of eating in obese children was implemented by Epstein, Masek, and Marshall (1978). Food intake was regulated for six lower-class black children, ages five and six, during breakfast and lunch meals in a Head Start Center. Each subject was at least 25% over his ideal weight. Techniques included increasing prelunch activity level in a withdrawal design, and improved food selection in a multiple-baseline fashion. During the eating treatment, foods were placed in three categories (red, yellow, and green) according to whether the subjects should decrease, maintain, or increase intake of these foods. For consuming appropriate foods children were rewarded with stars that could be exchanged for inexpensive toys. The study found a decrease in caloric intake as a function of either increasing activity or eating regulation procedures. Although each child gained weight, five of the six decreased the percentage they were overweight. The results were not maintained after the school year ended, but this study showed food selection and consumption behaviors to be modifiable, if only temporarily, with easily implemented behavioral procedures.

In summary, four case studies employed behavioral methodology to reduce weight in ten subjects with varying degrees of success with treatment ranging from 7 weeks to one year. The most successful programs involved behavioral contracting as a major component.

The first systematic group behavioral program for obese children was conducted by Rivinus, Drummond, and Combrinck-Graham in 1976. Therapy involved nine black, fatherless, lower-class children ranging from 8 to 13 years of age and averaging 71% overweight. Over 10 weeks, these subjects kept records of what they consumed and a "daily log" of their success in maintaining proper behavioral changes. Parents were trained in contracts, rewards, and the modeling of appropriate behavior. A weekly group supper consisted of instruction and reinforcement for proper eating behavior. Average weekly loss of the nine children that completed treatment was approximately 6.1 pounds, with children of normal weight mothers losing much more than children of obese mothers. A 1-month follow-up found that six children continued to lose or at least not gain weight, while two regained more weight than they had lost during treatment.

An early dissertation by Gillick (1973) combined parent training with record keeping and reinforcement procedures to reduce weight in 20 children aged 6 to 12. In addition a no-treatment control group and an effort-control group (in which subjects were told treatment would begin at a later date but to follow some instructions until that time) were assembled with 15 children in each group. Results in a 10-week program showed a significant difference between the weight loss of the experimental group and the other control groups, although these latter two groups did not differ from each other. One hundred percent of the treatment subjects experienced some weight loss. A 1-month follow-up showed continued weight loss in these children. The mothers in the treatment group lost more weight than other mothers.

Grace (1977) utilized self-monitoring in the modification of childhood obesity. Seventy-three children, aged eight to ten and at least 20 percent over the average weight for their age and height, were assigned to one of five conditions: a waiting-list, no-treatment control group (WL); a group-participation cell without self-monitoring (GP); a cell in which children self-monitored desired behavior (CD); a group in which children self-monitored undesired behavior (CU); and a condition in which children self-monitored desired and undesired behavior (CD + U). All treatment groups, including the group participation cell without self-monitoring, showed greater reduction in obesity than nontreated controls. However, none of these experimental conditions differed significantly from any other. But at follow-up 1 and 2 months later, the only condition that did not result in a decrease in the rate of weight loss involved self-monitoring of the desired behavior of exercise. One other encouraging finding was the absence of effects of age, sex, or social class.

Aragona, Cassady, and Drabman (1975) performed a controlled group study involving parental training and contingency contracting. Fifteen overweight girls, aged 5 to 11, were randomly assigned to one of three groups: response-cost plus reinforcement, response-cost alone, and a no-treatment control group. In the first group, parents contracted to facilitate their child's weight loss by carrying out stimulus control and reinforcement techniques, encouraging their children to exercise, and completing weekly charts and graphs. The parents paid a monetary fine if the child failed to lose weight, while the child was rewarded each week for losing the predetermined weight. The response-cost-only group did not contract to reinforce their child's performance. At the end of a 12-week treatment period composed of weekly meetings, both experimental groups had lost significantly more weight than the control group. A 31-week, no-contact follow-up failed to show a treatment effect but did show a trend toward lower weight gain by the response-cost-plus-reinforcement group.

Wheeler and Hess (1976) attempted to reduce juvenile obesity through a successive approximation of proper eating patterns. Forty children between 2 and 11 years of age had a median skinfold thickness three standard deviations above the mean for their age, sex, and race. Of the 28 subjects who did not drop out after three or fewer therapy sessions, 14 constituted the treatment group while the remaining 14 composed the no-treatment control group. The 7-month therapy involved mother-child pairs in individual half-hour sessions spaced out over long intervals. The actual treatment included detailed analysis and record keeping of stimuli and rewards associated with eating in the child's home environment, modification of inappropriate eating patterns, reinforcement of proper eating behavior, and approximations toward satisfactory weight. The experimental group dropped 5.5% in its mean percentage overweight, while the control group and dropouts increased 5.5 and 5.8%, respectively. Follow-up was not reported. The apparent strengths of this approach were the treatment of mothers and children in pairs, the emphasis on gradual changes and long-term involvement, and the attention to the needs of the individual child subsequent to careful behavioral analysis.

Epstein, Parker, McKoy, and McGee (1976) obtained a descriptive analysis of eating regulation in nonobese and obese children. Sip rate, bite rate, and concurrent activities of six, 7-year-old children, three obese and three nonobese, were observed at lunchtime over a 6-month period. A procedure for decreasing bite rate, putting eating utensils down between bites, was implemented in a multiple-baseline, across-subjects design. Concurrent activities and sip rates were also observed to assess behavioral covariations. Results indicated the control of bite rate across all subjects, with a significant reduction in amount of food consumed. Response classes were found to be at least partially independent, while differences in eating behavior of obese and nonobese subjects were observed. This study differs from other strategies in that it made no direct attempt to decrease obese subjects' weight levels, thereby demonstrating that systematic behavioral methods can slow eating rate.

Kingsley and Shapiro (1977) conducted a comparison of three behavioral programs. Forty 10 and 11 year olds from affluent homes took part in behavioral weight reduction groups composed of either children with their mothers (MC group), mothers alone (M group), children alone (C groups), or a no-treatment (NT) control group. The 8-week treatment for each group included information on nutrition and obesity, along with the provision of calorie-counting booklets and pocket diaries to record daily food intake. Weight loss did not differ among the experimental cells but was significantly greater in these conditions than for the control group. At 6 and 20-week follow-ups the rate of weight gain for the subjects in the three experimental groups was comparable to that of children their age. It was also reported that at the posttreatment and 6-week follow-up sessions the weight loss of the M group mothers remained significantly greater than that of mothers in any other group, although no intergroup differences between mothers were found at the 20-week follow-up.

Weiss (1977) conducted a controlled group study to evaluate the relative effectiveness of four methods for treating adolescent obesity. Eleven males and 35 females, ages 9.5 to 18 years, were placed into one of five groups: conventional diet (DNR), conventional diet plus self-reinforcement (DR), stimulus control (SC), diet with self-reinforcement and stimulus control (SCDR), or a no-treatment control group. All treatment groups lost some weight, while the control group gained a significant amount. Although a direct statistical analysis failed to show significant differences among the active-treatment groups, the author indicates that the SCDR group lost the most weight, decreased the most in its percentage overweight, and had the highest proportion of subjects who lost weight (6 of 8 or 75%). Moreover, at the one-year follow-up the groups involving stimulus control showed clear superiority; they were the only groups able to maintain weight loss and reduce their degree of overweight.

Rotatori, Parrish, and Freagon (1979) reported a controlled pilot study to evaluate the usefulness of a behavioral weight reduction and nutritional treatment package for use with mentally retarded children. The program included parental counseling, diet analysis and modification, as well as school, home, and self-reinforcement. During a 7-week treatment phase with three sessions per week, a school nurse trained six moderately to mildly retarded children to record their food intake, curb their urges to overeat, limit themselves to one helping per meal, reduce their rate of eating, leave some food on their plates, increase their energy expenditure, and eliminate snacking. The students attained a mean weight lost of 3.7 pounds with an average weekly weight loss of 0.6 pound per pupil. Thus the pilot program demonstrated that a school nurse with parental support can provide practical and effective behavioral/nutritional experiences for retarded children that produce weight loss. No follow-up data were reported.

Finally, Zakus, Chin, Keown, Herbert, and Held (1979) combined a number of behavior modification principles to treat five severely obese juvenile females in a medical setting. Therapy included record keeping, eating regulation, thought stopping, role-playing, stimulus control, peer group interaction, and instructional meetings for significant others. After 6 months three of the five girls had lost a net average of 8.3 pounds, while the other two girls gained a net average of 7.3 pounds. The authors concluded that this success rate was significant, compared with the same girls' weight gains during previous clinic contacts, but no adequate control procedure was used. Perhaps the most important finding of this study was the positive correlation between internal locus of control and success in losing weight. No follow-up data were reported.

In summary, seven controlled and three uncontrolled group studies were performed using a variety of behavioral treatments on over 270 subjects. The techniques included parent-training, contingency contracting, response-cost, eating regulation, self-control, self-monitoring, stimulus control, weight training, reinforcement, exercise, and successive approximations. Therapy ranged from 7 weeks to 7 months, while follow-up data were reported in six of the ten studies. Females constituted at least half of the subjects in all but one of the programs. The ages, number of dropouts, criteria for obesity, and average percent overweight of the subjects varied quite a bit across studies, making it difficult to compare the relative effectiveness of the strategies. All of these group studies reported at least partial success.

In all, four cases and ten group studies were reviewed. Nine of these employed appropriate control techniques. Almost all of the programs included some form of eating regulation and record keeping, while parent training and contingency contracting were also often employed. Over 280 children, mostly female ranging in age from 2 to 18, were used as subjects. Dropout rates were comparable to those of behavioral programs for other disorders. The minimum criterion for obesity, although often not reported, ranged from the mildly (10%) to the moderately (25%) obese, while some studies included severely obese (100%) children. Treatment ranged from 7 weeks to 7 months. Average weight losses within studies were as much as 47.5 pounds, and as many as 21 (of 26) subjects lost weight in any one design. Nine of the articles reported follow-up data, with five of these maintaining a good deal of their treatment effects.

Encouragingly all the studies succeeded to some extent. As with the research on behavioral treatment for adult obesity, these initial experiments with children delivered consistent though modest success rates.

However, at least five points must be kept in mind in order to make an accurate evaluation of these results. First, although many studies report statistical significance, they fail to approach true clinical significance. Second, the reports' promising results are tempered by the slim chances of less successful studies in getting published in competitive journals at all. Third, only 33% of the articles report significant maintenance of weight reduction, bringing the issue of long-term benefits into question. Fourth, many of the studies do not impart the average percent overweight for their subjects. A less comparable but often cited measure, such as loss of weight in pounds, fails to reflect developmental changes in the children.

Finally, many group studies use a waiting-list control group against which they compare their experimental cells. In all the no-treatment control groups cited, subjects gained weight. This is presented as evidence that the experimental subjects would have gained weight also if no treatment was employed. However, the control subjects may have gained weight because they anticipated receiving help in the near future. Perhaps they were less strict with their food intake, believing that they would be forced to eat less when therapy began. In other words, they may have feasted before the impending famine.

Childhood obesity is a prevalent condition which may have adverse physiological and psychological effects. Many factors are thought to be crucial in its inception and maintenance. Most of the early psychological research on the topic was psychoanalytic in nature and, with nonbehavioral treatments, met with little success. Behavioral treatments for adult obesity have been consistently but modestly successful. Behavioral techniques for childhood obesity began just over a one decade ago in a less than optimistic setting.

The 14 studies reviewed here suggest that the most effective way to combat childhood obesity involves the consistent, systematic application of behavioral techniques with emphasis on contracted, individualized attention focusing on long term commitment and expectations. The children's commitment must often be supplemented by significant others in home and school environments. A multimodal approach with components that continue outside of the specific therapy settings seems most promising.

The findings of two recent studies are also instructive. Epstein and Wing (1983) reported that behavior modification weight control procedures for children were more effective than a nutritional education program. Epstein et al. (1982) compared two exercise programs, both independent of dieting: (1) a "lifestyle change" program in which children increased their energy expenditure in a wide variety of common activities and games; and (2) an aerobic exercise program requiring daily performance of prescribed exercises. While all groups improved, the lifestyle change subjects maintained their improvements better than the aerobic group. This study suggests that children's improved weight status and physical fitness might be best maintained, with or without dieting, when the treatment involves lifestyle changes in energy expenditure.

Further research in the area should also attempt to discover safe and easily implemented methodology. It was refreshing not to see aversive techniques used as therapy for obese children in these initial behavioral studies. Research in the area will probably increase remarkably in the next few years because of the recent emphasis NIMH has given to children and behavioral medicine. We hope much of it will be focused on a third issue cited as a priority: prevention. If childhood obesity can be prevented, the need for behavioral or other treatments will decrease, as will the adverse consequences of this harmful disorder.

B. *Food Refusal*

Even under normal conditions children frequently refuse food, often to their parents' consternation. Much food refusal is well within normal limits and seems to be momentary, of low intensity, or perhaps too often even an appropriate response by an overstuffed child to an inappropriately insistent parent. At its extremes, however, food refusal by children and particularly by adolescents is a serious affair. The resulting weight loss and physical debilitation can breach life-threatening limits.

The term traditionally applied to extreme food refusal is *anorexia nervosa* meaning literally loss of appetite due to causes of "nervous" origin. "Nervous" is ordinarily taken to mean causes that are psychological as opposed to physiological in nature. The term is misleading and perhaps should be discarded. First, although psychological factors are clearly implicated in apparently major ways, it has yet to be determined that psychological factors are major causal agents (Bemis, 1978). Second, *anorexia* means "loss of appetite" and, as we are told by Stunkard and Mahoney (1976), a true loss of appetite does not seem to occur until the disorder is well advanced. Some researchers suggest that a more appropriate descriptive concept is fear of getting fat, "weight phobia" (Crisp, 1967; Morgan and Russell, 1975).

Severe food refusal is seen in children of both sexes and all ages, although the most frequent and dramatic cases are adolescent females. It is not clear if adolescent females constitute a true majority of anorexics or if unidentified selective factors have biased the known anorexic population in that direction. A rare condition, with recorded hospital cases at less than 1 in 100,000 (Tolstrup, 1975), there is some indication it may be significantly increasing (Duddle, 1973). This clinical rarity may be a major reason for the current lack of knowledge and the marked differences in explanatory models despite the hundred years since the disorder was first described by Gull and Lasegue (Tolstrup, 1975).

Clinically, the adolescent girl who becomes anorexic seems characterized by an unwillingness to admit she has any problem except that her parents and others do not leave her alone (Bemis, 1978), by disrupted menses, by extreme food refusal and dangerous weight loss, by interest in her own and others' intake of food, by often extremely energetic physical activity, and by a refusal to view herself as "thin" or "skinny" despite the bare-bones, often emaciated image that strikes everyone else who looks at the girl. Many have been noted to enjoy their mirror image, judging themselves to be "little" and beautiful, despite everyone else's perceptions. A considerable degree of perceptual distortion is clearly indicated.

By the time the anorexic is hospitalized the therapy of choice is usually medical, aimed at preventing death. High-calorie diets and intravenous feeding are used to bring the patient through the physical crisis. At a later point psychological treatment is begun to alleviate the psychological conditions that have presumably caused, exacerbated, or maintained the anorexia. Traditional psychological treatment has been psychodynamic, but the effectiveness of such treatment has not yet been demonstrated (Bemis, 1978). Since the mid-1960s there has been more use of behavioral approaches and the results have generated optimism among behavior modifiers, often criticism from others. Bruch (1975) for example, considers even "successful" cases of operant approaches to be instances of "brutal coercion."

A number of behavioral studies have reported success with single cases and small samples. Hallsten (1965) used systematic desensitization to successfully treat a 12-year-old girl. Lang (1965) reported success using relaxation procedures to reduce fears of disapproval. Effective use of varieties of contingent reinforcement were reported by Bachrach, Erwin, and Mohr (1965), Blinder, Freeman, and Stunkard (1970), Leitenberg, Agras, and Thompson (1968), and Azerrad and Stafford (1969). Informational feedback (e.g. calories consumed, weight gains) was found to be more important than positive reinforcement for weight gain (Agras et al., 1974). A combination of three factors, size of meals, positive reinforcement, and informational feedback was suggested by these researchers as potentially effective treatment.

Some of the larger studies were reported by Brady and Rieger (1975), 16 cases; Bhanji and Thompson (1974), 11 cases; and Halmi, Powers, and Cunningham (1975), 8 cases. Unlike many others each of these provided follow-ups on the patients at 23 months (Brady and Rieger), a mean of 32 months (Bhanji and Thompson) and a mean of 7 months (Halmi et al.). These follow-ups, like other studies, present a pessimistic picture for the maintenance of improvements as a result of hospital treatment. Bemis (1978) concludes that behavioral approaches appear to bring about weight gains and thus ease the medical crisis but have not yet demonstrated success in maintaining those gains. Some critics (e.g. Bruch, 1975) consider the failure of maintenance to be additional reason for rejecting behavioral approaches. Others, however, (Bemis, 1978) suggest that behavior modification has been used in too limited an application, focusing too specifically on bringing about weight gain in the acute or crisis situation. Rather than rejecting or further restricting the behavioral interventions, Bemis suggests, clinical researchers would do well to expand the behavioral approaches so as to study and gain control over those long-term, post hospital conditions in the patients' homes in order to bring about successful maintenance of gains, and even continued improvement. Four-year follow-ups are suggested by Bemis, far longer than the few months usually reported. Empirical study, Bemis noted, and not verbal clashes between psychodynamic and behavioral proponents, is potentially the most effective route for developing successful treatment and maintenance approaches to anorexia.

One of the most interesting studies of maintenance issues was reported by Rosen (1980). Twelve clearly diagnosed anorectic females, ages 11 to 21, successfully gained weight in a hospital behavior modification program and, their immediate crisis over, were discharged to their homes. Following discharge all developed abnormal, even bizarre, eating patterns, a common characteristic of anorectics. These included hoarding and hiding food, eating secretly, demanding special foods, refusing to eat with the family, etc. In four cases, bizarre eating patterns required rehospitalization for further nutritional treatment.

Rosen enlisted the aid of the patients' families in what was described as a "maladaptive eating program." That is, all patients at home were to be restricted to their own idiosyncratic, self-imposed eating patterns. This would require, for example, that they would be "permitted only foods they had secretly obtained or hidden; they were not to share mealtimes with their family; they were not to be seen eating by any member of their family, thus eating must always be done in private; they were to maintain their previously agreed-upon weight gain or stabilization" (p. 102).

The final two restrictions were that failure on any one of those demands would result in immediate rehospitalization, and "Permission to return to normal eating at home was contingent upon the patient totally rejecting inappropriate eating habits" (p. 102).

The results of this highly structured restriction to their own bizarre behavior were dramatic—reminiscent of J. Rosen's (1953) forced confrontations of psychotic patients with their own bizarre "symptoms." Five patients immediately dropped their idiosyncratic habits; after one day on the restrictions, three others gave up their idiosyncracies; before the end of the third day the last four resumed "their normal eating." Follow-ups for a mean of 3.2 years showed no relapses, and good maintenance of "stable weight, restoration of menses, and normal eating" (p. 103).

Rosen does not explain these surprising findings other than making two very tentative suggestions: (a) confronting one's own symptoms has some effective psychodynamic impact and (b) the social reinforcement value of the families' responses to the idiosyncratic behavior was eliminated when families markedly stopped trying to change those patterns. These results were impressive, and clearly warrant more research.

In nearly all cases the patient was seen as suffering primarily from the complex psychological and somatic condition, anorexia. In one paper, (Cairns and Altman, 1979) the patient's anorexia was a secondary and seriously complicating problem. The patient was a little girl, 11-year-old Jane, with a six year history of surgical and radiation treatment for cancer. During radiation therapy the child became anorexic, enuretic, withdrawn, and uncommunicative. Nonbehavioral psychological and psychiatric treatments failed to help, and the child continued to deteriorate.

Behavioral programming was instituted, using a continuous reinforcement schedule to reestablish eating. The child was first put on deprivation by removing all toys from her room and denying social contacts except for those she earned. In the initial phase of treatment each bite was rewarded by brief social interaction and access to toys. After eating had been reestablished, tokens were used as reinforcement during meals and snacks. Jane was helped to compile a "shopping list" of pleasant activities to be purchased with her earned tokens, such as use of the playroom. The token system was later installed at home, also. Cairns and Altman report a rapid and dramatic increase in eating, social interaction, and verbal communication, and significant weight gain. The improvements were maintained over an 8-month follow-up at home.

The authors caution that neither generalizations nor clear causality can be inferred from this case study, A-B design. But the dramatic improvements in the child that coincided with treatment are suggestive.

Overall, behavioral approaches to anorexia appear to have provided some of the most effective psychological treatment for bringing about rapid weight gain. There are still many uncertainties and weaknesses in these approaches and it appears that researchers are beginning to attend to them. The most important areas needing improvement are outlined in Bemis' (1978) critical evaluation of the research. Taken together these methodological criticisms indicate that to improve behavioral treatment of anorexia researchers should (a) increase their sample sizes; (b) more clearly and differentially diagnose anorexia so as to differentiate it from other major conditions such as schizophrenia and hysteria and in which similar behaviors are often seen; (c) include more effective controls so the relative contributions of behavioral programming can be identified in complex treatment packages often including drug and psychotherapy as well as behavior therapy; and (d) routinely include carefully planned maintenance programs, long-term monitoring, and evaluative follow-up examinations.

In addition Bemis (1978) and others suggest that behavior modification may be too narrowly focused on goals of rapid weight gain to the exclusion of other, possibly more important variables such as long-term social and emotional adjustment. As vague as such "adjustment" concepts may be, suggests Bemis, it is the long-term social and personal success of the patients that is the most important outcome for them. Concern for and measurement of such adjustment should be added to the behavioral interventions. On the same point the nearly exclusive focus on rapid weight gain, while perhaps useful in the crisis period of hospitalization, may have often resulted in negative effects, such as, heavy reinforcement of increased eating to the point of compulsivity and obesity and possible medical problems due to the drastic changes in food consumption and stored body fat.

A final problem area to be noted are the ethical issues involved in treating a condition the patient denies and clearly does not want treatment for, a response typical in anorexia. Any treatment, somatic, psychoanalytic, or behavioral, under such conditions of patient resistance, takes on coercive coloration. The patient is convinced to cooperate with treatment or is forced to receive treatment such as tube-feeding or unwanted visits of an insistent psychotherapist pressuring her to "talk about" her problems. Critics such as Bruch appear to believe that only behavior modification is coercive in that situation, while appearing quite thoroughly insensitive to the coercive nature of psychodynamic approaches. A more rational view, we suggest, is one that admits the coercive and external control aspects of all of our current treatments and then turns to the solution of four important questions: (1) What are the most effective treatments for anorexics? (2) Under what conditions are each of the treatments most appropriate? (3) If receiving treatment is not completely voluntary, what are the costs to the patient in terms of human rights, safety, comfort, psychological upset, and so on? (4) Who may properly serve as society's agent to make those costs-benefits ethical determinations for the patient—the child, the parents, the physician, the psychiatrist, the psychologist, an institutional ethics committee?

At this point successful treatment of anorexia is very uncertain. What seems clear is that somatic and psychological variables are involved, and that both somatic and psychological treatments are needed. The patient's condition varies from the depths of crises through a wide range of reactions, and the appropriate intervention at any one point must therefore be determined at that point and on an individual patient basis. As for psychological treatment, despite the growing evidence that behavioral approaches have been successful in achieving rapid weight gain, convincing demonstrations of maintenance through behavioral programs have not yet been reliably demonstrated. There is virtually no acceptable evidence to support the exclusive use of psychodynamic therapies in general or psychoanalysis in particular. Given the long period that these models have been applied to anorexia without demonstrable success, we must ask whether their continuation is either warranted or ethical.

C. *Chronic Rumination*

Chronic rumination is repeated vomiting, often voluntary, without nausea or retching. Seen most often in retarded and psychotic populations, it occurs also in otherwise normal infants. Serious physical breakdowns can result from chronic rumination—dehydration, malnutrition, emaciation, lowered resistance to disease, and, in some cases, death (Marholin, Luiselli, Robinson, and Lott, 1980; Sajwaj, Libet, and Agras, 1974; Toister, Condron, Worley, and Arthur, 1975), with death rates in ruminative infants of 12 to 20% (Marholin et al., 1980). Obvious personal and social problems can also ensue as the ruminative infant, smelling of both fresh and stale vomitus and perhaps about to regurgitate at any time, is not readily held, cuddled, or kissed by parents or other caretakers. In institutions for retarded adults, where rumination is not uncommon, staff, understandably stay away from ruminative patients, except to scold and clean them up, undoubtedly providing a great deal of negative attention. A brief paragraph (Blackwood et al., 1971) gives us some idea of the staff's task on a ward for profoundly retarded adults: "The attendants nominated (X) as the patient with the most repulsive behaviors. On returning from a meal, (X) almost invariably went to one side of the room, repeatedly vomited, and then consumed the vomitus. Other patients joined (X) in consuming the vomitus" (p. 91).

A variety of methods have been tried to control rumination. Among the most common (Marholin et al., 1980) are dietary changes, surgery, and drugs, including tranquilizers and anti-nauseants. Marholin et al. (1980) also list "mechanical restraints such as chin straps, oesophageal blocks, and arm straps" to prevent finger-induced vomiting. Surgical, drug, and mechanical restraints do not, however, help teach the patient to refrain from vomiting.

Behavioral approaches have been attempted at least since the early 1960s, with generally positive results. Because of the nature of the problem, nearly all reports have been case studies and, because of limited control possibilities in case studies the effectiveness and generalization of the various techniques are still open to question. The case studies do, however, describe a variety of procedures that seem to have been effective in a few cases and the clinician, faced with a ruminating patient, can select and try several.

Successful results have been reported by modifying feeding techniques (Ball, Hendrickson, and Clayton, 1974) and by feeding to satiation (Jackson, Johnson, Ackron, and Crowley, 1975; Foxx, Snyder, and Schroeder, 1979). In both sets of procedures the assumption was that feeding changes interrupted the learned behavioral chain that included ingestion, chewing, regurgitation, and, often, reingestion of vomit.

Extinction procedures were applied by Wolf, Birnbrauer, Williams, and Lawler (1965) through withholding attention to the vomiting or closely related behaviors. Although Wolf et al. (1965) reported success, the major potential danger in using extinction is that the many nonreinforced trials ordinarily required to bring about extinction may leave the patient vulnerable to injury due to the prolonged vomiting. A similar problem limits the use of extinction for other self-injurious behavior such as severe head-banging.

A variety of negative consequences have been employed as punishment contingencies: cayenne pepper (Blackwood et al., 1971), electric shocks (Lang and Melamed, 1969), and taste-aversive substances such as lemon juice (Sajwaj, Libet, and Agras, 1974). While the punishing stimuli (hot pepper, electric shock, and squirts of lemon juice) seem drastic, it should be noted that these severe and highly resistant problem behaviors were actually life threatening as noted by Lang and Melamed (1969) and Sajwaj et al. (1974).

Lang and Melamed's client was a 9-month-old boy for whom all other procedures had failed. The infant's ruminating had begun at 5 months, and worsened seriously until, at 9 months, he weighed only 12 pounds and was kept alive through nose-tube feeding. Lang and Melamed maintained electromyographic monitoring and, when the vomiting was about to occur, contingent shock to a thigh and a loud tone were presented. By the third 1-hour treatment session vomiting could be ended with only one or two presentations of the aversive stimulus. Vomiting decreased not only during treatment sessions but also at other times during the day. An interesting result was that nurses reported being able to interrupt imminent vomiting by loudly clapping their hands, suggesting the tone-shock pairing may have succeeded. Weight gain was noted, beginning with the start of treatment, and continued after discharge from the hospital. A 1-month follow-up showed a far healthier and more alert baby weighing 21 pounds. There appeared to have been no negative effects of this drastic—but possibly life-saving—treatment. A longer follow-up, preferably at least one or two years, would have been valuable.

Sajwaj et al. (1974) were also faced with a life-threatening problem for a 6-month-old, 8-pound girl suffering malnutrition and dehydration. The emaciated and socially unresponsive infant was seriously ill. Following each feeding abnormal tongue-thrusting movements were noted, followed by regurgitation of the formula. There appeared to be no particular pain or distress and, by examination, no physical disorder to account for the behavior.

The aversive treatment involved squirting 5-10 cubic centimeters of lemon juice into the baby's mouth at the first sign of postfeeding tongue-thrusting movements. After 12 treatment days the rumination ended, as did the abnormal tongue-thrusting movements. Normal tongue movements then began to occur. The child gained weight (to 12 pounds) was discharged from the hospital; a 10-month follow-up showed continued development.

The authors caution against two possible negative effects of this treatment: (1) because of its acidity the lemon juice may cause mild irritation in and around the mouth and (b) care must be taken to prevent the child from aspirating the juice into the lungs by keeping the head upright and reducing the force and amount of juice squirted into the mouth.

Other investigators have also used taste-aversion procedures to reduce rumination. Murray, Keele, and McCarver (1977) used tabasco sauce on the tongue of a normal 6-month-old infant; Becker, Turner, and Sajwaj (1978) successfully applied the lemon juice aversion to a retarded 36-month-old child. Marholin, Luiselli, Robinson, and Lott (1980), reported two case studies in which profoundly retarded institutionalized boys, aged 16 and 11, with severe rumination problems were successfully treated with taste-aversion procedures that employed lemon juice for one boy and tabasco sauce for the other.

The authors note that one serious limitation of the taste-aversion procedure—as with most contingent punishment procedures—is their highly situation-specific effects. Thus, they found that rumination at breakfast and lunch—where the taste-aversion procedure was applied—decreased. At dinner time, however, where the aversive procedure was not applied, rumination continued. It is necessary, then, to employ the procedures at each eating situation, since easy generalization of training will not occur across settings. Thus, as Marholin et al. caution, a child might be cured or significantly improved as a hospital inpatient but, unless the parents or other caretakers in the child's natural environment are instructed to also establish training at home, rumination might recur once the child is discharged.

In another single-case study O'Neil, White, King, and Carek (1979) reported equivocal success with the lemon juice taste-aversion procedure with a 26-month-old, retarded infant.

Overcorrection has been used as another aversive procedure by Azrin and Wesolowski (1975) and Duker and Sey (1977). In each case a prolonged clean-up procedure by the child was required. The necessary staff attention and time makes the overcorrection approach difficult to apply in most ward settings (Marholin et al., 1980).

Finally, three studies report success employing positive reinforcement rather than aversive procedures. Smith and Lyon (1976) reported limited success by positively reinforcing play as alternative behavior. Mulick, Schroeder, and Rojahn (1980) worked with an extremely difficult case, a 15-year-old, profoundly retarded boy who engaged in feces eating and self-induced rumination. The latter was not considered life threatening, but the two behaviors left his mouth and lips constantly raw and chapped and threatened by infection, and the noxious appearance, behavior, and odors caused his exclusion from educational and other programs. Feces-eating was quickly eliminated by overcorrection and by dressing him in snug-fitting pants and belt that discouraged reaching into his pants to extract feces to eat. Comparing four reinforcement conditions, the experimenters concluded that differential reinforcement of specified alternative play behavior was more effective in reducing rumination than either extinction alone or reinforcement of other, nonspecified behavior.

One of the most interesting case reports is by Barmann (1980), who worked with a six year-old, profoundly retarded, totally blind, nonambulatory boy who had no language or social skills. The behavior problem in question consisted of finger- and hand-sucking followed by ruminative vomiting some 30 times each day. The behavior had been occurring for 4½ years and the child was dehydrated, malnourished, and severely underweight at 23 pounds. It was medically a life-threatening situation.

Arguing against aversive controls, Barmann adopted a back-rubbing vibrator worn by the child in light harness. The mechanism (a standard J. C. Penney model) rested mostly on the back of the wheelchair and was no weight burden. To increase generalization, training sessions were held at random times, in many different places, wherever the wheelchair could be moved. The child was observed, and when his hands were not in his mouth (being either in his lap or engaged with toys or other appropriate activity) he was verbally reinforced, followed by 30 seconds of vibration. Using an ABAB reversal design, vomiting was reduced in 2 weeks from a mean of 30 times daily to a mean of 4.5 times daily. Follow-up observations made at 3-month intervals for one year showed the improvements had been maintained. The child also began to gain weight, going from 23 to 40 pounds at the year's follow-up.

Barmann concluded the procedure appeared to have been effective, entailed little cost, staff difficulty, no pain or discomfort, and had gains maintained for at least the year's follow-up. It would be instructive to have some replications of this procedure.

As noted earlier, these case reports describe different methods that can be adapted by clinicians and teachers for use with their own clients. Some, such as the aversive techniques, are severe, and consideration must be given to the severity of the disorder so as to justify punishing interventions. Use of contingent electric shock on children is an alternative to be carefully considered in life-threatening situations where other treatment attempts have failed. The case reports in which positive contingencies were applied (Barmann, 1980; Smith and Lyon, 1976; Mulick et al., 1980) offer possibilities for nonaversive control over rumination with even profoundly retarded children. Barmann's procedure appears to be the most promising in this group, and should be considered by workers facing these problems.

V. BOWEL AND BLADDER CONTROL PROBLEMS

Functional nocturnal enuresis is persistent bed-wetting without organic or urologic disorder (Campbell, 1970), a behavioral problem that occurs in twice as many boys as girls (Yates, 1970), affects some 20% of three year olds, 15% of six year olds, and approximately 3% of 14 year olds (Azrin and Thienes, 1978). A distinction has been made between primary or persistent enuresis, in which the child has never had nocturnal control over micturition, and secondary or acquired enuresis, in which 6 or more months of nocturnal continence had existed before enuresis began. This distinction, however, seems to have had no predictive value in treatment (Doleys, 1977).

It has been estimated (Campbell, 1970) that more than 50 different treatments including drugs and surgery have been applied to enuresis, with the choice of treatment guided by the clinician's theoretical position (Doleys, 1977). Surgery and drug treatment are used by those who view the problem in somatic terms. Long-term psychotherapy is used by psychodynamic clinicians who view enuresis as a symptom produced by unconscious, fundamentally more basic issues. A variety of teaching or training methods are applied by behavior modifiers who view enuresis as a behavioral deficit, a failure of the child to learn effective bladder control. Behavioral treatment of enuresis has become a large and well-researched area since Mowrer and Mowrer's (1938) development of their bell-and-pad training method. Several detailed reviews of behavioral treatment of enuresis have appeared (Jones, 1960; Lovibond, 1964; Yates, 1970; Doleys, 1977), so we will only briefly summarize recent research.

The major behavioral approaches are organized into three categories: urine-alarm systems, retention-control training, and operant-based methods.

A. *Urine-Alarm Procedures*

This has developed from Mowrer and Mowrer's (1938) bell-and-pad method in which a battery-operated alarm wakes the child whenever urination occurs. According to Mowrer and Mowrer, respondent conditioning occurred: the unconditioned stimulus (bell) elicits the unconditioned response (awakening). Bladder distention cues and other internal stimuli associated with the start of micturition immediately procede the US. With repeated CS/US pairings (reinforcements) the premicturition internal cues become conditioned stimuli, eliciting the now conditioned response of awakening. This original conditioning explanation has been questioned by more recent researchers (see Doleys, 1977), but the success of the treatment has held up well, having been demonstrated under various controlled conditions with several thousand subjects. Few areas in behavioral modification have been so thoroughly researched.

Forsythe and Redmond (1970) noted at least 11 different alarm systems, most of which were included in the various studies up to that time. A recent summary (Doleys, 1977) reviewed studies including 628 subjects. Summarizing the results presented by Doleys shows that of all the children treated with the urine-alarm system, approximately 42% were cured within 5 to 12 weeks' treatment, and showed no relapse at 6-month follow-up. Another 23% also met the criteria for "cure" but relapsed within 6 months, required another series of treatment, and were then also "cured." Another 10% of those treated met the criteria, but relapsed within 6 months and did not respond successfully to retraining. Finally 25% were not improved by the training procedures. Taken together the research over approximately the past ten years, added to the earlier research, continues to indicate that the urine-alarm procedure produces cures through one or two series (4 to 12 weeks) of treatments in approximately 65% of treated children, temporary or partial control in about 10%, and no success in 25 percent. These percentages are considerably higher than the estimated natural remission rates (Lovibond, 1964) that range from 25% for three year olds, down to 16% for 12 year olds.

It should be noted, too, that "relapse" after initial training success is usually stringently defined, ranging from the most liberal definition of three or more wet nights a week (Finley et al., 1973), to a demanding *any* nighttime wetting (Novick, 1966). Thus a child who had been wet every night before training, but only two nights weekly after having achieved some criterion such as 14 consecutive dry nights, would be considered a relapse. If the child did not respond to the second course of treatment but continued wetting once or twice weekly, then, despite the clear improvement from seven to one or two wet nights a week, the child would nevertheless be considered a failure.

Several attempts have been made to increase success rate, and reduce relapse rate and the time needed for training. Intermittent rather than continuous alarm schedules (Abelew, 1972; Turner, Young and Rachman, 1970; Finley et al., 1973; Finley and Wansley, 1976) did not appear to increase overall success rates but did reduce relapse rates. Finley, Wansley and Blenkarn (1977), using an intermittent, variable ratio schedule with 80 enuretic children, reported a lower relapse rate, and most interestingly achieved a 94% success rate in reaching the 14 consecutive dry-night criterion. Two recent papers (Finley et al. 1982; Fielding, 1982) point out that patterns of enuresis vary among children and individual functional analyses are necessary in order to determine the best mode of the urine-alarm procedure. Finely et al. found that children who were apparently more resistant to treatment and who wet several times nightly rather than only once, showed greatest resistance to relapses when a variable ratio schedule of 60 to 69% was used, rather than the standard 100% ratio.

Taylor and Turner (1975), using an overlearning procedure based on that described by Mowrer and Mowrer (1938), Freyman (1963), and Lovibond (1964) with 82 children treated at home, reported a small and not statistically significant reduction in relapse rate. An earlier study by Young and Morgan (1972) reported a substantial relapse rate reduction with their overlearning approach.

Reviewing studies that tried to reduce relapse rates through overlearning and/or intermittent reinforcement, Morgan (1978) concluded that both procedures appeared to have reduced relapses, and overlearning seems to be the more effective of the two. Morgan also suggested that the procedures may interact with patient variables such as age, and those possible interactions should be empirically studied in our search for more efficient and effective treatments.

In a study of 45 enuretic children Bollard and Nettlebeck (1981) found the conditioning method to be considerably better when the parents were supervised by a professional than when only initial instructions were given for the parents' unsupervised use. Thus contact with professionals enhanced the procedure's effectiveness.

Overall, the urine-alarm treatment appears highly effective; more so than either no-treatment or psychodynamic therapy (DeLeon and Mandell, 1966; Werry and Cohrssen, 1965), despite remaining empirical questions concerning the effective components and theoretical issues involved in explaining the continued success (Doleys, 1977). The relapse rate is still considered a problem, but research with partial reinforcement, overlearning procedures, and parent training to reinforce the maintenance of success appears promising. Finally, the criticism that symptom substitution would occur if enuresis were treated by conditioning methods (Salk, 1972; Sperling, 1965) has been discredited by a number of studies, most clearly by Baker (1969).

The urine-alarm treatment system was based upon the respondent-conditioning paradigm, although subsequent theoretical issues have been raised as to whether the conditioning was respondent or instrumental in nature. Mowrer and Mowrer's (1938) innovation and its adaptations resulted in continued reliable and impressive evidence that in the large majority of cases nocturnal enuresis is best treated as a learning problem—not as a symptom of underlying unconscious processes. Though a significant advance in children's treatment, the urine-alarm method has some drawbacks: the relapse rate of about 30 to 35% makes additional training time necessary; and the number of dropouts, although not a very large proportion, is a concern. Overall, as effective as it is, the method leaves some 25 percent of the children unimproved, either as dropouts or training failures. As noted earlier, research with intermittent reinforcement schedules and overlearning procedures appears promising in increasing successes and reducing relapses. However, the 5 to 12 weeks of training and persistent, if lowered, relapse rates remain unresolved drawbacks.

B. *Bladder Retention Control Training*

This alternate behavioral technique attempts to treat enuresis by increasing bladder capacity through gradual shaping procedures (Muellner, 1960; Kimmel and Kimmel, 1970). The child is instructed to drink large amounts of water during the day. When the bladder is full and urination is about to occur, the child delays urination for a few minutes for increasing periods daily. It is assumed that in this process the bladder retention capacity will increase and that increases will generalize to greater retention at night.

Some evidence to support the procedure has been presented in case studies by Kimmel and Kimmel (1970), Stedman (1972), and Miller (1973). Paschalis, Kimmel, and Kimmel (1972) trained 20 children and compared them with an untreated control group of 15 children. In their 20-day treatment 40% became dry to a criterion of seven consecutive dry nights and 23% showed no improvement. Three other studies (Rocklin and Tilker, 1973; Doleys et al., 1977; and Harris and Purohit, 1977) showed little or no difference between treated and untreated groups. At this point it appears that while bladder retention training is perhaps more effective than the 16 to 25% natural recovery rate estimated by Lovibond (1964), it is not nearly as effective as urine-alarm systems.

C. *Dry-Bed Training*

This fairly recent development is based on operant principles. Pointing out the continuing limitations of the urine-alarm method Azrin and his colleagues (Azrin, Sneed, and Foxx, 1973; 1974; Azrin, Thienes-

Hontos, and Besalel-Azrin, 1979) have developed and refined their approach, at first using it in conjunction with the urine-alarm system.

Azrin, Sneed, and Foxx (1973, 1974) introduced dry-bed training, a combination of bladder retention control training, the bell and pad, hourly wakings, and positive reinforcement and punishments, the latter involving an overcorrection clean-up process. A single night of intensive training is carried out in which all components are present. The bell and pad continues in use until seven consecutive dry nights are attained. Azrin et al. reported success with all their subjects, but also noted a 34 percent relapse rate—similar to that for the bell and pad alone.

In later studies reporting even greater success (Azrin and Thienes, 1978, Azrin et al., 1979), the urine alarm was eliminated and emphasis was put on the operant-based training, including one night's intensive training. Of particular note is their finding that parents apparently preferred the shorter, more intensive, treatment, in turn presumably reducing the dropout rate. In the latter study (Azrin et al., 1979), the procedure was made more efficient by substituting a single office visit for parent training in place of the home trainer's visit. The researchers reported that all of the 44 children stopped bed-wetting, there were no dropouts, and the relapse rate was only 7%. Azrin et al. concluded that enuresis can be effectively treated through a combination of a single office visit, one night of intensive training, and nightly practice for 1 or 2 weeks. These results are impressively superior to those with the urine alarm only. In another variation of the dry-bed training Bollard and Woodroffe (1977) trained parents to administer the all-night training program. All 14 of the children successfully achieved continence in a median time of 12 days. Only two relapses (14%) occurred over a 6-month follow-up.

Keating et al. (1983) tested dry-bed training of 23 children without the urine-alarm. The settings and therapist's contact with the child were varied: (a) in-home training of parent and child; (b) office-based training of parent and child; (c) office-based training of parent alone. They report improvement in the entire sample, regardless of setting and therapist's contact with the child.

However, not all tests of the dry-bed method have been this positive. Bollard and Woodroffe's study (1977) included a treatment group that did not use the urine alarm. Although bed-wetting was reduced, none of the ten children reached the criterion of continence. In Bollard and Woodroffe's work the urine alarm seems to have been a major part of the dry-bed training's success.

In a more completely controlled study Bollard and Nettlebeck (1981) conducted two separate experiments with enuretic children. The first, reported a few pages earlier, involved 45 children and found that professional supervision of the parents using the urine-alarm method, greatly enhanced effectiveness. The second experiment, with 120 children, compared urine-alarm conditioning treatment with dry-bed training administered under four different conditions. The major findings were that dry-bed training which included use of the conditioning apparatus was superior to the conditioning alone, but that dry-bed training without the conditioning apparatus was "only marginally better than no treatment at all" (p. 215). In effect, according to Bollard and Nettlebeck's findings, the effectiveness of the urine-alarm conditioning procedure can be increased by close professional supervision and by the addition of Azrin's dry-bed training—the latter, of course, includes close supervision. The combination of Mowrer's urine alarm and Azrin's dry-bed training appears to be quite powerful.

In a replication attempt of dry-bed training Doleys et al. (1977) reported success, but at a lower rate and requiring a longer treatment time, as compared with Azrin et al. (1979). It may be that the Bollard and Woodroffe and Doleys et al. studies did not include the same detail and completeness of training as did Azrin's later work.

Azrin and his colleagues support the effectiveness and efficiency of the dry-bed methods; the approach certainly deserves further research and application. Its high success and low relapse rates are clearly improvements over the urine-alarm used alone. Relatively brief training time is another indication of efficiency. Dry-bed training does not yet have the amount of research backing, including numerous replications, of the urine-alarm system. However, results to date certainly point to its potential superiority over the urine-alarm in terms of overall success, fewer relapses and dropouts, and less training time.

This brief summary has attempted to present enough of the contemporary literature to accurately represent the current state of the field. Numerous case studies suggest other, less well-designed methods. Several papers have reported on training in residential institutions. Young (1964) and Creer and Davis (1975) reported success with a "staggered wakening procedure" in which children are awakened several times during the night to go to the bathroom and urinate. Jehu, Morgan, Turner, and Jones (1977) successfully used a urine-alarm procedure with 19 institutionalized children. Successful treatment of enuresis, then, has been carried out in larger groups of children in institutions, as well as in individual homes.

Enuresis is clearly a problem readily cured in the large majority of cases. The urine-alarm and dry-bed procedures show 65–75% cure rates. The psychoanalytic criticism that symptom substitution will occur following conditioning treatment (Salk, 1972; Sperling, 1965) has been discredited, particularly in Baker's work (1969). Continuing research has pushed success rates higher, relapse and dropout rates lower. The urine-alarm and dry-bed training are highly effective; recent research is beginning to suggest higher cure rates for dry-bed training. Evaluated in light of the estimated natural recovery rate of 16 to 25 percent and contrasted with the failure of psychodynamic approaches, it appears clear and reasonable that our treatment of first choice with childhood enuresis must be one of the two conditioning methods.

The massive evidence is among the clearest in the mental health field for the elimination of one set of hypotheses about enuresis (psychodynamic) and support for another (conditioning). Given that, we must ask if clinicians dealing with enuretic children have discarded psychodynamic approaches and adopted conditioning methods as their treatment of first choice, and we have no clear answer. Some national surveys (Pailer and Graziano, 1972, reported in Graziano, 1975a) indicate that in the early 1970s clinical behavior modification was rarely practiced outside of universities or by professionals other than psychologists. That survey and other more indirect evidence (Brady, 1972; Birk et al., 1973; Franks and Wilson, 1974) suggest that while there has been increased activity and interest in behavior modification, it has had "little effect on clinical practice in traditional mental health settings, and is largely misunderstood by many mental health professionals, particularly those outside psychology" (Graziano, 1975a, p. 3). This apparent lack of impact on traditional clinicians has most recently been discussed by Wolpe (1981). Wolpe points out that despite massive evidence of the effectiveness of behavior therapy with adults, the psychoanalytic tradition still retains firm control over the field—clinicians seem not to have modified their practice in light of the weight of contemporary research. In an earlier paper Graziano (1969) raised the same issues and concluded that the traditional field's resistance to change was rooted in its politics—that is, a political power structure, such as exists in the traditional mental health field, will not be moved by science, rationality, or empirical evidence.

And here we return to enuresis and its treatment. If, in light of the evidence, clinicians persist in psychodynamic treatment of enuresis, we must raise questions about their professional judgement, responsibility, and ethics.

D. *Encopresis*

In introducing behavioral treatment of encopresis Ross (1981) pointed out important differences between this problem and enuresis. Most enuretic children wet at night and, however embarrassing or otherwise problematic that may be, their difficulties are usually known only within their immediate families. The encopretic child, however, may experience far more socially and personally disruptive effects because inappropriate bowel movements also occur during the day and are easily and quickly noticed by anyone near them. The reaction of others—social criticism, ostracism, and sometimes aggressive rejection—may lead to a deeply embarrassed, troubled, self-effacing, and solitary existence. Other children, vociferous about their disgust of the encopretic's behavior, often refuse to have him as a friend or companion. This problem cannot be easily hidden, as can nocturnal enuresis.

Further, Ross suggests, since the aversive consequences do not reduce the soiling behavior, encopresis appears not to be a problem of behavioral surplus but, rather, a skill deficit: a lack of bowel-control skills. The most appropriate treatment approaches should be those involving positive training of bowel-control skills.

Understandably, many parents, in their frustration and anger at the continuing problem, quickly resort to punishment: shaming, berating, spanking, taking away privileges, and so on. But if the essential problem is a skill deficit, punishment will have little positive effect, unless systematically associated with bowel-control skill-training.

That emphasis characterizes the behavioral literature on treating encopretic children. Through the 1960s and early 1970s a small number of studies utilized operant positive reinforcement (e.g. Browning and Stover, 1971; Keehn, 1965; Logan and Garner, 1971; McDonagh, 1971; Neale, 1963; Young and Goldsmith, 1972). Other earlier studies combined positive reinforcement for skills-training with punishments, such as brief time-outs, for inappropriate soiling (e.g. Edelman, 1971; Gelber and Meyer, 1965; Marshall, 1966; Tomlinson, 1970). The more recent studies have typically combined positive skills training with punishment, in differential reinforcement approaches (e.g. Ayllon, Simon, and Wildman, 1975; Bach and Moylan, 1975; Crowley and Armstrong, 1977; Plachetta, 1976; Wright and Walker, 1978).

Many earlier studies appear to have been carried out by professional or paraprofessional staff rather than parents although at the time of treatment most of the children reported on were living at home (Crowley and Armstrong, 1977). Given the daily, repetitive nature of this problem—children soiling several times daily at home and/or school, it seems most reasonable to provide interventions in the natural environment. This involves the parent-training, home-based approach seen in the most recent studies (e.g. Balson, 1973; Ashkenazi, 1975; Plachetta, 1976; Crowley and Armstrong, 1977). Ashkenazi trained local child health nurses who became the home instructors and monitors of the parents' efforts.

While the basic behavioral approach is one of differential reinforcement, it does not appear possible to utilize a standard approach for all children. Rather, it may be important to make some preliminary distinctions among children in terms of the basic issues involved. Ross (1981), for example, distinguishes three major issues: (1) Some children avoid defecation by good control for long periods until colonic pressure expels the feces or the feces may become impacted and require medical attention. (2) Some children have been insufficiently reinforced for proper toileting, although they do possess the skills. As parental reactions appear to be the major factor in maintaining the problems, training them in appropriate and consistent social-reinforcement skills seems indicated. (3) Some children were never trained and need systematic toilet skill-training.

Severe fears may also be causally involved in encopresis (Anthony, 1957). Some children may exhibit strong phobic avoidance of the toilet. Children in Ross's first group, for example, were living at home (Crowley and Armstrong, 1977). Many have experienced painful bowel movements and attempt to avoid the painful, feared event, by retaining feces. The younger children described by Ashkenazi (1975) were fearful. They refused to use the toilet, cried, and clung to their mothers. In these cases encopresis seems to have started with painful bowel movements because of constipation or diarrhea, and the toilet apparently became a conditioned aversive stimulus. In treating these children Ashkenazi (1975) first deconditioned the fear through gradual, reinforced approaches to the toilet to a criterion of sitting comfortably for several minutes. When the phobic behavior was eliminated, the training continued. It consisted of tangible reinforcers for appropriate defecation in the toilet, aided by rectal suppositories immediately after eating. The suppositories were discontinued after five consecutive days of appropriate toilet use. Prizes were then gradually faded, and verbal praise shifted to an intermittent schedule. Of 18 treated cases, 16 were successfully trained and maintained their new skills at 3- and 6-month follow-ups. A single-case study that also used positive reinforcement is reported by Plachetta (1976).

Many demonstrations show that a variety of behavioral techniques—punishment, overcorrection, desensitization, contingent reinforcement—have been successful in treating encopresis. Functional analyses in each case are important because several possible major issues appear to be involved; appropriate treatment is based on clear identification of these issues. Parent training and home behavioral intervention appear to be the treatments of choice for encopretic children.

VI. SLEEP DISTURBANCES

Mild sleep disturbances are common among children; it appears that many events can interrupt sleep. Delaying bedtime and fighting sleep through a variety of tactics—"Just let me see the rest of this program," a feigned stomachache, or calls for a drink of water—are familiar, and competent parents handle these with little difficulty.

More serious sleep disorders, however, do occur, and they include "night fears," nightmares, night terrors, somnambulism, and insomnia. It is not known how many children are affected by these sleep disturbances, but many single-case studies vividly suggest that such experiences can be severe. With only little data, we can speculate that severely interrupted sleep may have negative effects on a child's physical health and growth. Certainly the family social and psychological effects often appear to be quite debilitating.

Nightmares and night terrors are different phenomena, both involving frightening experiences during sleep. Like other dream activity, nightmares occur during lighter sleep periods (rapid eye movement), while night terrors like somnambulism, occur in deep, or non-REM sleep. The nightmare is a vividly frightening dream, often awakening the child who recalls the dream and remains frightened for some period of time. The dream content may be recurrent as in a case described by Clement (1970) of a seven year old boy who was repeatedly chased by a "big black bug."

In night terrors the deeply sleeping child, often wide-eyed, screaming or pleading, and sitting up or thrashing around in bed, appears to be in the throes of a literally terrifying experience. Such children are difficult to awaken and generally continue the episode despite parents' attempts to soothe or awaken them.

"Nightfears" is a syndrome suggested by the recent research of Graziano and colleagues. In four studies (Graziano, Mooney, Huber, and Ignasiak, 1979; Graziano and Mooney, 1980, 1981; Graziano, White, Kelly, Korytnyk, and Weidenbacher, 1981) "nightfears" were described as a severely fearful reaction to bedtime that disrupted the entire family for many hours virtually every night for at least two consecutive years. The researchers wrote:

> It is important to emphasize the reported severity of the children's nighttime fears. In each family "going to bed" had become a highly emotional and disruptive nightly event, with delays and battles often lasting well beyond midnight. Crying and severe panic behavior, crawling into parents' and siblings' beds, children's insistence on bright lights, radios, or televisions being left turned on in their rooms, restless nights continually interrupted in the early morning hours by frightened calling out to parents, and fatigue and difficulty in getting up to go to school in the mornings were common events. All parents reported having tried without success to reduce their children's fear. They had typically tried to patiently

> wait it out, to be reassuring, critical, and even punitive as the general levels of frustration rose. Night-lights, sitting up with the children, allowing them to sleep in another bed, letting them sleep with siblings or parents, soothing stories at bedtime, and, in one case, nightly medication prescribed by a pediatrician and, in another, psychotherapy were all tried, but without success. There is little doubt that the subjects presented severe and highly disruptive levels of fear (p. 222).

In all, 62 families have completed the 3-week training program. Training consisted of three group meetings for parent and child training, during 3 weeks of nightly home practice sessions of approximately 5 minutes. Practice consisted of relaxation, "pleasant thoughts," and verbal self-instructions about being "brave." Token reinforcement was given at four times during each daily practice. Overall the training was conceptualized as a cooperative parent-child, self-control, and problem-solving task.

After 3 weeks of training the experimental group, compared with delayed-treatment controls, was significantly less fearful as measured in terms of frequency, duration, and intensity of each occurrence, and their disruptive effects on the children, their siblings, and parents. In a three-year follow-up of 33 families Graziano and Mooney (1981) report impressive maintenance of the behavioral improvements in 31 of the families, with 2 others showing regression, but not back to baseline levels.

Insomnia is another sleep disorder experienced by children as well as adults. Case reports of behavioral treatment include that of an 11-year-old girl (Weil and Goldfried, 1973); a 13-year-old girl (Anderson, 1979); and a 7-year-old boy (Bergman, 1976). Relaxation procedures were used with the two older children, and a strict limit-setting procedure with the seven year old (i.e. he was no longer allowed to sleep in his parents' bed). In the latter case both insomnia and hyperactivity had been maintained by parental attention. Shifting the parents' contingent reinforcement quickly eliminated the insomnia and reduced the hyperactivity.

Children's sleep disturbances probably occur at a high rate, but there has been little systematic investigation of behavioral treatment methods. Clearly, more interest and research are needed.

VII. SEIZURES, TICS, HYPERACTIVITY

There appears to have been little work on the behavioral treatment of childhood neurological problems such as seizures and tics. In contrast, behavior modifiers have produced torrents of studies on what is generally considered a neurologically related problem: hyperactivity. In reviewing these papers it became evident that the hyperactivity is almost always defined by behavior modifiers within the social context of classrooms, where virtually all of the behavioral research on hyperactivity is carried out. This striking preponderance leads us to suspect that "hyperactive" may in large part be a situation-specific classroom problem in social behavior rather than a generalized, neurological problem of individual children. Until further clarification we will consider childhood hyperactivity a school problem, and refer the interested reader to Chapter 8.

Epilepsy is a somatic condition characterized by seizures believed to be caused by sudden, high neural discharges in the cerebral cortex. Epileptic patients are generally treated pharmacologically, so referrals for psychological treatment are rare, although it seems generally accepted that psychological factors can affect seizure activity. Patients referred for psychological treatment usually either suffer "false seizures" or are diagnosed as hysterical personalities (Balaschak, 1976).

Early attempts at behavioral treatment of epilepsy focused upon adult patients (e.g. Effron 1956, 1957; Forster, 1969). Relaxation training has been used in single-case studies of adults by Mostofsky and Vick (1973), Johnson and Meyer (1974), and Parrino (1971). The latter report relaxation as part of systematic desensitization. Operant-reinforcement approaches were reportedly successful with a 22-year-old, retarded epileptic (Flannery and Cautela, 1973). Despite extremely high, dangerous levels of medication, this patient's seizures had still not been brought under control. Flannery and Cautela created a positive reinforcement system, contingent upon periods of time free from seizures, and reduced seizures from a baseline of three per week, to one or less (13 of 28 weeks were seizure-free). Richardson (1972) reported improvements in two institutionalized patients with grand mal epilepsy by using a reward system for seizure-free days.

Only a few studies have reported behavioral approaches for controlling children's seizures. Three of them (Gardner, 1967; Balaschak, 1976; Ince, 1976) were single-case studies while one paper (Zlutnick, Mayville, and Moffat, (1975), was a multiple-case study of five children.

In Gardner's (1967) study a 10-year-old girl with no previous epilepsy or history of psychological or academic difficulties began to have seizures at home and in school. For several weeks the girl had increasingly complained of illness and had begun having temper outbursts. These behaviors culminated in her first seizure, which caused hospitalization and subsequent medical treatment. Gardner's analysis led him to speculate that a recent illness of the mother may have served as a model for the girl's growing complaints. Subsequently, several weeks of parental concern and growing attention to the girl's illness behavior appeared to have shaped an escalation to the first seizure. Subsequent seizures were presumably maintained by the continual high-level concern and attention of parents. Thus the seizures in this case appeared to be psychogenic, involving modeling, imitation, rehearsal, and shaping to escalated levels. It should be pointed out that neurological and other medical examinations had been negative.

Gardner's treatment intervention was with the parents alone. Seizure medication was witheld and the parents were counseled on nonreward of seizures, and differential, positive reinforcement of appropriate, nonillness behavior. Within 2 weeks seizures dropped to zero, while tantrums and complaints remained high but not below pretreatment levels. A planned reversal in the twenty-sixth week of treatment, in which illness behavior was again reinforced by parents, resulted in sharp increases and another seizure, convincing the parents of the controlling nature of their attention to the sick behavior.

Differential reinforcement was reestablished, seizures reduced to zero, and somatic complaints dropped. A one-year follow-up showed the child still free of seizures, none having occurred during the year's posttreatment.

Although conclusions drawn from a single-case study are tenuous, Gardner's report suggests that seizure like behavior was shaped, maintained, and subsequently eliminated through operant conditioning.

In another case study (Balaschak, 1976), seizures in an eleven year old epileptic girl were reduced through a teacher-administered contingency-management program. In this case the organically based epilepsy had been diagnosed in infancy. One parent and two siblings had also been diagnosed as epileptic, strengthening the assumption of an organic-based disorder. This child, long under medication, had shown social, psychological, and academic problems throughout school, although intellectually she tested at an average level. By age 11 she was in a special class, had many social and psychological problems, and was referred because of frequent, long-lasting seizures at school and at home.

Although organically based, the seizures appeared to be triggered by emotional stimuli such as high demands and school failure, thus appearing to have a strong "hysterical" component. Balaschak assumed that much of the seizure behavior was under operant control, stimulated by social pressures, and maintained by various forms of attention. In a procedure similar to that reported by Flannery and Cautela (1973) the teacher was taught to provide positive reinforcement for seizure-free time periods. A "good times" chart was kept of checkmarks for no seizures in each of three daily time periods. The girl appeared to become quite involved in the challenge to control seizures. The seizures decreased in school and, later, at home after the mother initiated a similar program.

This case is of interest not only because of what it suggests concerning the possible behavioral treatment of seizures in an epileptic child but also because of what it tells us about potential values clashes between behavior modifiers and other professionals. The child, after considerable improvement in the treatment, was absent from school because of mononucleosis. On her return, despite the apparent success of the earlier operant program, the teacher refused to reinstate the reward system in the last two months of the year and the number of seizures climbed back to pretreatment levels. Although the teacher's reasons were never made clear, Balaschak speculates that the teacher operated on some notion that returning their focus to the seizure-control program would divert the child's intellectual energy from the more important task of helping her make up all of her missed academic work.

A dramatic improvement was reported by Ince (1976) when a 12 year old epileptic boy completely eliminated both grand mal and petit mal seizures in a 3-month program, and remained seizure-free for a 6-month follow-up. Several seizures had been occurring daily, followed by his being taken to the nurse's office where he frequently slept for several hours. The problem was complicated psychologically because the boy had become fearful of school, and was reluctant to attend because of embarrassment, teasing by other children, and their refusal to play with him. Somatic problems began to increase—stomachaches, headaches, insomnia, and these became excuses to remain at home.

Ince's two-stage intervention began with a 4-week period during which deep muscle relaxation was taught, followed by imaginal desensitization to seizure-related items (e.g. sitting in a classroom and feeling an aura). By the end of five sessions he was no longer "nervous" about any of the items, and his somatic complaints ceased.

The second phase involved once weekly relaxation training sessions for 3 months. The child was taught to tell himself to "relax" and then to do so, associating the cue word with relaxation. He was taught to say the cue word repeatedly whenever he felt an aura. From a pretreatment level of 9 to 10 grand mal and 25 to 26 petit mal seizures a week, the intervention seemed to bring both types of seizures to zero, where they remained over a 9-month follow-up.

Although only suggestive, the results of this case are so striking that more controlled research is clearly indicated. The apparent success of what appears to be overlearning a relaxation response (a self-control strategy) with this child whose seizures were preceded by a definite aura may have important potential for other children, if supported by further research. Deep muscle relaxation was also used in a single-case study by Friedman (1980) in treatment of a child with Gilles de la Tourette syndrome.

Success was reported in a multiple-case study by Zlutnick, Mayville, and Moffat (1975). Five children, aged 4 to 14 with diagnoses that included psychoses and mental retardation in addition to epilepsy, were treated by institutional staff, teachers, or parents at home. Noting that a variety of preseizure behaviors can be reliably observed and many seizures thus predicted, Zlutnick et al. used a noxious interruption procedure for four of the children, a more positively reinforcing interruption procedure for the fifth child. The noxious procedure consisted of (1) a loudly shouted "No!" followed by (2) grasping the child by the shoulders and shaking him once, vigorously. The other procedure was used with the oldest child in the study, whose preseizure activity included raising her arms to shoulder height, body rigidity, clenched fists, snapping back of her head, and facial grimaces. When these occurred a staff member lowered the child's arms, waited 5 seconds, praised her "effusively" for keeping her arms down and gave her an M&M candy. These interventions presumably interrupted the children's behavioral chains that culminated in the seizures.

Pre- and posttreatment seizure frequencies per week for each of the five children are shown in the tabulation below. It appears that all but subject two showed a clinical decrease in weekly seizures. The greatest change (112 to 0 per week)

	Subjects				
	1	2	3	4	5
Pretreatment baseline	84	42	84	14	112
Posttreatment	14	35	49	2	0

occurred in the oldest child, the one treated with differential reinforcement interruption technique. Because of the case study nature of the findings we cannot draw conclusions about the relative effectiveness of the two variations in interruption. The researchers reported posttreatment maintenance checks for up to 12 months, indicating good maintenance for the four improved children.

The papers by Ince (1976) and by Zlutnick et al. (1975) describe working with children whose seizures are preceded by a detectable aura or preseizure behavior, and thus have fairly predictable behavior chains, possibly subject to interruption. In Ince's case the child, normal in other respects, developed self-control skills through relaxation when an aura began. Zlutnick et al. studied children who were intellectually or emotionally impaired as well as epileptic. In both studies clinical success was reported through various preseizure interruption procedures. These case studies should stimulate more controlled studies of behavioral reduction of seizures.

Another childhood condition believed to be organic in nature is Gilles de la Tourette's syndrome, a rare, severe, dramatic condition highly resistant to treatment that becomes progressively more severe. Major tics gradually develop, in some cases involving the child's entire body. Pronounced vocal tics appear, including frequent coughing and throat-clearing that may progress to grunting, sharp "barking" sounds and finally to coprolalia, the compulsive shouting or speaking of obscenities. Such vocal tics become a consistent form of behavior that is disruptive and intolerable in most childhood environments.

As reviewed by Kellman (1965), Tourette's syndrome has been attributed to both psychogenic and organic factors. A review by Shapiro, Shapiro, Wayne, and Clarkin (1973) concluded that psychological factors are unrelated and irrelevant to the etiology, diagnosis, and treatment of the condition. In their extensive review Shapiro, Shapiro, Brun, and Sweet (1978) concluded that behavior therapy was "largely ineffective" with this syndrome. Several recent studies have reported effective drug treatments and the current treatment of choice is haloperidol (Friedman, 1980).

Despite the apparent preference for a somatic model and treatment, some applications of behavior therapy to Tourette's syndrome report somewhat mixed results (Browning and Stover, 1971; Chapel, Brown, and Jenkins, 1964; Stevens and Blackly, 1966). Rosen and Wesner (1973) suggest an operant view of Tourette's syndrome in treatment of an institutionalized 12-year-old boy. The authors demonstrated the operant nature of the vocal tics and initiated a behavioral program that started with individual behavior therapy sessions, eventually involving the child's teacher as well as group classroom contingencies. The program included positive reinforcement for the suppression of tics and for alternative behavior, progressive relaxation training, self-monitoring, and, as noted above, social contingencies in the classroom. The tics were virtually eliminated in the classroom, but the improved behavior did not generalize to the residential setting, where the contingencies were carried out. It is not known whether the gains were maintained, since no follow-up was reported. At least in this instance Rosen and Wesner demonstrate that Tourette's syndrome is an operant under the control of external reinforcement contingencies and that appropriate operant methods may constitute effective treatment.

A self-control procedure was used by Hurtzell, Platzek, and Logue (1974) to help an 11-year-old boy reduce a variety of severe tics. Over a 6-month period the boy had developed a peculiar skipping walk, severe head-jerking, and a sharp "barking" sound. Previous use of medication and positive reinforcement for non tic behavior had not been successful. These obvious difficulties were creating social problems for the child who was eager to cooperate to gain control over the tics.

Treatment consisted of half-hour training sessions held twice weekly, in which the child was taught to accurately monitor his head jerks and "barks," recording their frequency on a hand-held counter. After 27 sessions both behaviors had been reduced to a low level, but not eliminated. At a one-year follow-up the boy, his parents, and teachers reported that he no longer displayed tic behavior, although observation at the clinic did show a low frequency of each. The authors suggested that the anxiety over returning to the clinic, although for only a follow-up, may have caused the apparently temporary and low-frequency return of the tics. This case report suggests that self-monitoring alone might effectively reduce severe tics.

A more recent case study by Friedman (1980) described a self-control treatment for an 11-year-old girl who for four years evidenced severe tics and frequently shouted obscene phrases. Baseline assessments by parents recorded these obscenities (verbal tics) at the rate of 150/hour. In the case investigation the girl, Susan, indicated that at times she tried self-control, trying to substitute "clean" words for the curses. At baseline these clean word substitutions were measured at 5 to 10 per hour. Friedman's treatment began by encouraging and reinforcing her attempts to substitute words like "fun." When cursing decreased over the next few weeks, relaxation training was begun in an attempt to control the severe neck, shoulder, arm, and leg twitches. Relaxation as well as "positive imagery" was practiced with the mother's support.

Treatment required 15 sessions over a 4-month period. Cursing decreased markedly, but the muscular tics remained a major problem, even at an 18-month follow-up. Drug treatment was then begun, and the tics decreased. Friedman suggests that the self-control approach succeeded in shifting to more socially acceptable words: when she felt compelled to curse, Susan would shout "fun." Although this change was probably of value, she remained a child with a high rate of muscular twitches and occasional explosive shouting, of nonshocking words. The behavioral approaches in this case were of apparently limited value, and drug therapy was eventually needed.

Primarily in single-case studies the use of deep muscle relaxation, self-monitoring, and contingency management in differential reinforcement procedures have been suggested as possibly effective interventions to reduce seizures and tics, even when the problems were organically based. In particular, overlearned deep muscle relaxation appears promising. Controlled experimental studies are needed to explore the tentative suggestions derived from case studies.

VIII. ADDITIONAL ISSUES

If we take seriously the notion that one's behavior may be critical in the creation, exacerbation, or maintenance of somatic illness, we begin to see that behavioral intervention may be effective in many more somatic conditions than those already acknowledged. For example, two large areas that are only beginning to be explored are the use of behavior modification in medical regimens, such as in the preparation of children for surgery, and methods to prevent illness-related behavior in the children of adolescents, such as the prevention of cigarette-smoking.

As noted in our section on fear reduction at least ten studies have reported modeling procedures to reduce fears of dental and medical procedures. One of those studies (Melamed and Siegel, 1975) used symbolic modeling—a 16-minute film of an initially fearful child who gradually copes with the situation and overcomes his or her own fears. Researchers found that children who viewed the modeling film, compared with control-group children, showed significantly less, "transitory situational anxiety" on all measures—sweat-gland activity, self-reported medical concerns, and overt, anxiety-related behavior. Their data also suggest that experimental group children had fewer postoperative behavior problems than the controls.

This group of ten studies is strongly suggestive that behavioral intervention, such as symbolic modeling, particularly for children undergoing medical/dental operative procedures for the first time, can be an important addition to the somatic treatment. Further research and the development of systematic programs that would become routine aspects of children's treatment appear to be important directions for future investigators and clinicians.

Dietary regulation is a critical component of some medical treatment, and the behavioral factors involved in maintaining the proper diets are of importance. Magrab and Papadopoulou (1977) reported success with a token-reinforcement program aimed at improving the dietary compliance of four children, aged 11-18, in hemodialysis treatment. Improvements were measured in terms of weight stability, potassium level, and blood urea nitrogen content.

The dietary regulation of phenylketonuria becomes problematic when the child resists the appropriate diet—one that severely restricts the intake of phenylalanine. In the PKU child, high levels of blood phenylalanine have severe affects on intellectual development. Untreated persons show retardation, with IQs below 50, while treated children are expected to show normal intellectual development.

The dietary control is achieved by providing the child with a special high-protein, low-phenylalanine formula. Some infants, however, find it unpalatable to the degree that they refuse it, thus increasing the probabilities of becoming retarded. Fox and Roseen (1977) report successful use of a parent-administered token-reinforcement program for a 3½ year old boy. The dietary compliance was improved and the improvement maintained at a one-year follow-up.

Loew and Lutzker (1979) report success with contingency-management procedures to improve dietary compliance of a juvenile diabetic. These three single-case or small-sample case studies suggest the potential importance of behavioral interventions as part of medical regimes requiring dietary compliance.

Children in intensive care units are often subjected to what may be traumatic conditions—isolation, experiencing and/or witnessing painful but necessary medical procedures, physical restraint because of connection to various vital-sign monitoring equipment, intravenous feeding, exposure to dying children, and so on (Cataldo et al., 1979). The resulting disruption of normal "age-appropriate behaviors and an increase in problem behaviors (may make) good medical care harder to provide and transition to home life more difficult" (Cataldo et al. 1979, p. 83). Little systematic behavioral research has been conducted on improving conditions in the pediatric intensive care unit and thus the behavior of child patients. Cataldo et al. (1979) report two studies of staff and patients in a pediatric intensive care unit. The first study indicated that "On the average, one-third of the patients were judged to be conscious and alert but markedly nonengaged with their environment" (p. 83). The second study was carried out to determine if fairly simple environmental manipulation, consisting of activities with toys and staff, could improve the child patients' behavior. They found increased attention, "engagement," and positive affect, as well as decreased inappropriate behavior. The researcher concluded that behavioral procedures can be effectively used as bases for designing intensive care unit procedures that will "provide quality medical care."

Because of the clearly established physical risks, smoking behavior is here viewed as an ideal prototype for studying illness-related behaviors. Though its reduction is important, its prevention is of even greater potential value and interest to researchers. The smoking literature is vast and, as yet, there is little optimism generated by results of behavioral studies of smoking cessation. In a recent review Leventhal and Cleary (1980) suggest that recently reported increases in smoking-cessation success rates may be due to changes in our social environment that "multiply the action of previously unsuccessful procedures." That is, they suggest that public campaigns, particularly those limiting smoking areas such as on airplanes and in restaurants, may be having some positive effects. Of particular importance for children, however, is their suggestion that habitual smoking behavior develops in stages, beginning in childhood. They infer a preparatory stage in which children develop attitudes, values, and understandings about smoking, an initiation phase of tentative attempts at smoking, and a stage that may take up to two years, of repeated and even sporadic experimentation, in which heavy smoking develops. Leventhal and Cleary suggest that, assuming the validity of their developmental analysis, different interventions will be appropriate at different stages. This suggestion and model provides researchers with many hints for future research on preventing cigarette smoking in children.

IX. CONCLUSIONS

It is clear that behavioral variables are in many ways related to somatic disorders. The fields of behavioral medicine and behavioral pediatrics are concerned with investigating the relationships between these two major sets of variables. As we learn more about behavioral influences on somatic disorders and their treatment we will also hopefully develop more interest in, and more sophisticated and effective methods to prevent the development of some disorders. A particularly intriguing potential seems to lie in the interaction of community psychology, public health, and behavioral medicine. We expect that a good deal of important and stimulating research will occur in these areas over the next decade.

10

Behavioral Community Psychology

I. POINTS OF INTERVENTION—INTERNAL-EXTERNAL EMPHASIS

After first developing in the mid-1920s as a clinical and educational model, behavior modification was eclipsed by Freud's successful popularization of the 100-year-old "Romantic Psychiatry" model (Graziano, 1975a). Freud's restatement, psychoanalysis, became the most influential personality theory and applied psychology model in the mental health field. It remains so today, at least in the applied mental health area, although it no longer enjoys its old exclusive status there and it has dropped to only secondary importance, at best, in its research achievements. In the late 1950s, with the continuing recognition of the limitations of psychoanalysis that had been made clear by its treatment failures during and after World War II, the behavioral model began to reemerge and it became well established, at least academically, by the mid-1960s.

That development did not entail a shift away from psychoanalysis by its practitioners but rather the addition of new psychologists to the applied mental health field, bringing with them their academic, behavioral background (Ullmann and Krasner, 1965). As the number and activities of psychologists grew, so too did the influence of one of academic psychology's major research areas of the time, behaviorism. From this renewed combination of behaviorism and the traditional, clinical mental health concerns, the elements of behavior modification were reassembled into applied clinical and educational models, and those models have continued to develop and influence the field.

But an even more basic development, integral to behavior modification but perhaps of greater ultimate importance in shaping our professional futures, was occurring—a growing disengagement from the Romantic Psychiatry notion that human behavior is primarily controlled by internal, motivational forces to the increasing acceptance of the belief that we are largely controlled by external events. That was a change of emphasis rather than complete negation of one or the other locus. Both internal (e.g., physiological, cognitive) and external (e.g., sociocultural, reinforcement contingencies) were viewed by both models as contributing factors but each model emphasized one over the other as its major, but not exclusive, point of intervention. This was a true shift in emphasis from the attribution of internal causes of psychological malfunctioning, to the attribution of external causes.

This emphasis on the power of the external environment has been stated many times and long before, even by the classical Greeks and Romans and it has periodically reappeared in history. We saw it again at the very beginning of the humanitarian reform movement in mental health in the 1700s, and it was made explicit a little later by Pinel, as it had been by Soranus, a first-century Roman physician, both of whom pointed out to their incredulous colleagues that dungeons and chains actually *contributed* to the severity of the condition they called "insanity" (Graziano, 1975a). Pinel's elegant question, here paraphrased, shows no signs of wearing thin after 170 years; "How are we," he asked, "to distinguish between the exasperation caused by the chains and the symptoms peculiar to the illness"? Pinel's question was a nineteenth-century recognition of the iatrogenic effects of at least some of our treatments of the mentally disturbed, a recognition that was again lost as we moved into the twentieth-century.

In the United States the early urban settlement house workers, before they became professional social workers and enamoured of nineteenth-century psychoanalysis, knew very well the realities of powerful external environments as casual factors in human behavior, thinking, and misery (Levine and Levine, 1970). The concept of environmental power to control human events is also central to the venerable public health field which has long sought to alter the physical conditions of human habitats so as to decrease disease and to promote health.

Surely the recognition of environmental influence has not been denied in any model of human behavior, even in psychoanalysis. But in each of these positions by Soranus, Pinel, settlement house workers, and others as we moved into the twentieth-century, the concept was not one to which only lip service was paid, but was the starting point for reform action. The commonality among these positions is their focus of clinical study and treatment, that is, what we have called their point of intervention. In each case then as now, clinicians calibrate, so to speak, and shift the clinical pointer along the internal-external dimension. For those external models the point of intervention was set just outside the client, thus pointing at the surrounding physical and social factors as major antecedent conditions that helped bring about disorder, and as concurrent conditions in maintaining it. Moral treatment from 1800 to 1850, for example (Bockoven, 1963), culminated in the construction of humane social environments that were considered to be necessary in the rehabilitation of clients. On the other hand, perhaps the most extreme example of an internal model was the late nineteenth-century and early twentieth-century medical model which focused intensively on seeking specific brain disorders as the major causes of insanity. In that model humane environments, although desirable from a political and human point of view, were perceived as having little to do with the psychological disorder. The point of intervention was internal, specifically on the brain, although no technology then existed for adequate study or treatment based on the model.

Thus in those early external models there was recognition that while psychological disorder was largely an individual, internal experience, important factors in the study, understanding, and treatment were to be found in external antecedent and concurrent events. The point of intervention shifted, and treatment, for Soranus, Pinel, and the moral therapists was largely that of altering the external environment so it would support integrative rather than disintegrative human functioning.

But in the twentieth century most of those emerging environmental threads were balled and tossed aside by the intrusion of psychoanalysis with its intense reassertion of the primacy of internal causes and its concomitant blindness to external reality. Freud was a major factor in shifting the point of intervention away from the still-young external focus, and back to an extreme internal focus such as had characterized the field for so long prior to the humanitarian reform movement. From the late 1920s through the late 1950s, psychoanalysis seems to have been an unfortunate, disruptive, and regressive diversion. Over the past two decades the primacy of psychoanalysis has decreased, and recent attempts such as that by Wachtel (1977) to attach psychoanalysis to the more contemporary and empirically successful behavior modification movement may be seen as some measure of the relative weakness into which psychoanalysis continues to fall. "When you can't beat'em, join 'em" is a frequent strategy in any shifting field and indeed has been a major strategy of both behavior modification and community psychology, as will be developed later. To whatever degree this strategy may prove successful for psychoanalysis, it will probably only delay that model's ultimate abandonment by the mental health field.

The 1960s reestablishment of a more environmental view in mental health assumed at least two forms: behavior modification and community psychology. At first viewed as distinctly different and even antagonistic developments, their important commonality seems clear now, with a bit of short-term hindsight, that is, they were both reactions against the internal psychodynamic focus and were both statements recognizing the power of external events to shape human functioning. This environmentally focused model in mental health had emerged before and, as noted, had served as the starting point for reform action; but now, for the first time, it was being taken seriously enough so that its systematic study was about to begin.

II. MAJOR LIMITATIONS OF THE CLINICAL FIELD

Behavior modification and community psychology are contemporaries. They grew from academic and social histories that were very different in many ways, but shared their reactions against the internal focus of inferred causality in human behavior and in their emphases on external physical and social events. They coemerged at about the same time, in the decade beginning about 1955. While they developed as alternatives to and therefore as different from, traditional helping systems, they nevertheless shared the major, general values and goals inherent in those systems. That is, they entered a mainstream of professional endeavor and became part of the existing commonalities toward the general goal of creating effective interventions to improve the quality of human existence. This common goal, however imprecise it may be, provides a directive reality that blunts the sharp differences that we, in our more partisan moments, seem to value so greatly. The mythical Martian visitor, upon hearing a contentious discussion among a group of cognitive behavior modifiers, operant behavior modifiers, respondent behavior modifiers, Freudians, social psychoanalysts, and Rogerians, would be hard-pressed to discern any important difference between them. Our Martian would be like a space-age Gulliver in some perplexity musing over the Lilliputians' heated conflicts between the Big-Endians and the Little-Endians. However new or radical behavior modification and community psychology present themselves as being, their overriding commitment to helping goals puts all the various models' adherents in the same arena, competing perhaps, but pursuing the same elusive ends.

At present there exists a variety of mental health procedures and models, to the point of some confusion. We have psychoeducation, psychoanalysis, psychotherapy, behavioral, cognitive, rational, biblio, and somatic therapy; social interventions, systems consultations, primary, secondary, and tertiary prevention; we have professionals, paraprofessionals, nonprofessionals, subprofessionals, and ancillary professionals; we provide services labeled clinical, community, inpatient, outpatient, outreach, halfway, crisis intervention, individual, group and family, to list only some. Our Martian visitor must conclude that with all of these alternatives, each with their enthused adherents, we surely must be achieving considerable success in doing away with mental disorders. Unfortunately the facts as we know them do not support so optimistic a conclusion.

Goodstein and Sandler (1978) offer a conceptual organization of our crowded field. They note four major health strategies currently in use: clinical psychology, community mental health, community psychology, and public policy psychology. Each major strategy encompasses various conceptual elements, which the authors identify as the targets of intervention, their content, their "process or style;" and their particular body of knowledge. The mental health strategies and conceptual elements are arranged in a 4 × 4 matrix and the resulting table is reproduced below.

Clinical psychology, even as it was first defined by Witmer some 50 years ago and immediately ignored by psychologists, involves the detailed study of and intervention with "troubled individuals" as clients. The clinician has a passive role, waiting in an office to be contacted by self-selected individuals. The treatment contract is between the clinician and the individual seeking help, to whom the clinician is accountable. A variety of psychodynamic, somatic, and behavior therapies are applied to individuals singly or to individuals brought together in small groups. Our often parochial professional and conceptual differences can be seen as relatively minor variations within these shared, individually focused, clinical strategies. Not only clinical psychology, but also psychiatry through most of its history, and modern social work embrace these traditional strategies. Goodstein and Sandler's organization of areas within psychology may thus be quite descriptive of the mental health field as a whole.

Not too long ago Alexander and Selesnick (1966) could write

> . . . the challenge will continue because today only a relatively small number of men, women, and children who need psychiatric help can obtain it. Lack of money, lack of facilities, and lack of enlightened public policy still conspire with man's ancient prejudices to keep the emotionally disturbed in chains of neglect and misery. Not until all people, whatever their wealth, race, creed, locale, or status, can find the help psychiatry can offer will the great psychiatric tradition truly come into its own (p. 404).

TABLE 10.1
A Conceptual Model for Using Psychology to Promote Human Welfare

	Conceptual elements			
Strategy	Target	Content	Process or style	Knowledge
Clinical psychology	Troubled individuals	Individual assessment and behavior change	Passive style; professional accountable to fulfill contract with individual client	Individual differences; personality; psychopathology; individual assessment and behavior change
Community mental health	Catchment area	Planning, organizing, delivering, and evaluating relevant services	Accountability to residents of catchment area and funding sources	Program planning and development; administration and management; facilitating community involvement; evaluation research; program evaluation; specialized clinical services; selection and training of paraprofessionals; supervision
	Troubled individual within catchment area	Clinical services relevant to catchment area	Active marketing of service; accountability to consumer groups	
	Significant others in catchment area	Consultation; training; education; coordination of effort	Role definition and clarification; professional gatekeeper	Methods of consultation and training in helping relationships; under-

				standing of other social agencies and community resources; organizational dynamics; psychopathology; cultural differences
Community psychology	Systems of deviance control	Analysis of system; technical advocacy; creation of settings; organizational development; evaluation research	Critic of system; advocate of change; facilitator of self-examination by system; developer of planned change strategies	Systems analysis; program design; evaluation research; consultation methods; advocacy strategies
	Systems of socialization and support	Restructuring organizations to facilitate healthy personal functioning	Organizational consultation outside of mental health; advocacy of social change; resolution of professional-client value discrepencies	Systems analysis; organizational theory; planned change strategies; social planning; environmental assessment; stress theory
Public policy psychology	Government policy makers, including administrators, legislators, and judges	Technical advice in formulation of public policy; social action on a broad front; program evaluation; expert witness	Adversary system; agent of control or countercontrol; participate in political process	Knowledge of policy formulation and implementation; broad knowledge of other relevant social sciences (e.g., economics); understanding of the political process and the law; evaluation research

Source: American Psychological Association, copyright 1978. Reprinted by permission of the publisher and authors.

This was an optimistic statement, for it assumed that psychiatry had, through long scientific development, arrived at a point where psychiatry knew what it was doing, that what psychiatry did, worked, and what was still needed to effectively deal with mental illness was more psychiatry, that is more psychiatrists, more ancillary professionals, more hospitals, more clinics, and more money.

The optimism flashed by Alexander and Selesnik is tarnished by two major limitations that are seemingly inherent in the clinical strategies. Indeed, several years before Alexander and Selesnik had restated their optimism regarding the clinical model, George Albee (1959), working with the Joint Commission on Mental Illness and Health (1961), had already discussed the clinical model's major limitations. Today, nearly a quarter of a century later, our field is still primarily focused upon the clinical model and barely catching up with Albee's concepts. Of all the limitations two seem most important. First, whatever may be the strengths of the various clinical disciplines and the different diagnostic and treatment models within the clinical area, the individual focus makes it impossible to provide clinical services to significantly reduce the massive numbers of "troubled individuals." It does not appear that *any* society can afford to consume so much of its financial, physical, human labor, and talent resources which would be required to provide individually focused clinical mental health services to all who need or desire them. In simpler times when only the affluent worried about or toyed with such things, there was enough psychoanalysis to meet the demands, and it apparently satisfied many of those relatively unsophisticated clients. But the world has changed, clients are different, and the professions must change with them.

Second, the therapeutic technologies (behavior therapy, psychotherapy, and somatic therapy) are, by definition and execution, after-the-fact approaches. As Cowen (1973) noted, "The core aim of (clinical) interventions has been to relieve the debilitating conditions, that is to rehabilitate an already disabled—sometimes chronically so—individual" (p. 424). Assuming that the spectrum of behavior therapy treatments are the most effective now available, it seems clear that however much behavioral or any therapy is made available to already troubled people, those services will not appreciably reduce the rate of occurrence of new cases. Clinical strategies have little prevention value.

Thus two of the major limitations of clinical strategies are that (1) we do not have and probably cannot create enough individually oriented services to meet demands and (2) even if we could, and if most interventions were completely successful, new cases would continue to occur.

III. POINTS OF INTERVENTION: DECISIONAL DIMENSIONS

In discussing various issues we have suggested that there are several dimensions along which we can "calibrate" and locate our professional points of intervention. We can choose to (1) intervene directly into the life of a single individual in order to change that person's functioning, or we can choose to intervene in social community systems without reference to any individual (an individual systems-social community systems dimension). If we choose to focus on the individual our interventions can be set on (2) internal issues, as is attempted in psychodynamic therapy, or on external events that immediately impinge on the individual, as is attempted in behavior modification (an internal-external individual dimension). While our interventions are always applied in the present, we can nevertheless also (3) calibrate along a temporal dimension by focusing our goals, or drawing our basic data or understanding from the past, present, or future (a temporal dimension). That is, we can focus our point of intervention after the fact as in rehabilitative, restorative approaches which by definition characterize virtually all present psychological therapies; concurrently, as is attempted in crisis intervention approaches; or before the disorder occurs, as is advocated by prevention strategies. Finally, another dimension on which we can locate our point of intervention concerns our focus on a range from pathology through health or optimum functioning (a pathology-health dimension).

When we consider clinical strategies we can see that the point of intervention has been set at fairly clear positions along these various dimensions, that is: (1) direct intervention in the life of a single individual; (2) a primary focus on individual internal or external events depending upon the clinician's psychodynamic-through-behavioral orientation; (3) in either model the temporal orientation is after the fact; and (4) clinical strategies are focused on psychopathology.

Every clinician makes these point-of-intervention decisions regarding every case. The decisions are not mutually exclusive; we are not presenting categorical differences but, rather, gradations along each dimension. Thus a behavior therapist employing systematic desensitization, for example, will range across a narrow band of intervention points on the internal-external dimension, considering both cognitions about one's anxiety feelings, and the external, stimulus-controlling events that elicit those anxiety responses. The psychoanalyst will range across narrow temporal bands from past to present, and from unconscious to conscious motivations across a small portion of the internal-external dimension, and so on. Each clinician operates within a fairly narrow band of intervention points on each dimension and the total pattern or profile constitutes that clinician's characteristic general point of intervention.

It is instructive to note that the point of intervention is most commonly *a characteristic of the clinician*, already determined by the clinician's training and preference and is almost irrespective of the characteristics of the client. It would appear most prudent for clinicians to make the point-of-intervention decisions only after some study of the individual client. Further, it seems wise for the clinician to be prepared to quickly shift the point(s) of intervention if needed as the client changes or fails to change. Thus we might conceptualize the most competent clinician as one who probes psychodynamically when needed, arranges reinforcement contingencies when needed, sits in an office talking and listening when appropriate, and moves out into the client's natural environment and even becomes the client's advocate when that is necessary, and so on. Such flexibility and breadth of skills, however, do not appear to be characteristic of professionals. Indeed, the differences between models may constitute paradigm clashes that make such integration difficult. Rather, we seem to have not only determined our points of intervention before seeing the client, but we apply the same points of intervention to every client and, once we begin with a client we seldom shift the interventions as the client changes. The predetermination and the fixity of each clinician's characteristic point of intervention may be one of our field's implacable rigidities. The result may be that what is offered by one clinician might not be what a given client can profit by while another clinician's package might be useful. Unless the client is carefully matched to the clinician's particular point of intervention profile—and the field spends very little time carefully making such matches—we will undoubtedly continue to have mismatched therapist-client diads forever adding to our failure rates.

We are not arguing here for an eclectic approach that assumes every model is as good as every other and they can somehow be integrated. Assessment of relative effectiveness is an empirical issue and if models or portions of them are ineffective or grossly inefficient, then they should be discarded. Rather we are arguing that if the clinical strategy is to be retained at all, then (1) better client-therapist matching is a major priority and (2) point-of-intervention decisions should be made explicitly and based on individual study of each client. If the clinician cannot provide the point of intervention needed for any given client, a referral should be made to another, more appropriate clinician. The rule now, however, seems to be to apply one's own characteristic point of interventions to whomever may come along, and to maintain it until there is success or the client quits.

IV. COMMUNITY PSYCHOLOGY, BEHAVIOR MODIFICATION, AND PREVENTION: THEIR FUTURE ORIENTATION

Community psychology and behavior modification, by virtue of their emphasis on external rather than internal causal events are potentially capable of addressing both of the major limitations of traditional clinical strategies: that is, they can be applied to large-scale physical and social systems interventions, and each is an appropriate base for generating preventive approaches. Community psychology describes a set of conceptual and applied strategies with two major focal points: (1) social systems analyses and interventions, aimed at (2) prevention rather than rehabilitation goals. "Ultimately," writes Cowen (1973), "the most important conceptual distinction should be the one between rehabilitative-restorative efforts and preventive-prophylactic ones" (p. 425).

Implicit in these two focal points is a little discussed but major characteristic of community psychology: its *necessary* future orientation. The essential task in this prevention-focused model is not that of ameliorating current pathology that reaches into the past for its substance but, rather that of identifying prevention goals that draw their substance from the present as they reach into the future. Beyond the values, goals, ethics, and professionalism shared by all of the helping professions, community psychology is distinguished primarily by its combination of prevention goals within natural social systems and its strong and necessary future orientation.

In contrast with this idealized and still little applied conception of community psychology, behavior modification over the past two decades has been very actively applied and its focus has been on the *current* behavior of *individual* clients, with rehabilitative-restorative goals. Behavior modification like psychoanalysis has remained well within the traditional arena of clinical strategies. However, *there is nothing in behavior modification paradigms that limits their applications to restorative goals concerning past behavioral pathologies.* Indeed, one of the advances offered by behavior modification over psychodynamic models is the behavior therapist's emphasis on the client's current rather than past functioning. This here-and-now emphasis compared with the psychodynamic absorption with memories, dreams, or other reconstructions of the past, moves us somewhat along the temporal dimension, to consideration of present issues. But in following behavioral paradigms we need not stop in the present; we can proceed to focus on future behavior. Indeed, when the behavior modifier creates a contingency-management program that includes the careful arrangement of successive approximations toward defined behavioral goals, he or she is engaged in a very future-oriented enterprise. Not only overt behavior but also future-oriented cognitions or "futurants" (Graziano, 1975) may be utilized in more cognitive behavioral approaches. Further, those future goals need not be limited to restorative ends, but can just as well focus on prevention. For example, school programs can be designed to help grammar school children to develop cognitive and behavioral skills to withstand future peer and commercial pressures to begin smoking cigarettes. In this example the goal is clearly preventive; the children represent normal age groups rather than pathological groups; the programs of successive approximations, contingent reinforcements, and defined behavioral goals utilize basic operant behavioral technologies. Finally, this intervention would be within and would utilize the characteristics of natural-environment social groups—it is a systems intervention utilizing behavioral technology and, in this instance, behavior modification has merged with community psychology.

It seems clear to us that behavior modification technology allows the possibilities of systematically manipulating probable futures. This is really no more than saying we may be able to predictably direct our own behavior with growing accuracy. At present our success in systematically directing future behavior has been limited to fairly simple issues of individual behavior, in which we have made predictions about issues such as academic functioning, fears, self-injury, and so on. The success seems to have been considerable within the clinical strategies model. However, we do not yet have much evidence that similar behavioral analyses and interventions can predictably affect large, natural social systems or that we can, in fact, validate the preventive value of such programs. Our current lack of validating data for such applications underscores the need for careful research along small-step successive approximations toward those behavioral community psychology goals, before we too enthusiastically begin trying to use them in ambitious, applied programs.

But once we take seriously the notion of using behavioral technology toward preventive goals, we can easily generate many more applications such as preventing poor nutrition and other illness-related behaviors; preventing anxiety on entering school and perhaps reducing future withdrawn behavior; preventing children's debilitating anxieties and crises that often occur when hospitalization, surgery, or dental treatment is needed, and so on.

As we continue generating ideas for behaviorally oriented prevention projects, two characteristics become clear: (1) the content areas appear limitless and (2) the ideas soon begin to confront an inherent limitation of the prevention model, and still another conceptual step is needed, as noted below.

V. PROMOTING HEALTH AND OPTIMUM FUNCTIONING

If we could—or, hopefully, when we do—develop the technologies needed to succeed at prevention goals such as reducing the incidence of brain damage in children by reducing the lead content of our environment, preventing serious aggressive, withdrawn, or fearful behavior in schoolchildren, and so on, we will indeed have achieved significant things. There is much of great value to be accomplished in this direction.

The limitation, of course, is that in order to succeed at prevention, we must focus upon the negative events, pathologies, that are to be prevented. The orbit of prevention is inherently a set of ideas that revolve around the central concept of pathology and those ideas cannot easily escape from the central concept's strong attractional grip. Prevention, then, by its very nature, must remain bound by the limits of our knowledge about pathological conditions. If that is so then if the concept, prevention, becomes more important and its methods more successful. Its very success, its expansion, and refinement will demand an even greater effort to understand pathology so as to extend those limits of knowledge and better define the area in which the increasingly precise prevention efforts are to operate. Ultimately, then, the prevention focus, now seen as a movement away from the constraints of the clinical rehabilitative model, might serve to bind us even more firmly to the old clinical focus on pathology and to define our professional aspirations in the negative terms of avoiding or preventing such pathology.

This is not to argue against pursuing preventive goals any more than we have argued against clinical goals. Both clinical and preventive strategies can contribute importantly but each, alone, is limited. The present remarks are intended only to sharpen our awareness of the limits of what we are about.

When we take the next conceptual step and move beyond the orbit of prevention while maintaining our future orientation, we begin to consider the development of strategies to bring about the future goals of augmenting and maximizing normal to optimal development. To use a somatic analogy, we might attempt to treat obesity once it has developed, and thus rehabilitate the individual (a clinical approach), prevent obesity from occurring at so high a rate in some identified population (a community psychology approach), or promote knowledge about good nutrition, food selection and preparation, physical exercise, and eating habits to generate and maintain good nutrition and health. The latter strategy goes beyond prevention and focuses upon the promotion of good health behavior. All three strategies are necessary in any conceptions of complete approaches to the problems of obesity. One of our points is to note the need for a reversal of priorities: at present our systematic attempts to deal with obesity and similar human problems are virtually all clinical in nature, with little concerted or systematic efforts at either prevention or promotion of optimum health behavior. The priorities, we believe, should be in the reverse order with our major professional efforts in research and applied strategies to promote optimum development. A complete approach would also provide prevention programs aimed at specific pathologies in targeted populations and clinical rehabilitative services for individuals for whom the other approaches have been too late or not effective.

To direct our professional efforts to the maximization of health and optimum development is a common idea and one that has long had a prominent place on the lip-service shelf of every discipline's professional cupboard. Recently, however, more serious attempts have been made to define issues and to move us closer to operationalizing that view. Goodstein and Sandler (1978) have argued that professional efforts to "enhance healthy human functioning" should be the major goal of community psychology. Sanford (1972), Cowen (1973), Iscoe (1974), Insel and Moos (1974), Zifferblatt and Hendricks (1974), and Zax and Cowen (1977), to name only a few, have all discussed aspects of systems interventions to maximize health and optimum human functioning. In Chapter 9, we quoted Matarazzo (1980) who, in his presidential address to the Division of Health Psychology of the American Psychological Association, made the same points specific to the task of moving behavior medicine away from its clinical strategies roots to focus on illness prevention, positive physical health, and maintenance. Arguing, as did Knowles (1977), that these positive health goals are individual, corporate, and public responsibilities, Matarazzo pointed out the need to define a field of systematic inquiry and practice in behavioral health. Matarazzo proposed "Behavioral health is an interdisciplinary field dedicated to promoting a philosophy of health that stresses *individual responsibility* in the application of behavioral and biomedical science knowledge and techniques to the *maintenance* of health and the *prevention* of illness and dysfunction by a variety of self-initiated individual or shared activities" (p. 813).

Clearly there is a growing consensus for the timeliness of our moving away from clinical psychology with its public identification as a *mental* health profession and its traditional focus on past-rooted pathologies of individuals, to a broader identity, that of systematically developing our psychological knowledge to enhance the general public's health and competence. We do not suggest the imminent demise of clinical psychology or the rapid abandonment of the strategy by its adherents. Rather, it appears reasonable to expect a very marked slowing of growth in clinical psychology generally and in psychodynamic scrutiny particularly, while this new, still amorphous field becomes one of psychology's major new growth areas.

Applying behavioral technology within the future-oriented, preventive view of community psychology, toward the goals of enhancing the public's health will simultaneously depend upon and help to create not only new functions for psychologists but also new forms of graduate education and training, new kinds of public health-oriented internships, and new directions and methods of research. We suggest that the next decade of applied psychology—a decade which, by the way, will bring us to the threshold of the twenty-first century—may be an exciting time of growth, discovery, and new achievements. Whether these developments ever mature will depend upon our profession's willingness to explore new areas; and whether those new areas prove to be important contributions to the public good can only be determined in time, by maintaining our research efforts.

VI. ADDITIONAL DATA BASES: DEVELOPMENTAL PSYCHOLOGY AND PUBLIC HEALTH

Applied psychology, in the public's view at least, has been identified as clinical psychology. The major data bases for clinical psychology, because of emphasis on pathology and postevent rehabilitation have been constructed primarily from observations of variously "disturbed" individuals. But if we are to explore concepts of competence, health, and optimum functioning, then the studies of normal human development from conception through the final stages of life appear to offer appropriate data. In a recent article Masterpasqua (1981) has proposed that the contemporaneous growth of community psychology and applied developmental psychology are related events. Both, he points out, are concerned with individual competence in real-life situations and the development of settings and environments to promote competence, health, and optimum development. Human ecology varies as stages of development are achieved and community psychology, focused on supportive settings, must include this facet within its temporal concepts—that is, must include not only static "end-state" goals projected into the future, but also an appreciation of the dynamic flow of myriad normal changes across time as humans progress toward those projected goals. With our current behavioral technology we are able to project specific goals, for example, of improved academic and social functioning in a group of 8-year-old, socially aggressive, boys. And with reasonably systematic care and a cooperative setting, a fair degree of success has been demonstrated in many applied attempts. But it will require a far more sophisticated model and technology than we now possess, to take into account the fluid, interactive, and significant changes that normally occur in each eight year old and in the group as a whole, during a single year. The children for whom behavioral goals are defined in October are, simply, not quite the same people as those children who are assessed 7 or 8 months later. Neither is the group as a whole. We cannot now incorporate the cognitive, physical, and social developmental changes which will occur *irrespective of our behavioral programming* and which may have significant effects on the process and outcome of behavioral change. Our usual tactic is to control for developmental changes in various experimental ways, as if they are extraneous, and thus exclude them from our plans and procedures. But in doing so we may be ignoring events of great significance for the children; events which, if adequately taken into account might very well cause major changes in the ways in which we plan and carry out our behavior modification programs for children. Our point here is this: if we are to more successfully apply clinical strategies (psychodynamic or behavioral) to individual children or to families, then the most appropriate data base for our intervention is knowledge from the child-development field. We will go so far as to argue that the pathology-oriented psychodynamic models which have been generated primarily from limited observations of adults are probably among the least appropriate models for use with children. We urge that child clinicians and child community practitioners study child development as a necessary part of their graduate education. A similar argument is proposed for both clinical and community psychology applications to adults, for whom the research area of human development is highly appropriate.

It appears to us that applied psychology over the next decade will continue to maintain, develop, and refine its clinical concepts and approaches, by utilizing modern studies of life-span human development as data bases, to make individual, post pathology, restorative interventions increasingly effective. We suggest, however, that the major developments will occur outside of the clinical strategies and will constitute advances in the development of a more sophisticated community psychology based heavily on developmental data and behavior modification technology. Community psychology will hopefully develop its focus on creation of settings to promote optimum development, competencies, and health. Community psychologists will hopefully have greater roles in issues such as population control, energy conservation, and environmental protection, and will take on roles of advocates in social action, legal involvements, and public policy as well as more traditional roles of teacher, researcher, and clinician. These expanded roles will require new data bases—not the abandonment of knowledge about pathology but rather, continued development of such knowledge with clear recognitions of the limits of the pathology view. Mainly our new roles will require significant expansion of our data base to include modern study of human life-span development.

Community psychology seems also to be moving toward the public health area. Concerns for disease prevention, optimum physical health, and modification of environmental systems to promote better life quality, are all areas in which public health workers by now have had ample experience. As community psychologists continue to move in similar directions it seems appropriate that we look to the public health field too, for much of our conceptual, procedural and data base.

We see, then, that community psychology may be developing across many disciplines and has potential application to a variety of social issues, which psychologists now seldom address, for example, the problems of human and environmental degradation due to the dumping of industrial wastes. In the Niagara Falls, New York, Love Canal disaster of 1978, for example, some 300 families have been forced to abandon their homes while 200 more families, who must remain there because they cannot afford to abandon their homes and know they have been abandoned by their local, state, and federal governments, feel constantly threatened by the pervasive toxins still buried there. The total costs to taxpayers for partial cleanup of this single chemical dump—only one of an estimated two thousand toxic dumps in the country—will be over 100 million dollars! The costs in cancer, miscarriages, respiratory and other diseases, and growth retardation of children, have not yet been fully determined. At the very least the total existence of hundreds of families—that is, thousands of people—has been traumatically dominated by their Niagara Falls experiences.

Throughout this Niagara Falls disaster, for that is what it is, the chemical companies that buried the estimated 88 thousand tons of chemical wastes and covered them over with landfill and pretty green grass; the Niagara Falls School Board officials who, despite warnings about the toxic potential, nevertheless accepted title to the poisoned land and decided to build a grammar school right over the center of the buried poisons; the Niagara Falls city officials who approved the construction of that school and many hundreds of new homes and apartments; the contractors and labor unions who profited from building them; and the local, state, and federal government agencies—all deny responsibility for what happened to those people. Indeed, one company official tried to dismiss it all as the irrational overreactions of hysterical women.

In this mix of tragic after-the-fact individual disabilities and large-scale social catastrophe, the need for cooperative and wise remedial action across a wide variety of disciplines and the need for action to prevent future Niagara Falls-Love Canal disasters in other toxic dumps are as much psychological problems as they are problems of chemical engineering, economics, and politics. Psychologists do have a potential role in bringing industry to accept responsibility for its behavior in such instances, in convincing industry and government to act wisely, now, and prevent future disasters, and in helping, as much as possible, these individual victims of disaster. Involvement in issues such as the Love Canal will take psychologists to advocacy positions, public action groups, newspapers, legislative offices, and law courts, all of which are far removed from our traditional roles (Levine, 1982).

The world is rapidly changing—a cliché, we know—but what is not a cliché because it is too important to ever become one no matter how often it may be repeated, is the recognition that many of the most significant changes occurring in modern society are not those we would easily label as "progress," but are severe disruptions of life quality that are occurring because of our past behavior, such as unrestrained industrial waste dumping. In this respect the behavioral future of 30 years ago has caught up with us; and if we are to seriously take part in today's "future" somewhere in the twenty-first century, then we must move to future-oriented, preventive, public health and optimum-development models. Disruptive changes resulting from our past technological, economic, and political behavior appear to be occurring at a high rate.

Characteristic of these modern disruptive events is their complex, interacting nature. Each issue, such as the Love Canal disaster, is not the result of some single force or event such as a natural tornado or drought. Rather the disaster is human constructed and, as such, is a result of the interactions of many factors of individual and social psychology, geologic characteristics, weather conditions, industrial development, politics, and local business goals, to name but some. It is the complex interaction of all of these which caused the tragedy. The problem, then, is complex and its solution demands understanding that totality of interactive events, that is, human ecology. For our modern social issues the simplicities of, for example, Freudian psychoanalysis are simply inadequate. An ecological understanding, a multidiscipline data base, and concern for a wide variety of modern social problems, seem to be the directions of growth for community psychology and, as a major technology within that field, for behavior modification as well.

To repeat our earlier cliché, the world is rapidly changing and our professions must change with it. If we cannot keep up with these events and their new ecological realities, then psychologists might remain as increasingly obvious anachronisms, quaint, perhaps, but none too important. Applied psychology will develop its ability to contribute to the general, increasingly complex goal of optimum life quality, or it will be left behind to tend Rorschachs and individual clients.

VII. REALITY, POLITICS, AND CONSTITUENTS: CONSTRAINTS ON DEVELOPING COMMUNITY PSYCHOLOGY

Politics, it has been said, is the art of compromise; applied mental health, at least according to some (Graziano, 1969), is the art of politics. In order to survive, the newly emerged or reemerged fields of behavior modification and community psychology compromised with the prevailing professional modes and values of the late 1950s. In that process behavior modification seems to have become a new technology in the service of old clinical values and community psychology seems to have all but disappeared.

In serving primarily clinical needs, behavior modification has made excellent contributions to the restorative approaches, and we do not suggest that such contributions are not worthwhile. But the problem has not been in what behavior modification has contributed but, rather, in what it has not contributed—the potential it has not developed. In becoming so thoroughly co-opted as part of the clinical establishment, behavior modification has failed to develop its potential contribution as a future-oriented technology that can merge with community psychology and advance toward the solution of larger, more compelling modern social issues. Behavior modification has been, overall, a set of clinical advances but its potential has been truncated, slowed, and co-opted by a common process of professional political entrapment (Graziano, 1977).

Community psychology appears to have undergone a similar development. In compromise with the clinical establishment, it became community mental health. In that development we can see the truncating effects of compromise. Community mental health adopts some of the community psychology concepts and direction by focusing on targeted populations, attempting to make its services available to large numbers of individuals, utilizing natural-environment supports such as local ministers, paraprofessionals, and community groups, and even assertively seeking out potential clients. But the actual services delivered to the individual have hardly changed. The community mental health clinic still has its psychodynamic testing, its one-to-one verbal psychotherapy, and its behavior therapy, all with their postevent rehabilitation goals which have no primary prevention thrust. As with behavior modification's contributions these are all recognized as important improvements in clinical services. But community psychology, like behavior modification, by virtue of stopping there, has failed to develop its potential that holds out the possibility of application to our more complex, modern world. We suggest that Goodstein and Sandler's (1978) two categories of strategies, community mental health and clinical strategies, are not operationally very different but in fact constitute a single category of clinical strategies.

Our own professional-political realities are further constrained by the nation's current political alignment. Our conservative federal government, with its emphasis on industrial-economic development, places little value on expenditures for social science development. It will be difficult for psychologists to develop new social action and community psychology roles, if there is little monetary or national political support. Our probable future, if we do not seek otherwise, may be to consolidate ourselves around our more traditional, accepted, clinical roles.

Another limiting reality is the difficulty in identifying and enlisting the support of an active constituency for community psychology. This is because its future and prevention orientation defines its general task as preventing and creating long-term future events that have not yet occurred and do not yet impinge upon people. It is easy enough to find a constituency of troubled people seeking help for themselves or family or friends. But how do we find a constituency for preventing disorders that people do not yet have? Who will be our constituency for what might be seen as Breughellian pie-in-the-sky goals of "optimum human functioning and quality of life"? It seems clear that one of the major immediate tasks of community psychology will be to develop methods applicable to the search for a supportive constituency. We may be in a position similar to public health workers of an earlier day and, again, we suggest that community psychologists turn to our public health colleagues for ideas and procedures.

VIII. BEHAVIORAL COMMUNITY PSYCHOLOGY: A BRIEF REVIEW OF RECENT EMPIRICAL STUDIES

We are a long distance from the applied community psychology that we have been describing, but there are trends toward integration of behavioral technology and community psychology. We note, for example, the inclusion in the 1981 American Psychological Association Convention of at least three special sessions devoted to behavioral research in energy conservation, environmental protection, and primary prevention. Another indication is the planned special issue of the *Journal of Community Psychology* for 1983, which will be devoted to behavioral community psychology. As tentatively defined by the guest editors for that issue, behavioral community psychology refers to "the application of behavioral methodology, analysis, and technology to community-based problems. It incorporates behavioral approaches which intersect with both a community mental health framework (e.g. characterized by an active intervention stance, use of paraprofessionals) and prevention-oriented, community psychology strategies (e.g. stress innoculation for youngsters, competency building, reduction of environmental irritants predisposing to difficulties in coping, and naturalistic observation of person-environment transactions)" (Jason and Glenwick, 1981, p. 19).

In our previous chapters on school, family systems, juvenile delinquency, and behavioral medicine, where prevention is potentially a major focus, we have seen some of the current moves toward behavioral community psychology. It seems reasonable to expect that those four areas of application will constitute a major portion of the future development of behavioral community psychology. In these areas can be seen steps in development from individual to group application and from clinical to community psychology strategies. The most critical aspect here is not so much the work with groups, since therapeutic groups have long been used in clinical strategies, but the nature of the groups worked with; that is, preexisting natural-environment social units rather than special-purpose, constructed therapy groups.

The remainder of this chapter will present briefly other areas of application in which we see the development from clinical to community behavior modification. They will be headed as follows: Problems of Entry; Community Mental Health Centers; Behavioral Paraprofessionals; Environmental Issues and Public Behavior.

A. *Problems of Entry*

During the 1960s there were many conflicts and points of resistance as the newer behavior modification approaches developed and became part of the clinical field. These problems of entry into the existing field were perhaps most marked when they aimed at a social or large-group approach such as in applications to hospital wards, children's institutions, classrooms, and within families. One of the earliest discussions of such entry problems (Graziano, 1969) described an early 1960s attempt to create a group behavior modification program for severely disturbed children in a medically and psychoanalytically dominated mental health community. One conclusion in that paper was that extra-scientific factors, ordinarily ignored by researchers and innovators, are critical in the implementation of new approaches. "The *conception* of innovative ideas in mental health depends upon creative scientific and humanitarian forces, while their implementation depends, not on science or humanitarianism, but on a broad spectrum of professional and social politics!" (1969, p. 12).

A few years later, discussing that early attempt to move behavior modification into a more social community stance, Sarason (1972) agreed with the conclusion about the importance of extrascientific factors but made the point that perhaps the most important of those issues was the innovator's failure to understand and to take into consideration the complex history of the preexisting clinical structure.

Reppucci and Saunders (1974) came to similar conclusions. They noted the early behavior modification directions toward community applications in the 1960s and saw this as a significant changing of "frontiers" for behavior modification as it shifted from clinical applications for individuals to applications to "populations larger than one in natural settings." While these trends seemed desirable, they noted, the reality of the field in the 1970s—that is, small-scale attempts to change the behavior of individuals in special settings—was far from what was being "imagined" as possible. The gap, they suggested, was "at least in part due to issues that fall outside the domain of behavioral psychology" and understanding these issues is necessary in order for behavior modification to grow into its community applications. We agree with these writers that a major area of difficulty in the further development of behavior modification is the extrascientific area of value conflicts. If a behavioral community psychology is to develop, we must anticipate and deal with such value conflicts.

B. *Community Mental Health Centers*

As we suggested earlier the community mental health movement seems to have been the resulting compromise between community and clinical strategies. When this compromise emerged in the 1960s, clinical strategies were dominated by psychodynamic models and it is not surprising that the new community mental health movement was also psychodynamically focused. Responsibility for the planning, development, and operation of the new community mental health centers was given to the same local professional leaders who had for so long operated in the traditional clinical manner (Graziano, 1969). The result, as noted by Gambrill (1975) was that "The so-called new programs often consisted of more of the same, that is, an emphasis on internal factors, on achieving change of verbal behavior as a prelude to change in actual behavior, and the carrying out of this focus within fairly traditional models of client-therapist contact, that is, once-a-week individual or group meetings. The environment was by and large still neglected" (p. 307). Thus problems of entry for behavioral models were similar in the community mental health area to the entry problems found in more traditional settings.

Gambrill urged that community mental health centers begin utilizing behavioral methods to focus on behavioral change within natural environments, utilizing the work of significant others such as parents and teachers. In other words the community mental health movement might better achieve its avowed goals, at least those with children, by utilizing concepts, approaches, and settings such as those described in the many research papers discussed in our chapters on families, schools, and juvenile delinquency.

At present however it appears that while some staff members of community mental health centers utilize various forms of behavior therapy, they do so in a fairly traditional, individual client manner (Nietzel et al., 1977). Thus in the community mental health center behavioral models have become part of clinical strategies but have not had much effect in generating more community-oriented programs.

Few mental health centers have attempted to develop a systematic behavioral community mental health approach. One, described at the 1975 American Psychological Association meetings (Turner, 1975) and by Rinn and Vernon (1975), was developed in the early 1970s at the Huntsville-Madison County Mental Health Center. One of their many programs was a series of classes for parents, dealing with child management issues (Rinn, Vernon, and Wise, 1975). Parents of "problem" children in which management issues included temper tantrums, school attendance, and enuresis, attended classes in which they followed a systematic course in behavioral interventions, including homework assignments. The program continued for three years and included at least 100 families. In this instance a mental health agency utilized a large-group teaching approach, behavioral analyses and interventions within families, and direct therapeutic work by parents. The goals were still restorative, therapeutic goals rather than prevention-oriented, but the entire program embodied behavioral community approaches.

While many service and research projects have explored behavioral community approaches, as seen in our chapters on families, schools, delinquency, and behavioral medicine, there are few reports of mental health centers adopting these approaches in a systematic fashion. Given their funding, their task, and knowledge of their own communities, mental health centers seem to be potentially important agents in developing behavioral community psychology.

C. *Behavioral Paraprofessionals*

One of the influences of the social community movement upon clinical practice is the paraprofessional development in mental health services. This development has occurred within community mental health strategies and has been viewed by many as a significant improvement over traditional clinical services. Initially these new staff were introduced to standard psychodynamic models but, in time, *behavioral paraprofessionals* emerged. This section will discuss mental health paraprofessionals in general, and behavioral paraprofessionals in particular.

As we noted several times, World War II accelerated many significant directions of change in mental health concepts and delivery of services. Among those important changes were (a) the influx of behaviorally oriented psychologists into the medically and psychoanalytically dominated mental health field; (b) development of the community mental health approach, largely spurred by the influence of the public health model; and (c) the postwar phenomenon of the rapid growth in numbers of paraprofessionals across nearly all human service areas, including the mental health professions. These three closely related directions of change are still evolving and, as best as we are able to judge, continue to have major influence on mental health research and applications. It is the third of the changes listed above, the growth in numbers of paraprofessionals, which will be considered by this section.

At first paraprofessional development was an attempt to reduce the personnel shortages that had been made so clearly evident by the demands of the war. Paramedics, nurse's aides, dental, laboratory, and x-ray technicians, and many others, soon formed a sizable cadre of ancillary, clinical-support personnel. Their function was to assist the various medical professionals by performing some of their more routine duties, thus releasing the professionals for more advanced, complex levels of function, that is, tasks requiring more knowledge, technical, teaching, and supervisory skills, and research and new creative problem solving for those issues where there were still no clear, technological solutions. Easing the "manpower problem" was the initial rationale for the massive paraprofessional development and, although additional rationales were put forward in the 1960s, it remains as the single, overriding reason for its continued development (Graziano and Katz, 1982).

In the mid-1960s, stimulated by the growing recognition of the failure of traditional mental health delivery systems, by a series of new federal laws that pushed the field toward community mental health concepts and services, and the 1960s enthusiastic "war on poverty," the mental health professions saw the rapid increase in numbers of "nontraditional personnel," or "paraprofessionals." These new paraprofessionals were recruited from unemployed housewives with college degrees, poverty groups, high school dropouts, and college and junior college students and graduates, and they filled positions from ward aides to intake interviewers and psychotherapists.

Enthusiasm, promise, and fine expectations ran high and the activity level of the field has been at least partly reflected in the annotated bibliography by Alley and Blanton (1978) that summarizes well over 1000 articles, books, and unpublished papers from 1966 to 1977, concerned with paraprofessionals. Cohen (1976) has estimated that some 400,000 paraprofessionals are employed across all human service areas and Levenson and Reff (1970) predicted that 40% of all positions in the mental health field would "eventually" be filled by paraprofessionals.

Looking back over those developments we see much more enthusiasm and commitment to beliefs and ideals than any substantial empirical support, in the confusing and often conflicting expectations, goals, professional-paraprofessional conflicts, people, and training programs. The paraprofessional movement was considered to be a "revolution" (Sobey, 1970) and this mixed cadre of new workers was going to ease manpower problems, create new services that the professionals had never thought of, and be superior—even without training—to professionals in understanding and in relating to special groups such as poor blacks. The new paraprofessionalism was even going to provide a significant number of jobs and career-ladder opportunities for the poor, and thus contribute to the well-being of the economy as well as the state of the nation's psychological health. Paraprofessionals' therapeutic work was to be two-edged, as those recruited to help others were expected to gain in personal ways through operation of the "helper-therapy" principle (Riessman, 1967).

With such creative diversity of beliefs, goals, people, settings, clients and activities, involving many thousands of people over nearly 20 years, it is entirely possible to reach in and pick out cases of paraprofessional successes. But, unfortunately, selective cases do not constitute validation and, to date, there is no overall evaluation with adequate representative sampling from the population of paraprofessionals and controlled, empirical tests, to enable anyone to claim that the paraprofessional endeavor has been, overall, a successful enterprise (Graziano and Katz, 1982).

The paraprofessional model is reasonably straightforward in its outline, that is, the professionals train the paraprofessionals to perform limited aspects of the professionals' traditional functions. The trained and supervised paraprofessionals then apply the newly learned skills in order to bring about improvement in clients. The savings in professional time and thus in financial resources should be significant.

To adequately test the paraprofessional model empirical research is needed on each of the critical variables: (1) selection of paraprofessionals and their backgrounds and characteristics; (2) the training procedures including the type, complexity, duration, and "sophistication" of the training, the theoretical models used, the operational skills taught, and the education, skills, and other characteristics of the professional trainers; (3) the clients to be served, their characteristics, and particular types of personal or clinical issues or problems they present; (4) the goals and procedures of the interventions to be used; (5) the outcomes for the clients as measured by their improved functioning; and (6) the nature of the service-delivery systems in which the paraprofessionals are to work, including the type and amount of supervision, the characteristics and training of the supervisors, the type of training and work setting and even political and professional issues operating between professionals and paraprofessionals. Despite some 20 years of development of paraprofessionalism in mental health, these variables and their interactions have, to date, been inadequately studied, and we seem to be still left with a promising but unproved field that, as it ages, is losing even its enthusiasm.

Instead of the general question of the effectiveness of paraprofessionals, the more meaningful questions should be posed to assess *what* paraprofessionals, with *what* kinds of training, are carrying out *what* specific functions, with *what* kinds of clients and problems and in *what* settings. Each of many different and interacting variables contributes to the overall function of paraprofessionals, and poses complex problems of evaluation. Taken together they present a formidable task, in view of which the overall and highly positive impressions of effectiveness so far formed in the field are of little continuing value.

Gartner (1971) has cleared some of the field's confusion by pointing out that, conceptualized in terms of their origins, three major groups of paraprofessionals have emerged across many human services areas. These are as follows.

The old paraprofessionals who form the traditional group of hospital-based workers such as psychiatric aides, typically perform routine, patient-care duties. They typically do not hold college degrees and are not recruited from the groups they serve.

The indigenous paraprofessionals have been recruited from the target population such as the poor, former drug addicts and other legal offenders, mental patients, and so on. The indigenous paraprofessionals do not hold college degrees, often have not completed high school and are usually employed in low-level positions in community mental health centers. Their particular strength is supposedly in their identification with the group to be served and they purportedly possess skills, independently of any new training, for good interactions with clients from that particular target population.

The *new middle-class paraprofessionals* include fairly well-educated middle-class persons such as housewives, many of whom hold college degrees, college students, and mental health Associate Degree graduates. Their socioeconomic backgrounds, their values, beliefs, social manners, and general behavior are quite similar to the middle-class professionals with whom they work.

In their review of paraprofessional training Graziano and Katz (1982) point out another distinct group of paraprofessionals who are different from the others because they focus specifically on children as clients, and they bear a special, prior, relationship to their child clients—*parents as paraprofessionals,* working with their own children. Although there are historical parent-training precedents from both psychoanalytic and client-centered models, the modern training of parents has been almost exclusively within the behavior modification field.

On evaluation, these four groups have functioned quite differently. Overall there has been general, even enthusiastic agreement that paraprofessionals' services are effective and useful. But as Heller and Monahan (1977) and many others point out many of the studies are so poorly controlled that their positive conclusions cannot be readily accepted. Neither can they be easily generalized to all paraprofessionals, all clients, or all settings. The better-controlled studies supporting the paraprofessionals' effectiveness, are primarily limited to two of the paraprofessional groups, the "middle-class" paraprofessionals, and the parents. Recent reviews of the better-controlled empirical studies (Durlak, 1979; Karlsruher, 1974) report studies that do support the claim of effectiveness of middle-class paraprofessionals working with limited segments of the adult population, such as with hospitalized psychotics and college students who seek counseling. There is little support for the expectation that either the "old" or the "indigenous" paraprofessionals have adequately demonstrated their effectiveness at operating in what were previously professional functions. Many disappointments have been noted by indigenous paraprofessionals who found their career ladder to be without rungs as their new and largely undefined roles gradually emerged as dead-ended at low levels. Individuals within these two groups might very well make significant contributions to patient care and to other aspects of the clinical enterprise, but we do not yet possess sufficient and acceptable data to validate their carrying out, even to limited degrees, professionals' therapeutic functions. Perhaps the lack of evidence is due to limitations in the research rather than in the paraprofessionals' potential, and perhaps future research will bear out the earlier claims and hopes. But at present it seems clear that it is the "new, middle-class" and the teacher and parent paraprofessionals, who have reliably held up over the years as potentially useful contributors to the mental health field. The field seems to have implicitly recognized this as there has been a noticeable decrease in interest in the indigenous and old paraprofessionals in new roles, a greater emphasis on training and employing the new middle-class group (Cohen, 1976), and growing development of didactic Associate Degree junior college programs for mental health workers (Becker, 1978; Young, True, and Packard, 1974), and a growing interest in training parents (Graziano, 1977). Further, the middle-class paraprofessionals, consisting of housewives and college students, have worked best with a limited array of adult clients, such as the college students who function as companions to hospitalized adult psychotics, and housewives working therapeutically with other housewives. The paraprofessionals' therapeutic work with children seems to have been carried out largely by teachers and parents, the two groups who carry a special, prior, and often very personal relationship to the child clients.

Paraprofessionals have been recruited from various populations, employed in many different settings and trained in—or at least introduced to—different theoretical models (e.g. behavioral, client-centered, psychodynamic). The theoretical models and didactic training have varied from near-zero conceptual rigor, such as those assuming that indigenous paraprofessionals enter the work system with sufficient "natural" skills so as to not require training, through some programs that include lengthy didactic and applied training. The training of paraprofessionals has been a large part of the behavior modification field since its reemergence in the late 1950s and early 1960s, and has included many parents, teachers, college students, and others.

It seems to have been commonly assumed by those earlier behavioral clinicians and researchers that the behavior modification principles and procedures, compared with those of the more traditional psychodynamic models, were more parsimonious and straightforward and thus much more readily taught to parents and to other nontraditional workers. Although this assumption was acted on in many programs in the 1960s and since, there has been little attention paid to validating predictions from that assumption, to the details of training procedures, and to evaluating the effectiveness of the behavioral training and the trained, behavioral paraprofessionals as they work with clients (Balch and Solomon, 1976). The limitations and criticisms of the paraprofessional field in general, and the major questions noted above that require research, apply as well to the development of behavioral paraprofessionals as they do to paraprofessionals in general. At this point it appears that behavioral paraprofessionals, like other paraprofessionals, are a promising, feasible group of new personnel, but their training needs to be explicated, and their effectiveness with clients validated.

The training of behavioral paraprofessionals has included all four of the paraprofessional groups. The old paraprofessionals, that is, psychiatric aides, have been trained as behavior modifiers for hospitalized adult patients. Aylion and Michael (1959) trained psychiatric aides and nurses as behavioral engineers, although the psychiatric nurses, like teachers, are not "para" or "non" professionals, in the same sense as are the aides. Aylion's work was among the first and most important of these training endeavors. The aides and nurses were taught in didactic meetings as well as through on-ward supervision, and were taught behavioral shaping skills to modify psychotic patients' behavior including improving and increasing speech, and reducing hoarding, food stealing, and overdressing. Other behavioral training programs include those with retarded patients (Watson, Gardner, and Sanders, 1971; Watson and Bassinger, 1973). The program described by Watson included didactic teaching, role-playing, and practice with an assigned patient, followed by a five-month internship. Guess, Smith, and Ensminger (1971) also trained aides in behavioral work with severely retarded patients.

Marks, Connolly, and Hallam (1973) provided 18 months of intensive behavioral training to five psychiatric nurses. Like some of the trainees in Ayllon's program, these nurses were not "paraprofessionals" in the usual sense. Mark et al. reported clinically significant improvement for 31 cases treated by the psychiatric nurses. Their use of systematic desensitization to treat clinical phobias was suggested to have been more effective than reports in the literature by professional therapists.

These and other early demonstrations strongly support the feasibility of training old paraprofessionals in the design and application of therapeutic programs of contingency management and systematic desensitization, to improve the behavior of hospitalized psychotic or retarded adults. By the mid-1970s, however, there was still considerably more research needed to progress beyond the level of demonstrating feasibility. The actual effectiveness of these paraprofessionals in bringing about improvement and maintaining that improvement across settings and in time, the selection and specific training procedures for best effectiveness, all are yet to be validated.

Examples of early programs that selected and trained indigenous paraprofessionals include those reported by Wetzel (1970) and Burkholder and Morris (1971). Wetzel selected and trained teachers, teachers' aides and volunteers, working in child-care centers. The aides and volunteers were from the poverty populations. Burkholder and Morris worked with southwestern American Indians, to train them as consultants to reservation youth programs. These researchers could not implement or evaluate their program because of problems of funding, but they did proceed through much of the training.

Some investigators have selected and trained retarded and schizophrenic patients to work with other patients (Whalen and Henker,

1971). The latter trained severely disturbed chronic schizophrenics to shape attention and other social behaviors of other, more disturbed, patients. Although they reported some success, this program required a good deal of intense professional supervision, and it is doubtful that it could become a feasible approach to easing the professional "manpower" problems.

As we noted above the training of paraprofessionals in behavioral work with children has involved primarily two groups of paraprofessionals, the middle-class paraprofessionals and the group composed of parents and teachers.

Through the mid-1970s there have been many reports of training and using new middle-class paraprofessionals, primarily college students, as behavior modifiers for disturbed and retarded children (e.g. Davison, 1965; Graziano, 1974; Keeley, Shemberg, and Ferber, 1973; Thorne and Shinedling, 1970). College students have been actively involved in many reports of research and clinical programs with disturbed children, although not always identified as paraprofessionals. Overall they seem to have provided a large source of reliable behavioral manpower readily trained and highly useful. The emphasis in the many papers reporting use of college students seems to have been on the behavioral methodology applied to the child clients, with little attention paid to the selection and training of the students. It appears almost as though the field tacitly agrees that college students can be trained, without examining in any detail just how such training can best be carried out. Although training details are lacking, there does appear to be a large component of didactic teaching as well as applied training, as reviewed by Balch and Solomon (1976). College students, although of considerable potential value, are a source of only temporary or short-term personnel. Their tenure as college students has a limited duration and once graduated, the former students probably move on to other, perhaps professional, pursuits. Thus, although the college student group constitutes a highly motivated and bright group of potential paraprofessionals, their higher aspirations make them, of necessity, a group with a high rate of turnover, and individuals will not long remain paraprofessionals.

If they are to be considered mental health paraprofessionals, then teachers and parents certainly stand out as being quite different from the rest of the paraprofessionals. Teachers are hardly paraprofessionals at all, as they already possess a professional identity, values, and skills. They have a prior relationship to the children—their pupils—with whom they are trained to work behaviorally. The training of teachers and teacher's aides in behavioral approaches to children in classrooms has been well reviewed elsewhere (e.g. O'Leary and O'Leary, 1976), and most of the training seems to have been focused upon educational goals, and will not be dealt with here. We will only repeat one of the points made by Graziano and Katz (1982) that teachers have often been included among the mental health paraprofessionals but, in fact, they are not paraprofessionals at all. Teachers are professionals and those teachers who learn specific behavioral approaches to children are professionals who are moving toward greater specialization, rather than paraprofessionals. To claim that successfully training professionals such as teachers (and, for that matter, psychiatric social workers or nurses) in behavioral management or any other segment of behavior modification adds credence to the paraprofessional notion of building a cadre of assistants from among nonprofessionals, is a misrepresentation of actual events.

As we noted in Chapter 7 training parents as behavior therapists for their own children has developed into a large and important area of research and clinical applications. We include parents in this section on paraprofessionals because as a group they seem to meet the field's generally accepted definition of the mental health paraprofessional—the parents are nonprofessionals, are trained in some limited functions as ancillary or aides to the therapist, and assume some of the therapeutic and other mental health tasks that were traditionally carried out by the professionals, thus making it possible for the professionals to work with a greater number of clients. To the degree that parents are successfully trained, that they successfully carry out "ancillary" roles, and effectively help reduce the manpower shortage, then indeed, they are "paraprofessionals."

It is clear, however, that parents are also significantly different from all of the other groups of mental health paraprofessionals, the "old," "indigenous," and the "new, middle-class" paraprofessionals. The most apparent differences are (a) their highly personal, complex and preexisting relationship with their "clients," and their own children and (b) their dual roles as both client and paraprofessional or assistant, in training. There are other important differences, too: the parents trained to work with their own children are ordinarily not interested in jobs or career ladders as mental health paraprofessionals, and they are not usually encouraged to continue in the field. There seems no reason, however, why many of those parents could not be encouraged. After all, many might receive training that is at least as good, and sometimes perhaps even better, that that given the other paraprofessionals in the field. Further, the complex roles might often create highly complex relationships among parent, child, and professional. In relation to the professional the parent is both paraprofessional trainee and a client receiving service. The parent both "works for" the supervising professional and, at the same time, "employs" or "retains" that professional, engaging the professional's services. In relation to the child the parent is both therapist and parent. The interaction of all of these varied roles and relationships may at times become highly complex indeed. These role complexities have not yet been adequately studied by behavior modifiers. On that point it is understandable that these complex and sophisticated issues have not been studied, since many of the more basic issues—such as, for example, the effective selection of which parents can best be trained—are still in need of proper study. In time, however, after more basic issues have been settled, those of the complex roles and relationships among parent-trainee, the trainer-therapist, and the child, will have to be researched.

It is clear that parent training has become a major area of research in behavior therapy with children. But what are some of the implications of these developments? Most obviously training parents to successfully solve child and child-parent problems in their own homes has important implications for community mental health programming. In every sense parent-training technologies involve sharing professional knowledge and skills, and disseminating them on a wide basis. Further, while parent behavior training has been almost exclusively an after-the-fact treatment of already existing problems, once parents are trained their new skills might very well serve preventive functions. Parent behavioral training holds considerable promise as a community mental health, preventive move, training parents in successful management of common issues, thus preventing the issues from becoming major issues later. Some of the research reported by Reisinger and Ora (1977) seems to be moving in this direction. Parent behavior training may be the behavioral area with the clearest potential for primary prevention programs on a large scale. It is, however, still "promise," and substantial work towards primary prevention goals is necesssary.

Other important implications of the growth of parent training have been discussed in Chapter 7. As we noted there, parent behavioral training may be far more than a technological development; it may have long-range implications for professional conduct and mental health policy making.

In summary, we have briefly discussed the development of mental health paraprofessionalism since World War II, and have focused primarily on behavioral paraprofessionals, that is, those trained in or working from social-learning models, and using some variations of behavioral interventions. Despite a voluminous and still growing literature there is little systematic information concerning the "old" and the "indigenous" paraprofessionals and still, at this point, meager data to validate their effectiveness.

It is with the new, middle-class paraprofessionals and the parent training that more systematic and empirical research has been carried out. Carefully selected and at least moderately trained nonprofessional middle-class adults have effectively worked with limited groups of adult clients such as college students and hospitalized schizophrenics. Many college students have been taught behavioral approaches to children, and have worked with issues ranging in severity from autism to mild conduct problems. Although information about the "new and middle-class" paraprofessionals is more substantial than that for the "old" and "indigenous" groups, it is still lacking needed research on issues of selection and training of paraprofessionals, and their effectiveness with clients.

Although reflective or client-centered models are employed in the training of the middle-class paraprofessionals, particularly in their work with adult clients, the parent-training literature is composed primarily of behavioral models and approaches. The research to date is promising and investigators are moving to increasing specificity. According to several reviews parents have been trained to work successfully with their children across a wide distribution of ages and problem-behavior areas. As with the rest of the paraprofessional training literature there are still many unresolved issues concerning the selection of parents to be trained, details of training, types of problems, ages and other characteristics of children, and the careful assessment of effectiveness of the parents' working with children.

At this point it appears that a promising area for continued investigation is the selection and training of middle-class adults, including college students, as paraprofessionals, and of parents as therapists for their own children. What appears to be happening in much of the paraprofessional field is a weakening of the old notions of selecting and employing relatively uneducated and trained people to carry out therapeutic work. Gradually replacing it are moves toward more careful selection and more formalized training of paraprofessionals, even to the extent of degree-granting programs. Child-behavior therapists should find a rich field of research and application in the selection and training of middle-class paraprofessionals and parents as therapists for their own children. In particular, we see the potential for developing a prevention focus in such training.

D. *Environmental Issues and Public Behavior*

Over the past decade there has been growing interest in research that attempts to study and modify environmentally related behaviors of the public. Most studies have been limited to adult subjects. For example, attempts to encourage home conservation of electricity and heating fuels, such as that by Winett and Nietzel (1975), focus on adults as the responsible family members. Children, with little control over payment of family bills, have apparently not been considered as having important impact upon families' energy use. But children and adolescents are important consumers of energy and it appears to us that helping parents to train their own children in energy-conservation behavior might be a potentially important environmental contribution. Indeed, there might be greater value in designing large-scale school programs that help *children* teach their *parents* better energy conservation skills. Such programs might have the dual effect of stimulating parents in the short term and teaching children long-term skills they might apply as adults. Such behavioral research does not yet seem to have been done but the idea raises interesting research possibilities.

Some studies that have been carried out with children involve attempts to reduce littering and to increase recycling of recoverable wastes. In a littering study at children's movie matinees, Burgess, Clark, and Hendee (1974) compared the effects of antecedent conditions such as prompts and availability of more trash cans in the lobby, with incentives for using litter bags (e.g. 10-cent payment or a free movie ticket). They found that incentive conditions were more effective than the manipulation of antecedent conditions. Chapman and Risley (1974) compared the effects of incentives on littering and clean-up behavior of children in a housing project. One condition was payment for litter collected and it was compared with a verbal-appeal condition, a payment-for-clean yard condition, and a no-payment condition. The payment for litter collected was associated with the greatest amount of litter turned in by the children.

Similar findings were reported by Hamad, Cooper, and Semb (1977). Ten elementary classrooms were included in a 9½-week paper-recycling experiment which compared the effectiveness of verbal appeals and contingent prizes. The contingent prize condition resulted in significantly more newspaper recycling, with 14,298 pounds compared with 792 pounds turned in by the children. In these studies it appears that manipulating antecedent conditions such as verbal appeals and greater availability of waste baskets might have some positive effects upon littering and recycling behavior. The application of contingent rewards, however, appears to be far more effective. While children's littering and recycling behavior can be altered, we have no data on either generalization or maintenance of the new, environmentally helpful behaviors. Neither do we know if the benefits of large-scale behavior change efforts, such as might be carried out in schools, are justified by the costs. With nearly two tons of wastes annually per capita in the United States, with waste disposal and management costs now beyond five billion dollars annually, and with the loss of millions of tons of recoverable resources each year, we can see that large-scale efforts at behavior change in this area may be potentially significant. While physical technology for waste recycling and recovery exists, we still have little tested behavioral technology with which to encourage such large-scale changes in public behavior. The potential importance of children's public behavior in such efforts has not yet been determined.

Our final two examples from the behavioral community literature will involve two quite different types of behaviors—children's safe street-crossing behavior and parents' and children's dental-care seeking. These will be considered together because they share a common problem. In both areas previous attempts at large-scale education have not been particularly successful. School programs to improve children's pedestrian behavior seem to have resulted in higher paper-and-pencil test scores, but have not influenced the actual street-crossing behavior of children. Likewise, public campaigns seem to have had little effect in altering actual dental care practices of children and their parents (Haefner, 1974). In both instances the attempts have been aimed toward increasing information, but not toward altering actual *behavior*. In the following two studies the experimenters have focused on actual behavior change.

Yeaton and Bailey (1978) noted the traffic hazards to millions of children who walk to and from school each day. Although crossing guards are stationed around many schools they do not serve an educational function. The children come to depend upon the guards' signals to stop or cross, but do not seem to learn critical, street-crossing skills. Martin and Heimstra (1973) and Salvatore (1974) suggested developmental aspects to child-pedestrian behavior, noting that younger children made more errors than did older children in judging the speed of oncoming cars. There have been few attempts to study developmental/perceptual factors in young children' pedestrian behavior or to modify that behavior.

In their study Yeaton and Bailey (1978) included 24 kindergarten through third-graders in two elementary schools. Behavioral targets included the acquisition of six "street-crossing skills: (1) wait at curbs, (2) look both ways, (3) watch vehicle distance, (4) walk, (5) continue to look, and (6) use cross-walk" (p. 315). After baseline observation of street-crossing behavior, an instructional package was used with two groups of six children. Training was carried out at the corner where the children normally crossed, and included verbal instructions, modeling, imitation, rehearsal, and verbal reinforcement.

The percentage of correct pedestrian behaviors of the two groups rose from 40 and 50% at baseline to 100 and 95% shortly after training. At a one-year follow-up the pedestrian skills were found to be still high, but somewhat decayed since posttraining. A single prompt session, however, brought the skills back to between 95 and 100%

The authors noted that few pedestrian skills programs for children had been implemented or evaluated. Some, taught in schools, may have resulted in higher scores on paper-and-pencil tests, but not improvements in actual street-crossing behavior. As Yeaton and Bailey suggest, much of the danger to children may not be in their lack of understanding, but in their poor skills in street-crossing behaviors. This behavioral program seems to provide a "field tested" procedure that can serve as prototype for larger applications and testing in other school settings.

In their study, Reiss, Piotrowski, and Bailey (1976) compared three approaches to "encourage low-income rural parents to seek dental care for their children" (p. 387). Fifty-one families were assigned to three treatment groups comparable on number of families and of students by grade levels, income, race, and children's dental condition.

The experimental conditions varied by the amount of prompting, that is, notes and telephone calls to parents, and incentives to seek dental care. It was noted that the usual procedure is to send a single reminder to the parents to bring children for examination. In this study a single reminder constituted the "one-prompt" condition, and was compared with a "three-prompt" condition (note, telephone call, and home visit) and a single-prompt, plus a five dollar incentive. Examining both behavioral effectiveness in terms of the number who responded by taking their children to the examinations, and cost effectiveness, the researchers concluded that the single-prompt plus incentive condition yielded significant behavioral compliance and was cost effective.

There are, of course, difficulties in applying money incentives on a large scale, regardless of how effective the procedure may be. Other incentives however, perhaps including some that might appeal to children, might be more appropriately tested. As the authors point out, the use of incentives such as coupons or rebates, while common in retail sales, may offer possibilities for use in health professions, to influence health-related behavior of prospective clients.

IX. SUMMARY AND CONCLUSIONS

Behavioral community psychology is a recently emerging, major departure from the traditional clinical psychology model. The clinical model has its focus on pathological conditions in individuals, carries out studies of the past development of disorder, and utilizes after-the-fact, restorative interventions. While relying primarily on psychodynamic and somatic models, the clinical approach has increasingly utilized an individual-client focused, behavior therapy model. In contrast the behavioral community views focus on development of healthy and optimum functioning and the prevention of future disorders. With this focus it carries a strong future orientation, and attempts to study and augment optimum functioning in naturally occurring groups such as families and neighborhoods. It emphasizes professional roles of researchers, educators, and consultants, in settings that range from an individual family, small classrooms, through large-scale public behavior areas and even to consultation and direct action with public policy-making bodies at all levels of government. The major conceptual bases include a growing combination of learning and behavior modification principles, and social community, organizational, and public health models.

Much of the recent behavioral research and applications in schools, juvenile justice systems, family training, and behavioral pediatrics is, in our view, part of this behavioral community trend. Other research areas, not yet so well-developed, are more specifically concerned with large-scale community behavior such as abuses of our physical environment. Together these areas of research and intervention share common, developing interests and goals that are beginning to define this new behavioral community psychology and to suggest its future.

In our judgment, while the clinical model will continue, behavioral community psychology will be the area of greatest discovery and excitement over the next several decades.

A Closing Note

This book reflects our views of a field in transition, developing a congruence with community psychology and mental health; public health and health psychology; and child development and education. An emerging interest common to these developments lies in the enhancement of normal, adaptive human functioning. In this shift we are not abandoning the more traditional clinical model with its pathology-amelioration focus, but are beginning to construct future-oriented alternatives to it. Both developments, *behavior therapy* and *behavioral enhancement*, have considerable potential for growth and as important contributions to human functioning. The degree to which the shifts that we perceive will in fact develop and reach the level of major contributions remains to be determined. We hope we have stimulated some of our colleagues and students to futher interest in these potentials.

Bibliography

Aaron, B. A., and Bostow, D. F. Indirect facilitation of on-task behavior produced by contingent free-time for academic productivity. *Journal of Applied Behavior Analysis*, 1978, *11*, 197.

Abbassi, V., Linscheid, T., and Coleman, M. Triiodothyronine concentration and therapy in autistic children. *Journal of Autism and Childhood Schizophrenia*, 1978, *8*, 383–388.

Abe, K. Phobias and nervous symptoms in childhood and maturity: Persistence and associations. *British Journal of Psychiatry*, 1972, *120*, 275–283.

Abelew, P. H. Intermittent schedules of reinforcement applied to the conditioning treatment of enuresis. *Dissertation Abstracts: International*, 1972, *33*, 2799-B–2800-B.

Abidin, R. R. (ed.). *Parent education and intervention handbook*. Springfield, Ill.: Charles C. Thomas, 1980.

Adams, J. Adaptive behavior and measured intelligence in the classification of mental retardation. *American Journal of Mental Deficiency*, 1973, *78*, 77–81.

Adelson, R., and Goldfried, M. R. Modeling and the fearful child patient. *Journal of Dentistry for Children*, 1970, *37*, 476–489.

Adelson, R., Liebert, R. M., Poulos, R. W., and Herskovitz, A. A. modeling film to reduce children's fears of dental treatment. *Journal of Dental Research*, 1972, *51*, 1708. (Abstract)

Agras, S. Foreword. In R. C. Katz and S. Zlutnik (eds.), *Behavior therapy and health care*. Elmsford, N.Y.: Pergamon Press, 1975.

Agras, W. H., Barlow, D. H., Chapin, H. N., Abel, G. G., and Leitenberg, H. Behavior modification of anorexia nervosa. *Archives of General Psychiatry*, 1974, *30*, 279–286.

Albee, G. W. *Mental health manpower trends*. New York: Basic Books, 1959.

Alexander, A. B. Systematic relaxation and flow rates in asthmatic children. Relationship to emotional precipitants and anxiety. *Journal of Psychosomatic Research, 1972, 16*, 405.

Alexander, A. B. The treatment of psychosomatic disorders: Bronchial asthma in children. In B. B. Lahey and A. E. Kazdin (eds.), *Advances in child clinical psychology*. New York: Plenum, 1980.

Alexander, A. B., Miklich, D. R., and Hershkoff, H. The immediate effects of systematic relaxation training on peak expiratory flow rates in asthmatic children. *Psychosomatic Medicine*, 1972, *34*, 388–394.

Alexander, A. B., Chai, H., Creer, T. L., Miklich, D. R., Renne, C. M., and De.A. Cardeso, R. R. The elimination of chronic cough by response suppression shaping. *Journal of Behavior Therapy and Experimental Psychiatry*, 1973, *4*, 75–80.

Alexander, A. B., Cropp, G. J. A., and Chai, H. Effects of relaxation training on pulmonary mechanics in children with asthma, *Journal of Applied Behavior Analysis*, 1979, *12*, 27–35.

Alexander, F. G., and Selesnik, S. T. *The history of psychiatry*. New York: Harper & Row, 1966.

Alexander, J. F., and Parsons, B. V. Short-term behavioral intervention with delinquent families: Impact on family processes and recidivism. *Journal of Abnormal Psychology*, 1973, *81*, 219–225.

Allen, K. E., and Harris, F. R. Elimination of a child's excessive scratching by training the mother in reinforcement procedures. *Behaviour Research and Therapy*, 1966, *4*, 79–84.

Alley, S., and Blanton, J. *Paraprofessionals in mental health: An annotated bibliography from 1966 to 1977*. Berkeley, Calif.: Social Action Res. Center, 1978.

Altman, K., Bondy, A., and Hirsch, G. Behavioral treatment of obesity in patients with Prader-Willi Syndrome. *Journal of Behavioral Medicine*, 1978, *1*, 403–412.

Alvord, J. R. The home token economy: A motivational system for the home. *Corrective Psychiatry and Journal of Social Therapy*, 1971, *17*, 6–13.

Alvy, K. T. Preventing child abuse. *American Psychologist*, 1975, *30*, 921–928.

Ambrose, S., Hazzard, A., and Haworth, J. Cognitive-behavioral treatment for abusive families. *Child Abuse and Neglect*, 1980, *4*, 119–125.

Anchor, K. N., and Johnson, L. G. The efficacy of EMG biofeedback in the treatment of hyperactivity. *Behavioral Engineering*, 1977, *4*, 39–43.

Anderson, D. R. Treatment of insomnia in a 13-year-old boy by relaxation training and reduction of parental attention. *Journal of Behavior Therapy and Experimental Psychiatry*, 1979, *10*, 263–265.

Anderson, L., Fodor, I., and Alpert, M. A comparison of methods for training self-control. *Behavior Therapy*, 1976, *7*, 649–685.

Angelino, H., and Shedd, C. Shifts in the content of fears and worries relative to chronological age. *Proc. of the Oklahoma Academy of Science*, 1953, *34*, 180–186.

Angelino, H., Dollins, J., and Mech, E. V. Trends in the "fears and wories" of schoolchildren as related to socio-economic status and age. *Journal of Genetic Psychology*, 1956, *89*, 263–276.

Anthony, E. J. An experimental approach to psychopathology of childhood: Encopresis. *British Journal of Medical Psychology*, 1957, *30*, 146–175.

Anthony, E. J. An experimental approach to psychopathology of childhood: Autism. *British Journal of Medical Psychology*, 1958, *31*, 211–225.

Anthony, W. Z. Brief intervention in a case of childhood trichotillomania by self-monitoring. *Journal of Behavior Therapy and Experimental Psychiatry*, 1978, *9*, 173–175.

Aragona, J., Cassady, J., and Drabman, R. S. Treating overweight children through parental training and contingency contracting. *Journal of Applied Behavior Analysis*, 1975, *8*, 269–278.

Ashkenazi, Z. The treatment of encopresis using a discriminative stimulus and positive reinforcement. *Journal of Behavior Therapy and Experimental Psychiatry*, 1975, *6*, 155–157.

Ayer, W. A. Use of visual imagery in needle-phobic children. *Journal of Dentistry for Children*, 1973, *40*, 125–127.

Ayllon, T., and Michael, J. The psychiatric nurse as a behavioral engineer. *Journal of the Experimental Analysis of Behavior*, 1959, *2*, 323–334.

Ayllon, T. D., and Roberts, M. D. Eliminating discipline problems by strengthening academic performance. *Journal of Applied Behavior Analysis*, 1974, *7*, 71–76.

Ayllon, T., and Skuban, W. Accountability in psychotherapy: A test case. *Journal of Behavior Therapy and Experimental Psychiatry*, 1973, *4*, 19–30.

Ayllon, T., Smith, D., and Rogers, M. Behavioral management of school phobia. *Journal of Behavior Therapy and Experimental Psychiatry*, 1970, *1*, 125–138.

Ayllon, T., Simon, S. J., and Wildman, R. W. Instructions and reinforcement in the elimination of encopresis: A case study. *Journal of Behavior Therapy and Experimental Psychiatry*, 1975, *6*, 235–238. (a)

Ayllon, T., Layman, D., and Kandel, H. A behavioral-educational alternative to drug control of hyperactive children. *Journal of Applied Behavior Analysis*, 1975, *8*, 137–146. (b)

Ayllon, T., Garber, S., and Pisor, K. Reducing time limits: A means to increase behavior of retardates. *Journal of Applied Behavior Analysis*, 1976, *9*, 247–252.

Azrin, N. H., and Besalel-Azrin, V. *Bedwetting eliminated through training*. New York: Simon & Schuster, 1979.

Azrin, N. H., and Foxx, R. M. Dry pants: A rapid method of toilet training children. *Behaviour Research and Therapy*, 1973, *4*, 435–442.

Azrin, N. H., and Foxx, R. M. *Toilet training in less than a day*. New York: Simon & Schuster, 1974.

Azrin, N. H., and Holz, W. Punishment. In W. K. Honig (ed.), *Operant behavior: Areas of research and application*. New York: Appleton-Century-Crofts, 1966, 380–447.

Azrin, N. H., and Thienes, P. M. Rapid elimination of enuresis by intensive learning without a conditioning apparatus. *Behavior Therapy*, 1978, *9*, 342–354.

Azrin, N. H., and Wesolowski, M. D. Eliminating habitual vomiting in a retarded adult by positive practice and self-correction. *Journal of Behavior Therapy and Experimental Psychiatry*, 1975, *6*, 145.

Azrin, N. H., Sneed, T. J., and Foxx, R. M. Dry-bed training; A rapid method of eliminating bedwetting (enuresis) of the retarded. *Behaviour Research and Therapy*, 1973, *11*, 427–434.

Azrin, N. H., Sneed, T. J., and Foxx, R. M. Dry-bed training: Rapid elimination of childhood enuresis. *Behaviour Research and Therapy*, 1974, *12*, 147–156.

Azrin, N. H., Gottleib, L., Hughart, L., Wesolowski, M. D., and Rahn, T. Eliminating self-injurious behavior by educative procedures. *Behaviour Research and Therapy*, 1975, *13*, 101–111.

Azrin, N. H., Thienes-Hontos, P., and Besalel-Azrin, V. Elimination of enuresis without a conditioning apparatus: An extension by office instruction of the child and parents. *Behavior Therapy*, 1979, *10*, 14–19.

Bach, R., and Moylan, J. J. Parents administer behavior therapy for inappropriate urination and encopresis: A case study. *Journal of Behavior Therapy and Experimental Psychiatry*, 1975, *6*, 239–241.

Bachman, J. A. Self-injurious behavior: A behavioral analysis. *Journal of Abnormal Psychology*, 1972, *80*, 211–224.

Bachrach, A. J., *Psychological Research: An introduction, 4th. Ed.* New York: Random House, 1981.

Bachrach, A. J., Erwin, W. J., and Mohr, J. P. The control of eating behavior in an anorexic by operant conditioning techniques. In L. Ullmann and L. P.

Krasner (eds.), *Case studies in behavior modification*. New York: Holt, Rinehart and Winston, 1965.

Bacon-Prue, A., Blount, R., Hosey, C., and Drabman, R. S. The public posting of photographs as a reinforcer for bedmaking in an institutional setting. *Behavior Therapy*, 1980, *11*, 417–420.

Baer, D. M., Wolf, M. M., and Risley, T. R. Some current dimensions of applied behavior analysis. *Journal of Applied Behavior Analysis*, 1968, *1*, 91–97.

Baer, F., Ascione, F., and Casto, G. Relative efficacy of two token economy procedures for decreasing the disruptive classroom behavior of retarded children. *Journal of Abnormal Child Psychology*, 1977, *5*, 135–146.

Bailey, J. S., Phillips, E. L., Phillips, E. A., Fixsen, D. L., and Wolf, M. M. Home-based reinforcement and the modification of pre-delinquents' classroom behavior. *Journal of Applied Behavior Analysis*, 1970, *3*, 223–233.

Baker, B. L. Symptoms treatment and symptom substitution in enuresis. *Journal of Abnormal Psychology*, 1969, *74*, 42–49.

Baker, B. L., Heifetz, L. J., and Murphy, D. M. Behavioral training for parents of mentally retarded children: One-year follow-up. *American Journal of Mental Deficiency*, 1980, *85*, 31–38.

Balaschak, B. S. Teacher-implemented behavior modification in a case of organically based epilepsy. *Journal of Consulting and Clinical Psychology*, 1976, *44*, 218–223.

Balch, P., and Solomon, R. The training of paraprofessionals as behavior modifiers: A review. *American Journal of Community Psychology*, 1976, *4*, 167–179.

Ball, T. S., Hendrickson, H., and Clayton, J. A special feeding technique for chronic regurgitation. *American Journal of Mental Deficiency*, 1974, *78*, 486–493.

Ballard, K. D., and Glynn, E. L. Behavioral self-management in story writing with elementary school children.*Journal of Applied Behavior Analysis*, 1975, *8*, 387–395.

Balson, P. M. Case study: Encopresis. A case with symptom substitution? *Behavior Therapy*, 1973, 4, 134–136.

Balthazer, E. E. Adaptive behaviour from a second order perspective. *British Journal of Mental Subnormality*, 1978, *24*, 74–80.

Bamber, J. H. The fears of adolescents. *Journal of Genetic Psychology*, 1974, *125*, 127–140.

Bandura, A. *Principles of behavior modification*. New York: Holt, Rinehart and Winston, 1969.

Bandura, A. Vicarious and self-reinforcement processes. In R. Glasser (ed.), *The nature of reinforcement*. New York: Academic Press, 1971, 228–278.

Bandura, A. Self-reinforcement: Theoretical and methodological considerations. *Behaviorsm*, 1976, *4*, 135–155.

Bandura, A. Self-efficacy: Toward a unifying theory of behavioral change. *Psychological Review*, 1977, *84*, 191–215. (a)

Bandura, A. *Social learning theory*. Englewood Cliffs, N.J.: Prentice-Hall, 1977 (b)

Bandura, A. The self-system in reciprocal determinism. *American Psychologist*, 1978, *33*, 344–358.

Bandura, A., and Barab, P. G. Conditions governing non-reinforced imitation. *Developmental Psychology*, 1971, *5*, 244–255.

Bandura, A., and Barab, P. G. Processes governing disinhibitory effects through symbolic modeling. *Journal of Abnormal Psychology*, 1973, *82*, 1–9.

Bandura, A., and Menlove, F. L. Factors determining vicarious extinction of avoidance behavior through symbolic modeling. *Journal of Personality and Social Psychology*, 1968, *8*, 99–108.

Bandura, A., and Perloff, B. Relative efficacy of self-monitored and externally-imposed reinforcement systems. *Journal of Personality and Social Psychology*, 1967, *7*, 111–116.

Bandura, A., and Walters, R. H. *Social learning and personality development*. New York: Holt, Rinehart and Winston, 1963.

Bandura, A., Grusec, J. E., and Menlove, F. L. Vicarious extinction of avoidance behavior. *Journal of Personality and Social Psychology*, 1967, *5*, 16–23.

Bandura, A., Ross, D., and Ross, S. Transmission of aggression through imitation of aggressive models. *Journal of Abnormal and Social Psychology*, 1973, *63*, 575–582.

Bandura, A., Jeffery, R. W., and Wright, C. L. Efficacy of participant modeling as a function of response induction aids. *Journal of Abnormal Psychology*, 1974, *83*, 56–64.

Banks, M., and Locke, B. J. *Self-injurious stereotypes and mild punishment with retarded subjects*. Working paper #123. Parsons Research Project, University of Kansas, 1966.

Barber, R., and Kagey, J. Modification of school attendance for an elementary population. *Journal of Applied Behavior Analysis*, 1977, *10*, 41–48.

Barkley, R. A. A review of stimulant drug research with hyperactive children. *Journal of Child Psychology and Psychiatry*, 1977, *18*, 137–165.

Barkley, R. A., Hastings, J. E., Tousel, R. E., and Tousel, S. E. Evaluation of a token system for juvenile delinquents in a residential setting. *Journal of Behavior Therapy and Experimental Psychiatry*, 1976, *7*, 227–230.

Barkley, R. A., Copeland, A., and Sivage, C. A self-control classroom for hyperactive children. *Journal of Autism and Developmental Disorders*, 1980, *10*, 75–89.

Barlow, D. H., Mavissakalian, M. R., and Schofield, L. D. Patterns of desynchrony in agoraphobia: A preliminary report. *Behaviour Research and Therapy*, 1980, *18*, 441–448.

Barmann, B. Use of contingent vibration in the treatment of self-stimulatory hand-mouthing and ruminative vomiting behavior. *Journal of Behavior Therapy and Experimental Psychiatry*, 1980, *11*, 307–311.

Barmann, B. C. Croyle-Barmann, C., and McLain, B. The use of contingent-interrupted music in the treatment of disruptive bus-riding behavior. *Journal of Applied Behavior Analysis*, 1980, *13*, 693–698.

Barnard, J. D., Christophersen, E. R., and Wolf, M. M. Teaching children appropriate shopping behavior through parent training in the supermarket setting. *Journal of Applied Behavior Analysis*, 1977, *10*, 49–59.

Baron, R. A. Aggression as a function of magnitude of victim's pain cues, level of prior arousal, and aggressor-victim similarity. *Journal of Personality and Social Psychology*, 1971, *18*, 48–54.

Barrera, R. D., Lobato-Barerra, D., and Sulzer-Azaroff, B. A simultaneous treatment comparison of three expressive language training programs with a mute autistic child. *Journal of Autism and Developmental Disorders*, 1980, *10*, 21–37.

Barrett, B. Behavior modification in the home: Parents adapt laboratory-developed tactics to bowel-train a 5 year old. *Psychotherapy, Theory, Research and Practice*, 1969, *6*, 172–176.

Barrios, B. A., Hartmann, D. P., and Shigetomi, C. Fears and anxieties in children. In E. J. Mash and L. G. Terdal (Eds.), *Behavioral assessment of childhood disorders*. New York: Guilford, 1981.

Barrish, H., Saunders, M., and Wolf, M. Good behavior game: Effects of individual contingencies for group consequences on disruptive behavior in the classroom. *Journal of Applied Behavior Analysis*, 1969, *2*, 119–124.

Barron, D. P., and Graziano, A. M. Parent participation in speech therapy. *Speech Journal*, 1968, *3*, 46–50.

Bartak, L., and Rutter, M. Differences between mentally retarded and normally intelligent autistic children. *Journal of Autism and Childhood Schizophrenia*, 1976, *6*, 109–120.

Barton, E., and Ascione, F. Sharing in preschool children: Facilitation, stimulus generalization, response generalization, and maintenance. *Journal of Applied Behavior Analysis*, 1979, *12*, 417–430.

Baruch, D. *New ways to discipline*. New York: McGraw-Hill, 1949.

Bauer, D. H. An exploratory study of developmental changes in children's fears. *Journal of Child Psychology and Psychiatry*, 1976, *17*, 69–74.

Baumeister, A. Mental retardation policy and research: The unfilled promise. *American Journal of Mental Deficiency*, 1981, *85*, 449–456.

Baumeister, A. A., and Muna, J. R. On defining mental retardation. *Journal of Special Education*, 1975, *9*, 293–306.

Beck, A. *Cognitive therapy and emotional disorders*. New York: International Universities Press, 1976.

Becker, H. J. Curricula of associate degree mental health/human services training programs. *Community Mental Health Journal*, 1978, *14*, 133–146.

Becker, J. V., Turner, S. M., and Sajwaj, T. E. Multiple behavioral effects of the use of lemon juice with a ruminating toddler-age child. *Behavior Modification, 1978, 2*, 267.

Begelman, D. A. Ethical and legal issues of behavior modification. M. Hersen, R. M. Eisler, and P. M. Miller (eds.), *Progress in behavior modification*, Vol. 5. New York: Academic Press, 1977, 159–189.

Begelman, D. A., and Hersen, M. Critique of Obler and Terwillinger's "Systematic desensitization with neurologically impaired children with phobic disorders." *Journal of Consulting and Clinical Psychology*, 1971, *37*, 10–13.

Bellamy, G. T., Peterson, L., and Close, D. Habilitation of the severely and profoundly retarded: Illustrations of competence. *Education and Training of the Mentally Retarded*, 1975, *10*, 174–187.

Bem, S. L. Verbal self-control: The establishment of effective self-instruction. *Journal of Experimental Psychology*, 1967, *74*, 485–491.

Bemis, K. M. Current approaches to the etiology and treatment of anorexia nervosa. *Psychological Bulletin*, 1978, *85*, 593–617.

Benaroya, S., Wesley, S., Ogilvie, H., Klein, L. S., and Meaney, M. Sign language and multisensory input training of children with communication and related developmental disorders. *Journal of Autism and Childhood Schizophrenia*, 1977, *7*, 23–31.

Benaroya, S., Wesley, S. Ogilvie, H., Klein, L., and Clarke, E. Sign language and multisensory input training of children with communications and related developmental disorders: Phase II. *Journal of Autism and Developmental Disorders*, 1979, *9*, 219–220.

Bender, N. N. Self-verbalization versus tutor verbalization in modifying impulsivity. *Journal of Educational Psychology,* 1976, *68,* 347–354.

Bentler, P. M. An infant's phobia treated with reciprocal inhibition therapy. *Journal of Child Psychology and Psychiatry,* 1962, *3,* 185–189.

Berecz, J. M. Phobias of childhood: Etiology and treatment. *Psychological Bulletin,* 1968, *74,* 694–720.

Berger, S. A clinical program for developing multimedia response with atypical deaf children. In J. McLean, D. Yoder, and R. Schiefelbusch (eds.), *Language intervention with the retarded.* Baltimore, Md.: University Park Press, 1972.

Bergin, A. E. Behavior therapy and ethical relativism: Time for clarity. *Journal of Consulting and Clinical Psychology,* 1980, *48,* 11–13.

Bergman, R. L. Treatment of childhood insomnia diagnosed as "hyperactivity." *Journal of Behavior Therapy and Experimental Psychiatry,* 1976, *7,* 199.

Berkowitz, B. P., and Graziano, A. M. Training parents as behavior therapists: A review. *Behavior Research and Therapy,* 1972, *10,* 297–317.

Berkson, G. Abnormal stereotyped movements of mental defectives: VI No effect of amphetamine or barbiturate. *Perceptual and Motor Skills,* 1965, *21,* 698.

Berkson, G. Abnormal stereotyped motor acts. In J. Zubin and H. F. Hunt (eds.), *Comparative psychopathology—animal and human.* New York: Grune & Stratton, 1967, 76–94.

Berkson, G., and Davenport, R. K. Stereotyped movements of mental defectives. I. Initial survey. *American Journal of Mental Deficiency,* 1962, *66,* 849–852.

Berkson, G., and Mason, W. A. Stereotyped movements of mental defectives. IV. The effects of toys and the character of the acts. *American Journal of Mental Deficiency,* 1964, *68,* 511–524. Berlin, I. N. (ed.), *Advocacy for child mental health.* New York: Brunner/Mazel, 1975.

Bernal, M. E. Behavioral feedback in the modification of brat behaviors. Journal of Nervous and Mental Disorders, 1969, *148,* 375–385.

Bernal, M. E. Behavioral treatment of a child's eating problem. *Journal of Behavior Therapy and Experimental Psychiatry,* 1972, *3,* 45–50.

Bernal, M. E. *Preliminary report of a preventive intervention project.* Paper read at the Rocky Mountain Psychological Association, Las Vegas, Nevada, May 1973.

Bernal, M. E., Duryea, J. S., Pruett, H. L., and Burns, B. J. Behavior modification and the brat syndrome. *Journal of Consulting and Clinical Psychology,* 1968, *32,* 447–455.

Bernal, M. E., Delfini, L. F., North, J. A., and Kreutzer, S. L. *Comparison of boys' behaviors in homes and classrooms.* Paper read at the Banff International Conference on Behavior Modification, Banff, Canada, 1974.

Bernal, M. E., Klinnert, M. D., and Schultz, L. A. Behavioral parent training and client-centered parent counseling for children with conduct problems. *Journal of Applied Behavior Analysis,* 1980, *13,* 677–691.

Besalel-Azrin, V., Azrin, N. H., and Armstrong, P. M. The student-oriented classroom: A method of improving student conduct and satisfaction. *Behavior Therapy,* 1977, *8,* 193–204.

Bhanji, S., and Thomson, J. Operant conditioning in the treatment of anorexia nervosa: A review and retrospective study of 11 cases. *British Journal of Psychiatry,* 1974, *124,* 166–172.

Biberdorf, J. R., and Pear, J. J. Two-to-one versus one-to-one student-teacher ratios in the operant verbal training of retarded children. *Journal of Applied Behavior Analysis*, 1977, *10*, 506.

Birk, L., Stolz, S. B., Brady, J. V., Lazaries, A. A., Lynch, J. J., Rosenthal, A. S., Skelton, W. D., Stevens, J. B., and Thomas, E. J. *Behavior therapy in psychiatry*. Washington, D.C.: American Psychiatric Association, 1973.

Birkimer, J. C., and Brown, J. H. The effects of student self-control on the reduction of children's problem behaviors. *Behavioral Disorders*, 1979, *4*, 131–136.

Birnbrauer, J. S. Generalization of punishment effects; A case study. *Journal of Applied Behavior Analysis*, 1968, *7*, 201–212.

Birnbrauer, J. S., Bijou, S. W., Wolf, M. M., and Kidder, J. D. Programmed instruction in the classroom. In L. P. Ullmann and L. Krasner (eds.), *Case studies in behavior modification*. New York: Holt, Rinehart and Winston, 1965, 358–363.

Blackwood, R. O. *Operant conditioning as a method of training the mentally retarded*. Unpublished doctoral dissertation, Ohio State University, 1962.

Blackwood, R. O., Horrocks, J. E., Keele, T. F., Hundziak, M., and Rettig, J. H. Operant conditioning of social behaviors in severely retarded patients. In A. M. Graziano (ed.), *Behavior Therapy with Children*. Chicago: Aldine-Atherton, 1971, 83–95.

Blanchard, E. B. Relative contributions of modeling, information influences, and physical contact in extinction of phobic behavior. *Journal of Abnormal Psychology*, 1970, *76*, 55–61.

Blanchard, E. B., and Young, L. D. Clinical applications of biofeedback training. *Archives of General Psychiatry*, 1974, *30*, 573–589.

Blanco, R. F. *Prescriptions for children with learning and adjustment problems*. Springfield, Ill.: Charles C. Thomas, 1972.

Blatt, B. The pariah industry: A diary from purgatory and other places. In G. Gerbner, C. J. Ross, and E. Zigler, (eds.), *Child abuse: An agenda for action*. New York: Oxford University Press, 1980, 185–203.

Blatt, B., and Kaplan, F. *Christmas in purgatory*. Boston: Allyn & Bacon, 1966.

Blechman, E. A., Olson, D. H. L., and Hellman, I. D. Stimulus control over family problem-solving behavior: The family contract game. *Behavior Therapy*, 1976, *7*, 686–692.

Blinder, B. J., Freeman, D. M. A., and Stunkard, A. J. Behavioral therapy of anorexia nervosa: Effectiveness of activity as a reinforcer of weight gain. *American Journal of Psychiatry*, 1970, *126*, 1093–1098.

Blum, R. W., and Runyan, C. Adolescent abuse: The dimensions of the problem. *Journal of Adolescent Health Care*, 1980, *1*, 121–126.

Bockoven, J. S. *Moral treatment in American psychiatry*. New York: Springer, 1963.

Bogartz, R. S., and Pederson, D. R. Variables influencing alternation prediction by preschool children: II. Redundant cue value and intertrial interval duration. *Journal of Experimental Child Psychology*, 1966, *4*, 211–216.

Bollard, R. J., and Woodroffe, P. The effect of parent-administered dry-bed training on nocturnal enuresis in children. *Behaviour Research and Therapy*, 1977, *15*, 159–165.

Bolman, W. M. A behavioral systems analysis of the school refusal syndrome. *American Journal of Orthopsychiatry*, 1967, *37*, 348–349.

Bolman, W. M. Systems theory, psychiatry and school phobia. *American Journal of Psychiatry*, 1970, *127*, 25–32.

Bolstad, O. D., and Johnson, S. M. Self-regulation in the modification of disruptive classroom behavior. *Journal of Applied Behavior Analysis,* 1972, *5,* 443–454.

Bonvillian, J. D., and Nelson, K. E. Sign language acquisition in a mute autistic boy. *Journal of Speech and Hearing Disorders,* 1976, *41,* 339–347.

Bonvillian, J. D., Nelson, K. E., and Rhyme, J. M. Sign language and autism. *Journal of Autism and Developmental Disorders.* 1981, *11,* 125–137.

Boring, E. G. *A history of experimental psychology.* New York: Appleton-Century, 1950.

Bornstein, B. Phobia in a two-and-a-half-year-old child. *Psychoanalytic Quarterly,* 1935, *4,* 93–119.

Bornstein, M., Bellack, A., and Hersen, M. Social-skills training for unassertive children: a multiple baseline analysis. *Journal of Applied Behavior Analysis,* 1977, *10,* 183–196.

Bornstein, P. H., and Hamilton, S. B. Positive parental praise: Increasing reactivity and accuracy of self-observation. *Journal of Abnormal Child Psychology,* 1978, *6,* 503–509.

Bornstein, P. H., and Quevillon, R. P. The effects of a self-instructional package on overactive preschool boys. *Journal of Applied Behavior Analysis,* 1976, *9,* 179–188.

Bornstein, S. A child analysis. *Psychoanalytic Quarterly,* 1935, *4,* 190–225.

Bowlby, J. *Attachment and loss,* Vol. 2. New York: Basic Books, 1973.

Braaten, S. The Madison school program: Programming for secondary level severely emotionally disturbed youth. *Behavioral Disorders,* 1979, *4,* 153–162.

Brady, J. P. Metronome-conditioned speech retraining for stuttering. *Behavior Therapy,* 1971, *2,* 129–150.

Brady, J. P. Research and training needs in behavior therapy. *Seminars in Psychiatry,* 1972, *4,* 185–189.

Brady, J. P., and Rieger, W. Behavioral treatment of anorexia nervosa. In T. Thompson and W. S. Dockens (eds.), *Applications of behavior modification: International symposium on behavior modification at Minneapolis, 1972.* New York: Academic Press, 1975.

Braud, W. The effects of frontal EMG biofeedback and progressive relaxation upon hyperactivity and its behavioral concomitants. *Biofeedback and Self-regulation,* 1978, *3,* 69–89.

Bray, N. W., Justice, E. M., and Simon, D. L. The sufficient conditions for directed forgetting in normal and educably mentally retarded adolescents. *Intelligence,* 1978, *2,* 153–167.

Brent, D., and Routh, D. Response cost and impulsive word recognition errors in reading-disabled children. *Journal of Abnormal Child Psychology,* 1978, *6,* 211–220.

Broden, M., Hall, R. V., and Mitts, B. The effect of self-recording on the classroom behavior of two eighth grade students. *Journal of Applied Behavior Analysis,* 1971, *4,* 191–199.

Broden, M. Bruce, C., Mitchell, A. M., Carter, V., and Hall, R. V. Effects of teacher attention on attending behavior of two boys at adjacent desks. *Journal of Applied Behavior Analysis,* 1975, *8,* 187–196.

Brotemarkle, R. A. (ed.). *Clinical psychology: Studies in honor of Lightner Witmer.* Philadelphia: University of Pennsylvania Press, 1931.

Brown, A. L., and French, L. A. The zone of potential development: Implications for intelligence testing in the year 2000. *Intelligence,* 1979, *3,* 255–273.

Brown, D. G. *Behavior modification in child and school mental health: An annotated bibliography on applications with parents and teachers.* DHEW Publication No. (HSM) 71-9043. Washington, D.C.: National Institute of Mental Health, 1971.

Brown, J. Prognosis from presenting symptoms of preschool children with atypical development. *American Journal of Orthopsychiatry,* 1960, *30,* 382–390.

Brown, J. Follow-up of children with atypical development (infantile psychosis). *American Journal of Orthopsychiatry,* 1963, *33,* 855–861.

Brown, L., and York, R. Developing programs for severely handicapped students: Teacher training and classroom instruction. *Focus on Exceptional Children,* 1974, *6,* 1–11.

Brown, P., and Elliot, R. Control of aggression in a nursery school class. *Journal of Experimental Child Psychology,* 1965, *2,* 103–107.

Brown, R. E., Copeland, R. E., and Hall, R. V. School phobia: Effects of behavior modification treatment applied by an elementary school principal. *Child Study Journal,* 1974, *4,* 125–133.

Brownell, K. D., Colletti, G., Ersner-Hershfield, R., Hershfield, S. M., and Wilson, G. T. Self-control in school children: Stringency and leniency in self-determined and externally imposed performance standards. *Behavior Therapy,* 1977, *8,* 442–455.

Browning, R. M. A same-subject design for simultaneous comparison of three reinforcement contingencies. *Behaviour Research and Therapy,* 1967, *5,* 237–243.

Browning, R. M. Treatment effects of a total behavior modification program with five autistic children. *Behaviour Research and Therapy,* 1971, *9,* 319–327.

Browning, R. M., and Stover, D. O. *Behavior modification in child treatment: An experimental and clinical approach.* Chicago: Aldine-Atherton, 1971.

Bruch, H. Juvenile obesity. *International Psychiatry Clinics,* 1970, *1,* 231–254.

Bruch, H. How to treat anorexia nervosa. *Roche Report: Frontiers of Psychiatry,* 1975, *5,* 1–2.

Bruch, H., and Touraine, G. Obesity in childhood: The family frame of obese children. *Psychosomatic Medicine,* 1940, *2,* 141–207.

Bucher, B., and King, L. W. Generalization of punishment effects in the deviant behavior of a psychotic child. *Behavior Therapy,* 1971, *2,* 68–77.

Bucher, B., and Lovaas, O. I. Use of aversive stimulation in behavior modification. In M. R. Jones (ed.), *Miami symposium on the prediction of behavior, 1967; Aversive stimulation.* Coral Gables, Fla: University of Miami Press, 1968, 77–145.

Bucher, B., Reykdal, B., and Albin, J. Brief physical restraint to control pica in retarded children. *Journal of Behavior Therapy and Experimental Psychiatry,* 1976, *7,* 137–140.

Bugelski, B. R., and Graziano, A. M. *The handbook of practical psychology.* Englewood Cliffs, N.J.: Prentice-Hall, 1980.

Bugental, D. B., Whalen, C. K., and Henker, B. Causal attributions of hyperactive children and motivational assumptions of two behavior-change approaches: Evidence for an interactionist position. *Child Development,* 1977, *48,* 847–884.

Bugental, D. B., Collins, S., Collins, L., and Chaney, L. A. Attributional and behavioral changes following two behavior management interventions with hyperactive boys: A follow-up study. *Child Development,* 1978, *49,* 247–250.

Burchard, J., and Tyler, V. O., Jr. The modification of delinquent behavior through operant conditioning. *Behaviour Research and Therapy,* 1965, *2,* 245–250.

Burgess, R. L., Clark, R. N., and Hendee, J. C. An experimental analysis of antilitter procedures. *Journal of Applied Behavior Analysis,* 1971, *4,* 71–75.

Burgio, L. D., Whitman, T. L., and Johnson, M. R. A self-instructional package for increasing attending behavior in educable mentally retarded children. *Journal of Applied Behavior Analysis*, 1980, *13*, 443–459.

Burkholder, R., and Morris, L. A. *Southwestern behavioral training center: Final report*. Unpublished manuscript, 1971.

Burlingham, D. T. Child analysis and the mother. *Psychoanalytic Quarterly*, 1935, *4*, 69–92.

Burney, J. D., Russell, B., and Shores, D. E. Developing social responses in two profoundly retarded children. *AAESPH Review*, American Association for the Education of the Severely/Profoundly Handicapped, 1977, *2*, 53–60.

Burnham, W. H. *The normal mind*. New York: Appleton-Century Crofts, 1924.

Butler, J. F. The toilet training success of parents after reading *Toilet training in less than a day*. *Behavior Therapy*, 1976, *7*, 185–191.

Butler, J. F. Treatment of encopresis by overcorrection. *Psychological Reports*, 1977, *40*, 639–646.

Cairns, G. F., and Altman, K. Behavioral treatment of cancer-related anorexia. *Journal of Behavior Therapy and Experimental Psychiatry*, 1979, *10*, 353–356.

Calhoun, K. S., and Matherne, P. The effects of varying schedules of time-out on aggressive behavior of a retarded girl. *Journal of Behavior Therapy and Experimental Psychiatry*, 1975, *6*, 139–143.

Cameron, N., and Robinson, V. Effects of cognitive training on academic and on-task behavior of hyperactive children. *Journal of Psychology*, 1980, *8*, 405–419.

Camp, B. W., Blom, G. F., Herbert, F., and VanDoorninck, W. J. "Think aloud": A program for developing self-control in young aggressive boys. *Journal of Abnormal Child Psychology*, 1977, *5*, 157–169.

Campbell, D. T., and Stanley, J. C. *Experimental and quasi-experimental designs for research*. Chicago: Rand-McNally, 1966.

Campbell, M. F. Neuromuscular uropathy. In M. F. Campbell and J. H. Harrison (eds.), *Urology*, Vol. 2. Philadelphia: Saunders, 1970.

Campbell, S. B. Cognitive styles in reflective impulsive and hyperactive boys and their mothers. *Perceptual and Motor Skills*, 1973, *36*, 747–752.

Canino, F. J., and Reeve, R. E. General issues in working with parents of handicapped children. In R. R. Abidin (ed.), *Parent education and intervention handbook*. Springfield, Ill.: Charles C. Thomas, 1980.

Cantor, N. L., and Gelfand, D. M. Effects of responsiveness and sex of children on adults' behavior. *Child Development*, 1977, *48*, 232–238.

Cantwell, D. P. *Clinical picture, epidemiology and classifications of the hyperactive child: Diagnosis, management, current research*. New York: Spectrum, 1975.

Cantwell, D. P. Hyperkinetic syndrome. In M. Rutter and L. Hersov (eds.), *Child psychiatry—modern approaches*. Oxford: Blackwell Scientific Co., 1977, 524–555.

Caplan, G. (ed.), *Prevention of mental disorders in children: Initial explorations*. New York: Basic Books, 1961.

Caplan, G. The role of pediatricians in community mental health with particular reference to primary prevention of mental disorders in children. In I. Bellak (ed.), *Handbook of community psychiatry and community mental health*. New York: Grune & Stratton, 1964, 287–299.

Caplan, G., and Grunebaum, H. Perspectives on primary prevention. *Archives of general psychiatry*, 1967, *17*, 331–346.

Carr, E. G. The motivation of self-injurious behavior: A review of some hypotheses. *Psychological Bulletin*, 1977, *84*, 800–816.

Carr, E. G. Teaching autistic children to use sign language: some research issues. *Journal of Autism and Developmental Disorders*, 1979, *9*.

Carr, E.G., Schreibman, L., and Lovaas, O. Control of echolalic speech in Psychotic children. *Journal of Abnormal Child Psychology*, 1975, *3*, 331–352.

Carr, E. G., Newsom, and Binkoff, J. Stimulus control of self-destructive behavior in psychotic child. *Journal of Abnormal Child Psychology*, 1976, *4*, 139–154.

Carr, E. G., Binkoff, J., Kologinsky, E., and Eddy, M. Acquisition of sign language by autistic children. I. Expressive labeling. *Journal of Applied Behavior Analysis*, 1978, *11*, 489–502.

Carr, E. G. Newsom, C. D., and Binkoff, J. A. Escape as a factor in the aggressive behavior of two retarded children. *Journal of Applied Behavior Analysis*, 1980, *13*, 101–117.

Carrera, F., and Adams, P. L. An ethical perspective on operant conditioning. *Journal of the American Academy of Child Psychiatry*, 1970, *9*, 607–623.

Carsrud, A. L., Carsrud, K. B., and Dodd, B. G. Randomly monitored staff utilization of behavior modification techniques: Long term effects on clients. *Journal of Consulting and Clinical Psychology*, 1980, *48*, 704–710.

Carter, D. B., Patterson, C. J., and Quasebarth, S. J. Development of children's use of plans for self-control. *Cognitive Therapy and Research*, 1979, *3*, 407–413.

Carter, J. L., Laz, B., and Russell, H. Effects of relaxation and EMG training on academic achievement of educably retarded boys. *Education and Training of the Mentally Retarded*, 1979, *14*, 39–41.

Casey, L. Development of communication behavior in autistic children: A parent program using manual signs. *Journal of Autism and Childhood Schizophrenia*, 1978, *8*, 45–60.

Cash, M., and Evans, I. M. Training pre-school children to modify their retarded siblings behavior. *Journal of Behavior Therapy and Experimental Psychiatry*, 1975, *6*, 13–16.

Cass, S., and Zimmer-Hart, C. L. Teaching a severely retarded child to stand by rewarding successive approximations. *Australian Journal of Mental Retardation*, 1978, *5*, 142–145.

Cataldo, M. F., Bessman, C. A., Parker, L. H., Pearson, J. E., and Rogers, M. C. Behavioral assessment for pediatric intensive care units. *Journal of Applied Behavior Analysis*, 1979, *12*, 83–97.

Catania, A. C. The myth of self-reinforcement. *Behaviorism*, 1975, *3*, 192–199.

Cautela, J. R. Covert conditioning. In A. Jacobs and L. B. Sachs (eds.), *The psychology of private events: Perspective on covert response systems*. New York: Academic Press, 1971.

Cavalier, A. R., and Ferretti, R. P. Stereotyped behaviour, alternative behaviour and collateral effects: A comparison of four intervention procedures. *Journal of Mental Deficiency Research*, 1980, *24*, 219–230.

Chapel, J. C. Treatment of a case of school phobia by reciprocal inhibition. *Canadian Psychiatric Association Journal*, 1967, *12*, 25–28.

Chapel, J. L., Brown N., and Jenkins, D. L. Tourette's disease: Symptomatic relief with holoperidol. *American Journal of Psychiatry*, 1964, *121*, 608–610.

Chapman, C., and Risley, T. R. Anti-litter procedures in an urban high-density area. *Journal of Applied Behavior Analysis*, 1974, *7*, 377–383.

Char, J., and Lubetsky, S. Childhood psychosis in the preschool child. *Journal of Autism and Developmental Disorders*, 1979, *9*, 271–276.

Chazan, M. School phobia. *British Journal of Educational Psychology*, 1962, *32*, 209–217.

Cheyne, J. A. Punishment and the "reasoning" in the development of self-control. In R. Parke, (ed.), *Recent trends in social learning theory*. New York: Academic Press, 1972, 77–91.

Christensen, A., Johnson, S. M., Phillips, S., and Glasgow, R. E. Cost effectiveness in behavioral family therapy. *Behavior Therapy*, 1980, *11*, 208–226.

Christophersen, E. R., and Rapoff, M. A. Behavioral pediatrics. In O. F. Pomerleau and J. P. Brady (eds.), *Behavioral Medicine: Theory and practice*. Baltimore, Md.: Williams & Wilkins, 1979.

Christopherson, E. R., Arnold, C. M., Hill, D. W., and Quilitch, H. R. The home point system: Token reinforcement procedures for application by parents of children with behavior problems. *Journal of Applied Behavior Analysis*, 1972, *5*, 485–497.

Christopherson, E. R., Kuehn, B. S., and Grinstead, J. D. A family training program for abuse and neglect families. *Journal of Pediatric Psychology*, 1976, *1*, 90–94.

Christy, P. R. Does use of tangible rewards with individual children affect peer observers? *Journal of Applied Behavior Analysis*, 1975, *8*, 187–194.

Churchill, D. W., Alpern, G. D., and DeMyer, M. K. (eds.) *Infantile autism*. Springfield, Ill.: Charles C. Thomas, 1971.

Clancy, H., and McBride, G. The autistic processes and its treatment. *Journal of Child Psychology and Psychiatry*, 1969, *10*, 233–244.

Clark, H. B., Boyd, S., and Macrae, J. A classroom program teaching disadvantaged youths to write biographical information. *Journal of Applied Behavior Analysis*, 1975, *8*, 67–76.

Clark, H. B., and Dameron, D. W. Using generalized imitation to expand verbal imitative repertoires in nonspeaking retarded children. *Behavior Therapy*, 1978, *9*, 966–967.

Clark, H. B., Rowbury, T., Baer, A. M., and Baer, D. M. Time-out as a punishing stimulus in continuous and intermittent schedules. *Journal of Applied Behavior Analysis*, 1973, *6*, 443, 455.

Clark, H. B., Greene, B. F., Macrae, J. W., McNees, P., Davis, J. L., and Risley, T. R. A parent advice package for family shopping trips: Development and evaluation. *Journal of Applied Behavior Analysis*, 1977, *10*, 605–624.

Clarke, A. D. B. Presidential address. From research to practice (A7-A-20). In P. Mittler (ed.), *Research to practice in mental retardation Vol. 1: Care and intervention*. Baltimore, Md.: University Park Press, 1977.

Cleary, T. A., Hymphreys, L. G., Kendrick, S. A., and Wesman, A. Educational uses of tests with disadvantaged students. *American Psychologist*, 1975, *30*, 15–41.

Cleland, C. C. *Mental retardation: A developmental approach*. Englewood Cliffs, N.J.: Prentice-Hall, 1978.

Clement, P. W. Elimination of sleepwalking in a seven-year old boy. *Journal of Consulting and Clinical Psychology*, 1970, *34*, 22-26. (a)

Clement, P. W. *Please mother, I'd rather you did it yourself: Training parents to treat their own children.* Paper read at the Western Psychological Association, Los Angeles, April 1970. (b)

Clement, P. W., Anderson, E., Arnold, J., Butman, R., Fantuzzo, J., and Mays, R. Self-observation and self-reinforcement as sources of self-control in children. Biofeedback and Self-regulation, 1978, *3*, 247–267.

Closurdo, J. S. Behavior modification and the nursing process. *Perspectives in Psychiatric Care*, 1975, *8*, 25–36.

Cloward, R. D. Studies in tutoring. *Journal of Experimental Education*, 1967, *36*, 14–25.

Coats, K. I. Cognitive self-instructional training approach for reducing disruptive behavior of young children. *Psychological Reports*, 1979, *44*, 127–134.

Cobb, H. V. *The forest of fulfillment.* New York: Teachers College Press, 1972.

Cohen, E. A., Gelfand, D. M., Dodd, D. K., Jensen, J., and Turner, C. Self-control practices associated with weight-loss maintenance in children and adolescents. *Behavior Therapy*, 1980, *11*, 26–37.

Cohen, H. C., *The P.I.C.A. project. Year 2, Project interim report: Programming interpersonal curricula for adolescents.* Silver Springs, Md.: Institute for Behavioral Research, 1970. (ERIC Document Reproduction Service No. ED 044717.)

Cohen, N. J. *Physiological concomitants of attention in hyperactive children.* Unpublished doctoral dissertation, McGill University, Montreal, 1970.

Cohen, N. J., Sullivan, N., Minde, K., Novak, C., and Helwig, C. Evaluation of the relative effectiveness of methylphenidate and cognitive behavior modification in the treatment of kindergarten-aged hyperactive children. *Journal of Abnormal Child Psychology*, 1981, *9*, 43–54.

Cohen, R. *New careers grow older: A perspective on the paraprofessionals' experience, 1965–1975.* Baltimore, Md.: Johns-Hopkins University Press, 1976.

Colby, K. M. Psychotherapeutic processes. *Annual Review of Psychology*, 1964, *15*, 347–370.

Colby, K. M. The rationale for computer-based treatment of language difficulties in non-speaking autistic children. *Journal of Autism and Childhood Schizophrenia*, 1973, *3*, 254–260.

Colby, K. M., and Smith, D. C. Computers in the treatment of nonspeaking autistic children. In J. H. Masserman (ed.), *Current psychiatric therapies.* New York: Grune & Stratton, 1971.

Cole, H. P., and Parsons, D. E. The Williams total creativity program. *Journal of Creative Behavior*, 1974, *8*, 187–207.

Coleman, J. C. *Abnormal psychology and modern life.* Glenville, Ill.: Scott, Foresman, 1972.

Coleman, P., and Blampied, N. M. Effects of self-monitoring token reinforcement and different back-up reinforcers on the classroom behaviour of retardates. *Exceptional Child*, 1977, *24*, 95–107.

Coleman, R., Frankel, F., Ritvo, E., and Freeman, B. J. The effects of fluorescent and incandescent illumination upon repetitive behaviors in autistic children. *Journal of Autism and Childhood Schizophrenia*, 1976, *6*, 157–162.

Coleman, R. I., Whitman, T. L., and Johnson, M. R. Suppression of self-stimulatory behavior of a profoundly retarded boy across staff and settings: An assessment of situational generalization. *Behavior Therapy*, 1979, *10*, 266–280.

Coleman, S. L., and Stedman, L. M. Use of a peer model in language training in an echolalic child. *Journal of Behavior Therapy and Experimental Psychiatry*, 1974, *5*, 275–279.

Colletti, G., and Harris, S. L. Behavior modification in the home: Siblings as behavior modifiers, parents as observers. *Journal of Abnormal Child Psychology,* 1977, *5,* 21–30.

Cone, J. D., and Sloop, E. W. Parents as agents of change. In A. Jacobs & W. W. Spradlin (eds.), *Groups as agent of change,* Chicago: Aldine, Atherton, 1971.

Conger, J. C. The treatment of encopresis by the management of social consequences. *Behavior Therapy,* 1970, *1,* 386–390.

Conley, D. S., and Wolery, M. R. Treatment by overcorrection of self-injurious eye gouging in preschool blind children. *Journal of Behavior Therapy and Experimental Psychiatry,* 1980, *11,* 121–125.

Conners, C. K., and Wells, K. Method and theory for psychopharmacology with children. In R. Trites (ed.), *Hyperactivity in children: Etiology, measurement and treatment implications.* Baltimore, Md.: University Park Press, 1979.

Conway, J., and Bucher, B. "Soap in the mouth" as an aversive consequence. *Behavior Therapy,* 1974, *5* 154–156.

Cook, J. W., Altman, K., Shaw, J., and Blaylock, M. Use of contingent lemon juice to eliminate public masturbation by a severely retarded boy. *Behaviour Research and Therapy,* 1978, *16,* 131–134.

Cooper, A. J. A case of bronchial asthma treated by behavior therapy. *Behaviour Research and Therapy,* 1964, *1,* 351.

Cooper, J. A. Application of the consultant role to parent-teacher management of school avoidance behavior. *Psychology in the Schools,* 1973, *10,* 259–262.

Corbett, J. Aversion for the treatment of self-injurious behaviour. *Journal of Mental Deficiency Research,* 1975, *19,* 79–95.

Cordle, C. J. and Long, C. G. The use of operant self-control procedures in the treatment of compulsive hair-pulling. *Journal of Behavior Therapy and Experimental Psychiatry,* 1980, *11,* 127–130.

Cornforth, A. R. T., Johnston, K., and Walter, M. Teaching sign language to deaf mentally handicapped adults. *Apex,* 1974, *2,* 23–35.

Corte, H. E., Wolf, M. M., and Locke, B. J. A comparison of procedures for eliminating self-injurious behavior of retarded adolescents. *Journal of Applied Behavior Analysis,* 1971, *4,* 201–213.

Cortes, J. *Delinquency and crime: A biophysical approach.* New York: Seminar Press, 1972.

Cowen, E. L. Social and community interventions. *Annual Review of Psychology,* 1973, *24,* 423–472.

Cowen, E. L., and Zax, M. Early detection and prevention of emotional disorder: Conceptualizations and programming. In J. W. Carter, (ed.), *Research contributions from psychology to community mental health.* New York: Behavioral Publications, 1969, 46–59.

Crahay, M. Analysis of the regulatory effect of three kinds of feedback (stereotype, specific, and feedback with self-control) on preoperational subjects. *Scientia Paedagogica Experimentalis,* 1977, *14,* 253–280.

Craig, M. M., and Furst, P. W. What happens after treatment? A study of potentially delinquent boys. *Social Service Review,* 1965, *39,* 165–171.

Craigie, F. C., and Garcia, E. E. Effects of child behavior change on teacher verbal behavior and rating of student behavior. *Journal of Applied Behavior Analysis,* 1978, *11,* 308–000.

Crane, V. and Ballif, B. L. Effects of black or white adult modeling with rule structure on adopting a standard for self-control in black boys. *Journal of Educational Research*, 1976, *70*, 96–101.

Crary, R. W. *Humanizing the schools: Curriculum development and theory*. New York: Knopf, 1969.

Creer, T. L. The use of a time-out positive reinforcement procedure with asthmatic children. *Journal of Psychosomatic Research*, 1970, *14*, 117–120.

Creer, T. L. *Asthma: psychological aspects and management*. Mimeographed paper, 1976.

Creer, T. L., and Davis, M. H. Using a staggered-wakening procedure with enuretic children in an institutional setting. *Journal of Behavior Therapy and Experimental Psychiatry*, 1975, *6*, 23–25.

Creer, T. L., and Miklich, D. R. The application of a self-modeling procedure to modify inappropriate behavior: A preliminary report. *Behaviour Research and Therapy*, 1970, *8*, 91–92.

Creer, T. L., and Renne, C. M. Training social agents in the rehabilitation of chronically ill children. In M. E. Bernal, (ed.), *Training in behavior modification*. Belmont, Calif.: Wadsworth, 1976.

Creer, T. L., Renne, C. M., and Christian, W. P. Behavioral contributions to rehabilitation and childhood asthma. *Rehabilitation Literature*, 1976, *37*, 266–232.

Crisp, A. H. The possible significance of some behavioral correlates of weight and carbohydrate intake. *Journal of Psychosomatic Research*, 1967, *11*, 117–131.

Croake, J. W. Fears of children. *Human Development*, 1969, *12*, 239–247.

Croake, J. W., and Knox, F. H. The changing nature of children's fears. *Child Study Journal*, 1973, *3*, 91–105.

Croghan, L., and Musante, G. J. The elimination of a boy's high building phobia by *in vivo* desensitization and game playing. *Journal of Behavior Therapy and Experimental Psychiatry*, 1975, *6*, 87–88.

Croll, W. L. Children's discrimination learning as a function of intertrial duration. *Psychonomic Science*, 1970, *18*, 321–322.

Crowley, C. P., and Armstrong, P. M. Positive practice, overcorrection and behavior rehearsal in the treatment of three cases of encopresis. *Journal of Behavior Therapy and Experimental Psychiatry*, 1977, *8*, 411–416.

Crozier, J., and Katz, R., Social learning treatment of child abuse. *Journal of Behavior Therapy and Experimental Psychiatry*, 1979, *10*, 213–220.

Cullinan, D., Epstein, M., and Silver, L. Modification of impulsive tempo in learning-disabled pupils. *Journal of Abnormal Child Psychology*, 1977, *5*, 437–444.

Cummings, J. D. The incidence of emotional symptoms in school children. *British Journal of Educational Psychology*, 1944, *14*, 151–161.

Cummings, J. D. A follow-up study of emotional symptoms in school children. *British Journal of Educational Psychology*, 1946, *16*, 163–177.

Cuvo, A. J., and Riva, M. T. Generalization and transfer between comprehension and production: A comparison of retarded and nonretarded persons. *Journal of Applied Behavior Analysis*, 1980, *13*, 315–331.

Cuvo, A. J., Veitch, V. D., Trace, M. W., and Konke, J. L. Teaching change computation to the mentally retarded. *Behavior Modification*, 1978, *2*, 531–548.

Darch, C. B., and Thorpe, H. W. The principal game: A group consequence procedure to increase on-task behavior. *Psychology in the Schools*, 1977, *14*, 341–347.

Davidson, W. S., and Seidman, E. Studies of behavior modification and juvenile delinquency: A review, methodological critique, and social perspective. *Psychological Bulletin*, 1974, *81*, 998–1011.

Davidson, W. S., and Wolfred, T. R. Evaluation of a community-based behavior modification program for prevention of delinquency. *Community Mental Health Journal*, 1977, *13*, 296–306.

Davis, A. B. L. Some experiences with two small groups of mothers in a child guidance clinic. *British Journal of Psychiatric Social Work*, 1947, *1*, 16–22.

Davis, D. J. NIAID initiatives in allergy research. *Journal of Allergy and Clinical Immunology*, 1972, *49*, 323.

Davis, M. H., Saunders, D. R., Creer, T. L., and Chai, H. Relaxation training facilitated by biofeedback apparatus as a supplemental treatment in bronchial asthma. *Journal of Psychosomatic Research*, 1973, *17*, 121.

Davis, K. V., Sprague, R. L., and Werry, J. S. Stereotyped behavior and activity level in severe retardates: The effect of drugs. *American Journal of Mental Deficiency*, 1969, *73*, 721–727.

Davison, G. C. A social learning therapy program with an autistic child. *Behaviour Research and Therapy*, 1964, *2*, 149–159.

Davison, G. C. The training of undergraduates as social reinforcers for autistic children. In L. P. Ullman, and L. Krasner (eds.), *Case studies in behavior modification*. New York: Holt, Rinehart and Winston, 1965.

Davison, G. C. Homosexuality: The ethical challenge. *Journal of Consulting and Clinical Psychology*, 1976, *44*, 157–162.

Dawson, B., Illsley, R., Horobin, G., and Mitchell, R. A survey of childhood asthma in Aberdeen. *Lancet*, 1969, *1*, 827.

Day, L., and Reznikoff, M. Preparation of children and parents for treatment at a children's psychiatric clinic through videotape modeling. *Journal of Consulting and Clinical Psychology*, 1980, *48*, 303–304.

de Coriat, L. F., Theslenco, L., and Waksman, J. The effects of psychomotor stimulation on the IQ of young children with Trisomy-21. In B. B. W. Richards (ed.), *Proceedings of the first congress of the international association for scientific study of mental deficiency*. Michael Jackson Publishing Co., 1968.

Deitz, S. M. An analysis of programming DRL schedules in educational settings. *Behaviour Research and Therapy*, 1977, *15*, 103–111.

Deitz, S. M., Repp, A., and Deitz, D. Reducing inappropriate classroom behavior of retarded students through three procedures of differential reinforcement. *Journal of Mental Deficiency Research*, 1976, *20*, 155–170.

Deitz, S. M., Slack, D. J., Schwarzmueller, E. B., Wilander, A. P., Weatherly, T. J., and Hillard, G. Reducing inappropriate behavior in special classrooms by reinforcing average interresponse times: Interval DRL. *Behavior Therapy*, 1978, *9*, 37–46.

Dekker, M. D., Pelser, H. E., and Groen, J. Conditioning as a cause of asthmatic attacks. *Journal of Psychosomatic Research*, 1957, *2*, 97–108.

DeLeon, G., and Mandell, W. A comparison of conditioning and psychotherapy in the treatment of functional enuresis. *Journal of Clinical Psychology*, 1966, *22*, 326–330.

DeLeon, G., and Sacks, S. Conditioning functional enuresis: a four year follow-up. *Journal of Consulting and Clinical Psychology*, 1972, *39*, 299–300.

deLorenzo, M. E. Early intervention, education, and training of preschool children. In P. Mittler (ed.), *Research to practice in mental retardation Vol. 2: Education and training*. Baltimore, Md.: University Park Press, 1977, 109–118.

DeMause, L. *The history of childhood*. New York: Psychohistory Press, 1974.

DeMyer, M. K., and Ferster, C. B. Teaching new social behavior to schizophrenic children. *Journal of the American Academy of Child Psychiatry*, 1962, *1*, 443–461.

DeMyer, M. K., Barton, S., DeMyer, W. E., Norton, J. A., Allen, J., and Steele, R. Prognosis in autism: A follow-up study. *Journal of Autism and Childhood Schizophrenia*, 1973, *3*, 199–246.

Denholtz, M. S. "At home" aversion treatment of compulsive fire-setting behavior: Case report. In H. Rudin (ed.), *Advances in behavior therapy: Proceedings of the 4th conference at the association for the advancement of behavior therapy*. New York: Academic Press, 1972.

Denicola, J., and Sandler, J. Training abusive parents in child management and self-control skills. *Behavior Therapy*, 1980, *11*, 263–270.

Denmark, J. C. Early profound deafness and mental retardation. *British Journal of Mental Subnormality*, 1978, *24*, 81–89.

Denny, M. R. A theoretical analysis and its application to training the mentally retarded. In N. R. Ellis (ed.), *International review of research in mental retardation*, Vol. 2. New York: Academic Press, 1966.

Despert, J. L. Schizophrenia in children. *Psychiatric Quarterly*, 1938, *12*, 366–371.

Devine, V. T., and Tomlinson, J. R. The "workclock": an alternative to token economics in the management of classroom behaviors. *Psychology in the Schools*, 1976, *13*, 163–170.

Dineen, J., Clark, H., and Risley, T. Peer tutoring among elementary students: Educational benefits to the tutor. *Journal of Applied Behavior Analysis*, 1977, *10*, 231–238.

Dinoff, M., Rickard, H. C., and Colwick, J. Weight reduction through successive contracts. *American Journal of Orthopsychiatry*, 1972, *42*, 110–113.

Dixon, M. *Juvenile delinquency prevention programs*. Washington, D.C.: National Science Foundation, 1974.

Doctor, R., and Singer, E. M. Behavioral intervention strategies with child abusing parents: A home-intervention program. *Child Abuse and Neglect*, 1978, *2*, 57–68.

Doleys, D. M. Behavioral treatments for nocturnal enuresis in children: A review of the recent literature. *Psychological Bulletin*, 1977, *84*, 30–54.

Doleys, D. M., Doster, J., and Cortelli, L. M. Parent training techniques: Effects of lecture-role playing followed by feedback and self-recording. *Journal of Behavior Therapy and Experimental Psychiatry*, 1976, *7*, 359–362. (a)

Doleys, D. M., Wells, K. C., Hobbs, S. A., Roberts, M. W., and Cartelli, L. M. The effects of social punishment on noncompliance: A comparison with time-out and positive practice. *Journal of Applied Behavior Analysis*, 1976, *9*, 471–482. (b)

Doleys, D. M., Ciminero, A. R., Tollison, J. W., Williams, S. C., and Wells, K. C. "Dry-bed" training and retention control training: A comparison. *Behavior Therapy*, 1977, *8*, 541–548.

Doll, E. A. *Vineland social maturity scale: Condensed manual of directions*. Circle Pines, Minn.: American Guidance Service, Inc., 1965.

Dollard, J., and Miller, N. E. *Personality and psychotherapy*. New York: McGraw-Hill, 1950.

Donofrio, A. F. Parent education vs. child psychotherapy. *Psychology in the Schools*, 1976, *13*, 176–180.

Dorsey, M. F., Iwata, B. A., Ong, P., and McSween, T. E. Treatment of self-injurious behavior using a water mist: Initial response suppression and generalization. *Journal of Applied Behavior Analysis*, 1980, *13*, 343–353.

Dorsey, M. F., Iwata, B. A., Reid, D. H., and Davis, P. A. Protective equipment: continuous and contingent application in the treatment of self-injurious behavior. *Journal of Applied Behavior Analysis*, 1982, *15*, 217–230.

Doughtery, E. H., and Lane, J. R. Naturalistic alternatives to extinction: An application to self-injurious bedtime behavior. *Journal of Behavior Therapy and Experimental Psychiatry*, 1976, *7*, 373–375.

Douglas, V. I. Are drugs enough? To train or to treat the hyperactive child. *International Journal of Mental Health*, 1975, *5*, 199–212.

Douglas, V. I., and Sanders, F. A. A pilot study of Rimland's diagnostic checklist with autistic and mentally retarded children. *Journal of Child Psychology and Psychiatry*, 1968, *9*, 105–109.

Douglas, V. I., Parry, P., Marton, P., and Carson, C. Assessment of a cognitive training program for hyperactive children. *Journal of Abnormal Child Psychology*, 1976, *4*, 389–410.

Dowrick, P. W., and Dove, C. The use of self-modeling to improve the swimming performance of spina bifida children. *Journal of Applied Behavior Analysis*, 1980, *13*, 51–56.

Dowrick, P. W., and Raeburn, J. M. Video editing and medication to produce a therapeutic self-model. *Journal of Consulting and Clinical Psychology*, 1977, *45*, 1156–1158.

Drabman, R. S., and Lahey, B. B. Feedback in classroom behavior modification: Effects on the target and her classmates. *Journal of Applied Behavior Analysis*, 1974, *7*, 591–598.

Drabman, R. S., and Spitalnik, R. Social isolation as a punishment procedure: A controlled study. *Journal of Experimental Child Psychology*, 1973, *16*, 236–249.

Drabman, R. S., Spitalnik, R., and O'Leary, K. D. Teaching self-control to disruptive children. *Journal of Abnormal Psychology*, 1973, *82*, 10–16.

Drabman, R. S., Jarvie, G. J., and Archbold, J. The use and misuse of extinction in classroom behavioral programs. *Psychology in the Schools*, 1976, *13*, 470–476.

Drabman, R. S., Cruz, G., Ross, J., and Lynde, S. Suppression of chronic drooling in mentally retarded children and adolescents: Effectiveness of a behavioral treatment package. *Behavior Therapy*, 1979, *10*, 46–56.

Dubey, D. R., Kent, R. N., O'Leary, S. G., Broderick, J. E., and O'Leary, K. D. Reactions of children and teachers to classroom observers: A series of controlled investigations. *Behavior Therapy*, 1977, *8*, 887–898.

Dubose, R. Identification. In M. Snell (ed.), *Systematic instruction of the moderately and severely handicapped*. Columbus, Ohio: Merrill, 1978.

Dubnoff, B. The habilitation and education of the autistic child in a therapeutic day school. *American Journal of Orthopsychiatry*, 1965, *35*, 385–386.

Duddle, M. An increase of anorexia nervosa in a university population. *British Journal of Psychiatry*, 1973, *123*, 711–712.

Duff, R., LaRocca, J., Lizzet, A., Martin, P., Pearce, L., Williams, M., and Peck, C. A comparison of the fears of mildly retarded adults with children of their mental age and chronological age matched controls. *Journal of Behavior Therapy and Experimental Psychiatry*, 1981, *12*, 121–124.

Duker, P. Intra-subject controlled time-out (social isolation) in the modification of self-injurious behaviour. *Journal of Mental Deficiency Research*, 1975 *19*, 107–112.

Duker, P. C., and Sey, D. M. Elimination of vomiting in a retarded female using restitutional correction. *Behavior Therapy*, 1977, *8*, 255.

Dunlap, G., and Koegel, R. L. Motivating autistic children through stimulus variation. *Journal of Applied Behavior Analysis*, 1980, *13*, 619–627.

Durlak, J. S. Comparative effectiveness of paraprofessional and professional helpers. *Psychological Bulletin*, 1979, *86*, 80–92.

Edelman, R. I. Operant conditioning treatment of encopresis. *Journal of Behavior Therapy and Experimental Psychiatry*, 1971, *7*, 71–73.

Edlund, C. V. A reinforcement approach to the elimination of a child's school phobia. *Mental Hygiene*, 1971, *55*, 433–436.

Edwards, K. A. An index for assessing weight change in children: Weight/height ratios. *Journal of Applied Behavior Analysis*, 1978, *11*, 421–429.

Effron, R. The effects of olfactory stimuli in arresting uncinate fits. *Brain*, 1956, *79*, 267–281.

Effron, R. The conditioned inhibition of uncinate fits. *Brain*, 1957, *80*, 251–262.

Egel, A. L., Richman, G. S., and Koegel, R. L. Normal peer models and autistic children's learning. *Journal of Applied Behavior Analysis*, 1981, *14*, 3–12.

Eimas, P. Multiple cue-discrimination in children. *Psychological Record*, 1969, *9*, 417–424.

Eisenberg, L. The autistic child in adolescence. *American Journal of Psychiatry*, 1956, *112*, 607–612.

Eisenberg, L. The course of childhood schizophrenia. *Archives of Neurology and Psychiatry*, 1957, *78*, 69–83.

Eisenberg, L., and Kanner, L. Early infantile autism, 1943–1955. *American Journal of Orthopsychiatry*, 1956, *26*, 556–566.

Eitzen, D. S. The effects of behavior modification on the attitudes of delinquents. *Behaviour Research and Therapy*, 1975, *13*, 295–299.

Elkisch, P. Simultaneous treatment of a child and his mother. *American Journal of Psychotherapy*, 1935, *7*, 105–130.

Ellis, N. R. The Partlow case: A reply to Dr. Roos. *Law and Psychology Review*, 1979, *5*, 15–49.

Ellis, N. R., Barrett, C. E., and Pryer, N. W. Operant behavior in mental defectiveness. *Journal of Behavior Therapy and Experimental Psychiatry*, 1960, *3*, 63–69.

Eme, R., and Schmidt, D. The stability of children's fears. *Child Development*, 1978, *49*, 1277–1279.

Emery, R. E., and Marholin, D. An applied behavior analysis of delinquency: The irrelevancy of relevant behavior. *American Psychologist*, 1977, *32*, 860–873.

Empey, L. T., and Ericson, M. L. *The provo experiment: Evaluating community control of delinquency*. Lexington, Mass.: Lexington Books, 1972.

Emshoff, J. G., Redd, W. H., and Davidson, W. S. Generalization training and the transfer of prosocial behavior in delinquent adolescents. *Journal of Behavior Therapy and Experimental Psychiatry*, 1976, *7*, 141–144.

Engeln, R., Knutson, J., Laughy, L., and Garlington, W. Behavioral modification techniques applied to a family unit—A case study. *Journal of Child Psychology and Psychiatry*, 1968, *9*, 245–252.

Epstein, L. H., and Wing, R. R., Reanalysis of weight changes in behavior modification and nutrition education for childhood obesity. *Journal of Pediatric Psychology,* 1983, *8,* 97–104.

Epstein, L. H., Wing, R. R., Koeske, R., Ossip, D., and Beck, S. A comparison of lifestyle change and programmed aerobic exercise on weight and fitness changes in obese children. *Behavior Therapy,* 1982, *13,* 651–666.

Epstein, L. H., Parker, L., McCoy, J. F., and McGee, G. Descriptive analysis of eating regulation of obese and non-obese children. *Journal of Applied Behavior Analysis,* 1976, *9,* 407–416.

Epstein, L. H., Masek, B. J., and Marshall, W. R. A nutritionally based school program for control of eating in obese children. *Behavior Therapy,* 1978, *9,* 766–778.

Epstein, M. H., Repp, A. C., and Cullinan, D. Decreasing "obscene" language of behaviorally disordered children through the use of a DRL schedule. *Psychology in the Schools,* 1978, *15,* 419–423.

Epstein, R., and Goss, C. M. Self-control procedure for maintenance of non-disruptive behavior in an elementary-school child. *Behavior Therapy,* 1978, *9,* 109–117.

Erickson, R. C. Walden III: Toward an ethics of changing behavior. *Journal of Religion and Health,* 1977, *16,* 7–14.

Etzel, B. C., and Le Blanc, J. M. The simplest treatment alternative: The law of parsimony applied to choosing appropriate instructional control and errorless learning procedures for the difficult-to-teach child. *Journal of Autism and Developmental Disorders,* 1979, *9,* 361–382.

Evans, B. A case of trichotillomania in a child treated in a home token program. *Journal of Behavior Therapy and Experimental Psychiatry,* 1976, *7,* 197–198.

Evers-Pasquale, W., and Sherman, M. The reward value of peers: A variable influencing the efficacy of filmed modeling in modifying social isolation in preschoolers. *Journal of Abnormal Child Psychology,* 1975, *3,* 179–190.

Evers, W. L., and Schwarz, J. C. Modifying social withdrawal in preschoolers: The effects of filmed modeling and teacher praise. *Journal of Abnormal Child Psychology,* 1973, *1,* 248–256.

Eyeberg, S. M., and Johnson, S. M. Multiple assessment of behavior modification with families: Effects of contingency contracting and order treatment problems. *Journal of Consulting and Clinical Psychology,* 1974, *42,* 594–606.

Eysenck, H. J. *Dimensions of personality.* London: Routledge & Kegan Paul, 1947.

Eysenck, H. J. *The scientific study of personality.* London: Routledge & Kegan Paul, 1952.

Eysenck, H. J. *The structure of human personality.* London: Methuen, 1960.

Eysenck, H. J., and Rachman, S. *The causes and cures of neuroses.* San Diego: Knapp, 1965.

Faillers, C. J. Treatment of asthma in a residential center: A fifteen year study. *Ann. Allergy,* 1970, *28,* 513.

Farb, J., Cottrell, A. W., Montague, J. C., and Thorne, J. M. Update on research into increasing intelligence levels of mentally retarded children. In P. Mittler (ed.), *Research to practice in mental retardation, Vol. 2: Education and training.* Baltimore, Md.: University Park Press, 1977, 129–136.

Farnum, M., and Brigham, T. A. The evaluation of study guides with middle school students. *Journal of Applied Behavioral Analysis,* 1978, *11,* 137–144.

Favell, J. E., McGimsey, J. F., and Jones, M. L. The use of physical restraint in the treatment of self-injury and as positive reinforcement. *Journal of Applied Behavior Analysis*, 1978, *11*, 225–241.

Fein, D., Tinder, P., and Waterhouse, L. Stimulus generalization in autistic and normal children. *Journal of Child Psychology and Psychiatry*, 1979, *20*, 325–335.

Feldman, G. M. The effect of biofeedback training on respiratory resistance of asthmatic children. *Psychosomatic Medicine*, 1976, *38*, 27–34.

Felixbrod, J. J., and O'Leary, K. D. Effects of reinforcement on children's academic behavior as a function of self-determined and externally imposed systems. *Journal of Applied Behavior Analysis*, 1973, *6*, 241–250.

Felixbrod, J. J., and O'Leary, K. D. Self-determination of academic standards by children: Toward freedom from external control. *Journal of Educational Psychology*, 1974, *66*, 845–850.

Fenichel, O. *The psychoanalytic theory of neurosis*. New York: Norton, 1945.

Ferenczi, S. The unwelcome child and his death instinct. *Final contributions to the problems and methods of psychoanalyses*. New York: Basic Books, 1956.

Ferritor, D. R., Buckholdt, D., Hamblin, R. L., and Smith, L. The non-effects of contingent reinforcement for attending behavior on work accomplished. *Journal of Applied Behavior Analysis*, 1972, *5*, 7–17.

Ferster, C. B. Reinforcement and punishment in the control of human behavior by social agencies. *Psychiatric Research Reports*, 1958, *12*, 101–118.

Ferster, C. B. Positive reinforcement and behavioral deficits of autistic children. *Child Development*, 1961, *32*, 437–456.

Ferster, C. B. Arbitrary and natural reinforcement. *The Psychological Record*, 1967, *17*, 341–347.

Ferster, C. B., and DeMeyer, M. K. The development of performances in autistic children in an automatically controlled environment. *Journal of Chronic Diseases*, 1961, *13*, 312–345.

Ferster, C. B., and DeMeyer, M. K. A method for the experimental analysis of the behavior of autistic children. *American Journal of Orthopsychiatry*, 1962, *32*, 89–98.

Feshback, S. Child abuse and the dynamics of human aggression. In G. Gerbner, C. J. Ross, and E. Zigler, (eds.), *Child abuse: An agenda for action*, N.Y.: Oxford University Press, 1980, 48–62.

Fielding, D. An analysis of the behavior of day- and night-wetting children: toward a model of micturition control. *Behaviour Research and Therapy*, 1982, *20*, 49–60.

Filipczak, J., and Wodarski, J. S. Behavioral intervention in public schools: Implementing and evaluating a model. In D. Safer, and R. P. Allen (eds.), *Alternative education programs for disruptive secondary school students*. Baltimore, Md.: University Park Press, 1980.

Finch, S. M. Psychophysiological disorders of children. In A. M. Freedman, and H. I. Kaplan (eds.), *The child: His psychological and cultural development*, Vol. 2. New York: Atheneum, 1972, 144–159.

Finley, W. W., and Wansley, R. A. Use of intermittent reinforcement in a clinical research program for the treatment of enuresis nocturna. *Journal of Pediatric Psychology*, 1976, *4*, 24–27.

Finley, W. W., Avie, J. R., and Johnson, G. Effect of varying alarm schedules on acquisition and relapse parameters in the conditioning treatment of enuresis. *Behaviour Research and Therapy*, 1982, *20*, 69–80.

Finley, W. W., Besserman, R. L., Bennett, L. F., Clapp, R. K., and Finley, P. M. The effect of continuous, intermittent and "placebo" reinforcement on the effectiveness of the conditioning treatment for enuresis nocturna. *Behavior Research and Therapy*, 1973, *11*, 289–297.

Finley, W. W., Wansley, R. A., and Blenkarn, M. M. Conditioning treatment of enuresis using a 70% intermittent reinforcement schedule. *Behaviour Research and Therapy*, 1977, *15*, 419–427.

Finnie, N. R. *Handling of the young cerebral palsied at home*. New York: Dutton, 1970.

Firestone, P. *The effects of reinforcement contingencies and caffeine on hyperactive children*. Unpublished Doctoral Dissertation, McGill University, Montreal, 1974.

Firestone, P., and Douglas, V. I. The effects of reward and punishment on reaction times and autonomic activity in hyperactive and normal children. *Journal of Abnormal Child Psychology*, 1975, *3*, 201–216.

Fischer, I., and Glanville, B. Programmed teaching of autistic children. *Archives of General Psychiatry*, 1970, *23*, 90–94.

Fischer, J., and Nehs, R. Use of a commonly available chore to reduce a boy's rate of swearing. *Journal of Behavior Therapy and Experimental Psychiatry*, 1978, *1*, 81–84.

Fishbein, M., and Wasik, B. Effect of the good behavior game on disruptive library behavior. *Journal of Applied Behavior Analysis*, 1981, *14*, 89–93.

Fixsen, D. L., Phillips, E. L., and Wolf, M. M. Achievement place: The reliability of self-reporting and peer-reporting and their effects on behavior. *Journal of Applied Behavior Analysis*, 1972, *5*, 19–30.

Fixsen, D. L., Phillips, E. L., and Wolf, M. M. Achievement place: Experiments in self-government with predelinquents. *Journal of Applied Behavior Analysis*, 1973, *6*, 31–47.

Flanagan, S., Adams, H. E., and Forehand, R. A. comparison of four instructional techniques for teaching parents to use time-out. *Behavior Therapy*, 1979, *10*, 94–102.

Flannery, R. B., and Cautela, J. R. Seizures: Controlling the uncontrollable. *Journal of Rehabilitation*, 1973, *39*, 34–36.

Fleischman, M. J. Using parenting salaries to control attrition and cooperation in therapy. *Behavior Therapy*, 1979, *10*, 111–116.

Fo, W. S., and O'Donnell, C. R. The buddy system: Relationship and contingency conditions in a community intervention programs for youth with non-professionals as behavior agents. *Journal of Consulting and Clinical Psychology*, 1974, *42*, 163–169.

Folstein, S., and Rutter, M. Infantile autism: A genetic study of 21 twin pairs. *Journal of Child Psychology and Psychiatry and Allied Disciplines*, 1977, *18*, 297–322.

Forehand, R., and Atkeson, B. M. Generality of treatment effects with parents as therapists: a review of assessment and implementation procedures. *Behavior Therapy*, 1977, *8*, 575–594.

Forehand, R., and King, H. E. Pre-school children's non-compliance: Effects of short-term behavior therapy. *Journal of Community Psychology*, 1974, *2*, 42–44.

Forehand, R., and King, H. E. Noncompliant children: *Effects of parent training on behavior and attitude change*. Unpublished manuscript, Univ. of Georgia, 1975.

Forehand, R., and Wells, K. C. Teachers and parents: Where have all the "good" contingency managers gone? *Behavior Therapy*, 1977, *8*, 1010.

Forehand, R., Cheney, T., and Yoder, P. Parent behavior training: Effects on the non-compliance of a deaf child. *Journal of Behavior Therapy and Experimental Psychiatry*, 1974, *5*, 281–283.

Forehand, R., King, H. E., Peed, S., and Yoder, P. Mother-child interactions:

Comparison of a non-compliant clinic group and a non clinic group. *Behavior Research and Therapy*, 1975, *13*, 79–84.

Forehand, R., Griest, D., and Wells, K. Parent behavioral training: An analysis of the relationships among multiple outcome measures. *Journal of Abnormal Child Psychology*, 1979, *7*, 229–242.

Forster, F. Clinical therapeutic conditioning in epilepsy. *Wisconsin Medical Journal*, 1969, *68*, 289–291.

Forsythe, W., and Redmond, A. Enuresis and the electric alarm. *British Medical Journal*, 1970, *1*, 211–213.

Foster, P. W. *Introduction to environmental science*. Homewood, Ill.: Irwin, 1972.

Fox, R. A., and Roseen, D. L. A parent-administered program for dietary regulation of phenylketanuria. *Journal of Behavior Therapy and Experimental Psychiatry*, 1977, *8*, 441–443.

Fox, S. J. *Juvenile courts*. St. Paul, Minn.: West Publishing Co., 1977.

Foxx, R. M. Attention training: the use of overcorrection avoidance to increase the eye contact of autistic and retarded children. *Journal of Applied Behavior Analysis*, 1977, *10*, 489–499.

Foxx, R. M., and Azrin, N. H. Restitution: A method of eliminating aggressive-disruptive behavior of retarded and brain-damaged patients. *Behaviour Research and Therapy*, 1972, *10*, 15–27.

Foxx, R. M., and Azrin, N. H. Dry pants: A rapid method of toilet training children. *Behaviour Research and Therapy*, 1973, *11*, 435–442. (a)

Foxx, R. M., and Azrin, N. H. The elimination of autistic self-stimulatory behavior by overcorrection. *Journal of Applied Behavior Analysis*, 1973, *6*, 1–14. (b)

Foxx, R. M., and Azrin, N. H. *Toilet training the retarded: A rapid program for day and nighttime independent toileting*. Champaign, Ill.: Research Press, 1973. (c)

Foxx, R. M., Synder, M. S., and Shroeder, F. A food-satiation and oral hygiene punishment program to suppress chronic rumination by retarded persons. *Journal of Autism and Developmental Disorders*, 1979, *9*, 399–412.

Frager, S., and Stern, C. Learning by teaching. *The Reading Teacher*, 1970, *23*, 403–417.

Francis, S. H. The effects of own home and institutional rearing on the behavioral development of normal and mongol children. *Journal of Child Psychology and Psychiatry*, 1971, *12*, 173–190.

Frank, S. M., Allen, D. A., Stein, L., and Myers, B. Linguistic performance in vulnerable and autistic children and their mothers. *American Journal of Psychiatry*, 1976, *133*, 909–915.

Frankel, F., Freeman, B., Ritvo, E., and Pardo, R. The effect of environmental stimulation upon the stereotyped behavior of autistic children. *Journal of Autism and Childhood Schizophrenia*, 1978, *8*, 389–394.

Franks, C., and Wilson, G. T. *Annual review of behavior therapy: Theory and practice*, Vol. II. New York: Brunner/Mazel, 1974.

Frazier, J. R., and Schneider, H. Parental management of innappropriate hyperactivity in a young, retarded child. *Journal of Behavior Therapy and Experimental Psychiatry*, 1975, *6*, 246–247.

Fredrickson, L. W., Jenkins, J. D., and Carr, C. R. Indirect modification of adolescent drug abuse using contingency contracting. *Journal of Behavior Therapy and Experimental Psychiatry*, 1976, *9*, 377–378.

Freeman, B. J., Behavior observation scale: Preliminary analysis of the similarities and differences between autistic and mentally retarded children. *Psychological Reports*, 1979, *44*, 519–524.

Freeman, B. J., Ritvo, E., and Miller, R. An operant procedure to teach an echolalic, autistic child to answer questions appropriately. *Journal of Autism and Childhood Schizophrenia*, 1975, *5*, 169–176.

Freeman, B. J., Roy, R. R., and Hemmick, S. Extinction of a phobia of physical examination in a seven year old mentally retarded boy—A case study. *Behaviour Research and Therapy*, 1976, *14*, 63–64.

French, T. M. Interrelations between psychoanalysis and the experimental work of Pavlov. *American Journal of Psychiatry*, 1933, *89*, 1165–1203.

French, T. M., and Alexander, F. Psychogenic factors in bronchial asthma. *Psychosomatic Medicine Monographs*, 1941, *4*, 2–94.

Freud, A. *The ego and the mechanisms of defense*. New York: International Universities Press, 1946.

Freud, S. Analysis of a phobia in a five year old boy. *Collected Papers*, Vol. 3. New York: Basic Books, 1959. (*Originally published in Jahrbuch für Psychoanalytische und Psychopathologische Forschungen, 8*, 1909).

Freyman, R. Follow-up of enuresis treatment with bell apparatus. *Journal of Child Psychology and Psychiatry*, 1963, *4*, 199–206.

Friebergs, V., and Douglas, V. I. Concept learning in hyperactive and normal children. *Journal of Abnormal Psychology*, 1969, *74*, 388–395.

Friedling, C., and O'Leary, S. G. Effects of self-instructional training on second- and third-grade hyperactive children: A failure to replicate. *Journal of Applied Behavior Analysis*, 1979, *12*, 211–219.

Friedman, S. Self-control in the treatment of Gilles de la Tourette's syndrome: Case study with 18-month follow-up. *Journal of Consulting and Clinical Psychology*, 1980, *48*, 400–402.

Friedman, S. B. The challenge in behavioral pediatrics. *Journal of Pediatrics*, 1970, *77*, 172–173.

Frith, V. Cognitive mechanisms in autism: Experiments with color and tone sequence production. *Journal of Autism and Childhood Schizophrenia*, 1972, *2*, 160–173.

Fuchs, N. R. Play therapy at home. *Merrill-Palmer Quarterly*, 1957, *3*, 89–95.

Fuller, P. R. Operant conditioning of a vegetative human organism. *American Journal of Psychology*, 1949, *62*, 587–590.

Fulwiler, R. L., and Fouts, R. S. Acquisition of American sign language by a noncommunicative autistic child. *Journal of Autism and Childhood Schizophrenia*. 1976, *6*, 43–51.

Furman, E. Treatment of under-fives by way of their parents. *Psychoanalytic Study of the Child*, 1957, *12*, 250–262.

Fyffe, C., and Prior, M. Evidence for language recoding in autistic, retarded, and normal children: A re-examination. *British Journal of Psychology*, 1978, *69*, 393–402.

Galloway, C., and Galloway, K. C. Parent groups with a focus on precise behavior management. Institute on Mental Retardation and Intellectual Development. *Imrid Papers and Reports*, 1970, *7*, 1.

Galloway, C., and Larsen, L. Associate teaching personnel. *Education and Training of the Mentally Retarded*, 1976, *11*, 273–280.

Gamble, A., and Strain, P. S. The effects of dependent and interdependent group contingencies on socially appropriate responses in classes for emotionally handicapped children. *Psychology in the Schools*, 1979, *16*, 253–260.

Gambrill, E. Role of behavior modification in community mental health. *Community Mental Health Journal, 11* (3), 1975, 307–315.

Garber, H., and Heber, F. R. The Milwaukee project. In P. Mittler (ed.), *Research to practice in mental retardation Vol. 1. Care and intervention*. Baltimore, Md.: University Park Press, 1977, 119–128.

Garcia, K. A. *Fears and phobias in childhood*. Unpublished manuscript, State University of New York at Buffalo, 1977.

Gardner, H., Forehand, R., and Roberts, M. Time-out with children: Effects of an explanation and brief parent training on child and parent behaviors. *Journal of Abnormal Child Psychology*, 1976, *4*, 277–288.

Gardner, J. E. Behavior therapy treatment approach to a psychogenic seizure case. *Journal of Consulting Psychology*, 1967, *31*, 209–212.

Gardner, J. E., Pearson, D. T., Berkovici, A. N., and Bricker, D. E. Measurement, evaluation, and modification of selected social interactions between a schizophrenic child, his parents, and his therapist. *Journal of Consulting and Clinical Psychology*, 1968, *32*, 537–542.

Gardner, J. M. Behavior modification in mental retardation: A review of research and analysis of trends. In R. D. Rubin, H. Fensterheim, A. A. Lazarus, and C. M. Franks (eds.), *Advances in behavior therapy*. New York: Academic Press, 1971, 37–59.

Gardner, R. A., and Gardner, B. T. Teaching sign language to a chimpanzee. *Science*, 1969, *165*, 664–672.

Gardner, W. I. Behavior therapy treatment approach to a psychogenic seizure case. *Journal of Consulting Psychology*, 1967, *3*, 209–212.

Gardner, W. I. Use of punishment procedures with the severely retarded: A review. *American Journal of Mental Deficiency*, 1969, *74*, 86–103.

Garrow, J. *Energy balance and obesity in man*. New York: Amer. Elsevier, 1974.

Gartner, A. *Paraprofessionals and their performance: A survey of education, health, and social service programs*. New York: Praeger, 1971.

Gartner, A., Kohler, M. C., and Riessman, F. *Children teach children: learning by teaching*. New York: Harper & Row, 1971.

Garvey, W. P., and Hegrenes, J. R. Desensitization techniques in the treatment of school phobia. *American Journal of Orthopsychiatry*, 1966, *36*, 147–152.

Gault, *In re*, 387U.S.1, 36 (1967).

Gaylin, W. On the borders of persuasion: A psychoanalytic look at coercion. *Psychiatry*, 1974, *37*, 1–9.

Geer, J. The development of a scale to measure fear. *Behaviour Research and Therapy*, 1965, *3*, 45–53.

Gelfand, D. M. Behavioral treatment of avoidance, social withdrawal and negative emotional states. In B. B. Wolman, J. Egan, and A. O. Ross (eds.), *Handbook of mental disorders in childhood and adolescence*. Englewood Cliffs, N.J.: Prentice-Hall, 1978.

Gelfand, D. M., and Hartman, D. P. Behavior therapy with children: a review and evaluation of research methodology. *Psychological Bulletin*, 1968, *79*, 204–215.

Gelber, H., and Meyer, V. Behavior therapy and encopresis: the complexities involved in treatment. *Behaviour Research and Therapy*, 1965, 2, 227–231.

Geller, M. I., and Scheirer, C. J. The effect of filmed modeling on cooperative play on disadvantaged preschoolers. *Journal of Abnormal Child Psychology*, 1978, *6*, 71–87.

Gerbner, G., Ross. C. J., and Zigler, E. *Child abuse: An agenda for action*. New York: Oxford University Press, 1980.

Gero-Heymann, E. A short communication on a traumatic episode in a child of two years and seven months. *Psychoanalytic Study of the Child*, 1955, *10*, 376–380.

Gillick, S. *Training parents as therapists in the treatment of juvenile obesity*. Unpublished doctoral dissertation, State University of New York at Buffalo, 1973.

Gladstone, B. W., and Sherman, J. A. Developing generalized behavior modification skills in high school students working with retarded children. *Journal of Applied Behavior Analysis*, 1975, *8*, 169–180.

Glenwick, D. S., and Barocas, R. Training impulsive children in verbal self-control by use of natural change agents. *Journal of Special Education*, 1979, *13*, 387–398.

Glowgower, F., and Sloop, E. W. Two strategies of group training of parents as effective behavior modities. *Behavior Therapy*, 1976, *7*, 177–184.

Glynn, E. L. Classroom applications of self-determined reinforcement. *Journal of Applied Behavior Analysis*, 1970, *3*, 123–132.

Glynn, E. L., and Thomas, J. D. Effect of cueing on self-control of classroom behavior. *Journal of Applied Behavior Analysis*, 1974, *7*, 299–306.

Glynn, E. L., Thomas, J. D., and Shee, S. M. Behavioral self-control of on-task behavior in an elementary classroom. *Journal of Applied Behavior Analysis*, 1973, *6* 105–114.

Goetz, E., Holmberg, M. and LeBlanc, J. Differential reinforcement of other behavior and non-contingent reinforcement as control procedures during the modification of a pre-schoolers compliance. *Journal of Applied Behavior Analysis*, 1975, *8*, 77–82.

Goetz, L., Schuler, A., and Sailor, W. Teaching functional speech to the severely handicapped: Current issues. *Journal of Autism and Developmental Disorders*, 1979, *9*, 325–342.

Gold, M. W. Stimulus factors in skill training of the retarded on a complex assembly task: Acquisition, transfer, and retention. *American Journal of Mental Deficiency*, 1972, *76*, 517–526.

Gold, M. W. Task analysis of a complex assembly task by the retarded blind. *Exceptional Children*, 1976, *42*, 76–84.

Goldenberg, H. Abnormal psychology: A social/community approach. Monterey, Calif.: Brooks/Cole, 1977.

Goldfarb, W. Saul Albert Memorial lecture, Corrective socialization: A rationale for the treatment of schizophrenic children. *Canadian Psychiatric Association Journal*, 1965, *10*, 481–496.

Goldiamond, I. Self-reinforcement. *Journal of Applied Behavior Analysis*, 1976, *9*, 509–514.

Goodstein, L. D., and Sandler, I. Using psychology to promote human welfare: A conceptual analysis of the role of community psychology. *American Psychologist*, 1978, *33*, 882–892.

Gottman, J. The effects of a modeling film on social isolation in preschool children: A methodological investigation. *Journal of Abnormal Child Psychology*, 1977, *5*, 69–78.

Gottman, J. M., and McFall, R. M. Self-monitoring effects in a program for potential high school dropouts: A time-series analysis. *Journal of Consulting and Clinical Psychology*, 1972, *39*, 273–281.

Gottman, J., Gonso, J., and Schuler, P. Teaching social skills to isolated children. *Journal of Abnormal Child Psychology*, 1976, *4*, 179–198.

Grace, D. L. *Self-monitoring in the modification of obesity in children*. Unpublished doctoral dissertation, State University of New York at Buffalo, 1975.

Grace, D. L. Self-monitoring in the modification of obesity in children. *Dissertation Abstracts International*, 1977, No. 77.

Graubard, P. S., Rosenberg, H., and Miller, M. Student applications of behavior modification to teachers and environments or ecological approaches to social deviancy. In E. A. Ramp and B. L. Hopkins (eds.), *A New Direction for Education: Behavior Analysis*, Vol. 1. Lawrence: University of Kansas, 1971.

Gray, J. J. Positive reinforcement and punishment in the treatment of childhood trichotillomania. *Journal of Behavior Therapy and Experimental Psychiatry*, 1979, *10*, 125–129.

Gray, J. S. A biological view of behavior modification. *Journal of Educational Psychology*, 1932, *23*, 611–620.

Graziano, A. M. *A description of a behavioral day-care and treatment program*. Report to the Connecticut State Department of Mental Health, Division of Children's Services, 1963.

Graziano, A. M. *Programmed psychotherapy: A behavioral approach to emotionally disturbed children*. Paper presented at the Eastern Psychological Association, Boston, 1967.

Graziano, A. M. Clinical innovation and the mental health power structure: A social case history. *American Psychologist*, 1969, *24*, 10–18.

Graziano, A. M. A group treatment approach to multiple problem behaviors of autistic children. *Exceptional Child*, 1970, *36*, 765–770. (a)

Graziano, A. M. An historical note on J. Stanley Gray's "A biological view of behavior modification." *Journal of the History of the Behavioral Sciences*, 1970, *6*, 156–158. (b)

Graziano, A. M. (ed.). *Behavior therapy with children*, Vol. 1. Chicago: Aldine, Atherton, 1971.

Graziano, A. M. In the mental health industry illness is our most important product. *Psychology Today*, 1972, *5*, 12–18.

Graziano, A. M. *Child without tomorrow*, Elmsford, N.Y.: Pergamon, 1974.

Graziano, A. M. *Behavior therapy with children*, Vol. II. Elmsford, N.Y.: Aldine, 1975. (a).

Graziano, A. M. Futurants, coverants and operants. *Behavior Therapy*, 1975, *6*, 421–422. (b)

Graziano, A. M. Reduction of children's fears. In A. M. Graziano (ed.), *Behavior therapy with children*, Vol. 2. Chicago: Aldine, 1975.

Graziano, A. M. Parents as behavior therapists. In M. Hersen, R. M. Eisler, and P. M. Miller (eds.), *Progress in behavior modification, Vol. III*. New York: Academic Press, 1977, 251–298.

Graziano, A. M., and DeGiovanni, I. S. The clinical significance of childhood phobias: A note on the proportion of child-clinical referrals for the treatment of children's fears. *Behaviour Research and Therapy*, 1979, *17*, 161–162.

Graziano, A. M., and Fink, R. Second-order effects in mental health treatment. *Journal of Consulting and Clinical Psychology*, 1973, *40*, 356–364.

Graziano, A. M., DeGiovanni, I. S., and Garcia, K. A. Behavioral treatment of children's fears: A review. *Psychological Bulletin*, 1979, *86*, 804–830.

Graziano, A. M., and Graziano, S. G. Children's liberation: Is now the time? In F. G. Esposito, Chairman, *Children's Liberation: Is Now the Time?*. Symposium presented at Eastern Psychological Association, Boston, Mass., 1972.

Graziano, A. M., and Katz, J. N. Training paraprofessionals. In M. Hersen, A. Bellack, and A. Kazdin (eds.), *International handbook of behavior modification and therapy*. New York: Plenum Press, In press, 1982.

Graziano, A. M., and Kean, J. Programmed relaxation and reciprocal inhibition with psychotic children. *Behaviour Research and Therapy*, 1968, *6*, 433–437.

Graziano, A. M., and Mooney, K. C. Family self-control instruction for children's nighttime fear reduction. *Journal of Consulting and Clinical Psychology*, 1980. *48*, 206–213.

Graziano, A. M., and Mooney, K. C. Behavioral treatment of children's "Nightfears": A three-year follow-up. *Journal of Consulting and Clinical Psychology*, 1982, *50*, 598–599.

Graziano, A. M., Hastrup, J., and Pearlson, H. *Behavioral treatment of an adolescent school phobic*. Unpubl. manu., State University of New York at Buffalo, 1975.

Graziano, A. M., Mooney, K. C., Huber, C., and Ignasiak, D. Self-control instruction for children's fear reduction. *Journal of Behavior Therapy and Experimental Psychiatry*, 1979, *10*, 221–227.

Graziano, A. M., White, R., Kelly, R., Korytnyk, N., and Weidenbacher, H. *Child-family "nightfears" reduction: A replication of extension*. Buffalo, N.Y.: State University of New York, Department of Psychology, Unpublished paper, 1981.

Graziano, A. M., Gallipeau, K. A., and Graziano, S. G. *Death, taxes and spanking*. Buffalo, N.Y.: State University, Department of Psychology, Unpubl. paper, 1981.

Greene, K. L., and Pranke, G. R. Preliminary report of the effects of biofeedback training on forced expiration volume in perennial asthmatics. *Journal of Biofeedback*, 1973, *1*, 69.

Greene, R., and Hoats, D. Aversive tickling: A simple conditioning procedure. *Behavior Therapy*, 1971, *2*, 389–393.

Gresham, F. M., and Nagle, R. J. Social skills training with children: Responsiveness to modeling and coaching as a function of peer orientation. *Journal of Consulting and Clinical Psychology*, 1980, *48*, 718–729.

Grey, S., Sartory, G., and Rachman, S. Synchronous and desynchronous changes during fear reduction. *Behaviour Research and Therapy*, 1979, *17*, 137–147.

Griffin, J. C., Locke, B., and Landers, W. Manipulation of potential punishment parameters in the treatment of self-injury. *Journal of Applied Behavior Analysis*, 1975, *8*, 458.

Griffith, E., Schnelle, J., McNess, M., Bissinger, C., and Huff, T. Elective mutism in a first grader: The remediation of a complex behavioral problem. *Journal of Abnormal Child Psychology*, 1975, *3*, 127–134.

Gross, A. M. The use of cost-effectiveness analysis in deciding on alternative living environments of the retarded. In P. Mittler (ed.), *Research to practice in mental retardation Vol. 1: Care and intervention*. Baltimore, Md.: University Park Press, 1977, 427–434.

Grossberg, J. M., and Wilson, H. K. A correlation comparison of the Wolpe-Lang Fear Survey Schedule and the Taylor Manifest Anxiety Scale. *Behaviour Research and Therapy*, 1965, *3*, 125–128.

Grossman, H. J. (ed.). *Manual on terminology and classification in mental retardation*. Washington, D.C.: American Association on Mental Deficiency, 1973.

Guerney, B. B. (ed.). *Psychotherapeutic agents: New roles for non-professionals, parents and teachers*. New York: Holt, 1969.

Guess, D., and Rutherford, G. Experimental attempts to reduce stereotyping among blind retardates. *American Journal of Mental Deficiency*, 1967, *71*, 984–986.

Guess, P., Smith, J. D., and Ensminger, E. E. The role of nonprofessional persons in teaching language skills to mentally retarded children. *Mental Retardation*, 1971, *9*, 27–33.

Gunn, P., Berry, P., and Andrews, R. Vocalization and looking behavior of Down's syndrome infants. *British Journal of Psychology*, 1979, *70*, 259–263.

Guthrie, E. R. *The psychology of learning*, New York: Harper, 1935.

Haberman, J. V. Probing the mind, normal and abnormal. First report. Feeling, association and the psychoreflex. *Medical Record*, 1917, *92*, 927–933.

Hackler, J. C. Boys, blisters and behavior: The impact of a work program in an urban central area. *Journal of Research in Crime and Delinquency*, 1966, *12*, 155–164.

Haefner, D. P. School dental health programs. *Health Education Monographs*, 1974, *2*, 212–219.

Hagman, E. A study of fears of children of preschool age. *Journal of Experimental Education*, 1932, *1*, 110–130.

Hale, G. A., and Morgan, J. S. Developmental trends in children's component selection. *Journal of Experimental Child Psychology*, 1973, *15*, 302–314.

Hall, R. V., and Broden, M. Behavior changes in brain-damaged children through social reinforcement. *Journal of Behavior Therapy and Experimental Psychiatry*, 1967, *5*, 463–474.

Hall, R. V., Cristler, C., Cranston, S. S., and Tucker, B. Teachers and parents as researchers using multiple baseline designs. *Journal of Applied Behavior Analysis*, 1970, *3*, 247–255.

Hall, R. V., Axelrod, S., Tyler, L., Grief, E., Jones, F. C., and Robertson, R. Modification of behavior problems in the home with a parent as observer and experimenter. *Journal of Applied Behavior Analysis*, 1972, *5*, 53–64.

Hallahan, D. P., Kauffman, J. M., and Ball, D. W. Selective attention and cognitive tempo of low achieving and high achieving sixth grade males. *Perceptual and Motor Skills*, 1973, *36*, 579–583.

Halle, J. W., Marshall, A. M., and Spradlin, J. E. Time delay: A technique to increase language use and facilitate generalization in retarded children. *Journal of Applied Behavior Analysis*, 1979, *12*, 431–439.

Halleck, S. L. Legal and ethical aspects of behavior control. *The American Journal of Psychiatry*, 1974, *131*, 381–385.

Hallsten, E. A. Adolescent anorexia nervosa treated by desensitization. *Behaviour Research and Therapy*, 1965, *3*, 87–91.

Halmi, K. A., Powers, P., and Cunningham, S. Treatment of anorexia nervosa with behavior modification. *Archives of General Psychiatry*, 1975, *32*, 93–95.

Hamad, D. C., Cooper, D., and Semb, G. Resource recovery: Use of a group contingency to increase paper recycling in an elementary school. *Journal of Applied Psychology*, 1977, *62*, 768–772.

Hamilton, J., and Standhal, J. Suppression of stereotyped screaming in a profoundly retarded institutionalized female. *Journal of Experimental Child Psychology*, 1969, *7*, 114–121.

Hamilton, J., Stephens, L., and Allen, P. Controlling aggressive and destructive behavior in severely retarded institutionalized residents. *American Journal of Mental Deficiency*, 1967, *71*, 852–856.

Hampe, E., Noble, H., Miller, L. C., and Barrett, C. L. Phobic children one and two years posttreatment. *Journal of Abnormal Psychology*, 1973, *82*, 446–453.

Handleman, J. S. Generalization by autistic-type children of verbal responses across settings. *Journal of Applied Behavior Analysis,* 1979, *12,* 273–284.

Handleman, J. S., and Harris, S. L. Generalization from school to home with autistic children. *Journal of Autism and Developmental Disorders,* 1980, *10,* 323–333.

Hanf, C. *Modifying problem behaviors in mother-child interaction: Standardized laboratory situations.* Paper read at the Association of Behavior Therapies, Olympia, Washington, April 1968.

Hanf, C. *A two-stage program for modifying maternal control during mother-child (m-c) interaction.* Paper read at the Western Psychological Association, Vancouver, April 1969.

Hanf, C., and Kling, J. *Facilitating parent-child interaction: A two stage training model.* Unpublished manuscript, University of Oregon Medical School, 1973.

Hannum, J. W., Thoresen, C. E., and Hubbard, D. R. Jr. A behavioral study of self-esteem with elementary teachers. In M. J. Mahoney, and C. E. Thoresen (eds.), *Self-control: Power to the people.* Monterey, Calif.: Brooks-Cole, 1974.

Hargrave, G. E., and Hargrave, M. C. A peer group socialization therapy program in the school: An outcome investigation. *Psychology in the Schools,* 1979, *16,* 546–550.

Hargrave, E., and Swisher, L. Modifying the verbal expressions of a child with autistic behaviors. *Journal of Autism and Childhood Schizophrenia,* 1975, *5,* 147–154.

Harper, D. C., and Richman, L. C. Pre-school screening for behavior problems. *Psychology in the Schools,* 1979, *16,* 38–42.

Harris, A., and Kapche, R. Behavioral modification in schools: ethical issues & suggested guidelines. *Journal of School Psychology,* 1978, *16,* 25–33.

Harris, L. S., and Purohit, P. Bladder training and enuresis: A controlled trial. *Behaviour Research and Therapy,* 1977, *15,* 485–490.

Harris, S. L. Teaching language to nonverbal children with emphasis on problems of generalization. *Psychological Bulletin,* 1975, *82,* 565–580.

Harris, S. L. and Ferrari, M., Developmental factors in child behavior modification. *Behavior Therapy,* 1983, *14,* 54–72.

Harris, S. L., and Ersner-Hershfield, R. Behavioral suppression of seriously disruptive behavior in psychotic and retarded patients: A review of punishment and its alternatives. *Psychological Bulletin,* 1978, *85,* 1352–1375.

Harris, S. L., and Romanczyk, R. G. Treating self-injurious behavior of a retarded child by overcorrection. *Behavior Therapy,* 1976, *7,* 235–239.

Harris, S. L., and Wolchik, S. A. Suppression of self-stimulation: Three alternative strategies. *Journal of Applied Behavior Analysis,* 1979, *12,* 185–198.

Harris, S. L., Wolchik, S. A. and Weitz, S., The acquisition of language skills by autistic children: can parents do the job? *Journal of Autism and Developmental Disabilities,* 1981, *11,* 373–384.

Harris, V. W., and Sherman, J. A. Effects of peer tutoring and consequences on the math performance of elementary classroom students. *Journal of Applied Behavior Analysis,* 1973, *6,* 587–597.

Harris, V. W., Sherman, J. A., Henderson, D. G., and Harris, M. Effects of peer tutoring on the spelling performance of elementary classroom students. In G. Semb (ed.), *Behavior analysis and education—1972.* Lawrence: University of Kansas, 1973, 222–231.

Hart, B. M., and Risley, T. R. Establishing use of descriptive adjectives in the spontaneous speech of disadvantaged preschool children. *Journal of Applied Behavior Analysis,* 1968, *1,* 109–120.

Hart, B. M., and Risley, T. R. The use of preschool materials for modifying the language of disadvantaged children. *Journal of Applied Behavior Analysis*, 1974, *7*, 243–256.

Hart, B. M., and Risley, T. R. Incidental teaching of language in the preschool. *Journal of Applied Behavior Analysis*, 1975, *8*, 411–420.

Hartig, M., and Kanfer, F. H. The role of verbal self-instructions in children's resistance to temptation. *Journal of Personality and Social Psychology*, 1973, *25*, 259–267.

Haskell, M. R., and Yablonsky, L. *Juvenile delinquency*, 2nd ed. Chicago: Rand McNally, 1978.

Hatcher, R. P. Treatment of food refusal in a two-year-old child. *Journal of Behavior Therapy and Experimental Psychiatry*, 1979, *10*, 363–367.

Hatzenbuehler, L. C., and Schroeder, H. E. Desensitization procedures in the treatment of childhood disorders. *Psychological Bulletin*, 1978, *85*, 831–844.

Havelkova, M. Follow-up study of 71 children diagnosed as psychotic in pre-school age. *American Journal of Orthopsychiatry*, 1968, *38*, 846–857.

Hawkins, R. P., Peterson, R. F., Schweid, E. L., and Bijou, S. W. Behaviour therapy in the home: Amelioration of problems parent-child relations with the parent in a therapeutic role. *Journal of Experimental Child Psychology*, 1966, *4*, 99–107.

Hay, W. M., Hay, L. R., and Nelson, R. O. Direct and collateral changes in on-task and academic behavior resulting from on-task versus academic contingencies. *Behavior Therapy*, 1977, *8*, 431–441.

Hayes, S. C. The role of approach contingencies in phobic behavior. *Behavior Therapy*, 1976, *7*, 28–36.

Heaton, R., Safer, D., Allen, R., Spinnoto, N., and Prumo, R. A motivational environment for behaviorally deviant junior high school students. *Journal of Abnormal Child Psychology*, 1976, *4*, 243–276.

Heller, K., and Monahan, J. *Psychology and community change*. Homewood, Ill.: Dorsey Press, 1977.

Helm, D. Psychodynamic and behavior modification approaches to the treatment of infantile autism: Empirical similarities. *Journal of Autism and Childhood Schizophrenia*, 1976, *6*, 27–42.

Henriksen, K., and Doughty, R. Decelerating undesirable behavior in a group of profoundly retarded boys. *American Journal of Mental Deficiency*, 1967, *72*, 40–44.

Herbert, E. W., and Baer, D. M. Training parents as behavior modifiers: Self-recording of contingent attention. *Journal of Applied Behavior Analysis*, 1972, *5*, 139–149.

Herbert, E. W., and Pinkston, E. M., Hayden, M. L., Sajwaj, T. E., Pinkston, S., Cordua, G., and Jackson, D. Adverse effects of differential parental attention. *Journal of Applied Behavior Analysis*, 1973, *6*, 15–30.

Hermelin, B., and O'Connor, N. *Psychological experiments with autistic children*. Oxford, England: Pergamon Press, 1970.

Herrnstein, R. J. Method and theory in the study of avoidance. *Psychological Review*, 1969, *76*, 49–69.

Hersch, C. The discontent explosion in mental health. *American Psychologist*, 1968, *23*, 497–506.

Hersen, M. Treatment of a compulsive and phobic disorder through a total behavior therapy program: A case study. *Psychotherapy: Theory, Research and Practice*, 1968, *5*, 220–225.

Hersen, M. Behavior modification approach to a school phobia case. *Journal of Clinical Psychology*, 1970, *26*, 128–132.

Hersen, M. The behavioral treatment of school phobia. *Journal of Nervous and Mental Disease*, 1971, *153*, 99–107.

Hersen, M. Token economies in institution settings. *Journal of Nervous and Mental Disease*, 1976, *162*, 206–211.

Hersen, M., and Barlow, D. H. Single-case experimental designs: Strategies for studying behavioral change. New York: Pergamon Press, 1976.

Hester, P. Evaluation and accountability in a parent-implemented early intervention service. *Community Mental Health Journal*, 1977, *13*, 261–267.

Hewett, F. M. Teaching reading to an autistic boy through operant conditioning. *American Journal of Orthopsychiatry*, 1964, *17*, 613–618.

Hewett, F. M. Teaching speech to autistic children through operant conditioning. *American Journal of Orthopsychiatry*, 1965, *35*, 927–936.

Hicks, D. Imitation and retention of film-mediated aggressive peer and adult models. *Journal of Personality and Social Psychology*, 1965, *2*, 97–100.

Hill, A. D., and Strain, P. S. The effects of teacher-delivered social reinforcement on the task persistent behavior of educable mentally retarded children. *Psychology in the Schools*, 1977, *14*, 207–212.

Hill, J., Liebert, R., and Mott, D. Vicarious extinction of avoidance behavior through film: An initial test. *Psychological Reports*, 1968, *12*, 192.

Hingtgen, J. N., and Bryson, C. Q. Recent developments in the study of early childhood psychoses: Infantile autism, childhood schizophrenia, and related disorders. *Schizophrenia Bulletin*, 1971, *5*, 8–53.

Hingtgen, J. N., Sanders, B. J., and DeMyer, M. K. Shaping cooperative responses in early childhood schizophrenics. In L. Ullman, and L. Krasner (eds.), *Case studies in behavior modification*. New York: Holt, Rinehart, and Winston, 1965, 130–137.

Hirsch, L., and Walder, L. Training mothers in groups as reinforcement therapists for their own children. *Proceedings, 77th Annual Convention, American Psychological Association*, 1969, *4*, 561–562.

Hobbs, S. A., Forehand, R., and Murray, R. G. Effects of various durations of timeout on the noncompliant behavior of children. *Behavior Therapy*, 1978, *9*, 652–657.

Hobbs, S. A. Moguin, L. E., Tyroler, M., and Lahey, B. B. Cognitive behavior therapy with children: has clinical utility been demonstrated? *Psychological Bulletin*, 1980, *87*, 147–165.

Hodges, P. M., and Deich, R. F. Teaching an artificial language to nonverbal retardates. *Behavior Modification*, 1978, *2*, 489–509.

Hogg, J., and Mittler, P. J. (eds.), *Advances in mental handicap research: Vol. 1*. Chichester: Wiley, 1980.

Holland, C. J. Elimination of fire-setting behavior in a 7-year-old boy. *Behaviour Research and Therapy*, 1969, *7*, 135–137.

Holland, C. J. Directive parental counseling: The parent's manual. *Behavior Therapy*, 1976, *7*, 123–127.

Hollis, J. H. Chlorpromazine: Direct measurement of differential behavioral effect. *Science*, 1968, *159*, 1487–1489.

Hollis, J. H., and Carrier, J. K. Research implications for communication deficiencies. *Exceptional Child*, 1975, *42*, 405–412.

Holmes, F. B. An experimental investigation of a method of overcoming children's fears. *Child Development*, 1936, *7*, 6–30.

Horne, A. M., and Patterson, G. R. Working with parents of aggressive children. In R. R. Abidan, (ed.), *Parent education and intervention handbook.* Springfield, Ill.: Charles C. Thomas, 1980, 159–184.

Horner, R. D. The effects of an environmental "enrichment" program on the behavior of institutionalized profoundly retarded children. *Journal of Applied Behavior Analysis*, 1980, *13*, 473–491.

Horner, R. H., and Brigham, T. A. The effects of self-management procedures on the study behavior of two retarded children. *Education and Training of the Mentally Retarded*, 1979, *14*, 18–24.

Horst, H. M. History of student tutoring at West High School, Akron, Ohio. *Junior Senior High School Clearinghouse*, 1931, *24*, 69–81.

Houts, A. C., and Krasner, L. Slicing the ethical gordian knot: A response to Kitchener. *Journal of Consulting and Clinical Psychology*, 1980, *48*, 8–10.

Howlin, P. A. The effectiveness of operant language training with autistic children. *Journal of Autism and Developmental Disorders*, 1981, *11*, 89–103.

Howlin, P. A., Marchant, R., Rutter, M., Berger, M., Hersov, L., and Yule, W. A home-based approach to the treatment of autistic children. *Journal of Autism and Childhood Schizophrenia*, 1973, *3*, 308–336.

Hugdahl, K. The three-system model of fear and emotion—a critical examination. *Behaviour Research and Therapy*, 1981, *19*, 75–85.

Humphrey, L. L., Karoly, P., and Kirschenbaum, D. S. Self-management in the classroom: Self-imposed response cost versus self-reward. *Behavior Therapy*, 1978, *9*, 592–601.

Humphrey, L., Forehand, R., McMahon, R., and Roberts, M. Parent behavioral training to modify child non-compliance: Effects on untreated siblings. *Journal of Behavior Therapy and Experimental Psychiatry*, 1978, *9*, 235–238.

Hundert, J. The effectiveness of reinforcement, response cost, and mixed programs on classroom behaviors. *Journal of Applied Behavior Analysis*, 1976, *9*, 107.

Hundert, J., and Bucher, B. Pupils' self-scored arithmetic performance: A practical procedure for maintaining accuracy. *Journal of Applied Behavior Analysis*, 1978, *11*, 304.

Hundert, J., Bucher, B., and Henderson, M. Increasing appropriate classroom behavior and academic performance by reinforcing correct work alone. *Psychology in the Schools*, 1976, *13*, 195–200.

Hung, D. Generalization of "curiosity" questioning behavior in autistic children. *Journal of Behavior Therapy and Experimental Psychiatry*, 1977, *8*, 237–246.

Hung, D. Using self-stimulation as reinforcement for autistic children. *Journal of Autism and Childhood Schizophrenia*, 1978, *8*, 355–366.

Hung, D. W. Teaching mute retarded children vocal imitation. *Journal of Behavior Therapy and Experimental Psychiatry*, 1976, *7*, 85–88.

Hutzell, R. R., Platzek, D., and Logue, P. E. Control of symptoms of Gilles de La Tourette's syndrome by self-monitoring. *Journal of Behavior Therapy and Experimental Psychiatry*, 1974, *5*, 71–76.

Ince, L. P. The use of relaxation training and a conditioned stimulus in the elimination of epileptic seizures in a child: A case study. *Journal of Behavior Therapy and Experimental Psychiatry*, 1976, *7*, 39–42.

Insel, P. M., and Moos, R. H. Psychological environments: Expanding the scope of human ecology. *American Psychologist*, 1974, *29*, 179–188.

Isaacs, C. D., Treatment of child abuse: A review of the behavioral interventions. *Journal of Applied Behavior Analysis,* 1982, *15,* 273–294.

Iscoe, I. Community psychology and the competent community. *American Psychologist,* 1974, *29,* 607–613.

Ives, C. C., Harris, S. L., and Wolchik, S. A. Food refusal in an autistic type child treated by a multi-component forced feeding procedure. *Journal of Behavior Therapy and Experimental Psychiatry,* 1978, *9,* 61–64.

Jackson, D. D. (ed.). *Communication, family and marriage.* Palo Alto, Calif.: Science and Behavior Books, 1968.

Jackson, G. M., Johnson, C. R., Ackron, G. S., and Crowley, R. Food satiation as a procedure to decelerate vomiting. *American Journal of Mental Deficiency,* 1975, *80,* 223–227.

Jacob, T. Family interaction in disturbed and normal families: A methodological and substantive review. *Psychological Bulletin,* 1975, *82,* 33–65.

Jacobson, E. *Progressive relaxation.* Chicago: University of Chicago Press, 1929.

Jakibchuk, Z., and Smeriglio, V. L. The influence of symbolic modeling on the social behavior of preschool children with low levels of social responsiveness. *Child Development,* 1976, *47,* 838–841.

Jason, L., and Glenwick, D. Announcement of special issue of *Journal of Community Psychology, Division 25 Recorder,* 1981, *16,* 19.

Jason, L. A., Ferone, L., and Soucy, G. Teaching peer-tutoring behaviors in first- and third-grade classrooms. *Psychology in the Schools,* 1979, *16,* 261–269.

Jeffery, R. W., Wing, R. R., and Stunkard, A. J. Behavioral treatment of obesity: The state of the art 1976. *Behavior Therapy,* 1978, *9,* 189–199.

Jehu, D., Morgan, R. T. T., Turner, R. K., and Jones, A. A controlled trial of the treatment of nocturnal enuresis in residential homes for children. *Behaviour Research and Therapy,* 1977, *15,* 1–16.

Jenkins, S., Bax, M., and Hart, H. Behavioral problems in pre-school children. *Journal of Child Psychology and Psychiatry,* 1980, *21,* 5–17.

Jersild, A. T. *Child psychology,* 6th ed. Englewood Cliffs, N.J.: Prentice-Hall, 1968.

Jersild, A. T., and Holmes, F. B. Children's fears. *Child Development Monograph,* No. 20, 1935. (a)

Jersild, A. T., and Holmes, F. B. Methods of overcoming children's fears. *Journal of Psychology,* 1935, *1,* 75–104. (b)

Jersild, A. T., Markey, F. U., and Jersild, C. L. Children's fears, dreams, wishes, daydreams, likes, dislikes, pleasant and unpleasant memories. *Child Development Monograph,* No. 12, 1933.

Jewett, J., and Clark, H. B. Teaching preschoolers to use appropriate dinnertime conversation: An analysis of generalization from school to home. *Behavior Therapy,* 1979, *10,* 589–605.

Johnson, C. A., and Katz, C. Using parents as change agents for their children: A review. *Journal of Child Psychology and Psychiatry,* 1973, *14,* 181–200.

Johnson, M., and Bailey, J. S. Cross-age tutoring: fifth graders as arithmetic tutors for kindergarten children. *Journal of Applied Behavior Analysis,* 1974, *7,* 223–232.

Johnson, M. R., Whitman, T. L., and Barloon-Noble, R. A home-based program for a pre-school behaviorally disturbed child with parents as therapists. *Journal of Behavior Therapy and Experimental Psychiatry,* 1978, *9,* 65–70.

Johnson, R., and Machen, J. B. Behavior modification techniques and maternal anxiety. *Journal of Dentistry for Children*, 1973, *40*, 272–276.

Johnson, R. K., and Meyer, R. G. Phased biofeedback approach for epileptic seizure control. *Journal of Behavior Therapy and Experimental Psychiatry*, 1974, *5*, 185–187.

Johnson, S. M. Self-reinforcement versus external reinforcement in behavior modification with children. *Developmental Psychology*, 1970, *6*, 147–148.

Johnson, S. M., and Brown, R. A. Producing behavior change in parents of disturbed children. *Journal of Child Psychology and Psychiatry*, 1969, *10*, 107–121.

Johnson, S. M., and Christensen, A. Multiple criteria follow-up of behavior modification with families. *Journal of Abnormal Child Psychology*, 1975, *3*, 135–154.

Johnson, S. M., and Martin, S. Developing self-evaluation as a conditioned reinforcer. In B. A. Ashem and E. G. Poser (eds.), *Adaptive learning: Behavior modification with children*. New York: Pergamon Press, 1973.

Johnson, S. M., Bolstad, O. D., and Lobitz, G. K. *The generalization of children's behavior and behavior change across settings*. Paper read at the International Conference of Behavior Modification, Banff, Canada, May 1974.

Johnson, S. M., Christensen, A., and Bellamy, T. Evaluation of family intervention through unobstrusive audio recordings: Experiences in "bugging" children. *Journal of Applied Behavior Analysis*, 1976, *9*, 213–219.

Joint Commission on Mental Health of Children. *Crisis in child mental health: Challenge for the 1970's*. New York: Harper, 1969.

Joint Commission on Mental Illness and Health. *Action for mental health*. New York: Basic Books, 1961.

Jones, H. G. The behavioral treatment of enuresis nocturna. In H. J. Eysenck (ed.), *Behaviour therapy and the neuroses*. Oxford, England: Pergamon Press, 1960.

Jones, M. C. The elimination of children's fears. *Journal of Experimental Psychology*, 1924, *7*, 382–390. (a)

Jones, M. C. Laboratory study of fear: The case of Peter. *Pedagogical Seminar*, 1924, *31*, 308–315. (b)

Jones, N. M., Loney, H., Weissenburger, F. E., and Fleischmann, D. J. The hyperkinetic child: what do teachers know? *Psychology in the Schools*, 1975, *12*, 388–392.

Journal of Programmed Instruction. Purpose. 1962, *1*, 2.

Kagan, J. Reflection-impulsivity: generality and dynamics of conceptual tempo. *Journal of Abnormal Psychology*, 1966, *71*, 17–24.

Kagan, J., Rosman, B. L., Day, D., Albert, J. J., and Phillips, W. Information processing in the child: Significance of analytic and reflective attitudes. *Psychological Monographs*, 1964, *78*m (whole no. 578).

Kandel, H., Ayllon, T., and Rosenbaum, M. Flooding or systematic exposure in the treatment of extreme social withdrawal in children. *Journal of Behavior Therapy and Experimental Psychiatry*, 1977, *8*, 75–81.

Kanfer, F. H. Issues and ethics in behavior manipulation. *Psychological Reports*, 1965, *16*, 187–196. (a)

Kanfer, F. H. Vicarious human reinforcements: A glimpse into the black box. In L. Krasner, and L. P. Ullmann (eds.), *Research in behavior modification*. New York: Holt, Rinehart and Winston, 1965. (b)

Kanfer, F. H. The maintenance of behavior by self-generated stimuli and reinforcement. In A. Jacobs and L. B. Sachs (eds.), *The psychology of private events*. New York: Academic Press, 1971.

Kanfer, F. H. *Behavior modification in education: A few opinions on critical issues.* Unpublished paper, University of Illinois, 1973.

Kanfer, F. H. and Busemeyer, J. R. The use of problem-solving and decision-making in behavior therapy. *Clinical Psychology Review,* 1982, *2,* 239–266.

Kanfer, F. H., and Grimm, L. G. Freedom of choice and behavioral change. *Journal of Consulting and Clinical Psychology,* 1978, *46,* 873–878.

Kanfer, F. H., and Karoly, P. Self-control: a behavioristic excursion into the lion's den. *Behavior Therapy,* 1972, *3,* 398–416.

Kanfer, F. H., and Phillips, J. S. *Learning foundations of behavior therapy.* New York: Wiley, 1970.

Kanfer, F. H., Cox, L. E., Greiner, J. M., and Karoly, P. Contracts, demand characteristics, and self-control. *Journal of Personality and Social Psychology,* 1974, *30,* 605–619.

Kanfer, F. H., Karoly, P., and Newman, A. Reduction of children's fear of the dark by competence-related and situational threat-related verbal cues. *Journal of Consulting and Clinical Psychology,* 1975, *43,* 251–258.

Kanner, L. Autistic disturbances of affective contact. *Nervous Child,* 1943, *2,* 217–250.

Kanner, L., and Eisenberg, L. Notes on the follow-up studies of autistic children. In P. H. Hock and J. Zubin (eds.), *Psychopathology of childhood.* New York: Grune & Stratton, 1955.

Karlsruher, A. E. The nonprofessional as a psychotherapeutic agent: A review of the empirical evidence pertaining to his effectiveness. *American Journal of Community Psychology,* 1974, *2,* 61–77.

Karnes, M. B., and Zehrbach, R. R. Early education of the handicapped: Program variables and components of an exemplary program. In P. Mittler (ed.), *Research to practice in mental retardation Vol. 1: Care and intervention.* Baltimore, Md.: University Park Press, 1977, 149–156.

Karoly, P. Behavioral self-management in children: Concepts, methods, issues, and directions. In M. Hersen, R. M. Eisler, and P. M. Miller (eds.), *Progress in behavior modification,* Vol. 5. New York: Academic Press, 1977.

Karoly, P., and Dirks, M. J. Developing self-control in preschool-children through correspondence training. *Behavior Therapy,* 1977, *8,* 398–405.

Karoly, P., and Kanfer, H. Effects of prior experiences on self-control in children. *Developmental Psychology,* 1974, *10,* 459–460.

Karoly, P., and Rosenthal, M. Training parents in behavior modification: Effects on perceptions of family interaction and deviant child behavior. *Behavior Therapy,* 1977, *8,* 406–410.

Katz, R. C. Single session recovery from a hemodialysis phobia: A case study. *Journal of Behavior Therapy and Experimental Psychiatry,* 1974, *5,* 205–206.

Kaufman, I. L., Heins, W., and Reiser, D. G. A re-evaluation of the psychodynamics of fire-setting. *American Journal of Orthopsychiatry, 1961, 31,* 123–137.

Kauffman, J., Hallahan, D. P., and Ianna, S. Suppression of a retardate's tongue protrusion by contingent imitation: A case study. *Behaviour Research and Therapy,* 1977, *15,* 196–198.

Kazdin, A. E. Response cost: The removal of conditioned reinforcers for therapeutic change. *Behavior Therapy,* 1972, *3,* 533–546.

Kazdin, A. E. The effect of vicarious reinforcement on attentive behavior in the classroom. *Journal of Applied Behavior Analysis,* 1973, *6,* 71–78.

Kazdin, A. E. Reactive self-monitoring: The effects of response desirability, goal setting, and feedback. *Journal of Consulting and Clinical Psychology*, 1974, *42*, 704–716. (a)

Kazdin, A. E. Self-monitoring and behavior change. In M. J. Mahoney and C. E. Thoresen (eds.), *Self-control: Power to the person*. Monterey, Calif.: Brooks/ Cole, 1974. (b)

Kazdin, A. E. The influence of behavior preceding a reinforced response on behavior change in the classroom. *Journal of Applied Behavior Analysis*, 1977, *10*, 299–310. (a)

Kazdin, A. E. Vicarious reinforcement and direction of behavior change in the classroom. *Behavior Therapy*, 1977, *8*, 57–63. (b)

Kazdin, A. E., and Bootzin, R. R. The token economy: An evaluative review. *Journal of Applied Behavior Analysis*, 1972, *5*, 343–372.

Kazdin, A. E., and Geesey, S. Enhancing classroom attentiveness by preselection of back-up reinforcers in a token economy. *Behavior Modification*, 1980, 98–114.

Kazdin, A. E., Silverman, N. A., and Sittler, J. L. The use of prompts to enhance vicarious effects of nonverbal approval. *Journal of Applied Behavior Analysis*, 1975, *8*, 279–286.

Keating, J. C., Butz, R. A., Burke, E. and Heimberg, R. G. Dry bed training without a urine-alarm: lack of effect of setting and therapist contact with child. *Journal of Behavior Therapy and Experimental Psychiatry*, 1983, *14*, 109–115.

Keehn, J. D. Brief case report: Reinforcement therapy of incontinence. *Behaviour and Research Therapy*, 1965, *2*, 239.

Keeley, S. M., Shemberg, K. M., and Ferber, H. The training and use of undergraduates as behavior analysts in the consultative process. *Professional Psychology*, 1973, *4*, 59–63.

Keller, M. F., and Carlson, P. M. The use of symbolic modeling to promote social skills in preschool children with low levels of social responsiveness. *Child Development*, 1974, *45*, 912–919.

Kelley, C. K. Play desensitization of fear of darkness in preschool children. *Behaviour Research and Therapy*, 1976, *14*, 79–81.

Kellman, D. H. Gilles de la Tourette's disease in children: A review of the literature. *Journal of Child Psychology and Psychiatry*, 1965, *6*, 219–226.

Kelly, E. W. School phobia: A review of theory and treatment. *Psychology in the Schools*, 1973, *10*, 33–42.

Kelly, J. A., and Drabman, R. S. Generalizing response suppression of self-injurious behavior through an overcorrection punishment procedure: A case study. *Behavior Therapy*, 1977, 468–472.

Kelly, J. A., Forman, W., Phillips, J., Hathorn, S., and Wilson, T. Teaching conversational skills to retarded adolescents. *Child Behavior Therapy*, 1979, *1*, 85–97.

Kelly, J. A., Wildman, B. G., and Berler, E. S. Small group behavioral training to improve the job interview skills repertoire of mildly retarded adolescents. *Journal of Applied Behavior Analysis*, 1980, *13*, 461–471.

Kempe, C. Approaches to preventing child abuse. *American Journal Disabled Child*, 1976, *30*, 941–947.

Kendall, P. C. On the efficacious use of verbal self-instructional procedures with children. *Cognitive Therapy and Research*, 1977, *1*, 331–341.

Kendall, P. C., and Finch, A. J. A cognitive-behavioral treatment for impulse control: A case study. *Journal of Consulting and Clinical Psychology*, 1976, *44*, 852–857.

Kendall, P. C., and Wilcox, L. E. Self-control in children: Development of a rating scale. *Journal of Consulting and Clinical Psychology*, 1979, *47*, 1020–1029.

Kendall, P. C., and Wilcox, L. E. Cognitive-behavioral treatment for impulsivity: Concrete versus conceptual training in non-self-controlled problem children. *Journal of Consulting and Clinical Psychology*, 1980, *48*, 80–91.

Kennedy, W. A. School phobia: Rapid treatment of fifty cases. *Journal of Abnormal Psychology*, 1945, *70*, 285–289.

Kent, R. N., and O'Leary, K. D. A controlled evaluation of behavior modification with conduct problem children. *Journal of Consulting and Clinical Psychology*, 1976, *44*, 586–596.

Khan, A. U., Staerk, M., and Bonk, C. Role of counterconditioning in the treatment of asthma. *Journal of Psychosomatic Research*, 1973, *17*, 389.

Kiernan, C. A strategy for research on the use of nonvocal systems of communication. *Journal of Autism and Developmental Disabilities*, 1981, *11*, 139–151.

Kimmel, H. D. Instrumental conditioning of autonomically mediated behavior. *Psychological Bulletin*, 1967, *67*, 337–345.

Kimmel, H. D., and Kimmel, E. C. An instrumental conditioning method for the treatment of enuresis. *Journal of Behavior Therapy and Experimental Psychiatry*, 1970, *1*, 121–123.

King, N. J. The behavioral management of asthma and asthma-related problems in children: A critical review of the literature. *Journal of Behavioral Medicine*, 1980, *3*, 169–189.

Kingsley, R. G., and Shapiro, J. A comparison of three behavioral programs for the control of obesity in children. *Behavior Therapy*, 1977, *8*, 30–36.

Kirschner, N. M., and Levin, L. A direct school intervention program for the modification of aggressive behavior. *Psychology in the schools*, 1975, *12*, 202–208.

Kissel, S. Systematic desensitization therapy with children: A case study and some suggested modifications. *Professional Psychology*, 1972, *3*, 164–168.

Kitchener, R. F. Ethical relativism, ethical naturalism, and behavior therapy. *Journal of Consulting and Clinical Psychology*, 1980, *48*, 14–16.

Klein, N. C., Alexander, J. F., and Parsons, B. V. Impact of family systems intervention on recidivism and sibling delinquency: A model of primary prevention and program evaluation. *Journal of Consulting and Clinical Psychology*, 1977, *45*, 469–474.

Klein, R. D. Modifying academic performance in the grade school classroom. In M. Hersen, R. M. Eisler, and P. M. Miller (eds.), *Progress in Behavior Modification*, 1979, *8*, 293–321.

Kleinknecht, R. A., and Bernstein, D. A. Short term treatment of dental avoidance. *Journal of Behavior Therapy and Experimental Psychiatry*, 1979, *10*, 311–315.

Klingman, A. and Weisner, E. The relationship of proximity to tension areas and size of settlement to fear levels of Israeli children. *Journal of Behavior Therapy and Experimental Psychiatry*, 1982, *13*, 321–323.

Klorman, R., Hilpert, P. L., Michael, R., LaGana, C., and Sveen, C. B. Effects of coping and mastery modeling on experienced and inexperienced pedodontic patients' disruptiveness. *Behavior Therapy*, 1980, *11*, 156–168.

Knapp, T. J., and Wells, Behavior therapy for asthma: A review. *Behaviour Research and Therapy*, 1978, *16*, 103–115.

Knapczyk, D. R., and Livingston, G. Self-recording and student teacher supervision: Variables within a token economy structure. *Journal of Applied Behavior Analysis*, 1973, *6*, 481–486.

Knight, M., and McKenzie, H. S. Elimination of bedtime thumbsucking in home settings through contingent readings. *Journal of Applied Behavior Analysis*, 1974, *7*, 33–38.

Knowles, J. H. The responsibility of the individual. In J. H. Knowles (ed.), *Doing better and feeling worse: Health in the United States*. New York: Norton, 1977.

Koegel, R. L., and Rincover, A. Treatment of psychotic children in a classroom environment: I. Learning in a large group. *Journal of Applied Behavior Analysis*, 1974, *7*, 45–59.

Koegel, R. L., and Rincover, A. Some detrimental effects of using extra stimuli to guide responding in autistic children and normal children. *Journal of Abnormal Child Psychology*, 1976, *4*, 59–71.

Koegel, R. L., and Rincover, A. Research on the difference between generalization and maintenance in extra-therapy responding. *Journal of Applied Behavior Analysis*, 1977, *10*, 1–12.

Koegel, R. L., and Schreibman, L. Teaching autistic children to respond to simultaneous multiple cues. *Journal of Experimental Child Psychology*, 1977, *24*, 299–311.

Koegel, R. L., and Wilhelm, H. Selective responding to the components of multiple visual cues by autistic children. *Journal of Experimental Child Psychology*, 1973, *15*, 442–453.

Koegel, R. L., and Williams, J. A. Direct versus indirect response-reinforcer relationships in teaching autistic children. *Journal of Abnormal Child Psychology*, 1980, *8*, 537–547.

Koegel, R., Russo, D., and Rincover, A. Assessing and training teachers in the generalized use of behavior modification with autistic children. *Journal of Applied Behavior Analysis*, 1977, *10*, 197–206.

Koegel, R. L., Glahn, T. J., and Nieminen, G. S. Generalization of parent-training results. *Journal of Applied Behavior Analysis*, 1978, *11*, 95–110.

Koegel, R. L., Schreibman, L., Britten, K., and Laitinen, R. The effects of schedule of reinforcement on stimulus overselectivity in autistic children. *Journal of Autism and Developmental Disorders*, 1979, *9*, 383–397.

Koegel, R. L., Dunlap, G., and Dyer, K. Intertrial interval duration and learning in autistic children. *Journal of Applied Behavior Analysis*, 1980, *13*, 91–99.

Kolansky, H. Treatment of a three-year-old girl's severe infantile neurosis: Stammering and insect phobia. *Psychoanalytic Study of the Child*, 1960, *15*, 261–285.

Kolb, D. A., and Boyatzis, R. E. Goal setting and self-directed behavior change. *Human Relations*, 1970, *23*, 439–458.

Kolko, D. J., Anderson, L., and Campbell, M. Sensory preference and overselective responding in autistic children. *Journal of Autism and Developmental Disorders*, 1980, *10*, 259–271.

Konstantareas, M. M., Oxman, J., and Webster, C. D. Simultaneous communication with autistic and other severely dysfunctional nonverbal children. *Journal of Communicative Disorders*, 1977, *10* 267–282.

Konstantareas, M. M., Webster, C. D., and Oxman, J. Manual language acquisition and its influence on other areas of functioning in four autistic-like children. *Journal of Child Psychology and Psychiatry*, 1979, *20*, 337–350.

Kornhaber, R. C., and Schroeder, H. E. Importance of model similarity on the extinction of avoidance behavior in children. *Journal of Consulting and Clinical Psychology*, 1975, *43*, 601–607.

Kozak, M. J., and Miller, G. A. Hypothetical constructs *vs.* intervening variables: a re-appraisal of the three-systems model of anxiety assessment. *Behavioral Assessment,* 1982, *4,* 347–358.

Kozlowski, N., and Richman, J. Operant training of head control and beginning language for a severely developmentally disabled child. *Journal of Behavior Therapy and Experimental Psychiatry,* 1977, *8,* 437–440.

Krug, D. A., Arick, J., and Almond, P. Behavior checklist for identifying severely handicapped individuals with high levels of autistic behavior. *Journal of Child Psychology and Psychiatry and Allied Disciplines,* 1980, *21,* 221–229.

Kubie, L. Resolution of a traffic phobia in conversations between a father and son. *Psychoanalytic Quarterly,* 1937, *6,* 223–226.

Kurtz, P. D., and Neisworth, J. T. Self-control possibilities for exceptional children. *Exceptional Children,* 1976, *42,* 212–217.

Kushner, M. The operant control of intractable sneezing. In D. Spielberger, B. Fox, and B. Masterson (eds.), *Contributions to general psychology.* New York: Appleton-Century-Crofts, 1968.

L'Abate, L. Early infantile autism: A reply to Ward. *Psychological Bulletin,* 1972, *77,* 49–51.

LaGreca, A. M., and Ottinger, D. R. Self-monitoring and relaxation training in the treatment of medically ordered exercises in a 12-year-old female. *Journal of Pediatric Psychology,* 1979, *4,* 49–54.

LaGreca, A. M., and Santogrossi, D. A. Social skills training with elementary school students: A behavioral group approach. *Journal of Consulting and Clinical Psychology,* 1980, *48,* 220–227.

Lal, H., and Lindsley, O. R. Therapy of chronic constipation in a young child by rearranging social contingencies. *Behaviour Research and Therapy,* 1968, *6,* 484–485.

Lally, M. Computer-assisted teaching of sight-word recognition for mentally retarded school children. *American Journal of Mental Deficiency,* 1981, *85,* 383–388.

Lamal, P. A. A simple technique for reducing self-stimulatory behavior of a retarded child. *Journal of Applied Behavior Analysis,* 1976, *9,* 140.

Lambert, N. M., and Sandoval, J. The prevalence of learning disabilities in a sample of children considered hyperactive. *Journal of Abnormal Child Psychology,* 1980, *8,* 33–50.

Lane, R. G., and Dormath, R. P. Behavior therapy: A case history. *Hospital and Community Psychiatry,* 1970, *21,* 150–153.

Lang, P. J. Behavior therapy with a case of nervous anorexia. In L. P. Ullman and L. Krasner (eds.), *Case studies in behavior modification.* New York: Holt, Rinehart, and Winston, 1965.

Lang, P. J. Imagery in therapy: An information processing analysis of fear. *Behavior Therapy,* 1977, *8,* 862–886.

Lang, P. J., and Lazovik, A. D. The experimental desensitization of an animal phobia. *Journal of Abnormal and Social Psychology,* 1963, *66,* 519–525.

Lang, P. J., and Melamed, B. G. Avoidance conditioning therapy of an infant with chronic ruminative vomiting. Case report: *Journal of Abnormal Psychology,* 1969, *74,* 1–8.

Lapouse, R., and Monk, M. An epidemiologic study of behavioral characteristics in children. *American Journal of Public Health,* 1958, *48,* 1134–1144.

Lapouse, R., and Monk, M. Fears and worries in a representative sample of children. *American Journal of Orthopsychiatry,* 1, *29,* 803–818.

Lassen, M. K., and Fluet, H. R. Elimination of nocturnal thumbsucking by glove wearing. *Journal of Behavior Therapy and Experimental Psychiatry*, 1978, *9*, 85.

Lasser, B. R. Teaching mothers of mongoloid children to use behavior modification procedures. *Dissertation Abstracts*, 1970, *30*, 5239A–5340A.

Latimer, P. R. The behavioral treatment of self-excoriation in a twelve-year-old girl. *Journal of Behavior Therapy and Experimental Psychiatry*, 1979, *10*, 349–352.

Lavigueur, H. The use of siblings as adjunct to the behavioral treatment of children in the home with parents as behavior therapists. *Behavior Therapy*, 1976, *7*, 602–613.

Lavigueur, H., Peterson, R. F., Sheese, J. G., and Peterson, L. W. Behavioral treatment in the home: Effects on an untreated sibling and long-term follow-up. *Behavior Therapy*, 1973, *4*, 431–441.

Lavoie, J. C. Punishment and adolescent self-control. *Developmental Psychology*, 1973, *8*, 16–24.

Lawrence, D. H. The transfer of discrimination along a continuum. *Journal of Comparative and Physiological Psychology*, 1952, *45*, 511–516.

Layne, C. C., Rickard, H. C., Jones, M. T., and Lyman, R. D. Accuracy of self-monitoring on a variable ratio schedule of observer verification. *Behavior Therapy*, 1976, *7*, 481–488.

Lazarus, A. A. The elimination of children's phobias by deconditioning. In H. J. Eysenck (ed.), *Behavior therapy and the neuroses*. New York: Pergamon, 1960.

Lazarus, A. A., and Abramovitz, A. The use of "emotive imagery" in the treatment of children's phobias. *Journal of Mental Science*, 1962, *108*, 191–195.

Ledwidge, B. Cognitive behavior modification: A step in the wrong direction? *Psychological Bulletin*, 1978, *85*, 353–375.

Leff, R. Behavior modification and the psychoses of childhood: A review. *Psychological Bulletin*, 1968, *69*, 396–409.

Lefkowitz, M. M., and Tesiny, E. P. Assessment of childhood depression. *Journal of Consulting and Clinical Psychology*, 1980, *48*, 43–50.

Leitenberg, H., and Callahan, E. J. Reinforced practice and reduction of different kinds of fears in adults and children. *Behaviour Research and Therapy*, 1973, *11*, 19–30.

Leitenberg, H., Agras, W. S., and Thomson, L. E. A sequential analysis of the effect of selective positive reinforcement in modifying anorexia nervosa. *Behaviour Research and Therapy*, 1968, *6*, 211–218.

Leon, G. R., and Roth, S. Obesity: Psychological causes, correlations, and speculations. *Psychological Bulletin*, 1977, *84*, 117–139.

Lepper, M., Sagotsky, J., and Mailer, J. Generalization and persistence of effects of exposure to self-reinforcement models. *Child Development*, 1975, *46*, 618–630.

Lerner, R. M. The development of personal space schemata toward body build. *The Journal of Psychology*, 1973, *84*, 229–235.

Levenson, A. J., and Reff, S. R. Community mental health center staffing patterns. *Community Mental Health Journal*, 1970, *6*, 118–125.

Leventhal, H., and Cleary, P. D. The smoking problem: A review of the research and theory in behavioral risk modification. *Psychological Bulletin*, 1980, *88*, 370–405.

Levine, A. G. *Love Canal: Science, politics, and people*. Lexington, Mass.: Heath, 1982.

Levine, F. M., and Fasnacht, G. Token rewards may lead to token learning. *American Psychologist*, 1974, *29*, 816–820.

Levine, F. M., Fasnacht, G., Funabiki, D., and Burkart, M. R. Methodological considerations regarding the evaluation of maintenance of gains due to token programs. *Psychology in the Schools,* 1979, *16,* 568–574.

Levine, M., and Graziano, A. M. Intervention programs in elementary schools, New York: 1968–1978. In S. E. Golan and C. Eisdorfer (eds.), *Handbook of community psychology, and mental health.* New York: Appleton-Century-Crofts, 1981.

Levine, M., and Graziano, A. M. Mental health approaches in elementary schools. In S. Golann and C. Eisdorfer (eds.), *Handbook of community psychology, and mental health.* New York: Appleton-Century-Crofts, 1972 (2nd ed., 1981).

Levine, M., and Levine, A. *A social history of helping services.* New York: Appleton-Century-Crofts, 1970.

Levine, R. A. Treatment in the home. *Social Work,* 1964, *9,* 19–28.

Levitt, E. E. The results of psychotherapy with children: An evaluation. *Journal of Consulting Psychology,* 1957, *21,* 189–196.

Lewis, B. L., and Strain, P. S. Effects of feedback timing and motivational content on teachers' delivery of contingent social praise. *Psychology in the Schools,* 1978, *15,* 423–429.

Lewis, S. A comparison of behavior therapy techniques in the reduction of fearful avoidance behavior. *Behavior Therapy,* 1974, *5,* 648–655.

Lichstein, K., and Schreibman, L. Employing electric shock with autistic children: A review. *Journal of Autism and Childhood Schizophrenia,* 1976, *6,* 163–174.

Lichstein, K., and Wahler, R. The ecological assessment of an autistic child. *Journal of Abnormal Child Psychology,* 1976, *4,* 31–54.

Lick, J. Statistical vs. clinical significance in research on the outcome of psychotherapy. *International Journal of Mental Health,* 1973, *2,* 26–37.

Lick, J., and Bootzin, R. Expectancy factors in the treatment of fear: Methodological and theoretical issues. *Psychological Bulletin,* 1975, *82,* 917–931.

Lick, J., and Unger, T. The external validity of laboratory fear assessment: Implications from two case studies. *Journal of Consulting and Clinical Psychology,* 1975, *43,* 864–866.

Liebert, R. M., Spiegler, M. D., and Hall, W. M. Effects of the value of contingent self-administered and non-contingent externally imposed reward on children's behavioral productivity. *Psychonomic Science,* 1970, *18,* 245–246.

Liebman, R., Minuchin, S., and Baker, L. An integrated program for anorexia nervosa. *American Journal of Psychiatry,* 1974, *131,* 432–435.

Lindsley, O. R. Direct measurement and prosthesis of retarded behavior. *Journal of Education,* 1964, *147,* 62–81.

Lindsley, O. R. An experiment with parents handling behavior at home. *Johnstone Bulletin,* 1966, *9,* 26–36.

Lindsley, O. R. An experiment with parents handling behavior at home. In F. A. Gargo, C. Bahrns, and P. Nolen (eds.), *Behavior modification in the classroom.* Belmont, Calif.: Wadsworth, 1970, 310–316.

Linscheid, T. R., Copeland, A. P., Jacobstein, D. M., and Smith, J. L. Overcorrection treatment for nighttime self-injurious behavior in two normal children. *Journal of Pediatric Psychology,* 1981, *6,* 29–38.

Logan, D. L., and Garner, D. Effective behavior modification for reducing chronic soiling. *American Annals of the Deaf,* 1971, *116,* 382–384.

London, P. *The modes and morals of psychotherapy.* New York: Holt, Rinehart and Winston, 1964.

London, P. *Behavior control.* New York: Harper & Row, 1971.

Lovaas, O. I. Cue properties of words: The control of operant responding by rate and content of verbal operants. *Child Development*, 1964, *35*, 245–256.

Lovaas, O. I. *The autistic child: Language development through behavior modification*. New York: Irvington, 1977.

Lovaas, O. I. Contrasting illness and behavior models for the treatment of autistic children: A historical perspective. *Journal of Autism and Developmental Disorders*, 1979, *9*, 315–322.

Lovaas, O. I., and Koegel, R. L. *Behavior modification in education, NSSE Yearbook*. Chicago: University of Chicago Press, 1973.

Lovaas, O. I., and Schreibman, L. Stimulus over selectivity of autistic children in a two stimulus situation. *Behaviour Research and Therapy*, 1971, *2*, 305–310.

Lovaas, O. I., Freitag, G., Kinder, M. I., Rubenstein, B. D., Schaeffer, B., and Simmons, J. Q. *Experimental studies in childhood schizophrenia. Developing behavior using electric shock*. Paper presented at the American Psychological Association, Los Angeles, 1964.

Lovaas, O. I., Freitag, G., Gold, V. J., and Kassorla, I. C. Experimental studies in childhood schizophrenia: Analysis of self-destructive behavior. *Journal of Experimental Child Psychology*, 1965, *2*, 67–84. (a)

Lovaas, O. I., Schaeffer, B., and Simmons, J. Q. Building social behavior in autistic children by use of electric shock. *Journal of Experimental Research in Personality*, 1965, *1*, 99–109. (b)

Lovaas, O. I., Berberich, J. P., Perloff, B. F., and Schaeffer, B. Acquisition of imitative speech in schizophrenic children. *Science*, 1966, *151*, 705–707.

Lovaas, O. I., Schreibman, L., Koegel, R., and Rehm, R. Selective responding by autistic children to multiple sensory input. *Journal of Abnormal Psychology*, 1971, *77*, 211–222.

Lovaas, O. I., Koegel, R., Simmons, J. Q., and Long, J. S. Some generalizations and follow-up measures on autistic children in behavior therapy. *Journal of Applied Behavior Analysis*, 1973, *6*, 131–166.

Lovaas, O. I., Schreibman, L., and Koegel, R. L. A behavior modification approach to the treatment of autistic children. *Journal of Autism and Childhood Schizophrenia*, 1974, *4*, 111–129.

Love, L. R. *Information feedback as a method of clinical intervention*. Paper read at the American Psychological Association, New York, September, 1966.

Lovibond, S. H. Conditioning and enuresis. New York: Pergamon Press, 1964.

Lovitt, T. C. Self-management projects with children with behavioral disabilities. *Journal of Learning Disabilities*, 1973, *6*, 15–28.

Lovitt, T. C., and Curtiss, K. A. Academic response rate as a function of teacher- and self-imposed contingencies. *Journal of Applied Behavior Analysis*, 1969, *2*, 49–53.

Lowe, K., and Lutzker, J. R. Increasing compliance to a medical regimen with a juvenile diabetic. *Behavior Therapy*, 1979, *10*, 57–64.

Ludlow, J. R. Study of a group of children in Kent suffering from Down's syndrome. *Journal of Mental Deficiency Research*, 1979, *23*, 29–44.

Ludwig, A., Marx, A., and Hill, P. Chronic schizophrenics and behavioral engineers. *Journal of Nervous and Mental Diseases*, 1971, *152*, 31–44.

Ludwig, A. M., Marx, A. J., Hill, P., and Browning, R. M. The control of violent behavior through faradic shock. *Journal of Nervous and Mental Disease*, 1969, *148*, 624–637.

Luiselli, J. Treatment of an autistic child's fear of riding a school bus through exposure and reinforcement. *Journal of Behavior Therapy and Experimental Psychiatry,* 1978, *9,* 169–172.

Luiselli, J. K., Helfen, C. S., Pemberton, B. W., and Reisman, J. The elimination of a child's in-class masturbation by overcorrection and reinforcement. *Journal of Behavior Therapy and Experimental Psychiatry,* 1977, *8,* 201–204.

Lundman, R. J., and Scarpitti, F. R. Delinquency prevention: Recommendations for future projects. *Crime and Delinquency,* 1978, *24,* 207–220.

Lundman, R. J., McFarlane, P. T., and Scarpitti, F. R. Delinquency prevention: A description and assessment of projects reported in the professional literature. *Crime and Delinquency,* July 1976, 297–308.

Luria, A. R. *The role of speech in the regulation of normal and abnormal behavior.* New York: Liveright, 1961.

Lyle, J. G. The effect of an institutional environment upon the verbal development of institutional children. I: Verbal intelligence. *Journal of Mental Deficiency Research,* 1959, *3,* 122–128.

Lysaught, T. V., and Burchard, J. D. The analysis and modification of a deviant parent-youth communication pattern. *Journal of Behavior Therapy and Experimental Psychiatry,* 1975, *6,* 339–342.

Maccoby, F. F., and Wilson, W. C. Identification and observational learning from films. *Journal of Abnormal and Social Psychology,* 1957, *55,* 76–87.

McCord, J. A. Thirty-year follow-up of treatment effects. *American Psychologist,* 1978, *33,* 284–289.

McCullough, J. P., Huntsinger, G. M., and Nay, W. R. Self-control treatment of aggression in a 16 year old male. *Journal of Consulting and Clinical Psychology,* 1977, *45,* 322–331.

McDonagh, M. J. Is operant conditioning effective in reducing enuresis and encopresis in children? *Perspective Psychiatric Care,* 1971, *9,* 17–23.

McDonald, J. E., and Trepper, T. Enuresis: An historical, cultural, and contemporary account of etiology and treatment. *Psychology in the Schools,* 1977, *14,* 308–314.

MacDonald, M. L. Multiple impact behavior therapy in a child's dog phobia. *Journal of Behavior Therapy and Experimental Psychiatry,* 1975, *6,* 317–322.

MacFarlane, J. W., Allen, L., and Honzik, M. P. *A developmental study of the behavior problems of normal children between twenty-one months and fourteen years.* Berkeley: University of California Press, 1954.

McGrath, P., Marshall, P. G., and Prior, K. A comprehensive treatment program for a fire-setting child. *Journal of Behavior Therapy and Experimental Psychiatry,* 1979, *10,* 69–72.

MacGregor, R., Ritchie, A., Serrano, A. C., Shuster, F. P., Macdonald, E. C., and Goolishian, H. A. *Multiple impact therapy with families.* New York: McGraw-Hill, 1964.

Machen, J. B., and Johnson, R. Desensitization, model learning, and the dental behavior of children. *Journal of Dental Research,* 1974, *53,* 83–87.

McKeethen, W. B. *Behavioral treatment of child-abusing parents.* Unpublished paper, State University of New York at Buffalo, 1981.

McKenzie, T. L., and Rushall, B. S. Effects of self-recording on attendance and performance in a competitive swimming training environment. *Journal of Applied Behavior Analysis,* 1974, *7,* 199–206.

McLaughlin, T. F. An analysis of self-control procedures in the maintenance of behavior. *Corrective and Social Psychiatry and Journal of Applied Behavior Technology*, 1975, *21*, 12–16.

McMahon, R. J., and Forehand, R. Nonprescription behavior therapy: Effectiveness of a brochure in teaching mothers to correct their children' inappropriate mealtime behaviors. *Behavior Therapy*, 1978, *9*, 814–820.

McMains, M., and Liebert, R. Influence of discrepancies between successively modeled self-reward criteria on the adoption of a self-imposed standard. *Journal of Personality and Social Psychology*, 1968, *8*, 166–171.

MacMillan, D. L., Meyers, C. E., and Morrison, G. M. System-identification of mildly mentally retarded children: Implications for interpreting and conducting research. *American Journal of Mental Deficiency*, 1980, *85*, 108–1158.

McNamara, E., and Heard, C. Self-control through self-recording. *Special Education Forward Trends*, 1976, *3*, 21–23.

MacNamara, M. Helping children through their mothers. *Journal of Child Psychology and Psychiatry*, 1963, *4*, 29–46.

Madsen, C. H. Positive reinforcement in toilet training of a normal child: A case report. In L. P. Ullman and L. Krasner (eds.), *Case studies in behavior modification*. New York: Holt, 1965, 305–306.

Madsen, C. H., Becker, W. C., and Thomas, D. R. Rules, praise and ignoring: elements of elementary classroom control. *Journal of Applied Behavior Analysis*, 1977, *10*, 465–478.

Magrab, P. R. (ed.). *Psychological management of pediatric problems, Vol. I: Early life conditions and chronic diseases*, Baltimore, Md.: University Park Press, 1978.

Magrab, P. R., and Calcagno, P. L. Psychological impact of chronic pediatric conditions. In P. R. Magrab, (ed.), *Psychological management of pediatric problems, Vol. I.*, Baltimore, Md.: University Park Press, 1978, 3–14.

Magrab, P. R., and Papadopoulou, Z. L. The effect of a token economy on dietary compliance for children on hemodialysis. *Journal of Applied Behavior Analysis*, 1977, *10*, 573–578.

Maher,-Loughan, G. P., MacDonald, N., Mason, A. A., and Fry, L. Controlled trial of hypnosis in the symptomatic treatment of asthma. *British Medical Journal*, 1962, *2*, 371–376.

Mahoney, M. J. Toward an experimental analysis of coverant control. *Behavior Therapy*, 1970, *1*, 510–521.

Mahoney, M. J. Terminal terminology: A self-regulated response to Goldiamond. *Journal of Applied Behavior Analysis*, 1976, *9*, 515–517.

Mahoney, M. J., and Mahoney, K. Self-control techniques with the mentally retarded. *Exceptional Children*, 1976, *42*, 338–339.

Mahoney, M. J., and Thoreson, C. E. *Self-control: Power to the person*. Monterey, Calif.: Brooks/Cole, 1974.

Main, G., and Munro, B. A token reinforcement program in a public junior high school. *Journal of Applied Behavior Analysis*, 1977, *10*, 93–94.

Malmquist, C. P. The delinquent and the insane: Right and adequacy of treatment. *American Journal of Orthopsychiatry*, 1970, *40*, 388–396.

Maloney, D. M., Harper, T. M., Braukmann, C. J., Fixsen, D. L., Phillips, E. L., and Wolf, M. M. Teaching conversation-related skills to predelinquent girls. *Journal of Applied Behavior Analysis*, 1976, *9*, 371.

Mann, J. Vicarious desensitization of test anxiety through observation of videotaped treatment. *Journal of Counseling Psychology*, 1972, *19*, 1–7.

Mann, J., and Rosenthal, T. L. Vicarious and direct counterconditioning of test anxiety through individual and group desensitization. *Behaviour Research and Therapy*, 1969, *7*, 359–367.

Manosevitz, M., and Lanyon, R. I. Fear survey schedule: A normative study. *Psychological Reports*, 1965, *17*, 699–703.

Marburg, C. C., Houston, B. K., and Holmes, D. S. Influence of multiple models on the behavior of institutionalized retarded children: Increased generalization to other models and behaviors. *Journal of Consulting and Clinical Psychology*, 1976, *44*, 514–519.

Margolies, P. J. Behavioral approaches to the treatment of early infantile autism: A review. *Psychological Bulletin*, 1977, *84*, 249–269.

Marholin, D., Luiselli, J. K., Robinson, M., and Lott, I. T. Response-contingent taste-aversion in treating chronic ruminative vomiting of institutionalized profoundly retarded children. *Journal of Mental Deficiency Research*, 1980, *24*, 47–56.

Marholin, D., II, Steinman, W., McInnis, E., and Heads, T. The effect of teacher's presence in the classroom behavior of conduct problem children. *Journal of Abnormal Child Psychology*, 1975, *3*, 11–24.

Marks, I. M. *Fears and phobias*. New York: Academic Press, 1969.

Marks, I. M., and Gelder, D. M. Different ages of onset in varieties of phobia. *American Journal of Psychiatry*, 1966, *123*, 218–221.

Marks, I. M., Connolly, J., and Hallam, R. S. Psychiatric nurse as therapist. *British Medical Journal*, 1973, *3*, 156–160.

Marlowe, R. H., Madsen, C. H. Jr., Bowen, C. E., Reardon, R. C., and Logue, P. E. Severe classroom behavior problems: teachers or counselors. *Journal of Applied Behavior Analysis*, 1978, *1*, 53–66.

Marshall, G. R. Toilet training of an autistic eight-year-old through operant conditioning therapy: A case report. *Behaviour Research and Therapy*, 1966, *4*, 242–245.

Martin, B. Brief family intervention: Effectiveness, and the importance of including the father. *Journal of Consulting and Clinical Psychology*, 1977, *45*, 1002–-1010.

Martin, B., and Kubly, D. Results of treatment of enuresis by a conditioned response method. *Journal of Consulting Psychology*, 1955, *19*, 71–73.

Martin, G. L., and Heimstra, N. W. The perception of hazard by children. *Journal of Safety Research*, 1973, *5*, 238–246.

Martin, R. *Legal challenges to behavior modification*. Champaign, Ill.: Research Press, 1975.

Martin, R. D., and Conway, J. B. Aversive stimulation to eliminate infant nocturnal rocking. *Journal of Behavior Therapy and Experimental Psychiatry*, 1976, *7*, 200–201.

Martin, S. *The comparability of behavioral data in laboratory and natural settings*. Paper read at the Banff International Conference on Behavior Modification, Banff, Canada, May, 1974.

Mash, E. J., and Hedley, J. Effect of observer as a function of prior history of social interaction. *Perceptual and Motor Skills*, 1975, *40*, 659–669.

Mastellone, M. Aversion therapy: A new use for the old rubber band. *Journal of Behavior Therapy and Experimental Psychiatry*, 1974, *5*, 311–312.

Masterpasqua, F. Toward a synergism of developmental and community psychology. *American Psychologist*, 1981, *36*, 782–786.

Masters, J., and Miller, D. Early infantile autism: A methodological critique. *Journal of Abnormal Psychology*, 1970, *75*, 342–343.

Masters, J. C., and Mokros, J. R. Self-reinforcement processes in children. In H. Reese (ed.), *Advances in child development and behavior*, Vol. 9. New York: Academic Press, 1974.

Masters, J. C., and Santrock, J. W. Studies in the self-regulation of behavior: Effects of contingent cognitive and affective events. *Developmental Psychology*, 1976, *12*, 334–348.

Mastria, E., Mastria, M., and Harkins, J. Treatment of child abuse by behavioral intervention: a case report. *Child Welfare*, 1979, *43*, 253–261.

Matarazzo, J. D. Behavioral health and behavioral medicine: Frontiers for a new health psychology. *American Psychologist*, 1980, *35*, 807–817.

Mathews, A. Fear-reduction research and clinical phobias. *Psychological Bulletin*, 1978, *85*, 390–404.

Mathis, M. I. Training of a "disturbed" boy using the mother as a therapist: A case study. *Behavior Therapy*, 1971, *2*, 233–239.

Matson, J. L., and Ollendick, T. H. Elimination of low-frequency biting. *Behavior Therapy*, 1976, *7*, 410–413.

Matson, J. L., Horne, A. M., Ollendick, D. G., and Ollendick, T. H. Overcorrection: a further evaluation of restitution and positive practice. *Journal of Behavior Therapy and Experimental Psychiatry*, 1979, *10*, 295–298.

Matson, J. L., Ollendich, T. H., and Martin, J. E. Overcorrection revisited: A long-term follow-up. *Journal of Behavior Therapy and Experimental Psychiatry*, 1979, *10*, 11–13.

Maurer, A. What children fear. *Journal of Genetic Psychology*, 1965, *106*, 265–277.

Measel, C. J., and Alfieri, P. A. Treatment of self-injurious behavior by a combination of reinforcement for incompatible behavior and overcorrection. *American Journal of Mental Deficiency*, 1976, *81*, 147.

Medland, M. B., and Stachnik, T. J. Good-behavior game: A replication and systematic analysis. *Journal of Applied Behavior Analysis*, 1972, *5*, 45–51.

Meichenbaum, D. Examination of model characteristics in reducing avoidance behavior. *Journal of Personality and Social Psychology*, 1971, *17*, 298–307.

Meichenbaum, D. Self-instructional methods. In F. H. Kanfer and A. P. Goldstein (eds.), *Helping people change*. New York: Pergamon Press, 1975.

Meichenbaum, D. *Cognitive-behavior modification*. New York: Plenum, 1977.

Meichenbaum, D. Teaching children self-control. In B. Lahey and A. Kazdin (eds.), *Advances in child clinical psychology*, Vol. 2. New York: Plenum, 1979.

Meichenbaum, D., and Goodman, J. The developmental control of operant motor responding by verbal operants. *Journal of Experimental Child Psychology*, 1969, *7*, 553–565.

Meichenbaum, D., and Goodman, J. Training impulsive children to talk to themselves: A means of developing self-control. *Journal of Abnormal Psychology*, 1971, *77*, 115–126.

Meichenbaum, D., and Turk, D. The cognitive-behavioral management of anxiety, anger, and pain. In P. O. Davidson (ed.), *The behavioral management of anxiety, depression and pain*. New York: Brunner/Mazel, 1976.

Melamed, B. G., and Siegel, L. J. Reduction of anxiety in children facing hospitalization and surgery by use of filmed modeling. *Journal of Consulting and Clinical Psychology*, 1975, *43*, 511–521.

Melamed, B. G., Hawes, R. R., Heiby, E., and Glick, J. The use of filmed modeling to reduce uncooperative behavior of children during dental treatment. *Journal of Dental Research*, 1975, *54*, 797–801. (a)

Melamed, B. G., Weinstein, D., Hawes, R., and Katin-Borland, M. Reduction of fear-related dental management problems using filmed modeling. *Journal of the American Dental Association*, 1975, *90*, 822–826. (b)

Melamed, B. G., Yurcheson, R., Fleece, E. L., Hutcheson, S., and Hawes, R. Effects of film modeling on the reduction of anxiety-related behaviors in individuals varying in level or previous experience in the stress situation. *Journal of Consulting and Clinical Psychology*, 1978, *46*, 1357–1367.

Menolascino, F. J., and Coleman, R. The pilot parent program: Helping handicapped children through their parents. *Child Psychiatry and Human Development*, 1980, *11*, 41–48.

Metz, J. R. Conditioning generalized imitation in autistic children. *Journal of Experimental Child Psychology*, 1965, *2*, 389–399.

Michael, J. Principles of effective usage. In R. Ulrich, T. Stachnik, and J. Mabry (eds.), *Control of human behavior*, Vol. II. Glenview, Ill.: Scott, Foresman, 1966.

Miklich, D. R. Operant conditioning procedures with systematic desensitization in a hyperkinetic asthmatic boy. *Journal of Behavior Therapy and Experimental Psychiatry*, 1973, *4*, 177–182.

Miller, A., and Miller, E. E. Cognitive developmental training with elevated boards and sign language. *Journal of Autism and Childhood Schizophrenia*, 1973, *3*, 65–85.

Miller, L. C. Louisville Behavior Check List for males 6–12 years of age. *Psychological Reports*, 1967, *21*, 885–896.

Miller, L. C., Barrett, C. L., Hampe, E., and Noble, H. Revised anxiety scales for the Louisville Behavior Check List. *Psychological Reports*, 1971, *29*, 503–511.

Miller, L. C., Barrett, C. L., Hampe, E., and Noble, H. Comparison of reciprocal inhibition, psychotherapy, and waiting list control for phobic children. *Journal of Abnormal Psychology*, 1972, *79*, 269–279. (a)

Miller, L. C., Barrett, C. L., Hampe, E., and Noble, H. Factor structure of childhood fears. *Journal of Consulting and Clinical Psychology*, 1972, *39*, 264–268. (b)

Miller, L. C., Barrett, C. L., and Hampe, E. Phobias of childhood in a prescientific era. In A. Davids (ed.), *Child personality and psychology: Current topics*, Vol. 1. New York: Wiley, 1974.

Miller, M. A., Cuvo, A. J., and Borakove, L. Teaching naming of coin values—comprehension before productions versus production alone. *Journal of Applied Behavior Analysis*, 1977, *10*, 735–736.

Miller, N. Learning of visceral and glandular responses. *Science*, 1969, *163*, 434–445.

Miller, N. E. *Comments on strategy and tactics of research*. In A. E. Bergin and H. H. Strupp (eds.), *Changing frontiers in the science of psychotherapy*. Chicago: Aldine, Atherton, 1972, 348–350.

Miller, P. M. The use of visual imagery and muscle relaxation in the counterconditioning of a phobic child: A case study. *Journal of Nervous and Mental Disease*, 1972, *154*, 457–460.

Miller, P. M. An experimental analysis of retention control training in the treatment of nocturnal enuresis in two institutionalized adolescents. *Behavior Therapy*, 1973, *4*, 288–294.

Miller, S., and Sloane, H. The generalization effects of parent training across stimulus settings. *Journal of Applied Behavior Analysis*, 1976, *9*, 355–370.

Miller, W. B. The impact of a "total community" delinquency control project. *Social Problems*, 1962, *10*, 168–191.

Minuchin, S. Conflict-resolution family therapy. *Psychiatry*, 1965, *28*, 278–286.

Mira, M. Results of a behavior modification training program for parents and teachers. *Behaviour Research and Therapy*, 1970, *8*, 309–311.

Mischel, W., and Ebbesen, E. B. Attention in delay of gratification. *Journal of Personality and Social Psychology*, 1970, *16*, 329–337.

Mischel, W., and Liebert, R. M. Effects of discrepancies between observed and imposed reward criteria on their acquisition and transmission. *Journal of Personality and Social Psychology*, 1966, *3*, 45–53.

Mischel, W., and Moore, B. Effects of attention to symbolically presented rewards upon self-control. *Journal of Personality and Social Personality*, 1973, *28*, 172–179.

Mischel, W., and Patterson, C. J. Substantive and structural elements of effective plans for self-control. *Journal of Personality and Social Psychology*, 1976, *34*, 942–950.

Mischel, W., Ebbesen, E. B., and Zeiss, A. R. Cognitive and attentional mechanisms in delay of gratification. *Journal of Personality and Social Psychology*, 1972, *21*, 204–218.

Mitford, J. *Kind and usual punishment: The prison business*. New York: Knopf, 1973.

Mittler, P. (ed.). *Research to practice in mental retardation, Vol. 1: Care and intervention*. Baltimore, Md.: University Park Press, 1977. (c)

Mittler, P., (ed.). *Research to practice in mental retardation, Vol. 2: Education and training*. Baltimore, Md.: University Park Press, 1977. (b)

Mittler, P. (ed.), *Research to practice in mental retardation Vol. 3: Biomedical aspects*. Baltimore, Md.: University Park Press, 1977. (c)

Montenegro, H., Lira, M. I., and Rodriquez, S. Early psychosocial stimulation program for infants (from birth to 24 months) of low socioeconomic class. In P. Mittler (ed.), *Research to practice in mental retardation Vol. 1: Care and intervention*. Baltimore, Md.: University Park Press, 1977, 195–204.

Moore, B. L., and Bailey, J. S. Social punishment in the modification of a preschool child's "autistic like" behavior with mother as therapist. *Journal of Applied Behavior Analysis*, 1973, *6*, 497–507.

Moore, D. J., and Shiek, D. A. Toward a theory of early infantile autism. *Psychological Review*, 1971, *78*, 451–456.

Moore, N. Behavior therapy in bronchial asthma: A controlled study. *Journal of Psychosomatic Research*, 1965, *9*, 257–276.

Moorefield, C. W. The use of hypnosis and behavior therapy in asthma. *American Journal of Clinical Hypnosis*, 1971, *13*, 162.

Moores, D. F. Issues in the modification of American Sign Language for instructional purposes. *Journal of Autism and Developmental Disorders*, 1981, *11*, 153–163.

Moores, D. F. Nonvocal systems of verbal behavior: In R. Schiefelbusch and L. Lloyd (eds.), *Language perspectives: Acquisition, retardation, and intervention*. Baltimore, Md.: University Park Press, 1974, 377–417.

Moreland, K. L. Verbal self-control in delay of gratification. *Psychological Reports*, 1978, *42*, 1202.

Morgan, G. A. V. Children who refuse to go to school. *Medical Officer*, 1959, *102*, 221–224.

Morgan, H. G., and Russell, G. F. M. Value of family background and clinical features as predictors of long-term outcome in anorexia nervosa: 4-year follow-up study of 41 patients. *Psychological Medicine*, 1975, *5*, 355–372.

Morgan, R. R. An exploratory study of three procedures to encourage school attendance. *Psychology in the Schools*, 1975, *12*, 209–215.

Morgan, R. T. T. "Paired reading" tuition: a preliminary report on a technique for cases of reading deficit. *Child: Care, Health, and Development*, 1976, *2*, 13–28.

Morgan, R. T. T. Relapse and therapeutic response in the conditioning treatment of enuresis: A review of recent findings on intermittent reinforcement, overlearning and stimulus intensity. *Behaviour Research and Therapy*, 1978, *16*, 273–279.

Morgan, R. T. T., and Lyon, E. "Paired reading"—a preliminary report on a technique for parental tuition of reading retarded children. *Journal of Child Psychology and Psychiatry*, 1979, *20*, 151–160.

Morrey, J. G. Parent training in precise behavior management with mentally retarded children. *Dissertation Abstracts*, 1971, *31*, 3376A.

Morris, H. H. Aggressive behavior disorders in children: A follow-up study. *American Journal of Psychiatry*, 1956, *112*, 991–997.

Morris, R. J., and Kratochwill, T. R. *Treating children's fears and phobias*: A behavioral approach. New York: Pergamon, 1983.

Mostofsky, D. I., and Vick, S. H. *The therapeutic value of muscle relaxation in seizure control: A case study*. Unpublished paper, Boston University, 1973.

Moustakas, C. W. *Psychotherapy with children*. New York: Harper, 1959.

Mowrer, O. H. Apparatus for the study and treatment of enuresis. *American Journal of Psychology*, 1938, *51*, 163–166.

Mowrer, O. H. A stimulus-response analysis of anxiety and its role as a reinforcing agent. *Psychological Review*, 1939, *46*, 553–565.

Mowrer, O. H., and Mowrer, W. M. Enuresis: A method for its study and treatment. *American Journal of Orthopsychiatry*, 1938, *8*, 436–459.

Muellner, S. A. Development of urinary control in children. *Journal of the American Medical Association*, 1960, *172*, 1256–1261.

Mulhern, T., and Baumeister, A. A. An experimental attempt to reduce stereotypy by reinforcement procedures. *American Journal of Mental Deficiency*, 1969, *74*, 69–74.

Mulick, J. A., Schroeder, S. R., and Rojahn, J. Chronic ruminative vomiting: A comparison of four treatment procedures. *Journal of Autism and Developmental Disorders*, 1980, *10*, 203–213.

Munford, P. R. Halopeidol and contingency management in a case of anorexia nervosa. *Journal of Behavior Therapy and Experimental Psychology*, 1980, *11*, 67–71.

Munro, D. M. G. An experiment in the use of group methods with parents in a child guidance clinic. *British Journal of Psychiatric Social Work*, 1952, *6*, 16–20.

Murphy, C. M., and Bootzin, R. R. Active and passive participation in the contact desensitization of snake fear in children. *Behavior Therapy*, 1973, *4*, 203–211.

Murphy, G. H., Steele, K., Gilligan, T., Yeow, J., and Spare, D. Teaching a picture language to a non-speaking retarded boy. *Behaviour Research and Therapy*, 1977, *15*, 198–201.

Murray, M. E., Keele, D. K., and McCarver, J. W. Treatment of rumination with behavioral techniques: A case report. *Behavior Therapy*, 1977, *8*, 999.

Myers, D. V. Extinction, DRO, and response-cost procedures for eliminating self-injurious behavior: A case study. *Behaviour Research and Therapy*, 1975, *13*, 189–191.

Nalven, F. B. Manifest fears and worries of ghetto versus middle class suburban children. *Psychological Reports*, 1970, *27*, 285–286.

Nash, R. T., Thorpe, H. W., Andrews, M. M., and Davis, K. A management program for elective mutism. *Psychology in the Schools*, 1979, *16*, 246–252.

Neale, D. H. Behavior therapy and encopresis in children. *Behaviour Research and Therapy*, 1963, *1*, 139–149.

Neisworth, J. T., and Moore, F. Operant treatment of asthmatic responding with the parent as therapist. *Behavior Therapy*, 1972, *3*, 95–99.

Nelson, D. L., Gergenti, E., and Hollander, A. C. Extra prompts versus no extra prompts in self-care training of autistic children and adolescents. *Journal of Autism and Developmental Disorders*, 1980, *10*, 311–321.

Nelson, R., Kapust, H., and Dorsey, B. Minimal reactivity of overt classroom observations on student and teacher behaviors. *Behavior Therapy*, 1978, *9*, 695–702.

Nelson, R. O., Lipinski, D. P., and Boykin, R. A. The effects of self-recorders' training and the obtrusiveness of the self-recording device on the accuracy and reactivity of self-monitoring. *Behavior Therapy*, 1978, *9*, 200–208.

Newstatter, W. L. The effect of poor social conditions in the production of neurosis. *Lancet*, 1938, *234*, 1436–1441.

Ney, P. G. Combined psychotherapy and deconditioning of a child's phobia. *Canadian Psychiatric Association Journal*, 1968, *13*, 293–294.

Ney, P. Operant conditioning of schizophrenic children. *Canadian Psychiatric Association Journal*, 1967, *12*, 9–13.

Nicol, A. R. Psychotherapy and the school. *Child Psychology and Psychiatry*, 1979, *20*, 81–86.

Nietzel, M. T., Winett, R. A., MacDonald, M. L., and Davidson, W. S. *Behavioral approaches to community psychology*. New York: Pergamon Press, 1977.

Nihira, K., Foster, R., Shellhaas, M., and Leland, H., *Adaptive behavior scales: Manual*. Washington, D.C.: American Association on Mental Deficiency, 1969.

Nocella, J., and Kaplan, R. M. Training children to cope with dental treatment. *Journal of Pediatric Psychology*, 1982, *7*, 175–183.

Nolan, D. J., and Pence, C. Operant conditioning principles in the treatment of a selectively mute child. *Journal of Consulting and Clinical Psychology*, 1970, *35*, 265–268.

Nordquist, V. M., and Wahler, R. G. Naturalistic treatment of an autistic child. *Journal of Applied Behavior Analysis*, 1973, *6*, 79–87.

Notz, W. W. Work motivation and the negative effects of extrinsic rewards. *American Psychologist*, 1975, *30*, 884–891.

Novick, J. Symptomatic treatment of acquired and persistent enuresis. *Journal of Abnormal Psychology*, 1966, *77*, 363–368.

Noyes, A. P., and Kalb, L. *Modern clinical psychiatry*, Philadelphia: Saunders, 1963.

Obler, M., and Terwilliger, R. F. Pilot study on the effectiveness of systematic desensitization with neurologically impaired children with phobic disorders. *Journal of Consulting and Clinical Psychology*, 1970, *34*, 314–318.

O'Connor, R. D. Modification of social withdrawal through symbolic modeling. *Journal of Applied Behavior Analysis*, 1969, *2*, 15–22.

O'Connor, R. D. Relative efficacy of modeling, shaping, and the combined procedures for modification of social withdrawal. *Journal of Abnormal Psychology,* 1972, *79,* 327–334.

O'Dell, S. L., Training parents in behavior modification: A review. *Psychological Bulletin,* 1974, *81,* 418–433.

O'Dell, S. L., Flynn, J., and Benlolo, L. A comparison of parent-training techniques in child behavior modification. *Journal of Behavior Therapy and Experimental Psychiatry,* 1977, *8,* 261–268.

O'Dell, S. L., Mahoney, N. D., Horton, W. G., and Turner, P. E. Media-assisted parent training: Alternative models. *Behavior Therapy,* 1979, *10,* 103–110.

Okovita, H. W., and Bucher, B. Attending behavior of children near a child who is reinforced for attending. *Psychology in the Schools,* 1976, *18,* 204–211.

O'Leary, K. D., and Drabman, R. S. Token reinforcement programs in the classroom: A review. *Psychological Bulletin,* 1971, *75,* 379–398.

O'Leary, K. D., O'Leary, S., and Becker, W. C. Modification of a deviant sibling interaction pattern in the home. *Behaviour Research and Therapy,* 1967, *5,* 113–120.

O'Leary, K. D., Becker, W. C., Evans, M. B., and Saudargas, R. A. A token reinforcement program in a public school: A replication and systematic analysis. *Journal of Applied Behavior Analysis,* 1969, *2,* 3–13.

O'Leary, S. G., and Dubey, D. R. Applications of self-control procedures by children: A review. *Journal of Applied Behavior Analysis,* 1979, *12,* 449–465.

O'Leary, S. G., and O'Leary, K. D. Behavior modification in the school. In, H. Leitenberg, (ed.), *Handbook of behavior modification and behavior therapy.* Englewood Cliffs, N.J.: Prentice Hall, 1976.

O'Leary, K., Pelham, W., Rosenbaum, A., and Price. G. Behavioral treatment of hyperkinetic children. *Behavior,* 1976. *15,* 510–515.

Ollendick, T. H., and Finch, A. J. Reflection-impulsivity in brain-damaged and normal children. *Perceptual and Motor Skills,* 1973, *36,* 654.

Ollendick, T. H., and Gruen, G. E. Treatment of a bodily injury phobia with implosive therapy. *Journal of Consulting and Clinical Psychology,* 1972, *38,* 389–393.

Ollendick, T. H., and Matson, J. L. Overcorrection: An overview. *Behavior Therapy,* 1978, *9,* 830–842.

Olsen, I., and Coleman, H. S. Treatment of school phobia as a case of separation anxiety. *Psychology in the Schools,* 1967, *4,* 151–154.

O'Neil, P. M., White, J. L., King, C. R., and Carek, D. J. Controlling childhood rumination through differential reinforcement of other behavior. *Behavior Modification,* 1979, *3,* 355.

Ora, J. *Instruction pamphlet for parents of oppositional children.* Regional Intervention Project for Preschoolers and Parents, Nashville, Tenn.: George Peabody College, 1971.

Orbach, I. Impulsive cognitive style: Three modification techniques. *Psychology in the Schools,* 1977, *14,* 353–359.

Orlando, R., and Bijou, S. Single and multiple schedules of reinforcement in developmentally retarded children. *Journal of Behavior Therapy and Experimental Psychiatry,* 1960, *3,* 339–348.

Page, D. P., and Edwards, R. P. Behavior change strategies for reducing disruptive classroom behavior. *Psychology in the Schools,* 1978, *15,* 413–418.

Pailer, B., and Graziano, A. M. *A national survey of behavior modification in clinical practice.* Unpublished paper, State University of New York at Buffalo, 1976.

Palkes, H., Stewart, M., and Kahana, K. Porteus maze performance of hyperactive boys after training in self-directed verbal commands. *Child Development*, 1968, *39*, 817–826.

Palkes, H., Stewart, M., and Freedman, J. Improvement in maze performance of hyperactive boys as a function of verbal-training procedures. *Journal of Special Education*, 1972, *5*, 337–342.

Palmer, S., Thompson, R. J., and Linscheid, T. R. Applied behavior analysis in the treatment of childhood feeding problems. *Developmental Medical and Childhood Neurosis*, 1975, *17*, 333–339.

Paloutzian, R. F., Hasazi, J., Streifel, J., and Edgard, C. L. Promotion of positive social interaction in severely retarded young children. *American Journal of Mental Deficiency*, 1971, *75*, 519–524.

Parmelee, A. H., Jr. Planning intervention for infants in high risk identified by developmental evaluation. In P. Mittler (ed.), *Research to practice in mental retardation, Vol. 1. Care and intervention*. Baltimore, Md.: University Park Press, 1977, 171–178.

Parrino, J. Reduction of seizures by desensitization. *Journal of Behavior Therapy and Experimental Psychiatry*, 1971, *2*, 215–218.

Parry, P. *The effect of reward on the performance of hyperactive children*. Unpublished doctoral dissertation, McGill University, Montreal, 1973.

Parsonon, B. S., and Baer, D. M. Training generalized improvisation of tools by preschool children. *Journal of Applied Behavior Analysis*, 1978, *11*, 363–381.

Parsons, B. V., and Alexander, J. F. Short-term family intervention: A therapy outcome study. *Journal of Consulting and Clinical Psychology*, 1973, *41*, 195–201.

Paschalis, A. P., Kimmel, H. D., and Kimmel, E. Further study of diurnal instrumental conditioning in the treatment of enuresis nocturna. *Journal of Behavior Therapy and Experimental Psychiatry*, 1972, *3*, 253–256.

Patterson, C. J., and Carter, D. B. Attentional determinants of children's self-control in waiting and working situations. *Child Development*, 1979, *50*, 272–275.

Patterson, C. J., and Mischel, W. Effects of temptation-inhibiting and task-facilitating plans on self-control. *Journal of Personality and Social Psychology*, 1976, *33*, 209–217.

Patterson, G. R. *Fathers as reinforcing agents*. Paper read at the Western Psychological Association, San Diego, April 1959.

Patterson, G. R. *State institutions as teaching machines for delinquent behavior*. Mimeographed paper. Child Study Center, University of Oregon, 1963.

Patterson, G. R. A learning theory approach to the treatment of the school phobic child. In L. P. Ullmann, and L. Krasner (eds.), *Case studies in behavior modification*. New York: Holt, 1965, 279–284.

Patterson, G. R. Interventions for boys with conduct problems: multiple settings, treatments, and criteria. *Journal of Consulting and Clinical Psychology*, 1974, *42*, 471–481.

Patterson, G. R. A performance theory for coercive family interaction. In R. Cairns (edl.), *Social interactional analysis: Methods and illustrations*. New York: Erlbaum Associates, 1979.

Patterson, G. R. *Coercive family processes*. Eugene, Or., Castalia, 1982.

Patterson, G. R., and Brodsky, G. A behavior modification programme for a child with multiple problem behaviours. *Journal of Child Psychology and Psychiatry*, 1966, *7*, 277–295.

Patterson, G. R., and Fleischman, M. J. Maintenance of treatment effects:

Some considerations concerning family systems and follow-up data. *Behavior Therapy*, 1979, *10*, 168–185.

Patterson, G. R., and Guillion, M. E. *Living with children: New methods for parents and teachers*, Champaign, Ill.: Research Press, 1968.

Patterson, G. R., and Reid, J. B. Intervention for families of aggressive boys: A replication study. *Behaviour Research and Therapy*, 1973, *11*, 383–394.

Patterson, G. R., Chamberlain, P., and Reid, J. B. A comparative evaluation of a parent-training program. *Behavior Therapy*, 1982, *13*, 638–650.

Patterson, G. R., McNeal, S., Hawkins, N., and Phelps, R. Programming the social environment. *Journal of Child Psychology and Psychiatry*, 1967, *8*, 181–195. (a)

Patterson, G. R., Littman, R. A., and Bricker, W. Assertive behavior in children: A step toward a theory of aggressions. *Monographs of the Society for Research in Child Development*, 1967, *32* (Serial No. 113). (b)

Patterson, G. R., Ray, R., and Shaw, D. Direct intervention in families of deviant children. *Oregon Research Institute Bulletin*, 1968.

Patterson, G. R., Shaw, D., and Ebner, M. Teachers, peers and parents as agents of change in the classroom. In F. A. M. Benson (ed.), *Modifying deviant social behaviors in various classroom settings*. Monograph No. 1. Eugene, Ore.: University of Oregon, 1969, 13–47.

Patterson, G. R., Cobb, J. A., and Ray, R. S. A social engineering technology for retraining aggressive boys. In H. E. Adams and I. P. Unikel (eds.), *Issues and trends in behavior therapy*. Springfield, Ill.: Charles C. Thomas, 1972, 139–224.

Patterson, G. R., Reid, J. R., Jones, R. R., and Conger, R. A. *A social learning approach to family intervention, Vol. 1. Families with aggressive children*. Eugene, Ore.: Castalia Publications, 1975.

Paul, G. L. Behavior modification research: Design and tactics. In C. M. Franks (ed.), *Behavior therapy: Appraisal and status*. New York: McGraw-Hill, 1969, 29–62.

Peacock, R., Lyman, R. D., and Rickard, H. C. Correspondence between self-report and observer-report as a function of task difficulty, *Behavior Therapy*, 1978, *9*, 578–583.

Pease, G. A., and Tyler, V. O. Self-regulation of time-out duration in the modification of disruptive classroom behavior. *Psychology in the Schools*, 1979, *16*, 101–105.

Pechey, B. M. The direct analysis of the mother-child relationship in the treatment of maladjusted children. *British Journal of Medicine and Psychology*, 1955, *28*, 101–112.

Peed, S., Roberts, M., and Forehand, R. *Generalization to the home of behavior modified in a parent training program for non-compliant children*. Unpublished manuscript, University of Georgia Psychological Clinic, 1975.

Peed, S., Roberts, M. W., and Forehand, R. Evaluation of the effectiveness of a standardized parent training program in altering the interaction of mothers and their noncompliant children. *Behavior Modification*, 1977, *1*, 233–250.

Peele, R. A., and Routh, D. K. Maternal control and self-control in 3-year-old child. *Bulletin of the Psychonomic Society*, 1978, *11*, 349–352.

Peine, H. A. *Programming the home*. Paper read at the Rocky Mountain Psychological Association, Albuquerque, N.M., May 1969.

Peine, H. A. *Effects of training models on the modification of parent behavior*. (Doctoral dissertation, University of Utah) Ann Arbor, Mich.: University Microfilms, 1971, No. 71-24641.

Peine, H. A., and Munro, B. *Training parents using lecture demonstration procedures and a contingency management program*. Unpublished manuscript, University of Utah, 1970.

Penney, R. K., Marcella, P., and Charlton, D. Classical and operant conditioning program for a fire-setting child. *Journal of the Ontario Association of Children's Aid Society*, 1974, 1–4.

Perloo, S. *Biofeedback in asthma: A review*. Unpublished paper, Los Angeles, Calif.: U.C.L.A., Neuropsychiatric Institute, 1976.

Peshkin, M. M. Intractable asthma of childhood rehabilitation at the institutional level with a follow-up of 150 cases. *International Archives of Allergy*, 1959, *15*, 91.

Petersen, C. R., and Hart, D. H. Use of multiple discriminant function analysis in evaluation of a state-wide system for identification of educationally handicapped children. *Psychological Reports*, 1978, *43*, 743–755.

Petersen, G. A., Austin, G. J., and Lang, R. P. Use of teacher prompts to increase social behavior: Generalization effects with severely and profoundly retarded adolescents. *American Journal of Mental Deficiency*, 1979, *84*, 82–86.

Peterson, L. and Shigetomi, C. The use of coping techniques in minimizing anxiety in hospitalized children. *Behavior Therapy*, 1981, *12*, 1–14.

Peterson, R. F., and Peterson, L. R. The use of positive reinforcement in the control of self-destructive behavior in a retarded boy. *Journal of Experimental Child Psychology*, 1968, *6*, 351–360.

Philip, R. C., Wilde, G. J. S., and Day, J. H. Suggestion and relaxation in asthmatics. *Journal of Psychosomatic Research*, 1972, *16*, 193–204.

Phillips, D. The family council: a segment of adolescent treatment. *Journal of Behavior Therapy and Experimental Psychiatry*, 1975, *6*, 283–287.

Phillips, E. L. Achievement place: Token reinforcement procedures in a home-style rehabilitation setting for pre-delinquent boys. *Journal of Applied Behavior Analysis*, 1968, *1*, 213–233.

Phillips, E. L., Phillips, E. A., Fixsen, D. L., and Wolf, M. M. Behavior shaping works for delinquents. *Psychology Today*, 1973, *7*, 75–79.

Piaget, J. *The child's conception of the world*. New York: Harcourt, Brace, 1929.

Piaget, J. *The child's conception of physical causality*. New York: Humanities Press, 1951.

Piggott, L. R. Overview of selected basic research in autism. *Journal of Autism and Developmental Disorders*, 1979, *9*, 199–218.

Pinkston, E. M., and Herbert, E. W. *Modification of irrelevant and bizarre verbal behavior using mother as therapist*. Paper presented at the 79th Annual Convention of the American Psychological Association, Washington, D.C., September, 1971.

Plachetta, K. E. Encopresis: A case study utilizing contracting, scheduling and self-charting. *Journal of Behavior Therapy and Experimental Psychiatry*, 1976, *7*, 195–198.

Plummer, S., Baer, D. M., and LeBlanc, J. M. Functional considerations in the use of time-out and an effective alternative. *Journal of Applied Behavior Analysis*, 1977, *10*, 689–705.

Polirstok, S., and Greer, R. Remediation of mutually aversive interaction between a problem student and four teachers by training the student in reinforcement techniques. *Journal of Applied Behavior Analysis*, 1977, *10*, 707–716.

Polsgrove, L. Self-control: Methods for child training. *Behavioral Disorders*, 1979, *4*, 116–130.

Pomerantz, P. B., Peterson, N. T., Marholin, D., and Stern, S. The *in vivo* elimination of a child's water phobia by a paraprofessional at home. *Journal of Behavior Therapy and Experimental Psychiatry*, 1977, *8*, 417–421.

Pomerleau, O. F. Behavioral medicine: The contribution of the experimental analysis of behavior to medical care. *American Psychologist*, 1979, *34*, 654–663.

Pomerleau, O. F., and Brady, J. P. Introduction: The scope and promise of behavioral medicine. In O. F. Pomerleau and J. P. Brady (eds.), *Behavioral medicine: Theory and practice*. Baltimore, Md.: Williams and Wilkins, 1979.

Porterfield, J. K., Herbert-Jackson, E., and Risley, T. R. Contingent observation: An effective and acceptable procedure for reducing disruptive behavior of young children in a group setting. *Journal of Applied Behavior Analysis*, 1976, *9*, 55–64.

Poser, E. G., and King, M. C. Strategies for the prevention of maladaptive fear response. *Canadian Journal of Behavioral Science*, 1975, *7*, 279–294.

Poznanski, E. O. Children with excessive fears. *American Journal of Orthopsychiatry*, 1973, *43*, 428–438.

Potter, H. W. Schizophrenia in children. *American Journal of Psychiatry*, 1933, *89*, 1253–1269.

Poulin, J. E., Levitt, J. L., Young, T. M., and Pappenfort, D. M. Juveniles in detention centers and jails: An analysis of state variations during the mid-seventies. *Reports of the National Juvenile Justice Centers*. Washington, D. C.: Government Printing Office, August 1980.

Poultin, K. T., and Algozzine, B. Manual communication and mental retardation: A review of research and implications. *American Journal of Mental Deficiency*, 1980, *85*, 145–152.

Pratt, K. C. The study of the "fears" of rural children. *Journal of Genetic Psychology*, 1945, *67*, 179–194.

Pressley, M. Increasing children's self-control through cognitive interventions. *Review of Educational Research*, 1979, *49*, 319–370.

Price, P. Overview of language remediation. *Australian Journal of Mental Retardation, 1978, 5*, 126–133.

Prior, M. R. Cognitive abilities and disabilities in infantile autism: A review. *Journal of Abnormal Child Psychology*, 1979, *7*, 357–380.

Prout, H. T., and Harvey, J. R. Applications of desensitization procedures for school related problems: A review. *Psychology in the Schools*, 1978, *15*, 533–541.

Purcell, K. The effect on asthma in children of experimental separation from the family. *Psychosomatic Medicine*, 1969, *31*, 144.

Purcell, K., Brady, K. Chai, H., Muser, J., Molk, L. Gordon, N., and Means, J. The effect on asthma in children of experimental separation from the family. *Psychomatic Medicine*, 1969, *31*, 144–164.

Rachman, S. Clinical applications of observational learning, imitation and modeling. *Behaviour Research and Therapy*, 1972, *3*, 379–397.

Rachman, S. The passing of the two-stage theory of fear and avoidance: Fresh possibilities. *Behaviour Research and Therapy*, 1976, *14*, 125–134.

Rachman, S. The conditioning theory of fear-acquisition: A critical examination. *Behaviour Research and Therapy*, 1977, *15*, 375–387.

Rachman, S. *Fear and courage*. San Francisco: Freeman, 1978.

Rachman, S., and Costello, C. G. The aetiology and treatment of children's phobias—A review. *American Journal of Psychiatry*, 1961, *118*, 97–105.

Rachman, S., and Hodgson, R. I. Synchrony and desynchrony in fear and avoidance. *Behaviour Research and Therapy*, 1974, *12*, 311–318.

Rachman, S., and Teasdale, J. *Aversion therapy and behavior disorders*. Coral Gables, Fla.: University of Miami Press, 1969.

Rainwater, N., and Ayllon, T. Increasing academic performance by using a timer as antecedent stimulus: A study of four cases. *Behavior Therapy*, 1976, *7*, 672–677.

Ramey, C. T., and Campbell, F. A. Prevention of development of retardation in high-risk children. In P. Mittler (ed.), *Research to practice in mental retardation Vol. 1: Care and intervention*. Baltimore, Md.: University Park Press, 1977, 157–164.

Rangell, L. A treatment of nightmares in a seven-year-old-boy. *Psychoanalytic Study of the Child*, 1952, *5*, 358–390.

Rapoff, M. A., Altman, K., and Christophersen, E. R. Suppression of self-injurious behaviour: Determining the least restrictive alternative. *Journal of Mental Deficiency Research*, 1980, *24*, 37–46.

Rapport, M., and Bostow, D. The effects of access to special activities on the performance in four categories of academic tasks with third grade students. *Journal of Applied Behavior Analysis*, 1976, *9*, 372.

Reavley, W., and Gilbert, M. The analysis and treatment of child abuse by behavioral psychotherapy. *Child Abuse and Neglect*, 1979, *3*, 509–514.

Redd, W. H. Effects of mixed reinforcement contingencies on adults' control of children's behavior. *Journal of Applied Behavior Analysis*, 1969, *4*, 249–254.

Reed, G. F. Elective mutism in children: A reappraisal. *Journal of Child Psychology and Psychiatry*, 1963, *4*, 99–107.

Reese, E. P. *The analysis of human operant behavior*. Dubuque, Iowa: Wm. Brown Co., 1966.

Reichle, J., Brubakken, D., and Tetreault, G. Eliminating perseverative speech by positive reinforcement and time-out in a psychotic child. *Journal of Behavior Therapy and Experimental Psychiatry*, 1976, *7*, 179–183.

Reid, J. B. A social learning approach to family interaction. *Observations in home settings*. Eugene, Ore.: Castalia, 1978.

Reid, J. B., and Patterson, G. R. The modification of aggression and stealing behavior of boys in the home setting. In E. Ribes and A. Bandura (eds.), *Analysis of delinquency and aggression*. Hillsdale, N.J.: Erlbaum Associates, 1976.

Reisinger, J. J., Frangia, G. W., and Hoffman, E. H. Toddler management training: Generalization and marital status. *Journal of Behavior Therapy and Experimental Psychiatry*, 1976, *7*, 335–340.

Reisinger, J. J., and Ora, J. P. Parent-child clinic and home interaction during toddler management training. *Behavior Therapy*, 1977, *8*, 771–786.

Reiss, M. L. Piotrowski, W. D., and Bailey, J. S. Behavioral community psychology: Encouraging low-income parents to seek dental care for their children. *Journal of Applied Behavior Analysis*, 1976, *9*, 387–397.

Repp, A. C., and Barton, L. E. Naturalistic observations of institutionalized retarded persons: A comparison of licensure decisions and behavioral observations. *Journal of Applied Behavior Analysis*, 1980, *13*, 333–341.

Repp, A. C., and Deitz, S. M. Reducing aggressive and self-injurious behavior of institutionalized retarded children through reinforcement of other behaviors. *Journal of Applied Behavior Analysis*, 1974, *7*, 313–325.

Reppucci, N. D., and Saunders, J. T. Social psychology of behavior modification: Problems of implementation in natural settings. *American Psychologist*, 1974, *29*, 649–660.

Resick, P. A., Forehand, R., and McWhorter, A. G. The effects of parental treatment with one child on an untreated sibling. *Behavior Therapy*, 1976, *7*, 544–548.

Resnick, L. B., Wang, M. C., and Kaplan, J. Task analysis in curriculum design: A hierarchically sequenced introductory mathematics curriculum. *Journal of Applied Behavior Analysis*, 1973, *6*, 679–710.

Revell, W. G., and Wehman, P. Vocational evaluation of severely and profoundly retarded clients. *Rehabilitation Literature*, 1978, *39*, 226–231.

Revill, S., and Blunden, R. A home training service for pre-school developmentally handicapped children. *Behaviour Research and Therapy*, 1979, *17*, 207–214.

Reynolds, B. S., Newsom, C. D., and Lovaas, O. I. Auditory overselectivity in autistic children. *Journal of Abnormal Child Psychology*, 1974, *2*, 253–263.

Rhines, W. B. Behavior therapy before institutionalization. *Psychotherapy: Theory, Research & Practice*, 1973, *10*, 281–283.

Rice, H. K., and McDaniel, M. E. Operant behavior in vegetative patients. *Psychological Record*, 1966, *16*, 279–281.

Richardson, R. A. *Environmental contingencies in seizure disorders*. Paper presented at Association for the Advancement of Behavior Therapy, New York, October 1972.

Richman, J. L., and Kozlowski, N. L. Operant training of head control and beginning language for a severely developmentally disabled child. *Journal of Behavior Therapy and Experimental Psychiatry*, 1977, *8*, 437–440.

Richman, J. S., Sonderby, T., and Kahn, J. V. Prerequisite vs. in-vivo acquisition of self-feeding skill. *Behaviour Research and Therapy*, 1980, *8*, 327–332.

Riessman, F. Strategies and suggestions for training nonprofessionals. *Community Mental Health Journal*, 1967, *3* (2), 103–110.

Rimland, B. *Infantile autism: The syndrome and its implications for a neural theory of behavior*. New York: Appleton-Century-Crofts, 1964.

Rimland, B. The differentiation of childhood psychoses: An analysis of checklists for 2,218 psychotic children. *Journal of Autism and Childhood Schizophrenia*, 1971, *1*, 161–174.

Rimland, B. Comment on Ward's "Early infantile autisms." *Psychological Bulletin*, 1972, *77*, 49–51.

Rimm, D. C., Janda, L. H., Lancaster, D. H., Nahl, M., and Dittmar, K. An exploratory investigation of the origin and maintenance of phobias. *Behaviour Research and Therapy*, 1977, *15*, 231–238.

Rimm, D. C., and Masters, J. C. *Behavior therapy: Techniques and empirical findings*. New York: Academic Press, 1974.

Rincover, A. Sensory extinction: A procedure for eliminating self-stimulating behavior in developmentally disabled children. *Journal of Abnormal Child Psychology*, 1978, *6*, 299–310. (a)

Rincover, A. Variables affecting stimulus fading and discriminative responding in psychotic children. *Journal of Abnormal Psychology*, 1978, *87*, 541–553. (b)

Rincover, A., and Koegel, R. L. Setting generality and stimulus control in autistic children. *Journal of Applied Behavior Analysis*, 1975, *8*, 235–246.

Rincover, A., and Koegel, R. L. Classroom treatment of psychotic children: II. Individualized instruction in a group. *Journal of Abnormal Child Psychology*, 1977, *5*, 113–126.

Rincover, A., Newsom, C. D., and Carr, E. G. Using sensory extinction procedures in the treatment of compulsive like behavior of developmentally disabled children. *Journal of Consulting and Clinical Psychology*, 1979, *47*, 695–701 (a)

Rincover, A., Cook, R., Peoples, A., and Packard, D. Sensory extinction and sensory reinforcement principles for programming multiple adaptive behavior change. *Journal of Applied Behavior Analysis*, 1979, *12*, 221–233. (b)

Rinn, R. C., and Vernon, J. C. Process of evaluation of outpatient treatment in a community mental health center. *Journal of Behavior Therapy and Experimental Psychiatry*, 1975, *6*, 5–11.

Rinn, R. C., Vernon, J. C., and Wise, M. J. Training parents of behaviorally disordered children in groups: A three-year's program evaluation. *Behavior Therapy*, 1975, *6*, 378–387.

Risley, T. R. The effects and side effects of punishing the autistic behaviors of a deviant child. *Journal of Applied Behavior Analysis*, 1968, *1*, 21–34.

Risley, T. R., and Wolf, M. M. Experimental manipulation of autistic behaviors and generalization in to the home. In R. Ulrich, T. Stachnick, and J. Mabry (eds.), *Control of human behavior*. Glenview, Ill.: Scott, Foresman, 1966, 187–198.

Ritter, B. J. The group treatment of children's snake phobias using vicarious and contact desensitization procedures. *Behaviour Research and Therapy*, 1968, *6*, 1–6.

Ritvo, E. R. Biochemical studies of children with the syndromes of autism, childhood schizophrenia and related developmental disabilities: A review. *Journal of Child Psychology and Psychiatry*, 1977, *18*, 373–379.

Rivinus, T. M., Drummond, T., and Combrinck-Graham, L. A group behavior treatment program for overweight children: Results of a pilot study. *Pediatric and Adolescent Endocrinology*, 1976, *1*, 55–61.

Roach, J. L. Some social-psychological characteristics of child guidance clinic caseloads. *Journal of Consulting Psychology*, 1958, *22*, 183–186.

Roberts, M. C., Wurtele, S. K., Boone, R. R., Ginther, J. J., and Elkins, P. D. Reduction of medical fears by use of modeling: A preventive application in a general population of children. *Journal of Pediatric Psychology*, 1981, *6*, 293–300.

Roberts, M. W., McMahon, R. J., Forehand R., and Humphreys, L. The effect of parental instruction-giving on child compliance. *Behavior Therapy*, 1978, *9*, 793–798.

Robertson, S., DeReus, D., and Drabman, R. Peer and college student tutoring as reinforcement in a token economy. *Journal of Applied Behavior Analysis*, 1976, *9*, 169–178.

Robertson, S. J., Simon, S. J., Pachman, J. S., and Drabman, R. S. Self-control and generalization procedures in a classroom of disruptive retarded children. *Child Behavior Therapy*, 1979, *1*, 347–362.

Robin, A., Schneider, M., and Dolnick, M. The turtle technique: an extended case study of self-control in the classroom. *Psychology in the Schools*, 1976, *13*, 449–453.

Robin, A. L., Armel, S., and O'Leary, K. D. The effects of self-instruction on writing deficiencies. *Behavior Therapy*, 1975, *6*, 178–187.

Robin, A. L., Kent, R., O'Leary, K. D., Foster, S., and Prinz, R. An approach to teaching parents and adolescents problem-solving communication skills: a preliminary report. *Behavior Therapy*, 1977, *8*, 639–644.

Robin, G. R. Anti-poverty programs and delinquency. *Journal of Criminal Law, Criminology, and Police Science*, 1969, *60*, 323–331.

Robins, L. N. *Deviant children grown up: A sociological and psychological study of sociopathic personality*. Baltimore, Md.: Williams & Wilkins, 1966.

Robinson, N. M., and Robinson, H. B. *The mentally retarded child*, 2nd ed. New York: McGraw-Hill, 1976.

Rocklin, H., and Tilker, H. Instrumental conditioning of nocturnal enuresis: A reappraisal of some previous findings. *Proceedings of the Annual Convention of the American Psychological Association*, 1973, *8*, 915–916.

Rodriguez, A., Rodriguez, M., and Eisenberg, L. The outcome of school phobia. *American Journal of Psychiatry*, 1959, *116*, 540–544.

Romanczyk, R. G. Intermittent punishment of self-stimulation: Effectiveness during application and extinction. *Journal of Consulting and Clinical Psychology*, 1977, *45*, 53–60.

Rondal, J. A., and Hoffmeister, R. J. Sign language as an alternative language system for the mentally retarded. *Philippine Journal of Mental Health*, 1976, *7*, 57–62.

Roos, P. Custodial care for the "subtrainable": Revisiting an old myth. *Law and Psychology Review*, 1979, *5*, 1–14.

Rose, S. D. A behavioral approach to the group treatment of parents. *Social Work*, 1969, *14*, 12–29.

Rose, S. D., Sundel, M., DeLange, J., Corwin, L., and Palumbo, A. The Hartwig project: A behavioral approach to the treatment of juvenile offenders. In R. Ulrich, R. Stachnik, and J. Mabry (eds.), *Control of human behavior*, Vol. 2. Glenville, Ill.: Scott, Foresman, 1970, 220–230.

Rosen, J. *Direct psychoanalysis*. N.Y.: Grune & Stratton, 1953.

Rosen, L. W. Modification of ritualized eating behavior in anorexia nervosa. *Journal of Behavior Therapy and Experimental Psychiatry*, 1980, *11*, 101–104.

Rosen, M., and Wesner, C. A behavioral approach to Tourette's syndrome. *Journal of Consulting and Clinical Psychology*, 1973, *41*, 308–312.

Rosenbaum, M., and Drabman, R. Self-control training in the classroom: A review and critique. *Journal of Applied Behavior Analysis*, 1979, *12*, 467–485.

Ross, A. O. *Psychological aspects of learning disabilities and reading disorders*. New York: McGraw-Hill, 1976.

Ross, A. O. *Child behavior therapy: Principles, procedures and empirical basis*. New York: Wiley, 1981.

Ross, D. M. Effect on learning of psychological attachment to a film model. *American Journal of Mental Deficiency*, 1970, *74*, 701–707.

Ross, D. M., and Ross, S. A. Cognitive training for the EMR child: Language skills prerequisite to relevant-irrelevant discrimination tasks. *Mental Retardation*, 1979, *17*, 3–7.

Ross, J. A. Parents modify thumbsucking: A case study. *Journal of Behavior Therapy and Experimental Psychiatry*, 1975, *6*, 248–249.

Rotatori, A. F., and Fox, R. The effectiveness of a behavioral weight reduction program for moderately retarded adolescents. *Behavior Therapy*, 1980, *11*, 410–416.

Rotatori, A. F., Parrish, P., and Freagon, S. Weight loss in retarded children—A pilot study. *Journal of Psychiatric Nursing and Mental Health*, 1979, *17*, 33–34.

Rowbury, T., Baer, A., and Baer, D. Interactions between teacher guidance and contingent access to play in developing preacademic skills of deviant preschool children. *Journal of Applied Behavior Analysis*, 1976, *9*, 85–104.

Rowe, J. A., and Rapp, D. L. Tantrums: Remediation through communication. *Child Care, Health and Development*, 1980, *6*, 197–208.

Ruben, M., and Thomas, R. Home training of instincts and emotions. *Health Education Journal*, 1947, *5*, 119–124.

Rudy, L. H., Himwich, H. E., and Rinaldi, F. A clinical evaluation of psychopharmacological agents in the disturbed mentally defective patient. *American Journal of Mental Deficiency*, 1958, *62*, 855–860.

Russell, G. W. Human fears: A factor analytic study of three age levels. *Genetic Psychology Monographs*, 1967, *76*, 141–162.

Russo, D., and Koegel, R. A method for integrating an autistic child into a normal public school classroom. *Journal of Applied Behavior Analysis*, 1977, *10*, 579–590.

Russo, D. C., Koegel, R. I., and Lovaas, O. I. A comparison of human and automated instruction of autistic children. *Journal of Abnormal Child Psychology*, 1978, *6*, 199–202.

Russo, S. Adaptations in behavioral therapy with children. *Behaviour Research and Therapy*, 1964, *2*, 43–47.

Rutter, M. Prognosis: Psychotic children in adolescence and early adult life. In J. K. Wing (ed.), *Early childhood autism*. London: Pergamon Press, 1966.

Rutter, M. Concepts of autism: A review of research. *Journal of Child Psychology and Psychiatry*, 1968, *9*, 1–25.

Rutter, M. The description and classification of infantile autism. In D. W. Churchill, G. D. Alpern, and M. K. DeMyer (eds.), *Infantile autism*. Springfield, Ill.: Charles C. Thomas, 1971, 8–28.

Rutter, M., and Bartak, L. Special educational treatment of autistic children: A comparative study—II. Follow-up findings and implications for service. *Journal of Psychology and Psychiatry*, 1973, *14*, 241–270.

Rutter, M., and Lockyer, L. A five to fifteen year follow-up study of infantile psychosis: I. Description of the sample. *British Journal of Psychiatry*, 1967, *113*, 1169–1182.

Rutter, M., Tizard, J., and Whitmore, K. *Education, health and behaviour*. New York: Wiley, 1970.

Ryall, M. R., and Dietiker, E. Fear word choice in preschoolers. *Journal of Behavior Therapy and Experimental Psychiatry*, 1978, *9*, 189–190.

Ryall, M. R., and Dietiker, K. E. Reliability and clinical validity of the children's fear survey schedule. *Journal of Behavior Therapy and Experimental Psychiatry*, 1979, *10*, 303–309.

Sacks, S., and DeLeon, G. Conditioning two types of enuretics. *Behaviour Research and Therapy*, 1973, *11*, 653–659.

Sagotsky, G., Patterson, C. J., and Lepper, M. R. Training children's self-control—Field experiment in self-monitoring and goal-setting in classroom. *Journal of Experimental Child Psychology*, 1978, *25*, 242–253.

Sajwaj, T., Libet, J., and Agras, S. Lemon-juice therapy: The control of life-threatening rumination in a six-month old infant. *Journal of Applied Behavior Analysis*, 1974, *7*, 557–563.

Sajwaj, T., Twardosz, S., and Burke, M. Side effects of extinction procedures in a remedial pre-school. *Journal of Applied Behavior Analysis*, 1972, *5*, 163–175.

Salk, L. *What every child would like his parents to know*. New York: McKay, 1972.

Salter, A. *Conditioned reflex therapy: The direct approach to the reconstruction of personality*. New York: Capricorn, 1949.

Salvatore, S. The ability of elementary and secondary school children to sense oncoming car velocity. *Journal of Safety Research*, 1974, *6*, 118–125.

Salzberg, C. L. Freedom and responsibility in an elementary school. In G.

Semb (ed.), *Behavior analysis and education—1972*. Lawrence: University of Kansas, Support and Development Center for Follow Through, 1972.

Salzinger, K., Feldman, R., Cowan, J., and Salzinger, S. Operant conditioning of verbal behavior of two young speech deficient boys. In L. Krasner and L. Ullman, (eds.), *Research in behavior modification*. New York: Holt, Rinehart and Winston, 1965.

Salzinger, K., Feldman, R. S., and Portnoy, S. Training parents of brain-injured children in the use of operant conditioning procedures. *Behavior Therapy*, 1970, *1*, 14–32.

Sanchez, V. Behavioral treatment of chronic hair pulling in a two year old. *Journal of Behavior Therapy and Experimental Psychiatry*, 1979, *10*, 241–245.

Sandler, J., VanDercar, C., and Milhoan, M. Training child abusers in the use of positive reinforcement practices. *Behaviour Research and Therapy*, 1978, *16*, 169–175.

Sanford, N. Is the concept of prevention necessary or useful? In S. E. Golann, and Eisdorder (eds.), *Handbook of community psychology*. New York: Appleton-Century-Crofts, 1972.

Sanok, R. L., and Striefel, S. Elective mutism: Generalization of verbal responding across people and settings. *Behavior Therapy*, 1979, *10*, 357–371.

Sanson-Fisher, R. W., Seymour, F. W., and Baer, D. M. Training institutional staff to alter delinquents' conversation. *Journal of Behavior Therapy and Experimental Psychiatry*, 1976, *7*, 243–247.

Santogrossi, D. A., O'Leary, K. D., Romanczyk, R. G., and Kaufman, K. F. Self-evaluation by adolescents in a psychiatric hospital school token program. *Journal of Applied Behavior Analysis*, 1973, *6*, 277–287.

Saposnek, D. T., and Watson, L. S. The elimination of the self-destructive behavior of a psychotic child: A case study. *Behavior Therapy*, 1974, *5*, 79–89.

Sarason, S. B. *The creation of settings and the future societies*. San Francisco: Jossey-Bass, 1972.

Sarason, S. B. An asocial psychology and a misdirected clinical psychology. *American Psychologist*, 1981, *36*, 827–847.

Sarason, S. B., Levine, M., Goldberg, I. I., Cherlin, D. L., and Bennett, E. M. *Psychology in community settings*. New York: Wiley, 1966.

Sattler, H. E., and Swoope, K. F. Teacher as token dispenser: Effect of an observer. *Psychology in the Schools*, 1976, *13*, 97–100.

Saudargas, R., Madsen, C., and Scott, J. Differential effects of fixed and variable timed feedback on production rates of elementary school children. *Journal of Applied Behavior Analysis*, 1977, *10*, 673–678.

Sawin, D. B., and Parke, R. D. Development of self-verbalized control of resistance to deviation. *Developmental Psychology*, 1979, *15*, 120–127.

Schaeffer, B., Kollinzas, G., Musil, A., and McDowell, P. Spontaneous verbal language for autistic children through signed speech. *Sign Language Studies*, 1977, *17*, 287–328.

Schepis, M. M., Reid, D. H., Fitzgerald, J. R., Faw, G. D., Van Den Pol, R. A. and Welty, P. A program for increasing manual signing by autistic and profoundly retarded youth within the daily environment. *Journal of Applied Behavior Analysis*, 1982, *15*, 363–379.

Scherer, M. W., and Nakamura, C. Y. A Fear Survey Schedule for Children (FSS-FC): A factor analytic comparison with manifest anxiety (CMAS). *Behaviour Research and Therapy*, 1968, *6*, 173–182.

Scherr, M. S., Crawford, P. L., Sergeant, C. B., and Scherr, C. A. Effect of biofeedback techniques on chronic asthma in a summer camp environment. *Ann. Alergy,* 1975, *35,* 289.

Schoenwetter, C. D. Case study: Weight control and retardation. *The Journal of School Health,* 1978, *3,* 166–167.

Schopler, E., Brehm, S., Kinsbourne, M., and Reichler, R. J. Effect of treatment structure on development in autistic children. *Archives of General Psychiatry,* 1971, *24,* 415–421.

Schover, L., and Newsom, C. D. Overselectivity, developmental level and overtraining in autistic and normal children. *Journal of Abnormal Child Psychology,* 1976, *4,* 289–298.

Schreibman, L. Effects of within- stimulus and extra-stimulus prompting on discrimination learning in autistic children. *Journal of Applied Behavior Analysis,* 1975, *8,* 91–112.

Schreibman, L., and Carr, E. Elimination of echolalic responding to questions through the training of a generalized verbal response. *Journal of Applied Behavior Analysis,* 1978, *11,* 453–464.

Schreibman, L., and Lovaas, O. I. Overselective response to social stimuli by autistic children. *Journal of Abnormal Child Psychology,* 1973, *1,* 152–168.

Schreibman, L., Koegel, R., and Craig, M. Reducing stimulus overselectivity in autistic children. *Journal of Abnormal Child Psychology,* 1977, *5,* 425–436.

Schreibman, L., Koegel, R. L., Charlop, M. H. and Egel, A. L. Autism. In A. S. Bellack, M. Hersen and A. E. Kazdin (Eds.) *International handbook of behavior modification and therapy.* N.Y.: Plenum Press, 1982, 891–915.

Schreibman, L., O'Neill, R. E. and Koegel, R. L. Behavioral training for siblings of autistic children. *Journal of Applied Behavior Analysis,* 1983, *16,* 129–138.

Schroeder, S. R., Petersen, C. R., Solomon, L. J., and Artley, J. J. EMG feedback and the contingent restraint of self-injurious behavior among the severely retarded: Two case illustrations. *Behavior Therapy,* 1977, *8,* 738–741.

Schulman, J., Suran, B., Stevens, T., and Kupst, M. Instructions, feedback, and reinforcement in reducing activity levels in the classroom. *Journal of Applied Behavior Analysis,* 1979, *12,* 441–447.

Schumaker, J., Hovell, M., and Sherman, J. An analysis of daily report cards and parent-managed privileges in the improvement of adolescents classroom performance. *Journal of Applied Behavior Analysis,* 1977, *10,* 449–464.

Schwartz, G. E., and Weiss, S. M. Yale conference on behavioral medicine. A proposed definition and statement of goals. *Journal of Behavioral Medicine,* 1978, *1,* 31–12.

Schwarz, H. The mother in the consulting room: notes on the psychoanalytic treatment of two young children. *Psychoanalytic study of the child,* 1950. *5,* 343–357.

Schwitzgebel, R. L. *Streetcorner research.* Cambridge, Mass.: Harvard University Press, 1964.

Schwitzgebel, R. L. Short-term operant conditioning of adolescent offenders on socially relevant variables. *Journal of Abnormal Psychology,* 1967, *72,* 134–142.

Schwitzgebel, R. L. Preliminary socialization for psychotherapy of behavior disordered adolescents. *Journal of Consulting and Clinical Psychology,* 1969, *33,* 71–77.

Schwitzgebel, R. L., and Kolb, D. A. Inducing behavior change in adolescent delinquents. *Behaviour Research and Therapy,* 1964, *1,* 297–304.

Scott, A. The value and practical use of behavior modification programmes: A nurse's viewpoint. *Australian Journal of Mental Retardation*, 1977, *4*, 14–17.

Scott, E. A desensitization program for the treatment of mutism in a seven year old girl: A case report. *Journal of Child Psychology and Psychiatry and Applied Disciplines*, 1977, *18*, 263–270.

Sears, R. R. Functional abnormalities of memory with special reference to amnesia. *Psychological Bulletin*, 1936, *33*, 229–274.

Sears, R. R. Experimental analysis of psychoanalytic phenomena. In J. McV. Hunt (ed.), *Personality and the behavior disorders*, Vol. I. New York: Ronald, 1944.

Sears, R. R. Social behavior and personality development. In T. Parsons and E. A. Shils (eds.), *Toward a general theory of action*. Cambridge, Mass.: Harvard University, 1951.

Seitz, S., and Hoekenga, R. Modeling as a training tool for retarded children and their parents. *Mental Retardation*, 1974, *12*, 28–31.

Seitz, S., and Terdal, L. A. A modeling approach to changing parent-child interactions. *Mental Retardation*, 1972, *10*, 39–43.

Sergeant, H. G. S., and Yorkston, N. J. Verbal desensitization in the treatment of bronchial asthma. *Lancet*, 1969, 1321–1323.

Serralde, A., DeScholz, H. C., and McDougall, D. Comparison of potential reinforcer ratings between slow learners and regular students. *Behavior Therapy*, 1978, *9*, 60–64.

Settle, D., and Patterson, C. Reported in lead-soldered cans: A serious hazard? *Science News*, 1980, *117*, 180–181.

Seymour, F. W., and Stokes, T. F. Self-recording in training girls to increase work and evoke staff praise in an institution for offenders. *Journal of Applied Behavior Analysis*, 1976, *9*, 41–54.

Shaffer, D. Drug treatment. In M. Rutter and L. Hersov (eds.), *Child psychiatry: Modern approaches*. Oxford: Blackwell Scientific Co., 1977.

Shaffer, D., and Greenhill, L. A critical note on the predictive validity of the hyperkinetic syndrome. *Journal of Child Psychology and Psychiatry*, 1979, *20*, 61–72.

Shapiro, A. K., Shapiro, E., Wayne, H., and Clarkin, J. Organic factors in Gilles de la Tourette's syndrome. *British Journal of Psychiatry*, 1973, *122*, 659–664.

Shapiro, A. K., Shapiro, E. S., Brun, R. D., and Sweet, R. D. *Gilles de la Tourette syndrome*. New York: Raven Press, 1978.

Shapiro, D., and Surwit, R. S. Learned control of physiological function and disease. In H. Leitenberg (ed.), *Handbook of behavior modification*. Englewood Cliffs, N.J.: Prentice-Hall, 1976.

Shapiro, D. H. Jr., and Zifferblatt, S. M. Zen meditation and behavioral self-control: Similarities, differences, and clinical applications. *American Psychologist*, 1976, July, 519–532.

Shapiro, E. S., and Kleinn, R. D. Self-management of classroom behavior with retarded/disturbed children. *Behavior Modification*, *4*, 83–97.

Shapiro, E. S., Barrett, R. P., and Ollendick, T. H. A comparison of physical restraint and positive practice overcorrection in treating stereotypic behavior. *Behavior Therapy*, 1980, *11*, 227–233.

Shearn, D. F., and Randolph, D. L. Effects of reality therapy methods applied in the classroom. *Psychology in the Schools*, 1978, *15*, 79–83.

Shenfeld, M. *The behavioral treatment of social withdrawal and isolation in children*. State University of New York of Buffalo, Unpublished manuscript, 1980.

Shepherd, M., Oppenheim, B., and Mitchell, S. *Childhood behavior and mental health*. London: University of London Press, 1972.

Sherman, T. M., and Cormier, W. H. An investigation of the influence of student behavior on teacher behavior. *Journal of Applied Behavior Analysis*, 1974, *7*, 11–21.

Shore, M. F., and Goldston, S. E. Mental health aspects of pediatric care: Historical review and current status. In P. R. Magrab (ed.), *Psychological management of pediatric problems, Vol. I. Early life conditions and chronic diseases*. Baltimore, Md.: University Park Press, 1978, 15–31.

Siegel, L. J., and Peterson, L. Stress reduction in young dental patients through coping skills and sensory information. *Journal of Consulting and Clinical Psychology*, 1980, *48*, 785–787.

Siegel, L. J. and Peterson, L. Maintenance effects of coping skills and sensory information on young children's response to repeated dental procedures. *Behavior Therapy*, 1981, *12*, 530–535.

Silberman, C. *Crisis in the classroom*. New York: Random House, 1970.

Silver, A. A. Progress in therapy with children. In L. E. Alt and B. F. Riess (eds.), *Progress in clinical psychology*, Vol. 5. New York: Grune & Stratton, 1963.

Simic, J., and Bucher, B. Development of spontaneous manding in language deficient children. *Journal of Applied Behavior Analysis*, 1980, *13*, 523–528.

Simon, A., and Ward, L. O. Variables influencing the sources, frequency and intensity of worry in secondary school pupils. *British Journal of Social and Clinical Psychology*, 1974, *13*, 391–396.

Simpson, D. D., and Nelson, A. E. Attention training through breathing control to modify hyperactivity. *Journal of Learning Disabilities*, 1974, *7*, 274–283.

Singh, N. N. The effects of facial screening on infant self-injury. *Journal of Behavior Therapy and Experimental Psychiatry*, 1980, *11*, 131–134.

Sirota, A. D., and Mahoney, M. J. Relaxing on cue: The self-regulation of asthma. *Journal of Behavior Therapy and Experimental Psychiatry*, 1974, *5*, 65.

Skeels, H. M. Adult status of children with contrasting early life experiences. *Monographs for Research in Child Development*, 1966, *31*, 105.

Skeels, H. M., and Dye, H. B. A study of the effects of differential stimulation on mentally retarded children. *Proceedings and Addresses of the American Association on Mental Deficiency*, 1939, *44*, 114–136.

Skinner, B. F. Contrived reinforcement. *Behavior Analyst*, 1982, *5*, 3–8.

Skinner, B. F. *Science and human behavior*. New York: Macmillan, 1953.

Skinner, B. F. The science of learning and the art of teaching. *Harvard Education Review*, 1954, *24*, 86–87.

Skinner, B. F. *Teaching machines*. Science, 1958, *128*, 3330, 969–977.

Skinner, B. F. *Cumulative record*. New York: MacMillan, 1961.

Skinner, B. F. Discipline, ethical behavior, and self-control. In B. Skinner, (ed.), *The technology of teaching*. New York: Appleton-Century-Crofts, 1968, 185–198.

Sloane, H. N., Johnston, M. K., and Bijou, S. W. Successive modification of aggressive behavior and aggressive fantasy play by management of contingencies. *Journal of Child Psychology and Psychiatry*, 1967, *8*, 217–226.

Small, M. M., Giganti, M., and Steinberg, D. A comparison of thermal biofeedback and relaxation training within a behavior management treatment program: A controlled single-subject experiment. *American Journal of Clinical Biofeedback*, 1978, *1*, 68–70.

Smeets, P. M., and Streifel, S. Acquisition and cross model generalization of receptive and expressive signing skills in a retarded deaf girl. *Journal of Mental Deficiency Research*, 1976, *20*, 251–259.

Smeets, P. M., Elson, L. E., and Clament, A. Eliminating nasal discharge in a multihandicapped deaf child. *Journal of Behavior Therapy and Experimental Psychiatry*, 1975, *6*, 264–266.

Smith, D., and Lyon, R. Eliminating vomiting behavior in a profoundly retarded resident. *Research and the Retarded*, 1976, *3*, 24–27.

Smith, J. M., and Burns, C. L. C. The treatment of asthmatic children by hypnotic suggestion. *British Journal of Dis. Chest*. 1960, *54*, 78.

Smith, M. B., and Hobbs, H. The community and the community health center. *American Psychologist*, 1966, *21*, 499–509.

Smith, M. M., Colebatch, H. J. M., and Clarke, P. S. Increase and decrease in pulmonary resistance with hypnotic suggestion in asthma. *American Review of Respiratory Disorder*, 1970, *102*, 236.

Smith, R. E., and Sharpe, T. O. Treatment of a school phobia with implosive therapy. *Journal of Consulting and Clinical Psychology*, 1970, *35*, 239–243.

Snell, M. E. (ed.). *Systematic instruction of the moderately and severely handicapped*. Columbus, Ohio: Merrill, 1978.

Sobey, F. *The non-professional revolution in mental health*. New York: Columbia University Press, 1970.

Solomon, R. L., and Turner, L. H. Discriminative classical conditioning in dogs paralyzed by curare can later control discriminative avoidance responces in the normal state. *Psychological Review*, 1962, *69*, 202–219.

Spates, C. R., and Kanfer, F. H. Self-monitoring, self-evaluation, and self-reinforcement in children's learning: A test of a multistage self-regulation model. *Behavior Therapy*, 1977, *8*, 9–16.

Spence, S. H., and Marzillier, J. S. Social skills training with adolescent male offenders: I. Short-term effects. *Behaviour Research and Therapy*, 1979, *17*, 7–16.

Sperling, M. Dynamic considerations and treatment of enuresis. *Journal of the American Academy of Child Psychiatry*, 1965, *4*, 19–31.

Spiegler, M., and Liebert, R. Some correlates of self-reported fear. *Psychological Reports*, 1970, *26*, 691–695.

Spiegler, M., Liebert, R., McMains, M., and Fernandez, L. Experimental development of a modeling treatment to extinguish persistent avoidance behavior. In R. D. Rubin and C. Franks (eds.), *Advances in behavior therapy, 1968*. New York: Academic Press, 1969.

Spinetta, J., and Rigler, D. The child-abusing parent: A psychological review. *Psychological Bulletin*, 1972, *77*, 296–304.

Spitalnik, R., and Drabman, R. A classroom timeout procedure for retarded children. *Journal of Behavior Therapy and Experimental Psychiatry*, 1976, *7*, 17–21.

Spitz, R. A. Aggression: Its role in the establishment of object relations. In R. C. Lowenstein (ed.), *Drives, affects, behavior*. New York: International Universities Press, 1953.

Spivack, G., and Shure, M. *Social adjustment of young children: A cognitive approach to solving real-life problems*. San Francisco: Jossey-Bass, 1974.

Spivack, G., and Swift, M. "High risk" classroom behaviors in kindergarten and first grade. *American Journal of Community Psychology*, 1977, *5*, 385–397.

Spradlin, J. E. Effects of reinforcement in severely mentally retarded children. *American Journal of Mental Deficiency*, 1962, *66*, 634–640.

Spradlin, J. E., and Girardeau, F. L. The behavior of moderately and severely retarded persons. In N. Ellis (ed.), *International Review of Research in Mental Retardation*, Vol. I. New York: Academic Press, 1966, 257–298.

Spradlin, J. E., Cromwell, R. L., and Foshee, J. G. Studies in activity level: III. Effects of auditory stimulation in organics, familials, hyperactives and hypoactives. *American Journal of Mental Deficiency*, 1960, *64*, 754–757.

Sprague, R. L., and Sleator, E. K. Methylphenidate in hyperkinetic children. Differences in dose effects on learning and social behavior. *Science*, 1977, *198*, 1274–1276.

Sreenivasan, U., Manocha, S. N., and Jain, V. K., Treatment of severe dog phobia in childhood by flooding: A case report, *Journal of Child Psychology and Psychiatry*, 1979, *20*, 255–260.

Stableford, W. Parental treatment of a child's noise phobia. *Journal of Behavior Therapy and Experimental Psychiatry*, 1979, *10*, 159–160.

Stahl, J. R., Fuller, E. J., Lefebvre, M. F., and Burchard, J. D. A token economy community youth center: A model for programming peer reinforcement. In J. Stumphauzer (Ed.), *Progress in behavior therapy with delinquents*. Springfield, Ill.: Charles C. Thomas, 1979.

Stanley, L. Treatment of ritualistic behavior in an eight-year-old girl by response prevention: A case report. *Journal of Psychology and Psychiatry*, 1980, *21*, 85–90.

Stawar, T. Fable-mod: Operantly structured fantasies as an adjunct in the modification of fire-setting behavior. *Journal of Behavior Therapy and Experimental Psychiatry*, 1976, *7*, 285–287.

Stedman, D. J. Important considerations in the review and evaluation of educational intervention programs. In P. Mittler (ed.), *Research to practice in mental retardation, Vol. 1: Care and intervention*. Baltimore, Md.: University Park Press, 1977, 99–108.

Stedman, J. M. An extension of the Kimmel treatment method for enuresis to an adolescent: A case report. *Journal of Behavior Therapy and Experimental Psychiatry*, 1972, *3*, 307–309.

Stevens, J. R., and Blachly, P. H. Successful treatment of the Maladies des Tics. *American Journal of Disease of Children*, 1966, *112*, 541–545.

Stevens-Long, J., Schwarz, J. L., and Bliss, D. The acquisition and generalization of compound sentence structure in an autistic child. *Behavior Therapy*, 1976, *7*, 397–404.

Stewart, W. The unmet needs of children. *Pediatrics*, 1967, *39*, 167.

Stokes, T. F., and Baer, D. M. Preschool peers as mutual generalization-facilitating agents. *Behavior Therapy*, 1976, *7*, 549–556.

Stokes, T. F., and Kennedy, S. H. Reducing child uncooperative behavior during dental treatment through modeling and reinforcement. *Journal of Applied Behavior Analysis*, 1980, *13*, 41–49.

Stokes, T. F., Doud, C., Rowbury, T., and Baer, D. Peer facilitation of generalization in a preschool classroom. *Journal of Abnormal Child Psychology*, 1978, *6*, 203–210. (a)

Stokes, T. F., Fowler, S. A., and Baer, D. M. Training preschool children to recruit natural communities of reinforcement. *Journal of Applied Behavior Analysis*, 1978, *11*, 285–303. (b)

Stokoe, W. Sign language structure: An outline of the visual communication system of the American deaf. Buffalo: University of Buffalo, Studies on Linguistics, Occasional Paper No. 8, 1958.

Stokoe, W. The study of sign language. *Sign language Studies*, 1976, *26*, 1–36.

Stoudenmire, J., and Salter, L. Conditioning prosocial behaviors in a mentally retarded child without using instructions. *Journal of Behavior Therapy and Experimental Psychiatry*, 1975, *6*, 39–42.

Strain, P. S. An experimental analysis of peer social initiations of the behavior of withdrawn preschool children: Some training and generalization effects. *Journal of Abnormal Child Psychology*, 1977, *5*, 445–456.

Strain, P. S., and Pierce, J. E. Direct and vicarious effects of social praise on mentally retarded preschool children's attentive behavior. *Psychology in the School*, 1977, *14*, 348–353.

Strain, P. S., and Timm, M. A. An experimental analysis of social interaction between a modificationally disordered preschool child and her classroom peers. *Journal of Applied Behavior Analysis*, 1974, *7*, 583–590.

Strain, P. S., Kerr, M. M., and Ragland, E. U. Effects of peer-mediated social initiations and prompting/reinforcement procedures on the social behavior of autistic children. *Journal of Autism and Developmental Disorders*, 1979, *9*, 41–54.

Strain, P. S., Shores, R. E., and Kerr, M. M. An experimental analysis of "spillover" effects on social interaction among behaviorally handicapped preschool children. *Journal of Applied Behavior Analysis*, 1976, *9*, 31–90.

Strain, P. S., Shores, R. E., and Timm, R. A. Effects of peer social imitations on the behavior of withdrawn preschool children. *Journal of Applied Behavior Analysis*, 1977, *10*, 289–298.

Strain, P. S., Steele, P., Ellis, T., and Timm, M. Long-term effects of oppositional child treatment with mothers as therapists and therapist trainers. *Journal of Applied Behavior Analysis*, 1982, *15*, 163–169.

Straughan, J. H. Treatment with child and mother in the playroom. *Behaviour Research and Therapy*, 1969, *2*, 37–41.

Straughan, J. H., Potter, W. K., and Hamilton, S. H. The behavioral treatment of an elective mute. *Journal of Child Psychology and Psychiatry*, 1965, *6*, 125–130.

Stromer, R. Modifying letter and number reversals in elementary school children. *Journal of Applied Behavior Analysis*, 1975, *8*, 211–212.

Stuart, R. B. *Trick or treatment: How and when psychotherapy falls*. Champaign, Ill.: Research Press, 1970.

Stuart, R. B. Behavioral contracting within families of delinquents. *Journal of Behavior Therapy and Experimental Psychiatry*, 1971, *2*, 1–11.

Stuart, R. B., Tripodi, T., Jayaratne, S., and Camburn, D. An experiment in social engineering in serving the families of predelinquents. *Journal of Abnormal Child Psychology*, 1976, *4*, 243–261.

Stumphauzer, J. S. Behavior modification with juvenile delinquents: A critical review. *Federal Correctional Institution Technical and Treatment Notes*, 1970, *1*, 1–22.

Stumphauzer, J. S. *Behavior therapy with delinquents*. Springfield, Ill.: Charles C. Thomas, 1973.

Stumphauzer, J. S. Elimination of stealing by self-reinforcement of alternative behavior and family contracting. *Journal of Behavior Therapy and Experimental Psychiatry*, 1976, *7*, 265–268.

Stumphauzer, J. S. (Ed.) *Progress in behavior therapy with delinquents*. Springfield, Ill.: Charles C. Thomas, 1979.

Stumphauzer, J. S., Aiken, T., and Veloz, E. East side story: behavioral analysis of a high crime juvenile crime community. *Behavioral Disorders*, 1977, *2*, 76–84.

Stumphauzer, J. S., Candelora, K., and Venema, H. A follow-up of probation officers trained in behavior modification. In J. S. Stumphauzer (Ed.), *Progress in behavior therapy with delinquents.* Springfield, Ill.: Charles C. Thomas, 1979.

Stumphauzer, J. S., Veloz, E., and Aiken, T. Behavioral analysis of communities: a challenge. *Psychological Reports*, 1981, *49*, 343–346.

Stunkard, A. J. Eating patterns of obesity. *Psychiatric Quarterly*, 1959, *33*, 284–295.

Stunkard, A. J., and Mahoney, M. J. Behavioral treatment of eating disorders. In H. Leitenberg (ed.), *Handbook of behavior modification and behavior therapy.* Englewood Cliffs, N.J.: Prentice-Hall, 1976, 45–73.

Sturgis, E. T., and Adams, H. E. The right to treatment: Issues in the treatment of homosexuality. *Journal of Consulting and Clinical Psychology*, 1978, *46*, 165–172.

Sulzer, B., Hunt, S., Ashby, E., Koniarski, C., and Krams, M. Increasing rate and percentage correct in reading and spelling in a class of slow readers by means of a token system. In E. A. Ramp and B. L. Hopkins (eds.), *New directions in education: Behavior analysis.* Lawrence: University of Kansas, 1971, 5–28.

Sulzer, E. S. Reinforcement and the therapeutic contract. *Journal of Counseling Psychology*, 1962, *9*, 271–276.

Surratt, P. R., Ulrich, R. E., and Hawkins, R. P. An elementary student as a behavioral engineer. *Journal of Applied Behavior Analysis*, 1969, *2*, 85–92.

Swanson, L. Removal of positive reinforcement to alter learning disabled adolescents' preacademic problems. *Psychology in the Schools*, 1979, *16*, 286–292.

Switzer, E., Deal, T., and Bailey, J. The reduction of stealing in second graders using a group contingency. *Journal of Applied Behavior Analysis*, 1977, *10*, 267–272.

Switzky, H. N., and Haywood, H. C. Motivational orientation and the relative efficacy of self-monitored and externally imposed reinforcement systems in children. *Journal of Personality and Social Psychology*, 1974, *30*, 360–366.

Szasz, T. S. The myth of mental illness. *American Psychologist*, 1960, *15*, 113–118.

Szasz, T. S. Psychoanalysis and the rule of law. *Psychoanalytic Review*, 1968, *55*, 248–258.

Szykula, S. A., and Hector, M. A. Teacher instructional behavior change through self-control. *Psychology in the School*, 1978, *15*, 87–94.

Tahmisian, J., and McReynolds, W. Use of parents as behavioral engineers in the treatment of a school-phobic girl. *Journal of Consulting Psychology*, 1971, *18*, 225–228.

Tal, A., and Miklich, D. R. Emotionally induced decreases in pulmonary flow rates in asthmatic children. *Psychosomatic Medicine*, 1976, *38*, 190–199.

Taplin, P. S., and Reid, J. B. Changes in parent consequences as a function of family intervention. *Journal of Consulting and Clinical Psychology*, 1977, *45*, 973–981.

Tasto, D. L. Systematic desensitization, muscle relaxation and visual imagery in the counter conditioning of a four-year-old phobic child. *Behaviour Research and Therapy*, 1969, *7*, 409–411.

Tate, B. G. Case study: Control of chronic self-injurious behavior by conditioning procedures. *Behavior Therapy*, 1972, *3*, 72–83.

Tate, B. G., and Baroff, G. S. Aversive control of self-injurious behavior in a psychotic boy. *Behaviour Research and Therapy*, 1966, *4*, 281–287.

Tavormina, J. B. Basic models of parent counseling: A review. *Psychological Bulletin*, 1974, *81*, 827–835.

Tavormina, J. B. Relative effectiveness of behavioral and reflective group counseling with parents of mentally retarded children. *Journal of Consulting and Clinical Psychology*, 1975, *43*, 22–31.

Taylor, P. D., and Turner, R. K. A clinical trial of continuous intermittent and overlearning bell and pad treatments for nocturnal enuresis. *Behaviour Research and Therapy*, 1975, *13*, 281–293.

Taylor, R. L. Use of the AAMD classification systems: A review of recent research. *American Journal of Mental Deficiency*, 1980, *85*, 116–119.

Terdal, L., and Buell, J. Parent education in managing retarded children with behavior deficits and inappropriate behaviors. *Mental Retardation*, 1969, *7*, 10–13.

Tharp, R. G., and Wetzel, R. J. *Behavior modification in the natural environment*. New York: Academic Press, 1969.

Thelen, M. H., Fry, R. A. Fehrenbach, P. A., and Frautschi, N. M. Therapeutic videotape and film modeling: A review. *Psychological Bulletin*, 1979, *86*, 701–720.

Thomas, E. G., and Walter, C. L. Guidelines for behavioral practice in the open community agency: Procedures and evaluation. *Behaviour Research and Therapy*, 1973, *11*, 193–205.

Thomas, J. D. Accuracy of self-assessment of on-task behavior by elementary school children. *Journal of Applied Behavior Analysis*, 1976, *9*, 209–210.

Thompson, G. A., Iwata, B. A., and Poynter, H. Operant control of pathological tongue thrust in spastic cerebral palsy. *Journal of Applied Behavior Analysis*, 1979, *12* 325–333.

Thoresen, C. E., and Mahoney, M. J. *Behavioral self-control*. New York: Holt, Rinehart and Winston, 1974.

Thoresen, C. E., and Wilbur, C. S. Some encouraging thoughts about self-reinforcement. *Journal of Applied Behavior Analysis*, 1976, *9*, 518–520.

Thorne, D., and Shinedling, M. Volunteer student behavioral engineers: Should they attempt to establish or eliminate target behaviors? *Mental Retardation*, 1970, *8*, 9–12.

Throne, J., and Farb, J. Can mental retardation be reversed? *British Journal of Mental Subnormality*, 1978, *24*, 67–73.

Timbers, G. D., Phillips, E. L., Fixsen, D. L., and Wolf, M. M. *Modification of the verbal interaction behavior of a pre-delinquent youth*. Paper presented at the American Psychological Association, Washington, D.C., September 1971.

Toepfer, C., Reuter, J., and Maurer, C. Design and evaluation of an obedience training program for mothers of preschool children. *Journal of Consulting and Clinical Psychology*, 1972, *39*, 194–198.

Toister, R. P., Condron, C. J., Worley, L., and Arthur, D. Faradic therapy of chronic vomiting in infancy: A case study. *Journal of Behavior Therapy and Experimental Psychiatry*, 1975, *6*, 55.

Tolstrup, K. The treatment of anorexia nervosa in childhood and adolescence. *Journal of Child Psychology and Psychiatry*, 1975, *16*, 75–78.

Tombari, M., and Bergan, J. Consultant cues and teacher verbalizations, judgments, and expectancies concerning children's adjustment problems. *Journal of School Psychology*, 1978, *16*, 212–219.

Tomlinson, J. R. The treatment of bowel retention by operant procedures: A case study. *Journal of Behavior Therapy and Experimental Psychiatry*, 1970, *1*, 83–85.

Toner, I. J., Moore, L. P., and Ashley, P. K. The effect of serving as a model of self-control on subsequent resistance to deviation in children. *Journal of Experimental Child Psychology*, 1978, *26*, 85–91. (a)

Toner, I. J., Parke, R. D., and Yussen, S. R. The effect of observation of model behavior on the establishment and stability of resistance to deviation in children. *Journal of Genetic Psychology*, 1978, *132*, 283–290. (b)

Toner, I. J., Moore, L. P., and Emmons, B. A. The effect of being labeled on subsequent self-control in children. *Child Development*, 1980, *51*, 618–621.

Tracy, J. J., and Clark, E. H. Treatment for child abusers. *Social Work*, 1974, *19*, 351–354.

Tretakoff, M. Counseling the parents of handicapped children—A review. *Mental Retardation*, 1969, *7*, 31–35.

Trojanowicz, R. C. *Juvenile delinquency: Concepts and control*, 2nd ed. Englewood Cliffs, N.J.: Prentice-Hall, 1978.

Tucker, D., Hollis, J., Sailor, W., Horner, D., Kelly, P., and Guess, D. Preparing paraprofessionals' personnel for education of the severely handicapped: The teaching associate. *Education and Training of the Mentally Retarded*, 1976, *11*, 274–280.

Turkewitz, H., O'Leary, K. D., and Ironsmith, M. Producing generalization of appropriate behavior through self-control. *Journal of Consulting and Clinical Psychology*, 1975, *43*, 577–583.

Turner, A. J. Behavioral community mental health centers: Development, management and preliminary results. In R. A. Winett (Chair), *Behavior modification in the community: Progress and problems*. Symposium presented at the 83rd Convention of the American Psychological Association, 1975.

Turner, R. K., Young, G. C., and Rachman, S. Treatment of nocturnal enuresis by conditioning techniques. *Behaviour Research and Therapy*, 1970, *8*, 367–381.

Ullmann, L. G., and Krasner, L. (eds). *Case studies in behavior modification*. New York: Holt, Rinehart and Winston, 1965.

Ullmann, L. P., and Krasner, L. A. *A psychological approach to abnormal behavior*. 2nd ed. Englewood Cliffs, N.J.: Prentice-Hall, 1975.

Ultee, C. A., Griffioen, D., and Schellekens, J. The reduction of anxiety in children: A comparison of systematic desensitization *in vitro* and systematic desensitization *in vivo*. *Behavior Research and Therapy*, 1982, *20*, 61–67.

Urbain, E. S., and Kendall, P. C. Review of social-cognitive problem-solving interventions with children. *Psychological Bulletin*, 1980, *88*, 109–143.

Vaal, J. J. Applying contingency contracting to a school phobic: A case study. *Journal of Behavior Therapy and Experimental Psychiatry*, 1973, *4*, 371–373.

Vachon, L., and Rich, E. S. Visceral learning in asthma. *Psychosomatic Medicine*, 1976, *38*, 122–130.

Vance, V. J., and Taylor, W. F. The financial cost of chronic childhood asthma. *Ann. Allergy*, 1971, *29*, 455.

Vanderheiden, H., Brown, W. P., Mackenzie, P., Reiner, S., and Schiebel, C. Symbol communication for the mentally handicapped. *Mental Retardation*, 1975, *13*, 34–36.

Van der Kooy, D., and Webster, C. D. A rapid and effective behavior modification program for an electively mute child. *Journal of Behavior Therapy and Experimental Psychiatry*, 1975, *6*, 149–152.

Van Hasselt, V. B., Hersen, M., Bellack, A. S., Rosenblum, N. D., and Lamparski, D. Tripartite assessment of the effects of systematic desensitization in a multiphobic child: An experimental analysis. *Journal of Behavior Therapy and Experimental Psychiatry*, 1979, *10*, 51–55.

VanHouten, R., and VanHouten, J. The performance feedback system in the special education classroom: An analysis of public posting and peer comments. *Behavior Therapy*, 1977, *8*, 366–376.

VanHouten, R., Morrison, E., Jarvis, R., and McDonald, M. The effects of explicit timing and feedback on compositional response rate in elementary school children. *Journal of Applied Behavior Analysis*, 1974, *7*, 547–555.

VanHouten, R., Hill, S., and Parsons, M. An analysis of a performance feedback system: The effects of timing and feedback, public posting, and praise upon academic performance and peer interaction. *Journal of Applied Behavior Analysis*, 1975, *8*, 449–457.

Vedder, C. B. *Juvenile offenders*, Springfield, Ill.: Charles C. Thomas, 1979.

Vernon, D. T. A., and Bailey, W. C. The use of motion pictures in the psychological preparation of children for induction of anesthesia. *Anesthesiology*, 1974, *40*, 68–72.

Verville, E. *Behavior problems of children*. Philadelphia: Saunders, 1967.

Vogrin, D., and Kassinove, H. Effects of behavioral rehearsal, audiotaped observation, and intelligence on assertiveness and adjustment in third grade children. *Psychology in the Schools*, 1979, *16*, 422–429.

Vygotsky, L. *Thought and language*. Cambridge, Mass.: MIT-Press, 1962.

Wachtel, P. L. *Psychoanalysis and behavior therapy: Toward an integration*. New York: Basic Books, 1977.

Wacker, D. P., Carroll, J. L., and Moe, G. L. Acquisition, generalization, and maintenance of an assembly task by mentally retarded children. *American Journal of Mental Deficiency*, 1980, *85*, 286–290.

Wade, T. C. Factor analytic approaches to the investigation of common fears: A critical appraisal and reanalysis. *Behavior Therapy*, *9*, 923–935.

Wagner, L., and Ora, J. *Parental control of the very young severely oppositional child*. Paper read at the Southeastern Psychological Association, Louisville, Ky., 1970.

Wagner, M. K. Parent therapist: An operant conditioning method. *Mental Hygiene*, 1968, *52*, 452–455.

Wahler, R. G. *Behavior therapy with oppositional children: Attempts to increase their parents' reinforcement value*. Paper read at the Southwestern Psychological Association, April 1967.

Wahler, R. G. Oppositional children: A quest for parental reinforcement control. *Journal of Applied Behavior Analysis*, 1969, *2*, 159–170. (a)

Wahler, R. G. Setting generality: Some specific and general effects of child behavior therapy. *Journal of Applied Behavior Analysis*, 1969, *2*, 239–246. (b)

Wahler, R. G. Parent insularity as a determinant of generalization success in family treatment. *The ecosystem of the sick kid: implications for classification and intervention*. New York: CUNY Graduate Center, 1980. (a)

Wahler, R. G. The insular mother: Her problems in parent-child treatment. *Journal of Applied Behavior Analysis*, 1980, *13*, 207–219. (b)

Wahler, R. G., and Erickson, M. Child behavior therapy: A community program in Appalachia. *Behaviour Research and Therapy*, 1969, *7*, 71–78.

Wahler, R. G., and Fox, J. Solitary toy play and time-out: A family treatment package for children with aggressive and oppositional behavior. *Journal of Applied Behavior Analysis*, 1980, *13*, 23–39.

Wahler, R. G., Winkel, G. H., Peterson, R. F., and Morrison, D. C. Mothers as behavior therapists for their own children. *Behaviour Research and Therapy*, 1965, *3*, 113–124.

Wahler, R. G., Leske, G., and Rogers, E. S. The insular family: a deviance support system for oppositional children. In L. A. Hamerlynck (ed.), *Behavioral systems for the developmentally disabled*: In *School and family environments*. New York: Brunner/Mazel, 1979.

Waksman, S. A. An evaluation of social learning procedures designed to aid students with conduct problems. *Psychology in the Schools*, 1979, *16*, 416–421.

Walder, L. O., Cohen, S. I., Breiter, D. E., Daston, P. G., Hirsch, I. S., and Liebowitz, J. M. *Teaching behavioral principles to parents of disturbed children*. Paper read at the Eastern Psychological Association, Boston, 1967.

Walder, L. O., Cohen, S. I., Breiter, D. E., Daston, P. B., Hirsch, I. S., and Leibowitz, J. M. Teaching behavioral principles to parents of disturbed children. In B. G. Guerney (ed.), *Psychotherapeutic agents: New roles for non-professionals, parents and teachers*. New York: Holt, Rinehart and Winston, 1969.

Walker, H. M., and Hops, H. Group and individual reinforcement contingencies in the modification of social withdrawal. In L. A. Hamerlynck, L. Handy, and E. Mash (eds.), *Behavior changes in methodology, concepts and practice*. Champaign, Ill.: Research Press, 1973.

Walker, H. M., Hops, H., and Johnson, S. M. Generalization and maintenance of classroom treatment effects. *Behavior Therapy*, 1975, *6*, 188–200.

Walker, H. M., Hops, H., and Fiegenbaum, E. Deviant classroom behavior as a function of combinations of social and token reinforcement and cost contingency. *Behavior Therapy*, 1976, *7*, 76–88.

Wall, S. M., and Bryant, N. D. Behavioral self-management of academic test performances in elementary classrooms. *Psychology in the Schools*, 1979, *16*, 558–567.

Wallick, M. M. Desentitization therapy with a fearful two-year old. *American Journal of Psychiatry*, 1979, *10*, 1325–1326.

Walter, H. I., and Gilmore, S. K. Placebo vs. social learning effects in parent training procedures designed to alter the behavior of aggressive boys. *Behavior Therapy*, 1973, *4*, 361–377.

Walton, D. The application of learning theory to the treatment of a case of bronchial asthma. In H. J. Eysenck (ed.), *Behavior therapy and the neuroses*. London: Pergamon Press, 1960.

Ward, A. J. Early infantile autism: Diagnosis etiology and treatment. *Psychological Bulletin*, 1970, *73*, 350–362.

Ward, A. J. Early childhood autism and structural therapy: Outcome after three years. *Journal of Consulting and Clinical Psychology*, 1978, *46*, 586–587.

Warner, S., Miller, R., and Cohen, M. Relative effectiveness of teacher attention and the "good behavior game" in modifying disruptive classroom behavior. *Journal of Applied Behavior Analysis*, 1977, *10*, 737.

Warner, V., and Jones, R. L. *Gifted elementary pupils as tutors of educable mental retardates*. Paper presented at the Annual Meeting of the Council for Exceptional Children, New York, 1968.

Wasserman, T. H., and Vogrin, D. J. Long-term effects of a token economy on target and off-task behaviors. *Psychology in the Schools*, 1979, *16*, 551–557.

Watson, J. Memory and "contingency analysis" in infant learning. *Merrill-Palmer Quarterly*, 1967, *13*, 55–76.

Watson, J. B., and Rayner, R. Conditioned emotional reactions. *Journal of Experimental Psychology*, 1920, *3*, 1–14.

Watson, L. S. Application of operant conditioning techniques to institutionalized severely and profoundly retarded children. *Mental Retardation Abstracts*, 1967, *4*, 1–18.

Watson, L. S., and Bassinger, J. F. *Behavior modification: Teacher's manual for programmed text for institutional staff*. Columbus, Ohio: Behavior Modification Technology, Inc., 1973.

Watson, L. S., Gardner, J. M., and Sanders, C. Program profiles: Shaping and maintaining behavior modification skills in staff members in an M.R. institution: Columbus State Institute behavior modification program. *Mental Retardation*, 1971, *9*, 39–42.

Watters, R. G., and Watters, W. E. Decreasing self-stimulatory behavior with physical exercise in a group of autistic boys. *Journal of Autism and Developmental Disorders*, 1980, *10*, 379–387.

Weber, H. An approach to the problem of fear in children. *Journal of Mental Science*, 1936, *82*, 136–147.

Webster, C. D., McPherson, H., Sloman, L., Evans, M. A., and Kuchar, E. Communicating with an autistic boy by gestures. *Journal of Autism and Childhood Schizophrenia*, 1973, *4*, 337–346.

Webster-Stratton, C. The long-term effects of a videotape modeling parent-training program: comparison of immediate and 1-year follow-up results. *Behavior Therapy*, 1982, *13*, 702–714.

Wehman, P., and Bates, P. Education curriculum for severely and profoundly handicapped persons. A review. *Rehabilitation Literature*, 1978, *39*, 2–14.

Weil, G., and Goldfried, M. R. Treatment of insomnia in an eleven-year-old child through self-relaxation. *Behavior Therapy*, 1973, *4*, 282–284.

Weiland, H., and Rudnik, R. Considerations of the development and treatment of autistic children. *The Psychoanalytic study of the child*. New York: International Universities Press, Vol. XVI, 1961, 549–563.

Weinberger, G., Leventhal, T., and Beckman, G. The management of a chronic school phobic through the use of consultation with school personnel. *Psychology in the Schools*, 1973, *10*, 83–88.

Weinrott, M. Garrett, B., and Todd, N. The influence of observer presence on classroom behavior. *Behavior Therapy*, 1978, *9*, 900–911.

Weinrott, M., Corson, J., and Wilchesky, M. Teacher mediated treatment of social withdrawal. *Behavior Therapy*, 1979, *10*, 281–294.

Weiss, A. R. A behavioral approach to the treatment of adolescent obesity. *Behavior Therapy*, 1977, *8*, 720–726.

Weiss, S. M. News and developments in behavioral medicine. *Journal of Behavioral Medicine*, 1978, *1*. 135–140.

Weiss, S. M. Support for research on aging in minority populations: National Institute on Aging. *Journal of Behavioral Medicine*, 1979, *2*, 103–108.

Welch, S. J., and Pear, J. J. Generalization of naming responses to objects in the natural environment as a function of training stimulus modality with retarded children. *Journal of Applied Behavior Analysis*, 1980, *13*, 629–643.

Wells, K. C., Forehand, R., and Hickey, K. Effects of a verbal warning and overcorrection on stereotyped and appropriate behaviors. *Journal of Abnormal Child Psychology*, 1977, *5*, 387–404. (a)

Wells, K. C., Forehand, R., Hickey, K., and Green, K. D. Effects of a procedure derived from the overcorrection principle on manipulated and non-manipulated behaviors. *Journal of Applied Behavior Analysis*, 1977, *10*, 679–687. (b)

Wells, K. C., Turner, S. M., Bellack, A. S., and Hersen, M. Effects of cue-controlled relaxation on psychomotor seizures. An experimental analysis. *Behaviour Research and Therapy*, 1978, *16*, 51–53.

Wells, K. C., Griest, D. L., and Forehand, R. The use of a self-control package to enhance temporal generality of a parent training program. *Behaviour Research and Therapy*, 1980, *18*, 347–353.

Welsh, R. S. *A highly efficient method of parental counseling*. Paper read at the Rocky Mountain Psychological Association, Albuquerque, N.M., May 1966.

Welsh, R. S. The use of stimulus satiation in the elimination of juvenile fire-setting behavior. In A. M. Graziano (ed.), *Behavior with children*, Vol. I. Chicago: Aldine-Atherton, 1971.

Werry, J. S., and Cohrssen, J. Enuresis: An etiologic and therapeutic study. *Journal of Pediatrics*, 1975, *67*, 423–431.

Wetzel, R. Use of behavioral techniques in a case of compulsive stealing. *Journal of Consulting and Clinical Psychology*, 1966, *30*, 367–374.

Wetzel, R., Baker, J., Roney, M., and Martin, M. Outpatient treatment of autistic behavior. *Behaviour Research and Therapy*, 1966, *4*, 169–177.

Wetzel, R. Behavior modification techniques and the training of teachers' aides. *Psychology in the Schools*, 1970, *7*, 325–330.

Whalen, C. K., and Henker, B. A. Creating therapeutic pyramids using mentally retarded patients. *American Journal of Mental Deficiency*, 1969, *74*, 331–337.

Whalen, C. K., and Henker, B. A. A pyramid therapy in a hospital for the retarded: Methods, program evaluation, and long-term effects. *American Journal of Mental Deficiency*, 1971, *75*, 414–434.

Whalen, C. K., and Henker, B. A. Psychostimulants and children: A review and analysis. *Psychological Bulletin*, 1976, *83*, 1113–1130.

Wheeler, L., and Levine, L. Observer-model similarity in the contagion of aggression. *Sociometry*, 1967,, *30*, 41–49.

Wheeler, M. E., and Hess, K. W. Treatment of juvenile obesity by successive approximation control of eating. *Journal of Behavior Therapy and Experimental Psychiatry*, 1976, *7*, 235–241.

White, W. C., Jr., and Davis, M. T. Vicarious extinction of phobic behavior in early childhood. *Journal of Abnormal Child Psychology*, 1974, *2*, 25–32.

White-Blackburn, G., Semb, S., and Semb, G. The effects of good-behavior contract on the classroom behaviors of sixth-grade students. *Journal of Applied Behavior Analysis*, 1977, *10*, 312–317.

Whitehill, M. B., Hersen, M., and Bellack, A. S. Conversation skills training for socially isolated children. *Behaviour Research and Therapy*, 1980, *18*, 217–225.

Whitman, T. L., Mercurio, S. R., and Caponigri, V. Development of social responses in two severely retarded children. *Journal of Applied Behavior Analysis*, 1970, *3*, 133–138.

Whitney, L. R., and Barnard, K. E. Operant learning theory and nursing care of the retarded child. *Mental Retardation*, 1966, *4*, 26–29.

Wiesen, A. E., and Watson, E. Elimination of attention seeking behavior in a retarded child. *American Journal of Mental Deficiency*, 1967, *72*, 50–52.

Wilbur, R. The linguistics of manual languages and manual systems. In L. Lloyd (ed.), *Communication assessment and intervention strategies*. Baltimore, Md.: University Park Press, 1976, 423–500.

Wilbur, R. *American Sign Language and Sign Systems*. Baltimore, Md.: University Park Press, 1979.

Wilhelm, H., and Lovaas, O. I. Stimulus overselectivity: A common feature in autism and mental retardation. *American Journal of Mental Deficiency*, 1976, *81*, 221–241.

Williams, C. D. The elimination of tantrum behaviors by extinction procedures. *Journal of Abnormal and Social Psychology*, 1959, *59*, 269–270.

Williams, H. E., and Phelan. *Respiratory illness in children*. London: Blackwell Scientific Publications, 1975.

Williams, J. A., Koegel, R. L., and Egel, A. L. Response-reinforcer relationships and improved learning in autistic children. *Journal of Applied Behavior Analysis*, 1981, *14*, 53–60.

Williams, R. L., and Long, J. D. *Toward a self-managed life-style*. Boston: Houghton-Mifflin, 1975.

Williams, W., Coyne, P., DeSpain, C., Johnson, F., Scheurman, N., Stengart, J., Swetlik, B., and York, R. Teaching math skills using longitudinal sequences. In M. Snell (ed.), *Systematic instruction of the moderately and severely handicapped*. Columbus, Ohio: Merrill, 1978.

Williamson, D., Sanders, S., Sewell, W., Haney, J., and White, D. The behavioral treatment of elective mutism: Two case studies. *Journal of Behavior Therapy and Experimental Psychiatry*, 1977, *8*, 143–149. (a)

Williamson, D., Sewell, W., Sanders, S., Haney, J., and White, D. The treatment of reluctant speech using contingency management procedures. *Journal of Behavior Therapy and Experimental Psychiatry*, 1977, *8*, 151–156. (b)

Willis, J. W., Morris, B., and Crowder, J. A remedial reading technique for disabled readers that employs students as behavioral engineers. *Psychology in the Schools*, 1972, *9*, 67–70.

Wilson, G. T. Methodological considerations in treatment outcome research in obesity. *Journal of Consulting and Clinical Psychology*, 1978, *46*, 687–702.

Wilson, G. T. Social desirability and sex differences in expressed fear. *Behaviour Research and Therapy*, 1967, *5*, 136–137.

Wiltz, N. A. *Modification of behaviors through parent participation in a group technique*. (Doctoral dissertation, University of Oregon) Ann, Arbor, Mich.: University Microfilms, 1969, No. 70-9482.

Wiltz, N. A., and Patterson, G. R. An evaluation of parent training procedures designed to alter inappropriate aggressive behavior of boys. *Behavior Therapy*, 1974, *5*, 215–221.

Winett, R. A., and Nietzel, M. T. Behavoral ecology: Contingency management of consumer energy use. *American Journal of Community Psychology*, 1975, *3*, 123–133.

Winett, R. A., and Winkler, R. C. Current behavior modification in the classroom: Be still, be quiet, be docile. *Journal of Applied Behavior Analysis*, 1972, *5*, 499–504.

Winett, R. A., Krasner, L., and Krasner, M. Child-monitored token reading program. *Psychology in the Schools*, 1971, *8*, 259–262.

Wing, L. The handicaps of autistic children: A comparative study. *Journal of Child Psychology and Psychiatry*, 1969, *10*, 1–40.

Wing, L. *Autistic children: A guide for parents*. New York: Brunner/Mazel, 1972.

Wish, P. A., Hasazi, J. E., and Jurgela, A. R. Automated direct deconditioning of a child phobia. *Journal of Behavior Therapy and Experimental Psychiatry*, 1973, *4*, 279–283.

Wodarski, J. S., Filipczak, J., McCombs, D., Koustenis, G., and Rusilko, S. Follow-up on behavioral intervention with troublesome adolescents. *Journal of Behavior Therapy and Experimental Psychiatry*, 1979, *10*, 181–188.

Wolfe, D. A., Aragona, J., Kaufman, K., and Sandler, J. The importance of adjudication in the treatment of child abusers: Some preliminary findings. *Child Abuse and Neglect,* 1980, *4,* 127–135.

Wolf, M. M., Birnbrauer, J. S., Williams, T., and Lawler, J. A note on the apparent extinction of the vomiting behavior of a retarded child. In L. P. Ullman and L. Krasner (eds.), *Case studies in behavior modification.* New York: Holt, Rinehart and Winston, 1965.

Wolf, M. M., Risley, T., Johnson, M., Harris, R., and Allen, E. Application of operant conditioning procedures to the behavior problems of an autistic child: A follow-up and extension. *Behaviour Research and Therapy,* 1967, *5,* 103–111.

Wolf, M. M., Risley, T. R., and Mees, H. Application of operant conditioning procedures to the behavior problems of an autistic child. *Behaviour Research and Therapy,* 1964, *1,* 305–312.

Wolpe, J. Reciprocal inhibition as the main basis of psychotherapeutic effects. *AMA Archives of Neurology and Psychiatry,* 1954, *72,* 205–226.

Wolpe, J. *Psychotherapy by reciprocal inhibition.* Stanford, Calif.: Stanford University Press, 1958.

Wolpe, J. *The practice of behavior therapy.* Elmsford, N.Y.: Pergamon Press, 1974.

Wolpe, J. Behavior therapy *vs* psychoanalysis: Therapeutic and social implications. *American Psychologist,* 1981, *36,* 159–165.

Wolpe, J., Brady, J. P., Serber, M., Agras, W. S., and Liberman, R. P. The current status of systematic desensitization. *American Journal of Psychiatry,* 1973, *130,* 961–965.

Wood, R., and Flynn, J. M. A self-evaluation token system versus an external evaluation token system alone in a residential setting with predelinquent youths. *Journal of Applied Behavior Analysis,* 1978, *11,* 503–512.

Wooden, K. *Weeping in the playtime of others: America's incarcerated children.* New York: McGraw-Hill, 1976.

Wooley, S. C., Wooley, O. W., and Dyrenforth, S. R. Theoretical, practical and social issues in behavioral treatments of obesity. *Journal of Applied Behavior Analysis,* 1979, *12,* 3–25.

Workman, E. A., and Hector, M. A. Behavioral self-control in classroom settings: A review of the literature. *Journal of School Psychology,* 1978, *16,* 227–236.

Wright, D. F., and Bunch, G. Parental intervention in the treatment of chronic constipation. *Journal of Behavior Therapy and Experimental Psychiatry,* 1977, *8,* 93–95.

Wright, L., and Walker, C. E. A simple behavioral treatment program for psychogenic encopresis. *Behaviour Research and Therapy,* 1978, *16,* 209–212.

Wright, L., Nunnery, A., Eichel, B., and Scott, R. Application of conditioning principles to problems of tracheostomy addiction in children. *Journal of Consulting and Clinical Psychology,* 1968, *32,* 603–606.

Wulbert, M., Nyman, B. A., Snow, D., and Owen, Y. The efficacy of stimulus fading and contingency management in the treatment of elective mutism: A case study. *Journal of Applied Behavior Analysis,* 1973, *6,* 434–441.

Wulfsohn, D., and Barling, J. From external to self-control: Behavioral treatment of trichotillomania in an eleven-year-old girl. *Psychological Reports,* 1978, *42,* 1171–1174.

Yates, A. J. *Behavior therapy,* New York: Wiley, 1970.

Yates, B. T. A cost-effectiveness analysis of a residential treatment program for behaviorally disturbed children. In P. Mittler (ed.), *Research to practice in mental retardation Vol. 1: Care and intervention.* Baltimore, Md.: University Park Press, 1977, 435–446.

Yates, B. T., and Mischel, W. Young children's preferred attentional strategies for delaying gratification. *Journal of Personality and Social Psychology,* 1979, *37,* 286–300.

Yeaton, W. H., and Bailey, J. S. Teaching pedestrian safety skills to young children: An analysis and one-year follow-up. *Journal of Applied Behavior Analysis,* 1978, *11,* 315–329.

Yorkston, N. J., McHugh, L., Brady, J., Serber, A., and Sergeant, H. Verbal desensitization in bronchial asthma. *Journal of Psychosomatic Research,* 1974, *18,* 371.

Young, C. E., True, J. E., and Packard, M. E. A national survey of associate degree mental health programs. *Community Mental Health Journal,* 1974, *10,* 466–474.

Young, G. A staggered-wakening procedure in the treatment of enuresis. *Med. Off.,* 1964, *111,* 142–143.

Young, G. C. The problem of enuresis. *British Journal of Hospital Medicine,* 1969, *2,* 628–632.

Young, G. C., and Goldsmith, A. O. Treatment of encopresis in a day treatment program. *Psychotherapy: Theory Research and Practice,* 1972, *9,* 231–235.

Young, G. C., and Morgan, R. T. T. Overlearning in the conditioning treatment of enuresis. *Behaviour Research and Therapy,* 1972, *10,* 147–151. (a)

Young, G. C., and Morgan, R. T. T. Overlearning in the conditioning treatment of enuresis—A long-term follow-up study. *Behaviour Research and Therapy,* 1972, *10,* 419–420. (b)

Yule, W., and Carr, J. (eds.), *Behavior modification for the mentally handicapped.* London: Croom Helm, 1980.

Zakus, G., Chin, M. L., Keown, M., Herbert, F., and Held, M. A group behavior modification approach to adolescent obesity. *Adolescence,* 1979, *14,* 481–490.

Zax, M., and Cowen, E. L. *Abnormal psychology: Changing conceptions.* New York: Holt, Rinehart and Winston, 1977.

Zegiob, L. B., and Forehand, R. Parent-child interactions: Observer effects and social class differences. *Behavior Therapy,* 1978, *9,* 118–123.

Zeilberger, J., Sampen, S. E., and Sloane, H. H. Jr., Modification of a child's problem behaviors in the home with the mother as therapist. *Journal of Applied Behavior Analysis,* 1968, *1,* 47–53.

Zentall, S., and Zentall, T. Activity and task performance of hyperactive children as a function of environmental stimulation. *Journal of Consulting and Clinical Psychology,* 1976, *44,* 693–697.

Zentall, S. S. Behavioral comparisons of hyperactive and normally active children in natural settings. *Journal of Abnormal Child Psychology,* 1980, *8,* 93–109.

Zifferblatt, S. M., and Hendricks, C. Applied behavioral analysis of social problems—Population change, a case in point. *American Psychologist,* 1974, *29,* 750–761.

Zigler, E. Controlling child abuse: Do we have the knowledge and/or the will? In G. Gerbner, C. J. Ross, E. Zigler (eds.), *Child abuse: An agenda for action.* New York: Oxford University Press, 1980, 3–32.

Zimberoff, S. J. Behavior modification with delinquents. *Correctional Psychologist,* 1968, *3,* 11–25.

Zlutnick, S. *The control of seizures by the modification of pre-seizure behaviors: The punishment of behavioral chain components.* Unpublished doctoral dissertation, University of Utah, 1972.

Zlutnick, S., Mayville, W. J., and Moffat, S. Modification of seizure disorders: the interruption of behavioral chains. *Journal of Applied Behavior Analysis*, 1975, *8*, 1–12.

Zuriff, G. E. Radical behaviorism and epistemology. *Psychological Bulletin*, 1980, *87*, 337–350.

Index